Best Racehorses of 2020

Volume 2

Great Britain & Ireland's Group 2 & Group 3 Winners

Dr SIEGLINDE McGEE

Set in 10.5 pt Garamond
Sleipnir Press

ISBN 978-1-8384331-1-6

Cover: Cadillac, a potential classic contender, was one of Europe's leading two-year-olds of 2020. The €40,000 Goffs Orby Sale graduate is a son of Lope de Vega and Seas of Wells, he was bred by Sunderland Holdings Inc, is owned by Alpha Racing 2000 and trained in Ireland by Jessica Harrington.
Photo: Healy Racing

Every effort has been made to ensure that the information in this book is accurate and up to date. Assessments of each horse reviewed are the personal opinion of the author, based on decades of experience examining the pedigrees, racing and stud careers of thoroughbreds.

ABOUT THE AUTHOR

Sieglinde discovered horse racing by chance on Grand National day 1982 and was instantly hooked, reading and watching everything she could about it. She started writing on the subject in the summer of 1983, began keeping personal databases on racing and pedigrees the following year, and got her first job in racing five years after that, doing course wires (tipping) and bloodstock sales reports for *The Sporting Life*, maintaining a small pedigree database, and producing press releases for a major stud. She has been widely published on racing and pedigrees over the past three decades, wrote and produced her own 'Timeform Annual-style' books for several years in the 1990s and has been writing for *The Irish Field* since the spring of 2000.

While still in secondary school, a well-known member of the British racing press joked that "with databases that detailed, you should almost be doing a degree in it!" So, she did, many years later, and in 2005, was conferred with a doctorate from Trinity College Dublin for a thesis titled *Behavioural Reactivity and Ensuing Temperamental Traits in Young Thoroughbred Racehorses (Equus caballus)*, the culmination of four years of postgraduate research.

Sieglinde is also a graduate of Dublin City University and of the world-famous Thoroughbred Breeding Course at the Irish National Stud. She taught in Trinity College Dublin and for Oscail (in DCU) for several years, has presented at academic conferences and given guest lectures.

OTHER BOOKS BY THE AUTHOR

Racing & bloodstock:
Best Racehorses of 2020 – Volume 1: European Group 1 Winners — print-on-demand paperback via Amazon
European Group 1 Winners of 2019 — print-on-demand paperback & eBook
New Sires of 2019 — print-on-demand-paperback & eBook via Amazon
Freshman Sires of 2019 — print-on-demand paperback via Amazon

European Group 1 Winners of 2018 — print-on-demand paperback & eBook via Amazon

Other:
Key Research & Study Skills in Psychology (SAGE, 2010) – hardback, paperback & eBook

Thank you for reading *Best Racehorses of 2020 – Volume 2: Great Britain & Ireland's Group 2 & Group 3 Winners.*

If you enjoy this book, please spread the word
and leave a review on Amazon, Goodreads or another book-review site.

Even a single line will do.

Reviews help authors!

CONTENTS

GROUP 2 & GROUP 3 WINNERS WHOSE ESSAY IS IN *BEST RACEHORSES OF 2020: VOLUME 1 – EUROPEAN GROUP 1 WINNERS*

Barney Roy (GB)
Battaash (IRE)

Campanelle (IRE)
Champers Elysees (IRE)

Dream of Dreams (IRE)

Enable (GB)

Gear Up (IRE)
Ghaiyyath (IRE)
Glen Shiel (GB)

Kameko (USA)

Lord North (IRE)

Mac Swiney (IRE)
Mishriff (IRE)

Mogul (GB)
Mohaather (GB)

Nazeef (GB)

One Master (GB)
Oxted (GB)

Pretty Gorgeous (FR)

Santiago (IRE)
Shale (IRE)
Space Blues (IRE)
Subjectivist (GB)
Supremacy (IRE)

Tarnawa (IRE)
Twilight Payment (IRE)

Wonderful Tonight (FR)

INTRODUCTION

The year 2020 was one for the history books and not just because of the races that ran and the horses that won them. It was a pandemic year, and as we get ready for the 2021 season it is still not known if or when any sense of the old normality will return. The Covid-19 virus, whose effect can be mild, moderate, long-term debilitating or lethal to those unlucky enough to catch it, is in its third wave in some parts of the world, a second wave in others. To date, over 106 million people have been confirmed as infected, with in excess of 2.3 million dead, and hundreds of thousands of new cases of infection are reported globally every day. And just as newly developed vaccines are being steadily rolled out there are reports that one of the most easily transportable ones is as little as ten per cent effective against a particular rapidly spreading strain. We all hope that we are near the end of this plague, but there could still be a long way to go.

The opening months of the 2020 season were unlike no other. Initially run behind closed doors, racing in Germany was suspended on March 16th, France halted its action from March 17th and Ireland's racing shutdown from March 25th. National Hunt racing's Cheltenham Festival went ahead as usual from March 10th to 13th but all further racing in Great Britain was then suspended from March 18th. The multi-million-dollar Dubai World Cup day at Meydan in the United Arab Emirates, due to be held on March 28th, was called off just six days before, and horses who had shipped over to compete made it out before a local lockdown. Many US tracks also shut down, as did racing in other jurisdictions, while Hong Kong, Japan, Australia, and New Zealand continued without spectators. For the northern hemisphere's flat sector, it would mean rescheduling of the early-season trials and classics, but for the National Hunt sector it meant the loss of the Grand National meeting at Aintree—which had been due to feature Tiger Roll's bid for a third victory in the feature event—plus both the Irish Grand National festival meeting at Fairyhouse and the Punchestown Festival.

The British Horseracing Authority (BHA) announced that the first four classics of the English season would be postponed to an as-yet unknown date. Soon afterwards, Ascot racecourse issued a statement that should the Royal Ascot festival go ahead on its scheduled dates in June then it would take place behind closed doors. At this point, both Horse Racing Ireland and France Galop remained hopeful that their countries' classic would go ahead on their usual dates.

The William Haggas-trained geldings Addeybb and Young Rascal were among those who had been overseas as the lockdowns spread, the pair having travelled to Australia with some big targets in mind. Both ran their races, with the former landing both the Group 1 Ranvet Stakes at Rosehill and Group 1 Longines Queen Elizabeth Stakes at Randwick and the latter taking a Group 3 contest at the first-named venue. The latter top-level win came hours after the Irish Taoiseach, Leo Varadkar, announced that Ireland's lockdown would be extended to May 5th.

In mid-April it was proposed to move the English mile classics to early June and the Derby and Oaks to July. Germany's racing officials hoped to be able to have a return to action as early as May 4th, and then the French announced plans to reopen their racing behind closed doors from May 11th, with no foreign-based horses or riders permitted entry until the end of that month. The answer to the question of whether or not foreign runners would be allowed was not yet available, so there was no guarantee that any could line-up for the rescheduled classics, which would be moved to a month later than their usual spot in the calendar. The French mile classics would run on June 1st, the Prix Saint-Alary and Prix Ganay on June 14th, the Prix du Jockey Club and Prix de Diane on July 7th, the Prix d'Ispahan on July 19th and for three-year-olds only, with the Grand Prix de Paris replacing the Prix Niel's slot in mid-September.

In April, there was also some speculation as to whether any restrictions on the ability of jurisdictions to accept international entries for their races would necessarily lead to a reduction in the pattern status of those races. Races that are restricted to horses who have been born in a specific country or only to horses trained in a particular region or nation have local pattern status only, for example, the Local Grade 1 of Canada's premier classic, the Queen's Plate, a race that counts only as listed status internationally. Thankfully, this remained no more than a short-lived discussion point.

The picture was clearer with regard to racecourse attendances by spectators. In Ireland, for example, this would be under restrictions until at least September, which meant that the Galway Festival, a famous week-long event with no pattern races but several top National Hunt handicaps, and which typically takes place around the same time as the Glorious Goodwood festival, would be without the massive crowds normally associated with it. In the end, the general public was still unable to attend a meeting in the country by the end of the year, whereas spectators were permitted on only a few days in Britain. The virus levels increased in the autumn and winter, necessitating further lockdowns.

Competition in France returned as planned, there was a flurry of stakes and pattern races, but just days later the region of Ile-de-France was one of those designated a 'red zone' and so racing was stopped again at ParisLongchamp, Chantilly, and a number of other tracks. The country's first classics of the year would instead be held at Deauville. Meanwhile, revised schedules for Ireland and Great Britain were being finalised, the latter despite an absence of any official confirmation that the sport would resume as hoped on June 1st. The Irish Derby and Irish Oaks would remain on their originally set day but the Guineas races would be held on June 12th and 13th, with the Tattersalls Gold Cup moving to July. That race is usually for older horses only, but for 2020 it would be open to three-year-olds too. Entries were made and declarations finalised for the proposed opening of the British flat season, in the expectation that the go-ahead would come in time, and that clearance was finally given on Saturday, May 30th, two days before a ten-race card at Newcastle was set to launch. A cap of twelve runners per race was one of the safety measures put in place. It had also been revealed that many of the major races would have their prize money cut due to the developing financial impact of the pandemic.

The first three weeks in June provided a feast of Group 1 and other pattern racing. The opening classics in France went ahead on the 1st, the Coronation Cup, 2000 Guineas and 1000 Guineas held at Newmarket on the 5th, 6th and 7th, the Irish 2,000

Guineas and Irish 1,000 Guineas the following Friday and Saturday, and then on to Royal Ascot where the running order was reorganised to create distance between the initial mile classics and the top three-year-old races, and to give as many two-year-old as possible the chance to qualify for a berth. Those initial couple of weeks were flooded with five- and six-furlong races for juveniles, with trainers given an opportunity to nominate the horse they'd rather not have balloted. With numbers restricted, qualification for Royal Ascot's juvenile contests would be based on wins and places obtained on the track before then, with unraced horses down the list but ahead of unplaced ones. There was also a flurry of such contests held in France from late May, and that country's freshman sire Goken (by Kendargent) made a quick impression by notching up five individual winners before the start of June. Adaay (by Kodiac), Dariyan (by Shamardal) and Twilight Son (by Kyllachy) all had a winner apiece on the continent too before racing began again in Britain or Ireland.

Finally, things were rolling, yet always under a cloud of doubt as to how much of a full season could take place. Victor Ludorum (by Shamardal), an undefeated top-level star at two but beaten on his seasonal reappearance before the lockdown, won the Group 1 Emirates Poule d'Essai des Poulains (French 2000 Guineas) on June 1st, Dream And Do (by Siyouni) had her nose in front on the line in the Group 1 Emirates Poule d'Essai des Pouliches (French 1000 Guineas) about 35 minutes later—both at Deauville—followed just over half an hour after that by Fearless King's (by Kingman) narrow victory against the previously undefeated juvenile champion Rubaiyat in the Group 2 Mehl-Mülhens-Rennen (German 2000 Guineas) at Cologne. It was strange to see well-known classic trials taking place after the classics with which they are associated.

There were two Group 3 races run before the March shutdown, one in England and one in Ireland, but it would be June 1st before any sort of race would be run again in Britain (the same date that the French and Germans held their first classics of the year), and June 8th before racing resumed in Ireland. The first British pattern race post lockdown was at Kempton on June 3rd, with the first Group 1, the Hurworth Bloodstock Coronation

Cup, taking place at Newmarket two days later. Ireland's second pattern event of the year took place at Leopardstown on June 9th.

Aside from a string of races at Meydan before the lockdown and an Australian Group 3 success for Young Rascal before he left the William Haggas team to join the Archie Alexander one 'down under', there was no British- or Irish-trained Group 2 or Group 3 winner outside of Britain and Ireland until Thursday June 25th when the Hughie Morrison-trained Telecaster landed the Group 3 La Coupe over ten furlongs at ParisLongchamp. The second one followed an hour and a half later when Charlie Appleby sent out Space Blues to take the Group 3 Prix de la Porte Maillot over seven furlongs at the same venue.

By the end of the year, after an almost complete if somewhat rejigged pattern-race schedule, 174 horses had won a Group 2 or Group 3 race in Britain and/or Ireland and/or been a British- or Irish-trained winner of such a race in another country, accumulating a total haul of 193 races at those levels. Of those, twenty-six won at least once at the highest level, and those horses are reviewed individually in *Volume 1: European Group 1 Winners.*

Multiple pattern winners

Although 174 horses won at either Group 2 or Group 3 level in 2020, only nineteen were multiple winners within those two grades, all successful in just two such races aside from a pair of them who also added a single Group 1 success to their tally. Twenty-four others who won a single Group 2 or Group 3 race did so in addition to securing either one, two or three Group 1 victories.

Barney Roy (by Excelebration), Ghaiyyath (by Dubawi) and Tarnawa (by Shamardal) were triple Group 1 stars who also got a single win at one of the lower pattern levels. Battaash (by Dark Angel), Nazeef (by Invincible Spirit) and Wonderful Tonight (by Le Havre) were dual Group 1 winners in addition to having one other pattern success, whereas Space Blues (by Dubawi) and Twilight Payment (by Teofilo) had one Group 1 win and two lower pattern wins to their name. Each of those horses is reviewed in *Volume 1*, as are the eighteen Group 2 or Group 3 winners who won once at the highest level.

In addition to Space Blues and Twilight Payment, the other horses who won two Group 2 and/or Group 3 races in 2020 were: A'Ali (by Society Rock), Angel Power (by Lope de Vega), Benbatl (by Dubawi), Dandalla (by Dandy Man), Enbihaar (by Redoute's Choice), Euchen Glen (by Authorized), Extra Elusive (by Mastercraftsman), Happy Power (by Dark Angel), Isabella Giles (by Belardo), Lemista (by Raven's Pass), Magic Lily (by New Approach), Manuela de Vega (by Lope de Vega), Pyledriver (by Harbour Watch), Safe Voyage (by Fast Company), Speak In Colours (by Excelebration), and Telecaster (by New Approach).

Breeders

There would be no horses without the breeders. Most of those who supplied three or more Group 2 or Group 3 winners include some of the perennial leaders in this area, but there were a few others who had an excellent year, especially if you add in their European Group 1 winners.

Godolphin's tally for the year was eleven plus two horses—Pinatubo (by Shamardal; Prix Jean Prat) and Victor Ludorum (by Shamardal; Poule d'Essai des Poulains)—who won only at Group 1 level during the year. Surprisingly, there were only two horses under their associated Darley banner: Benbatl (by Dubawi; Singspiel Stakes, Al Maktoum Challenge R2) and Glen Shiel (by Pivotal; British Champions Sprint Stakes, Phoenix Sprint Stakes). The eleven who won at least once at the lower levels were: Fanny Logan (by Sea The Stars; Hardwicke Stakes), Lazuli (by Dubawi; Dubai International World Trophy Stakes), Lord North (by Dubawi; Prince of Wales's Stakes, Brigadier Gerard Stakes), Loxley (by New Approach; Dubai City of Gold), Maamora (by Dubawi; Atalanta Stakes), Magic Lily (by New Approach; Cape Verdi Stakes, Balanchine Stakes), Master of The Seas (by Dubawi; Superlative Stakes), One Ruler (by Dubawi; Autumn Stakes), Royal Crusade (by Shamardal; Prix de Ris-Orangis), Space Blues (by Dubawi; Prix Maurice de Gheest, Lennox Stakes), and Zakouski (by Shamardal; Zabeel Mile).

Coolmore was listed as the breeder of six Group 2 and Group 3 winners, as part-breeder of Russian Emperor (by Galileo; Hampton Court Stakes), and also as the breeder of four horses who won only at the highest level: Fancy Blue (by Deep Impact; Prix de Diane, Nassau Stakes), Love (by Galileo; 1000 Guineas, Oaks, Yorkshire Oaks), Peaceful (by Galileo; Irish 1,000 Guineas), and Serpentine (by Galileo; Derby). The other six are Armory (by Galileo; Royal Whip Stakes), Delphi (by Galileo; Irish St Leger Trial Stakes), Divinely (by Galileo; Flame of Tara Stakes), Nobel Prize (by Galileo; Ballysax Stakes), Shale (by Galileo; Moyglare Stud Stakes, Silver Flash Stakes), and Tiger Moth (by Galileo; Paddy Power 'Is It 2021 Yet?' Stakes).

Lynch Bages Ltd and Orpendale, Chelston & Wynatt supplied three apiece, plus an additional horse each who won only in Group 1 company. The former company was responsible for Dawn Patrol (by Galileo; Loughbrown Stakes), Pista (by American Pharoah; Park Hill Stakes), Santiago (by Authorized; Irish Derby, Queen's Vase), plus Group 1 winner Even So (by Camelot; Irish Oaks), and they were part-breeder of Passion (by Galileo; Stanerra Stakes). Orpendale, Chelston & Wynatt, on the other hand, bred Anthony Van Dyck (by Galileo; Prix Foy), Battleground (by War Front; Vintage Stakes) and Military Style (by War Front; Tyros Stakes) plus the multiple Group 1 star Magical (by Galileo; Pretty Polly Stakes, Tattersalls Gold Cup, Irish Champion Stakes). O'Brien and his wife, former champion National Hunt trainer Anne-Marie, also breed horses under the Whisperview Trading Ltd banner and they had another good year. Rising star High Definition (by Galileo; Beresford Stakes) could become one of the standout performers of 2021, and it would be no surprise to see their 2020 top-level winners Order of Australia (by Australia; Breeders' Cup Mile) and Thunder Moon (by Zoffany; Vincent O'Brien National Stakes) hit the top again.

Jim Bolger had perhaps the most noteworthy year of all given he is not part of/fuelled by a major industrial machine, has had tremendous success with families he has been developing for many years and bred six pattern winners of 2020, three of them Group 1 stars and two of the sextet being by stallions who, it is fair to say, are not of a high profile. Also, he trains four of them. Twilight Payment (by Teofilo; Melbourne Cup, Curragh Cup, Vintage Crop Stakes), a former talented performer from his Coolcullen base, is now trained by Joseph O'Brien, whereas potential classic candidate Gear Up (by Teofilo; Criterium de Saint-Cloud) is trained by Mark Johnston. But the afternoon of Saturday, October 24th was a truly remarkable one for Bolger because Gear Up's Group 1 success in France came minutes before Mac Swiney (by New Approach; Vertem Futurity Trophy Stakes, Futurity Stakes) got his Group 1 win at Doncaster, and then Flying Visit (by Pride of Dubai) landed the Group 3 Eyrefield Stakes at Leopardstown. Bolger also bred and trained Gear Up's sire, Teofilo (by Danehill) and he trained Mac Swiney's sire, New Approach (by Galileo). New Treasure (by New Approach; Round Tower Stakes) and Poetic Flare (by Dawn Approach; Killavullan Stakes) were his other two pattern winners of 2020.

Seven other breeders were represented by at least three horses who either won a Group 1 race as a European-trained horse or won a Group 2 or Group 3 race as a British- or Irish-trained one.

Renowned classic producer Barronstown Stud struck with Lancaster House (by Galileo; Gladness Stakes), Royal Dornoch (by Gleneagles; Desmond Stakes) and Snow (by Galileo; Munster Oaks Stakes) plus Group 1 winner Van Gogh (by American Pharoah; Criterium International). Also based in Ireland, Ringfort Stud achieved the notable feat of having three Group 2-winning juveniles: Minzaal (by Mehmas; Gimcrack Stakes), Miss Amulet (by Sir Prancealot; Lowther Stakes) and Ubettabelieveit (by Kodiac; Flying Childers Stakes), whereas Tally-Ho Stud supplied A'Ali (by Society Rock; Coral Charge, Sapphire Stakes), Campanelle (by Kodiac; Prix Morny, Queen Mary Stakes), and Umm Kulthum (by Kodiac; Firth of Clyde Stakes).

Of British-based organisations, Bearstone Stud bred Lullaby Moon (by Belardo; Prix Miesque), Queen Jo Jo (by Gregorian; Summer Fillies' Stakes) plus dual top-level star Glass Slippers (by Dream Ahead; Flying Five Stakes, Breeders' Cup Turf Sprint). Cheveley Park Stud's trio consisted of Bowerman (by Dutch Art; Diamond Stakes), Molatham (by Night of Thunder; Jersey Stakes), and Regal Reality (by Intello; Sovereign Stakes); Rabbah Bloodstock Ltd had Century Dream (by Cape Cross; Celebration Mile Stakes, Diomed Stakes), Mighty Gurkha (by Sepoy; Sirenia Stakes), and Thunderous (by Night of Thunder; Dante Stakes), plus the Group 1 winners Addeybb (by Pivotal; Ranvet Stakes,

Queen Elizabeth Stakes, Champion Stakes) and Hello Youmzain (by Kodiac; Diamond Jubilee Stakes); whereas Shadwell Estate Company Ltd was responsible for Hukum (by Sea The Stars; Geoffrey Freer Stakes), Mujbar (by Muhaarar; Horris Hill Stakes), and Nazeef (by Invincible Spirit; Falmouth Stakes, Sun Chariot Stakes, Duke of Cambridge Stakes), plus Group 1 winner Tawkeel (by Teofilo; Prix Saint-Alary).

Trainers

The 174 horses who won a Group 2 or Group 3 race were split up among eighteen trainers in Ireland, forty-four in Great Britain and one in the United States of America. The latter was the Wesley Ward-trained Campanelle who won the Group 2 Queen Mary Stakes at the Royal Ascot meeting in June. They won a total of 193 Group 2 and/or Group 3 races between them distribution of the horses and races won among Irish and British trainers is shown in Table 1.

Table 1: Distribution of Irish- and British-trained Group 2 and Group 3 winners of 2020 (excluding one USA-trained horse)

Trained In	Trainers	Horses	Wins
Ireland	18	62	65
Great Britain	44	111	127
TOTAL	62	173	192

Eight trainers had six or more individual pattern winners in 2020. Aidan O'Brien's team at Ballydoyle, in Ireland, dominated again with twenty-two individual winners of Group 2 or Group 3 races plus an additional eight who won solely at Group 1 level. The latter group consisted of Circus Maximus (Queen Anne Stakes), Love (1000 Guineas, Oaks, Yorkshire Oaks), Magical (Pretty Polly Stakes, Tattersalls Gold Cup, Irish Champion Stakes), Order of Australia (Breeders' Cup Mile), Peaceful (Irish 1000 Guineas), Serpentine (Derby), St Mark's Basilica (Dewhurst Stakes) and Van Gogh (Criterium International). Those who won at Group 2 or Group 3 level (with or without an additional top-level score) were: Anthony Van Dyck (Prix Foy), Armory (Royal Whip Stakes), Battleground (Vintage Stakes), Cormorant (Derrinstown Stud Derby Trial Stakes), Dawn Patrol

(Loughbrown Stakes), Delphi (Irish St Leger Trial Stakes), Divinely (Flame of Tara Stakes), High Definition (Beresford Stakes), Lancaster House (Gladness Stakes), Love Locket (Leopardstown Fillies Trial Stakes), Magic Wand (Lanwades Stud Stakes), Military Style (Tyros Stakes), Mogul (Grand Prix de Paris, Hong Kong Vase, Gordon Stakes), Mother Earth (Fillies Sprint Stakes), Nobel Prize (Ballysax Stakes), Passion (Stanerra Stakes), Royal Dornoch (Desmond Stakes), Russian Emperor (Hampton Court Stakes), Santiago (Irish Derby, Queen's Vase), Snow (Munster Oaks Stakes), Tiger Moth (Paddy Power 'Is It 2021 Yet?' Stakes), and Wichita (Park Stakes).

Charlie Appleby sent out sixteen pattern winners for Godolphin during the year, only one of whom, the Group 1 Prix Jean Prat winner Pinatubo, was successful solely at the highest level. The Group 1 stars Barney Roy (Jebel Hatta, Grosser Dallmayr-Preis - Bayerisches Zuchtrennen; Grosser Preis von Berlin, Al Rashidiya), Ghaiyyath (Coral-Eclipse, Juddmonte International Stakes, Coronation Cup, Dubai Millennium Stakes), and Space Blues (Prix Maurice de Gheest, Lennox Stakes, Prix de la Porte Maillot) headed the rest, with Glorious Journey (Al Fahidi Fort), La Barrosa (Tattersalls Stakes), Lazuli (Dubai International Airport World Trophy Stakes), Loxley (Dubai City of Gold), Magic Lily (Cape Verdi Stakes, Balanchine Stakes), Master of The Seas (Superlative Stakes), One Ruler (Autumn Stakes), Royal Crusade (Prix de Ris-Orangis), Secret Advisor (Nad Al Sheba Trophy), Summer Romance (Princess Elizabeth Stakes), Volkan Star (Prix du Lys), and Zakouski (Zabeel Mile) the ones without a top-level win.

Three of the thirteen pattern winners for the John Gosden team won only at Group 1 level: Miss Yoda (Preis der Diana), Palace Pier (St James's Palace Stakes, Prix Jacques le Marois), and Stradivarius (Gold Cup, Goodwood Cup). The other ten featured the great Enable (King George VI and Queen Elizabeth Stakes, September Stakes), in her final season on the track, French classic scorer Mishriff (Prix du Jockey Club, Prix Guillaume d'Ornano), dual Group 1 star Nazeef (Falmouth Stakes, Sun Chariot Stakes, Duke of Cambridge Stakes), and Royal Ascot Group 1 winner Lord North (Prince of Wales's Stakes, Brigadier Gerard Stakes), and included an array of talented horses who got their best wins of the year at lower levels: Dubai Warrior (Winter Derby Stakes), Enbihaar (Lillie Langtry Stakes, Lonsdale Cup Stakes), Fanny Logan (Hardwicke Stakes), Frankly Darling (Ribblesdale Stakes), Indigo Girl (May Hill Stakes) and Terebellum (Dahlia Fillies' Stakes).

Joseph O'Brien, son of Aidan, brother of classic-winning trainer Donnacha, and the second-ranked of three Irish trainers who sent out six or more pattern winners, had a total of eleven, two of whom—Galileo Chrome (St Leger Stakes) and Thunder Moon (Vincent O'Brien National Stakes)—won only at Group 1 level. Pretty Gorgeous (Fillies' Mile, Debutante Stakes) and Twilight Payment (Melbourne Cup, Curragh Cup, Vintage Crop Stakes) also won at the highest level, and the rest consisted of Baron Samedi (Prix du Conseil de Paris), Buckhurst (Alleged Stakes), Crossfirehurricane (Gallinule Stakes), Patrick Sarsfield (Meld Stakes), Pista (Park Hill Fillies' Stakes), Speak In Colours (Greenlands Stakes, Ballycorus Stakes) and Thundering Nights (Snow Fairy Fillies Stakes).

Two trainers sent out eight pattern winners during the year: Andrew Balding and Jessica Harrington. Balding's juvenile Alcohol Free got her only pattern success in the Group 1 Cheveley Park Stakes but the stable also struck at the highest level with classic star Kameko (2000 Guineas, Joel Stakes). Berlin Tango (Classic Trial Stakes), Dashing Willoughby (Henry II Stakes), Foxtrot Lady (Sceptre Fillies' Stakes), Happy Power (Supreme Stakes), Spanish Mission (Doncaster Cup Stakes) and Tactical (July Stakes) were the team's other pattern winners.

Irish trainer Jessica Harrington is as capable of producing National Hunt champions as she is standouts in the flat sector and she added two more Group 1 winners to her haul in 2020: Alpine Star (Coronation Stakes) and Lucky Vega (Phoenix Stakes). The team's six other pattern winners were Cadillac (KPMG Champions Juvenile Stakes), Cayenne Pepper (Blandford Stakes), Leo de Fury (Mooresbridge Stakes), Millisle (Ballyogan Stakes), One Voice (Blue Wind Stakes) and Valeria Messalina (Brownstown Stakes).

Mark Johnston came next with a total of seven horses and his haul included Group 1 success with Gear Up (Criterium de Saint-Cloud, Acomb Stakes) and Subjectivist (Prix Royal-Oak, March Stakes). Dark Vision (Oettingen-Rennen), Elarqam (Legacy Cup Stakes), Nayef Road (Sagaro Stakes), Rose of Kildare (Musidora Stakes) and Thunderous (Dante Stakes) completed the roll of honour. He had an eighth one, briefly. King's Caper (by New Approach), who was a nose runner-up in the Group 2 Derby Italiano in July, was awarded the race in October following the disqualification of Tuscan Gaze on a technicality, but the original placings were reinstated in mid-December following an appeal.

William Haggas was the only other trainer with six or more pattern winners and one of those came with a horse who was running for the yard before switching to his new Australian connections. That was the Group 3 scorer Young Rascal (Iron Jack N E Manion Cup) who accompanied stable star Addeybb (Ranvet Stakes, Queen Elizabeth Stakes, Champion Stakes) on the trip 'down under'. The latter returned to Europe and added to his big-race haul at Ascot in October. The stable also notched up further Group 1 success with One Master (Prix de la Foret, Oak Tree Stakes), whereas Al Aasy (Bahrain Trophy Stakes), Nkosikazi (Hoppings Fillies' Stakes), Pablo Escobarr (Glorious Stakes) and With Thanks (Athasi Stakes) were their other pattern winners.

Owners
Godolphin had the highest number of pattern winners racing in their colours in 2020, followed by Hamdan Al Maktoum, but whether you put them at the top of the table or put Coolmore there depends on whether you put all of the various Coolmore partnerships together under the one umbrella rather than group them separately. Their horses are dealt with at the end of this section.

Godolphin recorded multiple Group 1 wins with Barney Roy (Jebel Hatta, Grosser Dallmayr-Preis - Bayerisches Zuchtrennen; Grosser Preis von Berlin, Al Rashidiya) and Ghaiyyath (Coral-Eclipse, Juddmonte International Stakes, Coronation Cup, Dubai Millennium Stakes), and additional Group 1 success with Pinatubo (Prix Jean Prat), Space Blues (Prix Maurice de Gheest,

Lennox Stakes, Prix de la Porte Maillot) and Victor Ludorum (Poule d'Essai des Poulains). They were also part-owners of Persian King (Prix d'Ispahan, Prix du Moulin de Longchamp). The rest were Benbatl (Singspiel Stakes, Al Maktoum Challenge R2), Dark Vision (Oettingen-Rennen), La Barrosa (Tattersalls Stakes), Lazuli (Dubai International Airport World Trophy Stakes), Loxley (Dubai City of Gold), Magic Lily (Cape Verdi Stakes, Balanchine Stakes), Master of The Seas (Superlative Stakes), One Ruler (Autumn Stakes), Royal Crusade (Prix de Ris-Orangis), Secret Advisor (Nad Al Sheba Trophy), Summer Romance (Princess Elizabeth Stakes), Terebellum (Dahlia Stakes), Volkan Star (Prix du Lys) and Zakouski (Zabeel Mile), bringing their overall total to twenty-one, of whom four won only at the highest level.

Thirteen horses carried the famous blue and white colours of Hamdan Al Maktoum to pattern and/or Group 1 victory, headed by the top-level successes of Battaash (King's Stand Stakes, Nunthorpe Stakes, King George Stakes), Mohaather (Sussex Stakes, Summer Mile Stakes), Nazeef (Falmouth Stakes, Sun Chariot Stakes, Duke of Cambridge Stakes) and Tawkeel (Prix Saint-Alary). Al Aasy (Bahrain Trophy Stakes), Alkumait (Mill Reef Stakes), Elarqam (Legacy Cup Stakes), Enbihaar (Lillie Langtry Stakes, Lonsdale Cup Stakes), Hukum (Geoffrey Freer Stakes), Minzaal (Gimcrack Stakes), Molatham (Jersey Stakes), Mujbar (Horris Hill Stakes) and Tabdeed (Hackwood Stakes) completed the roll of honour.

Two others had at least four individual pattern winners and/or Group 1 winners during the year: Mrs J S Bolger and King Power Racing Co Ltd. Potential classic contender Mac Swiney (Vertem Futurity Trophy Stakes, Futurity Stakes) was the most high-profile winner to carry the well-known white and purple colours of Jackie Bolger, all of them trained and bred by her husband, Jim. The other three, also juveniles, were Flying Visit (Eyrefield Stakes), New Treasure (Round Tower Stakes) and Poetic Flare (Killavullan Stakes). King Power Racing Co Ltd's blue and white colours have become instantly recognisable in recent seasons, and their quartet consisted of Angel Power (Pride Stakes, Premio Lydia Tesio), Art

Power (Lacken Stakes), Happy Power (Supreme Stakes) and Winter Power (Cornwallis Stakes).

Qatar Racing Ltd had four pattern winners in their ownership by the end of the year, headed by classic star Kameko (2000 Guineas, Joel Stakes), but Rose of Kildare (Musidora Stakes) was purchased privately by them after her pattern success, so only three carried their claret and gold colours to victory. Know It All (Derrinstown Stud Fillies Stakes) and The Lir Jet (Norfolk Stakes) were their other pair. Similarly, Mrs C.C. Regalado-Gonzalez, whose Thunder Moon (National Stakes) was a Group 1 winner, bought Steel Bull after his Molecomb Stakes victory, so also had three who were group-race winners in her well-known red and yellow colours. Patrick Sarsfield (Meld Stakes) and Speak In Colours (Greenlands Stakes, Ballycorus Stakes) were her other two.

So, on to the Coolmore horses. The various partnerships typically consist of Mrs John Magnier, Michael Tabor and Derrick Smith listed in various orders, with or without additional partners and, on occasion, the order switches about. Sometimes, as with Magical (Pretty Polly Stakes, Tattersalls Gold Cup, Irish Champion Stakes) there is just a single owner registered, in her case Derrick Smith.

The Magnier, Tabor, Smith (dark blue colours) horses were Anthony Van Dyck (Prix Foy), Armory (Royal Whip Stakes), Divinely (Flame of Tara Stakes), Love Locket (Leopardstown Fillies Trial Stakes), Military Style (Tyros Stakes), Passion (Stanerra Stakes), Serpentine (Derby), and Tiger Moth (Paddy Power 'Is It 2021 Yet?' Stakes). The purple and white colours of Smith, Magnier, Tabor were carried by Delphi (Irish St Leger Trial Stakes), Mother Earth (Fillies' Sprint Stakes), Shale (Moyglare Stud Stakes, Silver Flash Stakes), St Mark's Basilica (Dewhurst Stakes), and the sadly ill-fated Wichita (Park Stakes), as well as both High Definition (Beresford Stakes) and Order of Australia (Breeders' Cup Mile), both of whom have Anne-Marie O'Brien listed as a part-owner.

Tabor, Smith, Magnier horses race in the blue and orange colours and in addition to the Group 1 stars Fancy Blue (Prix de Diane, Nassau Stakes), Love (1000 Guineas, Oaks, Yorkshire

Oaks), Peaceful (Irish 1000 Guineas), Mogul (Grand Prix de Paris, Hong Kong Vase, Gordon Stakes) and Santiago (Irish Derby, Queen's Vase), they were carried to victory by Battleground (Vintage Stakes), Cormorant (Derrinstown Stud Derby Trial Stakes), Dawn Patrol (Loughbrown Stakes), Lancaster House (Gladness Stakes), Magic Wand (Lanwades Stud Stakes), Royal Dornoch (Desmond Stakes) and Snow (Munster Oaks Stakes), as well as Group 1 Criterium International scorer Van Gogh, whom they own in partnership with Mrs David Nagle.

Even So (Irish Oaks) raced in the sole ownership of Mrs John Magnier until after her classic success (then part-owned by Mrs Paul Shanahan), and she was a part-owner of Russian Emperor when he won the Group 3 Hampton Court Stakes.

Sires

Seven stallions were represented by four or more British- or Irish-trained horses who won at Group 2 or Group 3 level at least once in 2020 and one other stallion had three locally trained representatives plus a single US-trained horse that won an English pattern race. All eight are listed in Table 2 below along with the names of their Group 2- and/or Group 3-winning sons and daughters.

Table 2: Sires who had four or more British- or Irish-trained Group 2/3 winners worldwide in 2020, plus internationally trained Group 2/3 winners in Britain or Ireland

No.	Sire	Group 2 and Group 3 winners
18	Galileo	Anthony Van Dyck, Armory, Dawn Patrol, Delphi, Divinely, High Definition, Lancaster House, Lone Eagle, Magic Wand, Mogul, Nayef Road, Nobel Prize, Pablo Escobarr, Passion, Russian Emperor, Shale, Snow, Tiger Moth
11	Dubawi	Benbatl, Ghaiyyath, Glorious Journey, Indigo Girl, Lazuli, Lord North, Maamora, Master of The Seas, One Ruler, Secret Advisor, Space Blues
6	Sea The Stars	Al Aasy, Eagles By Day, Fanny Logan, Hukum, Terebellum, Volkan Star
5	Australia	Buckhurst, Cayenne Pepper, Epona Plays, Leo de Fury, Patrick Sarsfield
5	Lope de Vega	Angel Power, Antonia de Vega, Cadillac, La Barrosa, Manuela de Vega

No.	Sire	Group 2 and Group 3 winners
5	New Approach	Loxley, Mac Swiney, Magic Lily, New Treasure, Telecaster
4	Dark Angel	Art Power, Battaash, Happy Power, Top Rank
4	Kodiac	Campanelle, Nando Parrado, Ubettabelieveit, Umm Kulthum

When you expand the criteria to include all British- and Irish-trained pattern winners, including Group 1 level, plus all internationally trained horses who won any pattern race in Britain or Ireland during 2020, then the list of stallions with four or more winners grows to twelve members (see Table 3). The top three in the rankings remain the same but Australia moves into a clear fourth, ahead of Lope de Vega, whereas Kingman, Shamardal, Teofilo and Camelot join the list, bringing to a dozen the number of stallions who have four or more pattern-winning offspring reviewed in the two volumes of *Best Racehorses of 2020*. There are, of course, pattern winners of all levels not included for some of them because those were either not European-trained top-level scorers or they did not win a Group 2 or Group 3 in either Ireland or Great Britain.

Table 3: Sires who had four or more British- or Irish-trained pattern winners (all levels) worldwide in 2020, plus internationally trained pattern winners (all levels) in Britain or Ireland

No.	Sire	Group 2 and Group 3 winners
24	Galileo	Anthony Van Dyck, Armory, Circus Maximus, Dawn Patrol, Delphi, Divinely, High Definition, Lancaster House, Lone Eagle, Love, Magic Wand, Magical, Mogul, Nayef Road, Nobel Prize, Pablo Escobarr, Passion, Peaceful, Russian Emperor, Search For A Song, Serpentine, Shale, Snow, Tiger Moth
12	Dubawi	Benbatl, Ghaiyyath, Glorious Journey, Indigo Girl, Lazuli, Lord North, Maamora, Master of The Seas, One Ruler, Secret Advisor, Space Blues, The Revenant
8	Sea The Stars	Al Aasy, Eagles By Day, Fanny Logan, Hukum, Miss Yoda, Stradivarius, Terebellum, Volkan Star

No.	Sire	Group 2 and Group 3 winners
7	Australia	Buckhurst, Cayenne Pepper, Epona Plays, Galileo Chrome, Leo de Fury, Order of Australia, Patrick Sarsfield
6	Lope de Vega	Angel Power, Antonia de Vega, Cadillac, La Barrosa, Lucky Vega, Manuela de Vega
5	Kingman	Cormorant, Palace Pier, Persian King, Sinawann, Summer Romance
5	Kodiac	Campanelle, Hello Youmzain, Nando Parrado, Ubettabelieveit, Umm Kulthum
5	New Approach	Loxley, Mac Swiney, Magic Lily, New Treasure, Telecaster
5	Shamardal	Pinatubo, Royal Crusade, Tarnawa, Victor Ludorum, Zakouski
5	Teofilo	Donjah, Gear Up, Subjectivist, Tawkeel, Twilight Payment
4	Camelot	Current Option, Even So, Lady Wannabe, Sunny Queen
4	Dark Angel	Art Power, Battaash, Happy Power, Top Rank

Freshman Sires

Since the long-held restrictions on a stallion's book were abandoned, the freshman sires' championship often becomes heavily dependent on the matter of throwing as much as you can at the proverbial fan and seeing how much of it sticks. The increasing number of ultra-valuable sales and auction races muddy the picture some more and so the end-of-year table by prize money—the only way in which the title champion freshman sire, or any sire category, is actually earned—is not necessarily any indication of long-term potential. Stallions with what in the past would have been a normal-sized crop now have little chance of being crowned champion of that division or even of figuring prominently in the table. They could come up with a few stakes winners, with or without a Group 1 star, but will need to scoop some of those well-endowed lesser races to compensate for the smaller numbers.

Of course, just having a large crop to launch on the track is no guarantee of large numbers of winners. The stallion's progeny may be better suited to racing as three-year-olds and older horses for a variety of reasons, and contrary to an often-made misconception, sprinter neither equals precocious nor a potential source of many two-year-old winners. Freshman results are not a time to get wildly excited or to write off a horse either. Wait until their progeny have been tested in open company; you would not write someone off as a potential star athlete because they failed to excel at sport in primary school.

I am often reminded of the less than favourable comments some made about Galileo and Sea The Stars after their freshman season, when some were predicting failure for them because they "only" had one blacktype scorer among a low double-digit tally of winners, and, on the other hand, the raving about various flash-in-the-pan freshman "sensations" who never really amounted to anything.

In 2020, it was obvious by late summer that, barring a lucky run in the most valuable races, there was only one realistic candidate for champion freshman sire honours. Like many in the class, he benefitted from having a considerable amount to toss at that proverbial fan, and he broke new ground by having the largest number of individual winners ever seen by a freshman: fifty-six. They notched up eighty wins between them around the northern hemisphere and over £1 million in prize money, and a dozen of them earned blacktype. Two of those were listed winners but only two were pattern winners. He also got a listed winner in North America late in the year and just before shortly before this book went to print, he added a Grade 3 winner in California, bringing his total to six stakes winners. Five juvenile stakes winners plus several others who are placed at that level is a promising start for a freshman sire but a long way removed from 'sensational'; history does not eulogise about the number of maiden, conditions, novice, handicap or even seller and claiming winners that a stallion sires—just his stakes winners and long-term impact.

European champion freshman sire Mehmas (by Acclamation) supplied the Group 2 Gimcrack Stakes winner Minzaal and the Group 2 Richmond Stakes victor Supremacy, with the latter going on to add the Group 1 Middle Park Stakes, thereby making his sire the first of his cohort of stallions to get a winner at the highest level in Europe. However, Belardo (by Lope de Vega) was represented by three individual pattern winners including Isabella

Giles, who landed both the Group 2 Rockfel Stakes and Group 3 Prestige Stakes; he has also had a listed scorer in France and in New Zealand. The other freshmen with at least one pattern winner in Britain or Ireland were: Coulsty (by Kodiac), New Bay (by Dubawi), Pride of Dubai (by Street Cry) and Prince of Lir (by Kodiac). Of these, Pride of Dubai was also represented in Europe by Telepatic Glances (sic), an unbeaten listed and pattern winner in Italy and trained in that country, so not part of the data presented here.

Table 4: Freshman sires of 2020 with pattern winners in Great Britain and/or Ireland

No.	Sire	Group 2 and Group 3 winners
3	Belardo	Elysium, Isabella Giles, Lullaby Moon
2	Mehmas	Minzaal, Supremacy
2	New Bay	New Mandate, Saffron Beach
2	Pride of Dubai	Flying Visit, Star of Emaraaty
1	Coulsty	Santosha
1	Prince of Lir	The Lir Jet

Group 1-winning broodmares

Most of the focus on end-of-year breeding reviews focuses on stallions but, of course, there would not be any pattern winners to talk about if it were not for the mares who produced them. Fillies who win at the highest level on the track are among the most sought-after prospective broodmares, as you might imagine, and in 2020 there were fourteen Group 1-winning mares who supplied a British- or Irish-trained Group 2 or Group 3 winner somewhere in the world. They are listed in Table 5 along with the three who had one representative who won only at Group 1 level during the year; those mares are indicated with a *.

Table 5: Group 1-winning mares who were the dam of a British- or Irish-trained Group 2 or Group 3 winner and/or a European Group 1 winner in 2020 (* Group 1 only)

Group 1 winner	Group 2/Group 3 winners
Atlantic Jewel	Russian Emperor, by Galileo
Attraction	Elarqam, by Frankel
Chelsea Rose	Snow, by Galileo
Dancing Rain	Magic Lily, by New Approach
Fallen For You	Glorious Journey, by Dubawi

Group 1 winner	Group 2/Group 3 winners
Found	Battleground, by War Front
*Halfway To Heaven	Magical, by Galileo
Homecoming Queen	Shale, by Galileo
*Imagine	Van Gogh, by American Pharoah
*Iota	In Swoop, by Adlerflug
Lady Marian	Loxley, by New Approach
Mahbooba	Dubai Warrior, by Dubawi
Montare	Indigo Girl, by Dubawi
Nahrain	Benbatl, by Dubawi
Nightime	Ghaiyyath, by Dubawi
Red Evie	Divinely, by Galileo
Together Forever	Military Style, by War Front

Broodmare Sires

Eight broodmare sires were represented by at least four individual Group 2 or Group 3 winners during the year, all of them from a branch of the Northern Dancer (by Nearctic) line (see Table 6).

Dansili (by Danehill) led the way with ten horses by eight different sires. Only one of these was a two-year-old: Cadillac (by Lope de Vega). His sire made the table too, as did Danehill Dancer (by Danehill). Green Desert, who had four, has formed the other dominant branch of Danzig's (by Northern Dancer) line and he was joined on the list by his son Oasis Dream. Galileo (by Sadler's Wells) had nine winners by seven different sires, including the two-year-olds Battleground (by War Front) and Military Style (by War Front), whereas Montjeu (by Sadler's Wells) had four, each by a different stallion, two of them juveniles: Indigo Girl (by Dubawi) and La Barrosa (by Lope de Vega). Shamardal (by Giant's Causeway) was the other horse to make the table.

The order of merit changes slightly if you add in the European Group 1 winners sired by all of the stallions who had a British- or Irish-trained Group 2 or Group 3 winner during the year, with Galileo and Dansili swapping places at the top of the table. Sottsass (by Siyouni), St Mark's Basilica (by Siyouni) and Watch Me (by Olympic Glory) are the ones who make the difference for Galileo; only Galileo Chrome (by Australia) adds to Dansili's tally. Pivotal (by Polar Falcon), Cape Cross (by Green Desert) and Sadler's Wells (by Northern Dancer)—also all male-line descendants of Northern Dancer—join the list.

Table 6: Broodmare sires of four of more British- or Irish-trained Group 2 or Group 3 winners in 2020

No.	Sire	Group 2 and Group 3 winners
10	Dansili	Aspetar (Al Kazeem), Cadillac (Lope de Vega), Cormorant (Kingman), Dark Vision (Dream Ahead), Dream of Dreams (Dream Ahead), Glorious Journey (Dubawi), Magic Wand (Galileo), Pablo Escobarr (Galileo), Royal Crusade (Shamardal), Tilsit (First Defence)
9	Galileo	Barney Roy (Excelebration), Battleground (War Front), Certain Lad (Clodovil), Dame Malliot (Champs Elysees), Dubai Warrior (Dansili), Ghaiyyath (Dubawi), Military Style (War Front), Pista (American Pharoah), Secret Advisor (Dubawi)
8	Danehill Dancer	Armory (Galileo), Foxtrot Lady (Foxwedge), Helvic Dream (Power), Leo de Fury (Australia), Magic Lily (New Approach), Nayef Road (Galileo), Royal Dornoch (Gleneagles), Subjectivist (Teofilo)
6	Oasis Dream	Chindit (Wootton Bassett), Delphi (Galileo), Lancaster House (Galileo), Miss Amulet (Sir Prancealot), Twilight Payment (Teofilo), Ventura Tormenta (Acclamation)
4	Danehill	Bowerman (Dutch Art), Master of The Seas (Dubawi), Mogul (Galileo), Nobel Prize (Galileo)
4	Green Desert	Buckhurst (Australia), Minaun (Zoffany), Mother Earth (Zoffany), The Lir Jet (Prince of Lir)
4	Montjeu	Indigo Girl (Dubawi), La Barrosa (Lope de Vega), Nickajack Cave (Kendargent), Wonderful Tonight (Le Havre)
4	Shamardal	Al Aasy (Sea The Stars), Far Above (Farhh), One Ruler (Dubawi), Umm Kulthum (Kodiac)

Table 7: Broodmare sires of four of more British- or Irish-trained pattern winners (all levels) in 2020 including internationally trained pattern winners (all levels) in Britain or Ireland

No.	Sire	Pattern winners (all levels)
12	Galileo	Barney Roy (Excelebration), Battleground (War Front), Certain Lad (Clodovil), Dame Malliot (Champs Elysees), Dubai Warrior (Dansili), Ghaiyyath (Dubawi), Military Style (War Front), Pista (American Pharoah), Secret Advisor (Dubawi), Sottsass (Siyouni), St Mark's Basilica (Siyouni), Watch Me (Olympic Glory)

No.	Sire	Pattern winners (all levels)
11	Dansili	Aspetar (Al Kazeem), Cadillac (Lope de Vega), Cormorant (Kingman), Dark Vision (Dream Ahead), Dream of Dreams (Dream Ahead), Galileo Chrome (Australia), Glorious Journey (Dubawi), Magic Wand (Galileo), Pablo Escobarr (Galileo), Royal Crusade (Shamardal), Tilsit (First Defence)
10	Danehill Dancer	Armory (Galileo), Circus Maximus (Galileo), Foxtrot Lady (Foxwedge), Helvic Dream (Power), Leo de Fury (Australia), Magic Lily (New Approach), Nayef Road (Galileo), Royal Dornoch (Gleneagles), Serpentine (Galileo), Subjectivist (Teofilo)
8	Oasis Dream	Chindit (Wootton Bassett), Delphi (Galileo), Lancaster House (Galileo), Miss Amulet (Sir Prancealot), Siskin (First Defence), Tawkeel (Teofilo), Twilight Payment (Teofilo), Ventura Tormenta (Acclamation)
7	Danehill	Bowerman (Dutch Art), Even So (Camelot), Master of The Seas (Dubawi), Mogul (Galileo), Nobel Prize (Galileo), Order of Australia (Australia), Search For A Song (Galileo)
5	Pivotal	Golden Horde (Lethal Force), Love (Galileo), Magical (Galileo), Molatham (Night of Thunder), One Master (Fastnet Rock)
5	Shamardal	Al Aasy (Sea The Stars), Far Above (Farhh), Hello Youmzain (Kodiac), One Ruler (Dubawi), Umm Kulthum (Kodiac)
4	Cape Cross	Lucky Vega (Lope de Vega), Santiago (Authorized), Tarnawa (Shamardal), Thundering Nights (Night of Thunder)
4	Green Desert	Buckhurst (Australia), Minaun (Zoffany), Mother Earth (Zoffany), The Lir Jet (Prince of Lir)
4	Montjeu	Indigo Girl (Dubawi), La Barrosa (Lope de Vega), Nickajack Cave (Kendargent), Wonderful Tonight (Le Havre)
4	Sadler's Wells	Berlin Tango (Dansili), Enable (Nathaniel), Thunder Moon (Zoffany), Van Gogh (American Pharoah)

Auction prices

A total of 105 of the 174 horses who won a Group 2 or Group 3 race in Great Britain or Ireland in 2020 or who were a British- or

Irish-trained winner of such a race elsewhere in the world, were sold at least once in a public action ring. This excludes vendor buy-backs. Twenty-five of those were sold twice and three (Nkosikazi, Queen Jo Jo and Steel Bull) have been sold three times. Eleven were sold only as foals, nine were sold as breeze-up horses, and twelve as horses in training/older horses, five of whom (Breathtaking Look, Dubai Station, Nobel Prize, Queen Jo Jo, Royal Dornoch) changed hands after their 2020 pattern-race success. The lowest and highest prices for Group 2 and Group 3 winners from the various sales companies are shown in Table 8.

Table 8: Lowest and highest prices of Group 2 and Group 3 winners of 2020 who were sold by the various sales companies

Company	sold	lowest	highest
Arqana	10	€40,000	€1,400,000
DBS	3	£41,000	£70,000
Goffs	25	€1,000	€1,100,000
Goffs UK	11	£8,000	£135,000
Goresbridge	1	€100,000	€100,000
Keeneland	4	$85,000	$675,000
Osarus	1	€8,000	€8,000
Tattersalls	56	3,500gns	3,400,000gns
Tattersalls Ascot	2	£7,500	£15,000
Tattersalls Ireland	7	€3,000	€67,000
Tattersalls Ireland Ascot	1	£28,000	£28,000

The dual Group 1-placed Group 2 Lowther Stakes winner Miss Amulet (by Sir Prancealot) was the cheapest purchase, sold for €1,000 purchase at the 2018 Goffs November Foal Sale. She was one of nine who fetched a four-figure price in the ring among any age group. They are all shown in Table 9. There were other bargain-basement pattern winners elsewhere, notably the French juvenile Group 2 and Group 3 scorer Plainchant (by Gregorian) who cost just €4,000 at the 2019 Arqana October yearling sale, but only those who were either trained by a British- or Irish-based trainer or who won a pattern race in either of those countries have been included.

Table 9: Group 2 and Group 3 winners of 2020 who had been sold for a four-figure price at auction

Horse	Age	Sire	Won	Price	Sold
Ireland					
Goffs					
Laws of Indices	1c	Power	Gr3	€8,000	Autumn Yearling
Minaun	1f	Zoffany	Gr3	€8,000	Sportsman's Yearling
Miss Amulet	1f	Sir Prancealot	Gr2	€1,000	November Foals
Star of Emaraaty	1f	Pride of Dubai	Gr3	€3,500	Sportsman's Yearling
Tattersalls Ireland					
Rose of Kildare	1f	Make Believe	Gr3	€3,000	September Yearling
Steel Bull	fc	Clodovil	Gr3	€5,000	Flat Bloodstock
The Lir Jet	fc	Prince of Lir	Gr2	€9,500	November Flat Bloodstock
Great Britain					
Goffs UK					
The Lir Jet	1c	Prince of Lir	Gr2	£8,000	Premier Yearlings
Tattersalls					
Baron Samedi	fc	Australia	Gr2	3,500gns	December Foals

Horse	Age	Sire	Won	Price	Sold
Tattersalls Ascot					
Miss Amulet	1f	Sir Prancealot	Gr2	£7,500	Yearling
France					
Osarus					
Trueshan	1c	Planteur	Gr2	€8,000	September Yearlings

At the other end of the scale, Goffs sold Ghaiyyath (by Dubawi) for €1,100,000 as a foal, whereas made seven made seven-figure prices at yearlings. The seven-figure purchases are shown in Table 10.

Table 10: Pattern winners sold for a seven-figure sum at public auction. * Indicates a Group 1 winner at some point in their career

Name	Sire	Age	Amount	Venue
Cormorant	Invincible Spirit	1c	1,050,000gns	Tattersalls
Elarqam	Frankel	1c	1,600,000gns	Tattersalls
Ghaiyyath*	Dubawi	fc	€1,100,000	Goffs
Glorious Journey	Dubawi	1c	2,600,000gns	Tattersalls
Magic Wand*	Galileo	1f	€1,400,000	Arqana
Mogul*	Galileo	1c	3,400,000gns	Tattersalls
Snow	Galileo	1f	1,200,000gns	Tattersalls
Volkan Star	Sea The Stars	1c	1,000,000gns	Tattersalls

The auctions at which the 105 Group 2 and Group 3 winners were sold are listed in Table 11. Some horses may be counted in multiple events. Further details are provided in an index at the back of the book.

Table 11: Auctions at which Group 2 and Group 3 winners of 2020 were sold, showing the number sold plus the lowest and highest price at each venue

Auction	sold	lowest	highest
Ireland			
Goffs Autumn Yearling	2	€8,000	€15,000
Goffs November Foals	10	€1,000	€1,100,000
Goffs November Horses in Training	1	€200,000	€200,000
Goffs Orby	9	€25,000	€700,000
Goffs Sportsman's Yearling	4	€3,500	€55,000
Goresbridge Breeze-Up	1	€100,000	€100,000
Tattersalls Ireland Flat Bloodstock	1	€5,000	€5,000
Tattersalls Ireland September Yearling	3	€3,000	€67,000
Tattersalls Ireland September Yearlings Part 2	2	€12,000	€28,000
Tattersalls Ireland November Flat	1	€12,500	€12,500
Tattersalls Ireland November Flat Bloodstock	1	€9,500	€9,500

Auction	sold	lowest	highest
Great Britain			
DBS Premier Yearling	3	£41,000	£70,000
Goffs UK Breeze-Up	3	£28,000	£135,000
Goffs UK Premier Yearling	8	£8,000	£95,000
Goffs UK Spring Horses-in-Training	1	£45,000	£45,000
Tattersalls Ascot Yearling	2	£7,500	£15,000
Tattersalls Autumn Horses-in-Training	4	35,000gns	300,000gns
Tattersalls Craven Breeze-Up	2	68,000gns	90,000gns
Tattersalls Guineas Breeze-Up	2	31,000gns	105,000gns
Tattersalls Ireland Ascot September Yearling	1	£28,000	£28,000
Tattersalls July Horses-in-Training	3	52,000gns	230,000gns
Tattersalls October Book 1	21	50,000gns	3,400,000gns
Tattersalls October Book 2	15	15,000gns	200,000gns
Tattersalls October Book 3	4	13,000gns	42,000gns
Tattersalls December Foals	13	3,500gns	195,000gns
Tattersalls December Mares	3	30,000gns	400,000gns
France			
Arqana Deauville August Yearling	8	€35,000	€1,400,000
Arqana December Breeding Stock	1	€55,000	€55,000
Arqana May Breeze-Up	1	€800,000	€800,000
Osarus September Yearlings	1	€8,000	€8,000
United States of America			
Keeneland September Yearlings	4	$85,000	$675,000

Earliest career win

There is a large and seemingly growing segment of the industry that is obsessed with precocity and yet the majority of leading racehorses do not actually start winning before late summer or autumn of their juvenile year; some don't even win at that age. The two-year-old races of 2020 are a blip in that there was almost no racing before June 1st—Poetic Flare (by Dawn Approach; March 23rd) and Campanelle (by Kodiac; May 31st) achieved the feat—but that does not change the fact that of the Group 2 and Group 3 winners aged three and above, only two had got a juvenile win before May 1st: Romanised (by Holy Roman Emperor) and Ventura Rebel (by Pastoral Pursuits). Extend that to a first win before June 1st of their juvenile year and you can add only four more: Battaash (by Dark Angel; 18th), Rose of Kildare (by Make Believe; 20th), Certain Lad (by Clodovil; 21st), and Dream of Dreams (by Dream Ahead; 27th).

Compare that to the fourteen who got their first win in November or December of their juvenile season—Top Rank (by Dark Angel) got his first win on December 22nd—the forty-two British- or Irish-trained horses who won a Group 2 or Group 3 race somewhere in 2020 despite having being winless at two (some even unraced) and one pattern winner who was four when she recorded her first success.

Adding in this year's European Group 1 winner does not change the number who won before May 1st of their juvenile year, whereas you can add Pinatubo (by Shamardal; 10th), Siskin (by First Defence; 11th) and Sealiway (by Galiway; 12th) to those who had won before June 1st. You can also add two more to those whose maiden success came after November 1st, and twelve to those who got off the mark as three-year-olds.

Month of birth
An early foaling date is generally deemed favourable, but only eleven winners of a Group 2 or Group 3 race last year were born in January: Armory, Lemista, Pablo Escobarr, Happy Power, Ventura Rebel, Maamora, Tabdeed, One Voice, Barney Roy, Summer Romance, and Delphi, listed in order of birth. Fifty-seven were born in February, forty-eight in March, and forty-two in April. Those horses born in the month of May are mostly or all the result of coverings that took place in June, and sixteen May-born horses won at least one of those pattern races.

Those foaled in May were: Nayef Road, Art Power, New Mandate, Divinely, Santosha, Twilight Payment, Brad The Brief, Glen Shiel, Nobel Prize, Top Rank, Battleground, Millisle, Dawn Patrol, Tiger Moth, High Definition, and Anthony Van Dyck, with the latter pair arriving on the 18th and 19th respectively.

Note on suffixes in names
Readers may notice that some horses have not been given a suffix with their names in the pedigree charts or in the various indexes.

This is not an error or omission. The suffix indicates the country in which the horse was born, but those who were born in Ireland or Great Britain did not get suffixes until 1988. Therefore, horses born in those countries before that year do not have one as part of their official name. Some older Canadian-bred horses (pre-1967) do not have them either. There is at least one database out there that seem to have put a GB by default after the name of all horses without a suffix; this is an error. There is also another well-known racing website that has replaced many, if not all, of the GB suffixes with UK, whereas a well-known Australian one has all the IREs as IRL and the GBs as GBR; these are also incorrect. The latter has also changed NZ to NZL and GER to DEU, which may add further confusion for any readers from that region of the world.

To quote the International Federation of Horseracing Authorities (IFHA), "The suffix between brackets is taken from the International Code of Suffixes ... and constitutes part of the animal's registered name."

Having come across various sources that change the suffixes in horses' names to suit their own style, I have been reminded again and again just how important those two- and three-letter codes can be. Change it and you could be taking about a completely different horse; they are, in effect, like a surname. An example I give when talking to a class about the issue is that of Eva Luna. To which horse are they referring if someone tells you that their horse comes from the family of Eva Luna? There are five horses of that name registered with Weatherbys, and if it's the talented one you want then you are probably choosing between the two who were born in 1992.

Eva Luna (USA) was a daughter of Alleged (by Hoist The Flag) and the Oaks-placed Media Luna (by Star Appeal) and, as one might expect with such a pedigree, she showed stamina on the track and has been passing it on at stud. The Juddmonte Farms homebred won the Group 3 Park Hill Stakes and Listed Galtres Stakes, she is the dam of the Group 1 St Leger winner Brian Boru (by Sadler's Wells), his classic-placed Group 2-winning closer-than-half-brother Sea Moon (by Beat Hollow), and the Group 2 Prix de Royallieu winner Moon Search (by Rainbow Quest). She is also the grandam of the Group 1 Derby and Group 1 Prix de l'Arc de Triomphe star Workforce (by King's Best).

The other one born that same year was Eva Luna (IRE), a Jim Bolger trainee who was one of the top juvenile fillies of the crop. She won the Group 1 Phoenix Stakes, Group 3 Railway Stakes and Listed Silver Flash Stakes, she was third in the Group 1 Moyglare Stud Stakes, and she comes from a prolific blacktype family. The daughter of Double Schwartz (by Double Form) and Guess Again (by Stradavinsky) is inbred 3x3 to Fanghorn (by Crocket), a classic-placed mare from whom a string of notable winners descends. This Eva Luna disappointed as a broodmare, but she is the grandam of the Group 2 Flying Childers Stakes winner Beacon (by Paco Boy) and the Dişi Tay Deneme (Turkish 1000 Guineas, a local Group 1 only) scorer Luna Lovegood (by Kaneko) and ancestor of a couple of other high-profile Turkish horses.

The stallion Acclamation is another current example. In this part of the world, we are most likely referring to Acclamation (GB), the 1999-born son of Royal Applause (by Waajib) and Princess Athena (by Ahonoora) who was a high-class sprinter before going on to become a Group 1-producing sire for Rathbarry Stud. He has also earned a good reputation as a sire of stallions. However, if you are in North America then chances are you are talking about Acclamation (USA), the 2006-born son of Unusual Heat (by Nureyev) and Winning In Style (by Silveyville). He was an Eclipse Award winner in 2011, won the Grade 1 Pacific Classic Stakes, two editions of the Grade 1 Eddie Read Stakes and three back-to-back runnings of the Grade 1 Charles Whittingham Handicap, and he stands in California where he has sired several six-figure earners and some blacktype horses.

Conclusion

The pattern schedule has expanded considerably in recent years and while there are many benefits to that, there are also too many occurrences of sub-pattern-class horses picking up wins and placings at that level. Similarly, though not dealt with in this volume, there are too many horses who are below listed class yet picking up blacktype from those events. Perhaps—and as various other writers have also suggested—it is time to trim the calendar; these races are supposed to identify the elite members of the year's various crops—and for the most part they do—but there should not be what some call 'cheap blacktype'. A more condensed programme should also lead to stronger competition and reduce the number of low single-digit fields we've been seeing too often.

The 2020 season was certainly different in how we, as spectators, were able to view it, with the Covid-19 situation restricting or eliminating attendances, but how lucky that we live in an age where so much racing from around the world is available for viewing, live or via soon-posted replays. Think of what we would have missed last year were it not for such technology. Disruptions look set to continue until the summer of 2021, if not into the autumn—it depends on how quickly each country can roll out its vaccination programme and begin easing and lifting restrictions—but, fingers crossed, by the time the flat season of 2022 comes around we should all be able to attend as much racing as we can manage. That is something to look forward to with enthusiasm.

So too is the array of talent that will be back in action this coming season, both established stars and less exposed but promising contenders. The British and Irish horse racing authorities managed to host an almost complete schedule of pattern-race action in 2020, remarkable given the circumstances, and high praise is due to all who made it happen.

Sieglinde McGee
February 15th, 2021

A CASE OF YOU (IRE)

It is good to see the smaller yards having big-race winners and John McConnell, who trains in Stamullen in Co Meath, was talking of a potential Group 1 Commonwealth Cup challenge after sending out his first ever pattern winner, A Case of You, at the Curragh in October. He also owned the colt, a late-March-born bay who was a €3,000 vendor buy-back at the Goffs Sportsman's Yearling Sale but was sold privately before Christmas.

A Case of You finished third in a one-mile maiden at Bellewstown in late August, a venue whose juvenile races have thrown up some of talented horses in the past few years. He then dropped a furlong in trip and won a soft-ground maiden at Down Royal by almost three lengths from a newcomer, Earls Rock. That colt, a first-crop son of Fascinating Rock (by Fastnet Rock), did not run again in Ireland or at two, but shortly before this book went to print, he made it two out of two for US trainer Phil d'Amato, following an easy mile maiden success at Santa Anita with listed success over six and a half furlongs at the same venue. A Case of You, on the other hand, also dropped in trip after his maiden success, this time to six furlongs and sixty-three yards for the Group 3 Jebel Ali Racecourse and Stables Anglesey Stakes, one of the races moved to a different slot in the calendar in the Covid-induced restructuring.

End-of-season blacktype contests can be a little thin on quality, especially when the ground gets soft, but although third-placed Giuliana had only been placed in one of her three prior outings, this race looked solid for its type. New Treasure, who sprang a surprise in the Group 3 Round Tower Stakes on heavy ground at the same venue at the end of August, had a three-pound penalty for that success and finished fourth, and the runner-up was the smart Ballydoyle colt Lipizzaner. He had been fourth in the Group 2 Norfolk Stakes, only beaten by five and a quarter lengths when sixth to Supremacy in the Group 1 Middle Park Stakes and, two weeks after this Curragh second, won a six-furlong listed contest on heavy ground at Doncaster. A Case of You won by a length and a quarter in the hands of Gary Carroll.

Clearly a considerable amount of improvement will be required if this colt is going to win or go close in the Group 1 Commonwealth Cup in June, and his juvenile form combined with the track career of his young sire Hot Streak (by Iffraaj) raises a question as to his potential effectiveness on the sort of fast ground that often prevails at that Ascot meeting. However, he could be anything and the underfoot conditions might suit him just fine. He was given a wildcard entry in the Tattersalls Autumn Horses-in-Training Sale in late October but was withdrawn.

A Case of You is a half-brother to a seven-furlong Laytown winner who also came within a nose of landing a 14-furlong handicap on the Fibresand at Southwell, and he is out of Karjera (by Key of Luck), a mare who failed to win but was a half-length runner-up in a one-mile handicap at Dundalk as a three-year-old, off a mark of sixty-five. That mare's full sister Lock And Key won sprints at the Curragh and Sligo, for the Edward Lynam stable, and was beaten by between a short head and a neck in three pattern races—the Group 3 Round Tower Stakes, the Group 3 Brownstown Stakes and the Group 3 International Stakes— before crossing the Atlantic and finishing runner-up in a six-and-a-half-furlong Grade 3 handicap at Santa Anita.

Their full brother Akanti also had ability and following a three-length maiden win over seven furlongs at the Curragh at the end of May of his two-year-old season, he dropped to six furlongs to win the Listed Rochestown Stakes at the same venue. He was trained then by Ger Lyons but later moved to the USA where he notched up another five wins, eventually taking his career earnings to just short of $150,000.

Lock's Heath (by Topsider), the grandam of A Case of You, was a winning half-sister to a stakes winner called Big Brown Bear (by Strike The Gold) and she was a daughter of Lock's Dream (by Youth), a Grade 3-placed stakes winner in North America and out of 1978's Group 3 Princess Royal Stakes scorer Trillionaire (by Vaguely Noble). And although it has no bearing on his potential and is of academic interest only, the fifth dam of next year's potential sprint ace, the prolific blacktype mare Amerigos Fancy (by Amerigo), is also the fifth dam of the triple Group 1 Melbourne Cup heroine Makybe Diva (by Desert King) and fourth dam of the multiple US Grade 1 star Get Stormy, sire of the top mile filly Got Stormy.

A Case of You is an interesting prospect for 2021. Shortly before this book went to print, it was announced that the colt would now be trained by Ado McGuinness.

SUMMARY DETAILS
Bred: Limestone and Tara Studs
Owned: John C McConnell
Trained: John C McConnell
Country: Ireland
Race record: 311-
Career highlights: 2 wins inc Jebel Ali Racecourse And Stables Anglesey Stakes (Gr3)

A CASE OF YOU (IRE) – 2018 bay colt

Hot Streak (IRE)	Iffraaj (GB)	Zafonic (USA)
		Pastorale (GB)
	Ashirah (USA)	Housebuster (USA)
		Manwah (USA)
Karjera (IRE)	Key of Luck (USA)	Chief's Crown (USA)
		Balbonella (USA)
	Lock's Heath (CAN)	Topsider (USA)
		Lock's Dream (USA)

A'ALI (IRE)

Society Rock (by Rock of Gibraltar) was a top-class sprinter who won the Group 1 Golden Jubilee Stakes, Group 1 Sprint Cup and Group 2 Duke of York Stakes and achieved a Timeform rating of 126. He was a popular addition to the team at Tally-Ho Stud in Ireland but, sadly, died young, leaving behind only three crops. Some of his progeny have been prolific winners, his best daughter is the Group 1-placed Grade 2 scorer The Mackem Bullet and his other five stakes winners include two high-class sons. The Group 1 Prix Morny winner Unfortunately covered fifty-two mares in his first season at Cheveley Park Stud in Newmarket and moved to Oak Lodge Stud in Ireland for his second year, getting a similar-sized book in 2020. The likely future stallion A'Ali is the other son of note.

He was a runner-up on his only start before being pitched straight into pattern company as a two-year-old and quickly established himself as one of the best five-furlong horses of his crop. He beat Ventura Rebel by a neck in the Group 2 Norfolk Stakes at the Royal Ascot meeting that June, followed up with a three-quarter-length defeat of My Love's Passion in the Group 2 Prix Robert Papin over a half-furlong farther at Deauville and, two months later, landed the Group 2 Flying Childers Stakes by a length from Dream Shot at Doncaster.

His trainer, Simon Crisford, is among the first UK-based handlers to have their licence amended to a training partnership: it is now the Simon and Ed Crisford team. Their star colt disappointed when unplaced behind Dubai Station in the Group 3 Betway Pavilion Stakes on the Tapeta at Newcastle on his seasonal reappearance in early June but then bounced back to beat Liberty Beach in the Group 3 Coral Charge on good ground at Sandown a month later. He had been slowly into his stride but, having hit the front with around a quarter of a furlong to go, he won a shade cosily by a length.

He went to Ireland a fortnight later and, on ground described as good-to-yielding, added the Group 2 Holden Plant Rentals Sapphire Stakes at the Curragh. He and the eventual fourth-place finisher Punita Arora raced in their own small group nearer the stands' side of the track and, although not hitting the front until near the finish, there was an inevitability to the result from some way back. Popular five-year-old Make A Challenge had gone for home on the far side of the track but his younger rival was powering through that furlong with such gusto that he always looked likely to get there. The final margin of victory was a length and the mare Rapid Reaction was another length and three-quarters behind in third.

York was the next stop and A'Ali was one of only two horses that most punters saw as any potential danger to the odds-on favourite Battaash in the Group 1 Coolmore Nunthorpe Stakes. Victory would be unlikely against one of the most brilliant five-furlong horses of the modern era, but he and fellow three-year-old Art Power were the pair expected to take second and third, in either order. He ran a good race but could never challenge and had to settle for fourth as the lower-rated four-year-olds Que Amoro and Moss Gill became the pair who chased home the champion. His final run of the year came on a return trip to Ireland a month later but it was a hugely disappointing effort. He had been sent off the favourite for the Group 1 Derrinstown Stud Flying Five Stakes at the Curragh on Irish Champions Weekend but never looked like winning, eventually eased and trailing home last of the fourteen runners. Glass Slippers took the top prize from Keep Busy, Sonaiyla and Maid In India, with Make A Challenge, in fifth, the first male to cross the line; there was half a length between each of those placings.

A'Ali was bred by Tally-Ho Stud, who sold him for £35,000 at the Goffs UK Premier Yearling Sale in 2018, and he was picked up by his current connections for £135,000 at the Goffs UK Breeze-Up Sale eight months later. He is the second foal of Motion Lass (by Motivator), his older sibling, Slowmo (by Kodiac), has won over five and six furlongs, and his dam's two-year-old for 2021 is a first-crop Cotai Glory (by Exceed And Excel) filly who was a vendor buy-back at the most recent edition of the Goffs UK Premier Yearling Sale. She has been named Heartbreak Lass.

Motion Lass was runner-up in a mile maiden on her debut at Leicester but well-beaten in four subsequent outings over further, but several of her siblings were prolific winners. They include the sprinter Keep It Dark (by Invincible Spirit), the miler Uncle Brit (by Efisio), and middle-distance horse Enforcer (by Efisio), a nine-furlong Group 3 scorer who finished third to Youmzain in the Group 1 Preis von Europa over twelve furlongs at Cologne, third to Shirocco in the Group 1 Coronation Cup at Epsom and fourth to Hurricane Run in the Group 1 King George VI and Queen Elizabeth Stakes at Ascot.

Tarneem (by Zilzal), the grandam of A'Ali, got her sole win over a mile at Brighton and she was a daughter of Willowy Mood (by Will Win), a dual Grade 3 and prolific listed scorer in the USA whose placings featured third in the Grade 1 Mother Goose Stakes. There are plenty of other stakes winners to be found among that mare's relations, and if you go back farther on the page you will find that Forest Princess (by Fleet Nasrullah), the fifth dam of A'Ali, is also the grandam of Caressing (by Honour And Glory). That two-year-old champion won the Grade 1 Breeders' Cup Juvenile Fillies in 2000, she was a dual Grade 3 winner at three, and her progeny include 2017's US champion three-year-old male, West Coast (by Flatter). He won the Grade 1 Travers Stakes and Grade 1 Pennsylvania Derby, was placed in the Grade 1 Breeders' Cup Classic, Group 1 Dubai World Cup and Grade 1 Pegasus World Cup Invitational Stakes, and the young Lane's End Farm stallion's first foals arrived last year.

A'Ali is a high-class sprinter who represents the Danehill branch of the Danzig (by Northern Dancer) line. He is due to run at Meydan before returning to Europe and there should be more good prizes to be won with him before he eventually retires to stud.

SUMMARY DETAILS
Bred: Tally-Ho Stud
Owned: Shaikh Duaij Al Khalifa
Trained: Simon & Ed Crisford
Country: England
Race record: 211010-01140-
Career highlights: 5 wins inc Holden Plant Rentals Sapphire Stakes (Gr2), Wainwright Flying Childers Stakes (Gr2), Darley

Prix Robert Papin (Gr2), Norfolk Stakes (Gr2), Coral Charge (Gr3)

A'ALI (IRE) – 2017 bay or brown colt

Society Rock (IRE)	Rock of Gibraltar (IRE)	Danehill (USA)
		Offshore Boom
	High Society (IRE)	Key of Luck (USA)
		Ela's Gold (IRE)
Motion Lass (GB)	Motivator (GB)	Montjeu (IRE)
		Out West (USA)
	Tarneem (USA)	Zilzal (USA)
		Willowy Mood (USA)

AL AASY (IRE)

There are many factors that can bring about improvement in a racehorse and, in most cases, you can take your pick from any or some of maturity, physique, temperament, distance, track, underfoot conditions, tactics, pedigree, trainer, rider, experience. Al Aasy, who had finished third in a seven-furlong contest on soft ground on the Rowley Mile course at Newmarket in late October of his two-year-old season, made his second start in a ten-furlong listed race on fast ground at the same venue in June of 2020. He finished only fifth that day, beaten by a total of ten and a half lengths by the subsequent classic star Mishriff, but looked a different proposition on his third start, also over that course.

This was a twelve-furlong novice race on soft ground and although he had only four rivals of which one was sent off at odds of 300/1 and finished third, it was hard not to have been impressed with his performance. He was always going well, he hit the front over a quarter of a mile from home and stormed clear for a ten-length victory. The rank outsider was another eight lengths behind, four lengths clear of the fourth-place finisher.

That probably did his confidence a lot of good, but it was his next start that advertised his promise as a potential Cup horse. The distance of the Group 3 Bahrain Trophy Stakes on the July course at Newmarket was reduced to thirteen furlongs a few years ago, a move that has strengthened its quality, and Al Aasy won the 2020 edition comfortably by one and three-quarter lengths from Dawn Rising. That rival was also making his fourth career start, he too had been a runaway winner over twelve furlongs the time before, and the Ballydoyle representative finished one and three-quarter lengths in front of the third, Al Dabaran, who was representing the Godolphin team. Listed scorer and subsequent Group 1 Preis der Diana (German Oaks) heroine Miss Yoda was almost five lengths farther back in fourth.

The runner-up was gelded and not seen out again, but Al Aasy, now with an official handicap mark of 108, went to Goodwood for the Group 3 John Pearce Racing Gordon Stakes. This twelve-furlong contest, which was run on good ground, attracted a strong field, but Derby sixth English King and Derby runner-up Khalifa

Sat disappointed, finishing fourth and fifth, and Al Aasy went from cruising three out to weakening and finishing in last place. Both the winner and third, Mogul and Subjectivist, went on to subsequent Group 1 success, and they were split that day by the capable Highland Chief, the margins being three-quarters of a length and the same.

Al Aasy was not seen in action again. The 300,000-guinea Tattersalls October Book 1 graduate was bred by the Tsuis' Sunderlands Holdings Inc and he is a son of their great homebred Sea The Stars (by Cape Cross). The Timeform 140-rated superstar has just turned fifteen, he stands at Gilltown Stud in Ireland and his seventy-three stakes winners include fourteen who have won at least once at the highest level, notably standouts such as Crystal Ocean, Harzand, Sea of Class, Sea The Moon, Star Catcher, Stradivarius, and Taghrooda.

His William Haggas-trained son is the first foal of a mile winner named Kitcara (by Shamardal), and that half-sister to the Group 2-placed, ten-furlong French stakes winner Kapour (by Toylsome) is a daughter of the pattern-placed, stakes-winning miler Kitcat (by Monsun). That mare's siblings feature Konigstiger (by Tiger Hill), who won the Group 1 Gran Criterium over a mile at two, Group 2 and Group 3 races over middle-distances at three and finished fourth to Nicaron in the Group 1 Deutsches Derby. She is also a full sister to the classic-placed pattern winner and blacktype producer Karavel and to the Group 3 Prix Minerve scorer Halla, and she is out of Kittiwake (by Barathea), a daughter of the talented Gull Nook (by Mill Reef) and so a half-sister to the top-class middle-distance horse Pentire (by Be My Guest).

He short-headed Freedom Cry in the Group 1 Irish Champion Stakes at three, beat Classic Cliche by almost two lengths to take the Group 1 King George VI and Queen Elizabeth Stakes at four, having finished a neck runner-up to Lammtarra in the race twelve months before. He was third to Halling in the Group 1 Eclipse Stakes, fourth to Cigar in the Listed Dubai World Cup and like the other stallion sons of champion sire Be My Guest (by Northern Dancer), had mixed results in Europe. However, he did well in the southern hemisphere, got leading sprinters, milers, middle-distance horses and stayers, several horses who won in excess of £1 million in prize money, and a Group 1 roll of honour that included Xcellent, King Mufhasa, Rangirangdoo, and shock Melbourne Cup winner Prince of Penzance.

Al Aasy looks as though he will stay fourteen furlongs and potentially two miles, and if he can stay those trips and more in 2021 then there could be plenty of lucrative targets at which he can take aim.

SUMMARY DETAILS
Bred: Sunderland Holding Inc
Owned: Hamdan Al Maktoum
Trained: William Haggas
Country: England
Race record: 3-0110-
Career highlights: 2 wins inc Bahrain Trophy Stakes (Gr3)

AL AASY (IRE) – 2017 bay colt

Sea The Stars (IRE)	Cape Cross (IRE)	Green Desert (USA)
		Park Appeal
	Urban Sea (USA)	Miswaki (USA)
		Allegretta
Kitcara (GB)	Shamardal (USA)	Giant's Causeway (USA)
		Helsinki (GB)
	Kitcat (GER)	Monsun (GER)
		Kittiwake (GB)

ALKUMAIT (GB)

Group 2 winner and now fourteen-year-old Whitsbury Manor Stud stallion Showcasing (by Oasis Dream) is well-established as one of the top British-based sires. His fifty-one stakes winners include the Group 1 stars Advertise (National Stud, first foals in 2021), Quiet Reflection and Mohaather (new to Nunnery Stud in 2021) and no less than six of his eleven Group/Grade 2 scorers have been placed at least once at the highest level. They include the young stallions Soldier's Call (Ballyhane Stud, first foals in 2021) and Tasleet (Nunnery Stud, first foals in 2020). Quiet Reflection, of course, is female and both her now two-year-old son and yearling daughter are by the phenomenal Galileo (by Sadler's Wells).

It remains to be seen just how far up the pecking order Alkumait will go among his sire's progeny, but with the Group 2 Dubai Duty Free Mill Reef Stakes on his CV and a first-year rating of 113, he looks a fine prospect. He was bred by Whitsbury Manor Stud, who sold him for 150,000 guineas in Newmarket as a foal in 2018, and Hamdan Al Maktoum's Shadwell Estate Company had to go to 220,000 guineas to secure him from Book 1 of the Tattersalls October Yearling the following autumn. He is trained by Marcus Tregoning, finished a one-length fourth over six furlongs on his debut at Newbury in mid-July, then easily won a maiden over the same trip at Goodwood before his big-race success.

He went to the front about a furlong from home at Newbury, drifted from the centre of the track over towards the eventual runner-up, Fivethousandtoone, and although looking a bit green, won nicely by three-quarters of a length. There was a further gap of two and three-quarter lengths back to the third, Rhythm Master, and the time for the race, on good ground, was below standard. The third had filled the same position behind Campanelle in the Group 1 Prix Morny on his previous start, whereas the second, fourth and fifth had won easily shortly before the race, fifth-place Bahrain Pride having taken a listed contest at Ripon. Prior pattern scorer Cairn Gorm was sixth, beaten by a total of five lengths.

Ground conditions would appear to be an important key to him as the soft going at Newmarket the following month was put forward as an explanation for his disappointing performance in the Group 1 Darley Dewhurst Stakes. He had pulled hard early in the race, he was under pressure a quarter of a mile from home and weakened soon afterwards, eventually trailing home last of the fourteen runners.

It remains to be seen whether Alkumait is a sprinter or a miler or perhaps one of those horses that are equally effective in both divisions; both sides of his pedigree offer that potential. His lightly raced half-sister Praised (by Pivotal) won over six furlongs at Redcar in September, and half-brother Gloves Lynch (by Mukhadram) was beaten by less than two lengths when third in a seven-furlong listed contest on very soft ground at Chantilly as a two-year-old. The Broghie Man (by Cityscape) is the best of his siblings and although that gelding pipped Speak In Colours in an extended five-and-a-half-furlong listed contest at Navan as a three-year-old, he stays seven on the flat and has been runner-up several times in maiden hurdles.

His dam, Suelita (by Dutch Art), won four sprints in Italy, and both of her siblings are of interest. Outer Space (by Acclamation) has won eight times, mostly over seven furlongs and most recently at Leicester at the end of June 2020, and it is he who chased home Hot Streak in the Group 3 Cornwallis Stakes over five furlongs at Ascot when they were two-year-olds. Ayr Missile (by Cadeaux Genereux), on the other hand, ran only six times but was narrowly beaten over six furlongs at Haydock on her debut and was later placed over five at Beverley. She is the dam of Living In The Past (by Bungle Inthejungle), who beat Liberty Beach by three-quarters of a length in the Group 2 Lowther Stakes in 2019 and finished just over four lengths adrift of Millisle when fifth in the Group 1 Cheveley Park Stakes. They are the only three foals out of the unraced Venoge (by Green Desert).

Third dam Horatia (by Machiavellian) stayed farther, won the Grade 3 Matchmaker Stakes and was third in the Grade 2 Long Island Handicap. That mare's siblings include the multiple Group 1-placed, triple Group 2-winning stayer Opinion Poll (by Halling) and her progeny feature Moment In Time (by Tiger Hill), a Group

3 Pinnacle Stakes winner and Group 2 Lancashire Oaks runner-up who finished third in the Grade 1 E P Taylor Stakes on a trip Canada. This is also the family of the Timeform 130-rated miler Markofdistinction (by Known Fact), that Group 1 Queen Elizabeth II Stakes star being a half-brother to Ahead (by Shirley Heights), the Grade 2-placed fourth dam of Alkumait. The family also added blacktype in 2020 via Al Siq (by Acclamation), a two-year-old granddaughter of Horatia's stakes-placed half-sister Isadora (by Sadler's Wells). The €116,000 SGA September Selected Yearling Sale purchase and half-sister to juvenile nine-furlong Group 3 scorer Atom Hearth Mother (by Rock of Gibraltar), won a listed contest over seven and a half furlongs at San Siro in early July and was runner-up in a similar race two months later before finishing down the field behind Tiger Tanaka in the Group 1 Prix Marcel Boussac at ParisLongchamp in October.

A chestnut full sister to Alkumait was sold for 200,000 guineas from Book 1 of the Tattersalls October Yearling Sale barely three weeks after after his Group 2 success, and they have a younger Frankel (by Galileo) half-brother that Juddmonte Farms bought for 550,000 guineas at the Tattersalls December Foal Sale, whereas their Pivotal (by Polar Falcon) half-sister Praised has considerable broodmare potential. There could be plenty more updates to come for this family's record in the next few seasons.

SUMMARY DETAILS
Bred: Whitsbury Manor Stud
Owned: Hamdan Al Maktoum
Trained: Marcus Tregoning
Country: England
Race record: 4110-
Career highlights: 2 wins inc Dubai Duty Free Mill Reef Stakes (Gr2)

ALKUMAIT (GB) – 2018 bay colt

Showcasing (GB)	Oasis Dream (GB)	**Green Desert (USA)**
		Hope (IRE)
	Arabesque (GB)	Zafonic (USA)
		Prophecy (IRE)
Suelita (GB)	Dutch Art (GB)	Medicean (GB)
		Halland Park Lass (IRE)
	Venoge (IRE)	**Green Desert (USA)**
		Horatia (IRE)

ALOHA STAR (IRE)

Juvenile Group 1 star Millisle, the Cheveley Park Stakes heroine of 2019, represents the first full crop in the second phase of Starspangledbanner's European stud career (there was a single foal, a filly, born by him in Europe in 2016) and Aloha Star is from the second one. He had much-publicised fertility trouble in his early days, now resolved, and remained in his native Australia after just two shuttle seasons to Ireland. But those small crops featured the Group 1 Prix Morny scorer The Wow Signal, Group 2 Queen Mary Stakes winner and Group 1 Commonwealth Cup third Anthem Alexander, and multiple pattern winner Home of The Brave, so there were plenty who were keen to see how he might fare if returning to this side of the Equator. His global blacktype tally stands at fourteen stakes winners.

The mid-March-born Aloha Star is a €42,000 graduate of the Goffs November Foal Sale and made €67,000 when offered at the Tattersalls Ireland September Yearling Sale the following year. She was well-beaten in the maiden won by More Beautiful over five furlongs on fast ground at Navan in early June, fared better when a three-length third in a similar contest on yielding at Tipperary eleven days later and then got off the mark with a half-length success at Bellewstown at the start of July. That Co Meath venue has seen the profile of its two-year-old races rise considerably in recent seasons, a growing number of those winners going on to blacktype success.

Aloha Star added her name to the list just 17 days after win there, springing a 33/1 surprise in pipping Frenetic by a head in the Group 2 Airlie Stud Stakes over six furlongs at the Curragh. It was a four-runner race on ground described as good-to-yielding, the odds-on runner-up had run away with a listed contest at the same venue on her previous start, the front pair were trying the distance for the first time and they finished one and three-quarter lengths and three-quarters of a length ahead of the other pair, Mother Earth and Inner Beauty.

Her next task was a much more difficult one and she was again overlooked in the market only to outperform her odds in style. She was one of five members of the ten-strong field with a prior pattern win to her name—the others were Laws of Indices, Steel Bull, The Lir Jet, and Ventura Tormenta—but it was the Jessica Harrington-trained Lucky Vega who landed the spoils, showing a fine turn of foot inside the final furlong to take the Group 1 Keeneland Phoenix Stakes by three and a half lengths. Aloha Star, who had been racing on the far side of the track, leaned in on The Lir Jet as they made their challenge, and although she short-headed that colt for second, their placings were reversed following a stewards' enquiry. Laws of Indices was another half-length back in fourth, a neck in front of the subsequent Group 1 Darley Dewhurst Stakes winner St Mark's Basilica.

Eye Smiling (by Equiano), who won over six furlongs at Chelmsford and Hamilton for the David O'Meara stable in June, and Aloha Star were bred by Patrick Beirne (Jnr) and they are the first two foals of their dam, Zain Art (by Excellent Art). Their now two-year-old half-brother was sold to Italian trainer Stefano Botti for £20,000 at the Tattersalls Ireland September Yearling Sale in Newmarket and that son of Mastercraftsman (by Danehill Dancer) is followed by a first-crop daughter of Ribchester (by Iffraaj). The mare, who was sold to Camas Park Stud for €390,000 at the rescheduled Goffs Breeding Stock Sale in December, was unraced but has a talented half-brother in Battalion (by Authorized) who, as you might expect given his sire, is a middle-distance horse. He has won the Listed Foundation Stakes at Goodwood and two listed contests at Lingfield and the double-digit tally of races in which he has been placed include the Group 3 St Simon Stakes, Group 3 Diamond Stakes, Group 3 Winter Hill Stakes and Group 3 September Stakes.

Aloha Star's grandam did not race either but she, Zigarra (by Halling) is out of the Group 3 Prix Perth winner and Group 2 Prix d'Astarte runner-up Danzigaway (by Danehill) and that makes her a relation to a string of notable horses. Her half-brother Silent Name (by Sunday Silence) was a listed winner in France and a multiple Grade 1-placed Grade 2 scorer in the USA before going on to become champion sire in Canada, and her siblings also include Galiway (by Galileo), the pattern-placed stakes-winning young Haras de Colleville stallion who has achieved some eye-catching results in France. His first crop includes the Group 3 scorer Kenway and listed-race winner Wanaway, and his second crop is headlined by Sealiway, the colt who ran away with the Group 1 Prix Jean-Luc Lagardere at ParisLongchamp in October.

They also have another half-brother of note in Salto (by Pivotal). He didn't win a stakes race but he was runner-up in the Group 1 Criterium International at two, placed in a string of graded races at a mile in North America, and went to stud in Brazil where his stakes include the middle-distance Grade 1 stars Naomi Broadway and Oberyn. However, there won't be any stallion career for their relation Slalom (by Intello) as that Group 2 Prix Noailles winner and Group 1 Grand Prix de Paris runner-up (by half a length to Japan), who is out of Zigarra's half-sister Zagzig (by Selkirk), is now listed on France-Galop as a gelding.

If you look further back on the page then you find that Danzigaway is out of Blushing Away (by Blushing Groom), a stakes-placed daughter of the Grade 1-placed juvenile US Grade 2 scorer Sweet Revenge (by Raja Baba), and so she is a half-sister to the high-class miler and somewhat successful stallion Gold Away (by Goldneyev). He won the Group 2 Prix du Muguet and a trio of Group 3 contests, he was placed in the Group 1 Prix Maurice de Gheest, Group 1 Prix Jean Prat, Group 1 Prix d'Ispahan and two editions of the Group 1 Prix du Moulin de Longchamp, and he spent his stallion career at Haras du Quesnay in France. The Group 1 star Alexander Golden is easily his standout performer.

All of this makes Aloha Star an interesting three-year-old prospect for 2021. She is clearly effective at six furlongs and it is possible that she could be a Commonwealth Cup or Prix Jean Prat horse in the making, but if she has the sort of distance aptitude of many of the more notable members of her family, then there is the potential that a mile might be within her range too.

SUMMARY DETAILS

Bred: Patrick Beirne (jnr)
Owned: LNJ Foxwoods
Trained: Fozzy Stack
Country: Ireland
Race record: 03113-

Career highlights: 2 wins inc Airlie Stud Stakes (Gr2), 3rd Keeneland Phoenix Stakes (Gr1)

ALOHA STAR (IRE) 2018 bay filly

Starspangledbanner (AUS)	Choisir (AUS)	Danehill Dancer (IRE)
		Great Selection (AUS)
	Gold Anthem (AUS)	Made of Gold (USA)
		National Song (AUS)
Zain Art (IRE)	Excellent Art (GB)	Pivotal (GB)
		Obsessive (USA)
	Zigarra (GB)	Halling (USA)
		Danzigaway (USA)

ANGEL POWER (GB)

Dual French classic star Lope de Vega (by Shamardal) has just turned fourteen and the Ballylinch Stud team member is one of the most expensive stallions in Europe; his fee for 2021 is €125,000. His seventy-seven stakes winners include a dozen who have won at least once at the highest level, including a trio of his southern hemisphere-bred stock who have hit that target. His latest crop to race has already yielded two top-level winners, Aunt Pearl in the USA and Lucky Vega in Ireland, his classic-winning son Phoenix of Spain was one of the most popular new sires of 2020 and covered 148 mares in his debut season at the Irish National Stud, whereas first-crop son Belardo, a Group 1 winner at two and four years of age, was a leading freshman sire last year who already has three pattern winners and a listed scorer to his name.

Angel Power is further down the pecking order of the stallion's best runners but she is a filly with plenty of talent. The Roger Varian-trained bay can boast five wins and three placings from eight starts and after easily winning a handicap over the extended ten furlongs at York's Ebor Meeting in August, she reeled off a blacktype hat-trick. First came a listed contest at over ten and a half furlongs on good-to-soft at ParisLongchamp in early September, which she won by three-quarters of a length from Extreme Frost. The ground was soft at Newmarket a month later, as it had been when she finished third on her debut at that venue eleven months before, but she hit the front with just under a furlong to go in the Group 3 Darley Pride Stakes and then pulled away from the field to take the ten-furlong test by two and a half lengths from the strong-finishing Anna Nerium.

Her final outing of the year was in Italy in early November where, on good ground at Capannelle, she made all to beat the pattern-winning French mare Spirit of Nelson by two and a half lengths in the Group 2 Premio Lydia Tesio, also over ten furlongs. A group of five had flashed past the post together in a battle for the minor placings, the margins between second to sixth being a nose, short head, nose and nose. Three-year-old No Limit Credit, a German pattern winner who was runner-up in that country's

Group 2 1000 Guineas, picked up third ahead of the multiple blacktype-placed Santa Rita, pattern winner Elisa Again, and Grand Glory, a French Group 3 scorer who finished third to Channel in 2019's Group 1 Prix de Diane (French Oaks).

A 35,000-guinea Tattersalls December Foal Sale graduate who was sold on for 150,000 guineas from the Book 1 catalogue at the same venue the following October, Angel Power was bred by Anita Wigan who bought her dam, Burning Rules (by Aussie Rules), for 85,000 guineas in Newmarket as an in-foal four-year-old. Her year-younger half-sister Burkina Faso (by Mukhadram) has not yet raced and the now two-year-old sibling, also a filly, has been named Bellport (by Bated Breath). The mare did not have a foal in 2020 but was bred back to Lope de Vega.

Angel Power can be described as being a three-parts sister to the Group 3 Killavullan Stakes winner and Group 1 Irish 2,000 Guineas third Blue de Vega (by Lope de Vega). His dam, her grandam, is the placed Montjeu (by Sadler's Wells) mare Burning Heights, a half-sister to the Group 3 St Leger Italiano scorer Burma Gold and out of Bougainvillea (by Acatenango), a mare who has two celebrity siblings, both of whom won the Group 1 Deutsches Derby. Boreal (by Java Gold) added the Group 1 Coronation Cup to his classic success whereas champion filly Borgia (by Acatenango) added the Group 1 Grosser Preis von Baden and Group 2 Hong Kong Vase to hers. She was runner-up in the Grade 1 Breeders' Cup Turf and Group 2 Preis der Diana (German Oaks), third in the Group 1 Prix de l'Arc de Triomphe, and her string of blacktype descendants include her Group 1 Prix Vermeille-winning granddaughter Baltic Baroness (by Shamardal).

Britannia (by Tarim), the fourth dam of Angel Power, was also a champion, and the Group 2 Deutsches St Leger winner and Group 2 Preis der Diana runner-up was a half-sister to the Group 2-winning German middle-distance horse Buenos (by Aspros). This is a top German family and this will make her an exciting prospect she goes to stud. However, she is to remain in training as a four-year-old so there could be more good prizes to be won with her before that time comes.

SUMMARY DETAILS

Bred: Mrs Anita Wigan
Owned: King Power Racing Co Ltd
Trained: Roger Varian
Country: England
Race record: 3-1221111-
Career highlights: 5 wins inc Premio Lydia Tesio (Gr2), Darley Pride Stakes (Gr3), Prix de Liancourt (L)

ANGEL POWER (GB) – 2017 bay filly

Lope de Vega (IRE)	Shamardal (USA)	Giant's Causeway (USA)
		Helsinki (GB)
	Lady Vettori (GB)	Vettori (IRE)
		Lady Golconda (FR)
Burning Rules (IRE)	Aussie Rules (USA)	Danehill (USA)
		Last Second (IRE)
	Burning Heights (GER)	Montjeu (IRE)
		Bougainvillea (GER)

ANTHONY VAN DYCK (IRE)

The 2019 Group 1 Derby at Epsom produced a bunch finish and went to a well-exposed colt who not only did not end up the most highly rated runner in the race but failed to win again from five more starts that season. His end-of-year Timeform rating was low for a winner of the premier classic, but as noted in his essay here last year, there was reason to hope that he might be capable of better as a four-year-old. Why? He was a May 19th foal, which made him just thirteen days past his physical third birthday when he won his classic. Anthony Van Dyck, who was Timeform-rated 118 at two and 123 at three, reached a figure of 127 from that organisation at four. Sadly, he suffered a fatal injury in Australia in November.

The colt's good juvenile form and international three-year-old season were well-covered in last year's volume, as was an examination of his pedigree. To recap the latter, it is sufficient to point out that the late son of the prolific champion sire Galileo (by Sadler's Wells) was out of Believe'n'Succeed (by Exceed And Excel), an Australian juvenile Group 3 scorer whose other progeny include the classic-placed Group 1-winning sprinter Bounding (by Lonhro), a champion in New Zealand. The mare's siblings include two other stakes winners and one of those, the five-furlong Group 2 scorer Kuroshio, is at stud in Ireland. He did the reverse-shuttle trip from Australia to Overbury Stud in Gloucestershire in 2015, left behind a small crop, remained in his native land and only returned to Europe in 2019. He stands at Starfield Stud in Co Westmeath where he covered 132 mares in 2020. The reason for his return and newfound appeal was the results achieved from that initial European crop. He had four blacktype earners which include the Group 3 Coral Charge and Listed Scurry Stakes winner Kurious and the Group 2 Vintage Stakes runner-up Dunkerron. Despite the recent Australian connections, it is a North American family whose best include the Grade 1 stars Morning Line (by Tiznow) and November Snow (by Storm Cat), the latter the third dam of Anthony Van Dyck.

He kicked off his four-year-old campaign at Newmarket in June where he kept on well in the closing stages but never looked like catching the front-running Ghaiyyath in the Group 1 Hurworth Bloodstock Coronation Cup Stakes on ground described as good-to-firm. The race was run in track-record time, he was two and a half lengths down at the line and had star stayer Stradivarius that same margin behind him in third. He was again staying on at the finish at Ascot a fortnight later but had to settle for fifth to Fanny Logan in the Group 2 Hardwicke Stakes on soft ground, a disappointing effort given that, bar the 117-rated and ill-fated Defoe (third), those in front of him all had official handicap marks from 108 to 110.

However, his next two starts were excellent. He went to the front after a furlong of the Group 2 Qatar Prix Foy at ParisLongchamp in mid-September, set a steady gallop and turned the race into a bit of a sprint. Reducing the emphasis on stamina was a tactical move against Stradivarius, and although the chestnut ran on strongly, as you would expect, Anthony Van Dyck was always holding him. He won by a short neck, with Nagano Gold another length and a quarter back in third. He was in Australia a month later and carried top weight in the Group 1 Stella Artois Caulfield Cup over twelve furlongs on good-to-soft. After initially settling towards the rear, local star Hugh Bowman asked him for his effort two out, the colt quickened in the final furlong and ran on well, but he found the eight-pound weight concession to the outstanding New Zealand-bred mare Verry Elleegant just beyond him. The five-year-old, trained in Australia by Chris Waller, beat him by a head, The Chosen One (rec. 11lbs), Prince of Arran (rec. 9lbs), Finche (rec. 9lbs) and Avilius (rec. 3lbs) followed him home, with the Joseph O'Brien-trained Buckhurst (rec. 8lbs) crossing the line in seventh. It was arguably the best performance of his career.

Anthony Van Dyck again had top weight in the Group 1 Lexus Melbourne Cup at Flemington two and a half weeks later, meeting many of the same rivals he'd faced at Caulfield. Sadly, stumbled over a quarter of a mile from home and was immediately pulled up by Bowman; the fetlock injury proved fatal. Aside from the obvious loss to his connections, who also lost the classic-placed Group 2 scorer and future stallion prospect Wichita following complications after a work-related injury shortly after he arrived in Australia, there is also the loss to the breeding side too. As a notable two-year-old and a Derby-winning son of Galileo who came from a family that has produced several blacktype sires, including his dam's full brother Kuroshio, he would surely have been a popular and promising addition to the stallion ranks.

SUMMARY DETAILS

Bred: Orpendale, Chelston & Wynatt
Owned: Mrs John Magnier, Michael Tabor & Derrick Smith
Trained: Aidan O'Brien
Country: Ireland
Race record: 0111230-1120330-2012P-
Career highlights: 6 wins inc Investec Derby Stakes (Gr1), Qatar Prix Foy (Gr2), Galileo Irish EBF Futurity Stakes (Gr2), Japan Racing Association Tyros Stakes (Gr3), RaceBets Derby Trial Stakes (L), 2nd Stella Artois Caulfield Cup (Gr1), Hurworth Bloodstock Coronation Cup (Gr1), Dubai Duty Free Irish Derby (Gr1), Goffs Vincent O'Brien National Stakes (Gr1), 3rd Longines Breeders' Cup Turf (Gr1), Qipco Irish Champion Stakes (Gr1), Darley Dewhurst Stakes (Gr1)

ANTHONY VAN DYCK (IRE) – 2016 bay colt

Galileo (IRE)	Sadler's Wells (USA)	Northern Dancer
		Fairy Bridge (USA)
	Urban Sea (USA)	Miswaki (USA)
		Allegretta
Believe'n'Succeed (AUS)	Exceed And Excel (AUS)	Danehill (USA)
		Patrona (USA)
	Arctic Drift (USA)	Gone West (USA)
		November Snow (USA)

ANTONIA DE VEGA (IRE)

Antonia de Vega (by Lope de Vega) contributed to her sire's excellent season with two blacktype wins from four starts in 2020, both achieved by a half-length margin over twelve furlongs. First came the Listed Pontefract Castle Fillies' Stakes at Pontefract in mid-June where she hit the front a half a furlong from home and kept on well to hold off the late challenge of La Lune in a quick time. She followed up over three months later, adding the Group 3 Princess Royal Muhaarar Stakes at Newmarket. There were only four runners that day, but it was clearly a two-horse race from over two furlongs out. Antonia de Vega went past Sea of Faith and Katara quite easily and it was left to the three-year-old Alpinista, on the rails, to mount a challenge. That grey switched to her rival's outside after the furlong pole, changed her legs and kept on steadily to the finish, but the post came in time for the bay.

Both of those races were on good ground, as was her Group 3 Prestige Stakes success as a two-year-old, but it was soft at Ascot next time and heavy at Munich in November and she was well-beaten on both occasions. The first was the Group 1 Qipco British Champions Fillies & Mares Stakes, won by Wonderful Tonight, and the latter the Group 1 Allianz - Grosser Preis von Bayern, won by Stormy Queen. She had been a three-quarter-length fourth to Nancho on soft ground in that same German feature twelve months before. Her overall record stands at five wins and no placings from ten starts, and aside from her juvenile debut success over seven furlongs on fast ground at the July Course in Newmarket as a two-year-old, the only win not yet mentioned is her four-length score in a ten-furlong listed contest on soft ground at Newbury in June 2019.

Antonia de Vega is a €130,000 graduate of the Goffs Orby Sale, she was bred by Fermoir Ltd and has been trained throughout her career by Ralph Beckett. She is the first foal of Witches Brew (by Duke of Marmalade), who was runner-up in the Listed Platinum Stakes over a mile at Cork and third in the Listed Knockaire Stakes over seven furlongs at Leopardstown when trained by Edward Lynam in Ireland, and Beckett also has the mare's now two-year-old, a full sister to her multiple stakes-winning daughter. The mare's had another Lope de Vega filly in 2020 and was bred back to the stallion, whereas her half-brother Al Wukair (by Dream Ahead), who won the Group 1 Prix Jacques le Marois and finished third to Churchill and Barney Roy in the Group 1 2000 Guineas, stands at Haras de Bouquetot and will have his first runners in 2021. Caerlina (by Caerleon), the third dam of Antonia de Vega, won the Group 1 Prix de Diane (French Oaks), was runner-up in the Group 1 Prix Marcel Boussac and third in the Group 1 Poule d'Essai des Pouliches (French 1000 Guineas). Her descendants include the Group/Grade 2 scorers Tam Lin (by Selkirk) and Curren Mirotic (by Hearts Cry) and her relations feature Sri Putra (by Oasis Dream) and One World (by Captain Al), the latter a Grade 1 winner in South Africa and the former a Group 1 Coral-Eclipse-placed dual Group 2 winner.

The 109-rated Antonia de Vega has now retired to stud. She was a talented middle-distance filly who won on soft but seemed best suited to racing on good ground. She is well-related, is inbred 4x4x3 to Machiavellian (by Mr Prospector) and has the potential to become a broodmare of note.

SUMMARY DETAILS
Bred: Fermoir Ltd
Owned: Waverley Racing
Trained: Ralph Beckett
Country: England
Race record: 110-104-1100-
Career highlights: 5 wins inc Princess Royal Muhaarar Stakes (Gr3), Ladbrokes Prestige Stakes (Gr3), Pontefract Castle Fillies' Stakes (L), Johnnie Lewis Memorial EBF Stakes (L)

ANTONIA DE VEGA (IRE) – 2016 bay filly

Lope de Vega (IRE)	Shamardal (USA)	Giant's Causeway (USA)
		Helsinki (GB)
	Lady Vettori (GB)	Vettori (IRE)
		Lady Golconda (FR)
Witches Brew (IRE)	Duke of Marmalade (IRE)	Danehill (USA)
		Love Me True (USA)
	Macheera (IRE)	Machiavellian (USA)
		Caerlina (IRE)

ARMORY (IRE)

Armory has the odd distinction of having been beaten by a total of twenty-nine lengths while finishing second in two Group 1 races as a two-year-old. He chased home champion Pinatubo in the Group 1 Goffs Vincent O'Brien National Stakes over seven furlongs at the Curragh and was the twenty-length runner-up in a two-horse edition of the Group 1 Criterium International over the same trip on heavy at ParisLongchamp six weeks later. However, that does not tell his story; there is far more to this talented colt and it would not be a surprise to see him win at the highest level in 2021.

The Coolmore homebred ran seven times at two and five times in 2020 and his tally of four wins and six placings, plus two fourth-place finishes in Group 1 company, has yielded over €900,000 in prize money. He has done all of his racing from seven to ten furlongs, he seems to handle any surface other than heavy, and he has been among the best of his age group in both of his seasons to race. He won his maiden on his second start, followed that with a five-length score in the Group 3 Japan Racing Association Tyros Stakes at Leopardstown and followed-up with a three-quarter-length and one-length defeat of Rebel Tale and Geometrical in the Group 2 Galileo Irish EBF Futurity Stakes at the Curragh. It is fair to say that was a weak race for the grade and his third-place finish in the Group 1 Prix Jean-Luc Lagardere at ParisLongchamp in early October was much better. The ground was very soft that day, the mile represented his only time not running over seven furlongs that season, and he was only beaten by margins of three-quarters of a length and a short neck by Victor Ludorum and Alson. The latter is the colt who came home twenty lengths clear in the mud next time the pair met. His effort behind Pinatubo was also good. Few juveniles of any era could have lived with Godolphin's star that day, but Armory as a juvenile is better judged for having beaten his talented stablemate Arizona by a neck, the pair finishing two and a quarter lengths clear of their closest pursuer.

As a son of Galileo (by Sadler's Wells) and After (by Danehill Dancer)—she was placed in the Group 3 Ballyogan Stakes, Group

3 Anglesey Stakes and Group 3 Brownstown Stakes—there was every reason to hope that he could become a high-class mile-to-ten-furlong horse as a three-year-old. He has not disappointed. He began his season by matching one of his dam's feats, missing out on a classic placing by taking fourth in one. She filled that position in Beauty Parlour's Group 1 Poule d'Essai des Pouliches (French 1000 Guineas), whereas he ran behind Siskin in the Group 1 Tattersalls Irish 2,000 Guineas. Indeed, he is unlucky not to have a classic placing on his record as he met with some trouble in running, bumped and got bumped, but stayed on strongly only for the line to come a stride too soon. Siskin beat Vatican City by a length and three-quarters, and there was a gap of three-quarters of a length back to Lope Y Fernandez, whose nose hit the line just before Armory's. The placings remained unaltered after a stewards' enquiry.

He had a challenging task for his next start, which pitched him straight into all-aged Group 1 company. It was the Tattersalls Gold Cup over ten furlongs at the Curragh in late July, moved to that slot due to the Covid-19-enforced rejigging of the season. Magical made all for a comfortable two-and-a-quarter-length victory, beating the often-placed but subsequent Group 1 scorer Sir Dragonet, with that colt two lengths in front of the strong-finishing Search For A Song, winner of the previous season's Group 1 Irish St Leger. She would go on to a repeat victory in that fourteen-furlong test on her next start. Armory was half a length farther back in fourth, followed home by Leo de Fury and Buckhurst.

That was an adequate effort, as was his neck and one-length defeat of Numerian and Sinawann in the Group 3 Irish Field Celebrating 150 Years Royal Whip Stakes over the course and distance the following month, a race in which he again met with traffic problems, had to switch, quickened, but this time got up in time. However, it was his next two starts that showed his potential to win a big one. He and old rival Leo de Fury were the only non-top-level winners in the small but select line-up for the Group 1 Irish Champion Stakes at Leopardstown in mid-September, and although he never looked like getting to the star pair who dominated, Magical and Ghaiyyath, he was running on well in the closing stages and just managed to hold off Sottsass at the line, taking third place. The pair were four and a half lengths clear of Japan and a length and quarter adrift of Ghaiyyath who was, in turn, three-quarters of a length behind Magical. Sottsass, the previous year's Group 1 Prix du Jockey Club (French Derby) winner, won the Group 1 Prix de l'Arc de Triomphe a few weeks later.

Armory, on the other hand, went to Australia though had to pass a veterinary inspection on the morning before the Group 1 Ladbrokes Cox Plate at Moonee Valley due to a reported lameness issue that arose the previous day. He did. And, in the race itself, which was run on soft ground, he began to move forward from over two furlongs out, hit the front about a furlong later and got into a brief battle with his former stablemate Sir Dragonet who pulled away to win by a length and a quarter. He finished three-quarters of a length in front of the Irish-bred but Australian-trained classic star Russian Camelot with another ex-European, Mugatoo, fourth. A Henrythenavigator (by Kingmambo) gelding who had been a head runner-up in a Group 1 handicap on his previous start, Mugatoo rounded out a remarkable one-two-three-four in the race for horses carrying the IRE suffix. The first three were male-line descendants of the prolific champion sire Sadler's Wells (by Northern Dancer) and all four, in fact the first five home, were out of mares that represented branches of Danzig's (by Northern Dancer) male line.

All four of After's offspring are by Galileo with only the 2019 one being a filly. Bond Street won over a mile at Dundalk and seven furlongs at Leopardstown, was runner-up in a Premier Handicap over eight and a half furlongs at Galway and then exported to North America at the end of his three-year-old season. Hms Seahorse (it's punctuated as Hms, according to Weatherbys, and not as the HMS you'd expect) was fourth in Mac Swiney's maiden over seven furlongs on yielding ground at the Curragh in mid-July. He has not been seen out since but holds entries in several classics. After was covered again by Galileo in 2019 but there was no return, and she was bred back to him again last year.

Should Hms Seahorse or any of the mare's subsequent foals finish fourth in a classic then they would be keeping up something of a family tradition. The fourth-place finishes of After and Armory were noted above, but After's half-brother Temps Au Temps (by Invincible Spirit) did it too, in his case taking fourth, at 66/1, to Tin Horse in the Group 1 Poule d'Essai des Poulains (French 2000 Guineas). His best win came in a listed race. Their unraced half-sister Life of Pi (by Sea The Stars) also has a three-year-old this coming season although he, Bahrain Pride (by Kodiac), does not currently hold any classic entries. He beat Fivethousandtoone in a six-furlong maiden on his debut at Windsor in mid-August, followed up in the Listed Champion 2yo Trophy in similar conditions at Ripon a fortnight later, and was not disgraced when fifth to Alkumait in the Group 2 Mill Reef Stakes at Newbury or fourth to Winter Power in the Group 3 Cornwallis Stakes at Newmarket. This Simon and Ed Crisford-trained 300,000-guinea Tattersalls Craven Breeze-up graduate is bred to stay a mile but looks like he might be a sprinter.

Noahs Ark (by Charnwood Forest), the grandam of Armory, was listed-placed at the Curragh and Grade 1-placed at Belmont Park, she is a sister to Blueberry Forest, who won fifteen times in total and was multiple Group 3-placed in Germany. The third dam is Abstraction (by Rainbow Quest), a sister to the Group 2 Prix du Conseil de Paris scorer De Quest and his stakes-winning full brother Source of Light. Their half-sister Wandesta (by Nashwan) was a multiple Grade 1 star in California, whereas Valencia (by Kenmare), another sibling, is the non-winning dam of four talented speed horses and the grandam of two horses of note. That quartet consists of the Group 2 Flying Five Stakes winner Deportivo (by Night Shift), Group 3 Supreme Stakes scorer So Blessed (by Dansili), juvenile listed winner Irish Vale (by Wolfhound), and Cantabria (by Dansili) who was multiple pattern placed from seven to eight and a half furlongs.

Their half-sister Affluent (by Oasis Dream) got both of her wins over five furlongs and she is the dam of Daahyeh (by Bated Breath) and Saint Lawrence (by Al Kazeem). The latter was a pattern-placed stakes winner over seven furlongs in England in 2020 although does not hold any classic entries, whereas his year-older half-sister, who ran just once last season, was one of the juvenile stars of 2019. Daahyeh won the Group 2 Rockfel Stakes and Group 3 Albany Stakes and was runner-up in each of the Grade 1 Breeders' Cup Juvenile Filly Turf (to Sharing), Group 1 Moyglare Stud Stakes (to Love) and Group 2 Duchess of Cambridge Stakes (to Raffle Prize).

If you go back another step on the page then you will find that the fourth dam of Armory is De Stael (by Nijinsky), a winning full sister to the Group 1 Coronation Cup winner Quiet Fling. Her siblings also include the middle-distance pattern winners Armistice Day (by Rheingold) and Peacetime (by Nijinsky) as well as Intermission (by Stage Door Johnny), an Irish Cambridgeshire Handicap heroine who became a broodmare of influence. The mare's descendants include Group 1 July Cup and Group 1 Prix de l'Abbaye de Longchamp star Continent (by Lake Coniston), US Grade 1 scorer Midships (by Mizzen Mast), Group 1 Grand Prix de Paris victor Zambezi Sun (by Dansili), plus the Group/Grade 2 winners Bon Point (by Soviet Star), Invited Guest (by Be My Guest), Kalabar (by Kahyasi), Mission Boy (by Paco Boy) and Much Faster (by Fasliyev).

Armory finished his three-year-old season on an official handicap mark of 120. It would be no surprise to see him win at the highest level in 2021, and given his pedigree, connections, good juvenile form and excellent three-year-old season, it seems like that there will be a stallion career awaiting him at the end of his racing days.

SUMMARY DETAILS

Bred: Coolmore
Owned: Mrs John Magnier, Michael Tabor & Derrick Smith
Trained: Aidan O'Brien
Country: Ireland
Race record: 3111232-44132-
Career highlights: 4 wins inc Galileo Irish EBF Futurity Stakes (Gr2), Irish Field Celebrating 150 Years Royal Whip Stakes (Gr3), Japan Racing Association Tyros Stakes (Gr3), 2nd Ladbrokes Cox Plate (Gr1), Goffs Vincent O'Brien National Stakes (Gr1), Criterium International (Gr1), 3rd Irish Champion

Stakes (Gr1), Qatar Prix Jean-Luc Lagardere sponsorise par Manateq (Gr1)

ARMORY (IRE) 2017 bay colt

Galileo (IRE)	Sadler's Wells (USA)	Northern Dancer
		Fairy Bridge (USA)
	Urban Sea (USA)	Miswaki (USA)
		Allegretta
After (IRE)	Danehill Dancer (IRE)	Danehill (USA)
		Mira Adonde (USA)
	Noahs Ark (IRE)	Charnwood Forest (IRE)
		Abstraction (GB)

ART POWER (IRE)

The Group 1-winning miler Keltos (by Kendor) had a tiny first crop but the Kevin Prendergast-trained Evening Time was among those few foals. She won both of her starts at two, including a five-length score in the Listed Flame of Tara Stakes over six furlongs at the Curragh, she added a five-length win the Listed Sweet Mimosa Stakes over the same trip at Leopardstown the following summer and she was twice Group 3-placed. These, plus her nine-length debut win at Fairyhouse, were all on varying degrees of soft ground and her one time on a faster surface was also her sole attempt at a mile; it was an unplaced run in the Group 1 Matron Stakes.

Evening Time comes from a prolific blacktype family, all of her first eight foals have won at least once and four of them are blacktype horses. Shaan (by Iffraaj) has been listed placed at Gulfstream Park, Morning Frost (by Duke of Marmalade) was a six-and-a-half-furlong listed scorer in France, Penny Pepper (by Fast Company) won the Group 3 Ballyogan Stakes over six furlongs on soft-to-heavy at the Curragh, and Art Power easily beat Millisle in the Group 3 Coolmore Sioux Nation Lacken Stakes over the same trip at Naas in early July.

That two-and-a-half-length score, his fourth win in a row from five starts, a sequence achieved by an aggregate of sixteen and a half lengths, followed an impressive defeat of Keep Busy and nineteen other rivals in a five-furlong handicap at Royal Ascot. His sequence ended when he finished a six-length sixth to Battaash in the Group 1 Coolmore Nunthorpe Stakes on good ground at York in August, and although he was also out of the frame on his final two runs of the year, they were excellent fourth-place finishes on soft ground. He was only beaten by a total of two and a half lengths when fourth to Dream of Dreams in the Group 1 Betfair Sprint Cup Stakes at Haydock and by margins of a nose, half a length and half a length when fourth in the Group 1 Qipco British Champions Sprint Stakes at Ascot. Glen Shiel, Brando and One Master were the three that finished ahead of him, each of them at least twice his age.

Art Power, a Tim Easterby-trained €110,000 Goffs Orby Sale graduate who was bred by Owenstown Bloodstock Ltd, is among sixty-eight stakes winners by Yeomanstown Stud's standard-bearer Dark Angel (by Acclamation). He could be a leading player on the sprint scene in 2021 and given the number of his sire's sons who have already joined the ranks, he may have a stallion career ahead of him when his track days end.

SUMMARY DETAILS

Bred: Owenstown Bloodstock Ltd
Owned: King Power Racing Co Ltd
Trained: Tim Easterby
Country: England
Race record: 31-111044-
Career highlights: 4 wins inc Coolmore Sioux Nation Lacken Stakes (Gr3)

ART POWER (IRE) – 2017 grey colt

		Royal Applause (GB)
Dark Angel (IRE)	Acclamation (GB)	Royal Applause (GB)
		Princess Athena
	Midnight Angel (GB)	Machiavellian (USA)
		Night At Sea
Evening Time (IRE)	Keltos (FR)	Kendor (FR)
		Loxandra (GB)
	Shadow Casting (GB)	Warning
		Fanciful (FR)

ASPETAR (FR)

Aspetar's latest season took in just three races, two of them in England in July and the final one a disappointing effort on soft ground in Australia. That was the Group 1 Ladbrokes Cox Plate over ten furlongs at Caulfield in which he never threatened. Three months before that he had beaten Fox Chairman by one and a half lengths to add the Group 2 Sky Bet York Stakes to his two big wins from 2019. Lord Glitters was another half a length back in third and two and three-quarter lengths in front of Telecaster. Regal Reality, Elarqam and the disappointing King of Comedy completed the line-up. Fox Chairman had also been in opposition in the Listed Coral Gala Stakes over a few yards shorter at Sandown three weeks before, but that day the gap between them was only a neck as Aspetar finished runner-up, by the same margin, to Magny Cours, who was carrying an extra three pounds.

His career and pedigree were reviewed in detail in *European Group 1 Winners of 2019*, so a brief overview will suffice here. The Roger Charlton-trained gelding was unraced as a two-year-old, won a listed race over eleven furlongs at Goodwood from five starts at three and developed into a notable middle-distance performer at four, taking the Group 1 Preis von Europa by two and a half lengths from Amorella at Cologne, beating Ziyad by three-quarters of a length to win the Group 2 Grand Prix de Chantilly and, between those two runs, finishing a three-and-three-quarter-length fourth to Coronet in the Group 1 Grand Prix de Saint-Cloud.

Aspetar is a half-brother to the stakes-placed winner Qarasu (by Le Havre), he is out of a winning half-sister to the Group 2 scorers Alex My Boy (by Dalakhani) and Somehow (by Fastnet Rock) and to the seven-furlong Group 3 winner Happen (by War Front), and his grandam is Alexandrova (by Sadler's Wells), winner of the Group 1 Oaks, Group 1 Irish Oaks and Group 1 Yorkshire Oaks in 2006. His sire, Al Kazeem (by Dubawi), was a Timeform 128-rated star whose two wins in the Group 1 Tattersalls Gold Cup were separated by a spell at stud that found him to have fertility problems. Aspetar was one of the foals who resulted from that initial stint. He has had some more very small crops since returning to a stallion role, this time carefully managed small books at his owner-breeder's Oakgrove Stud, and he added three more stakes winners in 2020. The three-year-old gelding Usak won a mile listed contest at Toulouse, Harper won both his starts for the Andrea Marcialis stable in France, including the Listed Criterium de Bordeaux over a mile, whereas the Roger Varian-trained Saint Lawrence won the Listed Denford Stakes at Newbury, was third in the Group 3 Horris Hill Stakes over the same course and distance, and finished fourth to Master of The Seas in the Group 2 Superlative Stakes. Both that colt and Harper are now three-year-olds.

Aspetar is a capable middle-distance horse and there should be more good prizes to be won with him. He joined the Julian Smart stable in Qatar and was entered for the US$1 million H H Amir Trophy, due to be run over a mile and a half at the Al Rayyan Racecourse in Doha in late February.

SUMMARY DETAILS
Bred: HH Sheikh Mohammed Bin Khalifa Al Thani
Owned: HH Sheikh Mohammed Bin Khalifa Al Thani
Trained: Roger Charlton
Country: England
Race record: -11033-201410-210-
Career highlights: 5 wins inc 57th Preis von Europa (Gr1), Grand Prix de Chantilly (Gr2), Sky Bet York Stakes (Gr2), British Stallion Studs EBF Cocked Hat Stakes (L), 2nd Dubai Duty Free Finest Surprise (John Porter) Stakes (Gr3), Coral Gala Stakes (L), William Hill Doonside Cup Stakes (L)

ASPETAR (FR) – 2015 bay gelding

Al Kazeem (GB)	Dubawi (IRE)	Dubai Millennium (GB)
		Zomaradah (GB)
	Kazeem (GB)	Darshaan
		Kanz (USA)
Bella Qatara (IRE)	Dansili (GB)	Danehill (USA)
		Hasili (IRE)
	Alexandrova (IRE)	Sadler's Wells (USA)
		Shouk (GB)

BARON SAMEDI (GB)

Baron Samedi showed little in three starts as a juvenile and his first two outings of 2020, his fifth of fifteen in a nine-and-a-half-furlong Gowran Park handicap in late July his only time being beaten by a single-digit number of lengths. He was gelded soon after. That may have been the thing that brought about his transformation, or it could be that combined with other factors including general maturity, but this tall bay—his late sire, Harbour Watch (by Acclamation), was tall too—suddenly found a vein of form that deepened to such an extent that he wound up his year justifying favouritism in the Group 2 Prix du Conseil de Paris at ParisLongchamp.

The sequence began at Cork in late August when instead of going to the Tattersalls August Horses-in-Training Sale, for which he had been catalogued as lot 97, he was a short-head winner of a ten-furlong handicap, racing off a mark of sixty-five. Dylan Browne McMonagle's seven-pound claim reduced his impost to ten stone, three pounds for a low-grade handicap over an extended twelve and a half furlongs at Down Royal ten days later. The pair eased into the lead rounding the turn into the straight, a furlong and a half from home, went clear inside the final furlong and passed the post thirteen lengths in front of their closest pursuer. They followed up by four and three-quarter lengths over ten furlongs on good-to-yielding ground at Navan six days later and then, now rated ninety-seven, added a ten-furlong premier handicap on heavy ground at Listowel. Mickael Barzalona was in the saddle for his French outing. They hit the front a furlong out and had to fight to hold off the André Fabre-trained three-year-old Mare Australis by a head. That colt, in turn, was a length and a quarter in front of the five-year-old mare Eudaimonia, with gaps of four and a half lengths and a short neck back to Dariyma and Nagano Gold.

Baron Samedi was bred by Usk Valley Stud, was sold for just 3,500 guineas as a foal in Newmarket and as indicated above, is by Harbour Watch. That horse ran only as a two-year-old, winning all three of his races easily and completing his hat-trick in the Group 2 Richmond Stakes at Goodwood. The Timeform 121-

rated bay stood at Tweenhills Farm & Stud in Gloucestershire and has been getting winners over a wide range of distances. He comes from a branch of the famous Fall Aspen (by Pretense) family, so perhaps that's not really a surprise; there is an array of sprinters, milers, middle-distance horses and stayers in that line. The Hong Kong miler Waikuku gave him a first Group 1 winner at the start of 2020, Group 2 Prix Robert Papin scorer Tis Marvellous was an early stakes winner for him, the Australian-bred gelding Paret was a one-length runner-up in the Grade 1 United Nations Handicap at Monmouth Park in the USA in July, whereas Pyledriver was among the leading three-year-old colts in England last season. That Group 2 King Edward VII Stakes and Group 2 Great Voltigeur Stakes winner found his stamina stretched when finishing third to Galileo Chrome and Berkshire Rocco (margins were a neck and a length) in the Group 1 Pertemps St Leger Stakes at Doncaster in September.

Baron Samedi is a half-brother to the Swedish middle-distance winner Mukhaater (by Bahamian Bounty) and out of Dame Shirley (by Haafhd), a sister to the five-furlong Meydan pattern winner Fityaan and out of the mile Group 3 scorer Welsh Diva (by Selkirk). That mare, in turn, is a sister to the Group 3 Diomed Stakes winner and Group 1 Lockinge Stakes runner-up Trans Island, a horse who sired plenty of multiple winners, some of them prolific, some of them blacktype scorers, and some of them National Hunt horses.

An official handicap mark of 112 shows that although Baron Samedi improved by forty-seven pounds in the space of two months, he still has a long way to go to be rated of genuine Group 2 standard, and a penalty for his French success could be an added challenge to overcome. However, it would not be a surprise if this Joseph O'Brien-trained gelding does continue to progress, and it will be fascinating to see how his 2021 campaign turns out.

SUMMARY DETAILS
Bred: Usk Valley Stud
Owned: LECH Racing Ltd
Trained: Joseph O'Brien
Country: Ireland

Race record: 000-0011111-
Career highlights: 5 wins inc Prix du Conseil de Paris (Gr2)

BARON SAMEDI (GB) – 2017 bay gelding

Harbour Watch (IRE)	Acclamation (GB)	Royal Applause (GB)
		Princess Athena (IRE)
	Gorband (USA)	Woodman (USA)
		Sheroog (USA)
Dame Shirley (GB)	Haafhd (GB)	Alhaarth (IRE)
		Al Bahathri (USA)
	Welsh Diva (GB)	Selkirk (USA)
		Khuzba (GB)

BATTLEGROUND (USA)

A function of the international pattern system is to identify the elite members of each crop and, hence, the best candidates to become the top producers of future generations. There is, of course, no guarantee that any horse, no matter how great a celebrity on the track, will go on to excel at stud. It is easier for a stallion to succeed in that role than a mare—he can father more offspring in a month than a mare can produce in a lifetime—and so there is added pressure in selecting mates for the distaff side of the population. This is especially the case if she was a champion. For every Group 1 star like Dahlia, Highclere, Miesque or Urban Sea, standouts who became broodmares of considerable renown, there are many who disappoint, sometimes failing to get even a single stakes winner. It is too early to know where Found (by Galileo) will fit in given that she has just one racing-age foal to represent her so far, but that initial one is a Grade 1-placed, Group 2-winning son with classic prospects in 2021—a promising start.

Battleground made in his debut in the early-June six-furlong Naas maiden in which Lucky Vega beat Lipizzaner by half a length, but had to settle for fifth, beaten by a total of two and a half lengths on good-to-firm ground. It was soft at Ascot ten days later when he went to the front a furlong from home and stayed on for a two-and-a-half-length victory in what looks to have been an unremarkable edition of the Listed Chesham Stakes. Being a son of a mare who won the Group 1 Prix de l'Arc de Triomphe and Grade 1 Breeders' Cup Turf, it was to be expected that the seven-furlong trip at that time of the year would suit him well.

His final two runs were on good ground. First, he won the Group 2 Veuve Clicquot Vintage Stakes over seven furlongs at Goodwood. There are plenty of Group 1 winners who have that race on their CV, and there is every reason to hope that Battleground will follow in their hoof-prints this coming season, but the actual merit of what he achieved that day is open to question. Neither the third, Youth Spirit, nor fourth, Gorytus, ran again, whereas the second, fifth and sixth, Devious Company, Fountain Cross and Dark Lion, notched up four lesser-company placings from a total of twelve subsequent starts. The last-named was later gelded, as was the seventh-place finisher, and you have to go back to King Zain, who was eighth, to find a runner in the race who actually won a race afterwards. That Mark Johnston-trained colt was an odds-on four-length winner of a seven-furlong novice race at Lingfield on his only other outing.

The Group 1 Goffs Vincent O'Brien National Stakes was due to be his next start but he missed the engagement; he had a cough. Instead, he reappeared at Keeneland in early November where he was a leading contender for the Grade 1 Breeders' Cup Juvenile Turf presented by Coolmore America, run over a mile. He was not as quick to break as many of his rivals, he settled towards the back of the pack, stayed on over the final quarter mile and got up near the line for second place, three lengths adrift of Fire At Will. Outadore was a neck behind in third, there was another half a length back to the Jessica Harrington-trained Cadillac in fourth. Sealiway, who had been so impressive on heavy ground at ParisLongchamp the time before, was only fifth on this occasion.

Battleground, by Claiborne Farm's sprinter-miler War Front (by Danzig), is a grandson of the Group 1 Lockinge Stakes scorer Red Evie (by Intikhab), so a classic mile may suit him fine in the spring and summer of 2021. The way he stayed on at Keeneland suggests that he also has some of his dam's stamina, although how much of that quality he possesses remains to be seen. War Front, who has had twenty-three top-level scorers among an overall total of ninety-five stakes winners, is primarily associated with sprinters and milers. His nine-furlong Group 1-winning son Homesman was short-headed by Best Solution in the Group 1 Caulfield Cup over twelve, but the ideal trip for a middle-distance War Front tends to be ten furlongs (for example, Declaration of War, Lancaster Bomber).

Found stayed twelve well despite not being guaranteed to do so on pedigree, and her first-born may do so too. However, it is also possible that the colt could be an eight-to-ten-furlong horse at three rather than a Derby-type. He holds entries in the Group 1 Tattersalls Irish 2,000 Guineas and Group 1 Dubai Duty Free Irish Derby, as one would expect, plus the Group 1 Emirates Poule d'Essai des Poulains (French 2000 Guineas) and Group 1 Prix du Jockey Club (French Derby), and it catches the eye that among the early-closing races, he is not among those nominated for the twelve-furlong Group 1 Grand Prix de Paris.

SUMMARY DETAILS
Bred: Orpendale, Chelston & Wynatt
Owned: Michael Tabor, Derrick Smith & Mrs John Magnier
Trained: Aidan O'Brien
Country: Ireland
Race record: 0112-
Career highlights: 2 wins inc Veuve Clicquot Vintage Stakes (Gr2), Chesham Stakes (L), 2nd Breeders' Cup Juvenile Turf presented by Coolmore America (Gr1)

BATTLEGROUND (USA) – 2018 bay colt

		Northern Dancer
War Front (USA)	Danzig (USA)	Pas de Nom (USA)
	Starry Dreamer (USA)	Rubiano (USA)
		Lara's Star (USA)
Found (IRE)	Galileo (IRE)	Sadler's Wells (USA)
		Urban Sea (USA)
	Red Evie (IRE)	Intikhab (USA)
		Malafemmena (IRE)

BELIEVE IN LOVE (IRE)

Believe In Love is a late-April foal whose form improved as she stepped up in trip and as the year progressed. Placed in one of two starts as a juvenile and in a pair of ten-furlong handicaps on the Polytrack at Lingfield in February, she got off the mark by a nose in an eleven-furlong handicap at Kempton in March and followed that with a two-length score in a twelve-furlong handicap at Goodwood in late July, raising her official rating to eighty-eight. That rose to ninety-seven after she beat three rivals easily over fourteen furlongs on good-to-firm at the July Course at Newmarket in mid-August and to 107 after her ten-length romp over the same course and distance, on soft ground, a fortnight later. It was clearly time to step up into pattern company.

Her first attempt was the Group 2 bet365 Park Hill Fillies' Stakes over the St Leger course and distance in September, and although she hit the front briefly inside the final furlong, she was outstayed by Pista and Vivionn, eventually passing the post in third, beaten by margins of one and a half lengths and half a length. The lightly raced winner, who was completing a hat-trick that day, would go on to be the runner-up in the Group 1 Prix de Royallieu at ParisLongchamp on her next start. Believe In Love, on the other hand, went to Saint-Cloud in late October and, on heavy ground, went to the front over a furlong and a half from home and stayed there, beating Pontille and Palomba by three-quarters of a length and one and three-quarter lengths in the Group 3 Prix Belle de Nuit over a mile and six.

Believe In Love represents the first crop of the classic star and Ballylinch Stud stallion Make Believe (by Makfi), a horse whose five stakes winners feature the Group 1 Prix du Jockey Club (French Derby) winner Mishriff and the likeable and hard-working Rose of Kildare. The grandson of Dubawi (by Dubai Millennium) got his Group 1 wins at seven and eight furlongs but, with help from his mares, is getting horses who stay further than he tried; he was never asked to go beyond a mile.

The filly was bred in Ireland by Kenilworth House Stud, who sold her for 42,000 guineas in Newmarket as a foal, and she is a 55,000-guinea graduate of Book 1 of the Tattersalls October

Yearling Sale. The Roger Varian-trained bay is a half-sister to Top Trip (by Dubai Destination) and, like him, gets her stamina from the distaff side of her family. He won the Group 2 Prix Hocquart over eleven furlongs but was a nose runner-up in the Group 2 Yorkshire Cup and only beaten by a neck and a length when third to Estimate and Simenon in the Group 1 Gold Cup at Ascot. He stands as a National Hunt stallion in France and has already sired winners from a small number of runners; his eldest have just turned five. Topka (by Kahyasi), their dam, finished third in the Group 2 Prix de Mallaret over twelve furlongs and was, in turn, out of the multiple ten-furlong scorer Tipsy Topsy (by Ashkalani). That mare was a half-sister to the mile and dual seven-furlong pattern winner Salselon (by Salse) and related to the Timeform 130-rated mile star Markofdistinction (by Known Fact).

Believe In Love, who started the year rated seventy-one, is among the horses who made a considerable amount of improvement throughout the season, in her case measured as thirty-six pounds. She will make a promising addition to the broodmare ranks.

SUMMARY DETAILS
Bred: Kenilworth House Stud
Owned: Koji Maeda
Trained: Roger Varian
Country: England
Race record: 02-022111131-
Career highlights: 5 wins inc Prix Belle de Nuit (Gr3), 3rd bet365 Park Hill Fillies' Stakes (Gr2)

BELIEVE IN LOVE (IRE) – 2017 bay filly

Make Believe (GB)	Makfi (GB)	Dubawi (IRE)
		Dhelaal (GB)
	Rosie's Posy (IRE)	Suave Dancer (USA)
		My Branch (GB)
Topka (FR)	Kahyasi	Ile de Bourbon (USA)
		Kadissya (USA)
	Tipsy Topsy (GB)	Ashkalani (IRE)
		Heady (GB)

BENBATL (GB)

Benbatl's last two seasons have been as light as his first two were busy but he still did enough to confirm his position as one of the leading horses in training. Timeform-rated 129 in 2018, he had just two contrasting runs in 2019, a five-length victory in the Group 2 Shadwell Joel Stakes over a mile at Newmarket followed by a last-place finish on heavy ground in the Group 1 Queen Elizabeth II Stakes at Ascot. In 2020, he ran just once in Europe.

The son of Dubawi (by Dubai Millennium) began his six-year-old season with a pair of easy Group 2 wins at Meydan, one over nine furlongs on turf and the other over half a furlong farther on dirt, and then picked up a seven-figure cheque for his connections with a third-place finish in the inaugural Saudi Cup at Riyadh in late February, staying on well to pass the post three-quarters of a length and two lengths behind the US dirt specialists Maximum Security and Midnight Bisou and followed home by two more: Mucho Gusto and Tacitus. He was then off the track for seven months before chasing home Kameko and Regal Reality in the Group 2 Shadwell Joel Stakes, finishing half a length and half a length third having tried to make all.

He is the first foal of Nahrain (by Selkirk), who won the Group 1 Prix de l'Opera and Grade 1 Flower Bowl Invitational Stakes over ten furlongs and split Perfect Shirl and Misty For Me when runner-up in the Grade 1 Breeders' Cup Filly & Mare Turf over a furlong farther at Churchill Downs in 2011. She foaled a full sister to her Group 1 star in 2019, a Muhaarar (by Oasis Dream) half-brother in 2020, and she was then bred to Kingman (by Invincible Spirit). Her siblings include the dual mile listed scorer Baharah (by Elusive Quality) and her dam is Bahr (by Generous), the Group 2 Ribblesdale Stakes and Group 3 Musidora Stakes winner of 1998.

An unbeaten listed scorer at two with an eight-length debut win to her name, Bahr was runner-up to Shahtoush in the Group 1 Oaks at Epsom, third to Winona in the Group 1 Irish Oaks at the Curragh and third to Auntie Mame in the Grade 1 Flower Bowl Handicap over ten furlongs at Belmont Park. Bahr is a half-sister to the mile Group 3 scorer Clerio (by Soviet Star) and she is also notable as being the grandam of Dorraar (by Shamardal), the winning dam of Far Above (by Farhh). That lightly raced, Timeform 122-rated Group 3 Palace House Stakes winner is in his first season at Starfield Stud in Mullingar, Co Westmeath where he looks likely to prove popular.

Benbatl is a top-class eight-to-ten-furlong horse whose ten wins and six placings have netted over £5.8 million in prize money. He is by a stallion of potential long-term influence, is out of a Group 1-winning mare from a good blacktype family and has done more than enough to prove that he is worthy of a good berth at stud. However, he is not done with racing yet.

SUMMARY DETAILS

Bred: Darley
Owned: Godolphin
Trained: Saeed bin Suroor
Country: England
Race record: -1320100-112101012-10-1133-
Career highlights: 10 wins inc Dubai Turf sponsored by DP World (Gr1), Grosser Dallmayr Preis - Bayerisches Zuchtrennen (Gr1), Ladbrokes Stakes (Gr1), Al Maktoum Challenge R2 sponsored by Mubadala (Gr2), Singspiel Stakes presented by Longines Master Collection (Gr2), Al Rashidiya sponsored by Jebel Ali Port (Gr2), Shadwell Joel Stakes (Gr2), Hampton Court Stakes (Gr3), Singspiel Stakes presented by Longines Ladies Master Collection (Gr3), 2nd Ladbrokes Cox Plate (Gr1), Jebel Hatta sponsored by Emirates Airline (Gr1), Betfred Dante Stakes (Gr2), bet365 Craven Stakes (Gr3), 3rd Shadwell Joel Stakes (Gr2), Saudi Cup

BENBATL (GB) – 2014 bay horse

Dubawi (IRE)	Dubai Millennium (GB)	Seeking The Gold (USA)
		Colorado Dancer (IRE)
	Zomaradah (GB)	Deploy
		Jawaher (IRE)
Nahrain (GB)	Selkirk (USA)	Sharpen Up
		Annie Edge
	Bahr (GB)	Generous (IRE)
		Lady of The Sea

BERLIN TANGO (GB)

Berlin Tango had an official handicap mark of only ninety-eight when he went to Kempton at the start of June but that rose to 106 soon afterwards because he beat the subsequent classic-placed Group 2 star Pyledriver by a length and a quarter to take the Group 3 Unibet Classic Trial Stakes over ten furlongs. He was raised another four pounds after his third-place finish to Russian Emperor in the Group 3 Hampton Court Stakes at Ascot a fortnight later but was not seen out again in Europe.

He has been gelded and exported to Hong Kong where he is continuing his career as part of the Tony Cruz stable, although he finished well-beaten on both his first two starts for the new connections (owned by Siu Pak Kwan), in handicaps over seven furlongs and a mile at Sha Tin in November and December.

The former Andrew Balding-trained bay was bred by George Strawbridge, he is by the leading international sire Dansili (by Danehill) and out of the prolific blacktype earner Fantasia (by Sadler's Wells). Her six wins included the Grade 3 Modesty Handicap, Group 3 Nell Gwyn Stakes, Group 3 Prestige Stakes and two listed races, she was runner-up in the Grade 1 Just A Game Stakes and Group 1 Fillies' Mile and third in the Group 1 Poule d'Essai des Pouliches (French 1000 Guineas). Her now three-year-old daughter is named Fantalope (by Lope de Vega) and she had a Nathaniel (by Galileo) colt in February 2020.

Blue Symphony (by Darshaan), the winning grandam of Berlin Tango, is also responsible for two daughters who have become blacktype producers at stud. Her Group 3 Give Thanks Stakes winner Pink Symphony (by Montjeu) is the dam of last season's Group 2 Great Voltigeur Stakes runner-up Highland Chief (by Gleneagles), whereas Blue Rhapsody (by Cape Cross) did her part for the family by becoming the dam of the multiple Group 1-placed prolific pattern winner Western Hymn (by High Chaparral), a high-class performer at around ten furlongs.

This makes the juvenile champion Blue Duster (by Danzig) the third dam of Berlin Tango. She won the Group 1 Cheveley Park Stakes, Group 3 Queen Mary Stakes and Group 3 Princess Margaret Stakes, she was runner-up in the Group 1 Sprint Cup, and she was a full sister to the Group 1 Middle Park Stakes scorer and somewhat successful blacktype sire Zieten.

SUMMARY DETAILS
Bred: George Strawbridge
Owned: George Strawbridge (now Siu Pak Kwan)
Trained: Andrew Balding (now Tony Cruz)
Country: England (now Hong Kong)
Race record: 0133-21300-
Career highlights: 2 wins inc Unibet Classic Trial Stakes (Gr3), 3rd Hampton Court Stakes (Gr3), Weatherbys Global Stallions App Flying Scotsman Stakes (L), Longines Irish Champions Weekend EBF Stonehenge Stakes (L)

BERLIN TANGO (GB) – 2017 bay gelding

Dansili (GB)	Danehill (USA)	Danzig (USA)
		Razyana (USA)
	Hasili (IRE)	Kahyasi
		Kerali
Fantasia (GB)	Sadler's Wells (USA)	Northern Dancer
		Fairy Bridge (USA)
	Blue Symphony (GB)	Darshaan
		Blue Duster (USA)

BOWERMAN (GB)

Bowerman showed promise early in his career but by the time he appeared in the auction ring in Newmarket in July of his five-year-old season, he had made it to the track only six times. He had been a head runner-up to Stradivarius over a mile at Newcastle on his only start at two, won a one-mile maiden at Kempton and one-mile handicap at Chelmsford on his only runs at three, those two races separated by eight months, and was then off the track for almost a year and a half. He finished third in a Nottingham handicap on his turf debut in April 2019, won a mile contest on the Tapeta at Newcastle nineteen days later but then finished well-beaten over that same course and distance two months after that. Having been a 150,000-guinea Tattersalls Book 2 graduate as a yearling, he was knocked down for 52,000 guineas at the Tattersalls July Sale almost four years later. However, as was reported in an interview in *The Irish Field* last November, the new owners found out that he was a bleeder and returned him, so the underbidder, trainer Adrian (Ado) McGuinness, was offered the chance to buy him instead.

The horse has thrived in his new home. He was rated 103 when he arrived in Ireland, was runner-up over seven furlongs at Naas first time out for his new stable, won over a mile at Gowran Park but was unplaced in two blacktype contests. He was then gelded and, in 2020, has become a high-profile performer from a mile to ten and a half furlongs. He won easily over those two trips at Dundalk in January, beating the former Group 2 winner Princess Yaiza by three and three-quarter lengths in the longer race, was then runner-up in a mile listed contest at Cagnes-sur-Mer in France and, four months later, won the Paddy Power Irish Lincolnshire Handicap on good-to-firm turf at the Curragh, taking the prize by two and a half lengths. The now 106-rated bay was then runner-up to Ancient Spirit in a one-mile listed race at the same venue, disappointed at Leopardstown in July but then bounced back to finish third to Royal Dornach in the Group 3 Clipper Logistics Desmond Stakes there before returning to Dundalk for the Group 3 Al Basti Equiworld, Dubai Diamond Stakes over ten and a half furlongs. He hit the front inside the final furlong to win by half a length and two and a quarter lengths from Sky Seven and Gold Maze, with the high-profile three-year-olds Vatican City (seventh) and Crossfirehurricane (thirteenth) among those who finished farther behind.

Bowerman, who now has eight wins and six placings from eighteen starts, is a Cheveley Park Stud-bred son of Dutch Art (by Medicean) and he is the best of several winners out of Jamboretta (by Danehill). That dual winning mare is a half-sister to the speedy pattern-placed stakes winner Excusez Moi (by Fusaichi Pegasus) and she is out of Jiving (by Generous), a non-winning half-sister to the stakes winner and phenomenal broodmare Hasili (by Kahyasi).

That mare, who has been honoured with a statue at Banstead Manor Stud, was the dam of the Group/Grade 1 stars Banks Hill, Cacique, Champs Elysees, Heat Haze and Intercontinental—of those, only Heat Haze (by Green Desert) is not by Danehill (by Danzig)—as well as the Group 1-placed Group 2 scorer Dansili (by Danehill). Dansili became a leading international sire who has done well with stallion sons and broodmare daughters, whereas both Cacique and Champs Elysees have sired Group 1 winners. Hasili's descendants include her Group 1-winning granddaughter Romantica (by Galileo).

Of course, Hasili's stakes-winning full sister Arrive has also done her part for the family by coming up with the Group 1 Pretty Polly Stakes scorer Promising Lead (by Danehill), whereas stakes-placed Skiable (by Niniski) is the dam of the Grade 2-winning miler and former juvenile star Three Valleys (by Diesis) and grandam of Group 1 Fillies' Mile winner Quadrilateral (by Frankel). Others of note in the family include the classic sire and multiple Grade 1-winning miler Leroidesanimaux (by Candy Stripes) and the Group 1 Cheveley Park Stakes winner Sookera (by Roberto) who is the grandam of Hasili and fourth dam of Bowerman.

There is every reason to hope that Bowerman will be at least as good at the age of seven as he was as a six-year-old, and it will be disappointing if there are not more good prizes to be won with him. He is due to start his new campaign in a local Group 2 contest over a mile at Doha in Qatar on February 19th although was also entered in the Group 3 Betway Winter Derby Stakes, due to be run at Lingfield on February 27th.

SUMMARY DETAILS
Bred: Cheveley Park Stud Ltd
Owned: Total Recall Racing Club
Trained: Adrian (Ado) McGuinness
Country: Ireland
Race record: 2-11/3102010-11212031-
Career highlights: 8 wins inc Al Basti Equiworld, Dubai Diamond Stakes (Gr3), 2nd Dubai Duty Free Finest Surprise Celebration Stakes (L), Prix Saonois (L), 3rd Clipper Logistics Desmond Stakes (Gr3)

BOWERMAN (GB) – 2014 bay gelding

Dutch Art (GB)	Medicean (GB)	Machiavellian (USA)
		Mystic Goddess (USA)
	Halland Park Lass (IRE)	Spectrum (IRE)
		Palacegate Episode (IRE)
Jamboretta (IRE)	Danehill (USA)	Danzig (USA)
		Razyana (USA)
	Jiving (GB)	Generous (IRE)
		Kerali

BRAD THE BRIEF (GB)

Brad The Brief is an interesting member of the sprinters' division and a horse who could play a prominent role in 2021. A winner of three of his four starts as a two-year-old—finishing last of three to Lazuli on his second start was the sole defeat—and gelded before he made a winning return to action at three, he was then beaten twice before taking a listed contest at Newmarket in late August. That was the Close Brothers Hopeful Stakes on soft ground and if you'd paused the race a furlong and a half out you would likely have selected him as a likely candidate to finish out of the frame. However, he got going around the furlong marker, stayed on well, hit the front near the finish and just held on by a neck from the fast-finishing Summerghand.

He faced stronger opposition in the Group 3 Coral Bengough Stakes at York next time, also on soft ground, but although weakening in the final furlong acquitted himself quite well. He was the only three-year-old in the field and finished fourth, by margins of one and three-quarter lengths, three lengths and three-quarters of a length, beaten by Dakota Gold (who made all), The Tin Man and Brando. Kurious was over four lengths back in fifth, just ahead of old rival Summerghand. Three weeks later, he went to Chantilly where, on heavy ground, he hit the front over half a furlong from home and ran on well to beat Coeur de Pierre and Air de Valse by one and three-quarter lengths and a head in the Group 3 Prix de Seine-et-Oise.

Chasemore Farm's homebred son of the Cheveley Park Stud stallion Dutch Art (by Medicean) is trained by Tom Dascombe and, aside from his winning debut, which was over five furlongs on good ground at Bath in mid-August 2019, he has has raced only over six furlongs. He seems best suited to some ease in the ground, he has won on his sole attempt on an artificial track—his second juvenile win came on the Tapeta at Wolverhampton—and he holds an official handicap mark of 109.

He is the first foal of Kenzadargent (by Kendargent), a multiple pattern-placed stakes winner who stayed nine furlongs and had blacktype form on everything from very soft to firm ground. The mare's second foal is the €500,000 Arqana Deauville

August yearling sale graduate Taipan (by Frankel) who made a winning debut over a mile on heavy ground at Naas on November 1st; that Jessica Harrington-trained colt holds entries in the Group 1 Tattersalls Irish 2,000 Guineas, Group 1 Dubai Duty Free Irish Derby and Group 1 Investec Derby Stakes. She had a Siyouni (by Pivotal) colt in 2019. Quiza Bere (by Epistolaire), the grandam of Brad The Brief, won over nine furlongs on heavy ground in France and her siblings featured Bartex (by Groom Dancer), a prolific mile winner who picked up multiple pieces of blacktype from seven to nine and a half furlongs. This is a branch of the family of the Group 1 Premio Lydia Tesio winner Dubai Sunrise (by King's Best), of the dual Group 2 Prix de l'Opera winner Athyka (by Secretariat) and her classic-placed Grade 1-winning son Atticus (by Nureyev), plus various others of talent, but despite the relative stamina of many of his relations, the combination of Dutch Art with a daughter of Kendargent (by Kendor) yielded a sprinter.

Brad The Brief has been entered in an ultra-valuable six-furlong dirt race at Riyadh in late February. A good performance there would open up some other potential international targets.

SUMMARY DETAILS

Bred: Chasemore Farm
Owned: Chasemore Farm
Trained: Tom Dascombe
Country: England
Race record: 1311-130141-
Career highlights: 6 wins inc Prix de Seine-et-Oise (Gr3), Close Brothers Hopeful Stakes (L)

BRAD THE BRIEF (GB) – 2017 bay gelding

Dutch Art (GB)	Medicean (GB)	Machiavellian (USA)
		Mystic Goddess (USA)
	Halland Park Lass (IRE)	Spectrum (IRE)
		Palacegate Episode (IRE)
Kenzadargent (FR)	Kendargent (FR)	Kendor (FR)
		Pax Bella (FR)
	Quiza Bere (FR)	Epistolaire (IRE)
		Belisonde (FR)

BREATHTAKING LOOK (GB)

Many in the industry appear to have an obsession with early two-year-old speed, almost prepared to write-off a horse if it hasn't shown talent on the track before mid-summer. All too often it is the late-summer, autumn and even winter juvenile maiden winners who will go on to outperform their more precocious cohorts, and in plenty of cases horses can become high-to-top-class performers never having raced at two. No doubt some would have given up on Breathtaking Look as she hadn't even run before mid-summer of her three-year-old season, but she made a winning debut over six furlongs at Yarmouth that September and has barely looked back since. The six-time winner is pattern and listed scorer, a credit to all of her connections and also to her sire.

She got her first pattern win at the age of four when taking the Group 3 Japan Racing Association Sceptre Stakes over seven furlongs on fast ground at Doncaster. She has won only once from nine starts since then but that was the Group 3 Barriere Prix de Meautry over six furlongs on heavy ground at Deauville at the end of August. She beat Air de Valse by three and a half lengths that day having chased home runaway winner Dream of Dreams in the Group 2 Unibet Hungerford Stakes over a furlong farther at Newbury fifteen days before. She was only beaten by a neck when runner-up to Queen Jo Jo in the Group 3 William Hill Summer Fillies' Stakes on good ground at York in July and was not disgraced when finishing a three-length fourth to One Master in the Group 3 Saint Clair Oak Tree Stakes over seven on good-to-firm at Goodwood. Her 2020 form also included an eye-catching seasonal debut at Newmarket in early June when she chased home Oxted in the Group 3 Betway Abernant Stakes.

Breathtaking Look, who has an official BHA handicap mark of 106, was sold to Katsumi Yoshida for 400,000 guineas at the Tattersalls December Mare Sale. The combination of her race record, having a well-bred sire, lots of blacktype in the first few generations of her family and an eye-catching strike rate of winners to foals for some of her direct ancestors makes her a promising addition to the broodmare ranks.

She was bred by Ellis Stud and Bellow Hill Stud, has been trained throughout her career by Stuart Williams, and she is a daughter of the Timeform 125-rated stallion Bated Breath (by Dansili). He is a member of the Banstead Manor Stud team and got his first top-level winner when the Chad Brown-trained four-year-old Viadera, previously a pattern-placed stakes winner in Ireland for the Ger Lyons stable, had her nose in front where it mattered most in the Grade 1 Matriarch Stakes over a mile on turf at Del Mar in late November. Several of his sixteen blacktype scorers have also been placed at that level and they include the Group 2 winners Beckford and Daahyeh and the potential French classic prospect Makaloun. That Jean-Claude Rouget-trained Aga Khan homebred won a listed contest at Deauville in August, ran away with the Group 3 Prix de Conde over nine furlongs on heavy ground at Chantilly a month later and lost his unbeaten record when finishing a two-length third to Gear Up in the Group 1 Criterium de Saint-Cloud in late October, also on heavy ground.

Breathtaking Look is a 42,000-guinea graduate of Book 3 of the Tattersalls October Yearling Sale and she is the first foal of the dual stakes-placed three-time winner Love Your Looks (by Iffraaj). That mare's now three-year-old daughter French Braid (by Territories), an early May foal, made 145,000 guineas as a yearling, she had a Zoffany (by Dansili) colt in 2019 and she was bred to Invincible Spirit (by Green Desert) last year. Play Around (by Niniski), an Evry listed scorer, is the next dam and her tally of eight winners from a dozen offspring also includes the multiple stakes-placed dual French winner Priere (by Machiavellian). There is also plenty of blacktype to be found in the third generation of the pedigree, most notably by Play Around's half-sister multiple Group/Grade 2-placed stakes-winning half-sister Playact (by Hernando). Their dam, the listed-placed Play or Pay (by Play Fellow), produced seven winners from ten foals.

SUMMARY DETAILS
Bred: Ellis Stud and Bellow Hill Stud
Owned: J W Parry
Trained: Stuart Williams
Country: England

Race record: -101-3101010-20242100-
Career highlights: 6 wins inc Barriere Prix de Meautry (Gr3), Japan Racing Association Sceptre Stakes (Gr3), 2nd Unibet Hungerford Stakes (Gr2), William Hill Summer Fillies' Stakes (Gr3), Betway Abernant Stakes (Gr3)

BREATHTAKING LOOK (GB) – 2015 bay mare

Bated Breath (GB)	Dansili (GB)	Danehill (USA)
		Hasili (IRE)
	Tantina (USA)	Distant View (USA)
		Didina (GB)
Love Your Looks (GB)	Iffraaj (GB)	Zafonic (USA)
		Pastorale (GB)
	Play Around (IRE)	Niniski (USA)
		Play Or Pay (USA)

BUCKHURST (IRE)

Buckhurst was unraced at two but made a winning debut over a mile at Leopardstown in April of his three-year-old year before going on to prove himself to be a capable pattern-class colt. He was a half-length runner-up in the Group 3 Gallinule Stakes on his third start, defeated Blenheim Palace by a length and a half to take the Group 3 International Stakes and followed that by beating Leo de Fury by a head in the Group 3 Royal Whip Stakes, all three of those races over ten furlongs at the Curragh. He then chased home Norway in a twelve-furlong Group 3 contest at Leopardstown and so finished that initial campaign on an official handicap mark of 111. He looked a bright prospect for 2020 and it was no surprise to find that his dam was booked for a return visit to his sire.

His four-year-old campaign started off better than it finished, although he ended the year on a new handicap mark of 114. Ancient Spirit's nose was just ahead of his at the finish of the one-mile Listed Heritage Stakes on good-to-firm ground at Navan on his seasonal reappearance in June, but he gained some compensation two and a half weeks later when making all to beat the somewhat frustrating yet subsequent Group 1 scorer Sir Dragonet by a length and a half in a three-runner edition of the Group 3 Dubai Duty Free Jumeirah Creekside Hotel Alleged Stakes at the Curragh. The ground was good but the time 10.99 seconds slower than standard, highlighting that this was a tactical affair rather than a true reflection of relative merit. Listed scorer Numerian was the one who completed the line-up, passing the post a length and a quarter behind Sir Dragonet.

Buckhurst then finished last of six to Magical in the Group 1 Tattersalls Gold Cup, fifth to Tiger Moth in a twelve-furlong Group 3 contest at Leopardstown, a respectable three-and-a-half-length seventh to Verry Elleegant in the Group 1 Stella Artois Caulfield Cup over the same trip on good-to-soft in mid-October but then only tenth in the Group 1 Ladbrokes Cox Plate on soft ground at Moonee Valley a week later, the race in which Sir Dragonet finally got his first win at the highest level.

The Denford Stud-bred colt is a 70,000-guinea graduate of Book 1 of the Tattersalls October Yearling Sale where he was bought by his trainer, Joseph O'Brien. He represents the first crop of Australia (by Galileo) and that Coolmore Stud-based dual Derby winner made an overdue breakthrough as a Group 1 sire in 2020, represented by both the Group 1 St Leger Stakes winner Galileo Chrome and the surprise Grade 1 Breeders' Cup Mile scorer Order of Australia from his second crop. Cayenne Pepper, Epona Plays, Leo de Fury, and Patrick Sarsfield were also pattern winners for him last season.

Buckhurst is the sixth foal of Artful (by Green Desert), which makes him inbred 4x2 to her sire as well as having a 4x4 cross to Northern Dancer (by Nearctic). He is a half-brother to Duplicity (by Cadeaux Genereux). That gelding began his career with Richard Hannon, won the Listed Rose Bowl Stakes over six furlongs on soft ground at Newbury as a two-year-old back in 2009, achieved a peak handicap mark of 100, but later slid down through the ranks, had two other trainers, was beaten in several sellers and finished his track days on a handicap mark of forty-seven. The mare had a Zoffany (by Dansili) colt in 2019 and, as noted above, was bred to Australia in 2020. Her half-sister Fleece (by Daylami) is the dam of a classic-placed stakes winner in New Zealand: Savile Row (by Makfi). However, her siblings also include Chintz (by Danehill Dancer), the Group 3 C. L. Weld Park Stakes winner whose son The Gurkha (by Galileo) is a member of the Coolmore team.

He was unraced at two, was a nine-length winner of a mile maiden on very soft ground at Navan on his second start and impressed with a five-and-a-half-length victory in the Group 1 Poule d'Essai des Poulains (French 2000 Guineas) on good ground at Deauville a month later. He then chased home Galileo Gold in the Group 1 St James's Palace Stakes, was a half-length runner-up to Hawkbill in the Group 1 Coral-Eclipse Stakes at Sandown, both on soft ground, and got his revenge on his Ascot conqueror with a neck victory in the Group 1 Qatar Sussex Stakes on good-to-firm at Goodwood. He was not seen again, his earnings fell just short of £1 million, but the dual top-level star, who was the joint champion three-year-old miler of 2016, certainly earned his place at stud.

Although a horse whose pedigree and racing record suggested might get some promising results with autumn juveniles but not show his true worth until his three-year-olds are in action, The Gurkha had a large number of first-crop juvenile runners in 2020. Fourteen have them have won a race, including Group 3 Preis der Winterfavoriten success at Cologne for Best of Lips. He had only nineteen foals registered in 2020 (twenty-two 'no returns'), covered a book of fifty-seven mares and has his fee for 2021 cut to €5,000.

Gold Dodger (by Slew O' Gold), the grandam of Buckhurst, won a listed contest in France, and as she is a daughter of the Group 3 Prix Cleopatre winner and Group 2 Prix de Royallieu runner-up Brooklyn's Dance (by Shirley Heights), she is a half-sister to 2012's surprise Group 1 Prix de l'Arc de Triomphe winner Solemia (by Poliglote). Her siblings also include the Group 2 Prix Greffulhe winner and Group 1 Grand Prix de Paris runner-up Prospect Wells (by Sadler's Wells) and his classic-placed dual middle-distance pattern-winning full brother Prospect Park as well as being related to Silasol (by Monsun), the Group 1 Prix de Diane (French Oaks)-placed Group 1 Prix Saint-Alary and Group 1 Prix Marcel Boussac star who was France's joint champion juvenile filly of 2012.

Buckhurst is a talented performer who is effective from eight to twelve furlongs though possibly best suited by ten. He has good form on everything from good-to-firm to soft ground, and he is a well-bred colt who should be capable of picking up some more good prizes before his racing days end. He remained in Australia after his two runs there for the O'Brien stable.

SUMMARY DETAILS
Bred: Denford Stud Ltd
Owned: Lloyd J Williams
Trained: Joseph O'Brien
Country: Ireland
Race record: -102112-210000-

Career highlights: 4 wins inc Dubai Duty Free Jumeirah Creekside Hotel Alleged Stakes (Gr3), Royal Whip Stakes (Gr3), Dubai Duty Free Full Of Surprises International Stakes (Gr3), 2nd Paddy Power Betting Shop Stakes (Gr3), Kerrygold Gallinule Stakes (Gr3), Heritage Stakes (L)

BUCKHURST (IRE) – 2016 bay colt

Australia (GB)	Galileo (IRE)	Sadler's Wells (USA)
		Urban Sea (USA)
	Ouija Board (GB)	Cape Cross (IRE)
		Selection Board
Artful (IRE)	Green Desert (USA)	Danzig (USA)
		Foreign Courier (USA)
	Gold Dodger (USA)	Slew O' Gold (USA)
		Brooklyn's Dance (FR)

CADILLAC (IRE)

Dual classic winner Lope de Vega (by Shamardal) is the headliner at Ballylinch Stud and had someone declared in early July of 2020 that there would soon be a European Group 1 winner among his latest batch of two-year-olds, many would have predicted that Cadillac would be the one. His winning debut in a seven-furlong Leopardstown maiden on the first day of that month was visually stunning, a nine-length success that earned rave reviews. He'd swung into the straight in third place, going ominously well, was switched right to go outside the front pair rather than between them, then quickened up and went clear in the final half furlong, winning under a hands-and-heels ride.

The ground was good that day but was soft at the Curragh late the following month when eight went to post for the Group 2 Galileo Irish EBF Futurity stakes. Cadillac was backed as though defeat was out of the question but was being ridden along two out, was under pressure at the furlong pole and although staying on well in the closing stages, had to settle for second. There was half a length and half a length separating the first three, then a gap of one and a half lengths back to the fourth. It seemed disappointing on the day but doesn't look quite as much so now. The run of sixth-placed Van Gogh, who would go on to Group 1 success, cannot be considered as adding any shine to the result given his effort on the day landed him in front of the vet (he was found to be post-race normal), but the third, Oratorio, would go to be a runner-up in two of his three subsequent blacktype tries, whereas Jim Bolger's subsequent Group 1 Vertem Futurity Trophy Stakes scorer Mac Swiney was the winner.

There was a feeling that less ease in the ground would surely allow Cadillac to be seen to better effect, so when it was good at Leopardstown on the opening day of Irish Champions Weekend the following month, he was again sent off favourite, clear of Van Gogh in the market. The latter tried to make all, but when Cadillac moved up to join him a furlong and a half out, the result was inevitable. The Ballydoyle runner kept going to the line and held off third-place finisher Reve de Vol by two and three-quarter lengths, but he was no match for the Jessica Harrington-trained rising star who moved past him well inside the final furlong and pulled away for a three-and-a-half-length victory. The Group 1 stars Australia (2013), Johannes Vermeer (2015) and Mogul (2019) plus Derby runner-up Madhmoon (2018) feature on the recent roll of honour for that one-mile Group 2 KPMG Champions Juvenile Stakes—registered as the Golden Fleece Stakes—and although Cadillac lost his next two races, there remains every reason to hope that he can go on to succeed at the highest level.

The first of those races was the Group 1 Darley Dewhurst Stakes on soft ground at Newmarket where he finished a four-and-a-quarter-length fifth to St Mark's Basilica. He encountered some minor traffic issues, had to switch position, and was running on to the line but never looked like making the frame. The following month he ran about as well in the Grade 1 Breeders' Cup Juvenile Turf presented by Coolmore America, keeping on into fourth place while not threatening to get much closer. Fire At Will won that top prize by three lengths from the Aidan O'Brien-trained Battleground, with margins of half a length and the same separating that colt from Outadore and Cadillac. Sealiway, who had been so impressive on heavy ground at ParisLongchamp the time before, was another length back in fifth on this much faster ground.

Cadillac was bred by Sunderland Holdings Ltd—of Sea The Stars fame—and he is a €40,000 graduate of the Goffs Orby Yearling Sale. He is the second foal of Seas of Wells (by Dansili), a winning half-sister to a couple of winners out of a one-time scorer named Kiyra Wells (by Sadler's Wells). As only highly accomplished and/or very well-bred mares get to go to those horses' sires, you know it has to be a notable family without even looking it up to discover what celebrities are on the page. Kiyra Wells's three-parts sister Geminiani (by King of Kings) won the Group 3 Prestige Stakes and was runner-up in the Group 3 Musidora Stakes, whereas Damson (by Entrepreneur), another three-parts sister, is the closest of the Group 1 stars. She won the Group 1 Phoenix Stakes and Group 2 Queen Mary Stakes as a two-year-old, her grandson Last Kingdom (by Frankel) was a nine-furlong Group 3 scorer in France in 2017, whereas her son Requinto (by Dansili) won the Group 2 Flying Childers Stakes over five furlongs at Doncaster before going on to become a minor blacktype sire.

Tadkiyra (by Darshaan), their dam, got her only win in France and it is in that country that several of her better-known relations got their best wins. Half-brother Tassmoun (by Kalamoun) won the Group 3 Prix Messidor, 'nephew' Tiraaz (by Lear Fan) won the Group 1 Prix Royal-Oak, and unraced half-sister Takrana (by Misti) is the ancestor of both the Group 1 Prix Morny scorer Arcano (by Oasis Dream) and Group 1 Prix de l'Abbaye de Longchamp heroine Gilt Edge Girl (by Monsieur Bond). The mare's siblings also include Tashkourgan (by Shardari), who won a Group 3 contest in Italy, plus Tashtiya (by Shergar), the Group 3 Princess Royal Stakes winner whose descendants include the South African Grade 1 star and champion Whisky Baron (by Manhattan Rain) and the Group 1-placed Group 2 Prix de la Nonette winner Tasaday (by Nayef). If you go back farther you will find that the fifth dam of Cadillac is Tonnera (by Wild Risk), the Prix Saint-Alary winner and Poule d'Essai des Pouliches (French 1000 Guineas) runner-up of 1966; her dam, Texana (by Relic), won the Prix de l'Abbaye.

This is a pedigree with strong roots and it is likely the thin first two generations of it that contributed to the colt's price. It is his stable companion Lucky Vega who became that new juvenile Group 1 scorer for their sire, and the stallion added another when the Irish-bred but US-trained Aunt Pearl landed the Grade 1 Breeders' Cup Juvenile Fillies Turf at Keeneland in November. They are among a dozen top-level scorers that Lope de Vega has notched up among an overall total of seventy-seven stakes winners, and although he has just turned fourteen years old, he is well established as one of the world's leading sires. He covered a small number of mares to southern hemisphere time after no longer shuttling to Australia—his progeny there include Santa Ana Lane, at his peak one of the world's best sprinters—his top-priced yearlings of 2020 were 900,000 guineas, 825,000 guineas, 675,000 guineas, plus eight others who fetched at least a quarter of a million guineas, and his fee for our 2021 season has risen to €125,000.

Cadillac finished the year with an official rating of 114, just six pounds below the divisional champion, St Mark's Basilica. If he can avoid soft ground in 2021, there remains every reason to hope that he can fulfil that early promise and win at least once at the highest level. He holds entries in the Group 1 Tattersalls Irish 2,000 Guineas at the Curragh, the Group 1 Prix du Jockey Club at Chantilly and the Group 1 Derby Stakes at Epsom.

SUMMARY DETAILS
Bred: Sunderland Holdings Inc
Owned: Alpha Racing 2020
Trained: Jessica Harrington
Country: Ireland
Race record: 12104-
Career highlights: 2 wins inc KPMG Champions Juvenile Stakes (Gr2), 2nd Galileo Irish EBF Futurity Stakes (Gr2)

CADILLAC (IRE) – 2018 bay colt

	Shamardal (USA)	Giant's Causeway (USA)
Lope de Vega (IRE)		Helsinki (GB)
	Lady Vettori (GB)	Vettori (IRE)
		Lady Golconda (FR)
	Dansili (GB)	Danehill (USA)
Seas of Wells (IRE)		Hasili (IRE)
	Kiyra Wells (IRE)	Sadler's Wells (USA)
		Tadkiyra (IRE)

CAIRN GORM (GB)

Hunscote Stud's homebred chestnut Cairn Gorm made a two-and-a-half-length winning debut over six furlongs on good ground at Windsor in June, followed that with a narrow success over the same trip at Newbury and then completed his hat-trick with a one-length defeat of Jubilation in the Group 3 Darley Prix de Cabourg at Deauville. This was a promising start, but then he disappointed on his three subsequent outings, finishing unplaced in the Group 1 Prix Morny and Group 2 Mill Reef Stakes and, on his sole attempt at seven furlongs, last of five in the Group 1 Prix Jean-Luc Lagardere on heavy ground at ParisLongchamp in early October. The Mick Channon-trained colt has an official handicap mark of 101, down from a peak of 103.

He is a son of the Timeform 125-rated sprinter Bated Breath (by Dansili), who got his first top-level winner when Viadara landed the Grade 1 Matriarch Stakes over a mile at Del Mar in late November, and out of In Your Time (by Dalakhani), and so it could be that what he achieved at two is a bonus. His half-sister Time To Exceed (by Exceed And Excel) got her wins at three and four years of age, his unplaced dam is a half-sister to the Group 1 Prix de Diane (French Oaks)-placed pair Time Ahead (by Spectrum) and Time Away (by Darshaan), and his third dam is the brilliant Time Charter (by Saritamer).

Time Away, who won the Group 3 Musidora Stakes, is the dam of listed scorer Posted (by Kingman) and the Group 2 Prix de Mallaret winner Time On (by Sadler's Wells) and she is the grandam of the Group 1 Moyglare Stud Stakes winner Cursory Glance and the Group 3 Oh So Sharp Stakes winner Mot Juste, both daughters of Distorted Humor (by Forty Niner). But she is also notable as being the third dam of Digital Age (by Invincible Spirit). He has won five of his dozen starts, been runner-up twice and earned over $1.2 million, and he got his career-best win in 2020 when taking the Grade 1 Turf Classic Stakes over nine furlongs on turf at Churchill Downs. In 2019, he won the Grade 2 American Turf Stakes over a half-furlong less at the same venue, a listed contest over a mile at Tampa Bay Downs, was runner-up in the Saratoga Derby Invitational and missed out on Grade 1 placings when fourth in both the Belmont Derby Invitational Stakes and Hollywood Derby.

Time Charter, of course, was runner-up in the 1000 Guineas at Newmarket and won the Oaks at Epsom 1982 before going on to win the Group 1 Champion Stakes, Group 1 Coronation Cup and Group 1 King George VI and Queen Elizabeth Stakes, and she was fourth in the Arc. The Timeform 131-rated multiple champion was the dam of the Group 2 Jockey Club Stakes winners Zinaad (by Shirley Heights; classic sire) and Time Allowed (by Sadler's Wells) and she is the ancestor of a string of stakes and pattern winners in addition to the ones already noted here, including the classic-placed middle-distance Group 2 scorer Anton Chekhov (by Montjeu) and the speedy Best Terms (by Exceed And Excel) who won both the Group 2 Queen Mary Stakes and Group 2 Lowther Stakes in 2011.

This is a pedigree that would not look out of place on a miler, and although he started out by showing plenty of six-furlong speed and may indeed be a sprinter, it would be interesting to see how Cairn Gorm might get on if trying a mile on good ground in 2021.

SUMMARY DETAILS

Bred: Hunscote Stud
Owned: Hunscote Stud Ltd and Partner
Trained: Mick Channon
Country: England
Race record: 111000-
Career highlights: 3 wins inc Darley Prix de Cabourg (Gr3)

CAIRN GORM (GB) – 2018 chestnut colt

		Danehill (USA)
	Dansili (GB)	
		Hasili (IRE)
Bated Breath (GB)		Distant View (USA)
	Tantina (USA)	
		Didina (GB)
		Darshaan
	Dalakhani (IRE)	
		Daltawa (IRE)
In Your Time (GB)		Polish Precedent (USA)
	Not Before Time (IRE)	
		Time Charter

CAYENNE PEPPER (IRE)

There is a variety of types of inbreeding that find favour with some in the industry and doubling-up on an influential mare is one of those. Cayenne Pepper represents such a cross as she is inbred to two of the most influential mares of the modern era. The closer duplication is one of 4x3 to the hugely influential Allegretta (by Lombard), the mare who gave us King's Best (by Kingmambo), Urban Sea (by Miswaki) and so many more. The Jessica Harrington-trained filly is also inbred 5x4 to Special (by Forli), the dam of Nureyev (by Northern Dancer) and grandam of Sadler's Wells (by Northern Dancer). Whether or not this has had any impact on her ability as a racehorse is unprovable, but it is a pattern that will add an extra layer of interest to her prospects as a broodmare. Will there be attempts to add in further lines of either or both of those mares, or will those connections be avoided? It will be interesting to see her how future turns out.

The 195,000-guinea graduate of the Tattersalls December Foal Sale won three of her four starts as a juvenile, finishing the year on an official handicap figure of 110. She raised that to 115 as a three-year-old despite winning just once more. At two she had won the Group 3 Flame of Tara Stakes over a mile at the Curragh on her third start, beating So Wonderful by two and a half lengths, only to lose her unbeaten record next time with a three-length fourth to Quadrilateral in the Group 1 Fillies' Mile at Newmarket. Her first three starts of 2020 resulted in second-place finishes, but they were good efforts.

She had Fleeting a length and three-quarters behind when chasing home Magical in the Group 1 Alwasmiyah Pretty Polly Stakes over ten furlongs at the Curragh on her seasonal reappearance at the end of June, advertising her classic potential by staying on well in the closing stages, albeit never looking like catching the star Ballydoyle five-year-old who made all. The time for the Group 1 Juddmonte Irish Oaks three weeks later was a bit slower than one might expect for a race run on good-to-yielding and the winner failed to make the frame in two subsequent starts, adding to the overall feeling on the day that it was not a particularly strong edition of the classic. Cayenne Pepper was a two-length runner-up to Even So, she was half a length in front of the subsequent Group 1-placed pattern scorer Passion and the next two home were Laburnum and Snow. The first-named of those beaten horses won a listed race next time and was not disgraced in a pair of fourth-place finishes from her three other starts. Snow, who had tried to make all, came into the race following a Group 3 success over the trip at Cork, but she was a well-beaten last of three in the Group 2 Qatar Lillie Langtry Stakes and unplaced in the Group 2 bet365 Park Hill Fillies' Stakes on her next two runs. Both of those races are over farther, so perhaps she did not stay.

Cayenne Pepper passed the post three and three-quarter lengths clear of Passion when the pair met again in the Group 3 Irish Stallion Farms EBF Give Thanks Stakes over twelve furlongs on good ground at Cork in early August, but they had to settle for second and third respectively behind the Dermot Weld-trained four-year-old Tarnawa. That filly had won the same race in 2019 and followed it with Group 2 Blandford Stakes success, but the chestnut was about to raise her profile significantly, going on to complete a top-level hat-trick that culminated in her one-length defeat of Magical in the Grade 1 Breeders' Cup Turf at Keeneland in early November. Finishing a one-and-three-quarter-length runner-up to that filly was a good effort.

The three-year-old came down in trip for her final two outings of the year, the first one the Group 2 Moyglare 'Jewels' Blandford Stakes at the Curragh in mid-September. The ground was good, the Dermot Weld-trained Amma Grace tried to make all, but Cayenne Pepper hit the front over a furlong out and pulled four lengths clear by the line. The regally related runner-up finished a length and a half in front of the third, Thundering Nights, but the high-profile pair Magic Wand and One Voice—the latter also trained by Harrington—plus the early-season pattern scorer Lemista were well-beaten.

She then went to Keeneland for the Grade 1 Maker's Mark Breeders' Cup Filly & Mare Turf over nine and a half furlongs but, on firm ground, was one of three Europeans who disappointed in the race while the fourth representative, Audarya, stayed on well to take the top prize by a neck and a head from the local star Rushing Fall and the fast-finishing Harvey's Lil Goil.

She is the best of three winners out of Muwakaba (by Elusive Quality), a mare who made a winning debut over seven furlongs on the Polytrack at Kempton and finished third in a ten-furlong handicap on a similar surface at Lingfield on the final of her four starts. She is a half-sister to Morghim (by Machiavellian), a stakes-placed handicapper who won at up to ten furlongs, and out of Saleela (by Nureyev). That mare made all to take a twelve-and-a-half-furlong Warwick handicap on the last of her four races on the track, and in addition to being a half-sister to the aforementioned Group 1 stars King's Best (2000 Guineas; classic sire) and Urban Sea (Prix de l'Arc de Triomphe; dam of Galileo, Sea The Stars, etc.), she is also one to Allez Les Trois (by Riverman), the pattern-winning dam of the Group 1 Prix du Jockey Club (French Derby) scorer and blacktype sire Anabaa Blue (by Anabaa). Muwakaba had a first-crop Churchill (by Galileo) colt in 2019, a full brother to Cayenne Pepper in 2020 and was then bred to Galileo (by Sadler's Wells).

Cayenne Pepper stays twelve furlongs, as you might expect of a daughter of Australia (by Galileo) whose grandam is a half-sister to Urban Sea, but her Blandford success presents evidence that she may be better over ten. Of course, there is as yet insufficient data on which to make a definite statement, but hopefully there will be plenty of opportunities in 2021 to learn more about her as she is back in training for another year.

SUMMARY DETAILS
Bred: G H S Bloodstock & J C Bloodstock
Owned: Mrs S Kelly
Trained: Jessica Harrington
Country: Ireland
Race record: 1114-22210-
Career highlights: 4 wins inc Moyglare 'Jewels' Blandford Stakes (Gr2), Flame of Tara Irish EBF Stakes (Gr3), 2nd Juddmonte Irish Oaks (Gr1), Alwasmiyah Pretty Polly Stakes (Gr1), Irish Stallion Farms EBF Give Thanks Stakes (Gr3)

CAYENNE PEPPER (IRE) – 2017 chestnut filly

Australia (GB)	Galileo (IRE)	Sadler's Wells (USA)
		Urban Sea (USA)
	Ouija Board (GB)	Cape Cross (IRE)
		Selection Board
Muwakaba (USA)	Elusive Quality (USA)	Gone West (USA)
		Touch of Greatness (USA)
	Saleela (USA)	Nureyev (USA)
		Allegretta

CENTURY DREAM (IRE)

Century Dream is a talented horse who stays ten furlongs but is best over a mile. He has won on all types of ground from good to heavy, although seems at his best when there is some ease underfoot, and on his day, he is just short of Group 1 class. He is by the sire of Sea The Stars (by Cape Cross), he is a half-brother to a Group 1-winning miler and has done more than enough to demonstrate why he deserves a good place somewhere as a stallion. Yes, he had a wind procedure done in late 2019, but that was after he had already won seven of his twenty-three starts and been a Group 1-placed pattern winner with a peak Timeform end-of-year rating of 121. He performed at that 2018 level again in 2020 and added two more pattern wins to his tally. Plenty of less well-credentialed horses have been given the opportunity, so why not him?

The Rabbah Bloodstock-bred bay won the last of his three starts as a juvenile and worked his way up through the handicap ranks as a three-year-old, starting the year on eighty-six and running his final race of that season off 101, although his Timeform rating at that point stood at an eye-catching 116. He won a listed contest over a mile on soft ground at Ascot on his second outing as a four-year-old and followed that with a two-and-a-quarter-length defeat of Gabrial in the Group 3 Diomed Stakes at Epsom before stepping up in grade and acquitting himself well without winning. He missed out on blacktype placing in the first three of those runs, but not by much: he was fourth on each occasion.

His total margin of defeat was only three-quarters of a length when he filled that position behind Accidental Agent in the Group 1 Queen Anne Stakes, it was three and a half lengths when he was fourth to Beat The Bank in the Group 2 Summer Mile—both of those races over a mile on good-to-firm at Ascot, one the straight course, the other the round one—and then he was third past the post in the Grade 1 Arlington Million. Unfortunately, having tried to make all, he got tired, impeded the former Argentine Grade 1 scorer Catcho En Die in the final half furlong and had his placing with that gelding reversed. Robert Bruce won the race and had passed the post two and a half lengths in front of Century Dream. His final start of 2018 was one of particular note because he was only beaten margins of a neck and half a length when third to Roaring Lion and I Can Fly in the Group 1 Queen Elizabeth II Stakes on soft ground at Ascot.

He notched up two seconds and a fourth in blacktype company as a five-year-old before bouncing back at six, kicking off his latest campaign with a one-and-a-quarter-length defeat of King of Comedy in the Group 3 MansionBet's Beaten By A Head Diomed Stakes, this time run over a mile at Newbury rather than at its usual home, part of the early-season restructuring due to the Covid-19 situation. It was a bit disappointing that he finished a five-and-a-half-length fifth to Persian King in the Group 1 Prix d'Ispahan at Chantilly next time, but then he went to Goodwood for one of the best performances of his career. The ground was soft and having raced prominently throughout, he hit the front a quarter of a mile from home and went clear, passing the post four and a half lengths clear of Sir Busker and with Regal Reality another length and three-quarters behind in third.

That fine effort made his two subsequent performances a shade more disappointing. He was sent off the favourite for the Group 2 Clipper Logistics Boomerang Stakes at Leopardstown on the opening day of Irish Champions Weekend in September, but after being in front for much of the race, he came under pressure in the straight and could find no more, eventually losing fourth place on the line and finishing a total of six and three-quarter lengths adrift of the winner, Safe Voyage. He again raced prominently in the Group 1 Queen Elizabeth II Stakes at Ascot on his final start, but it was clear from around a quarter of a mile from home that a repeat of his prior good effort in the race was unlikely. He finished ninth, beaten by a total of eight lengths as The Revenant held off the strong challenge of Roseman by a head.

His Richard Hannon-trained half-brother King of Change (by Farhh) ran only six times but chased home Magna Grecia in the Group 1 2000 Guineas at Newmarket in 2019, followed that with listed success over a mile at Sandown and then beat The Revenant by a length and a quarter to take the Group 1 Queen Elizabeth II Stakes in the style of a horse who looked likely to play a major role in the mile division in 2020. Unfortunately, that Timeform 126-rated bay didn't make it back to the track and he has now joined the team at Derrinstown Stud in Ireland where he should prove popular in his new stallion role.

The brothers are the first and third foals of Salacia (by Echo of Light) and that granddaughter of Dubai Millennium (by Seeking The Gold) has had two other winners to back them up. Thawry (by Iffraaj), her second born, is a multiple scorer from nine and a half furlongs to twelve furlongs, he stays two miles and is trained by Antony Brittain. Banna (by Pivotal), on the other hand, can be described as being a three-parts sister to King of Change and, like Century Dream, she is trained by Simon and Ed Crisford. She didn't run as a two-year-old but got off the mark at the second attempt in 2020, winning a one-mile novice race on soft ground at Doncaster in early November. Their year-younger half-sister Royal Event (by Golden Horn) encountered some trouble in running when unplaced on her sole outing, over seven furlongs at Kempton three days earlier, and she should be capable of better in time. The mare's new two-year-old has been named Queen of Change (by Sea The Stars).

Salacia, who won once as a three-year-old, has a trio of stakes-placed horses among her siblings. However, more notable is that she is out of Neptune's Bride (by Bering), a Grade 2-placed winner of the Group 3 Prix Fille de l'Air and two listed races. That mare is a half-sister to Sea Dart (by Diesis), a former John Oxx-trained mile Group 2 scorer who was exported to Bahrain and won a similar contest at local level there before taking up stallion duties. Their dam, Wedding of The Sea (by Blushing Groom) also had plenty of ability and having been stakes placed as a two-year-old, she went on to become a smart sprinter. The Group 3 Prix de Ris-Orangis at Evry provided her with her best win whereas the races in which she was placed featured the Group 2 Prix du Gros-Chene at Chantilly and Group 2 Goldene Peitsche at Baden-Baden.

The next dam, Sweet Mover (by Nijinsky), was a stakes-placed winner in England and her siblings featured the prolific US graded scorer Hail Hilarious (by Fast Hilarious) and the Grade 1-placed multiple stakes winner Countess Fager (by Dr. Fager). The latter's trio of blacktype progeny included Reigning Countess (by Far

North), and that Grade 3 winner and mile track-record setter has a string of blacktype descendants, notably the middle-distance Group 1 scorer Mamool (by In The Wings). This is also a branch of the family of the Group 1-winning sprinter Sayf El Arab (by Drone)—his grandam, Sister Antoine (by Royal Serenade), is the sixth dam of Century Dream—and of fellow 2020 pattern scorer Dakota Gold (by Equiano).

SUMMARY DETAILS
Bred: Rabbah Bloodstock Ltd
Owned: Abdulla Belhabb
Trained: Simon & Ed Crisford
Country: England
Race record: 031-3411011-0114443-240020-10100-
Career highlights: 9 wins inc Ladbrokes Celebration Mile Stakes (Gr2), MansionBet's Beaten By A Head Diomed Stakes (Gr3), Investec Diomed Stakes (Gr3), Celebrating The Commonwealth Paradise Stakes (L), 2nd Zabeel Mile sponsored by Al Tayer Motors (Gr2), Price Bailey Ben Marshall Stakes (L), 3rd Queen Elizabeth II Stakes (Gr1)

CENTURY DREAM (IRE) – 2014 bay horse

Cape Cross (IRE)	Green Desert (USA)	Danzig (USA)
		Foreign Courier (USA)
	Park Appeal	Ahonoora
		Balidaress
Salacia (IRE)	Echo of Light (GB)	Dubai Millennium (GB)
		Spirit of Tara (IRE)
	Neptune's Bride (USA)	Bering
		Wedding of The Sea (USA)

CERTAIN LAD (GB)

Certain Lad was gelded after his juvenile season, in which he had won a listed contest over a mile at Lyon Parilly and finished third to Van Beethoven in the Group 2 Railway Stakes. He finished that campaign on an official handicap mark of 103, won handicaps over a mile at Haydock and ten furlongs at Ayr, and started the 2020 season rated 100. He had a busy season at four, taking in a trio of races at Meydan then five races spread around four tracks in England before heading to Bahrain in November where he finished a three-length sixth to the ex-Irish gelding Simsir in the valuable Bahrain International Trophy. Had he finished one place better in that ten-furlong conditions race at Sakhir, he would have picked up a cheque for £25,000; the winner earned £250,000.

He had given Simsir one pound plus a three-quarter-length beating when the pair finished one-two in a listed handicap over the same trip at Meydan in January and was outclassed when a distant fourth behind Ghaiyyath in the Group 3 Dubai Millennium Stakes the following month. His handicap mark was raised to 108 after his one-length second in the John Smith's Cup Handicap at York in mid-July, having been sent off at a generous 66/1 that day, and so it wasn't really surprising to see him chase home Extra Elusive in the Group 3 BetVictor Rose of Lancaster Stakes at Haydock three weeks later. Hollie Doyle was on board the winner there but took the mount on Certain Lad next time and the pair won the Group 3 Sky Bet and Symphony Group Strensall Stakes over nine furlongs at York. He was raised to 112 after that but later trimmed to 110 having finished down the field in the Cambridgeshire.

Certain Lad was bred by Barry Walters and made just 13,000 guineas when sold from Book 3 of the Tattersalls October Yearling Sale of 2017. He is a son of the now veteran Rathasker Stud sire Clodovil (by Danehill), the classic-winning miler whose three Group 1 scorers among an overall tally of twenty-five blacktype scorers includes Tiger Tanaka, winner of the Prix Marcel Boussac at ParisLongchamp in October. The stallion's runners in 2020 also included the Group 3 Molecomb Stakes scorer Steel Bull, and there were multiple blacktype wins for his

German sprinter Majestic Colt and for his Scandinavian star Duca Di Como.

Certain Lad's siblings include Brandon Castle (by Dylan Thomas), a multiple wide-margin handicap winner on the flat whose string of hurdle successes brings his overall career total to twelve wins and counting. Half-brothers Jack Regan (by Rock of Gibraltar) and The Statesman (by Zoffany) have also won under both codes, his now three-year-old half-brother Going Back To Cali (by Pride of Dubai) is a £40,000 graduate of the Goffs UK Premier Yearling Sale, and their dam had a Zoffany (by Dansili) filly in 2020 before being bred to U S Navy Flag (by War Front).

Chelsey Jayne (by Galileo) is the mare's name and although she was not a winner, she has a notable dam and four blacktype siblings. Her full sister Classic Legend won the Listed Montrose Stakes at Newmarket, half-brother Popmurphy (by Montjeu) was runner-up in the Listed Alleged Stakes, whereas Rawdaa (by Teofilo), who could be described as being her three-parts sister, achieved a Timeform rating of 118. She is not a stakes winner but was runner-up in the Group 2 Middleton Stakes and Group 2 Duke of Cambridge Stakes, third in both the Group 1 Nassau Stakes and Listed Snowdrop Stakes, and she was bred to Dubawi (by Dubai Millennium) in 2020. Their half-brother Jallotta (by Rock of Gibraltar), on the other hand, notched up seven wins and seventeen placings over the course of his career. He won the Group 3 Prix du Pin at Chantilly and Listed Guisborough Stakes at Redcar and the string of good races in which he was placed included the Group 1 Premio Vittorio di Capua, Group 2 Challenge Stakes, Group 2 bet365 Mile, and Group 2 Joel Stakes. You will see his fourth in the Group 1 Prix Morny on catalogue pages but, of course, that counts neither as being placed nor as a piece of blacktype.

Lady Lahar (by Fraam), the grandam of Certain Lad, won the Group 3 Futurity Stakes at the Curragh, was runner-up in the Group 3 Prix de la Nonette and third in the Group 2 Falmouth Stakes and Group 2 Cherry Hinton Stakes, and she is out of an unraced daughter of an unraced daughter of a minor two-year-old winner. The only other notable horse within the first four generations of Certain Lad's pedigree is the Grade 3-winning chaser and blacktype hurdles scorer Arctic Weather (by Montelimar), a half-brother to his third dam.

SUMMARY DETAILS
Bred: Barry Walters
Owned: C R Hirst
Trained: Mick Channon
Country: England
Race record: 11340310-004010421-134022100-
Career highlights: 7 wins inc Sky Bet And Symphony Group Strensall Stakes (Gr3), Zabeel Turf sponsored by Riviera 1 (L), Criterium de Lyon (L), 2nd BetVictor Rose of Lancaster Stakes (Gr3), 3rd GAIN Railway Stakes (Gr2), 32Red Casino Ascendant Stakes (L)

CERTAIN LAD (IRE) – 2016 bay gelding

Clodovil (IRE)	Danehill (USA)	Danzig (USA)
		Razyana (USA)
	Clodora (FR)	Linamix (FR)
		Cloche d'Or (GB)
Chelsey Jayne (IRE)	Galileo (IRE)	Sadler's Wells (USA)
		Urban Sea (USA)
	Lady Lahar (GB)	Fraam (GB)
		Brigadiers Bird (IRE)

CHINDIT (IRE)

If Chindit's season had stopped after his Group 2 bet365 Champagne Stakes victory he would have gone into winter quarters as unbeaten classic prospect boasting a Timeform rating of 117p. He still could become a Group 1 star, but his eighth-place finish behind St Mark's Basilica in the Group 1 Darley Dewhurst Stakes at Newmarket a month later tarnished the shine a little. The ground was soft that day, in contrast to his first three starts, he encountered some traffic problems en route but didn't pick up inside the final furlong. His rider, Pat Dobbs, reported that the colt had been hanging right-handed throughout the race. Something was clearly amiss.

All of his starts so far have been over seven furlongs and that could be his distance in 2020 but given that he is a son of Wootton Bassett (by Iffraaj) and the grandson of a half-sister to a Derby winner, there is a good chance that he will be effective at eight to ten furlongs. He won his maiden in good style at Doncaster in early July, followed that with a one-and-three-quarter-length defeat of Cobh in the Listed BetfredTV Pat Eddery Stakes on good-to-firm at Ascot and then went to the front inside the final furlong to beat Albasheer and State of Rest by a length and a short head in the Champagne. There was a seven-and-a-half-length gap back to the fourth, Mujbar. That colt, a seven-length winner on his previous start, was a seven-furlong Group 3 scorer at Newbury on his only subsequent run.

Chindit, a 65,000-guinea graduate of Book 2 of the Tattersalls October Yearling Sale and bred by J C Bloodstock and R Mahon, is the first foal of Always A Dream (by Oasis Dream), a mare whose sole win from eleven starts came in a seven-furlong apprentice handicap at Wolverhampton, off a mark of fifty-eight. She was then sold for just 16,000 guineas at the Tattersalls Autumn Horses-in-Training Sale. Her second foal is an Awtaad (by Cape Cross) colt who made 80,000 guineas from the 2019's Book 2 sale, she was bred to Profitable (by Invincible Spirit) in 2019 (no return) and to Bated Breath (by Dansili) last season. The mare is a half-sister to the middle-distance filly Goldie Hawk (by Golden Horn), who has won three of her five starts for the Chris

Wall stable, and she is out of Always Remembered (by Galileo), an unraced daughter of the listed scorer Out West (by Gone West).

That mare's star son Motivator (by Montjeu) won the Group 1 Racing Post Trophy in 2004, was an impressive winner of the Group 1 Derby at Epsom the following summer, and the brilliant classic and dual Prix de l'Arc de Triomphe heroine Treve is his standout among a total of thirty-one stakes winners. His full brother Macarthur won the Group 2 Hardwicke Stakes and was placed in the Group 1 Coronation Cup, half-sister Clear Skies (by Sea The Stars) was placed in the Group 3 Blue Wind Stakes, whereas Imperial Star (by Fantastic Light) is a pattern-placed stakes winner who has reportedly sired a winner of the Bahrain Oaks. Clear Skies, on the other hand, had a Camelot (by Montjeu) foal in January 2020 and was bred back to that colt's sire.

If you go farther back on the page then you will find some notable US and Brazilian horses appear under the fifth generation of the pedigree and its branches, but their connection to Chindit is remote and, at this point in his life, tell us nothing more than we already know about him and his prospects. Several of them stood as stallions, one of them achieving some notable results, and the time to consider them more closely will be if he goes on to Group 1 success and/or is assigned a place at stud. As for his own sire, Wootton Bassett is embarking on a new phase of his career as the long-time Haras d'Etreham stallion has joined the Coolmore Stud team, a move that, coinciding with the emergence of two new Group 1 stars for him among an overall career tally of sixteen stakes winners, has seen his fee soar from €40,000 to €100,000.

SUMMARY DETAILS
Bred: J C Bloodstock & R Mahon
Owned: Michael Pescod
Trained: Richard Hannon
Country: England
Race record: 1110-
Career highlights: 3 wins inc bet365 Champagne Stakes (Gr2), BetfredTV Pat Eddery Stakes (L)

CHINDIT (IRE) – 2018 bay colt

Wootton Bassett (GB)	Iffraaj (GB)	Zafonic (USA)
		Pastorale (GB)
	Balladonia (GB)	Primo Dominie
		Susquehanna Days (USA)
Always A Dream (GB)	Oasis Dream (GB)	Green Desert (USA)
		Hope (IRE)
	Always Remembered (IRE)	Galileo (IRE)
		Out West (USA)

CORMORANT (IRE)

Cormorant is a 135,000-guineas Tattersalls December Foal Sale graduate who became a 1,050,000-guinea Book 1 yearling but has not yet lived up to that potential. He won a one-mile Leopardstown maiden on his second attempt at two, finished fifth behind his stablemate Mogul in the Group 2 KPMG Champions Juvenile Stakes over the same course and distance before taking the runners-up spot in a ten-furlong conditions race at Chelmsford in early November. His three-year-old campaign began with a half-length defeat of Russian Emperor in the Group 3 Derrinstown Stud Derby Trial Stakes but he was only fourth to Thunderous in the Group 2 Dante Stakes at York a month later and fourth to Tiger Moth in a twelve-furlong Group 3 contest at Leopardstown on Irish Champions Weekend. He hit the front half a mile out in the latter but was under pressure turning into the straight and weakened in the closing stages. His stable companion won by four lengths from Silence Please, but there was only a neck back to Up Helly Aa in third and another head back to Cormorant. Buckhurst was fifth, three-quarters of a length farther behind.

The early March-born grey, who is inbred 4x4 to Danzig (by Northern Dancer), is the second foal of Shemya (by Dansili), a winning daughter of the talented Shemima (by Dalakhani). She won the Group 3 Prix Allez France and Group 3 Prix de Lutece, was runner-up in the Group 2 Prix Chaudennay and Group 2 Prix de Pomone and third in the Group 2 Prix Maurice de Nieuil, so it easy to see why her grandson has had a racing career geared towards middle distances, so far. Shemaka (by Nishapour), his third dam, won the Group 1 Prix de Diane (French Oaks) and her many blacktype descendants feature the Group 1 Grand Prix de Paris scorer Shakeel (by Dalakhani), Group 2 Prix Eugene Adam winner Shimraan (by Rainbow Quest), Grade 1 Premio El Derby victory Full of Luck (by Lookin At Lucky), and Group 1 Prix du Jockey Club runner-up Shamkiyr (by Sea The Stars).

Cormorant's sire, Kingman (by Invincible Spirit), was a Timeform 134-rated miler and although he has been getting his best winners mostly in the six-to-ten-furlong range, as expected, he has also been getting some who are effective over farther. Ten furlongs may be his trip, and there may still be some good prizes to be won with him, but it could be interesting to see how he would get on if brought back to the mile or even seven furlongs. Cormorant was gelded shortly before this book went to print and he has left Ballydoyle.

SUMMARY DETAILS
Bred: Michael E Wates
Owned: Michael Tabor, Derrick Smith & Mrs John Magnier
Trained: Aidan O'Brien
Country: Ireland
Race record: 4102-144-
Career highlights: 2 wins inc Derrinstown Stud Derby Trial Stakes (Gr3)

CORMORANT (IRE) – 2017 grey gelding

		Green Desert (USA)
Kingman (GB)	Invincible Spirit (IRE)	Green Desert (USA)
		Rafha
	Zenda (GB)	Zamindar (USA)
		Hope (IRE)
Shemya (FR)	Dansili (GB)	Danehill (USA)
		Hasili (IRE)
	Shemima (GB)	Dalakhani (IRE)
		Shemaka (IRE)

CROSSFIREHURRICANE (USA)

Kitten's Joy (by El Prado) has long been the top sire of turf horses in North America and it's somewhat of a surprise that larger numbers of his progeny have not been imported to Europe. The figures have been growing in recent seasons and Crossfirehurricane is among those who have won at pattern level. Judged on what we have seen of him so far, he is a long way behind the likes of Hawkbill, Roaring Lion and Kameko in terms of racing talent, and even on the merit of his early winning sequence it is hard to imagine him reaching those heights. That said, many of the offspring of his sire excel as older horses, so perhaps he can move past his two crushing defeats and pick up the pattern-winning thread again.

He won a seven-furlong Limerick maiden on yielding ground in mid-June of his two-year-old season and was not seen out again until Dundalk the following February. He took that seven-furlong contest on the Polytrack by three and a half lengths, followed up with a half-length score in a listed contest over a mile at the same venue three weeks later and, a few days after racing resumed in Ireland post-lockdown, landed the Group 3 Coolmore Ten Sovereigns Gallinule Stakes over ten furlongs at the Curragh. The Ballydoyle runner Toronto was still a long way clear three furlongs out, with Gold Maze being pushed along on the rail and Crossfirehurricane going well on the outside. The pair gradually reduced the colt's lead and joined him at the furlong pole. It was quickly evident that the front-runner was weakening and would not be placed, that Gold Maze was not going to hold on to the lead he had briefly taken, and that the unbeaten chestnut was going to complete his four-timer. It was a promising effort that raised his official handicap mark from ninety-six to 106. He finished a never-dangerous tenth behind Santiago in the Group 1 Dubai Duty Free Irish Derby two weeks later and was beaten by even farther behind Bowerman in the Group 3 Al Basti Equiworld, Dubai Diamond Stakes over the extended ten and a half furlongs at Dundalk in late September. A post-race veterinary report noted that the colt was coughing, possibly due to the kickback. His rating stands at 105 on Polytrack and 103 on turf.

Crossfirehurricane is out of Louvakhova (by Maria's Mon), a stakes-winning half-sister to Flotilla, the Grade 1 Breeders' Cup Juvenile Fillies Turf and subsequent Group 1 Poule d'Essai des Pouliches (French 1000 Guineas) heroine who was the joint champion juvenile filly in France in 2012. Their dam, Louvain (by Sinndar), won the Grade 3 Miesque Stakes and a pair of listed contests in California, is a half-sister to the Group 1 Sprint Cup scorer G Force (by Tamayuz) and out of Flanders (by Common Grounds). That is the Irish-bred Group 2-placed stakes-winning sprinter rather than the US-bred Grade 1 star of the same name, and, in human terms, she could be described as being an aunt to the dual Group 1-winning sprint champion Lethal Force (by Dark Angel), Group 1-placed Group 2 Prix Robert Papin scorer Family One (by Dubai Destination), and Group 2 Rockfel Stakes winner Juliet Capulet (by Dark Angel).

Crossfirehurricane has been a pattern winner over a mile and a quarter on fast ground and it will be interesting to see where his career goes from this point. Given how his sire's best horses tend to fare, it may be that he will be best suited to eight-to-ten furlongs rather than over further. He is now in the USA.

SUMMARY DETAILS
Bred: Glen Hill Farm & Scott C Heider
Owned: Scott C Heider
Trained: Joseph O'Brien
Country: Ireland
Race record: 1-11100-
Career highlights: 4 wins inc Coolmore Ten Sovereigns Gallinule Stakes (Gr3), Woodford Reserve Patton Stakes (L)

CROSSFIREHURRICANE (USA) – 2017 chestnut colt

Kitten's Joy (USA)	El Prado (IRE)	Sadler's Wells (USA)
		Lady Capulet (USA)
	Kitten's First (USA)	Lear Fan (USA)
		That's My Hon (USA)
Louvakhova (USA)	Maria's Mon (USA)	Wavering Monarch (USA)
		Carlotta Maria (USA)
	Louvain (IRE)	Sinndar (IRE)
		Flanders (IRE)

CURRENT OPTION (IRE)

Current Option notched up one win and four placings from five starts for the William Haggas stable, was sold for 85,000 guineas at the Tattersalls July Sale in Newmarket and joined the Ado McGuinness team in north Co Dublin. The gelding was placed over seven furlongs at Cork on his first outing for the new connections, was then a three-quarter-length runner-up in the Tote Irish Cambridgeshire over a mile at the Curragh before landing a premier handicap over seven furlongs at Leopardstown during Irish Champions Weekend. In 2020, he notched up three wins and a placing from seven starts, saw his handicap mark rise from ninety-four to 107, and became a dual stakes winner.

The bulk of his progression happened from the start of August when he won a premier handicap on soft ground at Galway by a neck from Njord, who would go on to win the Balmoral Handicap at Ascot in October. He followed up in a listed contest on good ground at Cork and, two months later, stepped up another half a furlong to take the Group 3 Coolmore U S Navy Flag Concorde Stakes at Tipperary, this time racing on going described as yielding-to-soft. He had led briefly in the early stages of the latter race, was prominent throughout and got back up in the final strides of the seven-and-a-half-furlong contest to pip Laughifuwant by a short head. The pair finished one and three-quarter lengths in front of the third-placed Soul Search, and she in turn was two lengths ahead of Could Be King in fourth. Albigna and Forever In Dreams disappointed, coming home seventh and tenth respectively.

Current Option is a son of Coolmore Stud's multiple classic star Camelot (by Montjeu), a stallion who had four top-level winners around the world in 2020: Even So (Irish Oaks), Russian Camelot (South Australian Derby, Underwood Stakes), Sir Dragonet (Cox Plate), and Sunny Queen (Grosser Preis von Bayern). He is the third foal of a placed mare called Coppertop (by Exceed And Excel), who is a half-sister to the mile listed scorer Canary Row (by Holy Roman Emperor). Despite how it looks on at least one catalogue page in which that six-time-winner appears, he was placed fifteen times, not twenty-eight, and has only one piece of blacktype: finishing fourth is not being placed (other than for betting purposes in a handicap with sixteen or more runners)—it is 'finishing out of the frame', 'missing out on the minor honours' or whichever similar expression you prefer—and it has not counted for blacktype for a very long time.

Valley of Song (by Caerleon), the third dam of Current Option, won her only start, she is a full sister to the Group 1 Moyglare Stud Stakes winner Preseli, half-sister to the Group 1 1000 Guineas runner-up Snowfire (by Machiavellian), and also a sibling of Group 3 scorer Kong (by Sadler's Wells) and listed winner Mount Kilimanjaro (by Sadler's Wells). White Star Line (by Northern Dancer), the multiple Grade 1-winning fifth dam, is the ancestor of a variety of other talented horses, notably the Group 1 Oaks d'Italia winner Valley of Gold (by Shirley Heights), Group 1 Deutsches Derby victor Dai Jin (by Peintre Celebre), Group 2 Derby Italiano scorer Worthadd (by Dubawi), Group 2 Prix de Pomone winner Whitehaven (by Top Ville), classic-placed pattern winner Musis Amica (by Dawn Approach) and that filly's Group 2-winning half-brother Harland (by Halling).

Current Option, who is inbred 3x3 to Sadler's Wells (by Northern Dancer) and 4x3 to Danehill (by Danzig), is a talented gelding who stays a mile but has got all of his best wins over up to a furlong less than that. He has been successful on ground ranging from good down to soft, and it will be interesting to see if he can raise his rating further in 2021. His dam foaled a full brother to him in February 2020 and she was then bred to U S Navy Flag (by War Front).

SUMMARY DETAILS
Bred: Grangecon Holdings Ltd
Owned: Dooley Thoroughbreds, Shamrock Thoroughbreds & B T O'Sullivan
Trained: Adrian (Ado) McGuinness
Country: Ireland
Race record: 23-321221-0201101-
Career highlights: 5 wins inc Coolmore U S Navy Flag Concorde Stakes (Gr3), Platinum Stakes (L)

CURRENT OPTION (IRE) – 2016 bay gelding

Camelot (GB)	Montjeu (IRE)	**Sadler's Wells (USA)**
		Floripedes (FR)
	Tarfah (USA)	Kingmambo (USA)
		Fickle (GB)
Coppertop (IRE)	Exceed And Excel (AUS)	Danehill (USA)
		Patrona (USA)
	Fresh Mint (IRE)	**Sadler's Wells (USA)**
		Valley of Song (GB)

DAKOTA GOLD (GB)

The final few months of the year have an added point of interest for pedigree analysts and breeders as it is then that the bulk of the stallion announcements are made for the following year. Aside from the fees for the new season and the revelation or confirmation of who has won a berth as a new addition to the ranks there are also a few notifications of a change in location for a horse who has already served at least one season. The switching of Wootton Bassett from Haras d'Etreham to Coolmore Stud, with an associated fee increase from €40,000 to €100,000, was the most high-profile move, but he was not the only Group 1 sire to make a change. He has only sixteen stakes winners to his name and is now thirteen years old. Equiano (by Acclamation), on the other hand, has had seventeen stakes winners and is three years older. The younger horse is a classic sire with three top-level winners his name, the older one a source of sprinters who has two top-level winners on his record. He looks sure to continue supplying talented performers mostly in the five-to-seven-furlong range, there's no reason why he couldn't get another smart miler like Grade 3 Florida Oaks scorer Baciami Piccola, and he looks sure to be very popular in his new home, the Irish National Stud, at a fee of €3,000.

Equiano's dozen pattern winners include the Grade 1 Breeders' Cup Turf Sprint heroine Belvoir Bay and the triple six-furlong Group 1 star The Tin Man. Dakota Gold was one of two who added their name to the stallion's group-race roster in 2020— Gustavus Weston was the other one—and his big day came when he beat The Tin Man by one and three-quarter lengths to take the Group 3 Coral Bengough Stakes over six furlongs at York in October. He added a three-and-a-half-length score in the five-furlong Listed Rous Stakes at Nottingham three days later and then completed a blacktype hat-trick when beating Aberama Gold by three-quarters of a length in the Listed Betfair Wentworth Stakes over six at Doncaster in early November. All three races were on soft ground, as was his earlier win in the Listed William Hill Beverley Bullet Sprint Stakes. Between that success and his first pattern win, he was placed in a pair of listed sprints on good ground.

He won a listed race and a valuable York handicap on good ground in 2019, as well as the Listed Rous Stakes on soft at its usual home, Ascot, and he was a half-length runner-up to Maid In India on good-to-firm in the Group 3 Dubai International Airport World Trophy Stakes over five furlongs at Newbury that September. Overall, this Michael Dods-trained bay, who was gelded before he ever raced, has notched up a total of thirteen wins and eleven placings from thirty-nine starts, earning almost £370,000 in prize money. That is a nice return on the 26,000 guineas for which Dods secured him from Book 2 of the Tattersalls October Yearling Sale in 2015.

Dakota Gold is the second foal of Joyeaux (by Mark of Esteem) and his trio of winning siblings includes Commanche Falls (by Lethal Force), a triple six-furlong winner for the Dods stable in 2020 and also winner of his two-year-old debut for the team in 2019. That gelding is an 11,000-guinea Tattersalls Book 3 graduate with a handicap mark of eighty-four. Their dam is a six-time winning half-sister to the Group 1 Premio Lydia Tesio winner Aoife Alainn (by Dr Fong) and to the prolific Adorabile Fong (by Dr Fong), an eighteen-time scorer who won at listed level and was third in the Group 2 Premio Parioli (Italian 2000 Guineas).

Divine Secret (by Hernando), the grandam of Dakota Gold, is an unraced half-sister to seven winners and out of Mysterious Plans (by Last Tycoon), a winning full sister to Monde Bleu. He won the Group 2 Prix du Gros-Chene, Group 3 Palace House Stakes and Group 3 Prix de Meautry, he was third in the Group 1 Prix de l'Abbaye de Longchamp and his nine winning siblings feature fellow sprint star Sayf El Arab (by Drone), winner of the Group 1 King's Stand Stakes in 1983. Their dam, Make Plans (by Go Marching), was unplaced but out of the talented and prolific US mare Sister Antoine (by Royal Serenade). Her dozen wins featured the Santa Margarita Handicap over nine furlongs at Santa Anita in 1961, a race that from the time the pattern system came into effect until 2019 was run as a Grade 1. Sister Antoine's descendants also include Group 1 star King of Change (by Farhh) and his high-class half-brother Century Dream (by Cape Cross), although she is the sixth dam of that pair. The latter is featured elsewhere in this volume.

Despite a preoccupation with early two-year-old speed in a large segment of the industry, many notable sprinters do not show their worth until they are three-year-olds or older horses, and some of them only from the age of five and upwards. Dakota Gold, whom Timeform rated 120 at five, had another outstanding year at the age of six, and there is every to hope that he will be at least as good again in 2021, especially when there is some ease in the ground. His official handicap mark is 111.

SUMMARY DETAILS

Bred: Redgate Bloodstock & Peter Bottowley Bloodstock
Owned: Doug Graham, Ian Davison & Alan Drysdale
Trained: Michael Dods
Country: England
Race record: 3100-121223-030002340100-0111121-0000123111-
Career highlights: 13 wins inc Coral Bengough Stakes (Gr3), Betfair Wentworth Stakes (L), Rous Stakes (L-twice), William Hill Beverley Bullet Sprint Stakes (L), LNER Supporting CALM Garrowby Stakes (L), 2nd Dubai International Airport World Trophy Stakes (Gr3), Al Basti Equiworld Dubai Garrowby Stakes (L), 3rd bet365 Scarborough Stakes (L)

DAKOTA GOLD (GB) – 2014 bay gelding

		Royal Applause (GB)
	Acclamation (GB)	
		Princess Athena
Equiano (FR)		
		Ela-Mana-Mou
	Entente Cordiale (IRE)	
		Mirmande (GB)
		Darshaan
	Mark of Esteem (IRE)	
		Homage (GB)
Joyeaux (GB)		
		Hernando (FR)
	Divine Secret (GB)	
		Mysterious Plans (IRE)

DAME MALLIOT (GB)

There is an increasing number of Group 1 scorers who got an early winning start on the artificial tracks and although Dame Malliot hasn't won at the highest level, she has been placed at it three times. Those were her final three outings of 2020 and they followed her two-and-a-quarter-length defeat of Communique in the Group 2 Princess of Wales's Tattersalls Stakes over twelve furlongs on soft ground at Newmarket in July.

She took a keen hold throughout the first few furlongs that day and was moved up to the lead at the seven-furlong pole. She seemed happier in front, although drifted across to the centre of the track, but bowled along until joined by Alounak and Communique at the four-furlong marker. Hollie Doyle began to ask her for more a furlong later and although headed by that named pair and being left for a while to race wide of the field by herself, the filly stayed on, got back in front inside the final furlong and went clear in the closing stages. By that point, Communique and third-placed Desert Encounter had drifted over to her side of the track. Enbihaar stayed on well into fourth, only missing out on a place by a head.

This was Dame Malliot's seasonal reappearance and, on the strength of this fine effort, she was sent off favourite to beat six rivals in the Group 1 Preis von Europa on soft ground at Cologne the following month. Doyle was again in the saddle, but this time, having tried to make all, they had to settle for third. They were only headed inside the final furlong but stayed on to the line and finished three-quarters of a length in front of Barney Roy but a neck and half-length behind Donjah and Kaspar. Frankie Dettori took the ride at ParisLongchamp in October and also tried to make all in the Group 1 Qatar Prix Vermeille. This time the filly lost her lead to the Dermot Weld-trained Tarnawa a furlong from home and lost second to Raabihah at the line. The margins were three lengths and a short head, with Laburnum, Wonderful Tonight and Even So the next three home, coming in at half-length margins.

Doyle and Dame Malliot were reunited at Ascot mid-October but again had to settle for minor honours. The filly took a keen hold but never went to the front. She was in second place three furlongs out, headed a furlong later, fought back, and passed the post a two-and-a-half-length runner-up to Wonderful Tonight, with the staying-on Passion a length back in third, two lengths ahead of Mehdaayih, the filly who had been second briefly in the straight. The Irish Oaks winner Even So disappointed again, this time finishing another two and three-quarter lengths adrift in fifth. The soft ground was likely a major factor in the spread-out nature of the field by the line, with the final four finishing between twenty-six and over eighty-one lengths behind the winner.

Dame Malliot is clearly effective on soft ground, and it was heavy when she won the Group 2 Prix de Pomone at Deauville as a three-year-old, but it was good when she ran away with a twelve-furlong listed contest at Newmarket the time before that and, as alluded to above, her sole start as a two-year-old was in an extended nine-furlong novice auction race on the Tapeta surface at Wolverhampton, which she won well. She has also been placed on Polytrack, which was in a ten-furlong novice race at Chelmsford first time out at three.

Anthony Oppenheimer's homebred is trained by Ed Vaughan and she is a daughter of the often underrated but sadly deceased Champs Elysees (by Danehill). That Group 1-winning full brother to leading international sire Dansili stood alongside his brother at Banstead Manor Stud for seven seasons before moving to Ireland to take up a dual-purpose role in 2017. He had served two seasons at Castlehyde Stud by the time of his death, aged just fifteen. His four Group 1 winners include 2020's Grand Prix de Saint-Cloud scorer Way To Paris and 2018's 1000 Guineas heroine Billesdon Brook, who added the Group 1 Sun Chariot Stakes as a four-year-old. Among his other pattern winners, Durance, Jack Naylor and Xcellence were placed in Group 1 classics.

Dame Malliot is the third foal of Stars In Your Eyes (by Galileo), a mare whose first four offspring have all won at least twice. She had a Lawman (by Invincible Spirit) colt in 2019—a full brother to Banksea, a triple winner from seven to ten furlongs—and she had a Kodiac (by Danehill) colt in late April of 2020. The mare is a half-sister to a juvenile mile listed scorer and to Group 2 Dante Stakes third Coordinated Cut (by Montjeu), grandam

Apache Star (by Arazi) is a stakes-placed half-sister to a stakes winner in California, and the next dam is an unraced half-sister to Nuryana (by Nureyev). This makes Dame Malliot a member of a branch of the family of Group 1 stars such as Golden Horn (by Cape Cross) and Rebecca Sharp (by Machiavellian) and of 2020's Oaks-placed Group 2 Ribblesdale Stakes scorer Frankly Darling (by Frankel). With this racing and pedigree profile, she clearly has considerable potential as a broodmare.

SUMMARY DETAILS
Bred: Hascombe and Valiant Studs
Owned: A E Oppenheimer
Trained: Ed Vaughan
Country: England
Race record: 1-2110-1332-
Career highlights: 4 wins inc Princess of Wales's Tattersalls Stakes (Gr2), Darley Prix de Pomone (Gr2), Ric and Mary Hambro Aphrodite Fillies' Stakes (L), 2nd Qipco British Champions Fillies & Mares Stakes (Gr1), 3rd 58th Preis von Europa (Gr1), Qatar Prix Vermeille (Gr1)

DAME MALLIOT (GB) – 2016 bay filly

Champs Elysees (GB)	Danehill (USA)	Danzig (USA)
		Razyana (USA)
	Hasili (IRE)	Kahyasi
		Kerali
Stars In Your Eyes (GB)	Galileo (IRE)	Sadler's Wells (USA)
		Urban Sea (USA)
	Apache Star (GB)	Arazi (USA)
		Wild Pavane (GB)

DANDALLA (IRE)

Nick Bradley has a remarkable record with horses purchased cheaply and Dandalla is one of the gems he uncovered from the bargain basement of the auction scene; Fev Rover is another. The filly is a €22,000 graduate of the Tattersalls Ireland September Yearling Sale having been sold previously by her breeder, as a foal in Goffs, for €15,500. She is clearly worth a great deal more than that now given her status as a dual pattern-winning juvenile filly in England in 2020.

The Karl Burke-trained bay, who has been ridden by Ben Curtis in all four of her races to date, began her career on the Tapeta at Newcastle on June 2nd, winning that five-furlong maiden by two lengths. She followed that with a visually impressive six-length victory in the Group 3 Albany Stakes over six furlongs at Royal Ascot seventeen days later. The runner-up that day, Setarhe, was listed placed next time but the finished out of the frame in four subsequent outings. Mother Earth, however, was a neck back in third and unlucky not to have been second given the trouble she encountered in the race and how well she was finishing at the end. Dandalla's next start resulted in a narrow defeat of Fev Rover in the Group 2 Duchess of Cambridge Stakes on soft ground at Newmarket, and she was not seen out again until the end of September when she could manage only fifth in the Group 1 Juddmonte Cheveley Park Stakes, ending the year on an official handicap mark of 105.

The ground was good on the Rowley Mile course for that famous six-furlong test and it was the Irish filly Miss Amulet who initially set off in front. That pattern-winning grey was headed after a quarter of a mile when the Andrew Balding-trained Alcohol Free took a narrow lead, and the bay would then remain in front all the way to the line. She had to fight back against Miss Amulet, who had briefly lost her place position only to reclaim it from Umm Kulthum in the final strides, and they left Happy Romance a length and a quarter behind. That filly was, in turn, three and a lengths clear of Dandalla who weakened inside the final half furlong. It will be interesting to see if she steps up in trip during 2021—she is entered in the Group 1 Emirates Poule d'Essai des

Pouliches (French 1000 Guineas)—although it's possible that sprinting will be her game.

The filly is a daughter of the high-class sprinter Dandy Man (by Mozart) and out of Chellalla (by Elnadim), which makes her inbred 4x3 to Danzig (by Northern Dancer). The mare won twice at seven and a half furlongs and once at a mile, and although she finished less than seven lengths seventh to Cherry Collect in the Group 3 Premio Regina Elena (Italian 1000 Guineas), she finished her track career on a handicap mark of sixty-five and was sold for just 7,500 guineas at the Tattersalls December Mare Sale of 2014. Cauthen (by Dandy Man), her first foal, won a seven-furlong Kempton handicap off a mark of fifty-five, her third foal is a daughter of Divine Prophet (by Choisir) who arrived in mid-April 2019, and she was bred to Kessaar (by Kodiac) in 2020.

Chellalla has two siblings who earned blacktype in Italy and Konkan (by Aussie Rules) is the more notable of them. She won three times as a two-year-old, including a listed contest over seven and a half furlongs at Capannelle and, in France, was listed-placed over six and a half furlongs at Maisons-Laffitte. Their dam, Cheloca (by Selkirk), is a half-sister to the Listed Prix de la Calonne scorer Canasita (by Zafonic) and out of City Centre (by Be My Guest), a half-sister to the Group 1 Prix du Cadran heroine Sought Out (by Rainbow Quest). That star stayer was, of course, the dam of the Group 1 Derby winner North Light (by Danehill), and her siblings included some broodmares of note.

Greektown (by Ela-Mana-Mou), for example, is the stakes-winning dam of the middle-distance Group 1 scorer Gamut (by Spectrum), Group 2 Geoffrey Freer Stakes winner Multicoloured (by Rainbow Quest), and listed scorer Athens Belle (by Groom Dancer), whereas her descendants include Grade 1 E. P. Taylor Stakes heroine Tannery (by Dylan Thomas), Group 2 Goodwood Cup and Group 2 Doncaster Cup winner Saddler's Rock (by Sadler's Wells), the sadly ill-fated St Leger and dual Derby-placed Galileo Rock (by Galileo), multiple stakes winner Allexina (by Barathea), and Tarfasha (by Teofilo), the Oaks-placed Group 2 Blandford Stakes and Group 3 Blue Wind Stakes winner of 2014. The last named has produced listed scorer Rakan (by Sea The Stars) and 2020's Group 3-placed juvenile winner and current

Group 1 Derby entrant Wuqood (by Dubawi) from her first three foals.

This is a famous Ballymacoll Stud family whose other notable members, also descended from Edinburgh (by Charlottown), include the dual Derby-placed Group 1 2000 Guineas and Group 1 King George VI and Queen Elizabeth Stakes winner Golan (by Spectrum), his dual Derby-placed, Group 2 Dante Stakes-winning full brother Tartan Bearer, Group 1 St Leger-placed Group 2 Great Voltigeur Stakes winner Bonny Scot (by Commanche Run), and the South African mile Grade 1 stars Front And Centre (by Dynasty) and Potala Palace (by Singspiel). Dandalla represents a comparatively weak branch of the family, one that has been cultivated towards sprinting rather than the classic range, and so she is remotely connected to those stars.

SUMMARY DETAILS

Bred: Robert Norton
Owned: Nick Bradley Racing 28 & E Burke
Trained: Karl Burke
Country: England
Race record: 1110-
Career highlights: 3 wins inc Duchess of Cambridge Stakes (Gr2), Albany Stakes (Gr3)

DANDALLA (IRE) – 2018 bay filly

		Danehill (USA)
Dandy Man (IRE)	Mozart (IRE)	Danehill (USA)
		Victoria Cross (USA)
	Lady Alexander (IRE)	Night Shift (USA)
		Sandhurst Goddess
Chellalla (GB)	Elnadim (USA)	Danzig (USA)
		Elle Seule (USA)
	Cheloca (GB)	Selkirk (USA)
		City Centre (IRE)

DARK VISION (IRE)

Dark Vision was a prominent member of his cohort as a two-year-old, winning three of his four starts including the Group 2 Qatar Vintage Stakes at Goodwood, earning an end-of-year rating of 111 on the official handicap. Godolphin had bought him after his pattern success and he'd been quite a disappointment when finishing a well-beaten last of six behind Too Darn Hot in the Group 2 Champagne Stakes but he was still a colt with the potential to run well in a Guineas. Although the son of a Timeform 133-rated multiple Group 1 star who excelled at six furlongs, the Mark Johnston-trained bay looked like a potential miler in the making.

He was a half-length third in a one-mile conditions race at Chelmsford on his seasonal reappearance, finished thirteen lengths behind Magna Grecia when running a never-dangerous twelfth in the Group 1 Qipco 2000 Guineas, and then dropped down in class, first to listed level and then into handicaps. He was beaten by less than two lengths when fourth in a valuable ten-furlong handicap at Newmarket in July, finished sixth to Lord North in the Cambridgeshire at that venue's Rowley Mile course in late September, but those were highlights among a disappointing eleven-race season; his handicap mark dropped to ninety-seven.

The colt's four-year-old season was quite a contrast, producing three big-race wins and a short-head second from six starts. His seasonal reappearance came in the Royal Hunt Cup over the straight mile at Ascot in June and, coming up the near side of the track, he made good progress through the final furlong and a half, hit the front in the final half furlong and won going away by a length and a quarter. Molatham (rec. 3lbs) was second, half a length in front of Pogo (gave 5lbs) who was, in turn, one and a quarter lengths ahead of Vale of Kent (gave 8lbs). There was a gap of over three lengths back to the fifth.

Montatham (rec. 6lbs) got his revenge less than three weeks later when short-heading Dark Vision in a mile handicap on good-to-firm going at Sandown; had the colt not started slowly and so raced in last place for much of the race, the result may have been different. He encountered some traffic problems in a five-runner listed contest at Pontefract eighteen days later, but this time fortune went his way. He got to the front well inside the final furlong and held on by a neck from the fast-finishing Beringer. In contrast, he never really looked like a contender at York the following month when finishing only sixth to Certain Lad in the Group 3 Sky Bet And Symphony Group Strensall Stakes over a few yard short of nine furlongs.

His other unplaced run of the year was when finishing seventh in the Group 1 Queen Elizabeth II Stakes on soft ground at Ascot in late October, beaten just over six lengths by The Revenant and Roseman, but he made a trip to Germany between those two outings and returned home with a new Group 2 success to his name. The race was the Kronimus Oettingen-Rennen over a mile on good ground at Baden-Baden and he stayed on strongly in the final furlong to catch his owner's slightly more fancied French-trained runner Half Light on the line. That filly was half a length in front of the German three-year-old Rubaiyat, with Runnymede a neck back in fourth and then a one-and-a-half-length gap back to the Group 3 winner and Group 2 German one-mile classic runner-up No Credit Limit in fifth.

Dark Vision, who was bred by S F Bloodstock LLC, was originally sold for just €15,000 in Goffs as a foal and snapped up by Mark Johnston for 15,000 guineas from Book 2 of the Tattersalls October Yearling Sale, yet another fine testament to his trainer's judgement of a horse. In striking contrast, his year-younger half-brother by Lope de Vega (by Shamardal) made €900,000 when sold by Arqana in Deauville as a yearling. That colt is the Aidan O'Brien-trained pattern winner Lope Y Fernandez, a horse who has been placed four times at the highest level from six and a half furlongs to a mile including the Irish 2,000 Guineas and Breeders' Cup Mile. The mare's other winners are also by Lope de Vega, her progeny include the multiple stakes-placed filly Al Hayyah, and she had a filly by the stallion in France in 2020.

Although starting out as a mere 5,000-guinea DBS October Yearling Sale graduate, Black Dahlia went to stud as a promising broodmare prospect. She was well-tested on the track, winning five of forty-two starts over four seasons, earning ten placings, and having briefly hit a career-high handicap mark of ninety-four on the artificial tracks as five-year-old, finished that phase of her career on a figure of eighty-nine on Polytrack, eighty-four on turf. She was then snapped up for 40,000 guineas at the Tattersalls December Mare Sale but failed to meet her reserve and was led out unsold (€145,000) at Deauville six years later while carrying Lope Y Fernandez in utero. Her half-brother Cold Turkey (by Polar Falcon) won sixteen times on the flat from ten furlongs to two miles, plus one of his two starts over hurdles. Her dam, South Rock (by Rock City), won a seven-furlong listed contest in France and three other races, whereas the next dam is South Shore (by Caerleon), a four-time middle-distance winner whose siblings feature the dual Group 1 Lockinge Stakes star Soviet Line (by Soviet Star).

Anything further back on the page is into remote territory, but this was a well-known family a few decades ago, so comment is warranted especially as there may be a stallion career ahead for either or both of the brothers. Shore Line (by High Line), the fourth dam of Dark Vision and Lope Y Fernandez, was a full sister to the Group 2 Park Hill Stakes winner Quay Line, Group 2 Premio Dormello scorer Ancholia, and Northumberland Plate victor Trade Line, and she was out of Dark Finale (by Javelot), a multiple winning half-sister to 1955's Irish 1,000 Guineas heroine Dark Issue (by Sayajirao), who was owned by Sir Winston Churchill.

Dark Vision is a son of Dream Ahead (by Diktat), who spent five years at Ballylinch Stud in Ireland before moving to Haras de Grandcamp in France where is now standing his fifth season, and the stallion has been represented by four Group 1 winners. Dream of Dreams and Glass Slippers achieved the feat in 2020, Glass Slippers also did so in 2019, and the other pair are his stallion sons Al Wukair (Haras de Bouquetot; 2yo in 2021) and Donjuan Triumphant (Haras de la Barbottiere; foals in 2021). Dark Vision is not at their level, but he is a capable miler who has two Group 2 wins to his name. He appears best suited to ground that is good or fast, and it will be interesting to see what the future holds for him.

SUMMARY DETAILS
Bred: S F Bloodstock LLC
Owned: Godolphin
Trained: Mark Johnston
Country: England
Race record: 1110-30404000030-2121010-
Career highlights: 6 wins inc 87th Kronimus Oettingen-Rennen (Gr2), Qatar Vintage Stakes (Gr2), Sky Bet Pomfret Stakes (L), Royal Hunt Cup

DARK VISION (IRE) – 2016 bay colt

Dream Ahead (USA)	Diktat (GB)	Warning
		Arvola (GB)
	Land of Dreams (GB)	Cadeaux Genereux
		Sahara Star (GB)
Black Dahlia (GB)	Dansili (GB)	Danehill (USA)
		Hasili (IRE)
	South Rock (GB)	Rock City
		South Shore

DASHING WILLOUGHBY (GB)

Meon Valley Stud has bred many notable racehorses over the years and although Dashing Willoughby would be down a bit in the order of merit, he is a talented stayer. Like an ever-increasing number of prominent runners, he made a winning start on an artificial track, in his case a narrow success in a maiden over the extended mile on the Tapeta surface at Wolverhampton in mid-August of his two-year-old season. He was runner-up in a conditions race over a mile at Newbury a month later, unplaced behind Magna Grecia in the Group 1 Vertem Futurity Trophy Stakes at Doncaster, placed on his first two starts at three but then stepped up to fourteen furlongs and won the Group 2 Queen's Vase at Royal Ascot.

He failed to make the frame in four subsequent outings that year, including when beating only one home behind Logician in the St Leger, and he was gelded before his return to action as a four-year-old. The new season started off well for him with listed success over twelve furlongs at Newmarket in June and a length-and-a-quarter defeat of Spanish Mission in the rescheduled and relocated Group 3 Coral Henry II Stakes over two miles at Sandown a month later. He had to settle for fourth in the Group 2 Weatherbys Hamilton Lonsdale Cup Stakes over the extended two miles at York in August, passing the post a total of two and a half lengths adrift of the winner, Enbihaar.

It had been announced shortly before that race that the high-profile New Zealand owner Sir Owen Glenn had bought a majority share in the gelding with the aim of targeting both the Caulfield Cup and Melbourne Cup before chasing after other top prizes. He would remain with Balding for the first two targets and then join an Australian trainer. Unfortunately, this has not yet gone as well as would have been hoped. The gelding was sent to the front after two furlongs of the twelve-furlong Group 1 Stella Artois Caulfield Cup in mid-October but was under pressure about three furlongs from home, weakened, and trailed home a long way last in the eighteen-runner field. He passed the post twenty-seven and a half lengths behind the winner, Verry Elleegant. He was then sent off at 100/1 for the Group 1 Lexus

Melbourne Cup seventeen days later and having always been at the rear of the pack, he beat only one horse home. Twilight Payment, Tiger Moth and Prince of Arran made it a one-two-three for the European contingent.

Dashing Willoughby is one of twenty-two stakes winners by the top-class middle-distance horse Nathaniel (by Galileo), the standard-bearer at Newsells Park Stud. He will forever be remembered as being the sire of the great Enable, and his tally also includes the Group 1 Premio Lydia Tesio scorer God Given, Group 1 Prix de Diane (French Oaks) heroine Channel and the Group 1-placed German Group 2 scorer Amorella.

Miss Dashwood (by Dylan Thomas), the dam of the talented gelding, won four times, the best of her siblings is the Group 1 Prix de l'Opera and Group 1 Prix Jean Romanet star Speedy Boarding (by Shamardal), and she is out of the Listed Warwickshire Oaks scorer Dash To The Front (by Diktat). That mare, in turn, is a half-sister to Dash To The Top (by Montjeu), the Group 1 Yorkshire Oaks-placed stakes winner whose daughter Anapurna (by Frankel) won both the Group 1 Oaks at Epsom and Group 1 Prix de Royallieu at ParisLongchamp in 2019. This makes Dashing Willoughby a direct descendant of Milligram (by Mill Reef), the Timeform 130-rated dual classic-placed miler who in winning the Group 1 Queen Elizabeth II Stakes at Ascot became one of the handful of horses who managed to beat the brilliant Miesque.

Dashing Willoughby is due to continue his career in Australia although he has not yet run since his Melbourne Cup disappointment. The obsession with breeding for speed has left races there from twelve furlongs and upwards tending to be weaker there than in Europe, so long as he is healthy, happy and injury free, he could do very well in his new home.

SUMMARY DETAILS
Bred: Meon Valley Stud
Owned: Sir Owen Glenn & Mick and Janice Mariscotti
Trained: Andrew Balding
Country: England
Race record: 120-2314000-11400-

Career highlights: 4 wins inc Queen's Vase (Gr2), Coral Henry II Stakes (Gr3), Betfair Exchange Buckhounds Stakes (L), 3rd MBNA Chester Vase Stakes (Gr3)

DASHING WILLOUGHBY (GB) – 2016 bay gelding

Nathaniel (IRE)	Galileo (IRE)	Sadler's Wells (USA)
		Urban Sea (USA)
	Magnificient Style (USA)	Silver Hawk (USA)
		Mia Karina (USA)
Miss Dashwood (GB)	Dylan Thomas (IRE)	Danehill (USA)
		Lagrion (USA)
	Dash To The Front (GB)	Diktat (GB)
		Millennium Dash (GB)

DAWN PATROL (IRE)

Many breeders prefer not to have their mare covered in the month of June, considering a May foaling date to be 'too late'. There is, of course, a very long list of pattern, Group 1 and classic stars who were born in the month of May. In 2019, for example, seven European-trained Group 1 stars were May foals: Hermosa (6th), Danceteria (7th), Defoe (8th), Millisle (11th), Holdthasigreen (14th), Magical (18th), Anthony Van Dyck (19th)—and both the first- and last-named on that list won classics. The latter, sadly ill-fated, was the latest-born pattern winner in Ireland or Great Britain in 2020, one of sixteen May-born horses who won a Group 2 or Group 3 contest in those countries during the year. You can find the full list of them in the appropriate index at the back of this volume. Three on that list also won at Group 1 level during the year, as did the two-year-old Thunder Moon who sneaks in having arrived on May 1st. Yes, of course there are some who may have been overdue from a late May covering, but that doesn't alter their status as a pattern winner who was born in that month. In 2018, by the way, the Group 1 Prix de l'Abbaye de Longchamp went to Mabs Cross, who was born on June 6th.

Dawn Patrol (by Galileo) was not only born on May 15th but he is the second of three consecutive May-born foals for his dam, Gwynn (by Darshaan). His older brother Ancient Mariner (6th) has been disappointing, whereas his André Fabre-trained sister Beluga (17th), who officially turned three on New Year's Day, has not yet raced.

Dawn Patrol was a well-beaten fourth over nine furlongs on soft-to-heavy ground at Tipperary on his only start at two, he was a half-length runner-up to stablemate Tiger Moth (born May 16th) in a ten-furlong Leopardstown maiden on good-to-firm on his seasonal reappearance in early June and then finished third in the Group 1 Dubai Duty Free Irish Derby. It was a one-two-three-four for the Ballydoyle team as Santiago beat Tiger Moth by a head, Dawn Patrol was five lengths behind them but was a length and a quarter clear of Order of Australia. The two younger colts had stayed on well in the closing stages, a promising sign for the future.

After picking up a ten-furlong maiden at Naas next time and finishing a one-length third to Pista in a listed contest over fourteen furlongs at Leopardstown, he made another bid for classic glory, this time in the Group 1 Pertemps St Leger Stakes at Doncaster. He was staying on at the finish but never looked dangerous, eventually passing the post sixth, a total of six and three-quarter lengths behind Galileo Chrome. The step up to two miles proved ideal as he hit the front inside the final furlong of the Group 3 Comer Group International Loughbrown Stakes at the Curragh later that month, staying on well to hold off the talented mare Barrington Court by three-quarters of a length. She went on to take a pair of twelve-furlong listed contests on her next two starts, whereas Dawn Patrol finished sixth behind runaway winner Trueshan in the Group 2 Qipco British Champions Long Distance Cup on soft ground at Ascot, albeit finishing only two and a quarter lengths behind the runner-up, Search For A Song.

In addition to those May-born siblings noted above, Dawn Patrol is a half-brother to the Derby winner and classic sire Pour Moi (by Montjeu), dual classic-placed dual pattern winner Gagnoa (by Sadler's Wells) and wide-margin Navan listed scorer Kissed (by Galileo). He looks like an ideal prospect for the 'Cup' races of 2021 and perhaps 2022 as well. Given his pedigree you'd have thought that there might be a possible career ahead of him as a National Hunt stallion, but that is now off the cards as he has been gelded since the end of the season. He has left Ballydoyle.

SUMMARY DETAILS
Bred: Lynch Bages Ltd
Owned: Michael Tabor, Derrick Smith & Mrs John Magnier
Trained: Aidan O'Brien
Country: Ireland
Race record: 4-2313010-
Career highlights: 2 wins inc Comer Group International Loughbrown Stakes (Gr3), 3rd Dubai Duty Free Irish Derby (Gr1), Vinnie Roe Stakes (L)

DAWN PATROL (IRE) – 2017 bay gelding

Galileo (IRE)	Sadler's Wells (USA)	Northern Dancer
		Fairy Bridge (USA)
	Urban Sea (USA)	Miswaki (USA)
		Allegretta
Gwynn (IRE)	Darshaan	Shirley Heights
		Delsy
	Victoress (USA)	Conquistador Cielo (USA)
		Royal Statute (CAN)

DELPHI (IRE)

Delphi could be a middle-distance horse or stayer of note in 2021. He was well-beaten on his only start as a two-year-old but won all four of his races at three, starting off with narrow wins in a mile maiden on good ground at the Curragh in late June and a ten-furlong Navan handicap on yielding a week later. Two weeks later, he added a four-and-a-half-length score in a twelve-furlong listed contest at Leopardstown, and that was a month before what turned out to be his final start of the year. The Group 3 Comer Group International Irish St Leger Trial, run over fourteen furlongs on good ground at the Curragh in mid-August, attracted an eight-runner field of mixed quality and experience, but Delphi made all and held on to take the top prize by a short head from Master of Reality. They were two and a half lengths clear of the lightly raced Micro Manage, who was third.

The colt is the second foal of the six-furlong juvenile Group 3 scorer Bye Bye Birdie (by Oasis Dream). I have seen the occasional online comment musing about the whether or not a horse out of an Oasis Dream (by Green Desert) mare can stay twelve furlongs or farther—seemingly focused on the fact that he was a sprint champion—but some of them do stay, and it's no surprise. There are stamina elements in his pedigree. Most of his brightest stars are sprinters or milers, but he has also proved that he can get Group 1-winning middle-distance racehorses too. Midday is the standout, so far, but Option got a Group 1 win over twelve furlongs in Australia and both Lady Jane Digby and Querari notched up one over ten furlongs. If he can sire them as racehorses then, with the right stallions, some of his daughters can produce them at stud too. Twilight Payment (by Teofilo), who won the Group 1 Melbourne Cup in November, is out of an Oasis Dream mare, for example.

Breeding a sprinter to Galileo (by Sadler's Wells) has yielded some top-class milers, but if she has some relative stamina in her family then there is the chance that she can pass that on rather than her short-track talent. Bye Bye Birdie is evidently such a mare and always had the potential to be one. She is out of Slink (by Selkirk), an unraced half-sister to Sulk, a Group 1 Prix Marcel

Boussac winner who went on to be placed in the Group 1 Yorkshire Oaks and Group 1 Prix Royal-Oak. That filly is one of three top-level winners out of Masskana (by Darshaan). Breeders' Cup Turf and dual Derby-placed ten-furlong Grade 1 scorer Eagle Mountain (by Rock of Gibraltar) and ten-furlong Grade 1 Breeders' Cup Filly & Mare Turf winner Dank (by Dansili) are the other pair. Delphi's year-older full sister Credenza was runner-up in the Group 3 Snow Fairy Stakes over nine furlongs, third in the Group 2 Blandford Stakes over ten but well-beaten on her sole try over twelve, looking that day like a non-stayer. Their younger brother, Matchless, holds an entry in the Group 1 Dubai Duty Free Irish Derby and he won the second of his two starts in 2020, a seven-furlong maiden on good ground at Listowel in late September where he made just about all of the running. The mare's fourth foal is a Galileo filly who was born in the first week of 2020.

Delphi is a pattern winner over fourteen furlongs. There is a shade of doubt, on pedigree, as to his ability to stay two miles and beyond and also a chance that his best distance could ultimately prove to be around twelve furlongs. He was rated 108 at the end of the year, so clearly has a lot of progress to make if he is going to be a top performer in 2021, but it's not impossible, and it will be interesting to see how his career progresses. He has left Ballydoyle.

SUMMARY DETAILS
Bred: Coolmore
Owned: Derrick Smith, Mrs John Magnier & Michael Tabor
Trained: Aidan O'Brien
Country: Ireland
Race record: 0-1111-
Career highlights: 4 wins inc Comer Group International Irish St Leger Trial Stakes (Gr3), Nijinsky Stakes (L)

DELPHI (IRE) – 2017 bay colt

Galileo (IRE)	Sadler's Wells (USA)	Northern Dancer
		Fairy Bridge (USA)
	Urban Sea (USA)	Miswaki (USA)
		Allegretta
Bye Bye Birdie (IRE)	Oasis Dream (GB)	Green Desert (USA)
		Hope (IRE)
	Slink (GB)	Selkirk (USA)
		Masskana (IRE)

DIVINELY (IRE)

Coolmore's homebred juvenile Divinely gave her already considerable future paddocks value a boost when winning one of her five starts last season. Although unplaced at Leopardstown on her debut, a well-beaten second on heavy ground at Roscommon next time and then only fourth over a mile at Cork, she opened her winning account on try number four, staying on well inside the final of eight furlongs to take the Group 3 Kilcarn Stud Flame of Tara Irish EBF Stakes by half a length and short head from Ahandfulofsummers and Ubuntu. The ground was heavy, which added to the stamina test. She was unplaced behind Shale in the Group 1 Moyglare Stud Stakes on her only subsequent outing and had an end-of-year official handicap mark of ninety-seven.

Divinely needs to show considerable improvement if she is going to play a prominent role as a three-year-old. Her entries in the Group 1 Tattersalls Irish 1,000 Guineas and Group 1 Juddmonte Irish Oaks are fanciful if judging her solely on the merit of what she has achieved so far. However, being a May 5th-born daughter of Galileo (by Sadler's Wells) and the Group 1 winning miler Red Evie (by Intikhab), she is bred not only to improve with time but potentially also with distance. She has also been entered in the Group 1 Emirates Poule d'Essai des Pouliches (French 1000 Guineas), Group 1 Saxon Warrior Coolmore Prix Saint-Alary and the Group 1 Prix de Diane Longines (French Oaks), so perhaps she has made significant progress over the winter months.

If she was an early foal of her dam there would be greater doubt about her potential to stay twelve furlongs given that the mare was a miler by a star miler and out of a daughter of Nordico (by Northern Dancer) and an Irish 1,000 Guineas-placed mare: Martinova (by Martinmas). However, she is Red Evie's eighth foal and so known to be a full sister to Best In The World, Magical Dream and, best by a long way, Found. The latter is the Arc and Breeders' Cup Turf-winning champion who won the Group 1 Prix Marcel Boussac at two, was placed in a long list of Group 1 races throughout her career, earned over £5 million in prize money and only failed to make the frame once in twenty-one starts. Found's first foal was one of the leading juveniles of 2020: the Breeders' Cup-placed Group 2 scorer Battleground (by War Front).

Best In The World won the Group 3 Give Thanks Stakes over twelve furlongs, was runner-up in the Group 2 Blandford Stakes over ten, was a one-mile listed scorer at two. Her first foal is the winning 2018-born Deep Impact (by Sunday Silence) filly Snowfall (one of the mixed-up pair in the Fillies' Mile), she had a colt by that same stallion in 2019, a son of Dubawi (by Dubai Millennium) on May 13th, 2020 and was bred back that Dalham Hall Stud standard-bearer. Magical Dream, on the other hand, got her good juvenile win in the Group 3 C. L. Weld Park Stakes over seven furlongs at the Curragh, she too was placed in the Group 2 Blandford Stakes at three and she was only beaten by a head when runner-up in the Group 3 Noblesse Stakes over twelve furlongs at Cork. Her first two foals are minor winners, her third is their unraced and now three-year-old full brother Urban War (by War Front), and she had daughters of American Pharoah (by Pioneerof The Nile) and Quality Road (by Elusive Quality) in 2019 and 2020 respectively.

It is not guaranteed that Divinely will stay beyond ten furlongs, but with what the best of her siblings have achieved over that and farther, the odds that she may not only stay but improve for the step up in distance look much better. It will be interesting to see how she turns out and, looking much further ahead, to see how the sisters ultimately compare in terms of broodmares and potential long-term impact.

SUMMARY DETAILS
Bred: Coolmore
Owned: Mrs John Magnier, Michael Tabor & Derrick Smith
Trained: Aidan O'Brien
Country: Ireland
Race record: 02410-
Career highlights: 1 viz inc Kilcarn Stud Flame of Tara Irish EBF Stakes (Gr3)

DIVINELY (IRE) – 2018 bay filly

Galileo (IRE)	Sadler's Wells (USA)	Northern Dancer
		Fairy Bridge (USA)
	Urban Sea (USA)	Miswaki (USA)
		Allegretta
Red Evie (IRE)	Intikhab (USA)	Red Ransom (USA)
		Crafty Example (USA)
	Malafemmena (IRE)	Nordico (USA)
		Martinova

DUBAI STATION (GB)

Leading Australian sprinter Brazen Beau, who was a half-length runner-up to the US raider Undrafted in the Group 1 Diamond Jubilee Stakes on his first of two starts in England, shuttled to Dalham Hall Stud in Newmarket for four years before remaining in Australia in 2020. He is a son of Invincible Spirit's (by Green Desert) outstanding Australian stallion I Am Invincible, and although awaiting his first winner at the highest level, his eleven stakes winners include a couple of Group 2 scorers from his initial southern hemisphere crop. Dubai Station is one of two stakes winners for him in Europe; the other one is the Italian juvenile listed scorer Avengers Queen.

Dubai Station won over five furlongs on soft ground at Haydock in early June of his juvenile season, finished a three-length third to A'Ali in the Group 2 Norfolk Stakes at Royal Ascot and then third to Earthlight in the Group 3 Prix de Cabourg over six at Deauville before disappointing in both the Group 2 Gimcrack Stakes at York and Listed Two Year Old Trophy at Redcar, the latter run on heavy ground. He was also unplaced twice at three, when down the field behind Golden Horde in the Group 1 Commonwealth Cup and behind Battaash in the Group 2 King George Stakes. However, he won the Group 3 Betway Pavilion Stakes on the Tapeta at Newcastle in early June and was only beaten by a length and a half when third to Royal Crusade in the Group 3 Prix de Ris-Orangis on good ground at Deauville in July. His final public appearance of the year was in the auction ring where he was sold for 150,000 guineas during the Tattersalls Autumn Horses in Training Sale in late October. He was bought by Middleham Park Racing and will be trained by Robert Cowell in Newmarket.

The colt is the first foal of Princess Guest (by Iffraaj), an unplaced mare whose six winning siblings including several prolific individuals, notably the stakes-winning six-time scorer Imperial Guest (by Imperial Dancer). Her dam, Princess Speedfit (by Desert Prince) also has a string of successful siblings, including the listed scorer Sibling Rival, who was runner-up in both the Group 2 Grand Prix de Deauville and Group 2 Grand Prix de

Chantilly. There is also some quality middle-distance stamina in the fourth generation of the pedigree too because third dam Perfect Sister (by Perrault) is a full sister to the Grade 1 San Luis Rey Stakes and Grade 1 Hollywood Gold Cup star Frankly Perfect, but Dubai Station is what you'd expect of a horse representing a Brazen Beau – Iffraaj (by Zafonic) cross: a sprinter.

It would be no surprise to see him start off his 2021 campaign in something like the Listed Abernant Stakes or Group 3 Palace House Stakes and, already on an official handicap mark of 108, there is every reason to hope that he can add to his blacktype tally for his new connections.

SUMMARY DETAILS
Bred: Hall Of Fame Stud
Owned: Ahmad Alshaikh & Co
Trained: Karl Burke
Country: England
Race record: 213300-1030-
Career highlights: 2 wins inc Betway Pavilion Stakes (Gr3), 3rd Norfolk Stakes (Gr2), Qatar Prix de Ris-Orangis (Gr3), Darley Prix de Cabourg (Gr3)

DUBAI STATION (GB) – 2017 bay colt

Brazen Beau (AUS)	I Am Invincible (AUS)	Invincible Spirit (IRE)
		Cannarelle (AUS)
	Sansadee (AUS)	Snaadee (USA)
		Sansapa (AUS)
Princess Guest (IRE)	Iffraaj (GB)	Zafonic (USA)
		Pastorale (GB)
	Princess Speedfit (FR)	Desert Prince (IRE)
		Perfect Sister (USA)

DUBAI WARRIOR (GB)

An examination of Dubai Warrior's racing record, up to the end of 2020, shows something of interest: he has won six of his seven starts on the artificial tracks but been unplaced on his two attempts on turf. Those two defeats were in blacktype contests and may not be entirely down to the ground, but still we are left with a clear picture that this talented colt is one of the best in Europe on Polytrack.

He was a four-and-a-half-length winner of a mile novice race at Chelmsford on his only start as a two-year-old and although it was nine months almost to the day when we next saw him in action, he won that one-mile Kempton contest by the same easy margin. His narrow defeat over two furlongs farther at Chelmsford a month later was a shock because the 2/5 favourite was beaten a neck by the vastly more experienced Desert Fire, with a five-length gap back to the third and with the future sprint star Glen Shiel further behind in fifth. This was followed by his first unplaced finish, in the Group 3 Prix du Prince d'Orange over ten furlongs on good ground at ParisLongchamp where, having gone right at the start and hit another rival, he spent some time on the lead but had little more to give after being headed a quarter of a mile from home, eventually passing the post in seventh as Soudania galloped to an easy three-length win.

He returned to Chelmsford in early November where he gave the year-older Kasbaan weight and a half-length beating in a ten-furlong handicap and then rounded off his campaign with an easy three-and-three-quarter-length success in the Listed Betway Quebec Stakes over the same trip at Lingfield just before Christmas, beating his older stable companion Court House.

The pair met again in the Group 3 Betway Winter Derby Stakes in late February 2020 and the result was the same. This time Dubai Warrior set off in front and was never headed, passing the post two and three-quarter lengths in front of Court House and with Bangkok another half a length back in third. The next horse home was almost five lengths adrift. It had not been a particularly strong gallop but the final time was quick. He led until a furlong out when finishing fifth to Magny Cours in the Listed Coral Gala

Stakes on good-to-firm turf at Sandown in early July. He was then off the track until mid-November when having raced prominently and not moved to the front until two out, he won the Listed Betway Churchill Stakes at Lingfield by three and a half lengths. This good effort saw him sent off at odds-on for the Listed Betway Quebec Stakes over the same course and distance a month later. He tried to make all and battled back when challenged in the final furlong but was caught in the final strides and lost out by a nose and a neck to Sangarius and Bangkok.

Dubai Warrior is a full brother to the former Hugo Palmer-trained Mootasadir, who won the Group 3 Diamond Stakes over ten and a half furlongs at Dundalk as a three-year-old and beat Extra Elusive by a half a length to take the Listed Magnolia Stakes at Kempton the following spring. The sons of the former Banstead Manor Stud standard-bearer Dansili (by Danehill) are out of Mahbooba, an Australian-bred daughter of Galileo (by Sadler's Wells) who excelled in South Africa and the United Arab Emirates. She was a Group 1 and Group 2 scorer over six furlongs as a two-year-old, was placed in both the Group 2 UAE Derby and Group 3 UAE Oaks and won the Group 2 Balanchine Stakes over nine furlongs at Meydan. She is out of a speedy triple winner called Sogha (by Red Ransom) and is a great-granddaughter of a half-sister to 1986's US champion and Horse of the Year, Lady's Secret (by Secretariat).

It will be interesting to see how Dubai Warrior gets on going forward. A repeat bid for the Group 3 Winter Derby looked likely to be on his schedule again, but just before this book went to print, he ran in a Group 2 contest on the dirt at Meydan, sweating up before the race, under pressure and going nowhere quite early and tailed off long before the nine-and-a-half-furlong contest came to an end. Mootasadir, his now Satish Seemar-trained full brother, showed little in the same race and was also tailed off, the only horse to finish behind him.

SUMMARY DETAILS

Bred: Essafinaat Ltd
Owned: Sheikh Mohammed Bin Khalifa Al Maktoum
Trained: John Gosden

Country: England
Race record: 1-12011-1013-0
Career highlights: 6 wins inc Betway Winter Derby Stakes
(Gr3), Betway Churchill Stakes (L), Betway Quebec Stakes (L)

DUBAI WARRIOR (GB) – 2016 bay colt

Dansili (GB)	Danehill (USA)	Danzig (USA)
		Razyana (USA)
	Hasili (IRE)	Kahyasi
		Kerali
Mahbooba (AUS)	Galileo (IRE)	Sadler's Wells (USA)
		Urban Sea (USA)
	Sogha (AUS)	Red Ransom (USA)
		Marple (USA)

EAGLES BY DAY (IRE)

Eagles By Day boosted his odds of finding a berth as a National Hunt stallion someday when beating Communique by half a length to win the Group 3 John Smith's Silver Cup Stakes over fourteen furlongs at York in July. He had been a twelve-furlong winner and third to Japan in the Group 2 King Edward VII Stakes the previous season. Why the potential sire appeal in that sector? He is by the Timeform 140-rated superstar and leading classic and Group 1 sire Sea The Stars (by Cape Cross)—has mostly flat-sire sons, but also Affinisea and Crystal Ocean who are covering large triple-digit books of National Hunt mares—and his blacktype hurdle-winning dam's relations include a National Hunt sire of note.

He is the first foal of the former Michael Winters-trained dual-purpose star Missunited (by Golan). Vanessa Hutch's homebred started out in bumpers, winning two from five, and won a maiden hurdle at Listowel on her sole start over obstacles before making her debut on the flat. She was short-headed in that Leopardstown maiden, won at Ballinrobe and Clonmel, reverted to obstacles to take a novice hurdle at Galway, won a fourteen-furlong flat race at Listowel and then chased home the runaway winner and subsequent Group 1 star Voleuse de Coeurs in the Irish Cesarewitch over two miles at the Curragh. She was fourth in a pair of graded hurdle races before winning one at Limerick, although was then tailed off behind Annie Power in the Grade 1 Irish Stallion Farms EBF Mares Novices' Hurdle Championship Final over two and a half miles at Fairyhouse; it was later reported that she scoped badly.

It is what she did over the next sixteen months that made her more widely known and identified her as a fascinating broodmare prospect. Almost two months after completing a sequence of three listed-race seconds on the flat, she won the famous Grade A Guinness Galway Hurdle by three and three-quarter lengths on heavy ground. It was to be her final race over jumps. Her remaining eight races are all on the flat, only one did not carry blacktype status, and she made the frame in seven. She won the Listed Oyster Stakes over a mile and a half at Galway, the Listed

Saval Beg Stakes over fourteen furlongs at Leopardstown and, on her final start, the Group 3 Lillie Langtry Stakes over that same trip on fast ground at Goodwood. She had picked up a Group 1 placing when third to Tac de Boistron in the Prix Royal-Oak at the end of her six-year-old season, but the race for which she is often best remembered—by flat fans anyway—is the one she ran on her penultimate start. She made classic star Leading Light and the previous year's winner Estimate fight to the line in the Group 1 Gold Cup at Ascot. The margins were a neck and a short head, and there was a four-and-a-half-length gap back to Brown Panther in fourth. Estimate's post-race sample was found to contain a prohibited substance, leading to her disqualification, so Missunited was moved up to second.

A pattern-winning colt by a leading international flat sire and out of a mare like Missunited looks like an ideal potential recruit as a National Hunt sire, and that is before you even take into account that his blacktype-producing but unraced third dam, Mombones, was a Lord Gayle (by Sir Gaylord) half-sister to the notable National Hunt sire King's Ride (by Rarity).

Eagles By Day is a 125,000-guinea Tattersalls December Foal Sale graduate who switched from the Michael Bell stable to David O'Meara's team shortly before his Group 3 success. He missed out on a Group 1 placing when only fourth to Stradivarius in the Goodwood Cup ten days after that win and was then unplaced in both the Group 2 Weatherbys Hamilton Lonsdale Cup Stakes and Group 2 bet365 Doncaster Cup, both of which were disappointing efforts. He finished the year on an official handicap mark of 111, and each of those runs from July through to September had been on good ground. It will be interesting to see how he gets on as a five-year-old.

SUMMARY DETAILS
Bred: Vanessa Hutch
Owned: Clipper Logistics
Trained: David O'Meara
Country: England
Race record: 2-21030-01400-

Career highlights: 2 wins inc John Smith's Silver Cup Stakes (Gr3), 3rd King Edward VII Stakes (Gr2)

EAGLES BY DAY (IRE) – 2016 bay or brown colt

Sea The Stars (IRE)	Cape Cross (IRE)	Green Desert (USA)
		Park Appeal
	Urban Sea (USA)	Miswaki (USA)
		Allegretta
Missunited (IRE)	Golan (IRE)	Spectrum (IRE)
		Highland Gift (IRE)
	Lets Clic Together (IRE)	Don't Forget Me
		Mombones

ELARQAM (GB)

Elarqam always had the potential to make an impact. He is a second-crop son of the great Frankel (by Galileo), out of Timeform 125-rated mile star Attraction (by Efisio) and having completed four seasons on the track is now embarking on a new career as a stallion. He is standing at Haras de Saint Arnoult in France and for a first-year fee of €6,000.

The 1,600,000 guineas he cost when his breeder, Floors Farming, consigned him to Book 1 of the Tattersalls October Yearling Sale is a testament to his combination of looks, physique and pedigree. He went into training with Mark Johnston and won his two juvenile starts by a combined margin of six lengths, a York novice race first time out and defeat of Tip Two Win in the Group 3 Tattersalls Stakes at Newmarket, both on good-to-soft ground and over seven furlongs. His next start was in the Group 1 Qipco 2000 Guineas the following May and he was one of only four members of the fourteen-strong field sent off at a single-digit price. He may have been a shade unlucky not to have been placed, but fourth in that edition of the classic was no disgrace. Saxon Warrior won it by a length and a half, a head, half a length and a neck from Tip Two Win, Masar, Elarqam and Roaring Lion. Gustav Klimt was sixth, with James Garfield (seventh) and Expert Eye (tenth) among those behind.

Many expected he would gain some compensation in the Group 1 Tattersalls Irish 2,000 Guineas three weeks later, but he was in trouble after halfway and came home sixth. Romanised, U S Navy Flag and Gustav Klimt filled the placings. He stepped up in trip two months later and only failed by two necks to make all in the Group 2 Sky Bet York Stakes over an extended ten furlongs. The five-year-old geldings Thundering Blue and Brorocco were the pair who headed him near the finish, whereas the former South African triple Grade 1 star Smart Call was two lengths behind him in fourth on what was the final start of her career. She was bred to Kingman (by Invincible Spirit) shortly afterwards and had a British-born filly, now named Call To Glory, on July 28th, 2019. Elarqam, on the other hand, ran once more that season, again trying unsuccessfully to make all the running. Once again it was against older horses, but it was disappointing that he had no more to give when headed a furlong out in the Group 3 Tattersalls Sovereign Stakes over a mile at Salisbury, eventually passing the post in fourth, four lengths behind the winner, Plumatic.

Elarqam had a wind procedure done not long after that, and while that is likely to have helped him to show his true ability more often, the physical maturity that comes with age probably also played a role. He won three of his seven races as a four-year-old, the best of his three blacktype successes being his three-and-a-quarter-length defeat of Addeybb in the Group 2 Sky Bet York Stakes on soft ground. That came three and a half weeks before the best performance of his life when, over the same course and distance and on good ground he finished a head and one-length third to Japan and Crystal Ocean in the Group 1 Juddmonte International Stakes. He had encountered some trouble in running in the final furlong and was unlucky not to have finished closer.

He was short-headed by Lord North in the Group 3 Betway Brigadier Gerard Stakes over ten furlongs at Haydock on his seasonal reappearance in early June 2020, but then produced a pair of disappointing efforts. He was only fifth to Fanny Logan in the Group 2 Hardwicke Stakes at Royal Ascot, his only try at twelve furlongs, and beat only one home behind Aspetar when bidding for a repeat success in the Group 2 Sky Bet York Stakes. However, he came back to his best for what turned out to be his career finale, the Group 3 Dubai Duty Free Legacy Cup Stakes over the unusual trip of eleven furlongs at Newbury in mid-September. He made most of the running and stayed on well to beat Desert Encounter and Extra Elusive by margins of one and a half lengths and a length and a quarter.

Elarqam, who achieved a peak handicap rating of 120 during his career, has now moved on to a new role. His lack of a Group 1 win or a pedigree that has proven strength in producing notable stallions may not put him high on many lists of exciting additions to the ranks, but he is well-bred, as you'd expect of a son of Frankel, and it would be no surprise to see him coming up with some progeny who are talented as himself.

His dam lit up the 2004 season with wins in the Group 1 1000 Guineas, Group 1 Irish 1,000 Guineas, Group 1 Coronation

Stakes, and Group 1 Sun Chariot Stakes. She was also runner-up in the Group 1 Falmouth Stakes and Group 1 Matron Stakes that summer, chasing home Soviet Song in both races, and she returned to training as a four-year-old to win that year's edition of the latter race, beating Chic by three-quarters of a length. She was also a star as a two-year-old, winning her five races by an aggregate of seventeen and a half lengths, a sequence that culminated in the Group 3 Queen Mary Stakes and Group 2 Cherry Hinton Stakes. She was, like her star son, trained by Mark Johnston.

Attraction is also the dam of Fountain of Youth (by Oasis Dream), who was a member of the Ballydoyle team at two and three. He was precocious and just missed out on blacktype when fourth in the Listed Windsor Castle Stakes on what would be his final of three runs as a juvenile. He was stepped up in trip upon his return, in an attempt to make him a Guineas horse but didn't stay, so he returned to the minimum trip in late June of that year and beat Extortionist by a head in a Group 3 contest on fast ground at the Curragh. He had been a 420,000-guinea Book 1 yearling, he has sired some multiple winners from his first two crops—including first-crop son Gravity Force, who was fourth (no blacktype) in the Group 3 Horris Hill Stakes—but his record does not necessarily detract from Elarqam's potential.

The two brothers are very different in terms of both their racing record and the male line that they represent. One is a precocious five-furlong specialist by a leading international sire who represents the Green Desert branch of Danzig's (by Northern Dancer) male line and has a mixed record as a sire of stallion sons. The other was a seven-furlong juvenile pattern scorer who went on to be best from eight to eleven furlongs, and he is by a leading sire son of Galileo (by Sadler's Wells) who can get speedy types but is mostly represented by those who excel at any point of the full classic range. Elarqam will also, therefore, be getting a different type of mare to the more speed-oriented ones that go to his brother.

Attraction's half-sister Titivation (by Montjeu) did her part for the family by coming up with the Group 2-placed stakes winner Titi Makfi (by Makfi), her dam Flirtation (by Pursuit of Love) is a half-sister to the middle-distance Group 2-placed listed scorer

Carmita (by Caerleon), and the international top-level winners that you will find under branches of the fourth generation of the family include Group 1 Prix de la Salamandre scorer and minor blacktype sire Lord of Men (by Groom Dancer) and Japanese filly champion Major Emblem (by Daiwa Major). It's a family with an established history of producing some talented and even top-class racehorses, and now it remains to be seen if Elarqam can write a new chapter in its legacy.

SUMMARY DETAILS
Bred: Floors Farming
Owned: Hamdan Al Maktoum
Trained: Mark Johnston
Country: England
Race record: 11-4034-4131130-2001-
Career highlights: 6 wins inc Sky Bet York Stakes (Gr2), Dubai Duty Free Legacy Cup Stakes (Gr3), Tattersalls Stakes (Gr3), Davies Insurance Services Gala Stakes (L), Betfair Best Odds On ITV Races Festival Stakes (L), 2nd Betway Brigadier Gerard Stakes (Gr3), 3rd Juddmonte International Stakes (Gr1), Sky Bet York Stakes (Gr2), Wolferton Stakes (L)

ELARQAM (GB) – 2015 bay horse

Frankel (GB)	Galileo (IRE)	Sadler's Wells (USA)
		Urban Sea (USA)
	Kind (IRE)	Danehill (USA)
		Rainbow Lake (GB)
Attraction (GB)	Efisio	Formidable (USA)
		Eldoret
	Flirtation (GB)	Pursuit of Love (GB)
		Eastern Shore

ELYSIUM (IRE)

Kildangan Stud's Belardo (by Lope de Vega) has made an eye-catching start to his stallion career and Elysium is one of four European stakes winners from his first crop of juveniles. Isabella Giles struck twice for him in pattern company, Lullaby Moon won the Group 3 Prix Miesque and Listed Two Year Old Trophy, and Belloccio won a listed contest in France. He has also had a listed scorer from the New Zealand half of his global first crop. It is, of course, too early to be getting overly excited about any stallion after just his freshman season results, but it is fair to say that this juvenile Group 1 scorer and subsequent Group 1 Lockinge Stakes winner remains one of the best long-term prospects among those stallions who had their first foals in Europe in 2018.

Elysium was well-beaten on her debut in a five-furlong Naas maiden on good-to-firm in early June but won a similar contest over 164 yards farther on yielding ground at Navan fifteen days later, scoring by one and three-quarter lengths. She stepped up to seven furlongs the following month but had to settle for third to Ebeko and State of Rest in a leg of the Foran Equine Irish EBF Auction Race series at Leopardstown, beaten by margins of one length and three and three-quarter lengths. She chased home Snapraeterea in another leg of that lucrative series over eighty yards farther on soft-to-heavy at Roscommon a month later and then went to the Curragh for the Group 3 Weld Park Stakes. She stayed on well in the closing stages of the seven-furlong contest, moving easily past the front-runners and quickly going clear for a length-and-a-half victory from Aunt Bridy, with Thinking of You and No Speak Alexander three-quarters of a length and a nose back in third and fourth.

The filly is the fourth foal of the six-furlong Pontefract maiden winner and Listed Chesham Stakes runner-up Sonning Rose (by Hawk Wing), has two winning siblings, and is related in varying degrees to a long list of horses who earned blacktype. The mare's first-crop Sioux Nation (by Scat Daddy) filly made €140,000 at the rescheduled Goffs November Foal Sale in late December. Sonning Rose's three blacktype siblings were placed in such company but you have to go back to fourth dam Gleam (by Spy

Well) to find a stakes winner. She was runner-up in the Criterium des Pouliches as a juvenile and is the horse got closest to the brilliant grey Humble Duty at the finish of the 1000 Guineas at Newmarket the following spring. The previous year's Cheveley Park Stakes winner was eased down to win the 1970 classic by seven lengths and she went on to add the Coronation Stakes and Sussex Stakes and earn a rating of 127 from Timeform. Gleam, on the other hand, then won the Prix Minerve and earned placings in the Prix de Mallaret and Prix de Royaumont. Many of her blacktype-earning descendants achieved the feat in North America and they include her Grade 3-winning granddaughter Upper Noosh (by Red Ransom).

Elysium, a €15,000 Goffs Autumn Yearling Sale graduate, is trained by Noel Meade and she was sold privately shortly after her final run of the year. In 2021, she will carry the famous white and green colours of George Strawbridge rather than the red and green of The London Racing Partnership. She holds an entry in the Group 1 Tattersalls Irish 1,000 Guineas, and while further improvement is required to be up to that standard, she did jump from eighty-five to 106 in the handicap because of her pattern success. You would expect a filly of her pedigree to make progress from two to three and that a Belardo filly out of a Hawk Wing (by Woodman) mare could be well-suited to a mile as a three-year-old.

SUMMARY DETAILS
Bred: Tullpark Ltd
Owned: The London Racing Partnership
Trained: Noel Meade
Country: Ireland
Race record: 01321-
Career highlights: 2 wins inc Weld Park Stakes (Gr3)

ELYSIUM (IRE) – 2018 bay filly

Belardo (IRE)	Lope de Vega (IRE)	Shamardal (USA)
		Lady Vettori (GB)
	Danaskaya (IRE)	Danehill (USA)
		Majinskaya (FR)
Sonning Rose (IRE)	Hawk Wing (USA)	Woodman (USA)
		La Lorgnette (CAN)
	Shinkoh Rose (FR)	Warning
		Sandpiper's Dream (USA)

ENBIHAAR (IRE)

Enbihaar is a mare that surely anyone hoping to breed middle-distance and Cup horses would love to have on their team. Unraced at two, she is by an outstanding Australian sire, from a notable blacktype family, and has notched up seven wins and three placings from a dozen starts. Her only times to finish out of the frame are when fourth in the Listed Noel Murless Stakes on her final start at three and when filling that same position behind Dame Malliot in the Group 2 Princess of Wales's Tattersalls Stakes at Newmarket in July. Her seven wins include five Group 2 contests, she has been placed once at the highest level and her career earnings stand at just over £500,000.

Yet another racehorse of note who got their early winning start on the artificial tracks, she finished third over ten furlongs at Chelmsford on her debut in early September of her three-year-old season, twelve days before she recorded a comfortable three-length victory over a furlong farther at Kempton. Her listed-race fourth came next, she was only beaten by a total of two and a quarter lengths on good ground, and it was an eye-catching turf debut. Her four-year-old season began with listed success over twelve furlongs at Goodwood in early May, she then failed by just half a length to beat Dramatic Queen in the Group 3 William Hill Bronte Cup Fillies' Stakes over a quarter of a mile farther on good-to-firm ground at York but reversed those placings at Haydock in early July, beating her old rival by a neck in the Group 2 bet365 Lancashire Oaks.

The ground was also good-to-firm on her next two starts but very soft at ParisLongchamp in October when her winning streak came to an end. She had trounced Manuela de Vega by five lengths to win the Group 2 Qatar Lillie Langtry Stakes over fourteen furlongs at Goodwood, short-headed Delphinia in the Group 2 DFS Park Hill Stakes over the St Leger course and distance in early September and despite considerably different underfoot conditions, she was sent off favourite for the Group 1 Qatar Prix de Royallieu. This was the first time the race had both its distance and status raised. Classic heroine Anapurna set a steady gallop, made all under Frankie Dettori and won comfortably by a length a quarter, keeping clear of the barging match that went on just behind her. Enbihaar and Delphinia made their challenges at the same time and they physically bumped into each other three times inside the final furlong. The younger filly short-headed the older one on the line and the placings remained unaltered following the inevitable stewards' enquiry. Lah Ti Dar was fourth, a further length and a half behind.

She was also the favourite for the aforementioned Princess of Wales's Stakes on her seasonal reappearance in 2020, but the ground was soft and although she did stay on in the closing stages, she had to settle for fourth. Dame Malliot beat Communique by two and a quarter lengths, with Desert Encounter and Enbihaar one and a half lengths and a head behind. Two runs on soft ground, two defeats. Her best runs had all been on good-to-firm and that was the going description too when she added a second edition of the Group 2 Qatar Lillie Langtry Stakes to her record at the start of August. It was an unsatisfactory race given that only a pair of capable but inferior three-year-olds showed up to take her on, both of whom would need to have shown a considerable amount of improvement to threaten her.

Snow set off in front and tried to make all. The Ballydoyle filly came into the race on an official rating of 106 having been a half-length runner-up to One Voice in the Group 3 Blue Wind Stakes over ten furlongs at Leopardstown before winning the Group 3 Munster Oaks at Cork and taking fifth behind Even So in the Group 1 Juddmonte Irish Oaks. Enbihaar joined her before three out, eased to the front a furlong later and went on, passing the post three and a half lengths clear of the other runner, Cabaletta. Snow weakened and was eased, passing the post a further ten lengths behind; she would be unplaced in first-time blinkers in the Group 2 Park Hill Stakes on her only subsequent outing. Cabaletta came into the race rated 103 following a narrow listed-race success at Newbury. She was well-beaten on her final two runs of the year despite one of those being a Group 3 placing at Goodwood.

Enbihaar's stamina over fourteen furlongs was well-established so it was worth a try stepping her up in trip, a move that was rewarded by providing her with a fifth Group 2 success. The ground at York was described as good on the day of the

Weatherbys Hamilton Lonsdale Cup Stakes, she was taking on some specialist stayers but proved up to the task. She came under some pressure from her regular partner, Jim Crowley, over two furlongs from home as Nayef Road led from Dashing Willoughby. The latter had no more to give and finished fourth, but the mare, drifting slightly to her right, eventually won her battle with Nayef Road and then held off the staying-on Stratum. The final margins were three-quarters of a length, the same, and a length, with Eagles By Day another three and a half lengths behind in fifth. The Prix de Royallieu was her stated target after this but instead York turned out to be her final run of the year.

The long-striding Enbihaar is a €500,000 Arqana Deauville August Yearling Sale graduate who was bred by Haras de Mezeray, trained by John Gosden, and has carried the famous blue and white colours of Sheikh Hamdan Al Maktoum throughout her career. She is a daughter of Redoute's Choice (by Danehill), champion racehorse, multiple champion sire and, with particular relevance to her future, now a multiple champion broodmare sire too. There have been thirty-eight Group 1 stars among his 177 stakes-winning offspring, including standouts success as Lankan Rupee, Miss Finland, Samantha Miss, and The Autumn Sun. His established stallion sons include the star trio Snitzel, Not A Single Doubt and Stratum, and the late long-time Arrowfields Stud resident shuttled to Haras de Bonneval in France in 2013 and 2014. Enbihaar and 2019's Group 1 Grosser Dallmayr-Preis - Bayerisches Zuchtrennen scorer Danceteria come from the latter crop. He also had a small number of horses born to Northern Hemisphere time back in 2008 and they included Elzaam. That horse began his career with Michael Jarvis, was a nose runner-up to Strong Suit in the Group 2 Coventry Stakes at Royal Ascot, ran away with a listed sprint at Newbury the following spring, and is now in his ninth season at Ballyhane Stud. His quartet of stakes winners features 2020's Group 1 Matron Stakes heroine Champers Elysees.

As a broodmare sire, Redoute's Choice's Group 1 roll of honour includes The Mission (by Choisir), Stay With Me (by Street Cry), Trekking (by Street Cry) and a string who are by Sadler's Wells-line stallions: Ace High (by High Chaparral), D'Argento (by

So You Think), Flit (by Medaglia d'Oro), Inference (by So You Think), and Super Seth (by Dundeel). Also, the star stallion Pierro (by Lonhro) is out of a mare who is by Daylami (by Doyoun) and out of a daughter of Sadler's Wells (by Northern Dancer), and his Group 1 stars out of Redoute's Choice mares are Arcadia Queen, Regal Power and Levendi. Tweenhills Farm & Stud's reverse-shuttle sire Zoustar (by Northern Meteor) also has Redoute's Choice as his broodmare sire and he is a grandson of Encosta de Lago, the standout racehorse and sire-son of Sadler's Wells' full brother Fairy King.

Enbihaar is a half-sister to a pair of stakes-placed handicappers: miler Silent Attack (by Dream Ahead) and middle-distance gelding King Bolete (by Cape Cross). Her dam, Chanterelle (by Trempolino), joined Rabbah Bloodstock after being sold for €340,000 at the 2019 Arqana December breeding stock sale, had a Wootton Bassett (by Iffraaj) colt just over three months later and was then bred back to Dubawi (by Dubai Millennium). The mare's two-year-old for this coming season is a Muhaarar (by Oasis Dream) filly who made €200,000 in Deauville in early September. Although unplaced on the track, Chanterelle's success as a broodmare is no surprise. She is a daughter of the Group 2 Prix Maurice de Gheest and Group 3 Prix du Palais Royal scorer Spectacular Joke (by Spectacular Bid) and has two siblings of particular note.

Cox Orange is a full sister to Chanterelle and like her 'niece' she was a tough and prolific blacktype performer who raced up to the age of five. She won the Group 3 Prix du Calvados and a listed contest in France before moving across the Atlantic, and her final career tally of ten wins included Grade 3 contests at Aqueduct and Gulfstream Park. Listed Masaka Stakes winner Vista Bella (by Diktat), who finished third to Virginia Waters in the Group 1 1000 Guineas at Newmarket, is the best of her nine winning offspring. Chanterelle's half-sister Amonita (by Anabaa) also raced from two to five years of age, she landed the Group 1 Prix Marcel Boussac as a juvenile and was a graded winner in the USA. Third dam No Joke (by Shecky Greene) won eleven of her seventeen starts in North America and that multiple stakes winner was a great-granddaughter of Test Stakes heroine Imperatrice (by Caruso), grandam of the great Secretariat (by Bold Ruler). His connection to Enbihaar is remote and has no bearing on her achievements or prospects, but there is clearly enough in her track record and immediate pedigree to explain why she will be a broodmare of considerable potential.

SUMMARY DETAILS

Bred: Haras du Mezeray
Owned: Hamdan Al Maktoum
Trained: John Gosden
Country: England
Race record: -314-121113-411-
Career highlights: 7 wins inc Weatherbys Hamilton Lonsdale Cup Stakes (Gr2), Qatar Lillie Langtry Stakes (Gr2-twice), DFS Park Hill Stakes (Gr2), bet365 Lancashire Oaks (Gr2), Unibet EBF Daisy Warwick Fillies' Stakes (L), 2nd William Hill Bronte Cup Fillies' Stakes (Gr3), 3rd Qatar Prix de Royallieu (Gr1)

ENBIHAAR (IRE) – 2015 bay mare

Redoute's Choice (AUS)	Danehill (USA)	Danzig (USA)
		Razyana (USA)
	Shantha's Choice (AUS)	Canny Lad (AUS)
		Dancing Show (USA)
Chanterelle (FR)	Trempolino (USA)	Sharpen Up
		Trephine (FR)
	Spectacular Joke (USA)	Spectacular Bid (USA)
		No Joke (USA)

EPONA PLAYS (IRE)

The 2020 season was an important one for Coolmore Stud stallion Australia (by Galileo) and after a steady start, his results strengthened from September onwards with classic success for Galileo Chrome at Doncaster and Breeders' Cup Mile victory for Order of Australia providing him with his first and much-needed Group/Grade 1 winners. Epona Plays is among five of his Irish- and British-trained offspring who won a Group 2 or Group 3 race in Ireland or Great Britain during the year: the others were Buckhurst, Cayenne Pepper, Leo de Fury, and Patrick Sarsfield.

Renzo Formi's homebred is trained by Willie McCreery, she was fourth and third on her only starts at two, didn't open her winning account until her fourth attempt in 2020 but then found a vein of form that raised her handicap mark from ninety-one to 104 and secured that all-important blacktype success. She missed out on her first attempt at that value-enhancer, finishing fourth to Laburnum in the Irish Stallion Farms EBF Hurry Harriet Stakes over nine and a half furlongs at Gowran Park. But she got it next time when staying on inside the final furlong to chase home Thundering Nights and Albigna in the Group 3 Snow Fairy Fillies Stakes over nine furlongs on soft ground at the Curragh. The margins were one and a half lengths and a neck.

Three weeks later she returned to Gowran Park for the Group 3 Denny Cordell Lavarack & Lanwades Stud Fillies Stakes, over the same distance as on her prior visit to the venue. She met with some minor traffic problems and had to be switched a couple of times, but when she got a clear run, drew level with Etneya and from there was always going to win. The margin was a neck and there was a five-length gap back to Cerro Bayo in third. She was unplaced behind Saltonstall in heavy ground at Naas on her final start in early November, but that does not detract from her standing. No matter what she does from this point forward, she has her place in the books as a pattern-winning half-sister to the Group 3 Athasi Stakes scorer Dolce Strega (by Zoffany).

The two are among four winning offspring of New Plays (by Oratorio), they have a stakes-placed half-sister in Bumbasina (by Canford Cliffs) and although their dam's 2018 Gleneagles (by

Galileo) colt died as a yearling, they do have a younger half-brother in the Muhaarar (by Oasis Dream) colt that arrived on February 16th, 2020. Their dam was then bred back to Gleneagles. Dolce Strega, on the other hand, wasn't covered last year after her third foal, a son of Australia, was born on May 12th. She had sons of Sea The Stars (by Cape Cross) in 2018 and 2019.

New Plays is a half-sister to the Group 2 Doncaster Cup runner-up Darley Sun (by Tiger Hill) and out of Sagamartha (by Rainbow Quest), a winning daughter of the Group 2 Falmouth Stakes runner-up Lovealoch (by Lomond). Her relationship to Darley Sun may sound sufficiently stout to raise a question of how Epona Plays could have so much stamina on both sides of the page and yet be better at under ten furlongs. Of course, all of her dam's blacktype offspring have so far been effective at somewhere in the seven-to-ten-furlong range, suggesting that their dam may have some speed to pass on rather than just stamina. Also, Lovealoch, who was Group 2 placed at a mile and sired by a Guineas winner, was the dam of juvenile filly champion Flashy Wings (by Zafonic).

That filly was by a juvenile star and excellent 2000 Guineas winner whose influence has been more for speed than stamina, and she likely got similar tendencies from her dam too. She won the Group 2 Queen Mary Stakes and Group 2 Lowther Stakes in 2005, both at York that year, was third in the Group 1 Cheveley Park Stakes, then stepped up to a mile at three and was placed in both the Group 1 Coronation Stakes and Group 1 Matron Stakes. You will also find several sprint blacktype winners under branches of the fifth generation of the pedigree, but those horses are too remote to have any bearing on any potential Epona Plays may have on the track this season or when she eventually goes to stud.

SUMMARY DETAILS
Bred: Renzo Forni
Owned: Renzo Forni
Trained: Willie McCreery
Country: Ireland
Race record: 43-02314310-

Career highlights: 2 wins inc Denny Cordell Lavarack & Lanwades Stud Fillies Stakes (Gr3), 3rd Snow Fairy Fillies' Stakes (Gr3)

EPONA PLAYS (IRE) – 2017 bay filly

Australia (GB)	Galileo (IRE)	Sadler's Wells (USA)
		Urban Sea (USA)
	Ouija Board (GB)	Cape Cross (IRE)
		Selection Board
New Plays (IRE)	Oratorio (IRE)	Danehill (USA)
		Mahrah (USA)
	Sagamartha (GB)	Rainbow Quest (USA)
		Lovealoch (IRE)

ETONIAN (IRE)

Etonian's first public appearance was as Lot 2 at the Goffs November Foal Sale in 2018 and the €14,000 colt's second was during the Book 4 session of the Tattersalls October Yearling Sale in Newmarket where he failed to change hands, a vendor buy-back at 10,000 guineas. Nine months later he went to Sandown for a seven-furlong maiden on good-to-firm ground, and although the middle of three long-priced representatives of the Richard Hannon stable in the line-up, he was an impressive winner. He beat One Ruler and Third Kingdom by three and a quarter lengths and a short head, with a further three-and-a-quarter-length gap back to the fourth. The third would be a wide-margin winner on his only subsequent outing, whereas the runner-up went on the land the Group 3 Autumn Stakes and chase home Mac Swiney in the Group 1 Vertem Futurity Trophy Stakes.

Etonian has not quite reached those heights yet but he did win a pattern race on his next start: the Group 3 Betway Solario Stakes over the same course and distance as his debut success. He lost his footing a bit on the bend half a mile from home but recovered, always looked to be going well in the straight, hit the front inside the final furlong and landed the spoils by a length and quarter and half a length from King Vega and Apollo One. This promising start made his final run more disappointing. He raced towards the rear of the field in the Group 1 Darley Dewhurst Stakes on soft ground at Newmarket in early October, was being pushed along at halfway, came under pressure soon afterwards and didn't pick up. He beat only two home in the fourteen-runner race, passing the post sixteen and a half lengths behind the winner, St Mark's Basilica.

The colt was bred by Emir Alkas and he represents the third crop of Haras de Bouquetot's top-class miler Olympic Glory (by Choisir). The stallion's blacktype figures are not as strong as one would have hoped at this point of his career but his six stakes winners include the mile dual Group 1 star Watch Me and classic-placed Group 3 scorer Grand Glory, whereas his nine blacktype-placed horses include Group 1 Australian Derby third Eric The Eel. Etonian is the third foal of an unraced mare called Naan (by

Indian Charlie), a daughter of the dual Group 3-placed Wingspan (by Silver Hawk). That mare is a half-sister to the US nine-furlong Grade 2 scorer Interactif (by Broken Vow)—a sire of winners and blacktype earners—whereas fourth dam Pennant Champion (by Mr Prospector) is a winning full sister two Grade 1 winners. Those top-level winners are but remote relations to Etonian but they certainly deserve a mention, as do their star half-sister and celebrity dam.

Traditionally won the Grade 1 Oaklawn Handicap as a four-year-old and spent time at stud in New Zealand and Ireland before being exported to Morocco. Miner's Mark won the Grade 1 Jockey Club Gold Cup and achieved some success at stud, although not at a level that would have been hoped. Their Grade 1-placed full brother Our Emblem secured his place in the history books by siring the Grade 1 Kentucky Derby and Grade 1 Preakness Stakes star War Emblem. He was more or less a one-hit-wonder in North America and was sent south where he added three top-level winners sired in Brazil. One of the trio, Sal Grosso, was champion three-year-old and Horse of the Year in that country.

Their half-sister My Flag (by Easy Goer) won the Grade 1 Breeders' Cup Juvenile Fillies at two, added the Grade 1 Coaching Club American Oaks, Grade 1 Ashland Stakes and Grade 1 Gazelle Handicap at three and went on to become the dam of the champion Storm Flag Flying (by Storm Cat). A triple Grade 1 star at two, she won the Grade 1 Personal Ensign Handicap at four, a race named in honour of her great grandam. The Ogden Phipps homebred, a daughter of Private Account (by Damascus), went undefeated in a thirteen-race career that included wins in the Grade 1 Frizette Stakes as a juvenile, two editions of the Grade 1 Beldame Stakes, plus a string of other top-level wins that culminated in her finale in the Grade 1 Breeders' Cup Distaff. An Eclipse Award champion, Broodmare of the Year and Hall of Fame inductee, Personal Ensign is the fifth dam of Etonian.

Etonian, who is an outcross—that is, no ancestors duplicated within the first five generations of his pedigree—looked full of promise in his first two starts and finished the year on an official rating of 109. He is bred to be better at three, so hopefully he can bounce back from that Newmarket disappointment and show us what he's capable of in 2021. He holds an entry in the Group 1 Derby Stakes at Epsom although, on pedigree, he looks more likely to be a miler who may stay ten furlongs. It will be interesting to see how he turns out.

SUMMARY DETAILS
Bred: Emir Alkas
Owned: Mrs J Wood
Trained: Richard Hannon
Country: England
Race record: 110-
Career highlights: 2 wins inc Betway Solario Stakes (Gr3)

ETONIAN (IRE) – 2018 bay colt

Olympic Glory (IRE)	Choisir (AUS)	Danehill Dancer (IRE)
		Great Selection (AUS)
	Acidanthera (GB)	Alzao (USA)
		Amaranthus
Naan (IRE)	Indian Charlie (USA)	In Excess
		Soviet Sojourn (USA)
	Wingspan (USA)	Silver Hawk (USA)
		Broad Pennant (USA)

EUCHEN GLEN (GB)

Owner-breeder William Johnstone has been experimenting with some close inbreeding in his horses and the project has yielded some good results. Euchen Glen is his most successful one so far, but he indicated in a *Racing Post* interview in November that Annandale could be even better. That Mark Johnston-trained Group 1 Investec Derby entrant has won two of his three starts to date, at Bath and Newcastle, and the son of Australia (by Galileo) is inbred 3x2 to Sadler's Wells (by Northern Dancer), the same pattern as in Enable's pedigree. Euchen Glen does not have such close duplication but is inbred 4x5x5x4 to Northern Dancer (by Nearctic), 5x4 to Special (by Forli), 4x5 to Raise a Native (by Native Dancer) and 4x3 to Nureyev (by Northern Dancer). Most of this duplication is on the distaff side, and the choice to send Jabbara (by Kingmambo), who is inbred 3x2 to Nureyev, to a Sadler's Wells-line horse was a deliberate one.

Euchen Glen is a son of the Derby winner Authorized (by Montjeu), a stallion who spent many years under the Darley banner until being sent to Turkey where he is now standing his second season. National Hunt fans are most familiar with him as being the sire of the dual Grade 3 Grand National hero Tiger Roll and the sadly ill-fated Grade 1 star Nichols Canyon, but he is primarily a flat sire. His son Santiago won the Group 1 Dubai Duty Free Irish Derby in 2020 and his other top-level winners include Seal of Approval, Complacent, and the multimillionaire Hartnell who went from being a Group 1-placed Group 3 scorer in England to a four-time Group 1 star in Australia. That gelding finished third to Magic Wand in the Group 1 Mackinnon Stakes on his final start in 2019, pushing his career earnings past the £4 million mark.

Jim Goldie trains Euchen Glen and done an outstanding job with the gelding who returned to training in 2020 after almost two full years out of action due to injury. The bay, who was a runner-up on his only start as a two-year-old, made fairly steady progression throughout his three-, four- and five-year-old seasons, notching up seven wins from ten furlongs to two miles and working his way up to a triple-digit handicap mark. That figure came after his eye-catching two-and-a-quarter-length defeat of Thundering Blue in the valuable and prestigious John Smith's Cup over the extended ten furlongs at York in July 2018. He made all under nine-stone-three, looking like a potential group-race winner in the making.

Timeform rated him 114 after that, his official handicap mark rose from ninety-nine to 107, but a tendon injury halted the horse's career. One year and eleven months later, he returned to the track to finish third to Red Verdon in a listed race over fourteen and a half furlongs at Doncaster, and although unplaced in his next four starts those included fifth to Fujaira Prince in the Sky Bet Ebor Handicap and fifth to Stradivarius in the Group 1 Al Shaqab Goodwood Cup Stakes. Then he won a valuable fourteen-furlong handicap on soft ground at Haydock, finished just over three lengths fourth to Addeybb in a listed contest at Ayr and made trips to York and Newbury that saw him end up a dual pattern winner. He beat Desert Encounter by half a length in the Group 3 Betsafe Cumberland Lodge Stakes over twelve furlongs on soft at the first of those venues and followed-up with a one-and-three-quarter-length defeat of Natural History in the Group 3 Pravha Stakes (registered as the St Simon Stakes) over the same trip on heavy ground at Newbury. Regular partner Paul Mulrennan was in the saddle for both races. The pair finished down the field in the Betfair November Handicap on Euchen Glen's final outing of the year, in which he was carrying nine-stone-ten. He now has a handicap mark of 110.

Euchen Glen is a full brother to two multiple winners of whom Sir Chauvelin is the more notable and prolific. Also trained by Goldie, he has won six times from twelve to fourteen furlongs on the flat and is a blacktype-placed four-time winner over hurdles. His flat wins include a £62,000-to-the-winner handicap at Goodwood, he has been runner-up in the Duke of Edinburgh Stakes at Royal Ascot and third in the Northumberland Plate at Newcastle. Their dam, who died in 2016 aged just thirteen, was a low-rated triple sprint winner for the Clive Brittain stable. She was out of Isle de France (by Nureyev), a Group 1-placed, middle-distance pattern-winning daughter of Stella Madrid (by Alydar), who won the Grade 1 Frizette Stakes, Grade 1 Spinaway Stakes and Grade 1 Matron Stakes as a two-year-old and added the Grade 1 Acorn Stakes at three. She was a full sister to Grade 1 Shuvee Handicap scorer Tis Juliet and out of the multiple Grade 1-winning US sprint champion and Hall of Fame inductee My Juliet (by Gallant Romeo).

Euchen Glen is a talented and consistent gelding who has progressed throughout his career and come back from injury to reach new heights at the age of seven. He is a credit to all of his connections and it will be interesting to see how he gets on in 2021.

SUMMARY DETAILS
Bred: W M Johnstone
Owned: W M Johnstone
Trained: Jim Goldie
Country: Scotland
Race record: 2-00100-00130101300-303121/3000014110-
Career highlights: 10 wins inc Pravha Stakes (registered as the St Simon Stakes) (Gr3), Betsafe Cumberland Lodge Stakes (Gr3)

EUCHEN GLEN (GB) – 2013 bay gelding

		Sadler's Wells (USA)
Authorized (IRE)	Montjeu (IRE)	Sadler's Wells (USA)
		Floripedes (FR)
	Funsie (FR)	Saumarez
		Vallee Dansante (USA)
Jabbara (IRE)	Kingmambo (USA)	Mr Prospector (USA)
		Miesque (USA)
	Isle de France (USA)	Nureyev (USA)
		Stella Madrid (USA)

EXTRA ELUSIVE (GB)

Extra Elusive created a favourable impression when winning a one-mile Newbury maiden on his sole start at two but it was not until his five-year-old season that he finally got a first pattern win to his name. Then he added a second one a few weeks later, both times ridden by Hollie Doyle. He won two of his four starts at three and although winless in four runs at four, finished that season on a handicap mark of 106. He had been a half-length runner-up to Mootasadir in a ten-furlong listed contest at Kempton, finished third to Crystal Ocean in the Group 3 bet365 Gordon Richards Stakes at Sandown and was only beaten by a head when runner-up to Elarqam in a ten-furlong listed contest over the latter's course and distance that July. He was gelded that autumn and returned to action in 2020 for the breakthrough season that would see him hit a peak handicap figure of 115.

He was unplaced in listed races at Lingfield and Ascot on his first two starts of the year but then chased home Global Giant in a similar contest at Newbury. It was then that Doyle, newly retained rider for owner Imad Alsagar, started her partnership with the horse. They went to the front after a furlong of the Group 3 BetVictor Rose of Lancaster Stakes over an extended ten furlongs at Haydock in early August, quickened the pace over two furlongs from home, the gelding responded well to pressure and pulled away to win by two and a quarter lengths from Certain Lad, who was three-quarters of a length in front of the odds-on favourite, Global Giant. The ground was good that day but soft at Windsor three weeks later when having raced prominently and not hit the front until over a furlong out, the pair won the ten-furlong Group 3 Gallagher Group Winter Hill Stakes by a length from Fox Chairman, with Sky Defender another two and three-quarter lengths behind in third. The gelding found the tough task of giving three pounds to Elarqam and Desert Encounter beyond him at Newbury in September, passing the post third to the pair at margins of one and a half lengths and one and a quarter lengths. It was an honourable effort. The Group 1 Qipco Champion Stakes was quite an ask on his final start of the year and he finished a nine-length sixth to Addeybb on soft ground.

Extra Elusive is a son of Coolmore Stud's classic winner and proven international classic sire Mastercraftsman (by Danehill Dancer), a horse who has so far supplied fifteen top-level winners among an overall tally of seventy-seven stakes winners. Seven of the elite winners are from his Irish-conceived crops and they include Alpha Centauri, Kingston Hill, and The Grey Gatsby. Extra Elusive is a half-brother to the unfortunate Group 2 Gimcrack Stakes scorer Ajaya (by Invincible Spirit). Although boasting a stallion's pedigree and getting a good berth at Rathbarry Stud in Ireland he was found to have poor fertility. His handful of offspring includes several winners, including the Archie Watson-trained dual six-furlong scorer Igotatext and the Johnny Murtagh-trained Fourhometwo, a ninety-eight-rated easy Galway maiden who just missed out on blacktype when fourth to Zaffy's Pride in a seven-furlong listed contest at Dundalk in early October.

Nessina (by Hennessy), the dam of Extra Elusive and Ajaya, is an unraced daughter of the Grade 1-placed Grade 2 scorer Didina (by Nashwan) and so is a half-sister to Tantina (by Distant View). That pattern-placed stakes winner is the dam of the Group 1 star and blacktype sire Cityscape (by Selkirk) plus Group 1-placed Group 2 scorer Bated Breath (by Dansili), who got his first top-level winner when Viadera landed the Grade 1 Matriarch Stakes over a mile at Del Mar in November. Tantina is also the grandam of Group 1 St Leger star Logician (by Frankel), multiple US graded winner Suffused (by Champs Elysees) and the talented sprinter Equilateral (by Equiano). This is a notable branch of the famous Best In Show (by Traffic Judge) family that has supplied so many Group/Grade 1 winners around the world.

Extra Elusive is a talented performer over ten furlongs and his best wins have been achieved on good and soft ground; his excellent run against Elarqam in 2019 came on good-to-firm. It will be interesting to see how he gets on as a six-year-old.

SUMMARY DETAILS
Bred: Saleh Al Homaizi & Imad Al Sagar
Owned: Imad Al Sagar
Trained: Roger Charlton
Country: England

Race record: 1-1210-2302-0021130-
Career highlights: 5 wins inc BetVictor Rose of Lancaster Stakes (Gr3), Gallagher Group Winter Hill Stakes (Gr3), 2nd bet365 Steventon Stakes (L), Davies Insurance Services Gala Stakes (L), Matchbook Magnolia Stakes (L), 3rd Dubai Duty Free Legacy Cup Stakes (Gr3), bet365 Gordon Richards Stakes (Gr3)

EXTRA ELUSIVE (GB) – 2015 chestnut gelding

Mastercraftsman (IRE)	Danehill Dancer (IRE)	Danehill (USA)
		Mira Adonde (USA)
	Starlight Dreams (USA)	Black Tie Affair
		Reves Celestes (USA)
Nessina (USA)	Hennessy (USA)	Storm Cat (USA)
		Island Kitty (USA)
	Didina (GB)	Nashwan (USA)
		Didicoy (USA)

FANNY LOGAN (IRE)

Fanny Logan ran only twice in 2020 but left no doubt as to her considerable talent. She also secured a footnote in the history books having become the first filly to win the Group 2 Hardwicke Stakes since Stanerra in 1983. She had taken a keen hold with Frankie Dettori, was asked for an effort a quarter of a mile from home, swept past the field while drifting to her right (she had been on the outside of the pack), hit the front well before the furlong marker and stormed clear, staying on to beat Alounak and Defoe by margins of two and a half lengths and one and three-quarter lengths. Hamish was another half-length back in fourth, a head and short head in front of the ill-fated Derby winner Anthony Van Dyck and the weakening Elarqam, who lost a shoe. It was her only run against males and the first time she did not wear a hood since she'd finished well-beaten behind Star Catcher in the Group 2 Ribblesdale Stakes over the course and distance twelve months before.

Her only other run in 2020 was when runner-up to the front-running Manuela de Vega in the Group 3 Betway Pinnacle Stakes over an extended eleven and a half furlongs on good-to-soft ground at Haydock on June 7th. In 2019, she had notched up a four-timer after her disappointing Ascot run, winning listed races at York, Salisbury (by seven lengths on soft ground) and Yarmouth (by three lengths on good-to-firm) and then the Group 3 Darley Pride Stakes on good-to-soft at Newmarket, beating Queen by a length on the Rowley Mile course. All four of those wins were over ten furlongs. However, her final outing was arguably her best effort that year, when she finished fourth to Iridessa in the Grade 1 Breeders' Cup Filly & Mare Turf on firm ground at Santa Anita.

The John Gosden-trained Fanny Logan was bred by Godolphin and she is among seventy-three stakes winners by Gilltown Stud's Timeform 140-rated superstar Sea The Stars (by Cape Cross). The prolific Group 1-winning half-brother to Galileo (by Sadler's Wells) has had fourteen Group 1 stars so far including standouts such as Crystal Ocean, Harzand, Sea of Class, Star Catcher, Stradivarius, Taghrooda, and Sea The Moon, the latter a Group 1 sire in 2020. It is early for him yet as a broodmare sire but he struck in 2020 with Group 3 scorer Love Locket (by No Nay Never), who is reviewed elsewhere in this volume.

Linda Radlett (by Manduro), Fanny Logan's stakes-placed dam, is a half-sister to the triple Group 1 scorer Hunter's Light (by Dubawi)—stands at Haras du Logis; had a first-crop three-year-old pattern winner in France in 2020—and out of Portmanteau (by Barathea), a winning half-sister to the middle-distance Group 2 winner Courteous (by Generous). That would already be more than enough to suggest that Fanny Logan has considerable potential as a broodmare, but then take into account that Dayanata (by Shirley Heights), her third dam, is an unraced full sister to the classic star and influential stallion Darshaan and half-sister to the Group 1 Prix Vermeille heroine and 'blue hen' mare Darara (by Top Ville). It will be quite a disappointment if she fails to produce at least one high-class son or daughter.

Darara is one of those exceptionally rare gems that have produced at least four individual top-level winners and one of her daughters is among the most valuable broodmares in Europe. Her son Diaghilev (by Sadler's Wells) got a Grade 1 win in Hong Kong under the name River Dancer, Darazari (by Sadler's Wells) got his top-level win in Australia, the sadly ill-fated Derby-placed Rewilding (by Tiger Hill) won the Group 1 Prince of Wales's Stakes in style, whereas Dar Re Mi (by Singspiel) won the Group 1 Pretty Polly Stakes, Group 1 Yorkshire Oaks and Group 1 Dubai Sheema Classic before going on to celebrity status at stud. Her first foal is the pattern-placed Haras du Mezeray stallion De Treville (by Oasis Dream) who is a freshman sire in 2021 and whose handful of yearlings offered included a €90,000 filly sold in Deauville in October.

So Mi Dar (by Dubawi) was number two and the Group 3 Musidora Stakes winner and Group 1 Prix de l'Opera third is now part of her owner-breeder Watership Down Stud's broodmare band. So Mi Dar had a Galileo (by Sadler's Wells) filly in 2019, a Sea The Stars colt in 2020 and was then bred to Frankel (by Galileo). Classic-placed Group 2 Middleton Stakes winner Lah Ti Dar (by Dubawi) is Dar Re Me's fourth foal and the Timeform 127-rated classic-placed triple Group 1 star Too Darn Hot (by

Dubawi) is number five. He covered 172 mares in his first season at Dalham Hall Stud and will be a much anticipated freshman of 2023. Darara's descendants also include the Group 1-placed dual Group 2-winning stayer Darasim (by Kahyasi), and her siblings include the Group 1-placed Group 2 Prix de Royallieu winner Dalara (by Doyoun), another broodmare of note in the family. Daliapour (by Sadler's Wells) is the more notable of that mare's two talented sons having won the Group 1 Coronation Cup and Group 1 Hong Kong Vase, been runner-up in both the Group 1 Derby and Group 1 Irish Derby and third in the Group 1 King George VI and Queen Elizabeth Stakes.

It is a pity that Fanny Logan did not get the chance to race again after June as she looked that day like a potential Group 1 star. However, she is back in training, and whether or not it is a gap on her CV that she can fill in 2021, she is a very well-bred individual could eventually go on to produce at least one son or daughter who will be as talented as she is.

SUMMARY DETAILS
Bred: Godolphin
Owned: HH Sheikha Al Jalila Racing
Trained: John Gosden
Country: England
Race record: 2-13011114-21-
Career highlights: 6 wins inc Hardwicke Stakes (Gr2), Darley Pride Stakes (Gr3), EBF Stallions John Musker Fillies' Stakes (L), British Stallion Studs EBF Upavon Fillies' Stakes (L), British Stallion Studs EBF Lyric Fillies' Stakes (L), 2nd Betway Pinnacle Stakes (Gr3), 3rd Arkle Finance Cheshire Oaks (L)

FANNY LOGAN (IRE) – 2016 bay filly

Sea The Stars (IRE)	Cape Cross (IRE)	Green Desert (USA)
		Park Appeal
	Urban Sea (USA)	Miswaki (USA)
		Allegretta
Linda Radlett (IRE)	Manduro (GER)	Monsun (GER)
		Mandellicht (IRE)
	Portmanteau (GB)	Barathea (IRE)
		Dayanata

FAR ABOVE (IRE)

Far Above made quite an impression in just five runs on the track and, by all accounts, has been doing so among those who have seen him at his new home, Starfield Stud near Mullingar in Co Westmeath. He made his debut in a seven-furlong maiden at Newmarket in April 2019, winning narrowly, but disappointed when only fourth to Jash in a listed contest over the same course and distance a month later, so he was dropped in distance. It was the right move. He trounced a dozen rivals in a six-furlong novice race on soft ground at Windsor and then travelled to France where he took a listed contest on good ground at Deauville, beating Duhail and We Go by a short neck and short head. Sprinting was clearly his game, but it was eleven months before he was seen in action again. He hit the front three furlongs from home in the Group 3 Betfair Supports Racing Welfare Palace House Stakes over the minimum trip at Newmarket in early June 2020 and then kept on well to the line to beat Judicial and Major Jumbo by three-quarters of a length and the same. Sadly, he finished lame and the injury ended his career.

Far Above looks likely to prove popular in his new role. The Timeform 122-rated bay is the fastest horse by the Group 1 Lockinge Stakes and Group 1 Champion Stakes star Farhh (by Pivotal), a stallion whose classic-placed mile Group 1 star King of Change (Derrinstown Stud) is also a new sire for 2021. He is the first foal of Dorraar (by Shamardal), and if he got the so-called 'speed gene' from both of his parents then his progeny will likely prove effective in the broad five-to-ten-furlong range, depending on the input from the mares. But if Far Above received the 'stamina gene' from either of them then do not be surprised to see him come up with some middle-distance winners too. His speed is the exception to his family's general rule and being able to sire winners over a wide range of distances boosts a stallion's prospects of taking high rank.

Dorraar won over seven furlongs at Salisbury as a three-year-old, her only season to race, she has several winning siblings and is out of Dorrati (by Dubai Millennium), a half-sister to Nahrain (by Selkirk). That former Roger Varian-trained star won the

Group 1 Prix de l'Opera at three and Grade 1 Flower Bowl Invitational Stakes at four, both over ten furlongs, and achieved further glory by becoming the dam of the top-class Benbatl (by Dubawi). That Godolphin entire, whose peak end-of-season rating from Timeform is the 129 he earned in 2018, is featured elsewhere in this volume having added a pair of Group 2s in 2020 to his prior Group 1 treble. He excels from eight to ten furlongs. Nahrain and her dual mile listed-winning half-sister Baharah (by Elusive Quality) are out of Bahr (by Generous). That Group 2 Ribblesdale Stakes and Group 3 Musidora Stakes winner was a three-quarter-length runner-up to Shahtoush in the Group 1 Oaks at Epsom, finished third to Winona in the Group 1 Irish Oaks and filled the same position behind Auntie Mame in the Grade 1 Flower Bowl Handicap at Belmont Park.

Far Above, a 105,000-guinea Tattersalls Guineas Breeze-Up graduate who was trained by James Tate, looked like a Group 1 horse in the making when he won at Newmarket. He is a fascinating addition to the stallion ranks and it would be no surprise to see him come up with some sons and daughters who can strike at higher levels than he had the chance to try.

SUMMARY DETAILS
Bred: Mohamed Abdul Malik
Owned: Sheikh Rashid Dalmook Al Maktoum
Trained: James Tate
Country: England
Race record: -1411-1-
Career highlights: 4 wins inc Betfair Supports Racing Welfare Palace House Stakes (Gr3), Qatar Prix Kistena (L)

FAR ABOVE (IRE) – 2016 bay colt

Farhh (GB)	Pivotal (GB)	Polar Falcon (USA)
		Fearless Revival
	Gonbarda (GER)	Lando (GER)
		Gonfalon (GB)
Dorraar (IRE)	Shamardal (USA)	Giant's Causeway (USA)
		Helsinki (GB)
	Dorrati (USA)	Dubai Millennium (GB)
		Bahr (GB)

FEV ROVER (IRE)

Fev Rover is one of a growing number of horses who have advertised Nick Bradley's eye for a bargain at the sales—Dandalla, reviewed elsewhere in this book, is another—and the Manister House Stud-bred bay cost just £20,000 at the Goffs UK Premier Yearling Sale in Doncaster. She went into training with Richard Fahey and finished her first season as a Group 2 and listed winner who picked up prize money in all five of her starts, accumulating a total of £78,205.

She chased home the wide-margin winner Method over six furlongs at Doncaster in late June, failed by just a head to beat Dandalla in the Group 2 Duchess of Cambridge Stakes on soft ground at Newmarket—a one-two in the race for Bradley—and then won a seven-furlong listed contest on good-to-firm at Sandown before showing that she could handle very soft underfoot conditions too with a neck defeat of Plainchant in the Group 2 Shadwell Prix du Calvados over seven furlongs at Deauville in late August. The runner-up that day, who had tried to make all, won a listed race on her previous start, ran away with a Group 3 over six at Chantilly next time and then added Group 2 success over that course and distance in October. Fev Rover, on the other hand, didn't make the frame or earn any blacktype on her only subsequent outing but still picked up a cheque for over £11,600: she was fourth in the Group 1 Qatar Prix Marcel Boussac - Criterium des Pouliches over a mile on heavy ground at ParisLongchamp. She had met with traffic problems, got a bump, but was running on in the closing stages. The margins were three-quarters of a length, one and a half lengths, and one and a quarter lengths, and the fillies ahead of her were Tiger Tanaka, Tasmania, and Rougir.

Her ability to stay the mile likely comes from her dam, Laurelita, as that mare is a daughter of the dual Derby and dual Breeders' Cup Turf star High Chaparral (by Sadler's Wells). The filly's sire, on the other hand, is the juvenile pattern winner Gutaifan (by Dark Angel) who started covering mares at three, as did his sire, but has not lived up to expectations. He has two listed winners and two pattern-placed runners in addition to his star daughter from two large crops of racing age and having spent five seasons at Yeomanstown Stud, he has moved to Haras des Faunes in France from 2021.

Fev Rover is her dam's third foal, her year-older half-brother Bill The Butcher (by Starspangledbanner), who won over seven furlongs at two, was gelded after a sole winning appearance in 2020, over a mile at Newbury in July. Laurelita, a seven-furlong winner who made the frame only twice in an eight-race career, had colts by El Kabeir (by Scat Daddy) and Starspangledbanner (by Choisir) in 2019 and 2020 and was then bred to Invincible Army (by Invincible Spirit). She is a half-sister to several winners out of the Juddmonte-bred six-furlong Lingfield maiden winner Chervil (by Dansili), a mare who can be described as being a three-parts sister to the Grade 1 Yellow Ribbon Stakes winner Light Jig (by Danehill). That ten-furlong ace is also notable as being the dam of the Grade 1 Hollywood Derby winner Seek Again (by Speightstown), mile Group 3 scorer Treble Jig (by Gone West) and ten-furlong listed winner Scottish Jig (by Speightstown).

There are plenty more talented horses to be found if you go back further, but at this stage in her career there is no need. There is more than sufficient evidence in the first few generations of her pedigree to illustrate why she was quite the bargain, especially now that she's got that Group 2 win to her name. You can guarantee she would attract a lot of attention now if she were to be offered for sale as a broodmare prospect. It remains to be seen whether or not she can make the sufficient improvement to be up to solid Group 1 company as a three-year-old, but it would not be a surprise to see her run well in a classic race or enhance her record with plentiful appearances in the better fillies' races at seven furlongs and a mile. She holds entries in both the Group 1 Tattersalls Irish 1,000 Guineas and Group 1 Emirates Poule d'Essai des Pouliches (French 1000 Guineas) as well as an eye-catching one in the ten-and-a-half-furlong Group 1 Prix de Diane Longines.

SUMMARY DETAILS
Bred: Manister House Stud
Owned: Nick Bradley Racing 43 & Partner

Trained: Richard Fahey
Country: England
Race record: 22114-
Career highlights: 2 wins inc Shadwell Prix du Calvados (Gr2), Irish Stallion Farms EBF Star Stakes (L), 2nd Duchess of Cambridge Stakes - sponsored by bet365 (Gr2)

FEV ROVER (IRE) – 2018 bay filly

		Acclamation (GB)
Gutaifan (IRE)	Dark Angel (IRE)	Midnight Angel (GB)
	Alikhlas (GB)	Lahib (USA)
		Mathaayl (USA)
Laurelita (IRE)	High Chaparral (IRE)	Sadler's Wells (USA)
		Kasora (IRE)
	Chervil (GB)	Dansili (GB)
		Nashmeel (USA)

FLYING VISIT (IRE)

Flying Visit rounded off an outstanding treble for his breeder and trainer, one achieved in under an hour on the afternoon of Saturday, October 24th, 2020. Jim Bolger bred Gear Up (by Teofilo), who won the Group 1 Criterium de Saint-Cloud for the Mark Johnston stable just minutes before Mac Swiney (by New Approach), a colt he both bred and trains, landed the Group 1 Vertem Futurity Trophy Stakes at Doncaster. Then Flying Visit, who was making his tenth start of the year, was a narrow winner of the Group 3 Eyrefield Stakes over nine furlongs at Leopardstown, beating Wuqood by a head. Like Mac Swiney, that bay carries the well-known white and purple colours of Bolger's wife, Jackie. What's more, Bolger also bred this gelding's dam, Fionnuar (by Teofilo), he bred and trained Teofilo (by Galileo) and he trained New Approach (by Galileo).

This was Flying Visit's second win—the other was a six-length maiden success over a mile on heavy ground at Listowel a month before—and he ran once more before the year ended, finishing down the field in the prestigious Tally-Ho Stud Irish EBF Birdcatcher Premier Nursery Handicap over six furlongs at Naas, also on heavy ground. That race was won by the Ken Condon-trained filly Colfer Kay, another first-crop representative of Flying Visit's sire, Pride of Dubai (by Street Cry).

That Coolmore stallion stood two shuttle seasons in Ireland, and has been notching up stakes winners, albeit ones that are not yet of high profile. The dual juvenile Group 1 star comes from the family of leading sires Invincible Spirit (by Green Desert) and Kodiac (by Danehill), the Australian half of his global first crop has yielded a listed winner and a Group 3 winner at the time of writing, whereas the European half has already thrown up five blacktype scorers. Star of Emaraaty won the Group 3 Sweet Solera Stakes at Newmarket, Fancy Man won the Listed Ascendant Stakes at Haydock, Zaffy's Pride took the Listed Star Appeal Stakes at Dundalk, and Telepatic Glances (sic) won the Group 2 Premio Dormello by two and three-quarter lengths on heavy ground at San Siro in late October, adding to her prior listed success.

Fionnuar, the dam of Flying Visit, won four of her nine starts from seven to twelve furlongs. She was placed at the latter distance and got her most valuable win in the Ulster Oaks Fillies Handicap over a few yards short of ten and a half furlongs at Down Royal, the middle leg of a hat-trick for her that month. Her 2019 colt has been named I Have A Voice (by Vocalised). She has a string of winning siblings and is out of Six Nations (by Danzig), a full sister to the US champion and prolific Grade 1 star Chief's Crown. Chief Bearhart, Chief Honcho, Erhaab and Grand Lodge are just four of the top-level standouts he sired at stud.

Flying Visit has an official handicap mark of 103. His pattern success could make things difficult for him in blacktype company, if he goes that route at three, but he clearly has ability and there may be some good prizes to be won with him in handicap company. He was gelded after his final start.

SUMMARY DETAILS
Bred: J S Bolger
Owned: Mrs J S Bolger
Trained: Jim Bolger
Country: Ireland
Race record: 03330122210-
Career highlights: 2 wins inc Eyrefield Stakes (Gr3)

FLYING VISIT (IRE) – 2018 bay gelding

Pride of Dubai (AUS)	Street Cry (IRE)	Machiavellian (USA)
		Helen Street
	Al Anood (AUS)	Danehill (USA)
		Eljazzi
Fionnuar (IRE)	Teofilo (IRE)	Galileo (IRE)
		Speirbhean (IRE)
	Six Nations (USA)	Danzig (USA)
		Six Crowns (USA)

FOXTROT LADY (GB)

Jeff Smith's homebred Foxtrot Lady was already a valuable broodmare prospect before last season but enhanced her profile with a one-and-a-quarter-length defeat of Althiqa in the Group 3 bet365 Sceptre Fillies' Stakes over seven furlongs on good ground at Doncaster in early September. Her half-sister Dancing Star (by Aqlaam) had won that same race two years before, a sole blacktype success in a six-win career that also featured the Stewards' Cup at Goodwood and a valuable six-furlong handicap on the July Course at Newmarket. Foxtrot Lady finished only sixth when she took her chance in a Stewards' Cup—the edition won by Gifted Master—but did match her sister's feat in that £62,000-to-the-winner Newmarket handicap. Dancing Star was bred to Night of Thunder (by Dubawi) in 2020; it will be fascinating to see how the broodmare career of both sisters will compare in time.

They are two of the early foals out of Strictly Dancing (by Danehill Dancer), a six-furlong Newbury winner who was placed twice over seven furlongs and retired with a BHA rating of ninety. The mare, whose overall strike rate stands at five winners from her first five foals, is a daughter of Lochangel (by Night Shift), the Group 1 Nunthorpe Stakes-winning half-sister to the brilliant sprinter Lochsong (by Song). It's hardly a surprise, therefore, that she has come up with two talented daughters. Her 2018 foal is an unraced colt named Dance At Night (by Dark Angel), that one's full sister, Silver Dawn, arrived in early May 2019 and the mare was among the large first book covered by Blue Point (by Shamardal) in 2020. Lochangel's five winners include the stakes-placed Verne Castle (by Sakhee's Secret) and she is the grandam of Norse King (by Norse Dancer), a Group 2 Prix du Conseil de Paris scorer who finished third in the Group 1 Prix Ganay. Lochsong, on the other hand, produced the listed scorer Loch Verdi (by Green Desert) and the Group 2-placed stakes winner Lochridge (by Indian Ridge), both sprinters.

Foxtrot Lady, an Andrew Balding-trained chestnut who was rated 105 after her pattern success, is by the talented Australian sprinter Foxwedge (by Fastnet Rock), which makes her inbred 3x3 to Danehill (by Danzig). He reverse-shuttled to Whitsbury Manor

Stud for four seasons, but Woodside Park Stud in Victoria, Australia, is his current home. His best representatives tend to be sprinters and milers, although his quartet of Group 1 scorers includes Urban Fox, surprise winner of the Pretty Polly Stakes over ten furlongs at the Curragh in 2018.

Like her half-sister, Foxtrot Lady promises to be a notable addition to her owner-breeder's broodmare band.

SUMMARY DETAILS
Bred: Littleton Stud
Owned: J C Smith
Trained: Andrew Balding
Country: England
Race record: 03223-221101021-04000300-4033010-
Career highlights: 5 wins inc bet365 Sceptre Fillies' Stakes (Gr3), 2nd EBF Stallions Highfield Farm Flying Fillies' Stakes (L), 3rd Sky Bet Pomfret Stakes (L), Bombardier British Hopped Amber Beer Midsummer Stakes (L), totepool Two-Year-Old Trophy (L)

FOXTROT LADY (GB) – 2015 chestnut mare

Foxwedge (AUS)	Fastnet Rock (AUS)	**Danehill (USA)**
		Piccadilly Circus (AUS)
	Forest Native (USA)	Forest Wildcat (USA)
		Miss Timebank (USA)
Strictly Dancing (IRE)	Danehill Dancer (IRE)	**Danehill (USA)**
		Mira Adonde (USA)
	Lochangel (GB)	Night Shift (USA)
		Peckitts Well

FRANKLY DARLING (GB)

Anthony Oppenheimer's homebred Frankly Darling looked a top-class prospect in her first two starts of the year but, sadly, didn't live up to that potential in three subsequent outings. Runner-up to Cabaletta over a mile at Yarmouth on her only start at two, she ran away with a ten-furlong maiden on the Tapeta at Newcastle on June 1st and followed that with victory in the Group 2 Ribblesdale Stakes at Royal Ascot fifteen days later. She took a keen hold with Frankie Dettori, moved into the lead at the two-furlong pole, was well clear of the field passing the furlong marker and a total of one and three-quarter lengths ahead of the staying-on Ennistymon at the line. Passion ran on for third, another two and a half lengths adrift, with Bharani Star an additional three-quarters of a length behind in fourth. In a topsy-turvy start to the season, she had just run what looked like a perfect trial for the Group 1 Investec Oaks. How odd to be able to describe the Ribblesdale Stakes in that way.

Unfortunately, she didn't handle the track at Epsom as well as hoped, and although Queen Daenerys and Passion were five lengths and a head behind her, she had to settle for third. Ennistymon, whose form petered out after this, made a bid for glory just before the two-furlong pole, but her turn in front was fleeting as Love swept past and ran away from the field for an impressive nine-length victory. Love was also a wide-margin winner of the Group 1 Darley Yorkshire Oaks in August, where Frankly Darling was struggling with over three furlongs to run and beat only one eased-down rival in a six-runner field. She was also beaten by about the same point of the race when finishing down the field behind Wonderful Tonight in the Group 1 Qipco British Champions Fillies & Mares Stakes at Ascot two months later.

As might be guessed from her name, the John Gosden-trained filly is among sixty stakes winners by Banstead Manor Stud's Timeform 147-rated superstar Frankel (by Galileo). That tally includes twelve who have won at the highest level, headed by the brilliant Cracksman. That Timeform 136-rated dual Group 1 Champion Stakes star stands at Dalham Hall Stud and his first foals arrived in 2020, including a chestnut half-brother to Frankly

Darling. The tally also includes the classic winners Anapurna, Logician, and Soul Stirring, as well as the Group 1-winning miler Without Parole who has returned from a stint racing in North America to take up stallion duties at Newsells Park Stud.

Frankly Darling is a half-sister to the Listed Galtres Stakes winner Our Obsession (by Shamardal) and so is very closely related to that mare's daughter Frankellina (by Frankel), who was runner-up in the Group 3 Tattersalls Musidora Stakes in 2019 and bred to Sea The Stars (by Cape Cross) in 2020. Hidden Hope (by Daylami), their dam, is out of the stakes winner Nuryana (by Nureyev) and that makes her a half-sister to several horses of note. Mystic Knight (by Caerleon) won the Group 3 Derby Trial Stakes at Lingfield, Rebecca Sharp (by Machiavellian) won the Group 1 Coronation Stakes and was runner-up in the Group 1 Queen Elizabeth II Stakes, and both she and her half-sister Fleche d'Or (by Dubai Destination) went on to success at stud. Rebecca Sharp's stakes-winning daughter Miss Pinkerton became the dam of the Group 2-placed middle-distance Group 3 scorer Precious Ramotswe, whereas Fleche d'Or is, of course, the dam of the Timeform 134-rated Derby and Arc hero Golden Horn (by Cape Cross). He also won the Group 1 Coral-Eclipse Stakes and the Group 1 Irish Champion Stakes, he stands at Dalham Hall Stud, his eldest are four-year-olds and he has been represented by three stakes winners plus nine others who have earned blacktype. The latter include the Group 1-placed Godolphin homebred Botanik, the André Fabre-trained colt who was a neck runner-up to Gear Up in the Criterium de Saint-Cloud in late October.

There are plenty of other stakes and pattern winners to be found within the first few generations of the pedigree, including 2020's Group 1-placed Group 2 Princess of Wales's Stakes heroine Dame Malliot (by Champs Elysees) and 2019's Group 1 Melbourne Cup scorer Vow And Declare (by Declaration of War), although their connection to Frankly Darling is remote. It would have been interesting to see her back in action as a four-year-old but she is no longer in training. She has the potential to become a significant broodmare.

SUMMARY DETAILS

Bred: Hascombe & Valiant Stud Ltd
Owned: A E Oppenheimer
Trained: John Gosden
Country: England
Race record: 2-11300-
Career highlights: 2 wins inc Ribblesdale Stakes (Gr2), 3rd Investec Oaks (Gr1)

FRANKLY DARLING (GB) – 2017 bay filly

Frankel (GB)	Galileo (IRE)	Sadler's Wells (USA)	
		Urban Sea (USA)	
	Kind (IRE)	Danehill (USA)	
		Rainbow Lake (GB)	
Hidden Hope (GB)	Daylami (IRE)	Doyoun	
		Daltawa (IRE)	
	Nuryana (GB)	Nureyev (USA)	
		Loralane	

GLORIOUS JOURNEY (GB)

Glorious Journey made headlines when sold for 2,600,000 guineas from Book 1 of the Tattersalls October Yearling Sale in 2017 and although he did go on to become a talented racehorse, it is fair to say that he has not lived up to those initial expectations. He was an unbeaten Group 3 winner at two but gelded after his three-year-old season yielded just one win and one place from six starts, all of those races in pattern-race company. He also won one from six as a four-year-old, that success coming in the Group 2 Hungerford Stakes over seven furlongs on soft ground at Newbury where he beat Librisa Breeze by half a length, after which his handicap mark rose from 108 to 113. In 2020, he won a listed contest on good ground over that same course and distance plus the Group 2 Al Fahidi Fort at Meydan in January, also over seven. His only placing in three starts between those two wins was third in a valuable conditions race in Saudi Arabia at the end of February, and he also made the frame in one final start after the Newbury success, taking third to Happy Power in the Group 2 Godolphin Stud & Stable Staff Awards Challenge Stakes on soft at Newmarket. He finished the year on a handicap mark of 111.

The Charlie Appleby-trained son of Dubawi (by Dubai Millennium) was bred by Normandie Stud and he is out of the Group 1 Coronation Stakes winner Fallen For You (by Dansili). One could have seen a horse with such parents prove best a mile and perhaps even stay ten furlongs, especially when the dam is out of a half-sister to the Group 1 Lockinge Stakes scorer Fly To The Stars (by Bluebird), but instead he appears to be a seven-furlong specialist. That adds an extra point of interest to his Roger Charlton-trained half-sister Love Is You (by Kingman). Now aged three, she won a mile maiden at Ascot in early September by only a neck but then dropped to seven furlongs at Newbury and, on heavy ground, landed a listed contest by three and a half lengths. Will she stay the mile in good company in 2021 or, like her sibling, prove best over the shorter trip?

Glorious Journey has ability and although well-exposed at this stage of his life, could be capable of picking up some more good prizes in 2021; he finished third in the Group 2 Al Fahidi Fort over seven furlongs at Meydan shortly before this book went to print, beaten by a total of one and a half lengths by the Saeed bin Suroor-trained winner, Land of Legends. His wins have all come on good through to soft ground—he has never run on heavy— and in 2019, he failed by just a neck to beat Limato in the Group 3 Criterion Stakes on good-to-firm at Newmarket.

SUMMARY DETAILS

Bred: Normandie Stud Ltd
Owned: HH Sheikha Al Jalila Racing
Trained: Charlie Appleby
Country: England
Race record: 11-430410-022010-130013-3
Career highlights: 6 wins inc Al Fahidi Fort sponsored by DP World UAE Region (Gr2), Unibet Hungerford Stakes (Gr2), Prix Daphnis Royal Palm Beachcomber Luxury (Gr3), Prix La Rochette (Gr3), Dubai Duty Free Cup Stakes (L), 2nd Randox Health Criterion Stakes (Gr3), Weatherbys Hamilton (Leisure) Stakes (L), 3rd Godolphin Stud & Stable Staff Awards Challenge Stakes (Gr2), Al Fahidi Fort (Gr2), Prix de Guiche (Gr3)

GLORIOUS JOURNEY (GB) – 2015 bay gelding

Dubawi (IRE)	Dubai Millennium (GB)	Seeking The Gold (USA)
		Colorado Dancer
	Zomaradah (GB)	Deploy
		Jawaher (IRE)
Fallen For You (GB)	Dansili (GB)	Danehill (USA)
		Hasili (IRE)
	Fallen Star (GB)	Brief Truce (USA)
		Rise And Fall

HAPPY POWER (IRE)

Yeomanstown Stud in Ireland not only bred and consigned Happy Power but they also stand his sire, Dark Angel (by Acclamation). The colt, a 625,000-guinea Tattersalls October Book 1 graduate, is not yet among the stallion's septet of top-level winners, but he has been successful in Group 2 company, missed out on a Group 1 placing when fourth to Too Darn Hot in 2019's edition of the Qatar Sussex Stakes at Goodwood, and holds an official rating of 115. His seven wins have come on everything from good-to-firm through to soft ground, his only run on heavy resulted in a sixth-place finish to King of Change in the Group 1 Queen Elizabeth II Stakes, also in 2019, and both of his pattern wins were achieved last season.

A Group 2-placed stakes winner going into his latest campaign, he finished third to Space Blues in a listed contest at Haydock in early June, chased home Limato in the Group 3 Betway Criterion Stakes at Newmarket and finished fourth to D'bai in a conditions race back at Haydock before getting off the mark for the year with a two-and-a-half-length defeat of the talented Anna Nerium in a conditions race on fast ground at Salisbury in early August. He followed that with victory in the Group 3 Ladbrokes Supreme Stakes on good-to-soft Goodwood, where he beat Toro Strike, Escobar and old rival D'bai by margins of a neck, a length and a length, and then completed his hat-trick by adding the Group 2 Godolphin Stud & Stable Staff Awards Challenge Stakes on soft ground on the Rowley Mile course at Newmarket in October. Pogo had tried to make all but had no more to give when Happy Power went by, the grey beating the chestnut by a length and a half. Glorious Journey was a further two and a quarter lengths back in third.

His final outing of the year, when unplaced in the Group 1 Qipco British Champions Sprint Stakes on soft ground at Ascot eight days later, was the only time during the year that he did not run over seven furlongs. He had tried a mile four times as a three-year-old, and in addition to his aforementioned good run in the Sussex Stakes, those runs yielded a listed success at York and a good third in the Group 2 Ladbrokes Celebration Mile at

Goodwood, beaten by just three-quarters of a length and a head by Duke of Hazzard and Turgenev and with the classic-placed Skardu three-quarters of a length behind in fourth.

The Andrew Balding-trained colt is the second foal out of an unraced mare called Tamarisk (by Selkirk) and he has a winning full brother called Melody of Life, now a three-year-old. That 425,000-guinea Book 1 graduate is also trained by Balding for King Power Racing Co Ltd, he was placed on both of his starts as a two-year-old and first time out at three and then got off the mark with victory over seven furlongs at Kempton on January 13th. All four of the colt's races to date have been on artificial tracks. The mare had another Dark Angel colt on February 14th, 2020, and was then bred back to the stallion, whereas their unraced three-parts sister Cold Comfort (by Gutaifan) was bred to Bungle Inthejungle (by Exceed And Excel) last year.

Happy Power's grandam is the Group 1 Cheveley Park Stakes runner-up Tanami (by Green Desert), his third dam is the Group 3 Queen Mary Stakes second Propensity (by Habitat), and so he comes from a family that has a long-standing record of producing talented horses. Cairns (by Cadeaux Genereux), who won the Group 2 Rockfel Stakes over seven furlongs as a two-year-old, is the best of his dam's siblings although another of them, Tanami Desert (by Lycius), is both the dam of the dual classic-placed Group 2 Prix Daniel Wildenstein winner Tamzirte (by Danehill Dancer) and grandam of Chachnak (by Kingman). That colt won both the Group 3 Prix de Guiche and Group 3 Prix du Prince d'Orange in France in 2020.

Wannabe (by Shirley Heights), a dual winner, is the most notable of Tanami's siblings and that's because of her record at stud. Her four stakes winners feature the Group 1 Cheveley Park Stakes heroine and Group 1 1000 Guineas runner-up Wannabe Grand (by Danehill) plus the pattern placed stakes winner Wannabe Better (by Duke of Marmalade). The latter is also notable as being the dam of 2020's Group 3 Darley Stakes winner and dual Irish listed scorer Lady Wannabe (by Camelot), who is reviewed elsewhere in this volume. The only inbreeding in Happy Power's pedigree is a single 5x5 cross of Northern Dancer (by Nearctic).

The early stallion sons of Dark Angel have not yet lived up to hopes and expectations, despite getting some blacktype results—for example, Group 1-winning sprinter Golden Horde is Lethal Force's sole stakes winner at the time of writing—but it is too early yet to judge how he will be viewed in that regard in the long-term. He has more sons in earlier stages of their stud careers and will have more going to stud in the coming years, so it is possible that one or more of them make an impact. Two years ago, one might have predicted a busy future stallion role for Happy Power, such was the popularity of his sire's sons, and while a berth at stud is certainly possible for this talented grey, he may need to achieve some more high-profile track success first.

SUMMARY DETAILS

Bred: Yeomanstown Stud
Owned: King Power Racing Co Ltd
Trained: Andrew Balding
Country: England
Race record: 4131-13104300-3241110-
Career highlights: 7 wins inc Godolphin Stud & Stable Staff Awards Challenge Stakes (Gr2), Ladbrokes Supreme Stakes (Gr3), equinITy Technology Ganton Stakes (L), 2nd Betway Criterion Stakes (Gr3), 3rd Ladbrokes Celebration Mile Stakes (Gr2), Betway Spring Trophy Stakes (L-twice)

HAPPY POWER (IRE) – 2016 grey colt

Dark Angel (IRE)	Acclamation (GB)	Royal Applause (GB)
		Princess Athena
	Midnight Angel (GB)	Machiavellian (USA)
		Night At Sea
Tamarisk (GER)	Selkirk (USA)	Sharpen Up
		Annie Edge
	Tanami (GB)	Green Desert (USA)
		Propensity

HAPPY ROMANCE (IRE)

The races restricted to graduates of particular sales can offer a lucrative pot for the less flashy members of a year's auction ring crop and, every now and then, those competitive events can reveal a stakes- or pattern-class horse. Happy Romance is a fine example. She is a £25,000 graduate of the Goffs UK Premier Yearling Sale in Doncaster, won two of those big pots, progressed successfully to pattern company and ended the year rated 106, placing her among the leading juvenile fillies of the year, just seven pounds below the trio that shared the championship title.

The Richard Hannon-trained bay was unplaced on her debut at Newmarket but showed the benefit of that first racecourse experience by trouncing two rivals at Sandown nine days later. She was beaten by just under five lengths when fifth to Campanelle in the Group 2 Queen Mary Stakes a week after that and then beat twenty-four rivals easily in the £84,965-to-the-winner Weatherbys Super Sprint Stakes at Newbury in mid-July. York a month later was the only time she encountered ground with any degree of soft in the description—it was good-to-soft—but once again she hit the front over a furlong from home and kept on well to the line. It was the Goffs UK Premier Yearling Stakes, her first attempt at six furlongs, and she beat the staying-on Devious Company by a length and a quarter.

She earned £88,524 for that win and yet her most important success with regard to her long-term future earned a prize of just £17,863. It was the Group 3 Shadwell Dick Poole Fillies' Stakes over six furlongs on good ground at Salisbury and, as in her previous two wins, she was in front over a furlong out and stayed there. This time her margin of victory was three-quarters of a length and Alcohol Free was the one who chased her home. That rival had been a Newbury winner on her only previous start, so lacked the experience of Happy Romance, and she reversed the placings when they met again on the Rowley Mile course at Newmarket three and a half weeks later. It was the Group 1 Juddmonte Cheveley Park Stakes, which the Andrew Balding-trained bay won by half a length and a head from Miss Amulet and Umm Kulthum, with the Hannon filly weakening in the final half furlong to finish another length and a quarter behind in fourth.

That latter filly, who had won the Group 3 Albany Stakes and Group 2 Duchess of Cambridge Stakes from three prior starts, is, like Happy Romance, a daughter of the Ballyhane Stud stallion Dandy Man (by Mozart). He has always seemed to have a higher reputation than his actual track results merit although, to be fair, he has sired a top-level winner in Canada, one in Hong Kong and one in California, and his two-year-olds did well in 2020. His career total of seventeen stakes winners also includes the pattern-winning sprinter and Group 1 Nunthorpe Stakes third Extortionist plus the sadly ill-fated classic-placed Group 3 scorer Lady Kaya. His blacktype horses are backed up by a long list of multiple winners, some of them prolific and several of them six-figure earners, with a long list of horses who have achieved a handicap mark of at least ninety. In short, he is a successful stallion who gives his supporters a good shot at producing a horse who can cover its costs and give its connections some fun and memorable days at the track, with a chance of blacktype too.

Happy Romance was bred by Redpender Stud, she is a half-sister to the lowly rated four-time sprint winner Red Tycoon (by Acclamation) and out of Rugged Up (by Marju), an unraced half-sister to two stakes winners but related to several others. Warsaw (by Danehill Dancer) and Meiner Eternal (by Tamayuz) got their blacktype wins at the age of two, one in Ireland and the other in Japan. Their dam, For Evva Silca (by Piccolo), was placed at that age but has some notable individuals among her nine winning siblings. Silca's Sister (by Inchinor) won the Group 1 Prix Morny, Green Manalishi's (by Green Desert) fourteen wins included a trio of listed sprints at Chester, whereas the stakes-placed pair Silca Legend (by Efisio) and Muso Corto (by Reprimand) won ten races between them.

Silca Chiave (by Pivotal) was placed in both the Group 1 Moyglare Stud Stakes and Group 1 Cheveley Park Stakes and became a blacktype producer, but Golden Silca was the most notable of all of the siblings. That daughter of Inchinor (by Ahonoora) was the top-rated two-year-old filly in Germany in 1998 and older female in Ireland two years later, and her eight wins featured the Group 2 Mill Reef Stakes, Group 3 Desmond Stakes, a Group 2 contest in Germany plus listed races at Newbury, Epsom and Newmarket. She was runner-up in the Group 1 Irish 1,000 Guineas, Group 1 Coronation Stakes and Group 2 Falmouth Stakes, third in the Group 1 Prix Morny, and became the dam of Calipatria (by Shamardal), an eleven-furlong Group 3 scorer in Germany. They are all out of Silca-Cisa (by Hallgate), who was runner-up in the Listed Cammidge Trophy and is the third dam of Happy Romance.

The filly holds entries in the Group 1 Tattersalls Irish 1,000 Guineas and Group 1 Emirates Poule d'Essai des Pouliches (French 1000 Guineas), so at least some consideration has been given to her prospect of staying a mile. Being out of a daughter of Marju (by Last Tycoon) may help her to get the trip, and her half-brother Feel This Moment (by Tamayuz) has won over the trip in Sweden, but it's also possible sprinting will be her game. With over £207,000 already accumulated from four wins out of seven starts, she has already repaid her purchase price multiple times over, plus she has a pattern victory to her name, so one could take the view that whatever she achieves at three and beyond is a bonus.

SUMMARY DETAILS
Bred: Redpender Stud Ltd
Owned: The McMurray Family
Trained: Richard Hannon
Country: England
Race record: 0101114-
Career highlights: 4 wins inc Shadwell Dick Poole Fillies' Stakes (Gr3)

HAPPY ROMANCE (IRE) – 2018 bay filly

		Danehill (USA)
	Mozart (IRE)	Danehill (USA)
Dandy Man (IRE)		Victoria Cross (USA)
	Lady Alexander (IRE)	Night Shift (USA)
		Sandhurst Goddess
	Marju (IRE)	Last Tycoon
Rugged Up (IRE)		Flame of Tara
	For Evva Silca (GB)	Piccolo (GB)
		Silca-Cisa (GB)

HELVIC DREAM (IRE)

Power was a leading two-year-old who won the Group 1 National Stakes and Group 2 Coventry Stakes and was runner-up in both the Group 1 Dewhurst Stakes and Group 1 Phoenix Stakes. He went on to take the Group 1 Irish 2,000 Guineas the following season, but despite being a son of Oasis Dream (by Green Desert) and out of a winning half-sister to Footstepsinthesand (by Giant's Causeway), he has not yet been as successful at stud as one might have hoped. He spent time on the Coolmore roster, Oaklands Stud in Queensland, Australia is home these days, and Helvic Dream is one of only fourteen stakes winners on his roll of honour. He has not yet got a winner at the highest level although two of his three Group 2 scorers, La Force and 2020 juvenile Laws of Indices, have been placed in that grade.

Helvic Dream is trained by Noel Meade, he beat the subsequent massive improver Champers Elysees by four and three-quarter lengths in an extended seven-furlong contest on heavy ground at Roscommon on his final start at two, then worked his way up through the rankings at three, finishing the year rated 110. He had come so close to a first blacktype success at Killarney in August when, having been in front from a quarter of a mile out, he was one of three horses that flashed past the post together in the Listed M D O'Shea & Sons Vincent O'Brien Ruby Stakes over a mile on heavy ground. The noses of So Wonderful and Up Helly Aa were just in front of his. Quizical, who had made the rest of the running, was a length and a quarter back in fourth.

He was third in a ten-furlong premier handicap at the Curragh on Irish Champions Weekend next time but then put up the performance that earned his high rating, trouncing old rival Up Helly Aa by seven and a half lengths to take the Group 3 Novi IT Services International Stakes over that same course and distance. The ground was soft, Raise You was another four and a half lengths behind in third and there was a further seven and a half lengths back to the fourth, Sonnyboyliston, the gelding who had won that premier handicap the time before. An unplaced finish behind Amma Grace in a listed contest at Leopardstown two weeks later did not lead to any alteration to his rating.

Helvic Dream will be an interesting contender for Ireland's better ten-furlong races in 2021 and it is possible he could rise a bit further in the rankings, especially if getting ground that's on the soft side of good. He is yet another fine example of the tremendous bargains that can be found in the auction ring, a €12,000 graduate of Part 2 of the Tattersalls Ireland September Yearling Sale. He was bred by the partnership of Tony O'Dwyer and Keith O'Brien, his younger half-sister Flirting Bridge (by Camelot) won a one-mile maiden at Dundalk in late November for the Henry de Bromhead stable, and they are the first two foals of an unraced mare called Rachevie (by Danehill Dancer). She was bred to Camelot (by Montjeu) in 2019 and to both Calyx (by Kingman) and Caravaggio (by Scat Daddy) in 2020. Challow Hills (by Woodman), the grandam of Helvic Dream, is out of a Nijinsky (by Northern Dancer) half-sister to the Timeform 126-rated and Group 1 St Leger-placed Group 1 Oaks, Group 1 Irish Oaks and Group 1 Yorkshire Oaks heroine Diminuendo (by Diesis), dam of the Group 1-placed mile pattern scorer Calando (by Storm Cat).

SUMMARY DETAILS
Bred: Tony O'Dwyer & Keith O'Brien
Owned: Mrs Caroline Hendron & Mrs M Cahill
Trained: Noel Meade
Country: Ireland
Race record: 3311-2303310-
Career highlights: 3 wins inc Novi IT Services International Stakes (Gr3), 3rd M D O'Shea & Sons Vincent O'Brien Ruby Stakes (L), Lenebane Stakes (L)

HELVIC DREAM (IRE) – 2017 bay gelding

Power (GB)	Oasis Dream (GB)	Green Desert (USA)
		Hope (IRE)
	Frappe (IRE)	Inchinor (GB)
		Glatisant (GB)
Rachevie (IRE)	Danehill Dancer (IRE)	Danehill (USA)
		Mira Adonde (USA)
	Challow Hills (USA)	Woodman (USA)
		Cascassi (USA)

HIGH DEFINITION (IRE)

Is this the Derby winner of 2021? There are many who think so. Right now, he is merely a twice-raced winner of two races at the Curragh, both over a mile, both by three-quarters of a length, and both when there was ease in the ground. However, the second of those was the Group 2 Alan Smurfit Memorial Beresford Stakes and a mere statement of the margin of victory says nothing about the remarkable performance.

If you had paused the race around three furlongs from home you would have thought him likely to finish well-beaten because he was being pushed along and seemingly going nowhere. But then he started to move forwards, coming down the centre of the track as Snapraeterea led along the far rail. He still had more of the field ahead of him than behind a furlong and a half out as the Kevin Prendergast-trained Monaasib moved up to challenge the long-time leader, seemingly set for victory. That pair were clear of the rest entering the final furlong, but High Definition was rapidly passing horses, just about third as he hit the furlong pole. Monaasib got the better of his rival and pulled away from him but the Ballydoyle colt's strong run was still in progress and carried him to the front in the dying strides. Snapraeterea was three lengths back in third, half a length in front of the winner's stablemate, Sir Lucan.

This was not the stunning turn of foot that some proclaimed in the heat of the moment but, instead, a strong staying-on finish, from an inexperienced horse, that was sustained over the course of over a furlong. It was an effort that suggested we may have seen a potential middle-distance Group 1 star of the future, although he will surely need to get involved in a race a bit sooner than he did there if he is going to hold his own or excel at the highest level. It is also worth considering what he beat.

Two of his closest pursuers ran again before the end of the year, but Monaasib didn't. That colt had won twice at around six furlongs and been short-headed in the valuable Irish EBF Ballyhane Stakes (an auction race) over six on soft ground at Naas on his previous start, carrying a rating of just ninety-nine into the Curragh race. He is a first-crop son of Bobby's Kitten (by Kitten's

Joy), the horse who beat No Nay Never in the Grade 1 Breeders' Cup Turf Sprint over six and a half furlongs at Santa Anita but was also a Grade 1-placed pattern winner at a mile. He later joined the Dermot Weld team and his sole run in Ireland was a runaway listed sprint success on heavy ground at Cork. Bobby's Kitten is a Lanwades Stud stallion, comes from the prolific Grade 1-producing family of the standouts such as Paradise Creek (by Irish River) and Theatrical (by Nureyev) and can be expected to get sprinters, milers and some who stay middle-distances. Monaasib's family contains everything from sprinters to stayers and so his entry in the Group 1 Tattersalls Irish 2,000 Guineas makes sense. Snapraeterea had been fourth to Mac Swiney in the Group 2 Futurity Stakes, was rated 102 before the race, 103 after it, and then finished fourth in the valuable Foran Equine Irish EBF Auction Race Final over seven furlongs on soft ground at Naas on his final start. Sir Lucan, on the other hand, had been last of five over a mile at Killarney on his only previous start but beat the well-exposed subsequent Group 3 scorer Flying Visit by a neck over a mile at Cork on his only run afterwards. He is a full brother to Sir Dragonet and holds multiple classic entries.

High Definition is certainly bred to achieve anything and, should he fulfil the hopes that many have for him, he would not be the first member of his family to win a classic.

His full brother Innisfree won 2019's edition of the Group 2 Beresford Stakes, beating Shekhem by a neck, the same colt he'd beaten by a neck in his maiden at Galway two months before. Then he chased home Kameko in the Group 1 Vertem Futurity Trophy Stakes at Newcastle. Neither he nor his twice-beaten rival ran again. Their dam, Palace (by Fastnet Rock), won the Listed Cairn Rouge Stakes over eight and a half furlongs at Killarney and was blacktype-placed over ten at Naas. She is also notable as being a half-sister to two classic-placed blacktype winners and to a filly who went to produce another such horse. The first pair are the Group 1 Irish Oaks third Lady Lupus (by High Chaparral) and ill-fated Group 1 Poule d'Essai des Poulains (French 2000 Guineas) third Furner's Green (by Dylan Thomas), and it is their stakes-winning half-sister Mystical Lady (by Halling) who gave us the

Group 1 Irish Derby runner-up Kingfisher (by Galileo). That dual stakes winner was also placed in the Group 1 Gold Cup at Ascot.

Lady Icarus (by Rainbow Quest), the grandam of High Definition, was unraced. Two of her siblings were pattern-winning milers, namely the full brothers Hazaam (by Blushing Groom) and Sharman, and another one was the stakes-winning sprinter Mudallel (by Machiavellian). However, it is on this part of the page that you find the three classic stars. Sonic Lady (by Nureyev) was the best of them and she was the dam of Lady Icarus and those talented siblings.

Timeform 129-rated Sonic Lady won the Group 1 Irish 1,000 Guineas, Group 1 Sussex Stakes and Group 1 Prix du Moulin de Longchamp, and was placed in the Group 1 1000 Guineas, Group 1 Queen Elizabeth II Stakes and Grade 1 Breeders' Cup Mile. She is also the third dam of both Japanese champion Logi Universe (by Neo Universe) and Deirdre (by Harbinger). The former won the Tokyo Yushun (Japanese Derby) in 2009, a time when many of Japan's top races were not yet listed in Part I of the International Cataloguing Standards and, hence, counted as listed status only. Deirdre, of course, is the popular Japanese mare who won the Group 1 Nassau Stakes at Goodwood in 2019 and her wins also include the Group 1 Shuka Sho at Kyoto, that ten-furlong contest being the third leg of the Japanese Fillies' Triple Crown. Sonic Lady is also the third dam of High Definition.

The colt, who was bred by Aidan and Anne-Marie O'Brien's Whisperview Trading Ltd, is unquestionably a colt of potential, one who is bred to achieve anything on the track. It will be fascinating to find out just how good he is. If he lives up to his promise then he will be among the leading middle-distance three-year-olds this coming season, likely staying twelve furlongs.

There is a chance that the Derby could come a bit soon for him, given that he was born on May 18th. He shares a birthday with Magical, and her form only really began to take off in the autumn of her three-year-old season. That said, she had been campaigned as a miler up to that point and her leap forward coincided with a step up to middle distances, so it could have been the latter or a combination of both maturity and running over a longer trip that was the key. Of course, the sadly ill-fated 2019

Derby winner, Anthony Van Dyck, was a May 19th foal, so we do not have to look far to find a case where the feat of winning an Epsom classic been achieved by a horse so close to its physical third birthday. Also, in 2019, Hermosa won the Group 1 Qipco 1000 Guineas the day before her physical third birthday. High Definition has also been entered in the Group 1 Prix du Jockey Club (French Derby) and Group 1 Grand Prix de Paris.

SUMMARY DETAILS

Bred: Whisperview Trading Ltd
Owned: Derrick Smith, Mrs John Magnier, Michael Tabor &
Mrs A M O'Brien
Trained: Aidan O'Brien
Country: Ireland
Race record: 11-
Career highlights: 2 wins inc Alan Smurfit Memorial Beresford Stakes (Gr2)

HIGH DEFINITION (IRE) – 2018 bay colt

		Northern Dancer
Galileo (IRE)	Sadler's Wells (USA)	Northern Dancer
		Fairy Bridge (USA)
	Urban Sea (USA)	Miswaki (USA)
		Allegretta
Palace (IRE)	Fastnet Rock (AUS)	Danehill (USA)
		Piccadilly Circus (AUS)
	Lady Icarus (GB)	Rainbow Quest (USA)
		Sonic Lady (USA)

HUKUM (IRE)

Hukum ran twice as a two-year-old, three times in 2020, and achieved an end-of-year handicap mark of 114. Yet another talented horse who got an early winning start on one of the artificial tracks—his maiden success came over a mile on the Polytrack at Kempton—he kicked off his second season with a half-length victory in the King George V Stakes (handicap) over twelve furlongs at Royal Ascot in June and followed that with an eye-catching effort in the Group 3 Irish Thoroughbred Marketing Geoffrey Freer Stakes at Newbury two months later. The ground was good-to-soft for that extended thirteen-furlong contest, he moved between the front-running Max Vega and the always-prominent Alignak to hit the front two out, kept the chestnut company as they pulled clear of the grey, then eased to the front at the furlong pole and soon asserted his authority. He won the race by a comfortable two and a half lengths, while Alignak held off the seven-year-old Morando for third, two and a quarter lengths behind Max Vega.

This good effort made the Group 1 Pertemps St Leger Stakes an obvious target. The ground was good at Doncaster that afternoon in September, and if you paused the race three out as the field fanned out in the centre of the course, positioning themselves for their classic bids, you might have identified him as the likely winner. Subjectivist was in front, Hukum was going well two horses to his left and had only Pyledriver, also going well, to his outside. Soon there were six horses in a row, closely pursued by the Irish Derby winner Santiago, and as the pace picked up two dropped back quickly—Subjectivist and Sunchart—leaving the remaining front-runners split into two groups. Hukum ultimately lost his battle with Pyledriver, the dark bay pulling almost three lengths clear in the final furlong while drifting considerably to his left. However, Galileo Chrome, Berkshire Rocco and Santiago made up the group initially racing closer to the rails. They gradually eased more towards the centre and the first two were separated by only a neck at the line. Pyledriver was a length back in third, denying Santiago another classic placing by a short-head. Hukum was fifth, not pressured in the final half-furlong when his chance was clearly gone but still keeping on to pass the post two and three-quarter lengths adrift of the Ballydoyle colt and almost the same margin clear of that rival's stable companion Dawn Patrol, who was sixth.

It will be interesting to see what sort of path this Owen Burrows-trained colt follows in 2021. A possible Cup campaign looks likely although he is not guaranteed on pedigree to stay two miles and beyond.

He is a son of the Timeform 140-rated standout Sea The Stars (by Cape Cross) whose best, aside from the great stayer Stradivarius and a few milers, tend to be middle-distance horses. His dam is a daughter of the influential triple Group 1-winning mile star Kingmambo (by Mr Prospector) and the two top-level winners who share that sire-broodmare/sire cross are Cloth of Stars and Zelzal—a middle-distance horse and a miler. Others whose broodmare sire represents a branch of the Mr Prospector (by Raise a Native) sire line are the dual Derby hero Harzand (dam by Xaar) and the Group 1 Prix Saint-Alary scorer Vazira (dam by Zafonic). Stradivarius, on the other hand, is out of a daughter of Bering (by Arctic Tern), a more noted source of stamina than Kingmambo.

Of course, it is not quite that simple. A sire/broodmare-sire cross can tell us plenty but says little about the amount of speed or stamina that the best horses in the family have shown, and that is generally the more reliable indicator of a horse's distance prospects. Hukum's half-brother Kasbaan (by Dansili) has won at ten furlongs but, more recently, twice at a mile. Aghareed, their dam, is a lightly raced winner of the Listed Prix de Liancourt over ten furlongs at ParisLongchamp, and that mare's siblings include Thibaan, a ten-furlong Doncaster winner in 2020 who was well-beaten when stepped up in trip. However, that would not be uncommon for a son of War Front (by Danzig). Their dam, Lahudood (by Singspiel), won the Grade 1 Breeders' Cup Filly & Mare Turf over eleven furlongs on soft ground at Monmouth Park and was only beaten by a head by the notable stayer Montare when runner-up in the Group 2 Prix de Royallieu over twelve and a half furlongs the year before. She surely got some of her stamina from her sire, but her Arazi (by Blushing Groom) dam Rahayeb also stayed twelve furlongs and was a granddaughter of the high-class middle-distance runner and influential broodmare Height of Fashion (by Bustino). This is the family of Nashwan (by Blushing Groom), Nayef (by Gulch) and Unfuwain (by Northern Dancer), and more distantly of Wind In Her Hair (by Alzao) and Deep Impact (by Sunday Silence). And, of course, it makes the King George-placed dual classic star Highclere (by Queens Hussar) the sixth dam of Hukum.

Hukum is clearly bred to be a top-class performer at around twelve furlongs. Whether or not he becomes an effective Cup horse may depend on what he's inherited from Kingmambo who, although the sire of St Leger winner Rule of Law and broodmare sire of Melbourne Cup scorer Cross Counter (by Teofilo), is not typically associated with stayers. It may mean nothing, but it is also eye-catching that he is inbred 4x3x5 to Mr Prospector, a noted speed influence. However, the manner in which he won at Newbury and then kept on to the line at Doncaster suggests that two miles will be within his compass. It will be very interesting to see how he turns out.

SUMMARY DETAILS
Bred: Shadwell Estate Company Ltd
Owned: Hamdan Al Maktoum
Trained: Owen Burrows
Country: England
Race record: 31-110-
Career highlights: 3 wins inc Irish Thoroughbred Marketing Geoffrey Freer Stakes (Gr3)

HUKUM (IRE) – 2017 bay colt

		Green Desert (USA)
	Cape Cross (IRE)	Park Appeal
Sea The Stars (IRE)		Miswaki (USA)
	Urban Sea (USA)	Allegretta
		Mr Prospector (USA)
	Kingmambo (USA)	Miesque (USA)
Aghareed (USA)		Singspiel (IRE)
	Lahudood (GB)	Rahayeb (GB)

INDIGO GIRL (GB)

This is a filly who may end up in Volume 1 of next year's annual. Her only defeat in three starts as a juvenile was when a half-length runner-up to Pretty Gorgeous in the Group 1 bet365 Fillies' Mile on soft ground at Newmarket in early October, and with her pedigree and connections there is every reason to hope that classic and/or other top-level success may lie in her future. On pedigree she is a middle-distance prospect, a potential Oaks star, but the recently emerged field of stride analysis paints a different story. Her entry on AtTheRaces.com shows that her cadence (stride frequency) in her first two starts was 2.43 and 2.45 respectively. This is indicative of a horse for whom a mile like likely to be the outer limit of distance range. For comparison, Too Darn Hot boasts similar pedigree credentials to Indigo Girl, in terms of being a Dubawi from a strong middle-distance family that has even yielded stayers, but his cadence of 2.4 in the Group 2 Champagne Stakes at two suggested he would be a miler who might be better suited to seven furlongs. And that is pretty much how he turned out.

Classic-winning miler and Dalham Hall Stud standard-bearer Dubawi (by Dubai Millennium) is one of the great English thoroughbred stallions of all time and on the verge of becoming one of the tiny handful of sires ever to notch up at least 200 individual stakes winners. His fee has been £250,000 every year since 2017, the year that Indigo Girl was conceived, so you know she has some elite relations. They are her full sister and her dam: Journey and Montare.

Six-time winner Journey landed the Group 1 British Champions Filly & Mare Stakes at Ascot, her tally also included the Group 3 Pinnacle Stakes at Haydock plus three listed races and in addition to another edition of that big Ascot feature, she was placed in the Group 1 Prix Vermeille. She is a promising young broodmare who has a now two-year-old son of Invincible Spirit (by Green Desert), a yearling daughter of Siyouni (by Pivotal) and was covered in 2020 by Sea The Stars (by Cape Cross). Montare (by Montjeu), on the other hand, won seven times including the Group 1 Prix Royal-Oak, the Group 2 Prix de

Royallieu and two editions of the Group 2 Prix du Conseil de Paris. She was runner-up in the Group 1 Prix Vermeille, multiple Group 2-placed, and her progeny also include the capable gelding Travelling Man (by Oasis Dream), who has been placed in the Group 2 Grand Prix de Deauville and Group 2 Prix Vicomtesse Vigier. Montare's now two-year-old full sister to Journey and Indigo Girl was born in early May, as was their younger Kingman (by Invincible Spirit) half-brother, and the mare was bred to Too Darn Hot (by Dubawi) in 2020. Montare's dual stakes-winning dam Contare is also the grandam of the Group 2 Dahlia Stakes and Group 3 Prix Minerve scorer Worth Waiting (by Bated Breath), and it catches the eye that Indigo Girl is inbred 4x3 to Contare's influential dual Derby-winning sire Shirley Heights (by Mill Reef).

Indigo Girl has worn a hood in all three of her starts, easily winning a mile maiden on soft ground at Yarmouth on her debut at the end of August and then beating Dubai Fountain by three-quarters of a length in the Group 2 bet365 May Hill Stakes on good ground at Doncaster, also over a mile. The automatic assumption most would make about a horse with this pedigree and juvenile form is that she will stay at least ten furlongs and likely the Oaks or even St Leger trip. Just a few years ago I would have said the same: 'here is a potential middle-distance star in the making; just look at what her relations have achieved'. And yet, if she is going to be typical of a horse with her cadence, she will not last those distances; the mile is likely to be as far as she wants to go. This arguably adds to her intrigue as a member of the latest classic generation. She is bred to stay but strides like a miler who could even be a Prix Jean Prat or Prix de la Foret contender.

She does not hold any entries in mile classics at the time of writing but is engaged in the Group 1 Saxon Warrior Coolmore Prix Saint-Alary, Group 1 Prix de Diane Longines (French Oaks) and Group 1 Juddmonte Irish Oaks and may start her campaign in the Listed Pretty Polly Stakes with a view to determining whether or not an Oaks route is viable. It will be fascinating to see how she turns out on the track and what her future offspring inherit.

SUMMARY DETAILS

Bred: George Strawbridge
Owned: George Strawbridge
Trained: John Gosden
Country: England
Race record: 112-
Career highlights: 2 wins inc bet365 May Hill Stakes (Gr2), 2nd bet365 Fillies' Mile (Gr1)

INDIGO GIRL (GB) – 2018 bay filly

Dubawi (IRE)	Dubai Millennium (GB)	Seeking The Gold (USA)
		Colorado Dancer
	Zomaradah (GB)	Deploy
		Jawaher (IRE)
Montare (IRE)	Montjeu (IRE)	Sadler's Wells (USA)
		Floripedes (FR)
	Contare (GB)	Shirley Heights
		Balenare

ISABELLA GILES (IRE)

Belardo (by Lope de Vega) has made a promising start to his stallion career. The Kildangan Stud resident, who won the Group 1 Dewhurst Stakes at two and Group 1 Lockinge Stakes at four, already has five stakes winners to his name, four of them from the European half of his global first crop. Isabella Giles heads the list. The Clive Cox-trained bay, yet another talented horse bred by Ballylinch Stud, has won four of her six starts and just missed out on a placing on one of the other two. That was in the Group 3 Princess Margaret Betfred Stakes over six furlongs at Ascot in July, a fourth-place finish to Santosha that ended her unbeaten record. Both of her first two starts were over six furlongs, a maiden and novice auction race at Leicester and Newbury respectively, and she resumed her winning ways and showed notable improvement in form when she stepped up to seven furlongs.

She was rated ninety-eight after her Ascot run but that was increased to a mark of 105 when she ran away with the Group 3 Ladbrokes Prestige Stakes on soft ground at Goodwood in late August. The seven-length runner-up, Prado, was unplaced on her only subsequent start and third-placed Seattle Rock, who was another head behind, did not run again, but the manner in which Isabella Giles won was impressive. She hit the front a quarter of a mile from home and was soon clear; she outclassed her four rivals. Old rival Santosha was among the four who lined-up against her in the Group 2 Shadwell Rockfel Stakes on the Rowley Mile course at Newmarket a month later but that filly was under pressure after halfway and finished a never-dangerous last of the five. Isabella Giles, on the other hand, raced with the early leader, Monday, for the first couple of furlongs, eased to the front after that, looked to have the race won from over a furlong out and kept on well to the line to beat the nursery-placed winner Nazuna and maiden winner Alba Rose by two lengths and three and a quarter lengths.

Her new rating of 110 was trimmed a point after her unplaced finish in the Group 1 bet365 Fillies' Mile on soft ground at the same venue a fortnight later. She had raced prominently but came under pressure three out and didn't pick up, eventually passing the post over thirteen lengths adrift of the winner, Pretty Gorgeous, and with just one of her nine rivals behind her.

The €45,000 Goffs Sportsman's Yearling Salle graduate is a daughter of the Group 3 Firth of Clyde Stakes winner Majestic Dubawi (by Dubawi), a mare who was unplaced on all three of her attempts beyond six furlongs and whose best son is the German-trained Majestic Colt (by Clodovil). He was a Group 3-placed triple stakes winner in 2020, the pattern-race performance being a two-length second over six furlongs and his blacktype wins coming over six-and-a-half furlongs and seven furlongs. The mare's new two-year-old, Novel Legend, looks likely to stay farther than some of his siblings given that he's a son of Nathaniel (by Galileo).

Tidal Chorus (by Singspiel), the grandam of Isabella Giles, is a half-sister to South Rock (by Rock City), who was a seven-furlong listed scorer that stayed a mile, whereas the next dam is South Shore (by Caerleon), a half-sister to the dual Group 1 Lockinge Stakes victor Soviet Line (by Soviet Star). There is some middle-distance stamina further back in her family but speed is the more typical trait in the first couple of generations of her pedigree and so it would be no surprise to see Isabella Giles prove best at seven furlongs or a mile, perhaps even six and a half furlongs. She holds entries in both the Group 1 Tattersalls Irish 1,000 Guineas and Group 1 Emirates Poule d'Essai des Pouliches (French 1000 Guineas).

SUMMARY DETAILS
Bred: Ballylinch Stud
Owned: Paul & Clare Rooney
Trained: Clive Cox
Country: England
Race record: 114110-
Career highlights: 4 wins inc Shadwell Rockfel Stakes (Gr2), Ladbrokes Prestige Stakes (Gr3)

ISABELLA GILES (IRE) – 2018 bay filly

Belardo (IRE)	Lope de Vega (IRE)	Shamardal (USA)
		Lady Vettori (GB)
	Danaskaya (IRE)	Danehill (USA)
		Majinskaya (FR)
Majestic Dubawi (GB)	Dubawi (IRE)	Dubai Millennium (GB)
		Zomaradah (GB)
	Tidal Chorus (GB)	Singspiel (IRE)
		South Shore

JUDICIAL (IRE)

This admirable campaigner was better than ever at the age of eight, achieving a career-high mark of 111 after a near three-length win in a listed sprint at Chester in August. It was his second blacktype success of the year, adding to his length-and-a-half defeat of Brando in the Group 3 Betfair Backs Racing Welfare Chipchase Stakes on the Tapeta at Newcastle in late June, and brought his career tally to sixteen wins of which, surprisingly, only five have been in blacktype contests. This gelding has consistently held a triple-digit rating since being raised to 102 after a handicap success over five furlongs at Pontefract in April 2017.

He beat the subsequent Group 1 star Profitable on his racecourse debut as a two-year-old, was unbeaten in all three of his starts that season and gelded before the end of that year. He ran only twice at three, leaving the Roger Charlton yard after the first run and joining Julie Camacho's team a couple of months before the second one. The Elite Racing Club's popular homebred had a wind procedure done after his unplaced finish behind Blue Point in the Group 1 King's Stand Stakes at Royal Ascot in 2019, by which point he was an eleven-time winner who had been successful in Group 3 company, and he added two listed race wins to his tally before the end of that campaign.

He kicked off 2020 with a good second to Far Above in the Group 3 Betfair Supports Racing Welfare Palace House Stakes at Newmarket in early June, his only run of the year over five furlongs. The winner, who beat him by three-quarters of a length, looked like a potential Group 1 contender that day but picked up a career-ending injury and is now at stud in Ireland. Judicial, on the other hand, got his aforementioned Group 3 and listed-raced successes and missed out on further placings when taking fourth twice and fifth once, all in blacktype contests. His final two defeats saw his handicap mark trimmed to 108.

The gelding is a son of the Dalham Hall Stud veteran Iffraaj (by Zafonic), a stallion whose seventy-three stakes winners include ten Group 1 stars of whom Chriselliam, Ribchester, Rizeena, and Wootton Bassett stand out in Europe. The latter is now among the most sought-after sires in these parts, his addition to the

Coolmore Stud team for 2021, having spent many years at Haras d'Etreham in France, accompanied by a hike in his fee from €40,000 to €100,000. Ribchester, of course, stands at Kildangan Stud, his yearlings made up to 350,000 guineas in 2020 and he is potentially going to be among the leading freshman sires this coming season.

Judicial, the first foal of the five-furlong listed scorer Marlinka (by Marju), is the year-older half-brother to sprint star Marsha (by Acclamation) whom the Elite Racing Club sold to Coolmore for 6,000,000 guineas at the 2017 Tattersalls December Mare Sale. The Group 1 Nunthorpe Stakes and Group 1 Prix de l'Abbaye de Longchamp heroine had her first foal in January 2020, a daughter of the prolific champion sire Galileo (by Sadler's Wells). Marlinka, on the other hand, is out of the four-time sprint winner Baralinka (by Barathea), a mare who has three contrasting siblings of note. Penzance (by Pennekamp) won the Grade 1 Triumph Hurdle, Sister Act (by Marju) is the winning dam of Group 1 Prix Jean Romanet and Group 2 Blandford Stakes heroine Ribbons (by Manduro) and Group 2-placed miler Tribute Act (by Exceed And Excel), but Soviet Song (by Marju) was talented on the track as she was unlucky at stud.

The James Fanshawe-trained star notched up nine wins and eight places from a twenty-four-race career that spanned five seasons, earning £1,168,370 in prize money. She won the Group 1 Sussex Stakes, Group 1 Matron Stakes, Group 1 Fillies' Mile and two editions of the Group 1 Falmouth Stakes, her tally also included clear-cut wins in the Group 2 Windsor Forest Stakes at Royal Ascot and Group 2 Ridgewood Pearl Stakes at the Curragh, and she just missed out on being classic placed when fourth to Russian Rhythm in the Group 1 1000 Guineas at Newmarket. Soviet Song died in 2015, aged fifteen. Her unplaced daughter Roubles (by Speightstown) was bred to both Dawn Approach (by New Approach) and Teofilo (by Galileo) in 2018 but didn't have her first foal until January 2020, a daughter of Mayson (by Invincible Spirit). She was then bred to Cable Bay (by Invincible Spirit).

Judicial is a talented listed-to-Group 3-class sprinter who has given his many owners plenty of fun days. If he's fit, happy and well in 2021 then there could be more good prizes to be won with him.

SUMMARY DETAILS
Bred: Elite Racing Club
Owned: Elite Racing Club
Trained: Julie Camacho
Country: England
Race record: 111-01-40100103-000111420-201100-0010101-214140-
Career highlights: 16 wins inc Betfair Backs Racing Welfare Chipchase Stakes (Gr3), Coral Charge (Gr3), #chestertogether Queensferry Stakes (L), Betway Golden Rose Stakes (L), William Hill Beverley Bullet Sprint Stakes (L), 2nd Betfair Supports Racing Welfare Palace House Stakes (Gr3), Longholes Palace House Stakes (Gr3), Total Fitness Queensferry Stakes (L)

JUDICIAL (IRE) – 2012 bay gelding

Iffraaj (GB)	Zafonic (USA)	Gone West (USA)
		Zaizafon (USA)
	Pastorale (GB)	Nureyev (USA)
		Park Appeal
Marlinka (GB)	Marju (IRE)	Last Tycoon
		Flame of Tara
	Baralinka (IRE)	Barathea (IRE)
		Kalinka (IRE)

KNOW IT ALL (GB)

The best Japanese horses routinely race until they are five years old and some of them for another season or two beyond that. Lord Kanaloa (by King Kamehameha) won his only start at two, a Group 3 sprint at three, landed the Group 1 Sprinters Stakes at Nakayama and Group 1 Longines Hong Kong Sprint at Sha Tin as a four-year-old and retired at the end of a glittering five-year-old season which saw him crowned champion sprinter, champion miler and Horse of the Year in Japan. He scored repeat wins in the aforementioned Group 1s and added the Group 1 Takamatsunomiya Kinen over six furlongs at Chukyo and Group 1 Yasuda Kinen over a mile at Tokyo. Overall, he won thirteen of his nineteen starts, was placed in the other six, and earned over £3.95 million in prize money.

Lord Kanaloa is a member of the powerful team at Shadai Stallion Station and his first crop, born in 2015, is headed by the superstar Almond Eye. The nine-time Group 1 winner retired at the end of November after landing her second Japan Cup, this time beating the previously undefeated Triple Crown champions Contrail and Daring Tact. The £13.1 million-earner is the best of five top-level winners by her sire so far: the others are classic scorer Saturnalia, miler Stelvio, Hong Kong Sprint winner Danon Smash and the Australian-bred Tagaloa.

Know It All is also among the stallion's twenty-four stakes winners and the first thing that catches the eye when you see her name on the list is that her suffix is GB: the Qatar Racing-homebred was born in Great Britain. Common Knowledge (by Common Grounds), her dam, had previously produced the five-furlong pattern winner Astrophysical Jet (by Dubawi) and seven-furlong juvenile Group 3 scorer Coral Wave (by Rock of Gibraltar), so she is now the dam of three pattern-winning daughters. She also produced a filly in 2020, a mid-January-born member of the sole crop by the late and lamented Roaring Lion (by Kitten's Joy).

Know It All won the Group 3 Derrinstown Stud Fillies Stakes over a mile on good ground at Leopardstown at the start of July. The Johnny Murtagh-trained filly, who had been a pattern-placed winner over seven furlongs a two-year-old and chased home Love Locket in a Group 3 over that trip at Leopardstown on her seasonal reappearance, then finished a close third to Watch Me and Half Light in the Group 1 Prix Rothschild over a mile at Deauville, beaten by three-quarters of a length and a short head. She finished an honourable fourth to her stablemate Champers Elysees in the Group 1 Coolmore America 'Justify' Matron Stakes at Leopardstown on the opening day of Irish Champions Weekend six weeks later, and that was her final outing of the year. The filly, who is rated 110, led that accomplished field a furlong and a half from home at the Dublin venue and it was only in the final strides that she lost third position. It was a highly popular result for the Murtagh stable, taking first and fourth in a Group 1 contest. The classic stars Peaceful and Fancy Blue filled the minor placings, the margins between the top four being one and a quarter lengths, one and a half lengths and a head. Albigna was another length and a half behind in fifth.

She promises to have a notable future as a broodmare because she comes from one of the most famous families in the Stud Book. Her dam's siblings include the Grade 1-placed middle-distance Group 2 scorer Blueprint (by Generous) and Fairy Godmother (by Fairy King), the pattern-placed, stakes-winning dam of the Australian ten-furlong Group 1 scorer Kingdom of Fife (by Kingmambo). Request (by Rainbow Quest) is another sibling of note, a non-winner on the track but dam of the Group 1 Coronation Cup and Group 1 Prix Royal-Oak scorer Ask (by Sadler's Wells). Know It All's grandam, therefore, is the Group 2 Ribblesdale Stakes runner-up Highbrow (by Shirley Heights), a daughter of 1000 Guineas and Prix de Diane (French Oaks) heroine Highclere (by Queen's Hussar) and so a half-sister to Height of Fashion (by Bustino). That Group 2 Princess of Wales's Stakes winner is, of course, the dam of the multiple Group 1 stars Nashwan (by Blushing Groom) and Nayef (by Gulch) and their top-class yet Group 2-winning half-brother Unfuwain (by Northern Dancer)—each of them the sires of Group 1 winners— and she is the ancestor of many other horses of note.

Know It All's three-year-old half-brother Mindpower (by Gleneagles), a May 17th foal, made 120,000 guineas from

Tattersalls' Book 1 sale as a yearling but was snapped up by Irish trainer Denis Hogan for just £5,000 as an unraced juvenile at the Goffs UK December (Mixed) Sale. He could be one to watch in 2021. The colt was consigned by Godolphin, as was the unfortunate Sceptical, the £2,800 Goffs UK purchase in 2019 that Hogan transformed from unraced and Godolphin-sold three-year-old gelding into one of the top sprinters in training.

SUMMARY DETAILS
Bred: Qatar Bloodstock Ltd
Owned: Qatar Racing Ltd
Trained: Johnny Murtagh
Country: Ireland
Race record: 4103-2134-
Career highlights: 2 wins inc Derrinstown Stud Fillies Stakes (Gr3), 2nd Leopardstown Fillies Trial Stakes (Gr3), 3rd Prix Rothschild (Gr1), Weld Park Stakes (Gr3)

KNOW IT ALL (GB) – 2017 bay filly

Lord Kanaloa (JPN)	King Kamehameha (JPN)	Kingmambo (USA)
		Manfath (IRE)
	Lady Blossom (JPN)	Storm Cat (USA)
		Saratoga Dew (USA)
Common Knowledge (GB)	Rainbow Quest (USA)	Blushing Groom (FR)
		I Will Follow (USA)
	Highbrow (GB)	Shirley Heights
		Highclere

LA BARROSA (IRE)

La Barrosa didn't have the clearest of passages in the Group 3 Tattersalls Stakes at Newmarket in late September but there was plenty to like about the way he ran and won, eventually getting to the line one length and three-quarters of a length ahead of Dark Lion and Qaader. The latter had held the winner in two furlongs out and then raced close to him as Godolphin's colt began to assert, even getting a bump at one point. He had been runner-up in the Group 2 Coventry Stakes earlier in the year but was well-beaten on his next start. La Barrosa, on the other hand, had made a winning debut over seven furlongs at Ascot nineteen days before this success and then disappointed behind Van Gogh in the Group 1 Criterium International on heavy ground at Saint-Cloud a month later. That may have been more to do with the ground than the distance as one would expect that a Lope de Vega (by Shamardal) colt out of a Montjeu (by Sadler's Wells) mare would not find a mile to be too far.

Of course, pedigrees are not that simple. If both parents have the so-called 'speed gene' to pass on then they could get a sprinter rather than ten-to-twelve-furlong horse. In this colt's case, however, he looks more like being a miler who may stay ten furlongs. His sire is a leading source of top-class international talent, mostly in the five-to-ten-furlong range, and his dam, Bikini Babe, is a mare who can produce winners in a similar range. Her lightly raced daughter Rkaya (by Exceed And Excel), for example, has won at five and six furlongs. Of those born before La Barrosa, her runners have been by sprinters. Her only win came over seven furlongs as a two-year-old and she was Group 3-placed over the same trip that year, but she was also a half-length runner-up in the Group 3 Prix de Psyche over ten furlongs at Deauville the following summer.

Bikini Babe has a string of blacktype siblings of whom three are more closely related than the others. The prolific Combat Zone (by Refuse To Bend) was a Group 2-winning miler, Royal Empire (by Teofilo) won the Group 3 Geoffrey Freer Stakes over the extended thirteen furlongs at Newbury, whereas Group 3 Strensall Stakes winner Scottish (by Teofilo) was runner-up in the

Group 1 Caulfield Cup over twelve furlongs. All three of those geldings are, of course, representatives of the Sadler's Wells (by Northern Dancer) male line. Zut Alors, in contrast, is a daughter of Pivotal (by Polar Falcon), and while that outstanding stallion is a grandson of Nureyev (by Northern Dancer), the famous three-parts brother to Sadler's Wells, that's typically more often a speed line, not a middle-distance stamina one. This filly was multiple stakes-placed from five and a half to seven furlongs, her best son is Baccarat (by Dutch Art), whose string of sprint wins featured the Wokingham Handicap at Royal Ascot, whereas the Group 1 Poule d'Essai des Pouliches (French 1000 Guineas) scorer Precieuse (by Tamayuz) is her most notable daughter.

Zeiting (by Zieten), the grandam of La Barrosa, also had speed rather than stamina, winning a listed contest over six furlongs on heavy ground at Maisons-Laffitte as a two-year-old and earning a listed-race placing over a mile at three. Being out of a daughter of the Irish Derby winner Law Society (by Alleged), it's likely that her pace came from her sire, a Middle Park Stakes-winning son of Danzig (by Northern Dancer). The same is true of Zeiting's half-sister Madany (by Acclamation), the dual six-furlong Haydock winner who has given us the Group 1 Commonwealth Cup victor Eqtidaar (by Invincible Spirit), classic-placed seven-furlong Group 2-winner Massaat (by Teofilo), and 2020's Group 3 Horris Hill Stakes scorer Mujbar (by Muhaarar). Eqtidaar covered seventy-four mares in his first season at Nunnery Stud (2020), and Massaat, whose first foals arrived in 2020, is a popular member of the team at Mickley Stud where he has covered over eighty mares in both of his first two seasons. As for Bikini Babe, Knocktoran Stud's mare has a now two-year-old filly named Once (by Tamayuz) and she was bred to Belardo (by Lope de Vega) in 2020.

These family connections make La Barrosa an interesting prospect for 2021. Whether or not the 750,000-guinea Tattersalls Book 1 graduate justifies his entry in the Group 1 Tattersalls Irish 2,000 Guineas remains to be seen, but it would no surprise to see this Charlie Appleby-trained colt become one of the more high-profile members of his age group this coming season.

SUMMARY DETAILS

Bred: Knocktoran Stud
Owned: Godolphin
Trained: Charlie Appleby
Country: England
Race record: 110-
Career highlights: 2 wins inc Tattersalls Stakes (Gr3)

LA BARROSA (IRE) – 2018 bay colt

Lope de Vega (IRE)	Shamardal (USA)	Giant's Causeway (USA)
		Helsinki (GB)
	Lady Vettori (GB)	Vettori (IRE)
		Lady Golconda (FR)
Bikini Babe (IRE)	Montjeu (IRE)	Sadler's Wells (USA)
		Floripedes (FR)
	Zeiting (IRE)	Zieten (USA)
		Belle de Cadix (IRE)

LADY BOWTHORPE (GB)

Lady Bowthorpe gave her future paddocks value a tremendous boost in 2020 when winning the Group 3 Betfred Valiant Fillies' Stakes over a mile on good ground at Ascot in late July. It was a career-best effort which she won by four and three-quarter lengths from Farzeen. It was also her sole placing from four attempts in stakes company. She not only has blacktype to her name but those all-important blocked capitals too. This a feat that her half-brother Speak In Colours (by Excelebration), her 'uncle' Tullius (by Le Vie Dei Colori) and various other relations have also achieved and so she will, like them, stand out on catalogue pages rather than being lost among a sea of more notable family members.

She was fourth on her sole start at two and only fifth on her return to action about ten and a half months later, but then got her first win, a seven-furlong novice race at Lingfield and was runner-up in a pair of mile handicaps at Sandown and Newmarket. Her end-of-year rating was eighty-one, that soared to 108 after her Ascot success and remained there despite two subsequent defeats. She was beaten by less than four lengths on both occasions, behind Maamora in the Group 3 Betway Atalanta Stakes at Sandown and then, on heavy ground, behind Nazeef in the Group 1 Kingdom of Bahrain Sun Chariot Stakes on the Rowley Mile.

The 82,000-guinea Tattersalls Book 2 graduate is a daughter of Newsells Park Stud's stallion Nathaniel (by Galileo), forever to be remembered as the sire of the great Enable but also, at the time of writing, responsible for twenty other stakes winners including Group 1 Prix de Diane (French Oaks) winner Channel and the Group 1 Premio Lydia Tesio scorer God Given. Her half-brother Speak In Colours, a likely future stallion, has won the Group 2 Greenlands Stakes and three other pattern races. His placings include third in the Group 1 Prix de la Foret and before he joined the Joseph O'Brien stable, he was a stakes-winning two-year-old for Marco Botti's team. Botti also acquired blacktype for the family when another of the siblings, Pretty In Grey (by Brazen Beau), who followed a Kempton hat-trick with handicap success over a mile at Newmarket in July, picked up third place in the

Listed Irish Stallion Farms EBF Cooley Fillies & Mares Stakes over a mile at Dundalk in mid-November.

They are out of the five-time winner Maglietta Fina (by Verglas) and were followed by a 2018 Mayson (by Invincible Spirit) filly and early-May 2019 Muhaarar (by Oasis Dream) colt; she was bred to Holy Roman Emperor (by Danehill) last season. The mare's siblings include the aforementioned Tullius, a Group 1 Lockinge Stakes runner-up whose eleven wins featured the Group 2 bet365 Mile and Group 2 Sky Bet York Stakes, and prolific win totals can be found in the next generation of the family too. Whipped Queen (by Kingmambo), the grandam of Lady Bowthorpe, won 'only' two races but she was out of Meringue Pie (by Silent Screen), whose fourteen wins includes several blacktype contests, and her siblings include Pie In Your Eye (by Spend A Buck), whose tally of twenty-nine included a mile Grade 3 contest at Garden State and a listed contest at Arlington; stakes-winning nine-time scorer Pie's Lil Brother (by Roar); and the stakes-placed thirteen-time winner Sweet Wager (by Bet Twice). Monsagem (by Nureyev), another of the siblings, was arguably more talented than some of them. His four wins included a listed contest at Leicester, he was third in the Group 1 Prix Jean Prat and Group 2 Lockinge Stakes and placed in various other good races.

Family connections like these make Lady Bowthorpe an excellent prospect as a broodmare, one who may produce plenty of winners including some who notch up eye-catching totals. Her pattern success and the exploits of her star brother (who is featured elsewhere in this volume) should widen the options for potential mates and will look attractive on catalogue pages of any future progeny that might go through the auction ring.

SUMMARY DETAILS

Bred: Scuderia Archi Romani
Owned: Ms E L Banks
Trained: William Jarvis
Country: England
Race record: 4-0122-104100-

Career highlights: 3 wins inc Betfred Valiant Fillies' Stakes (Gr3)

LADY BOWTHORPE (GB) – 2016 bay filly

Nathaniel (IRE)	Galileo (IRE)	Sadler's Wells (USA)
		Urban Sea (USA)
	Magnificient Style (USA)	Silver Hawk (USA)
		Mia Karina (USA)
Maglietta Fina (IRE)	Verglas (IRE)	Highest Honor (FR)
		Rahaam (USA)
	Whipped Queen (USA)	Kingmambo (USA)
		Meringue Pie (USA)

LADY WANNABE (IRE)

Lady Wannabe enhanced her paddocks value with a pair of blacktype successes in 2020 and she will go to stud as a pattern winner following her win in the Group 3 Darley Stakes over nine furlongs on soft ground at Newmarket in October. It was the third blacktype win of her career, coming a few weeks after victory in a nine-furlong listed contest on good ground at Listowel and adding to a one-mile listed success on good-to-yielding at Killarney in August 2019. Coincidentally, all three of those wins were achieved by a margin of one and three-quarter lengths. Indeed, she came within a short-head of having a fourth stakes win to her name because she was pipped by Viadera over the latter-named course and distance as a three-year-old. That rival, a Juddmonte homebred who had been trained by Ger Lyons, joined the Chad Brown stable in 2020 and narrowly won the Grade 1 Matriarch Stakes over a mile at Del Mar in late November.

Lady Wannabe has twice been fourth in stakes company, neither of which counts as being placed or awards any blacktype. The first of those was also in 2019, when she crossed the line two and a half lengths adrift of Buckhurst in the Group 3 International Stakes over ten furlongs at the Curragh, and the other was a last-place finish in the Group 2 Lanwades Stud Stakes over a mile at the same venue on her seasonal reappearance in 2020, a race won by Magic Wand. Her final start was in the valuable Bahrain International Trophy at Sakhir in Bahrain in late November but she finished a long way last of the fourteen runners in that ten-furlong conditions race.

The filly is one of twenty-two pattern winners among an overall tally of thirty-three stakes winners by Coolmore Stud's multiple classic star Camelot (by Montjeu). Four of the stallion's seven top-level scorers achieved the feat in 2020, with classic success for Even So in Ireland and Russian Camelot in Australia, a Group 1 win in Germany for Sunny Queen and Group 1 Cox Plate victory for Sir Dragonet. He is a well-bred horse who has been receiving well-bred mares, so there is every reason to hope that at least some of his daughters will excel as broodmares.

This daughter is the first foal of Wannabe Better (by Duke of Marmalade), a dual mile stakes winner who also landed the Group 3 Ballycorus Stakes at Leopardstown. The mare's siblings include the mile listed scorer Pirateer (by Danehill Dancer) and the Listed Galtres Stakes winner and Group 3 Noblesse Stakes third Wannabe Posh (by Grand Lodge; dam of mile Group 3 winner Wannabe Yours, by Dubawi). However, Wannabe Grand (by Danehill) is the most notable of these offspring of Wannabe (by Shirley Heights). She won the Group 1 Cheveley Park Stakes, Group 2 Cherry Hinton Stakes and Listed Empress Stakes as a juvenile, added the Listed Flying Fillies' Stakes over six furlongs at Pontefract the following summer, and was the half-length runner-up to Wince in the Group 1 1000 Guineas at Newmarket. Sadly, she disappointed as a broodmare. Estrela (by Authorized) is the only one of her winners to have earned any blacktype, and she achieved the field when finishing a well-beaten third in the Listed Oaks Trial at Lingfield, but there is potential for an update on the page in 2021. Estrela's daughter One Journey (by Mastercraftsman), who is trained by Roger Charlton, was a two-and-a-half-length winner of a one-mile novice race on soft ground at Newbury in late October, her only start to date.

There are other blacktype horses to be found in the branches of these closest generations of the family, including the stakes-placed Tannaaf (by High Chaparral), who won the (local Grade 1) Qatar Derby at Doha in 2015, and more if you go back a little further on the page. For example, Propensity (by Habitat), a daughter of the Prix Imprudence runner-up Kalamac (by Kalamoun), was runner-up in the Group 3 Queen Mary Stakes and is the third dam of Lady Wannabe. The fifth and sixth dams were minor blacktype winners and are too remote to have any real influence on the current-day filly, but Propensity's daughter Tanami (by Green Desert) has more relevance. She had been beaten by a total of three and a half lengths when fourth to Gay Gallanta in the Group 3 Queen Mary Stakes but closed that gap to just half a length when runner-up to that same chestnut in the Group 1 Cheveley Park Stakes almost four months later. Nine years after that, her daughter Cairns (by Cadeaux Genereux) won the Group 2 Rockfel Stakes. Tanami also has a stakes-placed daughter called Tanamia (by Nayef) and that one's daughter Tansania (by Sea The Moon) was listed-placed in Germany in 2020.

Wannabe Better has had three daughters of Galileo (by Sadler's Wells) since Lady Wannabe was born and she was bred to Camelot last year. Propriety, the eldest, made headlines when sold for 1,200,000 guineas from Book 1 of the Tattersalls October Yearling Sale in 2018 but showed little aptitude for racing in three starts over middle-distances last year. Higher Truth, now aged three, made 500,000 guineas at the same auction twelve months later. She was an early-May foal, reportedly went to North America but she is, as yet, unraced. The mare's 2019 foal also arrived in early May.

Lady Wannabe is one of the best horses within the first few generations of her pedigree. There is every reason to hope that she can do at least as well at stud and perhaps even outperform the other females on her page in that second career.

SUMMARY DETAILS

Bred: Churchtown House Stud
Owned: Mrs T Gaffney & Mrs Barbara Murphy
Trained: James (Fozzy) Stack
Country: Ireland
Race record: 0-1024210-4000110-
Career highlights: 4 wins inc Darley Stakes (Gr3), Edmund & Josie Whelan Memorial Listowel Stakes (L), Dunloe Hotel & Gardens Vincent O'Brien Ruby Stakes (L), 2nd Irish Stallion Farms EBF Cairn Rouge Stakes (L)

LADY WANNABE (IRE) – 2016 bay filly

Camelot (GB)	Montjeu (IRE)	Sadler's Wells (USA)
		Floripedes (FR)
	Tarfah (USA)	Kingmambo (USA)
		Fickle (GB)
Wannabe Better (IRE)	Duke of Marmalade (IRE)	Danehill (USA)
		Love Me True (USA)
	Wannabe (GB)	Shirley Heights
		Propensity

LANCASTER HOUSE (IRE)

Barronstown Stud has bred many top-class horses over the years and appeared to have another potential star for their roll of honour when Lancaster House made a winning debut at Galway in early August 2019. The Aidan O'Brien-trained three-year-old ran away with a maiden of a little short of eight and a half furlongs on good ground, clocking a quick time. He followed up with defeat of three rivals over nine furlongs at Tipperary nearly four weeks later and then took a listed contest easily over the same trip on soft ground at Listowel before heading to Leopardstown five days later for the Group 2 Clipper Logistics Boomerang Stakes over a mile on the opening day of Irish Champions Weekend. It was perhaps a big ask of an inexperienced colt, four races in the space of a month and a half, and the initial reaction to his seventh-place finish was disappointment. However, it emerged that he was lame on his left foreleg, so the performance could be excused.

His first two races of 2020 were excellent, both of them over seven furlongs, but the latter two were very disappointing, both over a mile. He was receiving three pounds from Speak In Colours in the Group 3 Coolmore Calyx Gladness Stakes at the Curragh in mid-June and made the most of it, beating that high-class entire by two and a quarter lengths on ground described as good-to-firm, with the 103-rated Smash Williams another one and three-quarter lengths back in third. Lancaster House had made almost all of the running and tried to repeat the feat over the same course and distance the following month, this time in the Group 2 Paddy Power Minstrel Stakes. However, the classic-winning miler Romanised went to the front inside the final furlong and had his young rival's measure to the line, passing the post with one and three-quarter lengths to spare. The capable mare Surrounding was another two and a quarter lengths adrift in third, with Love Locket almost two lengths behind that one in fourth. He was in second position as the field swung for home at Leopardstown for the 2020 edition of the Group 2 Clipper Logistics Boomerang Stakes but instead of picking up, he seemed to find nothing, almost looking like a non-stayer. He finished last of ten there and last of fourteen in the Group 1 Queen Elizabeth II Stakes on his final start.

He stays nine furlongs on soft ground but, given how he ran last season, perhaps seven furlongs on good or fast ground is what he needs to be seen to best effect. It would be a little surprising for a son of Galileo (by Sadler's Wells) but not impossible, especially if he has inherited the speed of his dam's sire, Oasis Dream (by Green Desert). However, his dam, the Grade 2 Royal Heroine Mile winner Quiet Oasis, is out of Silent Heir (by Sunday Silence), a mare whose dam is a three-parts sister to New Approach (by Galileo). Not only is Lancaster House closely related to that juvenile star turned Derby and runaway Champion Stakes star, but his fourth dam is the Group 1 Phoenix Champion Stakes heroine Park Express (by Ahonoora).

There are many more notable horses in this famous family, including the Group 1 Oaks winner Was (by Galileo) whose dam, Alluring Park (by Green Desert) is bred similar lines to Quiet Oasis, making that classic heroine another somewhat close relation of the young Ballydoyle horse. There are some in the family who excelled at a mile or less, like Park Express's classic-placed daughter Dazzling Park (by Warning) who was a runaway Group 3 scorer over the distance, and Shinko Forest (by Green Desert) who was a top-level sprint winner in Japan at a time when that country's races were not yet listed in Part I of the International Cataloguing Standards and, hence, counted only for listed success.

On balance, everything seems to point to Lancaster House being bred to be a miler who stays ten furlongs and possibly a bit further. It could be worth trying a step up in distance for him, and yet, despite that listed success in 2019, his initial performances in 2020 suggest that speed rather than stamina may be his forte and that it could even be interesting to try a seven-furlong route with him.

SUMMARY DETAILS
Bred: Barronstown Stud
Owned: Michael Tabor, Derrick Smith & Mrs John Magnier
Trained: Aidan O'Brien

Country: Ireland
Race record: -1110-1200-
Career highlights: 4 wins inc Coolmore Calyx Gladness Stakes (Gr3), Edmund & Josie Whelan Memorial Listowel Stakes (L), 2nd Paddy Power Minstrel Stakes (Gr2)

LANCASTER HOUSE (IRE) – 2016 bay colt

Galileo (IRE)	Sadler's Wells (USA)	Northern Dancer
		Fairy Bridge (USA)
	Urban Sea (USA)	Miswaki (USA)
		Allegretta
Quiet Oasis (IRE)	Oasis Dream (GB)	Green Desert (USA)
		Hope (IRE)
	Silent Heir (AUS)	Sunday Silence (USA)
		Park Heiress (IRE)

LAWS OF INDICES (IRE)

Different sales cater for different markets and it is fair to say that those typically offered at the Goffs Autumn Yearling Sale would not be viewed as potential classic or Group 1 stars, not that one could not emerge from among them. Laws of Indices may not be up to winning at the highest level—significant improvement is required—but he has been Group 1-placed. The Ken Condon-trained Group 2 GAIN Railway Stakes winner cost only €8,000 in the 2019 edition of that auction, known then as Lot 5. He has already earned more than ten times that purchase price from just six starts.

He was unplaced first time out in the maiden won by Lucky Vega over six furlongs on good-to-firm ground at Naas in early June but got off the mark at Navan two weeks later, scoring by a short head over a few yards less. He then sprang that 66/1 Group 2 shock, beating Lucky Vega by half a length before finishing fourth to that colt in the Group 1 Keeneland Phoenix Stakes over the same course and distance in early August. The ground was described as good-to-yielding that day and yielding for both of his wins. He stepped up to seven furlongs for his final two runs, first finishing almost six lengths behind Thunder Moon when seventh in the Group 1 Goffs Vincent O'Brien National Stakes at the Curragh and then picking up third in the Group 1 Qatar Prix Jean-Luc Lagardere - Grand Criterium on heavy ground at ParisLongchamp in early October. He was only three-quarters of a length behind the Coventry Stakes winner Nando Parrado and a neck in front of the filly Libertine, but this was the race that Sealiway won by eight lengths.

Laws of Indices is a son of Power (by Oasis Dream), a leading juvenile who went on to take the Group 1 Irish 2,000 Guineas. He spent time on the Coolmore roster but although out of a half-sister to Footstepsinthesand (by Giant's Causeway), the now Oaklands Stud (in Australia) horse has disappointed as a stallion. This colt and 2020 Group 3 scorer Helvic Dream, who is featured elsewhere in this volume, are among a total of only fourteen stakes winners for him and, so far, none has won at the highest level.

It will be interesting to see how the career of this young colt moves forward. There is some middle-distance stamina in his family but his three successful siblings, who have won eighteen races between them, are all sprinters. Sampers Seven (by Anjaal) has notched up all three of her wins over five furlongs, Spirit of Zebedee's (by Zebedee) nine are over six furlongs, whereas Spirit of Wedza (by Footstepsinthesand) has won over both trips. His dam, Sampers (by Exceed And Excel), who was also bred by Nick Hartery, was a triple winner at Dundalk, once over five and twice over six. Perhaps it is these horses on whom we should focus rather than looking at the milers and middle-distance horses who appear in the second and third generation of the family, especially as its tendency has been for speed sires to get sprinters.

Laws of Indices is rated 104 and holds an entry in the Group 1 Tattersalls Irish 2,000 Guineas. He may indeed stay a mile, as his sire did, but it's also possible that he could be a sprinter. Holding his own in pattern company would likely require at least some degree of further improvement, but if he fails to make the necessary progression then he could be one to note in the various premier handicaps, at anywhere from six furlongs to a mile.

SUMMARY DETAILS
Bred: N Hartery
Owned: Miss C R Holmes
Trained: Ken Condon
Country: Ireland
Race record: 011403-
Career highlights: 2 wins inc GAIN Railway Stakes (Gr2), 3rd Qatar Prix Jean-Luc Lagardere - Grand Criterium (Gr1)

LAWS OF INDICES (IRE) – 2018 bay colt

Power (GB)	Oasis Dream (GB)	Green Desert (USA)
		Hope (IRE)
	Frappe (IRE)	Inchinor (GB)
		Glatisant (GB)
Sampers (IRE)	Exceed And Excel (AUS)	Danehill (USA)
		Patrona (USA)
	Gujarat (USA)	Distant View (USA)
		Privity (USA)

LAZULI (IRE)

Lazuli is talented sprinter who could be a more prominent member of that division in 2021. He had a wind procedure done shortly after finishing down the field behind Good Vibes in the Group 3 Cornwallis Stakes on his final start as a two-year-old, was gelded not long after that and went on to become a dual stakes winner over five furlongs last season. He was runner-up under nine-stone-seven in a Newmarket handicap on his seasonal reappearance and fourth to Maystar in a listed contest at Deauville in early August on his only starts over six furlongs—the trip over which he had won twice at two—but won two of his three tries over the minimum distance.

The first of those was in mid-June, one week after his handicap second, and he made all to beat Keep Busy and Dream Shot in fine style in the Listed Unibet Scurry Stakes on good ground at Sandown. The margins were three and a half lengths and three and a quarter lengths. It was a performance that looked sure to prelude pattern success and he achieved that feat at Newbury three months later. He hit the front a furlong from home in the Group 3 Dubai International Airport World Trophy Stakes, drifting to his left both before and after that point, and he got to the post a length and nose in front of Tiz Marvellous and Equilateral, with Glamorous Anna another half-length back in fourth. It was his final run of the year.

Lazuli, a Godolphin homebred, is a son of the outstanding Dalham Hall Stud stallion Dubawi (by Dubai Millennium), a classic-winning miler who has proved that he can get notable winners over any distance. Floristry (by Fasliyev), his dam, completed a hat-trick of sprint wins as a two-year-old, culminating in a six-furlong listed contest at Doncaster, and she has done well as a broodmare. Her stakes-winning sprinter Inspiriter (by Invincible Spirit) is the dam of pattern-placed sprinter Leading Spirit (by Exceed And Excel), and her other winners include the listed-placed Bouquet de Flores (by Street Cry). That filly's full brother, Moving Forward, has never been tried at less than a mile and the more recent of his two wins came in a ten-and-a-half-furlong handicap at Dundalk in late October.

Zibelina (by Dansili), a half-sister to Floristry, was a ten-length winner on her debut over seven furlongs as a three-year-old, followed that with listed success over a mile at Ascot and completed her hat-trick with a narrow win in the Group 3 Prix de Lieurey over the same trip at Deauville just under three weeks later. She was beaten on her final four starts but has made an eye-catching start to her broodmare career as each of her first three foals is a winner. They include the Group 2 Champagne Stakes runner-up Royal Crusade (by Shamardal), who beat Glen Shiel to win the Group 3 Prix de Ris-Orangis over six furlongs at Deauville in July—he is reviewed elsewhere in this volume—and Royal Fleet (by Dubawi), who made a winning juvenile debut over seven furlongs at Kempton in late November.

Zaeema (by Zafonic) is Lazuli's grandam. She won over seven furlongs at two, her only racecourse appearance, she is a daughter of the Group 2 Sun Chariot Stakes winner (over ten furlongs) and Group 3 Lancashire Oaks runner-up Talented (by Bustino) and so is a half-sister to the Group 2 Dante Stakes winner Carlton House (by Street Cry). He also won the Group 3 Brigadier Gerard Stakes, he was runner-up in the Group 1 Prince of Wales's Stakes and a Group 1 contest in Australia and, from a small number of Australian-born progeny, has sired Too Close The Sun, a dual stakes winner who was runner-up in a one-mile Group 1 handicap at Ascot, Australia, in late November. There are many other stakes and pattern winners to be found if you go back further into the pedigree, a mixture of everything from sprinters to stayers.

Lazuli finished the year on an official handicap mark of 110, which has been trimmed a pound following his third-place finish in a five-furlong Meydan handicap in January 2021. All bar one of his races to date have been on either good ground or good-to-firm, and it would be no surprise to see him take high rank among the sprinters' division this coming season.

SUMMARY DETAILS
Bred: Godolphin
Owned: Godolphin
Trained: Charlie Appleby
Country: England

Race record: 110-21041-3
Career highlights: 4 wins inc Dubai International Airport
World Trophy Stakes (Gr3), Unibet Scurry Stakes (L)

LAZULI (IRE) – 2017 bay gelding

Dubawi (IRE)	Dubai Millennium (GB)	Seeking The Gold (USA)
		Colorado Dancer
	Zomaradah (GB)	Deploy
		Jawaher (IRE)
Floristry (GB)	Fasliyev (USA)	Nureyev (USA)
		Mr P's Princess (USA)
	Zaeema (GB)	Zafonic (USA)
		Talented (GB)

LEMISTA (IRE)

Lemista is a credit to her connections. She won her maiden over a mile on heavy ground on her final start as a two-year-old and reeled off a blacktype hat-trick in 2020, including two pattern events, despite reaching a career-peak handicap mark of just 104. She was raised to that figure after her two-length defeat of Come September in a nine-and-a-half-furlong listed contest at Gowran Park in mid-June where she hit the front two out and was not headed. The ground was yielding that day but it had been described as soft-to-heavy when she landed the Group 3 Lodge Park Stud Irish EBF Park Express Stakes over a mile at Naas in March, just before everything shut down due to the Covid-19 situation. She had reached the front a furlong out that day and kept on well to hold off four-year-old Hamariyna and subsequent classic scorer Even So by three-quarters of a length and a neck.

She is clearly effective when there is ease in the ground, and her trainer stressed that point in post-race interviews at the Curragh in mid-July, but her victory there, in the Group 2 Kilboy Estate Stakes over nine furlongs, was on good ground. It produced a slow time for the distance and conditions, which suggests that the form may not be reliable, and certainly the performance of the favourite, One Voice, can be forgiven as she encountered significant trouble in running. That Group 1-placed filly passed the post in fifth as Lemista stayed on well to beat Lovelier, Kiss For A Jewel and the front-running Crotchet by three-quarters of a length, half a length and half a length. Lemista's debut fourth over seven furlongs at Leopardstown as a two-year-old was also on good ground, as was her final start, in the Group 2 Moyglare 'Jewels' Blandford Stakes over ten furlongs at the Curragh on the second day of Irish Champions Weekend in mid-September. She was never dangerous that day, being pushed along from a quarter of a mile from home and eased when her chance was clearly gone.

Her sire got his most famous win over ten furlongs and her third dam's siblings include a Kentucky Derby star, so one might expect that the distance would not present her with any problem. It would be interesting to see her try it again. It is also possible, however, that it may be a little beyond where she's most comfortable. Her sire has had plenty who show speed rather than stamina, whereas her dam is a half-sister to a sprinter of note, is by a sprinter and out a daughter of a sprint champion.

The mid-January-born bay was bred by Drumlin Bloodstock and made just €16,000 when sold at the 2017 edition of the Goffs Foal Sale but was sold privately to Peter Brant before her Curragh success. She is a daughter of Kildangan Stud resident Raven's Pass (by Elusive Quality), a stallion who has not achieved the level of success that might have been hoped for given his high-profile racing career yet has compiled a decent record with three top-level winners among thirty-five blacktype scorers. Two members of the trio achieved the feat in 2019: juvenile Royal Marine and Japanese sprinter and seven-figure earner Tower of London (new to Darley Japan in 2021). The former Mark Johnston-trained Matterhorn, who sadly died shortly before this book went to print, was a wide-margin winner of the Group 1 Emirates Airline Al Maktoum Challenge R3 over ten furlongs at Meydan in March 2020.

Lemista is the second foal of Shortmile Lady (by Arcano). Her younger half-sister Mummy Bear (by Kodi Bear) finished out of the frame at Chelmsford in late November on her only juvenile start for the Richard Hannon stable but has been placed twice at Lingfield in 2021. The mare had sons of Australia (by Galileo) and Zoffany (by Dansili) in 2019 and 2020 and was bred to Exceed And Excel (by Danehill) last season, so the talented filly is unlikely to remain her dam's only winner for long. The mare's half-sister Indian Maiden (by Indian Ridge) was an accomplished racehorse and has produced two stakes winners both of whom, like her, are sprinters. Maid In India's (by Bated Breath) seven wins include the Group 3 Dubai World Trophy Stakes over five furlongs at Newbury, pattern-placed Love Spirit's (by Elusive City) eight wins included a pair of listed races, whereas Indian Maiden won fifteen times including the Group 3 Prix de Meautry and seven listed contests.

Jinsiyah, grandam of Lemista and by the dual US Eclipse Award-winning sprinter Housebuster (by Mt. Livermore)—who was also effective at a mile—is a stakes-placed granddaughter of the Grade 1-placed multiple stakes winner All Rainbows (by Bold

Hour). That makes her third dam, Minifah (by Nureyev), a half-sister to the 1988 US three-year-old filly champion and Kentucky Derby heroine Winning Colors (by Caro). That famous grey also won the Grade 1 Santa Anita Derby and Grade 1 Santa Anita Oaks, and her siblings also include a one-time winner, All Dance (by Northern Dancer), who became the dam of Grade 1 Japan Cup scorer Tap Dance City (by Pleasant Tap).

Those stars are too distantly connected to Lemista to indicate what she might achieve in the future, but with what she and her closest relations have achieved there is every reason to hope that she will have a notable stud career ahead of her. She has been exported to the USA and at the time of writing, is in training in Florida.

SUMMARY DETAILS
Bred: Drumlin Bloodstock
Owned: Peter M Brant
Trained: Ger Lyons
Country: Ireland
Race record: 401-1110-
Career highlights: 4 wins inc Kilboy Estate Stakes (Gr2), Lodge Park Stud Irish EBF Park Express Stakes (Gr3), Irish Stallion Farms EBF Victor McCalmont Memorial Stakes (L)

LEMISTA (IRE) – 2017 bay filly

		Gone West (USA)
	Elusive Quality (USA)	Touch of Greatness (USA)
Raven's Pass (USA)		Lord At War (ARG)
	Ascutney (USA)	Right Word (USA)
	Arcano (IRE)	Oasis Dream (GB)
		Tariysha (IRE)
Shortmile Lady (IRE)		Housebuster (USA)
	Jinsiyah (USA)	Minifah (USA)

LEO DE FURY (IRE)

Last season was an important one for Coolmore Stud's Australia. The Derby-winning son of the Epsom classic stars Galileo (by Sadler's Wells) and Ouija Board (by Cape Cross) had an unexpectedly quiet time with his first crop, plenty of blacktype horses and a few who performed with credit at the highest level but nothing that managed to step forward and win in the top grade. In 2020, he made the breakthrough with two members of his second crop: Group 1 Pertemps St Leger winner Galileo Chrome and Grade 1 Breeders' Cup Mile scorer Order of Australia.

Leo de Fury represents his first crop. He was unraced at two, won a pair of ten-furlong contests by a combined margin of ten lengths to kickstart his career but then finished out of the frame in three of his next four outings. The exception was the Group 3 Royal Whip Stakes at the Curragh where he failed by just a head to beat Buckhurst, another son of Australia. Two of the defeats had been over twelve furlongs and the third, back over ten but on very soft ground at ParisLongchamp, saw him finish fourth to Skalleti in the Group 2 Qatar Prix Dollar. Aside from his first start, which was over a half-furlong farther, all of his runs at four were over a mile and a quarter.

He looked set for greater things following his comeback success at the Curragh in mid-June, an impressive three-length defeat of Fleeting in the Group 2 Coolmore Magna Grecia Irish EBF Mooresbridge Stakes on good-to-firm ground. He was going well on the outside three out, made steady progress to hit the front over a furlong later and stayed on well for a comfortable success. His official rating rose to 114 but was later trimmed to 111 following three disappointing runs in stronger company. He finished fifth to Magical in the Group 1 Tattersalls Gold Cup in late July, was a never-dangerous last of five to Armory in the Group 3 Irish Field Celebrating 150 Years Royal Whip Stakes nineteen days later and then trailed home last of six in the Group 1 Irish Champion Stakes at Leopardstown.

The Jessica Harrington-trained chestnut is a €25,000 Goffs Orby Sale graduate and both of his younger siblings have been winners for the Joseph O'Brien stable. Sense of Style (by Zoffany) is one of them and that Naas maiden winner, who has run six times to date, was short-headed in a one-mile listed contest at the Curragh on her final start. She holds entries in both the Group 1 Tattersalls Irish 1,000 Guineas and Group 1 Juddmonte Irish Oaks. Their dam, Attire (by Danehill Dancer), is a full sister to the middle-distance stakes winner Forgotten Voice and a half-sister to Australie (by Sadler's Wells), the Group 3 Prix de Flore-winning dam of two stakes winners. Their grandam, Asnieres (by Spend A Buck), is among the double-digit tally of winners produced from the Group 2 Prix de l'Opera third Albertine (by Irish River), a tally that is headlined by the shock Grade 1 Breeders' Cup Classic star Arcangues (by Sagace). He also won the Group 1 Prix d'Ispahan, and although he disappointed at stud, several of his siblings produced major winners.

Agathe (by Manila) was the most talented racehorse among those siblings, she gave us the US Grade 1 scorer Artiste Royal (by Danehill) and his champion full sister Aquarelliste and she is the grandam of Ziyad (by Rock of Gibraltar), the Group 2 Grand Prix de Deauville winner who has been placed in the Grade 1 Canadian International and two editions of the Group 1 Grand Prix de Saint-Cloud. Aquarelliste, of course, won the Group 1 Prix de Diane (French Oaks), Group 1 Prix Vermeille and Group 1 Prix Ganay and she was runner-up to Sakhee in the Group 1 Prix de l'Arc de Triomphe, among other performances of note. Afrique Bleu Azur (by Sagace) and Ange Bleu (by Alleged) are the other notable daughters of Albertine, minor track performers but successful at stud. The former is the dam of the impressive Group 1 1000 Guineas heroine Cape Verdi (by Caerleon), who also had the distinction being sent off favourite for the Derby at Epsom, whereas Ange Bleu is the dam of the dual US Grade 1 star Angara (by Alzao) and Group 2 Prix Corrida winner Actrice (by Danehill).

Leo De Fury was gelded after his last run. He seems well-suited to ten furlongs on fast ground, could be worth trying at nine or even eight furlongs, and it will be interesting to see how 2021 goes for him.

SUMMARY DETAILS

Bred: B V Sangster
Owned: Zhang Yuesheng
Trained: Jessica Harrington
Country: Ireland
Race record: -110204-1000-
Career highlights: 3 wins inc Coolmore Magna Grecia Irish EBF Mooresbridge Stakes (Gr2), 2nd Royal Whip Stakes (Gr3)

LEO DE FURY (IRE) – 2016 chestnut gelding

Australia (GB)	Galileo (IRE)	Sadler's Wells (USA)
		Urban Sea (USA)
	Ouija Board (GB)	Cape Cross (IRE)
		Selection Board
Attire (IRE)	Danehill Dancer (IRE)	Danehill (USA)
		Mira Adonde (USA)
	Asnieres (USA)	Spend A Buck (USA)
		Albertine (FR)

LIMATO (IRE)

There is plenty about Limato's pedigree that could have seen him prove to be an effective miler, but despite finishing fourth to Belardo in the Group 1 Lockinge Stakes and being beaten by only three and a half lengths when sixth to Tourist in the Grade 1 Breeders' Cup Mile, his best form was over six and seven furlongs. Gelded before he ever ran, he was an unbeaten dual stakes winner as a two-year-old and a rising star at three, a season in which he won the Group 3 Pavilion Stakes over six, the Group 2 Park Stakes over seven, and was runner-up in the Group 1 Prix de la Foret, Group 1 Commonwealth Cup, and Group 2 Sandy Lane Stakes. He won the Group 1 July Cup and Group 1 Prix de la Foret at four and chased home Mecca's Angel in the Group 1 Nunthorpe Stakes on what was, remarkably, the only time in his career that he ran over five furlongs.

He won the Group 2 Challenge Stakes and chased home Harry Angel in the Group 1 July Cup as a five-year-old, won a second Challenge Stakes plus two listed races at six, was a Group 3 scorer from five runs at the age of seven, and added another pattern success to his tally in 2020, aged eight. It was the Group 3 Betway Criterion Stakes over seven furlongs on fast ground at Newmarket in late June and he looked like the force of old in easily beating Happy Power by three and a half lengths. He was raised to 115 from 114 following this fine effort, a remarkable figure for a horse of his age; he was on 122 at his peak as a four- and five-year-old. His only other run was in the Group 2 bet365 Park Stakes at Doncaster in mid-September and that seven-furlong contest was to be his finale. He had some talented horses behind at the line but had been unable to challenge the principals, going out on a fifth-place finish. The sadly ill-fated Wichita short-headed the history-maker One Master to win the race, with Molatham and Urban Icon third and fourth.

Limato's thirty-three-race career spanned seven seasons and took in fourteen wins and seven placings, netting over £1.4 million in prize money. Not bad for a horse who cost just £41,000 as a yearling. The Doncaster Premier Yearling Sale graduate was bred by Seamus Phelan and is one of two standout sons sired by the juvenile Group 1 scorer and Rathbarry Stud veteran Tagula (by Taufan). The classic-winning miler Canford Cliffs is the other one and they are among an overall total of thirteen stakes winners for the stallion. The tally includes three Group 2 scorers of whom the prolific sprinter Tax Free is most notable. He has sixteen others who have been blacktype placed, and a long list of horses who have been multiple winners, some of them prolific. He has had small crops in recent years, covered only six mares in 2020 and, now aged twenty-eight, is listed as private for 2021.

Come April, the dam of Limato, won over ten furlongs. That was no surprise for a daughter of the top international performer Singspiel (by In The Wings) and So Admirable (by Suave Dancer), an unraced sibling of the Group 1 stars Compton Admiral (by Suave Dancer) and Summoner (by Inchinor). The former won the Group 1 Coral-Eclipse Stakes and Group 3 Craven Stakes, whereas the latter landed the Group 1 Queen Elizabeth II Stakes at Ascot. Their half-sister Twyla Tharp (by Sadler's Wells) didn't win at blacktype level, but she was runner-up in the Group 2 Ribblesdale Stakes, third in a listed contest at Yarmouth and later became the dam of the four-time Group 1 star The Fugue (by Dansili). That John Gosden-trained celebrity won the Irish Champion Stakes, Prince of Wales's Stakes, Yorkshire Oaks, and Nassau Stakes. She was Group 1-placed in Hong Kong, twice placed at the Breeders' Cup and earned over £1.9 million in prize money. Her daughters Fughetta and Counterpoint have not raced, and their 1,000,000-guinea full brother Mahomes (by Dubawi) finished third in a ten-furlong Bath novice race from three juvenile starts in 2020. She had a Shamardal (by Giant's Causeway) colt at the end of January last year and was bred back to Sea The Stars (by Cape Cross).

There are plenty of other blacktype horses in the family, including the Group 1 Prix Saint-Alary third and US Grade 2 scorer Arvada (by Hernando)—a winner-producing broodmare in Japan—whose dam, Lalindi (by Cadeaux Genereux), is a seven-time winning half-sister to Limato's third dam Sumoto (by Mtoto). It would have been hard to imagine when seeing her finishing well-beaten in all four of her attempts in blacktype company that Sumoto, a Sir Philip Oppenheimer homebred, would go on to become such a mare of influence: four Group 1 winners among her descendants and the potential for more. Of course, she did have ability and she won both of her other two starts, comfortably beating the subsequent classic and multiple Group 1 star Sayyedati by two lengths on their juvenile debut over six furlongs at Ascot and then pipping Queen's View in a seven-furlong conditions race on soft ground at Lingfield the following year.

Limato, who was trained by Henry Candy, is now in what will hopefully be a long, happy and healthy retirement. He will be fondly remembered.

SUMMARY DETAILS

Bred: Seamus Phelan
Owned: Paul G Jacobs
Trained: Henry Candy
Country: England
Race record: 1111-12212-41210-03241-0001110-41002-10-
Career highlights: 14 wins inc Darley July Cup (Gr1), Qatar Prix de la Foret (Gr1), Godolphin Stud And Staff Stable Awards Challenge Stakes (Gr2-twice), Saint Gobain Weber Park Stakes (Gr2), Betway Criterion Stakes (Gr3-twice), Merriebelle Stable Pavilion Stakes (Gr3), Ryedale House Garrowby Stakes (L), Price Bailey Chartered Accountants Hopeful Stakes (L), totepool Two-Year-Old Trophy (L), Rose Bowl Stakes - sponsored by Compton Beauchamp Estates Ltd (L), 2nd Darley July Cup (Gr1), Coolmore Nunthorpe Stakes (Gr1), Qatar Prix de la Foret (Gr1), Commonwealth Cup (Gr1), Godolphin Stud And Staff Stable Awards Challenge Stakes (Gr2), 888sport Sandy Lane Stakes (Gr2), 3rd Diamond Jubilee Stakes (Gr1)

LIMATO (IRE) – 2012 bay gelding

Tagula (IRE)	Taufan (USA)	Stop The Music (USA)
		Stolen Date (USA)
	Twin Island (IRE)	Standaan (FR)
		Jolly Widow
Come April (GB)	Singspiel (IRE)	In The Wings
		Glorious Song (CAN)
	So Admirable (GB)	Suave Dancer (USA)
		Sumoto (GB)

LONE EAGLE (IRE)

The two-year-old division of 2020 lacked stars and created a somewhat muddled picture of the order of relative merit. Sometimes the principals from an unexciting year remain near or at the top again as three-year-olds, but often those years are also ones in which some of the less exposed or even unraced horses overtake them. On occasion those who surge forward can come from among horses who took a quieter path during their juvenile season. It is likely that few had noticed or heard of Lone Eagle before October 10th and yet he ended the year as a 110-rated pattern winner and quoted at 33/1 in the ante-post market for the Group 1 Derby Stakes at Epsom.

Lone Eagle had looked like a potential middle-distance horse in the making in his first three runs, all over a mile, the latter a nursery in which he had received five pounds from the top-weight while running off a mark of eighty-four. He was raised six pounds for that win. A step up to ten furlongs for his final run was no surprise and although the target may have seemed ambitious on the strict merit of what he had achieved to that point, he was sent off second favourite and came away an impressive winner.

The race was the Group 3 Godolphin Flying Start Zetland Stakes. Once an all-too-often purveyor of so-called 'cheap blacktype', it has developed into an important two-year-old contest in recent years, one from which plenty of Group 1 performers have emerged. Highland Chieftain, who took the prize back in 1985, was a rare one to go on to Group 1 success, the Premio Roma headlining a string of pattern wins for the sixteen-time scorer, but Hartnell (2013), Coronet (2016) and Kew Gardens (2017) are among its recent winners. The ill-fated Permian and subsequent Derby star Wings of Eagles were third and fourth respectively in 2016, Dee Ex Bee was runner-up in 2017, Irish Derby third Norway landed the prize in 2018, and it was Miss Yoda (Group 1 Preis der Diana [German Oaks]) and Berkshire Rocco (neck runner-up in the Group 1 St Leger) who chased home Max Vega in 2019.

It is possible that some of those who disappointed that day might emerge as talented performers in 2021. However, the first two finished a long way clear of the third, Mystery Angel, making it a one-two-three on the day for nursery winners. That first-crop Kodi Bear (by Kodiac) filly went on to be runner-up in a pair of one-mile listed races on her final two starts, raising her rating to ninety-five. The runner-up, Recovery Run, an Andrew Balding-trained son of Nathaniel, has a record of two wins and four seconds from six starts, was raised to 107 after this pattern performance and is the colt that Lone Eagle beat narrowly in a Sandown maiden on good-to-firm in early August. The margin between them was one and three-quarter lengths on the soft ground at Newmarket. Lone Eagle made most of the running in the Zetland and, racing beside the rail, stayed on strongly to the line after a battle with Recovery Run.

Lone Eagle is a son of the phenomenal and prolific champion sire Galileo (by Sadler's Wells) and he is the first foal out of Modernstone (by Duke of Marmalade), a dual stakes-placed multiple twelve-furlong winner in England who went on to become a Grade 3-placed stakes winner in Kentucky. She is a half-sister to the Saint-Cloud listed scorer Chasing Stars (by Observatory) and out of Post Modern (by Nureyev), an unraced full sister to 1997's Group 1 Oaks heroine Reams of Verse. That classic star is a blacktype producer, the grandam of the Group 1-placed mile Group 2 scorer Zacinto (by Dansili)—a classic sire in New Zealand—and third dam of the Group 3 March Stakes scorer Maid Up (by Mastercraftsman).

Reams of Verse was among pattern winners out of an unraced mare named Modena (by Roberto) and that string of talented siblings included the Group 1 Coral-Eclipse Stakes and Group 1 Phoenix Champion Stakes ace Elmaamul (by Diesis)—sire of the top-level winners Muhtathir (sire of Group 1 winners) and Sweet Return—and the Group 2 Yorkshire Cup scorer Manifest. High Walden (by El Gran Senor) and Midsummer (by Kingmambo) are notable among the mare's eleven winners who did not succeed at pattern level, the first-named a Grade 2-placed stakes winner who is the grandam of stakes winners and the latter-named being the stakes-placed dam of Midday (by Oasis Dream) and her Group 1-placed, pattern-winning half-sisters Sun Maiden (by Frankel) and Hot Snap (by Pivotal).

Midday's nine wins featured the Grade 1 Breeders' Cup Filly & Mare Turf, the Group 1 Yorkshire Oaks and a record three editions of the Group 1 Nassau Stakes, whereas the races in which she was placed included her runner-up spots in the Group 1 Oaks and Group 1 Coronation Cup at Epsom and the Group 1 Juddmonte International Stakes at York. Her progeny include the Group 2-placed dual middle-distance pattern winner Midterm (by Galileo) and listed scorer Mori (by Frankel) who was a neck runner-up to Coronet in the Group 2 Ribblesdale Stakes at Royal Ascot.

This is a branch of the family of the brothers Zafonic (by Gone West) and Zamindar—their pattern-winning dam, Zaizafon (by The Minstrel), was a half-sister to Modena—and that could make Lone Eagle an interesting stallion prospect if he earns such a role upon completion of his racing career. In the shorter term, he has the potential to make an impact from ten furlongs and upwards, making him a possible candidate for both the Derby and St Leger. In addition to Epsom, he also holds entries in the Group 1 Prix du Jockey Club (French Derby) and Group 1 Grand Prix de Paris. The 500,000-guinea Tattersalls Book 1 graduate is trained by Martyn Meade, was bred by Ballylinch Stud in Ireland and races in partnership with them and Aquis Farm. His dam had a Lope de Vega (by Shamardal) colt in 2019 and was bred back to that stallion last year.

SUMMARY DETAILS
Bred: Ballylinch Stud
Owned: Ballylinch Stud & Aquis Farm
Trained: Martyn Meade
Country: England
Race record: 2111-
Career highlights: 3 wins inc Godolphin Flying Start Zetland Stakes (Gr3)

LONE EAGLE (IRE) – 2018 bay colt

Galileo (IRE)	Sadler's Wells (USA)	Northern Dancer
		Fairy Bridge (USA)
	Urban Sea (USA)	Miswaki (USA)
		Allegretta
Modernstone (GB)	Duke of Marmalade (IRE)	Danehill (USA)
		Love Me True (USA)
	Post Modern (USA)	Nureyev (USA)
		Modena (USA)

LOVE LOCKET (IRE)

Love Locket has only had two wins and a single placing from eight starts, but she gave her future paddocks value a tremendous boost in early June when winning the Group 3 Leopardstown Fillies Trial Stakes. She was always prominent through the seven-furlong contest, was marginally in front as the field swung into the straight and then kept on well to the line, pulling clear to win by a length and a half from Know It All. The runner-up, who would go on to become a Group 1-placed pattern winner over a mile, finished a head and a head in front of Precious Moments and Unforgetable (sic). The winner, who had won a maiden and been runner-up in a nursery from four starts at two, did not progress. She beat only one home when unplaced behind Alpine Star in the Group 1 Coronation Stakes at Royal Ascot, put up a better effort when finishing a five-and-three-quarter-length fourth to Romanised in the Group 2 Paddy Power Minstrel Stakes over seven at the Curragh and then finished last of eleven in the Group 1 Coolmore America 'Justify' Matron Stakes at Leopardstown in mid-September.

Her best form has been over seven furlongs, she appears to go on any ground and she could do better at stud than she did on the track. The daughter of No Nay Never (by Scat Daddy) was bred by Dermot Weld's Springbank Way Stud, also the breeder of Ghaiyyath, the world's top-rated horse of 2020. She was bought by Ciaran Conroy's Glenvale Stud for €52,000 at the Goffs November Foal Sale and sold on for a massive €700,000 at the following year's Goffs Orby Sale. She is the second foal of her dam, her older half-brother Raakib Alhawa (by Kingman) has won a listed race over eleven and a half furlongs at Windsor, and her younger half-sister Geminga (by Awtaad) finished third in a one-mile novice race at Kempton in November, her only start at two. That filly is a Lord Halifax-homebred as her dam, Starlet (by Sea The Stars) was sold for 160,000 guineas at the Tattersalls December Mare Sale in 2017.

Starlet was a five-length winner of a twelve-furlong maiden at Leopardstown on her second start but then finished last in a pair of listed races. She had a Lope de Vega (by Shamardal) colt in

2019, a Mastercraftsman (by Danehill Dancer) filly in 2020 and was then bred to Iffraaj (by Zafonic). Her half-brother Treasure The Ridge (by Galileo) is a six-time middle-distance flat winner, whereas her dam, Treasure The Lady (by Indian Ridge), is a stakes-placed half-sister to High Chaparral (by Sadler's Wells). That dual Derby and dual Breeders' Cup Turf star was a leading international sire, a shuttler, whose 130 stakes-winning offspring feature twenty-three who won at least once at the highest level. His full brother Black Bear Island won the Group 2 Dante Stakes and was runner-up in the Grade 1 Secretariat Stakes.

His full sister Chenchikova's stakes-winning progeny are headed by 2020's Group 1 Prix de Diane (French Oaks) and Group 1 Nassau Stakes heroine Fancy Blue (by Deep Impact), whereas half-sister Mora Bai (by Indian Ridge) is the dam of the Group 1-placed Group 2 scorers Hunting Horn (by Camelot)—new sire in Ireland in 2021—and David Livingston (by Galileo). Kozana (by Kris), the fourth dam of Love Locket, won the Group 2 Prix de Mallaret and Group 3 Prix de Sandringham and was runner-up in the Group 1 Prix du Moulin de Longchamp, and she was out of Koblenza (by Hugh Lupus), the Poule d'Essai des Pouliches (French 1000 Guineas) winner of 1969.

With these pedigree connections it would not be a surprise to see Love Locket become a Group 1 producer for the Coolmore team.

SUMMARY DETAILS
Bred: Springbank Way Stud
Owned: Mrs John Magnier, Michael Tabor & Derrick Smith
Trained: Aidan O'Brien
Country: Ireland
Race record: 4012-1040-
Career highlights: 2 wins inc Leopardstown Fillies Trial Stakes (Gr3)

LOVE LOCKET (IRE) – 2017 bay filly

No Nay Never (USA)	Scat Daddy (USA)	Johannesburg (USA)
		Love Style (USA)
	Cat's Eye Witness (USA)	Elusive Quality (USA)
		Comical Cat (USA)
Starlet (IRE)	Sea The Stars (USA)	Cape Cross (IRE
		Urban Sea (USA)
	Treasure The Lady (IRE)	Indian Ridge
		Kasora (IRE)

LOXLEY (IRE)

Loxley won the Group 2 Grand Prix de Deauville in the summer of 2018, was a half-length runner-up to Alignement (sic) in the Group 2 Prix Dollar shortly afterwards but was well-beaten on his return to action in Meydan as a four-year-old, was gelded and picked up three listed-race seconds over twelve furlongs, from four starts. It was a disappointing campaign. He was well-beaten on his first two runs of 2020 too but made it third time lucky when, stepped back up to a mile and a half, he short-headed the unfortunate Defoe in the Group 2 Dubai City of Gold at Meydan in early March.

He was then off the track until late September when he finished a well-beaten last of six in a listed contest at Newmarket having taken a keen hold and raced prominently for much of the race. The gelding was more amenable to restraint at Kempton next time, hit the front inside the final furlong and won a listed contest by two lengths from Palavecino, with the fillies Kirstenbosch and Tribal Craft one and a quarter lengths and a short head behind in third and fourth. The valuable Bahrain International Trophy, over ten furlongs at Sakhir, was his only subsequent race of the year and, having raced keenly, he finished a three-length seventh to Simsir.

His Dalham Hall Stud-based sire, New Approach (by Galileo), has sired eight Group 1 winners—including classic stars Dawn Approach, Masar and Talent, and 2020 juvenile Mac Swiney—and is listed as private for 2021. His dam, Lady Marian (by Nayef), won the Group 1 Prix de l'Opera and was a neck runner-up in the Group 1 Preis der Diana (German Oaks) as a three-year-old and her sole placing at four came when short-headed by Alpine Rose in the Group 1 Prix Jean Romanet at Deauville. She is a half-sister to the mile Group 3 scorer Lucidor (by Zafonic) and from the immediate family of the Group 1 stars Laveron (by Konigsstuhl), Lavirco (by Konigsstuhl), and Lomitas (by Niniski).

Loxley finished the year on a handicap mark of 109, down from a seasonal best of 111 and a career-high figure of 112. He is a Godolphin homebred, has earned over £430,000 and presuming he's happy and well again this coming season, he should be capable of adding to that sum in 2021.

SUMMARY DETAILS
Bred: Godolphin
Owned: Godolphin
Trained: Charlie Appleby
Country: England
Race record: 10-121102-00222-041010-
Career highlights: 6 wins inc Dubai City of Gold sponsored by Emirates SkyCargo (Gr2), Lucien Barriere Grand Prix de Deauville (Gr2), Unibet 3 Uniboosts A Day Floodlit Stakes (L), Prix Nureyev (L), 2nd Qatar Prix Dollar (Gr2), Bahrain Trophy Stakes (Gr3), 32Red Wild Flower Stakes (L), Matchbook Floodlit Stakes (L), Mukhadram Godolphin Stakes (L)

LOXLEY (IRE) – 2015 bay gelding

New Approach (IRE)	Galileo (IRE)	Sadler's Wells (USA)
		Urban Sea (USA)
	Park Express	Ahonoora
		Matcher
Lady Marian (GER)	Nayef (USA)	Gulch (USA)
		Height of Fashion (FR)
	La Felicita (GB)	Shareef Dancer (USA)
		La Concordia (GER)

LULLABY MOON (GB)

Lullaby Moon raced for three different trainers in her first season, kicking off her career with a winning debut over five furlongs at Goodwood for the Joseph Tuite team. She was then unplaced in the valuable Weatherbys Super Sprint at Newbury for the Michael Bell yard before notching up three wins from four starts for Ralph Beckett. The 16,000-guinea Tattersalls Book 2 graduate was a wide-margin winner over six furlongs on heavy ground at Goodwood in late August, finished third to Umm Kulthum in the Group 3 Scotty Brand Firth of Clyde Fillies' Stakes over the same trip on good-to-soft at Ayr three weeks later, and then became a dual stakes winner.

The first-crop daughter of Kildangan Stud's dual Group 1 star Belardo (by Lope de Vega) beat twenty rivals to take the Listed William Hill Two Year Trophy on soft ground at Redcar in early October before stepping up to seven furlongs at Chantilly where she beat Asterella by two lengths, on heavy ground, to take the Group 3 Prix Miesque.

She is a half-sister to several multiple winners out of dual five-furlong scorer Bold Bidder (by Indesatchel), which makes her inbred 3x4 to Danehill (by Northern Dancer). The mare's stakes-placed half-sister Right Answer (by Lujain) is the dam of the dual listed-placed triple sprint winner Galtymore Lad (by Indesatchel), whereas their dam is Quiz Show (by Primo Dominie), a winning half-sister to sprint star and blacktype sire Mind Games (by Puissance). Lullaby Moon's fifth dam is 1968's Irish 1000 Guineas winner Front Row (by Epaulette), a half-sister to 1970's winner of that same classic: Black Satin (by Linacre). So, this is also the family of US Grade 1 star and blacktype sire Czaravich (by Nijinsky) and 1991's Group 1 Irish Oaks and Group 1 Oaks d'Italia heroine Possessive Dancer (by Shareef Dancer), among various other talented performers.

Lullaby Moon's now two-year-old half-brother has been named Bold Ribb (by Ribchester) and that £82,000 Goffs UK Premier Yearling Sale graduate is to be trained by Roger Varian. Their dam's 2020 Washington DC (by Zoffany) colt made 58,000 guineas when sold in Newmarket in late November.

It will be interesting to see if Lullaby Moon tries a mile this coming season, a distance over which her promising young sire got the second of his Group 1 wins. She holds an entry in the Group 1 Emirates Poule d'Essai des Pouliches (French 1000 Guineas) so her connections are clearly considering such a move. Her best wins came when there was plenty of ease in the ground but given that her debut success came on good, she is clearly not inconvenienced by a sounder surface. She finished her first season on an official handicap mark of 104 and it would be no surprise to see her rise further in the rankings.

SUMMARY DETAILS
Bred: Bearstone Stud
Owned: Amo Racing Ltd & Co
Trained: Ralph Beckett
Country: England
Race record: 101311-
Career highlights: 4 wins inc Prix Miesque (Gr3), William Hill Two Year Old Trophy (L), 3rd Scotty Brand Firth of Clyde Fillies' Stakes (Gr3)

LULLABY MOON (GB) – 2018 bay filly

Belardo (IRE)	Lope de Vega (IRE)	Shamardal (USA)
		Lady Vettori (GB)
	Danaskaya (IRE)	Danehill (USA)
		Majinskaya (FR)
Bold Bidder (GB)	Indesatchel (IRE)	Danehill Dancer (IRE)
		Floria (IRE)
	Quiz Show (GB)	Primo Dominie
		Aryaf (CAN)

MAAMORA (IRE)

Maamora was runner-up in a listed contest over a mile in Sweden in September 2019 and sprang a surprise when finishing third to Magic Lily in a Group 2 race over a furlong farther at Meydan in mid-February, a performance for which her handicap mark rose to 102. But she put up the best effort of her career on her only subsequent outing, earning an end-of-year figure of 108. The race came after a six-month gap, it was the Group 3 Betway Atalanta Stakes over a mile on good ground at Sandown, and she made all to beat the dual Group 1 star Billesdon Brook and the talented Lavender's Blue by half a length and three-quarters of a length, with the classic-placed Group 1 scorer Quadrilateral a neck back in fourth, just holding on from the strong-finishing Posted.

The daughter of leading international sire Dubawi (by Dubai Millennium) is a half-sister to a pair of multiple winners, one of whom is her younger half-brother Boosala (by Dawn Approach). That colt looked a potential pattern-calibre horse in the making following wins at Windsor and York as a two-year-old but was not seen out again until the end of December 2020 when he finished a half-length third in a six-furlong conditions race at Wolverhampton. Their dam, Zoowraa (by Azamour), who had a No Nay Never (by Scat Daddy) filly in 2020, disappointed as a three-year-old but won her only two starts at two, including the Listed Radley Stakes over seven furlongs at Newbury, by a combined margin of over eight lengths. That mare is, in turn, a daughter of Beraysim (by Lion Cavern), a pattern-placed seven-furlong stakes winner whose stakes-winning dam, Silk Braid (by Danzig), was a half-sister to the champion and dual US classic star Risen Star (by Secretariat).

Maamora has raced mostly over a mile although she came within a short head of scoring over ten furlongs at Chelmsford on her fourth start. The Group 2-placed pattern winner has notched up four wins and five placings from thirteen starts and earned just over £90,000. She is by the broodmare sire of the Group 1 winners Blair House (by Pivotal), Dream Castle (by Frankel) and Nazeef (by Invincible Spirit) and Group 2 scorers such as Amorella (by Nathaniel), Isabella Giles (by Belardo), Liberty

Heights (by King Kamehameha) and Royal Julius (by Royal Applause), and she promises to become a notable addition to the paddocks.

SUMMARY DETAILS
Bred: Godolphin
Owned: Sheikh Ahmed Al Maktoum
Trained: Simon & Ed Crisford
Country: England
Race record: 00-22210112-031-
Career highlights: 4 wins inc Betway Atalanta Stakes (Gr3), 2nd Lanwades Stud Stakes (L), 3rd Balanchine sponsored by Gulf News (Gr2)

MAAMORA (IRE) – 2016 bay filly

Dubawi (IRE)	Dubai Millennium (GB)	Seeking The Gold (USA)
		Colorado Dancer
	Zomaradah (GB)	Deploy
		Jawaher (IRE)
Zoowraa (GB)	Azamour (IRE)	Night Shift (USA)
		Asmara (USA)
	Beraysim (GB)	Lion Cavern (USA)
		Silk Braid (USA)

MAGIC LILY (GB)

Many would have been tempted to retire a horse like Magic Lily to the paddocks a couple of years back and more would have considered the decision one year ago. She had been an impressive debut winner over a mile at Newmarket, followed that eight-length score with a close third-place finish to Laurens and September in the Group 1 Fillies' Mile over the same course and distance, but was then off the track for two years before finishing runner-up in a ten-furlong listed contest on very soft ground at Saint-Cloud. That showed she still retained some ability but then she finished unplaced in a listed contest over the same trip on the Polytrack at Lingfield. She hit the front a quarter of a mile from home that day but weakened a furlong out and passed the post four and a half lengths behind the winner, Scentasia.

However, Godolphin's homebred was kept in training as a five-year-old and it was a decision that reaped notable reward. She short-headed Nisreen to take the Group 2 Cape Verdi over a mile at Meydan in January, extended her margin of superiority over that rival to a length and a quarter in the nine-furlong Group 2 Balanchine Stakes a month later and then chased home Barney Roy in the Group 1 Jebel Hatta over that course and distance in early March. She disappointed on her final two starts of the year, when finishing well-beaten behind Nazeef in the Group 2 Duke of Cambridge Stakes over a mile at Royal Ascot and behind Angel Power in the Group 3 Darley Pride Stakes over ten on soft ground at Newmarket in October but had run quite well when third in the Group 2 Betfair Dahlia Stakes over that same course and distance in early June. The ground was good-to-firm and she had the fourth six lengths adrift when chasing home Terebellum and Queen Power, the margins one and a quarter lengths and one and a half lengths.

The gamble of keeping her in training was arguably greater given her superb pedigree. The daughter of Dalham Hall Stud's classic sire New Approach (by Galileo) is a full sister to the Group 1-placed stakes winner Jalmoud and out of Dancing Rain (by Danehill Dancer). That chestnut completed a unique classic double by following her Group 1 Oaks success with a three-length score in the Group 1 Preis der Diana (German Oaks). She also won the 2011 edition of the Group 2 British Champions' Fillies & Mares Stakes at Ascot. Her fourth foal, Sakura Petal (by Dubawi), won the second of her two starts for the Charlie Appleby stable in 2020, that now four-year-old is followed by Galileo (by Sadler's Wells) colts who arrived in 2019 and 2020 and the mare was among the small but select final book covered by the late Shamardal (by Giant's Causeway) last season.

Dancing Rain's dam, Rain Flower (by Indian Ridge), was unraced, as was her grandam, Rose of Jericho (by Alleged), but the latter achieved fame through the exploits of four of her sons and several more of her descendants. Dr Devious (by Ahonoora) won the Group 1 Derby at Epsom, the Group 1 Irish Champion Stakes by fraction of a nostril at Leopardstown and the Group 1 Dewhurst Stakes at two, he was runner-up in the Group 1 Irish Derby and later sired winners at all levels without making a lasting impact or achieving high profile in that role. His half-brother Royal Court (by Sadler's Wells) won the Group 3 Ormonde Stakes, Shinko King (by Fairy King) was a good winner in Japan, but Archway (by Thatching) took after his sire by becoming a leading sprinter. He won the Group 3 Greenlands Stakes, was placed in the Group 2 King's Stand Stakes, and although never a major sire and generally remembered here as being responsible for the dual Grade 1 Champion Hurdle star Hardy Eustace, he came up with several Group 1 winners in Australia include Oaks heroines Grand Archway and Rose Archway and fellow top-level middle-distance filly She's Archie who chased home Makybe Diva in a Group 1 Melbourne Cup.

Rose of Jericho's daughter Breeze Hill (by Danehill) is the dam of 2020's Group 1 Juddmonte Irish Oaks winner Even So (by Camelot), Rose of Suzuka (by Fairy King) is the dam of the Japanese Group 1 scorer Suzuka Phoenix (by Sunday Silence), and Band of Angels (by Alzao) is an ancestor of the Group 1 Mackinnon Stakes winner Awesome Rock (by Fastnet Rock), but we need to return to Rain Flower.

Dancing Rain is not her only notable daughter. Just as her dam had a talented sprinter among all that middle-distance talent, Rain Flower came up with Sumora (by Danehill), a three-parts sister to

Dancing Rain but who got her blacktype success over five furlongs. She has produced a Group 2 Queen's Vase runner-up in Barbados (by Galileo) but, so far, it is speed she has been passing on rather than middle-distance talent. Her daughter Promise To Be True (by Galileo) won the Group 3 Silver Flash Stakes and was placed in both the Group 1 Prix Marcel Boussac and Group 1 Criterium International as a two-year-old, whereas that one's full sister Maybe was Europe's juvenile filly champion of 2011 when she won the Group 1 Moyglare Stud Stakes at the Curragh. That filly went on to be third in the Group 1 1000 Guineas and her second foal is the juvenile and classic star Saxon Warrior (by Deep Impact).

He won all three of his starts at two, all over a mile and featuring the Group 2 Beresford Stakes at Naas and Group 1 Racing Post Trophy at Doncaster. The stamina in his pedigree combined with his clear-cut Group 1 2000 Guineas success and his powerful connections saw him go off odds-on at Epsom, but he had to settle for fourth to Masar. He finished closer to victory in the Group 1 Irish Derby at the Curragh next time, but that was third place to Latrobe and Rostropovich. So, he dropped back to ten furlongs, failed by only a neck to beat Roaring Lion in the Group 1 Coral-Eclipse Stakes, was a slightly disappointing five-length fourth to that same star in the Group 1 Juddmonte International Stakes next time and then lost out to that colt yet again in the Group 1 Irish Champion Stakes at Leopardstown, again going down by a neck. However, it quickly emerged that he had sustained a tendon injury there and he was retired to Coolmore Stud. Four of the eighteen members of his large first-crop of foals that went through the auction ring in 2020 fetched six-figure prices.

There are no guarantees in this business, but there will be not a shred of surprise if Magic Lily becomes the dam of a classic star or other racehorse(s) of note.

SUMMARY DETAILS
Bred: Godolphin
Owned: Godolphin
Trained: Charlie Appleby

Country: England
Race record: 13/20-112300-
Career highlights: 3 wins inc Balanchine sponsored by Gulf News (Gr2), Cape Verdi sponsored by Creek Views (Gr2), 2nd Jebel Hatta sponsored by Emirates Airline (Gr1), Prix Dahlia - Fonds Europeen de l'Elevage (L), 3rd bet365 Fillies' Mile (Gr1), Betfair Dahlia Stakes (Gr2)

MAGIC LILY (GB) – 2015 chestnut mare

New Approach (IRE)	Galileo (IRE)	Sadler's Wells (USA)
		Urban Sea (USA)
	Park Express	Ahonoora
		Matcher
Dancing Rain (IRE)	Danehill Dancer (IRE)	Danehill (USA)
		Mira Adonde (USA)
	Rain Flower (IRE)	Indian Ridge
		Rose of Jericho (USA)

MAGIC WAND (IRE)

Magic Wand's career and pedigree were reviewed in detailed in *European Group 1 Winners of 2019* and so, aside from a quick recap of some highlights, the focus this time is how her final season on the track went. The horse who gave Galileo (by Sadler's Wells) the outright world record for the number of individual Group 1 winners when she won the Mackinnon Stakes at Flemington in November 2019—Danehill had eighty-three of them, according to Weatherbys' data, not eighty-four as has been widely reported—she added just one more win to her tally in 2020. That was the Group 2 Lanwades Stud Stakes over a mile on good-to-firm ground at the Curragh in mid-June where, having hit the front around halfway, she was always in command, outclassing three rivals to win easily. For the record, Haraiyna passed the post in second, four and a half lengths adrift but two and a quarter lengths in front of the third, Silk Forest. Lady Wannabe was last of the quartet.

Chasing home Zula Alpha in the Grade 1 Pegasus World Cup Turf Invitational Stakes over nine and a half furlongs at Gulfstream Park in January was the only other time she made the frame during the year. She was well-beaten behind Maximum Security in the ultra-valuable Saudi Cup at Riyadh in February, fourth to Ghaiyyath in the Group 1 Coral-Eclipse Stakes at Sandown in July, fifth to Fancy Blue in the Group 1 Qatar Nassau Stakes at Goodwood and then well-beaten behind Cayenne Pepper in the Group 2 Moyglare 'Jewels' Blandford Stakes at the Curragh in mid-September.

The Group 1 Cox Plate at Moonee Valley was her next intended target but she was found to have a foot abscess just days before the race, so she missed the ten-furlong feature, leaving her stable companion Armory to represent the Ballydoyle team instead. Her retirement from racing was announced a few days later, so her final tally reads as four wins and eleven places from twenty-eight races and she accumulated career earnings in excess of £3.7 million (€4.1 million).

Magic Wand is now a member of the all-powerful Coolmore Stud broodmare band. She is a full sister to the pattern-placed Je

Ne Regretterien and half-sister to Chicquita (by Montjeu), the Group 1 Irish Oaks winner who chased home Treve in the Group 1 Prix de Diane (French Oaks). Chicquita is the dam of 2018's Group 3 Silver Flash Stakes third Secret Thoughts (by War Front) and her third foal is the Donnacha O'Brien-trained and classic-entered Nicest (by American Pharoah) who made a winning debut over a mile at Leopardstown in July but finished fifth in a Group 3 contest on heavy ground at the Curragh on her only other outing. She had daughters of Dubawi (by Dubai Millennium) in 2019 and 2020 and was bred back to that stallion last season.

As noted last year, Magic Wand's stakes-winning dam, Prudenzia (by Dansili), is out of listed scorer Puce (by Darshaan) and related to a long list of stakes and pattern winners that includes Group 1 Melbourne Cup winner Rekindling (by High Chaparral), classic-placed pattern scorer Golden Sword (by High Chaparral), juvenile Group 1 winner Magical Romance (by Barathea), middle-distance Group 1 scorer Aspetar (by Al Kazeem), and classic stars Alexandrova (by Sadler's Wells) and Channel (by Nathaniel). In 2020, the family saw listed success and Derby favouritism for Prudenzia's half-brother English King (by Camelot), Group 3 Prix de Lutece victory for Paix (by Muhaarar), who is out of Prudenzia's pattern-winning half-sister Pacifique (by Montjeu), plus both listed success and two pattern placings for Alkandora (by Nathaniel), who shares with Magic Wand the aforementioned Puce as a third dam. There was also further listed success in Australia for Alkandora's "uncle" Drill (by Dansili), now racing under the name Dr Drill.

Magic Wand has many of the big-name stallions within the first few generations of her pedigree and that adds to the intrigue of decisions regarding potential mates. On November 1st, it was announced that as the US Triple Crown winner Justify (by Scat Daddy) was in Australia for the southern hemisphere season, Magic Wand would be bred to him there. As she is reportedly going to be based in Ireland, going to that celebrity in her first season suggests that No Nay Never (by Scat Daddy) could be on the shortlist for 2022 or later. Indeed, with Wootton Bassett (by Iffraaj) now on the stud's roster it would not be a surprise to see him on her card at some point, a mating that would produce a foal inbred 3x4 to the juvenile star and classic-winning miler Zafonic (by Gone West). She is a fascinating prospect and it would be no surprise to see her price at least one or two offspring who share her considerable talent.

SUMMARY DETAILS

Bred: Ecurie Des Monceaux & Skymarc Farm Inc
Owned: Michael Tabor, Derrick Smith, Mrs John Magnier
Trained: Aidan O'Brien
Country: Ireland
Race record: 0-314100224-203220224012-201400-
Career highlights: 4 wins inc Seppelt Mackinnon Stakes (Gr1), Lanwades Stud Stakes (Gr2), Ribblesdale Stakes (Gr2), Arkle Finance Cheshire Oaks (L), 2nd Qipco Irish Champion Stakes (Gr1), Longines Hong Kong Cup (Gr1), Pegasus World Cup Turf Invitational Stakes (Gr1-twice), Arlington Million XXXVII Stakes (Gr1), Juddmonte Pretty Polly Stakes (Gr1), Prix de l'Opera Longines (Gr1), Qatar Prix Vermeille (Gr1), Wolferton Stakes (L), 3rd Man O' War Stakes (Gr1)

MAGIC WAND (IRE) – 2015 bay mare

Galileo (IRE)	Sadler's Wells (USA)	Northern Dancer
		Fairy Bridge (USA)
	Urban Sea (USA)	Miswaki (USA)
		Allegretta
Prudenzia (IRE)	Dansili (GB)	Danehill (USA)
		Hasili (IRE)
	Platonic (GB)	Zafonic (USA)
		Puce (GB)

MANUELA DE VEGA (IRE)

Manuela de Vega comes from a family noted for speed and she is by a stallion who has become a noted source of sprinters and milers, but both she and her full sister, Isabel de Urbina, relish twelve furlongs and have form over farther. Two of Lope de Vega's (by Shamardal) dozen top-level winners have shown their best form beyond a mile, albeit nine and ten furlongs, but he did win the Group 1 Prix du Jockey Club over ten and a half at Chantilly and is by a grandson of Irish Oaks winner Helen Street (by Troy), so with the right mare it is possible he could get a star over the Derby distance.

Roscoff would not seem like an obvious choice to be 'the right mare' and in truth her star offspring are talented without being stars, but it would appear that she may have inherited stamina from her sire, Daylami (by Doyoun), and passed that on. If so, she didn't display it on the track, although to be fair, she was campaigned at around a mile and was listed-placed at that trip. That said, she is out of the blacktype sprinter Traou Mad (by Barathea) who is out of the classic-placed, pattern-winning sprinter Pont-Aven (by Try My Best) and so is a half-sister to the star French sprinter Sainte Marine (by Kenmare) and the smart Josr Algarhoud (by Darshaan) who stayed a mile but was arguably best at seven furlongs. Yes, even noted stamina influence Darshaan (by Shirley Heights) got a speed horse from this family. Stamina appears to be a recessive trait in this distaff line. It pops up from time to time—there's a Cheshire Oaks winner in a branch—but you don't see if very often. Roscoff has bucked the family's trend and that adds another layer of interest to the broodmare careers of her talented daughters.

Traou Mad, Josr Algarhoud and Group 1-placed Group 2 Prix du Gros-Chene ace Sainte Marine can also count Cap Coz (by Indian Ridge) among their siblings, a pattern-placed stakes winner who was best at around seven furlongs and who has achieved some notable results at stud. Her son Biniou (by Mozart) was a multiple stakes-winning sprinter, listed scorer Reply (by Oasis Dream) was placed in the Group 3 Greenlands Stakes, Group 1 Irish 2,000 Guineas and Group 1 Middle Park Stakes, but Indian

Days got his best wins over twelve furlongs. The Group 3 John Porter Stakes and dual Group 2 Bosphorus Trophy scorer is by Daylami and so can be described as being a three-parts brother to Roscoff. So, it would appear that the 'Daylami factor' did indeed make Roscoff 'the right mare'.

Her Iffraaj (by Zafonic) gelding Auxerre looked a high-class miler in the making, winning four in a row from five starts for Godolphin, but sadly he died young. Hero Look, a full brother to Manuela de Vega and Isabel de Urbina, won the Group 2 Gran Criterium at two and Group 3 Premio Parioli (Italian 2000 Guineas) at three but went on to an undistinguished career from six to eight furlongs in Hong Kong. Their younger sibling Thai Power (by Kingman), who was gelded in November, won over twelve furlongs at Kempton in June before being a runner-up three times, twice at fourteen furlongs.

Isabel de Urbina won twelve-furlong listed races at Goodwood and Pontefract and missed out on further blacktype placing when fourth in the Group 3 Bronte Cup Fillies' Stakes over a quarter-mile farther at York. The Merriebelle Irish Farm Ltd-homebred had her first foal in 2020, a daughter of Siyouni (by Pivotal) who has already been named Canila Lucinda. Manuela de Vega, on the other hand, was sold by the fillies' breeder at the Goffs Orby Sale, but the €100,000 bay has been trained, like her sister, who had been a Tattersalls Book 1 buy-back, by Ralph Beckett.

She was an unbeaten mile stakes winner at two and chased home Mehdaayih in the Listed Cheshire Oaks before finishing fourth to Anapurna in the Group 1 Oaks and fifth to Star Catcher in the Group 1 Irish Oaks. She chased home Enbihaar in the Group 2 Lillie Langtry Stakes and finished third to Sir Ron Priestley in the Group 3 March Stakes, both over fourteen furlongs at Goodwood, before taking the runners-up spot in both a listed contest at Chester and the Group 1 Grosser Preis von Bayern at Munich. The latter was a neck defeat by Nancho on soft ground, and she finished the year on a mark of 107.

Manuela de Vega kicked off her four-year-old season in style, first beating Fanny Logan by two lengths in the Group 3 Betway Pinnacle Stakes over an extended eleven and a half furlongs on good-to-soft at Haydock in early June, one month before trouncing Makawee and three other rivals in the Group 2 bet365 Lancashire Oaks over a few yards farther on soft ground at the same venue. Taking on Love in the Group 1 Darley Yorkshire Oaks next time was a big ask but she gave it a good try, setting off in front and remaining in front until the champion took over three out. Her younger rival strode home to another impressive win whereas Manuela de Vega kept on to the line but could only manage fourth. Sadly, her final three runs were disappointing as she finished well-beaten in Group 1s at ParisLongchamp (heavy ground), Ascot (soft) and Munich (heavy), after which her 110 rating was clipped to 108.

Manuela de Vega is a fascinating broodmare prospect: will her progeny show her stamina or might some of them follow the family's trend for speed at up to and around a mile? It will likely depend on the stallions to whom she is sent. Her final racing record stands at four wins and five placings from fifteen starts and earnings of over £270,000.

SUMMARY DETAILS

Bred: Merriebelle Irish Farm Ltd
Owned: Waverley Racing
Trained: Ralph Beckett
Country: England
Race record: 11-2402322-114000-
Career highlights: 4 wins inc bet365 Lancashire Oaks (Gr2), Betway Pinnacle Stakes (Gr3), ebfstallions.com Silver Tankard Stakes (L), 2nd Grosser Preis von Bayern (Gr1), Qatar Lillie Langtry Stakes (Gr2) Sportpesa Stand Cup Stakes (L), Arkle Finance Cheshire Oaks (L), 3rd Ladbrokes March Stakes (Gr3)

MANUELA DE VEGA (IRE) – 2016 bay filly

Lope de Vega (IRE)	Shamardal (USA)	Giant's Causeway (USA)
		Helsinki (GB)
	Lady Vettori (GB)	Vettori (IRE)
		Lady Golconda (FR)
Roscoff (IRE)	Daylami (IRE)	Doyoun
		Daltawa (IRE)
	Traou Mad (IRE)	Barathea (IRE)
		Pont-Aven

MASTER OF THE SEAS (IRE)

This colt could be a horse of note in 2021 and although he holds entries in the Group 1 Dubai Duty Free Irish Derby, Group 1 Prix du Jockey Club (French Derby) and Group 1 Grand Prix de Paris it may be that his other big entries, the Group 1 Tattersalls Irish 2,000 Guineas and Group 1 Poule d'Essai des Poulains (French 2000 Guineas), are the more suitable option. He is a son of the classic-winning miler and outstanding Dalham Hall Stud stallion Dubawi (by Dubai Millennium), who gets good winners over everything from five furlongs to two miles but comes from a family that is noted for speed at up to a mile. He may stay ten furlongs but his pedigree casts a shade of doubt over his ability to be as effective beyond that distance. It is certainly not impossible that he will stay twelve furlongs: it may depend on whether he has inherited some of the stamina influence that his dam's sire, Danehill (by Danzig), could pass on or his speed.

Master of The Seas had to work on his debut at Newmarket in mid-June, eventually getting the better of a determined William Bligh to win by three-quarters of a length, but the pair left their other two rivals a very long way behind on the soft ground. It was his next performance, however, that identified him a potentially top-class colt in the making. He was fractious in the stalls and didn't have the smoothest of breaks but was soon going well and having hit the front over a furlong from home, he went clear for a three-length win. Devious Company chased him home, followed by Seventh Kingdom, Saint Lawrence and Ventura Tormenta in what was a useful-looking edition of the Group 2 bet365 Superlative Stakes.

The ground was good there and also at the Curragh when he lined up for the Group 1 Goffs Vincent O'Brien National Stakes two months later. He was sent off joint-favourite with the Jessica Harrington-trained Lucky Vega, who had been so impressive in the Group 1 Keeneland Phoenix Stakes in August, but in what was a somewhat messy contest, he had to settle for fourth. He had avoided some of the traffic trouble that afflicted several of his rivals but had fought for his head in the early part of the race, eventually settled, hit the front a furlong from home only to have three pass him in the closing stages. Thunder Moon beat Wembley and St Mark's Basilica by one and a half lengths and a short head, with the latter passing the post half a length in front of Master of The Seas.

He was not seen out again, but the first three would go on to fill the first three placings in the Group 1 Darley Dewhurst Stakes, albeit in a different order—St Mark's Basilica beat Wembley and Thunder Moon that day—and fifth-placed Lucky Vega, who had some of the worst traffic problems at the Curragh, failed by only half a length to beat Supremacy in the Group 1 Juddmonte Middle Park Stakes two weeks later. Master of The Seas finished the year on an official rating of 112, placing him among the leaders of his age group and eight pounds behind the divisional champion, St Mark's Basilica.

He is a half-brother to the seven-furlong stakes winner and Group 1 St James's Palace Stakes runner-up Latharnach (by Iffraaj), seven-furlong listed scorer Etive (by Elusive Quality) and Group 3 UAE Oaks (nine and a half furlongs) heroine Falls of Lora (by Street Cry), the dam of the talented Cascadian (by New Approach). That gelding was a short-neck runner-up to Intellogent in the Group 1 Prix Jean Prat at Deauville but has since won a seven-and-a-half-furlong Group 3 contest at Rosehill in Australia and been a head runner-up to Yulong Prince in a Group 1 handicap over a mile. Tipstaff, a full brother to Falls of Lora, won over ten furlongs at Navan and finished third to Brendan Brackan in a listed contest over an extended mile at Cork but was well down the field when tried over twelve furlongs.

They are all out of Firth of Lorne (by Danehill), the French mile winner who chased home Zenda in the Group 1 Poule d'Essai des Pouliches (French 1000 Guineas) and later picked up third place in a nine-furlong Grade 2 handicap at Santa Anita. Her dam Kerrera (by Diesis) chased home Musical Bliss in a steadily run edition of the Group 1 1000 Guineas at Newmarket and spent the rest of her career in sprints. She beat Thorn Dance in the Listed Sandy Lane Stakes over six furlongs at Haydock shortly after her classic run and was fourth to Cadeaux Genereux in the Group 1 July Cup. At two, Kerrera had run away with the Group 3 Cherry Hinton Stakes and been runner-up to Shuttlecock

Corner in the Group 2 Flying Childers Stakes over five furlongs. Her half-brother Rock City (by Ballad Rock) was a high-class performer from six furlongs to a mile, easily winning the Group 2 Gimcrack Stakes, Group 3 Coventry Stakes and Group 3 July Stakes at two and adding the Group 3 Criterion Stakes and Group 3 Greenham Stakes, both over seven furlongs, at three. He was runner-up in the Group 1 St James's Palace Stakes, Group 1 Middle Park Stakes and Group 2 Prix Maurice de Gheest, third in the Group 1 July Cup and fourth to Tirol in the Group 1 2000 Guineas.

Master of The Seas is a highly promising colt and he could be one of the year's leading performers from seven to nine furlongs. It would be no surprise to see him strike at the highest level and to be Group 1-placed at ten furlongs, but whether or not he can win well-run races at that distance or beyond depends in part on the factors outlined above. He is one of the more interesting members of the current three-year-old crop that took part in the better juvenile races of 2020.

SUMMARY DETAILS
Bred: Godolphin
Owned: Godolphin
Trained: Charlie Appleby
Country: England
Race record: 114-
Career highlights: 2 wins inc bet365 Superlative Stakes (Gr2)

MASTER OF THE SEAS (IRE) – 2018 bay colt

Dubawi (IRE)	Dubai Millennium (GB)	Seeking The Gold (USA)
		Colorado Dancer
	Zomaradah (GB)	Deploy
		Jawaher (IRE)
Firth of Lorne (IRE)	Danehill (USA)	Danzig (USA)
		Razyana (USA)
	Kerrera	Diesis
		Rimosa's Pet

MIGHTY GURKHA (IRE)

This Archie Watson-trained colt had a busy first season on the track, kicking off with a seven-and-a-half-length score on his debut over six furlongs at Lingfield on June 5th and finishing when failing by just a nose to give seven pounds to Victory Heights over the same trip at Wolverhampton six months later. He finished fifth to Tactical in the Listed Windsor Castle Stakes at Royal Ascot, chased home Method in the Listed Rose Bowl Stakes over six at Newbury and won the Group 3 Sirenia Stakes by a nose at Kempton in early September. He made all that day and just held on from Cloudbridge, a Godolphin runner who hung to his left in the final half-furlong. The runner-up was gelded shortly after the race and not seen out again, and third-placed Mystery Smiles, who had been a length behind, was also running for the final time of the season. That Andrew Balding-trained colt had finished third to Minzaal in the Group 2 Al Basti Equiworld Dubai Gimcrack Stakes on his previous start.

Mighty Gurkha, a 14,000-guinea vendor buy-back at the Tattersalls Book 3 sale, is a son of the Australian juvenile champion and sprint star Sepoy (by Elusive Quality), a horse who reverse-shuttled to Dalham Hall Stud for five seasons. His twenty stakes winners are headed by the Australian champion and triple Group 1-winning sprint ace Alizee, whereas his European progeny include the Group 2 German 1000 Guineas winner Unforgetable Filly (sic), US Grade 1-placed German Group 3 scorer Indian Blessing, and the Group 1-placed English Group 3 winner Dabyah.

He is the first foal of Royal Debt (by Royal Applause), a mare who has several winning siblings and whose third dam is the pattern-placed, stakes-winning Irish miler Rua d'Oro (by El Gran Senor). Her half-brother Rewarding Hero (by Exceed And Excel) was a Group 1-placed mile stakes winner in Hong Kong, her Ed Vaughan-trained full brother Dance And Dance won seven times in England and was runner-up in each of the Group 3 Diomed Stakes, Group 3 Sovereign Stakes and the Royal Hunt Cup in a fifty-nine-race career, and her dam is the Group 3-placed dual five-furlong winner Caldy Dancer (by Soviet Star). Royal Debt had a Slade Power (by Dutch Art) colt in 2019, a first-crop daughter of Jungle Cat in 2020 and was then bred to that Group 1-winning stallion's sire, Iffraaj (by Zafonic).

Mighty Gurkha is rated 103 and, shortly before this book went to print, he made a winning reappearance in a six-furlong conditions race at Kempton, scoring by a neck from the stakes-placed Zamaani while giving five pounds to all of his rivals He led until a furlong out there, was headed, fought back, and hit the front again a half furlong from the line. His record on synthetic tracks reads 1121 versus 02000 on turf, so it will be interesting to see how his career pans out. It would not be a surprise to see him pick up more blacktype and/or to win some valuable sprint handicaps.

SUMMARY DETAILS
Bred: Rabbah Bloodstock Ltd
Owned: Mohammed Rashid
Trained: Archie Watson
Country: England
Race record: 10201002-1
Career highlights: 3 wins inc Unibet 3 Uniboosts A Day Sirenia Stakes (Gr3), 2nd bet365 Rose Bowl Stakes (L)

MIGHTY GURKHA (IRE) – 2018 bay colt

		Gone West (USA)
	Elusive Quality (USA)	Touch of Greatness (USA)
Sepoy (AUS)		Danehill (USA)
	Watchful (AUS)	Canny Miss (AUS)
		Waajib
	Royal Applause (GB)	Flying Melody
Royal Debt (GB)		Soviet Star (USA)
	Caldy Dancer (IRE)	Smile Awhile (USA)

MILITARY STYLE (USA)

There was a time when it seemed that the Ballydoyle team dominated two-year-old races and that most of their good horses would not only win first time out at that age but be expected to do so. In recent seasons, however, it has become commonplace for the stable's juveniles to be placed or finish out of the frame on their first and sometimes even second start. It may in part be due to the increasing competitiveness of racing in Ireland. Military Style is one of the stable's youngsters who made a winning debut in 2020, in his case by a neck over six furlongs on good-to-yielding ground at Naas in late June. He was odds-on for the Group 3 Marble Hill Stakes at Cork two weeks later and finished only third, beaten by a neck and three-quarters of a length by the Henry de Bromhead-trained Minaun and the Paddy Twomey-trained Artician.

The colt stepped up to seven furlongs for his final two starts, first making all to beat the subsequent Group 1 scorer Van Gogh by a neck in the Group 3 Japan Racing Association Tyros Stakes at Leopardstown, in what was a somewhat bunched finish. He again tried to make all in the Group 1 Goffs Vincent O'Brien National Stakes at the Curragh the following month but was headed a quarter of a mile from home and weakened soon afterwards, eventually finishing ninth and with only Masen, who had been a close third to him in the Tyros, behind. He was entered in the Group 1 Vertem Futurity Trophy Stakes at Doncaster but did not make the journey.

The 106-rated Military Style is bred to be a top-class performer but has a considerable amount of improvement to make if he is going to be among his stable's leading three-year-olds. The son of Claiborne Farm standard-bearer War Front (by Danzig), he is the second foal of the Group 1 Fillies' Mile winner Together Forever (by Galileo). She missed out on a classic placing when only fourth to Covert Love in the Group 1 Irish Oaks, but her full sister Forever Together beat Wild Illusion by four and a half lengths to take the Group 1 Oaks at Epsom and, on her final start, was a neck runner-up to the sadly ill-fated Sea of Class in the Group 1 Irish Oaks. Their half-brother Lord Shanakill (by Speightstown) was well-beaten behind Sea The Stars at Newmarket on his sole classic attempt but later won the Group 1 Prix Jean Prat over a mile at Chantilly. The Group 1 Prince of Wales's Stakes winner and young Irish stallion My Dream Boat is the better of his two European stakes winners by a very wide margin.

Green Room (by Theatrical), the unraced second dam of Military Style, is one of those somewhat rare mares who have produced at least three top-level winners at stud, but she is not the only Group 1 producer in her family. Her late half-sister Spanish Fern (by El Gran Senor) won at the highest level in California, her unraced half-sister Rusty Back (by Defensive Play) gave us the US Grade 1 scorer Heatseeker (by Giant's Causeway), and winning half-sister Dayville (by Dayjur) is the grandam of the juvenile Group 1 winner Hearts of Fire (by Firebreak). Chain Fern (by Blushing Groom), the third dam of Military Style, was an unraced full sister to the Group 1 Irish 1,000 Guineas heroine Al Bahathri, the mare who gave us the Group 1 2000 Guineas and Group 1 Champion Stakes star Haafhd (by Alhaarth).

Military Style is a full brother to the stakes-placed winner King of Athens and an as-yet unnamed two-year-old, and a half-brother to a first-crop Justify (by Scat Daddy) colt on March 8th, 2020. He is among ninety-six stakes winners by his sire, a stallion who has had twenty-three Group/Grade 1 scorers and whose best tend to shine in the five-to-ten-furlong range. It remains to be seen how good he is, and it is possible that he may improve when stepped up to a mile or even ten furlongs.

SUMMARY DETAILS
Bred: Orpendale, Chelston & Wynatt
Owned: Mrs John Magnier, Michael Tabor & Derrick Smith
Trained: Aidan O'Brien
Country: Ireland
Race record: 1310-
Career highlights: 2 wins inc Japan Racing Association Tyros Stakes (Gr3), 3rd Marble Hill Stakes (Gr3)

MILITARY STYLE (USA) – 2018 bay colt

War Front (USA)	Danzig (USA)	Northern Dancer
		Pas de Nom
	Starry Dreamer (USA)	Rubiano (USA)
		Lara's Star (USA)
Together Forever (IRE)	Galileo (IRE)	Sadler's Wells (USA)
		Urban Sea (USA)
	Green Room (USA)	Theatrical
		Chain Fern (USA)

MILLISLE (IRE)

Millisle was one of the top two-year-olds in Europe in 2019 but had a less notable season this time around, winning just once from six starts. That was a four-length score in the Group 3 Yeomanstown Stud Ballyogan Stakes over six furlongs on good ground at Naas in late July and it followed her second-place finish to Art Power in the Group 3 Coolmore Sioux Nation Lacken Stakes over the same course and distance eighteen days before. These were the only times she made the frame in 2020. She was seventh behind Love in the Group 1 Qipco 1000 Guineas on her seasonal reappearance in early June, finished a six-length sixth to Golden Horde in the Group 1 Commonwealth Cup at Royal Ascot, and was then unplaced in blacktype sprints at the Curragh and Newmarket in August and October respectively.

Her pedigree and juvenile record were examined in detail in *European Group 1 Winners of 2019*, so a brief recap is sufficient this time. She is among fourteen stakes winners for Coolmore Stud's reverse-shuttler Starspangledbanner (by Choisir), a star sprinter-miler who has overcome the fertility problems he had in his early years at stud. The tally includes his first-crop son The Wow Signal, who won the Group 1 Prix Morny and Group 2 Coventry Stakes but died young at stud, and his latest juveniles feature the Group 1-placed Group 2 winner Aloha Star and listed scorer Dickiedooda.

Millisle, the twelfth foal of Green Castle (by Indian Ridge), has a string of winning siblings of whom three earned minor blacktype. Her dam is out of listed scorer and Group 1 Irish Oaks third Green Lucia (by Green Dancer), a mare whose siblings featured the runaway dual classic star Old Vic (by Sadler's Wells). The Group 1 Irish Derby and Group 1 Prix du Jockey Club standout sired pattern winners from his early flat-bred crops but later made his name as one of the premier sources of staying chasers.

Millisle appears to have inherited the speed of her sire and maternal grandsire rather than any of the miler or stamina influences on either side of the family. That would suggest that the stallions to whom she is sent during her stud career could determine her progeny's best racing distance; those who pass on speed will likely yield a sprinter, while those who pass on stamina could get a miler that stays ten furlongs. Her final track record stands at four wins and three seconds from eleven starts and with total earnings of over £245,000.

SUMMARY DETAILS
Bred: Stonethorn Stud Farms Ltd
Owned: Stonethorn Stud Farms Ltd
Trained: Jessica Harrington
Country: Ireland
Race record: 12121-002100-
Career highlights: 4 wins inc Juddmonte Cheveley Park Stakes (Gr1), Yeomanstown Stud Ballyogan Stakes (Gr3), Ryan Cleaning Event Specialist Curragh Stakes (L), 2nd Coolmore Sioux Nation Lacken Stakes (Gr3), Shadwell Dick Poole Fillies' Stakes (Gr3)

MILLISLE (IRE) – 2017 chestnut filly

Starspangledbanner (AUS)	Choisir (AUS)	Danehill Dancer (IRE)
		Great Selection (AUS)
	Gold Anthem (AUS)	Made of Gold (USA)
		National Song (AUS)
Green Castle (IRE)	Indian Ridge	Ahonoora
		Hillbrow
	Green Lucia	Green Dancer (USA)
		Cockade

MINAUN (IRE)

Henry de Bromhead is well known as being one of the top National Hunt trainers, so it was a mild surprise to see him send out a pattern-winning two-year-old. Minaun is an €8,000 graduate of the Goffs Sportsman's Yearling Sale, despite being a daughter of Zoffany (by Dansili) and out of a famously related Green Desert (by Danzig) mare, and the value of this late February-born bay soared after her second start. She was a one-and-a-half-length runner-up to Oodnadatta in a seven-furlong fillies' maiden at Leopardstown on her debut in late June and then beat Artician and Military Style by a neck and three-quarters of a length to take the Group 3 Marble Hill Stakes over six furlongs at Cork. The ground was good on both occasions and she was not seen out again.

Her late Coolmore Stud-based sire has the Group 1 winners Albigna, Thunder Moon and Ventura Storm among an overall tally of thirty-eight stakes winners, so far, and she is the most notable of five winners out of Bee Eater, a stakes-placed four-time six-furlong winner in a six-race career in England. The mare's half-brother Expedition (by Oasis Dream) was third in the Group 3 Round Tower Stakes as a Ballydoyle two-year-old in 2013, whereas her winning half-sister Swift Action (by Invincible Spirit) is the dam of last year's Group 3 Prix d'Aumale winner and Group 2 Prix du Calvados third King's Harlequin (by Camelot). The Group 1 Moyglare Stud Stakes third and four-time sprint winner Littlefeather (by Indian Ridge) is the grandam of Minaun and that makes the brilliant Marwell (by Habitat) her third dam.

That Timeform 133-rated multiple Group 1 star (July Cup, Prix de l'Abbaye de Longchamp, King's Stand Stakes, Cheveley Park Stakes) finished a non-staying fourth in the 1000 Guineas and was the dam of the Group 1 winners Marling (by Lomond) and Caerwent (by Caerleon). The latter, who was trained by Vincent O'Brien, achieved the feat in the National Stakes at the Curragh, was runner-up in both the Group 1 Irish 2000 Guineas and Group 1 Prix de l'Abbaye de Longchamp, but had only minor success as a stallion. Marling, on the other hand, was a Timeform 124-rated and Geoff Wragg-trained four-time top-level star whose tally included the Irish 1,000 Guineas at the Curragh and that unforgettable battle with Selkirk in the Sussex Stakes at Goodwood. Mugharreb (by Gone West), a pattern-placed sprint stakes winner, was the best of her offspring on the track.

Minaun has the pedigree to be a sprinter or miler and eventually to become a broodmare of note. It will be fascinating to see how she turns out. Noel Meade bought her now two-year-old half-brother Beescatty (by El Kabeir) for €29,000 at the Goffs Autumn Online Yearling Sale in November. However, she has been exported to North America and, at the time of writing, is in training in Florida.

SUMMARY DETAILS

Bred: Sir E J Loder
Owned: Stephen E McCarthy
Trained: Henry de Bromhead
Country: Ireland
Race record: 21-
Career highlights: 1 win viz Marble Hill Stakes (Gr3)

MINAUN (IRE) – 2018 bay filly

Zoffany (IRE)	Dansili (GB)	Danehill (USA)
		Hasili (IRE)
	Tyranny (GB)	Machiavellian (USA)
		Dust Dancer (GB)
Bee Eater (IRE)	Green Desert (USA)	Danzig (USA)
		Foreign Courier (USA)
	Littlefeather (IRE)	Indian Ridge
		Marwell

MINZAAL (IRE)

Minzaal showed himself to be a leading juvenile sprinter with the potential to become a Group 1 Commonwealth Cup contender at three, winning two of his four starts and being placed in one. His sole time out of the frame was his debut fourth at Ascot in late July. He won a novice race by almost four lengths at Salisbury two weeks later, caught the eye with a two-length defeat of Devilwala in the Group 2 Al Basti Equiworld Dubai Gimcrack Stakes at York and then finished third in the Group 1 Juddmonte Middle Park Stakes at Newmarket, beaten by margins of half a length and two and a quarter lengths by Supremacy and Lucky Vega. Tactical was three-quarters of a length behind in fourth.

The Owen Burrows-trained colt was bred by Ringfort Stud, also the breeders of 2020's juvenile Group 2 winners Miss Amulet and Ubettabelieveit. They sold him for 85,000 guineas at the Tattersalls December Foal Sale, and he is also a 140,000-guinea graduate of Tattersalls' Book 2 Sale. His dam, Pardoven (by Clodovil), is an unraced half-sister to four blacktype-placed horses and out of the Listed Oaks Trial Stakes third Dancing Prize (by Sadler's Wells), a mare whose relations include the Group 1-placed trio Polar Bear (by Polar Falcon), Dance To The Top (by Sadler's Wells) and Bankable (by Medicean). The first-named won listed contests at York and Flemington and was runner-up in the Group 1 Underwood Stakes. The other pair are mother and son, the former having finished second in the Group 1 Fillies' Mile and the latter a Group 2 Al Fahidi Fort winner who was runner-up in the Group 1 Dubai Duty Free Stakes, both at Meydan.

Aim For The Top (by Irish River), the third dam of Minzaal, was a pattern placed stakes winner at two plus a listed scorer in England and Group 3 winner in Italy at three. In addition to being a half-sister to 1992's Group 2 Gimcrack Stakes winner and Group 1 Prix de la Salamandre third Splendent (by Shadeed), she comes from a prolific blacktype family whose success goes back over many generations. Those notable relations include the July Cup and Champion Stakes star and classic sire Honeyway (by Fairway), who was a half-brother to Aim For The Top's talented third dam, Run Honey (by Hyperion). The connection of those horses to Minzaal is, of course, so remote as to have no bearing on the horse he is and his prospects for the future.

Minzaal represents the first crop of juvenile Group 2 scorer and Tally-Ho Stud stallion Mehmas (by Acclamation), a horse who had more runners as a freshman sire in 2020 than similarly credentialed stallions of just a few decades ago would have had from two or three crops combined. That enabled him to sire a large number of winners and accumulate a large number of races won, with five stakes winners, including one over a mile in California on New Year's Eve, and seven others who were blacktype-placed. That is a promising start. He will likely continue to supply stakes and pattern winners in the coming years—Going Global became number six for him when winning a Grade 3 sprint at Santa Anita shortly before this book went to print—and the Group 1 Middle Park Stakes and Group 2 Richmond Stakes star Supremacy is unlikely to remain his only top-level winner for long.

Minzaal could achieve the feat if he lives up to his potential and depending on what he has inherited from the distaff side of his family, there is a chance that this likely sprint prospect could be effective at seven furlongs and a mile.

SUMMARY DETAILS
Bred: Ringfort Stud
Owned: Hamdan Al Maktoum
Trained: Owen Burrows
Country: England
Race record: 4113-
Career highlights: 2 wins inc Al Basti Equiworld Dubai Gimcrack Stakes (Gr2), 3rd Juddmonte Middle Park Stakes (Gr1)

MINZAAL (IRE) – 2018 bay colt

Mehmas (IRE)	Acclamation (GB)	Royal Applause (GB)
		Princess Athena
	Lucina (GB)	Machiavellian (USA)
		Lunda (IRE)
Pardoven (IRE)	Clodovil (IRE)	Danehill (USA)
		Clodora (FR)
	Dancing Prize (IRE)	Sadler's Wells (USA)
		Aim For The Top (USA)

MISS AMULET (IRE)

A horse who sells for as little as €1,000 as a foal rarely amounts to much as a racehorse. Miss Amulet fetched that price at the 2018 Goffs November Foal Sale, changed hands for £7,500 at the following September's Tattersalls Ascot Yearling Sale, and joined the Ken Condon stable in Ireland. She is now worth considerably more and no doubt yielded a substantial profit for her connections when sold privately to Doreen Tabor after winning the Group 2 Sky Bet Lowther Stakes at York in August. The filly remained in the same yard, ran twice in her new colours and picked up a pair of top-level placings. She was a half-length runner-up to Alcohol Free in the Group 1 Juddmonte Cheveley Park Stakes at Newmarket in late September and finished a two-and-three-quarter-length third to Aunt Pearl in the Grade 1 Breeders' Cup Juvenile Fillies Turf over a mile at Keeneland in early November, just a neck behind the Irish-trained runner-up Mother Earth but two lengths in front of Group 1 Prix Morny and Group 2 Queen Mary Stakes star Campanelle. Barely noticed in her earliest public appearances, this grey filly now turns heads, has earned almost £200,000 in prize money and is a potential classic contender for 2021.

She was seventh and fourth on her first two starts but got off the mark with a five-length score over five furlongs at Cork in early July and was runner-up over the same trip at Down Royal before springing a surprise in the Listed Arqana Irish EBF Marwell Stakes at Naas. That came just seventeen days before her one-length defeat of Sacred at York and was the last time she has run over the minimum trip. She holds entries in the Group 1 Tattersalls Irish 1,000 Guineas and Group 1 Emirates Poule d'Essai des Pouliches (French 1000 Guineas), and should she make the frame in either of those races or in another Group 1 classic, she would not be the first in her family to achieve the feat.

Miss Amulet was bred by Ringfort Stud, also the breeders of 2020's Group 1-placed juvenile Group 2 scorers Minzaal and Ubettabelieveit. She is out of Shena's Dream (by Oasis Dream), a Kilcarn Stud-bred four-time winner who had two winners from her first two foals but changed hands for only 1,200 guineas at

2019's Tattersalls December Mare Sale. The mare had been offered in foal to Haatef (by Danzig), had a filly a few months later and was returned to the 2020 edition of the December Mare Sale without a new covering. Her daughter's success, however, saw her price soar to 280,000 guineas, a remarkable profit.

Shena's Dream has six winning siblings and her dam, the one-time scorer Sallanches (by Gone West), is a half-sister to nine, four of whom won at pattern level. Mill Native (by Exclusive Native) was the standout performer among them, taking the Grade 1 Arlington Million plus two French Group 3s and a trio of listed races. His half-brother French Stress (by Sham) was a triple pattern-winning miler who was placed in the Group 1 Poule d'Essai des Poulains (French 2000 Guineas), Group 1 Prix Jacques le Marois and Group 1 Prix d'Ispahan. Their dam was the stakes-placed winner Stresa (by Mill Reef), daughter of the Falmouth Stakes winner Ileana (by Abernant) and granddaughter of Romantica (by Never Say Die), a Princess Royal Stakes and Galtres Stakes winner from the family of Prix Lupin and Grand Criterium scorer and successful Claiborne Farm stallion Ambiorix (by Tourbillon).

It is, of course, the most recent generations of the pedigree that have the greatest impact on a current horse, and those indicate that Miss Amulet could be a high-class miler in the making. Her sire, a Group 2 Flying Childers Stakes winner who retired as a two-year-old, spent five seasons at Tally-Ho Stud but was in residence in Australia when secured by Rancho San Miguel in California where he is now in his second season. He has only had nine stakes winners to date and thirteen others who have been blacktype-placed, but Sir Prancealot (by Tamayuz) is the sire of the Grade 1 American Oaks winner Lady Prancealot, the multiple Grade 1-placed multiple Grade 2 scorers Beau Recall and Madam Dancealot, four-time English seven-furlong Group 2 winner Sir Dancealot, and now Miss Amulet. His fee for 2021 is advertised as being $15,000.

Miss Amulet's now two-year-old half-sister, also grey, has been named Between The Sheets (by El Kabeir) and the 45,000-guinea Tattersalls Ascot Yearling Sale graduate is in training with Michael Bell, due to race in the well-known yellow and blue colours of

Christopher Wright. Their younger Haatef half-sister was born in Italy and has already been named Contagion.

SUMMARY DETAILS
Bred: Ringfort Stud
Owned: Doreen Tabor
Trained: Ken Condon
Country: Ireland
Race record: 04121123-
Career highlights: 3 wins inc Sky Bet Lowther Stakes (Gr2), Arqana Irish EBF Marwell Stakes (L), 2nd Juddmonte Cheveley Park Stakes (Gr1), 3rd Breeders' Cup Juvenile Fillies Turf (Gr1)

MISS AMULET (IRE) – 2018 grey filly

Sir Prancealot (IRE)	Tamayuz (USA)	Nayef (USA)
		Al Ishq (FR)
	Mona Em (IRE)	Catrail (USA)
		Moy Water (IRE)
Shena's Dream (IRE)	Oasis Dream (GB)	Green Desert (USA)
		Hope (IRE)
	Sallanches (USA)	Gone West (USA)
		Stresa (IRE)

MOLATHAM (GB)

It is somewhat surprising, given the start he has made to his stallion career, that Kildangan Stud's classic-winning miler Night of Thunder (by Dubawi) is awaiting his first Group 1 winner. He has had fifteen stakes winners from his first two crops in Europe plus four more in Australia, and an additional eleven horses who have been placed at least once in blacktype company. This a promising beginning to what could be a significant career. Perhaps the elusive top-level wins will start to come in 2021.

Molatham is among his sire's notable representatives. He beat the sadly ill-fated Wichita in a listed contest at Doncaster as a two-year-old and kicked off his three-year-old campaign with a half-length defeat of Monarch of Egypt in the Group 3 Jersey Stakes at Royal Ascot. The ground was soft that day, as it was when he was a well-beaten fourth in the Group 3 Dubai Autumn Stakes on his final start at two and when beaten by even farther in the Group 1 Queen Elizabeth II Stakes at Ascot twelve months later. Perhaps the problem was the distance: both races are over a mile. His other two runs in 2020 were over seven furlongs on good ground: a fifth-place finish to Pinatubo in the Group 1 Prix Jean Prat at Deauville and then a two-length third to Wichita and One Master in the Group 2 bet365 Park Stakes.

The colt is bred to achieve anything on the track and, if he earns the opportunity, at stud. His third dam is the dual French classic winner East of The Moon (by Private Account), her star sibling is the multiple Group 1 star and influential stallion Kingmambo (by Mr Prospector) and their dam is the brilliant miler Miesque (by Nureyev). What's more closely related to him may the key to him distance-wise. His half-sister Perfection (by Dutch Art) got her listed wins over six furlongs at Pontefract and Newmarket but was a neck runner-up to Billesdon Brook in the Group 3 Oak Tree Stakes at Goodwood, a head runner-up to Pretty Baby in the Group 3 Chartwell Fillies' Stakes at Lingfield and a one-length second to Surrounding in the Group 3 Brownstown Stakes at Fairyhouse, all over seven furlongs.

Their dam Cantal (by Pivotal), also bred by Cheveley Park Stud, got her sole win and two of her three placings over seven furlongs—the other one was over a mile at Goodwood—and she is a half-sister to Evasive (by Elusive Quality). He won his maiden and the Group 3 Horris Hill Stakes over seven, was fourth to Mastercraftsman in the Group 1 St James's Palace Stakes before becoming a blacktype sire in France; he now stands in Norway. Their half-brother Autocratic (by Dubawi) was campaigned as a middle-distance horse in England and Australia and won a pair of pattern races over ten furlongs, the latter under the name Captain Cook. Canda (by Storm Cat), the grandam of Molatham, was a stakes-placed sprinter in France and half-sister to the pattern-winning sprinter Moon Driver (by Mr Prospector), but also to Helike (by Rahy), a listed scorer who followed his dam in winning at up to ten and a half furlongs.

Molatham may do well over a mile as a four-year-old, or perhaps he will prove to be a seven-furlong specialist. He clearly has ability and he remains an interesting prospect. His now two-year-old half-brother, an early May-foaled first-crop son of Ulysses (by Galileo), has been named Gastronomy.

SUMMARY DETAILS
Bred: Cheveley Park Stud
Owned: Hamdan Al Maktoum
Trained: Roger Varian
Country: England
Race record: 2114-1030-
Career highlights: 3 wins inc Jersey Stakes (Gr3), Weatherbys Global Stallions App Flying Scotsman Stakes (L), 3rd bet365 Park Stakes (Gr2)

MOLATHAM (GB) – 2017 chestnut colt

Night of Thunder (IRE)	Dubawi (IRE)	Dubai Millennium (GB)
		Zomaradah (GB)
	Forest Storm (GB)	Galileo (IRE)
		Quiet Storm (IRE)
Cantal (GB)	Pivotal (GB)	Polar Falcon (USA)
		Fearless Revival
	Canda (USA)	Storm Cat (USA)
		East of The Moon (USA)

MOTHER EARTH (IRE)

Mother Earth was involved in one of the most bizarre incidents of 2020, a year that was strange in so many ways. It appeared that she had finished down the field in the Group 1 bet365 Fillies' Mile at Newmarket in early October, disappointing in eighth place as her 50/1 stablemate Snowfall ran the race of her life to finish third. But then an eagle-eyed viewer spotted a problem and raised the alarm.

With Covid-19 restrictions in place everywhere, the Aidan O'Brien stable had a small team based in England so those horses and staff could move around more easily, and so it was not he who saddled the two runners. Someone inadvertently got the fillies mixed up, putting the wrong number cloths on. This led to the wrong jockeys getting the leg up and the wrong names being called in the race. There was speculation that both fillies would be disqualified, thereby moving Dubai Fountain up a spot and into Group 1 placing. However, the enquiry found that in what was a level-weights race, no advantage had been gained and there was nothing in the rules that would lead to the pair being thrown out. Instead, the correct names were listed in the placings in which they had actually finished: Mother Earth was third and Snowfall eighth. Pretty Gorgeous had won the race by half a length from Indigo Girl, with the first of the Ballydoyle fillies a length and a half back in third, a neck in front of Dubai Fountain.

Mother Earth had started her season over an extended five furlongs at Navan in June, chasing home Frenetic. She was then a six-and-a-quarter-length third to Dandalla in the Group 3 Albany Stakes at Royal Ascot before scoring a four-length victory in the Group 3 Coolmore Stud Irish EBF Fillies' Sprint Stakes at Naas, the only race she has won to date. She was a two-length third to Aloha Star in the Group 2 Airlie Stud Stakes at the Curragh two weeks later and then stepped up to seven furlongs, first finishing third in the Group 2 A.R.M. Holding Debutante Stakes on soft ground at the Curragh, beaten two and a half lengths and the same by Pretty Gorgeous and Shale, staying on well from behind. However, then she tried to make all in the Group 1 Moyglare Stud Stakes and it was the only time she failed to make the frame. She lost her lead a quarter of a mile from home and weakening soon afterwards, eventually finished eleventh as Shale and Pretty Gorgeous took the top two placings.

Her final start was arguably her best performance and the one that highlighted her potential as a high-class mile-to-ten-furlong filly in 2021. She never looked like catching the front-running two-and-a-half-length winner Aunt Pearl in the Grade 1 Breeders' Cup Juvenile Fillies Turf over the mile at Keeneland in early November, but she stayed on strongly, beat Miss Amulet by a neck for second, with Campanelle another two lengths back in third.

The €150,000 Goffs Orby Sale graduate was bred by Grenane House Stud and her siblings include Night Colours (by Night of Thunder) who won the Group 2 Premio Dormello over a mile on heavy ground at San Siro at the end of her two-year-old campaign. They are out of the Group 3-placed, nine-furlong listed scorer Many Colours (by Green Desert), their fourth dam is the stakes-winning sprinter Sandhurst Goddess (by Sandhurst Prince), and so their third dam, Star Profile (by Sadler's Wells), is a half-sister to Lady Alexander (by Night Shift). That filly won the Group 3 Anglesey Stakes and Group 3 Molecomb Stakes as a two-year-old and her star daughter was the Group 2 Queen Mary Stakes winner Anthem Alexander (by Starspangledbanner), who was placed in the Group 1 Commonwealth Cup and Group 1 Cheveley Park Stakes. But her standout son is the sprinter and stallion Dandy Man (by Mozart).

That Ballyhane Stud veteran won the Group 3 Palace House Stakes and a trio of listed races, he was placed in the Group 1 Nunthorpe Stakes, Group 2 King's Stand Stakes and a string of other blacktype races, and he is among the busiest sires in Ireland. He covered over 200 mares in 2019, 159 in 2020, his yearlings (excluding vendor buy-backs) made up to 75,000 guineas last year and his standout auction foal, a half-brother to One Voice (by Poet's Voice), made 190,000 guineas in Newmarket at the end of November. He gets a lot of prolific winners and horses rated ninety and upwards, his latest juveniles included Dandalla and Happy Romance (who are featured elsewhere in this volume) and his trio of top-level winners among an overall total of seventeen stakes winners includes River Boyne, the US miler now starting his stallion career at Tara Stud in Ireland.

Mother Earth, who is inbred 4x3 to Danzig (by Northern Dancer), is among thirty-eight stakes winners by Coolmore Stud's late Zoffany (by Dansili). He has had three Group 1 winners so far, including 2020 juvenile Thunder Moon, and his latest batch of two-year-olds to race also included the Group 3 Marble Hill Stakes winner Minaun, who is reviewed elsewhere in this volume. Sadly, the stallion died due to liver failure at the start of January, aged just 13. His daughter holds entries in the Group 1 Tattersalls Irish 1,000 Guineas, Group 1 Emirates Poule d'Essai des Pouliches (French 1000 Guineas), Group 1 Saxon Warrior Coolmore Prix Saint-Alary, Group 1 Prix de Diane Longines (French Oaks) and Group 1 Juddmonte Irish Oaks, so she is clearly held in high regard. Ten furlongs looks likely to be within her range although given the amount of speed in the distaff side of her family, it is possible that twelve furlongs may be a bit too far.

SUMMARY DETAILS

Bred: Grenane House Stud
Owned: Derrick Smith, Mrs John Magnier & Michael Tabor
Trained: Aidan O'Brien
Country: Ireland
Race record: 23133032-
Career highlights: 1 win inc Coolmore Stud Irish EBF Fillies' Sprint Stakes (Gr3), 2nd Breeders' Cup Juvenile Fillies Turf (Gr1), 3rd bet365 Fillies' Mile (Gr1), A.R.M. Holding Debutante Stakes (Gr2), Airlie Stud Stakes (Gr2), Albany Stakes (Gr3)

MOTHER EARTH (IRE) – 2018 bay filly

Zoffany (IRE)	Dansili (GB)	Danehill (USA)
		Hasili (IRE)
	Tyranny (GB)	Machiavellian (USA)
		Dust Dancer (GB)
Many Colours (GB)	Green Desert (USA)	Danzig (USA)
		Foreign Courier (USA)
	First of Many (GB)	Darshaan
		Star Profile (IRE)

MUJBAR (GB)

Muhaarar has made a slower-than-expected start to his stallion career, but that is not uncommon with some of the sons of Oasis Dream (by Green Desert) and there is plenty of time for him to turn it around and notch up the string of stakes and pattern winners one would hope to see. Nine of his progeny had earned blacktype by the end of 2020 but only two of those have won at that level, one from his first crop and one from his second. The former is the French filly Paix, who won the Group 3 Prix de Lutece in early September having been a pattern-placed stakes winner before that. She appears to have inherited the middle-distance stamina of the distaff side of her family rather than her sire's speed. Indeed, there is some evidence that Muhaarar may be passing on more stamina than expected, possibly the influence of his dam's sire, Linamix (by Mendez), and so do not be surprised if he becomes more of a classic-type sire than a sprint one.

Mujbar represents his second crop. The Shadwell homebred was a disappointing favourite on his debut over six furlongs at Newbury in July but looked potentially pattern class next time, powering home seven lengths clear of his closest pursuer in a seven-furlong novice contest on soft ground on the July course at Newmarket. That made his first foray into that level all the more disappointing. He was keen in the early stages of the Group 2 bet365 Champagne Stakes at Doncaster in September, came under pressure a quarter of a mile from home and weakened. He finished two and a half lengths and neck in front of the useful pair Devious Company and Saint Lawrence, but seven and a half lengths adrift of third-placed State of Rest and runner-up Albasheer, with Chindit another length in front of those two.

The ground was good that day but heavy at Newbury the following month when Mujbar beat eleven rivals to take the Group 3 Molson Coors Beverage Company Stakes—registered as the Horris Hill Stakes—over seven furlongs. It looked like hard work for all of them in the conditions, but Mujbar took over the lead from the front-running Percy's Lad inside the final furlong and stayed on well to beat that colt by a length. Saint Lawrence and Nastase were a length and a half and a nose back in third and fourth.

Mujbar's half-brother Eqtidaar (by Invincible Spirit) won the Group 1 Commonwealth Cup and covered seventy-four mares at Nunnery Stud in 2020, his first year at stud, whereas Hathiq (by Exceed And Excel) carried high weights to victory in five-furlong handicaps at the Curragh and Tipperary in 2019. The colt is by a sprint champion and out of a daughter of noted speed influence Acclamation (by Royal Applause) but neither his juvenile form nor the way he moves suggests that this is the route he will take. Massaat (by Teofilo), the eldest of his siblings, won the Group 2 Hungerford Stakes over seven furlongs and was placed in the Group 1 2000 Guineas, Group 1 Prix du Moulin de Longchamp, Group 1 Dewhurst Stakes and Group 2 Challenge Stakes before taking up stallion duties at Mickey Stud. There are sixty-eight registered foals in his first crop and his second will come from the book of eighty-three mares he covered in 2020.

Mujbar may be a miler too, but it is also possible that he will stay a bit further. His dam, Madany, is a winning daughter of one-time scorer Belle de Cadix, a mare by the Irish Derby winner and stamina influence Law Society (by Alleged). She, in turn, is out of an unraced mare called Gourgandine (by Auction Ring) and related to a string of big-race winners in India, one a classic-winning mile champion and another a champion stayer. Her own produce record and that of her daughters also shows a mixture of speed and stamina. One daughter, Dolled Up (by Whipper), won the Group 3 Prix du Bois and was placed in both the Group 2 Prix Robert Papin and Group 2 Criterium de Maisons-Laffitte. That one's multiple stakes-winning half-sister Zeiting (by Zieten), on the other hand, is the dam of the Group 2-winning miler Combat Zone (by Refuse To Bend), Group 3 Geoffrey Freer Stakes scorer Royal Empire (by Teofilo) and that one's Group 3 Strensall Stakes-winning full brother Scottish who was runner-up in the Group 1 Caulfield Cup. Their pattern-placed half-sister Bikini Babe (by Montjeu) has done her part by coming up with 2020's juvenile seven-furlong Group 3 scorer La Barrosa (by Lope de Vega), whereas another half-sister, Zut Alors (by Pivotal), is the pattern-placed dam of Group 1 Poule d'Essai des Pouliches (French 1000 Guineas) heroine Precieuse (by Tamayuz).

If you go back the fourth generation of the pedigree then you will find the middle-distance Group 1-placed Group 2 scorer Fortune's Wheel (by Law Society), his classic-placed Group 2-winning half-sister Libertine (by Hello Gorgeous), the juvenile mile Group 1-placed pattern winner Harmless Albatross (by Pas de Seul), Group 2-placed and stakes-winning stayer Kahtan (by Nashwan) as well as the Group 1-placed Group 2 scorers Volochine (by Soviet Star) and Red Tea (by Sakhee), plus the Group 2 Lowther Stakes winner Infamous Angel (by Exceed And Excel). Those horses are between distantly to remotely connected to Mujbar.

Mujbar may be capable of making the frame in an early-season seven-furlong classic trial, but the 102-rated colt looks likely to prove best when stepped up another one to three furlongs. He holds an entry in the Group 1 Emirates Poule d'Essai des Poulains (French 2000 Guineas).

SUMMARY DETAILS
Bred: Shadwell Estate Company Ltd
Owned: Hamdan Al Maktoum
Trained: Charles Hills
Country: England
Race record: 0141-
Career highlights: 2 wins inc Molson Coors Beverage Company Stakes (registered as the Horris Hill Stakes) (Gr3)

MUJBAR (GB) – 2018 bay colt

Muhaarar (GB)	Oasis Dream (GB)	Green Desert (USA)
		Hope (IRE)
	Tahrir (IRE)	Linamix (FR)
		Miss Sacha (IRE)
Madany (IRE)	Acclamation (GB)	Royal Applause (GB)
		Princess Athena
	Belle de Cadix (IRE)	Law Society (USA)
		Gourgandine

NANDO PARRADO (GB)

The compressed start to the 2020 season made it likely that we might see some surprising results in early pattern races, but it's fair to say that nothing like the odds at which Nando Parrado won the Group 2 Coventry Stakes would have been imagined. The colt had finished a five-length fifth in a six-furlong Newmarket maiden on his debut sixteen days before but shocked the Ascot viewers with his one-length defeat of Qaader, paying odds of 150/1. It is a record for the Royal meeting. Horses who figure at those types of odds frequently fail to reproduce that type of form—500/1 Derby runner-up Terimon, a subsequent Group 1 scorer, was a notable exception—but this Clive Cox-trained colt went on to be a Group 1 runner-up in his only two subsequent outings.

The ground was good at Ascot but soft at Deauville two months later when he chased home the two-length winner Campanelle in the Darley Prix Morny. She had won the Group 2 Queen Mary Stakes on her previous start and was fourth in the Grade 1 Breeders' Cup Juvenile Fillies Turf at Keeneland on the only time she has been seen in action since. The underfoot conditions were heavy at ParisLongchamp on the first weekend of October, so the seven furlongs of the Group 1 Qatar Prix Jean-Luc Lagardere (Grand Criterium) would put an increased emphasis on stamina. Nando Parrado kept on in the final furlong to beat the Irish pattern winner Laws of Indices and the French-trained Libertine by three-quarters of a length and a neck but never looked like posing any sort of danger to the winner, Sealiway, who stormed clear over the final furlong and a half for an eight-length victory.

Nando Parrado, a son of Tally-Ho Stud's notably successful stallion Kodiac (by Danehill)—he had a particularly good year with his two-year-olds in 2020—is a 165,000-guinea graduate of the Tattersalls December Foal Sale, which speaks volumes for his physique and the amount of blacktype in his family. He has a pair of Irish-born half-brothers who have been blacktype placed and notched up fourteen wins between them, but the rest of the family's blacktype is with its Argentine-breds. His Grade 1-placed, Grade 3-winning dam Chibola (by Roy) is a full sister to the juvenile Grade 1 sprint winner Chollo and half-sister to a pair of listed-race winners, and she is out of Choice (by Confidential Talk), a winning half-sister to the Argentine champion and middle-distance classic star Cheyenne (by Pepenador). Two of their siblings have produced Grade 1 horses at stud, one of those horses having also won at that level: El Charleta (by Missionary).

Muntadab (by Invincible Spirit), the more prolific of Nando Parrado's siblings, is a seven-furlong specialist who has been a winner at ten furlongs and a stakes-placed winner at a mile; the other one is triple ten-furlong winner Dubai Horizon (by Poet's Voice) who was a one-length runner-up in a fourteen-furlong listed contest at Meydan in January 2020 and third in a Group 3 race over that course and distance a month later. Their dam stayed a mile too, so it is possible that the distance will also be within his range.

He also has two younger siblings who may be worth watching for in the next few seasons. His now two-year-old half-sister has been named Orzo. She is a first-crop daughter of Aclaim (by Acclamation) and was a vendor buy-back at Tattersalls' Book 2 sale but their Showcasing (by Oasis Dream) half-sister was sold for 110,000 guineas at the December Foal Sale at that venue just over six weeks later.

Nando Parrado was entered in the Group 1 Vertem Futurity Trophy Stakes at Doncaster and is in both the Group 1 Tattersalls Irish 2,000 Guineas at the Curragh and Group 1 Emirates Poule d'Essai des Poulains (French 2000 Guineas) at ParisLongchamp, so his connections have also considered his potential to stay a mile. But whether he is a sprinter or a miler or a horse who is effective in both disciplines, the 111-rated colt clearly has plenty of ability. The popularity of his sire, how some of that horse's sons fared as freshmen in 2020, plus the juvenile record of the colt also suggest that, in this era of over-obsession with speed and precocity, there may also be a stallion role ahead for Nando Parrado regardless of how 2021 turns out for him.

SUMMARY DETAILS
Bred: Mrs Anita Wigan
Owned: Marie McCartan

Trained: Clive Cox
Country: England
Race record: 0122-
Career highlights: 1 win inc Coventry Stakes (Gr2), 2nd Qatar Prix Jean-Luc Lagardere - Grand Criterium (Gr1), Darley Prix Morny (Gr1)

NANDO PARRADO (GB) – 2018 bay colt

Kodiac (GB)	Danehill (USA)	Danzig (USA)
		Razyana (USA)
	Rafha	Kris
		Eljazzi
Chibola (ARG)	Roy (USA)	Fappiano (USA)
		Adlibber (USA)
	Choice (ARG)	Confidential Talk (USA)
		Che Constanza (ARG)

NAYEF ROAD (IRE)

Nayef Road is a capable horse who worked his way up from handicaps to become a classic-placed pattern winner at three and, although winning just once at four, he reached a career-best rating of 115 in 2020. He kicked off the year with a three-quarter-length defeat of Mildenberger in the Group 3 Betway Sagaro Stakes over an extended two miles on the Tapeta at Newcastle in early June, chased home runaway winner Stradivarius in the Group 1 Gold Cup on soft ground at Ascot and was only beaten a length by that champion next time, in the Group 1 Al Shaqab Goodwood Cup Stakes over two miles. He had tried to make all that day, was joined by the Irish Derby winner Santiago a quarter of a mile from home but had no extra to give when the star chestnut moved past him near the finish. Santiago finished a length and a quarter back in third, three lengths in front of Eagles By Day.

His final result of the year was a shade disappointing: third in the Group 2 Weatherbys Hamilton Lonsdale Cup Stakes over the extended two miles at York. The ground was good, as it had been at Goodwood. The colt reared in the stalls and came out awkwardly, then raced keenly against the rail, rapidly making up several placings. He later moved off the rail but was still keen, made a move forward with half a mile to go, soon hit the front, now towards the centre of the track, with Enbihaar chasing on his outside. He started tiring a little a furlong out, hardly surprising given how he'd run throughout the race, and as the mare went on to win, Stratum also stayed on past him in the closing stages. The margins were three-quarters of a length and the same, with Dashing Willoughby another length back in fourth, a further three and a half lengths clear of Eagles By Day. It was his last run.

The chestnut is a 100,000-guinea Tattersalls Book 1 graduate out of the pattern-placed six- and seven-furlong listed scorer Rose Bonheur (by Danehill Dancer) and his siblings include Middle East (by Frankel), a dual French mile winner whose blacktype came from a third-place finish in a seven-furlong listed contest at Dusseldorf. His grandam, Red Feather (by Marju), won her maiden by ten lengths over seven furlongs at Limerick as a two-year-old and was runner-up in the Group 1 Moyglare Stud Stakes before going on to win a mile Group 3 contest at the Curragh the following summer, a contrast to her half-brother Frankies Dream (by Grand Lodge) who was pattern-placed at twelve furlongs and stayed two miles. This is a branch of the family of the top-level winners Kitwood (by Nureyev), Miss Oceana (by Alydar) and Sabin (by Lyphard), among others of note.

Nayef Road is a son of the prolific champion sire Galileo (by Sadler's Wells) and he has notched up five wins and eight places from nineteen starts, amassing over £420,000 in prize money. It would not be a surprise to see him find a home as a National Hunt stallion somewhere, but first there are likely to be more good prizes to be won with him. Given he won the Group 3 Gordon Stakes and was third in the Group 1 St Leger at three, and that he can run keenly, it would be interesting to see him run over fourteen furlongs, in races such as the Group 2 Yorkshire Cup and Group 1 Irish St Leger.

SUMMARY DETAILS
Bred: B V Sangster
Owned: Mohamed Obaida
Trained: Mark Johnston
Country: England
Race record: 201103-100321030-1223-
Career highlights: 5 wins inc Betway Sagaro Stakes (Gr3), Qatar Gordon Stakes (Gr3), 2nd Gold Cup (Gr1), Al Shaqab Goodwood Cup Stakes (Gr1), Bahrain Trophy Stakes (Gr3), 3rd William Hill St Leger Stakes (Gr1), Weatherbys Hamilton Lonsdale Cup Stakes (Gr2), Queen's Vase (Gr2)

NAYEF ROAD (IRE) – 2016 chestnut colt

Galileo (IRE)	Sadler's Wells (USA)	Northern Dancer
		Fairy Bridge (USA)
	Urban Sea (USA)	Miswaki (USA)
		Allegretta
Rose Bonheur (GB)	Danehill Dancer (IRE)	Danehill (USA)
		Mira Adonde (USA)
	Red Feather (IRE)	Marju (IRE)
		Galyph (USA)

NEW MANDATE (IRE)

New Bay (by Dubawi), an Arc-placed classic star in France, stands at Ballylinch Stud in Ireland and has made an eye-catching start to his stallion career. He was among the leading freshmen of 2020, a noteworthy achievement given he had been a runner-up in a one-mile contest in November on his only run as a two-year-old. He comes from the family of Beat Hollow (by Sadler's Wells), Oasis Dream (by Green Desert) and Kingman (by Invincible Spirit) and got two pattern winners among his first crop of juveniles.

Saffron Beach is an unbeaten winner of the Group 3 Oh So Sharp Stakes at Newmarket, whereas New Mandate followed his Listed bet365 Flying Scotsman Stakes success over seven furlongs at Doncaster with a three-quarter-length defeat of Ontario in the Group 2 Juddmonte Royal Lodge Stakes over a mile at Newmarket in late September. That one's other win came in a seven-furlong nursery at Sandown in August, which he won by two and a half lengths under nine-stone-eight, but it all went wrong at Keeneland in November and, having been eased in the final quarter mile, he trailed home last of the fourteen runners in the Grade 1 Breeders' Cup Juvenile Turf.

The Royal Lodge has been won by some standout horses in the past, with Frankel, Roaring Lion and the Australian mile Group 1 scorer Best of Days among its recent winners. New Mandate looked full of promise as he added his name to the race's roll of honour—Cobh was third and the subsequent Group 1 winner Gear Up fourth—but he will not have some of the traditional paths open to him this coming season. He was gelded before he ever raced and that rules him out of all of the European Group 1 classics, plus a variety of other races too, but there are still plenty of options open to this €35,000 Arqana Deauville August yearling sale graduate, especially when he turns four.

Although he ran six times as a two-year-old, there are grounds to believe that he may be capable of plenty of improvement. He is an early May foal, is by a horse who excelled as a three-year-old and out of a daughter of the Derby winner Authorized (by Montjeu) who comes from a top family that has produced stars in all age groups. Mishhar, his dam, was only placed but is a half-sister to Puggy (by Mark of Esteem), the stakes-placed dam of the dual French classic star Avenir Certain (by Le Havre). His grandam, Jakarta (by Machiavellian), is a winning half-sister to the dual Group 1-placed multiple middle-distance pattern winner Blue Monday (by Darshaan), whereas third dam Lunda (by Soviet Star) is out of listed winner and Cheshire Oaks third Lucayan Princess (by High Line).

That mare is the one who gave us the multiple middle-distance Group 1 stars Luso (by Salse) and Warrsan (by Caerleon), the Group 2 Gallinule Stakes winner and Group 1 St James's Palace Stakes second Needle Gun (by Sure Blade), and their Group 1 Prix Vermeille-placed, Group 3 Nell Gwyn Stakes-winning half-sister Cloud Castle (by In The Wings). The latter's Group 3-winning daughter Queen's Best (by King's Best) is the dam of 2016's Grade 1 Breeders' Cup Filly & Mare Turf heroine Queen's Trust (by Dansili). This is also the family of the Group 1-placed dual juvenile Group 2 scorer and champion freshman sire Mehmas (by Acclamation), a son of Jakarta's unraced full sister Lucina.

All of this, plus the 2.34 cadence he recorded at Doncaster, suggests that New Mandate could be a high-class prospect at around ten-to-twelve furlongs. There are plenty of opportunities these days for a talented gelding and it is possible that this one could be a prominent player in the middle-distance division for the next few years.

SUMMARY DETAILS
Bred: Mishhar Syndicate
Owned: Marc Chan
Trained: Ralph Beckett
Country: England
Race record: 331110-
Career highlights: 3 wins inc Juddmonte Royal Lodge Stakes (Gr2), bet365 Flying Scotsman Stakes (L)

NEW MANDATE (IRE) – 2018 bay gelding

New Bay (GB)	Dubawi (IRE)	Dubai Millennium (GB)
		Zomaradah (GB)
	Cinnamon Bay (GB)	Zamindar (USA)
		Trellis Bay (GB)
Mishhar (IRE)	Authorized (IRE)	Montjeu (IRE)
		Funsie (FR)
	Jakarta (IRE)	Machiavellian (USA)
		Lunda (IRE)

NEW TREASURE (IRE)

Every season produces some shock results but there seemed to be more of them than usual in 2020. The victory of New Treasure in the Group 3 Heider Family Stables Round Tower Stakes on heavy ground at the Curragh in late August was one of them. He had been unplaced in a seven-furlong maiden at the venue on his only previous start, and so he was returned at odds of 66/1 after beating Teresa Mendosa by half a length.

It wasn't even close to the largest odds on a juvenile pattern winner during the year, but unlike the 150/1 Coventry Stakes shocker Nando Parrado, who was a Group 1 runner-up in his two subsequent starts, New Treasure did not really progress or show himself capable of holding his own in stronger company. You would have hoped that the son of a classic sire would, having won a Group 3 on his second start, have been able to move up to Group 2 or even Group 1 company by the end of the season.

Including the sex allowance for fillies, he was carrying ten pounds more than most of his rivals in the Listed Ballyhane Blenheim Stakes on good ground at Fairyhouse next time out and failed by only a length and a quarter to beat Lady Princess. There was another four-and-a-half-length gap back to the third, Bell I Am. A drop to five furlongs for a listed contest at Dundalk in early October didn't prove an ideal move—he beat only three home in a fourteen-runner contest—but had a clearer run and produced a better effort in the Group 3 Jebel Ali Racecourse and Stables Anglesey Stakes on his final start. That race is run over the unusual distance of six furlongs and sixty-three yards, he again had a penalty for his prior pattern success, and he finished fourth, three and a half lengths behind the winner, A Case of You. The runner-up, Lipizzaner, went on to win a listed contest at Doncaster shortly afterwards.

New Treasure, on the other hand, went to Newmarket where he was sold for 90,000 guineas at the Tattersalls Autumn Horses-in-Training Sale in late October, holding an official handicap mark of 104, and bought by Voute Sales for the Riyadh-based Najd Stud. He was gelded shortly afterwards and he is now in training with John Gosden. It will be interesting if he remains in sprints or steps up in trip, although the latter seems likely.

He was bred by his initial trainer, Jim Bolger, and is out of Maoineach (by Congaree), a mare who won the Group 3 Round Tower Stakes at two and the Group 3 Leopardstown 1000 Guineas Trial Stakes over seven furlongs at three for the same stable. She disappointed on her only attempt at farther, although that was in Group 1 company and on just her second start, and you would imagine that, on pedigree, her talented son would stay a mile.

Indeed, it would not be a surprise to see him prove effective at nine or even ten furlongs. He is a son of juvenile star and Derby hero New Approach (by Galileo), who is a proven classic sire, and out of a smart seven-furlong scorer whose siblings include a Grade 2-placed US stakes winner who stayed nine furlongs: Tiz Now Tiz Then (by Tiznow). It is true that Maoineach's five-time winning full sister Givhans Ferry got her blacktype placing over six furlongs, although their 'nephew' Just Right (by Into Mischief) was third in the eight-and-a-half-furlong Listed New York Derby in 2019, and you will find some more notable individuals if you go back further on the page.

The Argentine nine-furlong Grade 2 scorer Norimberga (by Exchange Rate), whose grandam, Troubling (by Storm Cat), is the third dam of New Treasure, is not making any contribution other than being of academic interest, and the fifth dam is too remote to be making an impact on her distant descendant, but it would be remiss not to mention her. That's because she is the four-time nine-furlong US Grade 1 star Dispute (by Danzig) and she also happens to be the third dam of 2020's Group 1 Criterium de Saint-Cloud winner and potential Derby candidate Gear Up (by Teofilo) who, like New Treasure, was bred by Bolger.

SUMMARY DETAILS
Bred: J S Bolger
Owned: Mrs J S Bolger (now HRH Prince Faisal Bin Khaled)
Trained: Jim Bolger (now John Gosden)
Country: Ireland (now England)
Race record: 01204-

Career highlights: 1 win inc Heider Family Stables Round Tower Stakes (Gr3), 2nd Ballyhane Blenheim Stakes (L)

NEW TREASURE (IRE) – 2018 chestnut gelding

New Approach (IRE)	Galileo (IRE)	Sadler's Wells (USA)
		Urban Sea (USA)
	Park Express	Ahonoora
		Matcher
Maoineach (USA)	Congaree (USA)	Arazi (USA)
		Mari's Sheba (USA)
	Trepidation (USA)	Seeking The Gold (USA)
		Troubling (USA)

NICKAJACK CAVE (IRE)

The Group 1-placed miler Kendargent (by Kendor) was not an obvious candidate to become a sire of note, but he has built a strong profile in his native France and is a valuable member of the team at Haras de Colleville. He has not yet got a winner at the highest level but three of his four Group 2 scorers have been placed in that grade, most recently the Group 1 Qipco Champion Stakes runner-up Skalleti, a dual winner of the Group 2 Prix Dollar. He has several sons at stud, including the notably successful 2020 freshman Goken and the talented Jimmy Two Times, that talented sprinter-miler now in his first season in France having spent two years in Germany. Nickajack Cave is also among his sire's dozen pattern winners—the stallion's overall tally of blacktype scorers stands at thirty-three—but like Skalleti and the triple English middle-distance pattern scorer Morando, he is a gelding.

He moved to Australia shortly after his pattern success, now based with the Peter Moody team although as yet unraced, but all of his form in Ireland was as a member of the Ger Lyons stable. He made a winning debut in a ten-furlong Cork maiden in April of his three-year-old year, won a handicap over the same trip at Navan two starts later and was a runner-up at the Curragh before a trio of defeats in stronger company, two of them blacktype contests. The last of those was Listed Martin Molony Stakes over twelve and a half furlongs on heavy ground at Limerick and he finished a two-length third to Dadoozdart. That rival is also now in Australia.

Although finishing a five-length fourth to Numerian in a ten-furlong listed contest at Navan in late March, just before the lockdown, he won his only other two races of 2020. He beat the subsequent Group 1 Melbourne Cup hero Twilight Payment by one and a half lengths at level weights in the Listed Saval Beg Levmoss Stakes over fourteen furlongs in mid-June, the pair finishing well clear of third-placed Falcon Eight. Then he rounded off the European phase of his career with that two-length defeat of Fresnel in the Group 3 Bahrain International Ballyroan Stakes over twelve at the same venue. Both races were on good ground.

The filly had set a steady gallop, she quickened into a slightly larger lead as the field swung into the straight and although keeping on well to the end, Nickajack Cave was a half-length too good at the line. Two and a half lengths covered the entire five-runner field.

The £65,000 Goffs UK Premier Yearling Sale graduate is out of an unraced daughter of an unraced half-sister to the top-class mare Pride (by Peintre Celebre), the Arc-placed winner of the Group 1 Champion Stakes, Group 1 Grand Prix de Saint-Cloud and Group 1 Hong Kong Cup. That champion's star son is One Foot In Heaven (by Fastnet Rock), the Group 1-placed winner of the Group 2 Grand Prix de Chantilly and Group 2 Prix du Conseil de Paris. Pride's Group 1-placed half-sister Fate (by Teofilo) won the Group 3 Prix de Flore, and her siblings also include Specifically (by Sky Classic), the dam of 2006's Group 1 1000 Guineas heroine Speciosa (by Danehill Dancer). They are out of the Listed George Stubbs Stakes winner Specificity (by Alleged), a half-sister to the Derby-placed Group 1 St Leger and Group 1 Irish St Leger star Touching Wood (by Roberto). This is a branch of the family of Test Stakes winner Miss Disco (by Discovery) and her champion and hugely influential son Bold Ruler (by Nasrullah).

Nickajack Cave could be just the sort of horse to do well in Australia and it will be fascinating to see how this new phase of his career turns out. He has been entered in the Group 1 Queen Elizabeth Stakes over ten furlongs at Randwick on April 10th, one of the big-race targets for which his old rival Dadoozdart has also been nominated.

SUMMARY DETAILS
Bred: SCEA Team Hogdala France
Owned: David Spratt, Sean Jones & Mrs Lynne Lyons
Trained: Ger Lyons (now Peter Moody)
Country: Ireland (now Australia)
Race record: -1212003-411-
Career highlights: 4 wins inc Bahrain International Ballyroan Stakes (Gr3), Saval Beg Levmoss Stakes (L), 3rd Martin Molony Stakes (L)

NICKAJACK CAVE (IRE) – 2016 grey gelding

Kendargent (FR)	Kendor (FR)	Kenmare (FR)
		Belle Mecene (FR)
	Pax Bella (FR)	Linamix (FR)
		Palavera (FR)
Could You Be Loved (IRE)	Montjeu (IRE)	Sadler's Wells (USA)
		Floripedes (FR)
	Light My Way (IRE)	Polish Precedent (USA)
		Specificity (USA)

NKOSIKAZI (GB)

Nkosikazi was well placed by her connections to pick up a Group 3 win in 2020, a feat that would have seemed unlikely for much of her career. Unraced at two and a maiden when well-beaten at 100/1 behind Alpha Centauri in the Group 1 Coronation Stakes at Ascot on her third start, the grey won a one-mile handicap easily that summer but finished the year on a handicap mark of eighty-five. She was sold for 30,000 guineas at the Tattersalls December Mare Sale, joined the William Haggas stable and fetched 220,000 guineas when re-offered in Newmarket twelve months later. She had added no wins but four placings from six starts to her record and one of those was third in a listed contest over thirteen furlongs at Lingfield. The well-bred filly had blacktype.

She ran three times as a five-year-old, giving the runner-up twenty-one pounds and a neck beating in a slowly run ten-furlong handicap on good ground at Redcar in mid-June and then, nine days later, the ninety-four-rated grey raised her rating to 102 with victory in the Group 3 Betfair Exchange Hoppings Fillies' Stakes over the same trip on Tapeta at Newcastle. It was a fine ride by Tom Marquand who set a steady gallop on Nkosikazi, was joined just before two out by the favourite, Virgin Snow, battled with that filly for a furlong and then asserted, pulling clear for a two-and-a-half-length win. Look Around was another length and a half back in third and the other two runners were well beaten. Her only other run was in a ten-furlong handicap at Goodwood in late July where she looked awkward from over a quarter of a mile from home and eventually finished a well-beaten sixth.

Nkosikazi, who was bred by David and Trish Brown of Furnace Mill Stud, is a daughter of the mile Group 1 winner and influential stallion Cape Cross (by Green Desert) and a half-sister to Juan Elcano (by Frankel), a triple Group 2-placed chestnut who finished fifth in the 2000 Guineas at Newmarket in June. Her dam, Whatami (by Daylami), was placed once over twelve furlongs from three runs, and is out of Eljazzi's (by Artaius) daughter Wosaita (by Generous). The young grey is somewhat closely related to Group 1 winner and leading international sire Invincible Spirit (by Green Desert), a son of Wosaita's classic-winning half-sister Rafha (by Kris). That Group 1 Prix de Diane (French Oaks) heroine is also responsible for the blacktype-placed Kodiac (by Danehill), another stallion of considerable note.

There are many other talented horses in the various branches of the family and they include Rathbarry Stud's speedy Group 1-placed Group 2 winner James Garfield (by Exceed And Excel) whose first foals arrived in 2020. He is out of Whazzat, the stakes-winning full sister to Nkosikazi's dam. This is also the family of Group 1 stars such as Chinese White (by Dalakhani), Mishriff (by Make Believe; classic winner in 2020); Nayarra (by Cape Cross), Pinatubo (by Shamardal; new to Dalham Hall Stud in 2021); Pride of Dubai (by Street Cry; a leading freshman sire in 2020), and Uni (by More Than Ready), whereas others of note include the pattern winners and young stallions Gustav Klimt (by Galileo) and Master Carpenter (by Mastercraftsman) who stand at Castlehyde Stud and March Hare Stud respectively and had their first foals in 2020.

All of this makes Nkosikazi an exciting broodmare prospect and it would not be a surprise to see her produce one or more offspring that are even more talented than her.

SUMMARY DETAILS
Bred: D J & Mrs Brown
Owned: Olivia Hoare
Trained: William Haggas
Country: England
Race record: -43031000-224330-110-
Career highlights: 3 wins inc Betfair Exchange Hoppings Fillies' Stakes (Gr3), 3rd Ladbrokes Football Acca Boosty EBF River Eden Fillies' Stakes (L)

NKOSIKAZI (GB) – 2015 grey mare

Cape Cross (IRE)	Green Desert (USA)	Danzig (USA)
		Foreign Courier (USA)
	Park Appeal	Ahonoora
		Balidaress
Whatami (GB)	Daylami (IRE)	Doyoun
		Daltawa (IRE)
	Wosaita (GB)	Generous (IRE)
		Eljazzi

NOBEL PRIZE (IRE)

Nobel Prize is a full brother to two Group 1 stars and also to a classic-placed Group 2 scorer but he has not yet reached their heights. He finished unplaced behind Mogul on his debut in a mile maiden at the Curragh in late August of his juvenile season, was runner-up in a similar contest at Leopardstown nearly two months later and then narrowly won a seventeen-runner contest on heavy ground at Naas, also over a mile.

His three-year-old season at Ballydoyle also consisted of one win from three starts, winning a ten-and-a-half-furlong Group 3 contest on the Polytrack at Dundalk in mid-July. He was well-beaten on his other two starts, when behind Santiago in the Group 2 Queen's Vase on his seasonal reappearance at Ascot in June and behind Mogul in the Group 1 Juddmonte Grand Prix de Paris on good ground at ParisLongchamp three months later. His next public appearance was in the sales ring in Newmarket where he was sold for 170,000 guineas during the Tattersalls Autumn Horses in Training Sale in late October. The good-looking colt was bought by John Walsh Bloodstock as a stallion prospect. Exact details were not available on the day, but Walsh was quoted as saying that there was "interest in him from various countries" while confirming that the colt would not race again. The horse is standing in Turkey and with his pedigree, he could make quite an impact there.

Nobel Prize is a son of the phenomenal Galileo (by Sadler's Wells) and he is out of the Group 1-placed Hveger (by Danehill). That makes him a full brother to the multiple middle-distance Group 1 star Highland Reel, to Australian Group 1 scorer Cape of Good Hope and to the dual Derby-placed Group 2 Great Voltigeur Stakes and Group 2 Hardwicke Stakes winner Idaho. The latter is a Beeches Stud stallion whose first foals made up to €28,000 in 2020, whereas the first-named had a mixed reception with his initial yearlings. He had a 320,000-guineas colt in Tattersalls' Book 1, a 110,000-guinea one in Book 2, sons that fetched £72,000 and £65,000 at the Goffs Orby Sale (held in Doncaster in 2020) but, excluding vendor buy-backs, only seven that made 50,000 guineas or more at any auction.

Hveger is a full sister to the multiple middle-distance Group 1 winner Elvstroem and half-sister to the similarly talented miler Haradasun (by Fusaichi Pegasus), neither of whom has had anything the sort of success that might have been hoped for as stallions. Elvstroem, who moved to Haras du Petit Tellier in France in 2016 after many years in Australia, has sired more than 320 winners of around 1,000 races. He was born in November 2000, so is considered to be twenty-one years old here, and yet has just a dozen stakes winners to his name of whom one, Hucklebuck, winner of the Group 1 Cantala Stakes over a mile at Flemington in 2014, has struck at the highest level. He is also responsible for the Group 2 winner and Group 1 Caulfield Guineas runner-up Carrara. Haradasun has also had small numbers of stakes winners and his standout performer has been the sadly ill-fated South African champion Harry's Son.

SUMMARY DETAILS
Bred: Coolmore
Owned: Coolmore, Moffitt & Meduri Syndicate
Trained: Aidan O'Brien
Country: Ireland
Race record: 021-010-
Career highlights: 2 wins inc Woodford Reserve Ballysax Stakes (Gr3)

NOBEL PRIZE (IRE) – 2017 bay colt

Galileo (IRE)	Sadler's Wells (USA)	Northern Dancer
		Fairy Bridge (USA)
	Urban Sea (USA)	Miswaki (USA)
		Allegretta
Hveger (AUS)	Danehill (USA)	Danzig (USA)
		Razyana (USA)
	Circles of Gold (AUS)	Marscay (AUS)
		Olympic Aim (NZ)

One Ruler was one of the leading two-year-olds of 2020 and he may take high rank again at three and four years of age. The son of Dalham Hall Stud's outstanding stallion Dubawi (by Dubai Millennium) finished his initial season on a rating of 114 following his second-place finish to Mac Swiney in the Group 1 Vertem Futurity Trophy Stakes over a mile on heavy ground at Doncaster in late October. That's just six pounds below the divisional champion, St Mark's Basilica. He had beaten the subsequent Group 1 winner Van Gogh by one and three-quarter lengths in the Group 3 Emirates Autumn Stakes over the same trip on soft ground at Newmarket a fortnight before. His maiden win came over seven furlongs on good at Sandown in August, a month after he had chased home Etonian over the same course and distance, and his only other run is his third-place finish to New Mandate in a listed contest at Doncaster in September.

A Godolphin homebred trained by Charlie Appleby, the mid-April-born colt is the second foal of the high-class miler Fintry (by Shamardal). She won five of her eleven starts, including the Group 2 Prix de Sandringham and Group 3 Prix Bertrand du Breuil Bertrand at Chantilly—the latter a half-length defeat of the dual classic star Avenir Certain—and the Group 3 Atalanta Stakes at Sandown in which she beat Odeliz by a length and a quarter. She also won a listed contest by six lengths, was third to Integral in the Group 1 Sun Chariot Stakes and got her wins on everything from good ground to very soft. Fintry had a Fastnet Rock (by Danehill) colt in 2020 and then visited Kingman (by Invincible Spirit).

The mare is a half-sister to the Group 2 Prix Daniel Wildenstein runner-up Lochinver (by Kingmambo) and out of Campsie Fells (by Indian Ridge), a Grade 1-placed Group 3 winner over nine furlongs whose grandam, Mill Path (by Mill Reef), was a half-sister to the Group 1 Irish Oaks star Give Thanks (by Relko). In addition to being the dam of the classic-placed Group 2 Falmouth Stakes winner Alshakr (by Bahri), Give Thanks is the grandam of 1995's Group 1 1000 Guineas heroine Harayir (by Gulch) and third dam of 2016's Group 1 Jebel Hatta scorer Tryster (by Shamardal). One Ruler is bred on similar lines to that nine-furlong top-level scorer. This is a family that represents a branch of the famous Moller family that began with Horama (by Panorama).

It is possible that One Ruler may stay ten furlongs, but the immediate generations of his pedigree combined with the 2.40 cadence he recorded on good ground at Doncaster in September suggest that a mile might be his best trip, possibly even seven furlongs. It would not be a surprise to see him strike at the highest level. He holds entries in both the Group 1 Tattersalls Irish 2,000 Guineas and Group 1 Dubai Duty Free Irish Derby.

SUMMARY DETAILS

Bred: Godolphin
Owned: Godolphin
Trained: Charlie Appleby
Country: England
Race record: 21312-
Career highlights: 2 wins inc Emirates Autumn Stakes (Gr3), 2nd Vertem Futurity Trophy Stakes (Gr1), 3rd bet365 Flying Scotsman Stakes (L)

ONE RULER (IRE) – 2018 bay colt

Dubawi (IRE)	Dubai Millennium (GB)	Seeking The Gold (USA)
		Colorado Dancer
	Zomaradah (GB)	Deploy
		Jawaher (IRE)
Fintry (IRE)	Shamardal (USA)	Giant's Causeway (USA)
		Helsinki (GB)
	Campsie Fells (UAE)	Indian Ridge
		Queen's View (FR)

ONE VOICE (IRE)

Poet's Voice (by Dubawi) was a top-class miler whose early produce proved popular in auction ring. Blacktype success did not come as quickly as hoped or at the expected levels, the early years establishing him as sire of Group 3 and Group 2 classic winners in Italy and Germany. Then the European middle-distance champion Poet's Word emerged, Trap For Fools won at the highest level in Australia, but their sire was unable to capitalise on their success. He died in 2018, aged just eleven, and his final crop of just sixteen foals arrived the following year. Hopes that his dual Group 1-winning son—who is related to the Group 1 sire Inchinor (by Ahonoora)—might be able to do for him what his sire, Dubawi, did for Dubai Millennium (by Seeking The Gold) were dashed when the stallion attracted only thirty mares in his maiden season. He was immediately moved to the National Hunt sector and received 229 mares in his second year at stud.

One Voice is among the twenty-one stakes winners sired by Poet's Voice and she came within a neck of giving him another top-level scorer when runner-up to Fancy Blue in the Group 1 Qatar Nassau Stakes over ten furlongs at Goodwood at the end of July. The Jessica Harrington-trained bay had been a nose runner-up in a listed contest at Navan and half-length winner of the Group 3 Irish Stallion Farms EBF Blue Wind Stakes at Leopardstown, both also over that distance, and her initial top-level placing was something of a surprise. It was also perhaps unlucky not to have been a winning effort as she had been short of room at a key stage of the race and, once clear, finished strongly, just failing to catch her classic-winning rival. The pair finished two and three-quarter lengths clear of the third, four-year-old Nazeef, with Queen Power and Magic Wand the next two home.

Another Group 1 placing was a strong possibility next time, a race in which likely only considerable misfortune would have prevented the odds-on favourite, Love, from adding another big win to her tally. That brilliant chestnut duly took the Darley Yorkshire Oaks by five lengths, and although One Voice ran well and briefly looked like taking second place, the grey Alpinista went past her a furlong out, eventually passing the post two lengths clear. Manuela de Vega and Frankly Darling were fourth and fifth. It is the only time that One Voice has tried twelve furlongs. Her only subsequent run was a disappointing one as she finished seventeen and a half lengths behind her stable companion Cayenne Pepper in the Group 2 Moyglare 'Jewels' Blandford Stakes over ten furlongs at the Curragh in mid-September, that filly having won the race by four lengths from the regally related long-shot Amma Grace.

One Voice, a €55,000 graduate of the Goffs Sportsman's Yearling Sale, has a now yearling half-brother by Dandy Man (by Mozart) who made 190,000 guineas at the Tattersalls December Foal Sale, and she is the best of three winners out of Zaaqya (by Nayef). That mare is a half-sister to the Grade 2-placed Californian listed scorer Double Touch (by Dutch Art) and they are out of the lightly raced Classical Dancer (by Dr Fong) who was placed in eight- and ten-furlong listed contests in England. Third dam Gorgeous Dancer (by Nordico) earned her blacktype when placed in a listed Oaks Trial at the Curragh but is better remembered as being the dam of the prolific Imperial Dancer (by Primo Dominie). His eleven wins featured the Group 1 Premio Roma, Group 3 Meld Stakes, Group 3 St Simon Stakes, Group 3 Scottish Classic and a pair of listed contests, and his long list of blacktype placings included the Group 1 Premio Roma and two editions of the Group 1 Grosser Dallmayr Preis Bayerisches Zuchtrennen.

There are plenty of other blacktype horses on the page and all of this makes One Voice a potential broodmare of note.

SUMMARY DETAILS

Bred: J Lenihan
Owned: Craig Bernick
Trained: Jessica Harrington
Country: Ireland
Race record: 21-210230-
Career highlights: 2 wins inc Irish Stallion Farms EBF Blue Wind Stakes (Gr3), 2nd Qatar Nassau Stakes (Gr1), Irish Stallion Farms EBF Salsabil Stakes (L), 3rd Darley Yorkshire Oaks (Gr1)

ONE VOICE (IRE) – 2017 bay filly

Poet's Voice (GB)	Dubawi (IRE)	Dubai Millennium (GB)
		Zomaradah (GB)
	Bright Tiara (USA)	Chief's Crown (USA)
		Expressive Dance (USA)
Zaaqya (GB)	Nayef (USA)	Gulch (USA)
		Height of Fashion (FR)
	Classical Dancer (GB)	Dr Fong (USA)
		Gorgeous Dancer (IRE)

PABLO ESCOBARR (IRE)

Pablo Escobarr had potential classic aspirations at one stage but having chased home Anthony Van Dyck in the Listed Derby Trial at Lingfield he bypassed Epsom in favour of Ascot. He was only fifth to Japan there in the Group 2 King Edward VII Stakes and had a wind procedure done shortly afterwards but returned to track in good form late in the year. He chased home the rising star Lord North in a ten-furlong listed contest on heavy ground at Newmarket in early November before making the most of the four pounds he was receiving from Loxley to win the Listed 32Red Wild Flower Stakes over a quarter-mile farther at Kempton in December.

His four-year-old campaign began on January 2nd and ended in late August and although he won only once, that was a three-quarter-length defeat of Desert Encounter in the Group 3 L'Ormarins Queen's Plate Glorious Stakes over a mile and a half on good-to-firm ground at Goodwood in late July. He had been third in listed contests at Newmarket and Newbury on his two previous outings—the first two runs after he had been gelded—and had run well in two races over the same trip at Meydan earlier in the year. The first of those was a runners-up spot in a listed contest and the second was a fourth-place finish to his old rival Loxley in the Group 2 Dubai City of Gold. Indeed, he was staying on at the finish and may have taken third had there been another few strides to go, the final margins being a short head, one and a quarter lengths and a head, with Defoe and Mountain Hunter filling the placings. His only other run of the year was when finishing down the field behind Fujaira Prince in the Ebor at York in August, his first time trying the fourteen-furlong trip and his first time on soft ground since that run against Anthony Van Dyck.

Pablo Escobarr (by Galileo), a half-brother to 2020's Group 1 Moyglare Stud Stakes third Oodnadatta (by Australia), is out of the four-time pattern-winning sprinter Bewitched (by Dansili), a filly who missed out on Group 1 placing when an eight-length fourth to Dream Ahead in the Prix de la Foret on her penultimate start. She had a full brother to Oodnadatta in 2019—he has been named Luis Fernando—a first-crop daughter of Saxon Warrior (by Deep Impact) last April and was then among the first book covered by the classic-winning miler Magna Grecia (by Invincible Spirit). The mare's unraced half-sister Attachante (by Teofilo) also had a notable result in 2020 as she is the dam of Aviateur (by Intense Focus), a Group 3 scorer over a few yards short of nine furlongs at Dortmund and runner-up in the Group 2 Badener Mile.

Abbatiale (by Kaldoun), the grandam of Pablo Escobarr, was a talented filly in France, winning the Group 3 Prix Penelope and Listed Prix Rose de Mai, both at Saint-Cloud, and chasing home Zainta in the Group 1 Prix de Diane (French Oaks) at Chantilly. Her full sister, Aubergade, won the same listed contest twelve months later but was placed in both the Group 3 Prix Penelope and Group 2 Prix de Pomone. Their siblings also include Alta Anna (by Anabaa), the unraced dam of the former Ballydoyle horse Southern France (by Galileo). A now six-year-old who is inbred 3x4x4 to Northern Dancer (by Nearctic), he won the Group 3 Irish St Leger Trial Stakes, was runner-up in the Group 2 Queen's Vase and Group 2 Yorkshire Cup and third in both the Group 1 St Leger at Doncaster and Group 1 Irish St Leger at the Curragh before going on to take the Group 2 Zipping Classic over twelve furlongs at Sandown in Australia.

Pablo Escobarr, a €200,000 graduate of the Arqana Deauville August yearling sale, is a capable middle-distance runner. Presuming the 108-rated gelding is happy and healthy in 2021, there should be some more good prizes to be won with him.

SUMMARY DETAILS

Bred: R Scarborough & Carradale
Owned: Hussain Alabbas Lootah
Trained: William Haggas
Country: England
Race record: 2421-22021-243310-
Career highlights: 3 wins inc L'Ormarins Queen's Plate Glorious Stakes (Gr3), 32Red Wild Flower Stakes (L), 2nd Dubai Racing Club Classic sponsored by Emirates NBD Wholesale Banking (L), Weatherbys TBA James Seymour Stakes (L),

RaceBets Derby Trial Stakes (L), 3rd bet365 Steventon Stakes (L), Betway Fred Archer Stakes (L)

PABLO ESCOBARR (IRE) – 2016 bay gelding

Galileo (IRE)	Sadler's Wells (USA)	Northern Dancer
		Fairy Bridge (USA)
	Urban Sea (USA)	Miswaki (USA)
		Allegretta
Bewitched (IRE)	Dansili (GB)	Danehill (USA)
		Hasili (IRE)
	Abbatiale (FR)	Kaldoun (FR)
		Anna Edes (FR)

PASSION (IRE)

Passion was a valuable broodmare prospect before she ever ran but has enhanced her profile considerably following a three-year-old season in which she showed herself to be talented without being top class. Her final end-of-year rating was 111 but that hardly matters with regard to her stud prospects. The 800,000-guinea Tattersalls October Book 1 graduate is part of the Coolmore/Ballydoyle team and presumably will be afforded the best opportunities in her stud career.

The daughter of prolific champion sire Galileo (by Sadler's Wells) won a one-mile Cork maiden from three starts as a juvenile and kicked off her second season with a fourth-place finish in a listed contest over ten furlongs at Navan in June. Six days later, she picked up her first piece of blacktype when taking third to Frankly Darling and Ennistymon in the Group 2 Ribblesdale Stakes at Royal Ascot, beaten by margins of one and three-quarter lengths and two and a half lengths. Rejigging of the early part of the season, delayed due to the Covid-19 pandemic, meant that this race was position as a trial for the Group 1 Investec Oaks rather than as a perceived consolation for those beaten at Epsom or who missed the classic. However, although the two that finished ahead of her at Ascot took third and second respectively at Epsom, albeit finishing a long way behind the runaway winner Love, there was an additional five-length gap back to Passion who finished only fifth this time.

The race traditionally serves as a good trial for the Group 1 Juddmonte Irish Oaks at the Curragh and Passion ran in that classic a fortnight after her trip to England. She finished well but passed the post in third, beaten two lengths and half a length by Even So and Cayenne Pepper. The latter's margin of superiority was extended to three and three-quarter lengths when they met at Cork three weeks later, the pair finishing second and third to Tarnawa in the Group 3 Irish Stallion Farms EBF Give Thanks Stakes. The winner, who was making her seasonal reappearance that day, would go on to become a triple Group/Grade 1 star. Passion, on the other hand, stepped up in trip and won the Group

3 Irish Stallion Farms EBF Stanerra Stakes over fourteen furlongs on soft ground at Naas.

She was then fifth in both the Group 1 Comer Group International Irish St Leger on good at the Curragh and Group 1 Qatar Prix de Royallieu on heavy at ParisLongchamp before going to Ascot in mid-October and picking up her second Group 1 placing. The ground was soft, Wonderful Tonight won in good style from Dame Malliot, and Passion stayed on into third, a length behind, passing the tiring Mehdaayih in the final half-furlong. Even So was a disappointing fifth, followed home by Manuela De Vega and Thundering Nights.

Passion is a full sister to the Group 1 Irish Derby and Group 1 St Leger star Capri, who covered 158 mares in his first season as a National Hunt stallion at Grange Stud in 2020. Their full brother Cypress Creek won the Group 3 Loughbrown Stakes over two miles, their now two-year-old full sister made 850,000 guineas at the Tattersalls October Book 1 Sale, and their dam, Dialafara (by Anabaa), had another Galileo colt on May 15th last year. The mare is a winning daughter of Diamilina (by Linamix), a talented middle-distance performer who won the Group 2 Prix de Mallaret and Group 3 Prix de la Nonette and was runner-up to Aquarelliste in the Group 1 Prix Vermeille.

That talented grey had a sister who looked set for potential Group 1 stardom after her first two starts but, sadly, the runaway Group 3 Prix Cleopatre winner Diamonixa (by Linamix) died before having the chance to run again. Their winning full sister Dali's Grey became the dam of the Group 3 Geelong Cup winner and Group 1 Melbourne Cup runner-up Bauer (by Grand Lodge), whereas half-brother Diamond Green (by Green Desert) was a high-class miler. He won the Group 3 Prix la Rochette at two, was placed in the Group 1 Poule d'Essai des Poulains (French 2000 Guineas), Group 1 Prix du Moulin de Longchamp and Group 1 St James's Palace Stakes, and he spent time as a stallion at Ballyhane Stud in Ireland and several locations in France before his death in 2020, aged nineteen. His standout representative, by some way, is his daughter Watdachances, the Grade 1-placed Grade 3 scorer who was second past the post to Secret Gesture in the Grade 1 Beverly D Stakes at Arlington but got the race in the stewards' room.

There are plenty of other talented horses to be found in various branches of the family, including the Irish Oaks winner Pampalina (by Bairam; sixth dam of Passion) and her Irish 2,000 Guineas-winning son Pampapaul (by Yellow God), but they are only distant to remote connections to last season's classic-placed pattern winner and tell us nothing more than we already know about her prospects as a potential broodmare of repute. Passion is still in training, so we should see her in action as a four-year-old.

SUMMARY DETAILS

Bred: Lynch Bages Ltd & Camas Park Stud
Owned: Mrs John Magnier, Michael Tabor & Derrick Smith
Trained: Aidan O'Brien
Country: Ireland
Race record: 010-4300331003-
Career highlights: 2 wins inc Irish Stallion Farms EBF Stanerra Stakes (Gr3), 3rd Juddmonte Irish Oaks (Gr1), Qipco British Champions Fillies & Mares Stakes (Gr1), Ribblesdale Stakes (Gr2), Irish Stallion Farms EBF Give Thanks Stakes (Gr3)

PASSION (IRE) – 2017 bay filly

Galileo (IRE)	Sadler's Wells (USA)	Northern Dancer
		Fairy Bridge (USA)
	Urban Sea (USA)	Miswaki (USA)
		Allegretta
Dialafara (FR)	Anabaa (USA)	Danzig (USA)
		Balbonella (FR)
	Diamilina (FR)	Linamix (FR)
		Diamonaka (FR)

PATRICK SARSFIELD (FR)

Coolmore Stud's Derby winner Australia (by Galileo) had a breakthrough season as a stallion with a string of stakes winners that included his first ones to strike at the highest level: Galileo Chrome and Order of Australia. Patrick Sarsfield was on the list and finished the year as a 114-rated Group 1-placed pattern winner.

He was placed in the maidens won by Madhmoon and Sydney Opera House on his only starts as a two-year-old, both for the Edward Lynam stable, and he joined the Joseph O'Brien team before the first of two runs as a three-year-old. He was placed in that Cork race but then won a mile maiden by four lengths at the Curragh next time and was gelded before returning to action in 2020. He kicked off the season with a five-length win in a nine-furlong handicap at Leopardstown in June, added a valuable handicap over ten furlongs at Navan twelve days later and then, having been raised to a rating of 109, he stepped up into pattern company.

First stop was the Group 3 'Green Room' Meld Stakes over nine furlongs at Leopardstown. He was going well as the field was about to swing into the straight, was asked for his effort when they rounded the bend, gradually moved past the front-running Ancient Spirit and stayed on well to beat that entire by two lengths. Fort Myers was three-quarters of a length back in third, with Trais Fluors fourth and Zabeel Prince fifth. He went to Germany two weeks later but although staying on well in the closing stages, he had to settle for third, beaten a neck and one and a quarter lengths by Barney Roy and Quest The Moon, and it was only in the final strides that he denied Durance of that placing.

He was positioned to strike as the field rounded the final bend at Leopardstown on Irish Champions Weekend in September but was unable to pick up in the straight and passed the post only seventh behind Tiger Moth in the Group 3 Paddy Power 'Is It 2021 Yet?' Stakes. This was his first attempt at twelve furlongs and it looked as though he didn't stay the trip. That might seem a bit strange for a son of Australia who comes from the family of Fame And Glory (by Montjeu), but the branch he represents includes a lot of milers, which lessens the surprise. His final outing of the year was in the Group 2 Qatar Prix Dollar over an extended nine and a half furlongs on heavy ground at ParisLongchamp in early October, and although he looked like he might win when he went to the front a furlong from home, Skalleti went past him in the final half furlong to win by a length and a quarter, with a further two-and-a-half-length gap back to Dariyma in third.

Patrick Sarsfield is a €140,000 Arqana Deauville August yearling sale graduate who joined O'Brien after being sold on for 230,000 guineas at the 2019 Tattersalls July Sale. He is the best of four winners from the first four foals of Ultra Appeal (by Lawman), who had a son of Dark Angel (by Acclamation) last year and was bred back to Australia. The mare is a non-winning half-sister to three more stoutly bred stakes winners one of whom is the Group 2-placed middle-distance pattern scorer and blacktype producer Goathemala (by Black Sam Bellamy). Global World (by Big Shuffle), the stakes-placed grandam of Patrick Sarsfield, has seven blacktype-earning siblings and they include the pattern-winning miler Global Thrill (by Big Shuffle) and juvenile Group 2 scorer Global Dream (by Seattle Dancer).

Third dam Goonda (by Darshaan) achieved a tally of eight blacktype offspring among a total of thirteen winners from sixteen foals. She had only been a one-time winner on the track but had obvious broodmare potential because she was not only a daughter of a hugely influential stallion but was out of the German mile classic winner and Group 2 Preis der Diana (German Oaks) third Grimpola (by Windwurf). That mare, a full sister to a stakes winner, produced five winners from eight foals, a tally that included her Group 3-placed daughter Gryada (by Shirley Heights). It is that three-parts sister to Goonda who gave us the aforementioned Group 1 Irish Derby, Group 1 Tattersalls Gold Cup, Group 1 Coronation Cup and Group 1 Gold Cup star Fame And Glory. He died young but the early indicators are that the progeny he left behind will propel him to the top end of the National Hunt sires' championship for at least a few seasons. His winning full sister Yummy Mummy is the dam of the Group 1 1000 Guineas heroine and narrow Group 1 Investec Oaks runner-up Legatissimo (by Danehill Dancer), a star who also won the

Group 1 Nassau Stakes and Group 1 Matron Stakes and was second in the Group 1 Pretty Polly Stakes and Grade 1 Breeders' Cup Filly & Mare Turf. That star has visited Galileo each season since she retired to stud and the older of her daughters has just turned two.

Only one of Grimpola's offspring did not race, her 1989 Slip Anchor (by Shirley Heights) foal. However, that filly, who was named Gonfalon, became the dam of several talented racehorses of whom Gonbarda (by Lando) and Gonfilia (by Big Shuffle) stand out on two counts. Gonbarda had her sire's stamina, won both the Group 1 Deutschlandspreis and Group 1 Preis von Europa and was runner-up in the Group 1 Grosser Preis von Baden. She had a Dubawi (by Dubai Millennium) filly in 2019 and a son of Shamardal (by Giant's Causeway) in 2020 but it is two of her older sons of Pivotal (by Polar Falcon) who are, right now, her standard-bearers. Racing History won the Group 3 Winter Hill Stakes and was twice Group 1-placed in Germany, but his older brother Farhh is the Group 1 Lockinge Stakes and Group 1 Champion Stakes star whose mostly small crops have yielded the Group 1-winning miler King of Change (new to Derrinstown Stud in 2021), the Derby-placed stayer Dee Ex Bee, and high-class sprinter Far Above (new to Starfield Stud in 2021) among others of note. Gonfilia, on the other hand, got her best win in the Group 3 Princess Elizabeth Stakes and, in 2020, her son Glen Shiel (by Pivotal) won the Group 1 Qipco British Champions Sprint Stakes at Ascot shortly after finishing as runner-up in the Group 1 Sprint Cup at Haydock.

There is obviously no prospect of a stallion career for Patrick Sarsfield, but presuming he's healthy and happy, this talented gelding should be capable of winning more good prizes for his connections.

SUMMARY DETAILS
Bred: China Horse Club International Ltd
Owned: Mrs C C Regalado-Gonzalez
Trained: Joseph O'Brien
Country: Ireland
Race record: 32-21-111302-

Career highlights: 4 wins inc "Green Room" Meld Stakes (Gr3), 2nd Qatar Prix Dollar (Gr2), 3rd Grosser Dallmayr-Preis Bayerisches Zuchtrennen (Gr1)

PATRICK SARSFIELD (FR) – 2016 bay gelding

Australia (GB)	Galileo (IRE)	Sadler's Wells (USA)
		Urban Sea (USA)
	Ouija Board (GB)	Cape Cross (IRE)
		Selection Board
Ultra Appeal (IRE)	Lawman (FR)	Invincible Spirit (IRE)
		Laramie (USA)
	Global World (GER)	Big Shuffle (USA)
		Goonda (GB)

PISTA (USA)

US Triple Crown and Breeders' Cup Classic hero American Pharoah (by Pioneerof The Nile) is an understandably in-demand member of the team at Ashford Stud in Kentucky and he has made a promising start to his stallion career. His first two crops have yielded a dozen stakes winners, at the time of writing, plus eleven others who have been blacktype placed, with his first batch headlined by the Breeders' Cup-placed Grade 1 winner Harvey's Lil Goil and his second by the Irish-trained juvenile Van Gogh. That regally related colt put up an impressive performance on heavy ground in late October to take the Group 1 Criterium International over a mile at Saint-Cloud. Many are obviously keen to give the stallion every chance to become a leading sire of turf horses as well as dirt ones and it is striking that, so far, all five of his progeny who have won at Group/Grade 2 level or above have achieved the feat on grass. Pista is one of them.

The $675,000 Keeneland September Yearling Sale graduate did not run until late June when she was unplaced in a ten-furlong Leopardstown maiden. She was stepped up in trip and the result was an eye-catching six-and-a-half-length score on soft ground at Galway, so blacktype company was a logical next move. She was only in fourth place a furlong from home in the Listed Vinnie Roe Stakes at Leopardstown eleven days later but stayed on strongly to take the race by half a length and the same from Sunchart and Group 1 Irish Derby third Dawn Patrol. The latter went on to pattern success over two miles, whereas Pista stayed at around the fourteen furlongs. First, she went to Doncaster where, despite running about a bit in the closing stages, drifting left and then right, she won the Group 2 bet365 Park Hill Fillies' Stakes over the St Leger course and distance. Vivionn was the length-and-a-half runner-up, with Believe In Love a half-length back in third.

The ground had been good for both of those winning starts but it was heavy at ParisLongchamp at the start of October and that made the Group 1 Qatar Prix de Royallieu, being run over its fairly new distance of 2800 metres (fourteen furlongs), additionally testing. Pista again hung in the final half furlong but it did not affect the finishing order as Wonderful Tonight, who hung in the opposite direction, landed the spoils by one and a quarter lengths. Ebaiyra passed the post third, five lengths behind Pista.

The Joseph O'Brien-trained bay comes from one of the most famous families in the stud book and that, combined with her race record, will make her a very valuable broodmare. Her stamina also makes her a potential source of middle-distance stars and Cup horses, so it will be fascinating to see what sort of stallions she visits. She could have been a Cup horse if remaining in training, and it may also have been worth a shot trying her back over twelve furlongs, but she has moved on to the next phase of her career.

Pista is the first foal of Mohini (by Galileo), who was placed twice at around nine furlongs in a lowly rated five-race career in Ireland. Her siblings include Beta Leo (by A.P. Indy), who is the dam of 2017's Group 1 Prix de Diane (French Oaks) winner Senga (by Blame), whereas her dam is Denebola (by Storm Cat), the Group 1 Prix Marcel Boussac-winning daughter of Machiavellian's (by Mr Prospector) Group 1-winning full sister Coup de Genie. She has a year-younger, Japan-born full sister named Ishtar, her dam had a Kitasan Black (by Black Tide) filly in 2019 and a son of Duramente (by King Kamehameha) last year.

SUMMARY DETAILS
Bred: Lynch Bages Ltd
Owned: Scott C Heider
Trained: Joseph O'Brien
Country: Ireland
Race record: -01112-
Career highlights: 3 wins inc bet365 Park Hill Fillies' Stakes (Gr2), Vinnie Roe Stakes (L), 2nd Qatar Prix de Royallieu (Gr1)

PISTA (USA) – 2017 bay filly

American Pharoah (USA)	Pioneerof The Nile (USA)	Empire Maker (USA)
		Star of Goshen (USA)
	Littleprincessemma (USA)	Yankee Gentleman (USA)
		Exclusive Rosette (USA)
Mohini (IRE)	Galileo (IRE)	Sadler's Wells (USA)
		Urban Sea (USA)
	Denebola (USA)	Storm Cat (USA)
		Coup de Genie (USA)

POETIC FLARE (IRE)

Dawn Approach (by New Approach) was one of the stars of his Derby-winning sire's first crop, a juvenile champion who went on to classic success over a mile at three. He has had thirteen stakes winners plus a dozen others who have been blacktype placed, and although without a top-level winner to his name, Madhmoon was runner-up in the Group 1 Derby at Epsom, Dawn Patrol has been second in the Group 1 New Zealand 2000 Guineas at Riccarton Park, Musis Amica was a runner-up in both the Group 1 Prix de Diane (French Oaks) at Chantilly and Group 1 Prix Vermeille at ParisLongchamp, and the sadly ill-fated Mary Tudor was third in a Group 1 Irish Oaks at the Curragh. They have all won at listed or pattern level although Alyaasaat, who has been Grade 1-placed in South Africa, has not.

Jim Bolger, who bred and trained Dawn Approach, has been supporting him well at stud and in addition to being listed as the breeder of eleven of the stallion's forty-strong foal crop in 2020, he supplied him with twenty-one of his book of thirty-two mares last season. He is also the breeder and trainer of his promising son Poetic Flare, who holds entries in the Group 1 Tattersalls Irish 2,000 Guineas and Group 1 Emirates Poule d'Essai des Poulains. So, it was no surprise to learn that the stallion, who began his career at Kildangan Stud and shuttled to Australia, is now a member of the team at Redmondstown Stud in Co Wexford.

Poetic Flare beat Lipizzaner by half a length on their debut over five furlongs on soft-to-heavy ground at Naas in March, the latter finishing four and a quarter lengths clear of third-placed The Blue Panther. The former went on to become a pattern-placed stakes winner, the latter a ninety-four-rated one-time winner whose busy season featured the runners-up spot in the valuable Foran Equine Irish EBF Auction Race Final over seven furlongs at Naas in October. Poetic Flare, on the other hand, was not seen out again until October. The Group 1 Darley Dewhurst Stakes was a big ask and he looked understandably a bit green among his more experienced rivals, always behind and finishing tenth, a total of eight and three-quarter lengths behind the winner, St Mark's Basilica.

However, he showed the benefit of that experience just one week later when at Leopardstown for the Group 3 Killavullan Stakes. The ground was yielding-to-soft, he led in the early stages of the race, then raced prominently, was going easily when moving back into the lead on the rails rounding the final bend and soon went clear, staying on to the line to win by two and a half lengths. Zaffy's Pride, who had won a listed race at Dundalk on her previous start, was the one who chased him home and she finished three and a quarter lengths clear of the third, maiden Mexico City. That colt, who was sold for 60,000 guineas in Newmarket a few days later to go to Spain, is one of three reported survivors of a dreadful accident where the lorry in which he was travelling with nine other horses caught fire on a motorway in France.

After the Leopardstown race, assistant trainer Una Manning said that the colt's lengthy absence had been down to him "growing all year" and that he would be aimed at the Guineas. The mile should not present him with any difficulty and, given that he is out of Maria Lee (by Rock of Gibraltar) and so can be described as being a three-parts brother to Glamorous Approach (by New Approach), there has to be a chance that he will also stay ten furlongs. That filly got both of her listed wins over ten furlongs, she was a pattern-placed handicap winner over twelve, a listed runner-up over fourteen furlongs, although perhaps found the two miles a stretch when third in a handicap over that trip at the Curragh. She had chestnut Lope de Vega (by Shamardal) colts in 2019 and 2020 and was bred back to him last season; the two-year-old has been named Glam de Vega. Maria Lee, on the other hand, had a full brother to Poetic Flare in 2019—named Frazil—a U S Navy Flag (by War Front) filly at the end of March last year and was then bred to Magna Grecia (by Invincible Spirit). Bolger sold her for €65,000 at the 2018 edition of the Goffs November Mare Sale.

The mare is a half-sister to a few winners, one of them the Grade 2-winning juvenile hurdler Fiscal Focus (by Intense Focus), although she was unplaced over twelve furlongs on her only start. Her dam, Elida (by Royal Academy), won a seven-furlong maiden and nine-furlong handicap, both at Tipperary, and is also notable as being the grandam of the Listed Eyrefield Stakes winner Dubai

Sand (by Teofilo). She is a half-sister to two stakes winners that Bolger bred from her regally related dam, Saviour (by Majestic Light). Elida's full brother Graduated won a listed handicap at Leopardstown but half-sister Speirbhean (by Danehill) is the stakes winner from whom Bolger bred the undefeated two-year-old champion and notable classic sire Teofilo (by Galileo). That mare is also responsible for the pattern-winning fillies Bean Feasa (by Dubawi) and Poetic Charm (by Dubawi).

Teofilo had been talked of as a potential Triple Crown contender but, sadly, did not race beyond his juvenile year due to injury. The Kildangan Stud veteran has sired twenty-one Group 1 winners among an overall tally of ninety-four blacktype scorers, and in addition to the Hong Kong star Exultant (who was classic-placed in Ireland under the name Irishcorrespondent), his Melbourne Cup winners Cross Counter and Twilight Payment, his Group 1-siring son Havana Gold, Bolger's own stallion Parish Hall, and 2020 Group 1 scorers Donjah, Gear Up (two-year-old), Subjectivist and Tawkeel, his roll of honour includes the likes of Irish St Leger winner Voleuse de Coeurs, Irish 1,000 Guineas heroine Pleascach and the sadly ill-fated Irish Derby victor Trading Leather. Bolger bred and trained the latter pair, whereas Dermot Weld trained the Irish National Stud-bred Voleuse de Coeurs.

Poetic Flare has some way to go yet if he's going to hit the top, but there is no doubt that he is bred to do so, and it would not be a surprise to see this 107-rated colt make the necessary improvement to win at the highest level at anywhere from a mile and upwards. Should he fulfil that potential then it is reasonable to think that he will earn a place at stud whenever his racing days come to an end, and his relationship to Teofilo could make that an interesting second career. His initial classic target will depend on his stable companion Mac Swiney. One of the pair will run in the Group 1 Qipco 2000 Guineas on May 1st and if that's Mac Swiney then Poetic Flare is going to head to ParisLongchamp and the Curragh. But if the Group 1 Vertem Futurity Trophy Stakes winner misses Newmarket then that colt will likely be rerouted to the Derrinstown Stud Derby Trial at Leopardstown before going to Epsom, with Poetic Flare taking his place at Newmarket instead. It will be fascinating to see how the two colts compare at the end of the year.

SUMMARY DETAILS
Bred: J S Bolger
Owned: Mrs J S Bolger
Trained: Jim Bolger
Country: Ireland
Race record: 101-
Career highlights: 2 wins inc Killavullan Stakes (Gr3)

POETIC FLARE (IRE) – 2018 bay colt

Dawn Approach (IRE)	New Approach (IRE)	Galileo (IRE)
		Park Express
	Hymn of The Dawn (USA)	Phone Trick (USA)
		Colonial Debut (USA)
Maria Lee (IRE)	Rock of Gibraltar (IRE)	Danehill (USA)
		Offshore Boom (IRE)
	Elida (IRE)	Royal Academy (USA)
		Saviour (USA)

PYLEDRIVER (GB)

Harbour Watch was undefeated in a three-race career, winning at Salisbury, Newmarket and Goodwood, a hat-trick achieved by an aggregate margin of ten and a half lengths and headlined by the Group 2 Richmond Stakes. The big son of Acclamation (by Royal Applause) came from a branch of the famous Fall Aspen (by Pretense) family and he spent his stallion career at Tweenhills Farm & Stud in Gloucestershire. Unfortunately, he had an arthritis problem, was pensioned from covering duties in 2017 and died in 2019, aged just ten. Waikuku, a Group 1-winning miler in Hong Kong who began his career with the John Oxx stable in Ireland, is the stallion's standout performer and was one of three horses keeping their late sire's name in lights in 2020. The other pair were three-year-olds, members of his penultimate crop.

Baron Samedi was one. That Joseph O'Brien-trainee showed little in three starts at two and in his first two outings of 2020, was gelded, won a ten-furlong handicap at Cork and kept going, completing his five-in-a-row with a head success in the Group 2 Prix du Conseil de Paris over eleven furlongs on heavy ground at ParisLongchamp in late October. Pyledriver was the other one and it would not be a surprise if this William Muir-trained colt goes on to win at the highest level in 2021.

The dark bay sprang a 50/1 shock on his debut as a two-year-old, taking a seven-furlong Salisbury maiden on firm ground that July. He was only fourth to Thunderous in a listed contest at Newbury a month later but then stepped up to a mile and, on soft ground at Haydock, won the Listed Ascendant Stakes by a length and a quarter from Sound of Cannons. The subsequent pattern-placed stakes winner Tammani finished third that day, almost two lengths in front of 2020's Group 1-winning stayer Subjectivist in fourth. Pyledriver's final run that year was disappointing, trailing home last of eight in the Group 2 Juddmonte Royal Lodge Stakes at Newmarket, but his trainer was reported as noting that the colt had been growing throughout the summer and had lost some of his strength. With time, therefore, it was likely that we would see improvement.

He chased home Berlin Tango in the Group 3 Unibet Classic Trial Stakes over ten furlongs at Kempton on his seasonal reappearance in early June and then advertised his classic potential with a two-length victory in the Group 2 King Edward VII Stakes at Royal Ascot, this twelve-furlong test acting as a potential Derby trial in 2020 rather than a 'consolation' given the rejigged and delayed early-season schedule. It was an impressive performance. He hit the front a quarter of a mile from home and stayed on well to the line, never looking like being caught by Arthur's Kingdom. Mohican Heights stayed on into third, another two lengths adrift, with the odds-on favourite and subsequent dual Group 1 star Mogul a disappointing fourth.

His Derby performance was disappointing but he bounced back at York the following month, again hitting the front a quarter of a mile out and staying on well to win in style despite giving three pounds to all of his rivals. He wandered around a bit while clear in the final furlong but passed the post three and a half lengths in front of Highland Chief, with Mogul and Berkshire Rocco half a length and head back in third and fourth. The Group 1 Pertemps St Leger is the obvious target for most Great Voltigeur winners and Pyledriver duly lined up at Doncaster. His pedigree had cast a shade of doubt over his prospects of staying twelve furlongs well, which he does, so the extra near two and a half furlongs was a journey into the unknown. His enthusiasm in the early stages of the race was a concern with regard to his ability to stay the distance, and although racing wide of the others—the principals drifted towards him in the closing stages—and again failing to run in a totally straight line, he kept on the line without being able to find the bit extra that could have made a significant difference. Galileo Chrome won the classic by a neck from Berkshire Rocco, who was a length and short head in front of Pyledriver and Santiago.

Pyledriver had one final start in 2020, the Group 1 Qipco Champion Stakes over ten furlongs on soft ground at Ascot in mid-October. He was widest of the field as they swung into the straight, again did not keep a straight line, and although passing a few tiring rivals in the closing stages was a never-dangerous seventh to Addeybb. He had won on soft as a two-year-old and it was good-to-soft at Ascot in June, but he is a big horse and the underfoot conditions may have been deeper than ideal for him that last day.

The way he wanders about in the closing stages of his races is curious and could have a variety of potential causes including maturity or learned behaviour. He had eased left from behind horses on his juvenile debut and then his rider switched him between rivals, two jinks his right as he was making his challenge and after which he no doubt received a rewarding response from his various connections; perhaps the colt made a link between moving off a straight line when being asked for maximum effort. Positive reinforcement is one of the ways in which horses learn. He kept fairly straight in his Ascot win: when he's drifted it's often been to his left.

If Pyledriver does become a Group 1 winner then he will be latest member of the most recent generations of his family to achieve the feat. He is the first foal of a dual French winner La Pyle (by Le Havre), his two-year-old half-brother has been named Stockpyle (by Oasis Dream) and that mid-April-born colt was followed by a May 1st, 2020 daughter of Frankel (by Galileo). His dam a full sister to the Group 3 Park Express Stakes winner Normandel and half-sister to Mont Ormel (by Air Chief Marshal) who won the Group 1 Grand Prix de Paris before moving to Hong Kong where he was blacktype placed under the name Helene Charisma. Their winning dam Lidana (by King's Best) is a half-sister to the notably versatile and talented Linngari (by Indian Ridge) and out of a half-sister to the Group 1 Tattersalls Gold Cup runner-up and multiple stakes winner Livadiya (by Shernazar). Linngari won the Group 2 Goldene Peitsche over six furlongs and was a neck runner-up to Caradak in the Group 1 Prix de la Foret over seven before stepping up in distance to take the Group 1 Premio Vittorio di Capua over a mile, two editions of the Group 2 Al Fahidi Fort at Meydan and a win in the Group 1 Grosser Dallmayr Preis Bayerisches Zuchtrennen over ten furlongs.

If you go back farther on the page, heading into the remote territory, then you will find that Licara (by Caro), the sixth dam of Pyledriver, was a half-sister to the Group 1 stars Acamas (by Mill

Reef), Akarad (by Labus) and Akiyda (by Labus). Acamas won the Group 1 Prix du Jockey Club (French Derby) and Group 1 Prix Lupin, Akarad won the Group 1 Grand Prix de Saint-Cloud and became a classic sire, whereas Akiyda was runner-up in the Group 1 Prix de Diane (French Oaks) and Group 1 Prix Vermeille before beating Ardross by a head in the Group 1 Prix de l'Arc de Triomphe.

Pyledriver is a talented middle-distance colt for whom Group 1 success may await. Should he fulfil that potential then he may be able to secure a good berth at stud someday, and it would be fascinating to see what he might do with such an opportunity.

SUMMARY DETAILS

Bred: Knox & Wells Ltd & R Devlin
Owned: La Pyle Partnership
Trained: William Muir
Country: England
Race record: 1410-210130-
Career highlights: 4 wins inc Sky Bet Great Voltigeur Stakes (Gr2), King Edward VII Stakes (Gr2), Read Ryan Moore Exclusively At betfair.com Ascendant Stakes (L), 2nd Unibet Classic Trial Stakes (Gr3), 3rd Pertemps St Leger Stakes (Gr1)

PYLEDRIVER (GB) – 2017 bay colt

Harbour Watch (IRE)	Acclamation (GB)	Royal Applause (GB)
		Princess Athena
	Gorband (USA)	Woodman (USA)
		Sheroog (USA)
La Pyle (FR)	Le Havre (IRE)	Noverre (USA)
		Marie Rheinberg (GER)
	Lidana (IRE)	King's Best (USA)
		Lidakiya (IRE)

QUEEN JO JO (GB)

Queen Jo Jo, a filly who comes from the family of two Kentucky Derby and Preakness Stakes winners, began her public life as an £11,000 Goffs UK Premier Yearling Sale graduate. The Bearstone Stud-bred grey was sold on for 68,000 guineas at the Tattersalls Craven Breeze-Up Sale the following April, went into training with Kevin Ryan and quickly established herself as a talented performer. She chased home Que Amoro over five furlongs at Beverley on her debut that July, won over that course and distance seventeen days later and then finished an honourable third to Fairyland in the Group 2 Sky Bet Lowther Stakes at York. Her only other start that year was in the Group 3 William Hill Firth of Clyde Stakes at Ayr in late September and, on heavy ground—in contrast to the good-to-firm on which she had only raced previously—she finished fourth to Queen of Bermuda.

She was only fifth to Dandhu over seven furlongs on her seasonal reappearance at three but returned to six and won a listed contest on soft at Nottingham before a trip to Ireland that yielded a third-place finish in a Group 3 sprint at the Curragh, beaten a neck and half a length by the four-year-olds Soffia and Dan's Dream and with the fourth another four and a half lengths adrift. It was a good effort. It was also a year to the day before the filly was next seen in action. She chased home Liberty Beach in a listed contest at Haydock that afternoon, ran poorly at the Curragh three weeks later—might it have been the so-called 'bounce effect'— before notching up the biggest win of her career. She hit the front half a furlong from home and kept on well to beat Breathtaking Look by a neck in the Group 3 William Hill Summer Fillies' Stakes on good ground at York.

Queen Jo Jo ran twice more before returning to Tattersalls where she was sold for 360,000 guineas at the December Mare Sale, bought by Hurworth Bloodstock. The first of those runs was in the Group 2 Sky Bet City of York Stakes over seven furlongs and she was certainly not disgraced in finishing third to Safe Voyage and One Master, beaten by three and a half lengths and three-quarters of a length. Her final outing was a tough ask, highlighted by her 50/1 odds, and she finished well down the field behind Dream of Dreams in the Group 1 Betfair Sprint Cup Stakes on soft ground at Haydock.

The talented grey is a daughter of Group 2 Hungerford Stakes winner Gregorian (by Clodovil), who spent four seasons at the National Stud in Newmarket before returning to his breeders' Rathasker Stud in Ireland where his fee this year is €5,000. Eleven of his offspring have earned blacktype, four of those are stakes winners and his only pattern scorer aside from Queen Jo Jo is Plainchant, one of the leading two-year-olds in France in 2020. She is out of a daughter of stamina influence Doyen (by Sadler's Wells) and has won four of her six starts. The talented youngster was a neck runner-up to Fev Rover in the Group 2 Shadwell Prix du Calvados at Deauville in August, took a listed contest over six furlongs at La Teste de Buch on her previous start, and went on to win the Group 3 Prix Eclipse by five lengths from Legal Attack and the Group 2 Criterium de Maisons-Laffitte at Chantilly, that one by three-quarters of a length from Go Athletico. Plainchant, a €4,000 Arqana October Yearling Sale graduate, is trained by Maurizio Guarnieri and could be a notable performer again this year at anywhere from six to nine furlongs.

Queen Jo Jo has three winning siblings and is out of the stakes-placed sprint winner River Song (by Siphon). She also has two younger ones waiting in the wings. The £65,000 Goffs UK Premier Yearling Sale graduate Insomnia (by Due Diligence) is an unraced three-year-old in the Richard Spencer yard, whereas their two-year-old half-sister, a 40,000-guinea Tattersalls Book 3 graduate, has been named Intoxicated (by Fountain of Youth). She is also a half-sister to Romany Gypsy (by Indesatchel) who, although unplaced in three starts, is the dam of the five-times stakes-placed winner Gypsy Spirit (by Gregorian).

River Song, on the other hand, is a half-sister to Allied Forces (by Miswaki), a Group 2 Queen Anne Stakes winner and Group 1 Sussex Stakes third whose tally also included a couple of Grade 2 handicaps in the USA. They are out of Mangala (by Sharpen Up) and although her half-sisters include the stakes-winning dam of a Grade 1-placed Grade 2 scorer and the pattern-placed fourth dam of the Group 1 Pretty Polly Stakes heroine Nezwaah (by Dubawi), it is not to them that the eye is drawn first.

Mangala is a half-sister Really Blue (by Believe It), a filly who won three of her twenty-three starts before going on to become the dam of 1998's Grade 1 Kentucky Derby and Grade 1 Preakness Stakes star Real Quiet (by Quiet American); he was runner-up in the Belmont Stakes in his bid to sweep the US Triple Crown. That Eclipse Award winner landed the Grade 1 Hollywood Futurity at two and went on to take the Grade 1 Hollywood Gold Cup and Grade 1 Pimlico Special at four. He was only fifteen when he died following a paddock accident and he left behind only twenty-three stakes winners, which was a disappointing figure, but they included the Grade 1 Coaching Club American Oaks winner Wonder Lady Anne L, triple Grade 1 star Pussycat Doll, and Eclipse Award winner Midnight Lute, winner of the Grade 1 Forego Stakes and back-to-back editions of the Grade 1 Breeders' Cup Sprint. That star son stands at Hill 'N' Dale Farm in Kentucky, four of his thirty-three stakes winners have won at the highest level to date and they are headed by the champion and prolific Grade 1 star Midnight Bisou.

Meadow Blue (by Raise a Native), the dam of Mangala and Really Blue, was unraced but had two famous full brothers. Crowned Prince won the Dewhurst Stakes and Champagne Stakes in England as a two-year-old in 1971, two years after his full brother Majestic Prince went close to US Triple Crown glory. The Belmont Stakes, in which he was runner-up to Arts and Letters, was the only time he lost in a ten-race career that had seen him take the Kentucky Derby, Preakness Stakes and Santa Anita Derby. He went on to sire thirty-two stakes winners from 362 foals, five of them top-level winners including the Belmont Stakes winner Coastal, classic-placed Eternal Prince, and classic sire Majestic Light.

All of this makes Queen Jo Jo a fascinating broodmare prospect, one who could produce sprinters, milers and even classic horses depending on the type of stallion to which she is sent.

SUMMARY DETAILS
Bred: Bearstone Stud Ltd
Owned: Roger Peel & Clipper Logistics

Trained: Kevin Ryan
Country: England
Race record: 2134-013-20130-
Career highlights: 3 wins inc William Hill Summer Fillies' Stakes (Gr3), EBF Weatherbys General Stud Book Kilvington Stakes (L), 2nd Betway EBF Cecil Frail Fillies' Stakes (L), 3rd Sky Bet City of York Stakes (Gr2), Sky Bet Lowther Stakes (Gr2), TRM - Excellence In Equine Nutrition Ballyogan Stakes (Gr3)

QUEEN JO JO (GB) – 2016 grey filly

Gregorian (IRE)	Clodovil (IRE)	Danehill (USA)
		Clodora (FR)
	Three Days In May (GB)	Cadeaux Genereux
		Corn Futures (GB)
River Song (USA)	Siphon (BRZ)	Itajara (BRZ)
		Ebrea (BRZ)
	Mangala (USA)	Sharpen Up
		Meadow Blue (USA)

RED VERDON (USA)

Red Verdon was sixth to Harzand in the Group 1 Derby at Epsom, fourth behind that same star in the Group 1 Irish Derby at the Curragh and chased home Mont Ormel (later known as Helene Charisma) in the Group 1 Grand Prix de Paris at Saint-Cloud. That was in 2016, and the latter race took place sixteen months before he finally won a stakes race. That twelve-furlong listed victory at Kempton preceded a string of pattern-race seconds, including chasing home Crystal Ocean in the Group 2 Hardwicke Stakes at Royal Ascot, and he was gelded in December 2018. Since then, he has won four of his sixteen starts including the Group 3 John Smith's Silver Cup Stakes over fourteen furlongs at York in July 2019, a listed contest over half a furlong farther at Doncaster last June and, one month after that, the Group 2 Prix Maurice de Nieuil over 2,800 metres (fourteen furlongs) at ParisLongchamp.

He beat Called To The Bar by a length and a quarter that day but finished a well-beaten fourth to Telecaster in the Group 2 Lucien Barriere Grand Prix de Deauville next time and was last of seven in the Group 2 bet365 Doncaster Cup Stakes. He picked up third place in the Group 2 Premio Jockey Club - Sire Trofeo Pio Bruni over twelve furlongs on heavy ground at San Siro in late October, beaten a total of six and a quarter lengths by the winner, Walderbe, and then finished only fourth to Johnny Drama, to whom he was giving seven pounds, in the Listed Unibet Wild Flower Stakes over the same trip at Kempton in early December. Since then, he has been placed in handicaps at Chelmsford (fourteen furlongs) and Wolverhampton (nine and a half furlongs) and shortly before this book went to print, he was last of five in a ten-furlong listed contest won by Bangkok at Lingfield. His overall record stands at nine wins and thirteen places from forty-two starts with over £583,000 in prize money.

The Ed Dunlop-trained chestnut is an \$85,000 graduate of the Keeneland September Yearling Sale who made 90,000 guineas at the following April's Tattersalls Craven Breeze-Up Sale. He is a son of the classic winner and long-time Lane's End Farm resident Lemon Drop Kid (by Kingmambo) who has supplied nine

Group/Grade 1 winners among an overall tally of ninety-eight blacktype scorers; he is on the verge of reaching that notable career landmark of a triple-digit stakes-winner tally. Red Verdon's dam, on the other hand, is the sprinter Porto Marmay (by Choisir), who was a stakes winner on both sides of the Atlantic. She has produced three other winners, including the six-figure earner Portando (by Bertrando), and she is out of Nordicolini (by Nordico), a winning half-sister to the great Hong Kong champion River Verdon (by Be My Native), a Triple Crown winner and multiple champion at a mile and upwards.

Red Verdon has earned a triple-digit handicap mark each season from three to seven, with two pattern wins and multiple blacktype placings. His latest end-of-year mark of 108 compares well to his peak of 113 and it seems likely that, presuming he's happy and well, he will be capable of enhancing his CV further this coming season at the age of eight. He holds an entry in the ultra-valuable Red Sea Turf Handicap over fifteen furlongs at Riyadh in late February.

SUMMARY DETAILS
Bred: Liberty Road Stables
Owned: The Hon R J Arculli
Trained: Ed Dunlop
Country: England
Race record: 21-211042-000420321-142222000-100100-
411403433-0
Career highlights: 9 wins inc Prix Maurice de Nieuil (Gr2), John Smith's Silver Cup Stakes (Gr3), Betway Grand Cup Stakes (L), 32Red Wild Flower Stakes (L), 2nd Juddmonte Grand Prix de Paris (Gr1), Hardwicke Stakes (Gr2), Dunaden Jockey Club Stakes (Gr2), Bombay Sapphire Glorious Stakes (Gr3), Matchbook VIP Henry II Stakes (Gr3), 32Red Floodlit Stakes (L), 3rd Premio Jockey Club - Sire Trofeo Pio Bruni (Gr2)

RED VERDON (USA) – 2013 chestnut gelding

Lemon Drop Kid (USA)	Kingmambo (USA)	Mr Prospector (USA)
		Miesque (USA)
	Charming Lassie (USA)	Seattle Slew (USA)
		Lassie Dear (USA)
Porto Marmay (IRE)	Choisir (AUS)	Danehill Dancer (IRE)
		Great Selection (AUS)
	Nordicolini (IRE)	Nordico (USA)
		Tuyenu

REGAL REALITY (GB)

Regal Reality, a Cheveley Park Stud homebred, has not quite reached the peak he has promised to hit on occasion, but he is highly talented and just about good enough that, if things fell his way and principals met with trouble or other disappointment, he could snatch a big race. He has been placed once at the highest level, when third to Enable and Magical in the Group 1 Coral-Eclipse Stakes in 2019, but all three of his pattern wins have come at Group 3 level. The most recent of those was the AJN Steelstock Sovereign Stakes on good-to-firm ground at Salisbury in early August when, in a first-time visor, he defeated Beat Le Bon by three and a half lengths. He then finished just over six lengths third to Century Dream in the Group 2 Ladbrokes Celebration Mile Stakes at Goodwood and failed by just a neck to beat Kameko in the Group 2 Shadwell Joel Stakes at Newmarket a month later.

The now six-year-old is a gelded son of Intello (by Galileo), the Group 1 Prix du Jockey Club winner who has been serving alternate double seasons at Cheveley Park Stud and Haras du Quesnay. He is at the latter venue in 2021, standing for a fee of €10,000. He is a superbly bred stallion, as one might imagine given the sort of mare that goes to his sire, but he has been somewhat disappointing so far. The Group 1 Prix Jean Prat scorer Intellogent is his sole top-level winner among a total of just thirteen blacktype scorers, and Regal Reality is among the five others who have won at pattern level, all of them Group 3s. Of course, the stallion is only eleven years old, he is supported by an array of top breeders and so there is every reason to hope that his profile will strengthen considerably over the coming seasons.

His foals of 2020 include a filly out of the Group 3 Oak Tree Stakes and Group 3 Prestige Stakes winner Regal Realm (by Medicean), and that mid-February-born bay is a full sister to Regal Reality. He is the second foal of his dam and is the younger half-brother to Regal Splendour (by Pivotal), the unraced dam of Recovery Run (by Nathaniel). That Andrew Balding-trained colt notched up two wins and four seconds from six starts last season and had the third seven lengths behind when chasing home Lone

Eagle in the Group 3 Godolphin Flying Start Zetland Stakes over ten furlongs on soft ground at Newmarket in October.

Regal Realm has some prolific siblings but is the best of her dam's five winners. She is out of Regal Riband (by Fantastic Light), who is a winning daughter of the Group 1 Cheveley Park Stakes scorer Regal Rose (by Danehill), a filly who was closely related to her dam's half-brother Shaadi (by Danzig). He won the Group 1 Irish 2,000 Guineas, Group 2 St James's Palace Stakes and Group 3 Craven Stakes in 1989 but disappointed as a stallion.

Regal Reality has spent a large chunk of his career racing over ten furlongs, including the extended distance at York, but his last three outings of 2020 were over a mile, a trip over which he was a Group 2-placed pattern winner as a three-year-old. Perhaps it is over that distance that we may see him being campaigned in 2021, and so it could be a very interesting year for him.

SUMMARY DETAILS
Bred: Cheveley Park Stud Ltd
Owned: Cheveley Park Stud
Trained: Sir Michael Stoute
Country: England
Race record: 1-0133-313400-300132-
Career highlights: 4 wins inc AJN Steelstock Sovereign Stakes (Gr3), Matchbook Brigadier Gerard Stakes (Gr3), Bonhams Thoroughbred Stakes (Gr3), 2nd Shadwell Joel Stakes (Gr2), 3rd Coral-Eclipse Stakes (Gr1), Ladbrokes Celebration Mile Stakes (Gr2), bet365 Mile (Gr2), Shadwell Joel Stakes (Gr2), Unibet Mile (registered as the Superior Mile) (Gr3), Wolferton Stakes (L)

REGAL REALITY (GB) – 2015 bay gelding

Intello (GER)	Galileo (IRE)	Sadler's Wells (USA)
		Urban Sea (USA)
	Impressionnante (GB)	Danehill (USA)
		Occupandiste (IRE)
Regal Realm (GB)	Medicean (GB)	Machiavellian (USA)
		Mystic Goddess (USA)
	Regal Riband (GB)	Fantastic Light (USA)
		Regal Rose (GB)

ROMANISED (IRE)

Romanised's pedigree and race record were reviewed in detail in *European Group 1 Winners of 2019* and there is not much to add here. The classic-winning miler, now a stallion in France, started off his final racing season in good style when beating Lancaster House by almost two lengths to take the Group 2 Paddy Power Minstrel Stakes at the Curragh. Although that race had been a prelude to Group 1 success the year before, he finished well-beaten in all three of his subsequent blacktype outings this time around. His sole placing was a disappointing third at Dundalk where, in a one-mile conditions race, he was slowly away, expended a lot of energy early in the contest and then weakened in the closing stages. Saltonstall beat Harpocrates by three-quarters of a length with a similar gap back to Romanised. He had been giving a lot of weight to all of his rivals, but this was a dual Group 1 star in amongst mostly handicappers.

It had been said often that the entire's final race would be in the Group 1 Longines Hong Kong Mile and that he would then be going to stud, and it was mid-December, and after his crushing defeat at Sha Tin—where he missed the break, made up ground but had nothing more to give when it mattered—that details of his new career were revealed. He is standing at Haras de Bouquetot in France with a first-season fee of €7,000.

His other unplaced finishes in 2020 were fifth behind Palace Pier in the Group 1 Prix Haras de Fresnay-le-Buffard Jacques le Marois on heavy ground at Deauville and last of six behind Persian King in the Group 1 Prix du Moulin de Longchamp. When assessing his merit as a racehorse, it is best to overlook his final four starts; he was a very good miler at his best. His final handicap mark was 117, down only two pounds on the career-peak 119 he achieved after his classic success. Timeform, on the other hand, had him on 121 as a three-year-old and 123 at four.

Romanised, who could be described as being a three-parts brother to the four-time Hong Kong Group 1 star Designs On Rome, is one of thirteen Group 1 winners among the eighty-nine stakes winners by the Coolmore veteran and multiple classic sire Holy Roman Emperor (by Danehill) and he is the best of three stakes winners out of Romantic Venture (by Indian Ridge). He was bred by Monica Aherne, comes from a family that did well for Moyglare Stud, and has as his fourth dam a mare who was a half-sister to the Group 1 sire Taufan (by Stop The Music). That long-time Rathbarry Stud resident was only a Group 2-placed winner on the track but came up with Tagula, Taufan's Melody and twenty-one other stakes winners, with Tagula going on to sire a couple of Group 1 stars of his own.

This is also the family of the hugely influential mare Best In Show (by Traffic Judge)—she is a half-sister to Romanised's fifth dam— and there are many Group 1-siring stallions and even champion sires who have descended from her. He is a promising addition to the stallion ranks in France, one who, depending on what his mares contribute, get his best winners in the broad six-to-twelve-furlong range.

SUMMARY DETAILS

Bred: Monica Aherne
Owned: Robert Ng
Trained: Ken Condon
Country: Ireland
Race record: 1002-01000-044112-10030-
Career highlights: 5 wins inc Prix du Haras de Fresnay-le-Buffard Jacques le Marois (Gr1), Tattersalls Irish 2,000 Guineas (Gr1), Paddy Power Minstrel Stakes (Gr2-twice), 2nd Prix du Moulin de Longchamp (Gr1), BetBright Solario Stakes (Gr3)

ROMANISED (IRE) – 2015 bay horse

		Danzig (USA)
Holy Roman Emperor (IRE)	Danehill (USA)	Danzig (USA)
		Razyana (USA)
	L'On Vite (USA)	Secretariat (USA)
		Fanfreluche (CAN)
Romantic Venture (IRE)	Indian Ridge	Ahonoora
		Hillbrow
	Summer Trysting (USA)	Alleged (USA)
		Seasonal Pickup (USA)

ROSE OF KILDARE (IRE)

Rose of Kildare is an admirable filly. She is no star and seems unlikely to have much improvement in her given how many times she has raced, but this €3,000 Tattersalls Ireland September Yearling Sale graduate is another fine testament to Mark Johnston's judgement of a horse. She is also a horse that many would surely love to own. The triple Group 3 scorer has notched up six wins and six placings from eighteen starts, been placed in a Group 2 classic, earned almost £170,000 in prize money, and was sold privately to Qatar Racing Ltd shortly before her final start. She is going to be a fascinating broodmare prospect, but she is not done with racing yet.

She won five of her twelve starts as a two-year-old and was already running for the sixth time when finishing down the field behind Pinatubo in the Listed Chesham Stakes at Royal Ascot. Her Group 3 William Hill Firth of Clyde victory came on her eleventh outing, eighteen days before she added the Group 3 Godolphin Lifetime Care Oh So Sharp Stakes, and she finished that busy season on a rating of 103. She was well down the field behind Love in the Group 1 Qipco 1000 Guineas on her seasonal reappearance in June but then finished third in the Group 2 Wempe 100th German 1000 Guineas at Dusseldorf and filled the same position behind Summer Romance in the Group 3 Princess Elizabeth Stakes at Epsom before stepping up to middle-distances.

The early-March-born bay is by a classic-winning miler, out of a ten-furlong listed scorer and from a family whose best include an Irish St Leger victor and an Oaks-placed Yorkshire Oaks heroine, so it is not really a surprise that she was suited by the move. She made most of the running in the Group 3 Tattersalls Musidora Stakes five days later and ultimately won it going away from her quintet of rivals in style, passing the post two and a half lengths clear of Albaflora, with Ricetta and Dubai Love another half-length and the same back in third and fourth. That race is usually a classic trial, but in the odd year that was 2020 it came in early July and several days after the Oaks. Instead, this filly used it as springboard for her ambitious tilt at the Group 1 Juddmonte International Stakes.

There was never a moment where one might have thought she could sneak into the frame in that extended ten-furlong feature, but although weakening in the final furlong she managed to keep fairly close contact with the field, and that was a creditable effort. Ghaiyyath made all for a three-length win from Magical, who was a length and a quarter in front of Lord North. Kameko's stamina had appeared to ebb and he was another three-quarters of a length back in fourth, but the gap back to Rose of Kildare was only an additional two and three-quarter lengths. She tried twelve furlongs on her final start but lost second place on the line, finishing two and a half lengths and a nose third to Zamrud and Virginia Joy in a Group 2 contest for fillies and mares. The fourth, Sunny Queen, went on to Group 1 success over the trip later in the year.

Rose of Kildare represents the first crop of Make Believe (by Makfi), the Group 1 Poule d'Essai des Poulains (French 2000 Guineas) and Group 1 Prix de la Foret star who stands at Ballylinch Stud in Ireland. He has made a promising start to his stallion career, four of his five stakes winners have achieved the feat in pattern company, and the Group 1 Prix du Jockey Club (French Derby) winner Mishriff is among them. The filly is the second foal of the Listed Ballymacoll Stakes winner and Listed Chesham Stakes runner-up Cruck Realta (by Sixties Icon). Her half-brother Western Alliance (by Kingman) finished third in an eight-and-a-half-furlong novice race on his debut at Wolverhampton in early December, the mare had a Make Believe colt in April 2019—he was sold for 175,000 guineas from Book 2 of the Tattersalls October Yearling Sale; his sire's only six-figured lot of that age group in 2020—no return to Dandy Man (by Mozart) after that and was then bred to Fastnet Rock (by Danehill).

The first three or four generations are the most important when reviewing a pedigree—anything farther back is in the distant to remote range—and if you were to put only the first four generations of her pedigree on the catalogue page then there would be a lot of white space available for making notes. Aside from her and her dam, there is nothing there but a few minor winners under each generation. That would have likely been a factor in her bottom-of-the-market yearling price. When you even glance at the fifth generation, however, it becomes clear that it is not a poor family from which she comes but a weak branch of a strong one, albeit one so light it's almost akin to a twig.

Rosia Bay (by High Top) is her fifth dam and that dual winning half-sister to Teleprompter (by Welsh Pageant), Chatoyant (by Rainbow Quest) and Selection Board (by Welsh Pageant) is the dam of the middle-distance Group 1 stars Ibn Bay (by Mill Reef) and Roseate Tern (by Blakeney). Rosia Bay's other descendants include a variety of horses, from Group 2 winner and dual Group 1 Prix de l'Abbaye de Longchamp runner-up Rangali (by Namid) to the juvenile mile Group 1 scorer Red Bloom (by Selkirk) and her classic-placed dam Red Camellia (by Polar Falcon). Teleprompter, of course, won the Grade 1 Arlington Million and Group 2 Queen Elizabeth II Stakes among other races of note and, along with Bedtime, was one of those whose talent helped to bring about a lifting of the bar on geldings taking part in most Group 1 races in England. Chatoyant won the Group 3 Brigadier Gerard Stakes and was placed in the Group 2 Prince of Wales's Stakes, whereas Selection Board made her name at stud.

Most of those horses have only a remote connection to Rose of Kildare, as has Selection Board's outstanding daughter Ouija Board (by Cape Cross) and that champion's Derby-winning and classic-sire son Australia (by Galileo). There is a chance that she and her dam will remain the highlights in this part of the family, but it is also possible that we may be seeing a resurgence in what has been, from a blacktype perspective, a dormant line. It will be fascinating to see how their broodmare records unfold in the coming years and what impact they might have in the long-term.

SUMMARY DETAILS
Bred: Wansdyke Farms Ltd
Owned: Qatar Racing Ltd
Trained: Mark Johnston
Country: England
Race record: 241120013411-033103-

Career highlights: 6 wins inc Tattersalls Musidora Stakes (Gr3), Godolphin Lifetime Care Oh So Sharp Stakes (Gr3), William Hill Firth of Clyde Stakes (Gr3), 3rd T von Zastrow Stutenpreis (Gr2), Wempe 100th German 1000 Guineas (Gr2), Princess Elizabeth Stakes - sponsored by Investec (Gr3)

ROSE OF KILDARE (IRE) – 2017 bay filly

Make Believe (GB)	Makfi (GB)	Dubawi (IRE)
		Dhelaal (GB)
	Rosie's Posy (IRE)	Suave Dancer (USA)
		My Branch (GB)
Cruck Realta (GB)	Sixties Icon (GB)	Galileo (IRE)
		Love Divine (GB)
	Wansdyke Lass (GB)	Josr Algarhoud (IRE)
		Silankka (GB)

ROYAL CRUSADE (GB)

This colt is an intriguing prospect and something of a dark horse. He was only sixth to Golden Horde in the Group 1 Commonwealth Cup at Royal Ascot in June but then beat Glen Shiel by a length and a quarter to take the Group 3 Prix du Ris-Orangis over six furlongs on good ground at Deauville in mid-July. He was not seen out again, but the gelding he beat that day went on to Group 1 glory in the autumn and a future rematch could go either way.

The Godolphin homebred started out over seven furlongs, the sort of juvenile campaign you expect to see in a colt being considered as a classic prospect. He kicked off with a narrow success on the July Course at Newmarket, failed by only a neck to beat Threat in the Group 2 Pommery Champagne Stakes at Doncaster—both of those races on good-to-firm ground—and was then a beaten favourite in the Group 3 Prix Thomas Bryon on very soft ground at Saint-Cloud that October. His stablemate King's Command made all to beat him by three and a half lengths, with Wooded, the Group 1 Prix de l'Abbaye de Longchamp star of 2020, finishing a neck behind in third. Now it seems as though he may be slotting into the sprinters' division, and that could set up the possibility of him meeting one of his talented relations on the track.

Royal Crusade is a son of the late and much-missed Shamardal (by Giant's Causeway) and both of his other racing-age siblings are winners. Severanaya (by Dubawi) ran only as a three-year-old, was a wide-margin winner over a mile at Newcastle and seven furlongs at Chepstow before finishing third in a mile handicap at Newmarket on her final start. She was bred to Lope de Vega (by Shamardal) in 2020. Royal Fleet (by Dubawi), on the other hand, is a promising prospect for this season having won a seven-furlong novice race at Kempton in late November, his only race to date. Like Royal Crusade, he is trained by Charlie Appleby. They are out of the mile Group 3 scorer Zibelina (by Dansili), who is a half-sister to the juvenile listed winner Floristry (by Fasliyev). Lazuli (by Dubawi), who is also reviewed in this volume, is the better of that sprinter's stakes winners having won the Group 3

Dubai International Airport World Trophy Stakes and Listed Unibet Scurry Stakes last season.

These horses may paint a picture of this being a speed family, and it is certainly true that they represent a branch that is producing some quick horses, but the third dam, Talented (by Bustino), won the Group 2 Sun Chariot Stakes when it was run over ten furlongs, she was runner-up in the Group 3 Lancashire Oaks and produced two middle-distance stakes-winning sons. Carlton House (by Machiavellian) is the more notable. He won the Group 2 Dante Stakes and Group 3 Brigadier Gerard Stakes, was runner-up in the Group 1 Prince of Wales's Stakes and in a Group 1 contest in Australia and, from a small number of Australian-born progeny, is the sire of the dual stakes winner Too Close The Sun, who was runner-up in a one-mile Group 1 handicap in late November and beaten by only three and a half lengths when finishing fourth to the Dundeel (by High Chaparral) gelding Truly Great in the nine-furlong Group 1 Kingston Town Classic at Ascot, Australia, in early December.

Talented was out of an unraced mare named Triple Reef, that one a daughter of Mill Reef (by Never Bend) and Triple First (by High Top), winner of the Group 2 Nassau Stakes, Group 2 Sun Chariot Stakes (ten furlongs), Group 3 Musidora Stakes, Group 3 May Hill Stakes and fourth in the Group 1 Oaks at Epsom. That sounds pure middle-distance, although Triple First was by a 2000 Guineas winner and out of a daughter of Grey Sovereign (by Nasrullah) and so perhaps it is not such as surprise that some of her descendants have shown more speed than stamina. Triple Reef is an ancestor of the Group 1 Irish St Leger winner Duncan (by Dalakhani), Group 2 Doncaster Cup scorer Samuel (by Sakhee) and Group 2 Park Hill Stakes heroine Gretchen (by Galileo)—that trio is out of her miler great-granddaughter Dolores (by Danehill)—but also of the pattern-winning sprinters Presto Shinko (by Shinko Forest) and Three Points (by Bering), the latter having also finished second in the Group 1 Prix Maurice de Gheest.

Royal Crusade is clearly talented and, like Lazuli, he could play a prominent role in the sprinters' division in 2021. His two-year-old form and pedigree suggest that he may stay a mile, although the cadence of 2.43 that he recorded at Doncaster as a juvenile catches the eye. The distance could be within his range but six to seven furlongs may suit better. As for his dam, she had no return from her breeding to Lope de Vega in 2019 and she was covered by both Shamardal and his sprint-star son Blue Point last season.

SUMMARY DETAILS
Bred: Godolphin
Owned: Godolphin
Trained: Charlie Appleby
Country: England
Race record: 122-01-
Career highlights: 2 wins inc Qatar Prix de Ris-Orangis (Gr3), 2nd Pommery Champagne Stakes (Gr2), Prix Thomas Bryon Jockey Club de Turquie (Gr3)

ROYAL CRUSADE (GB) – 2017 bay colt

Shamardal (USA)	Giant's Causeway (USA)	Storm Cat (USA)
		Mariah's Storm (USA)
	Helsinki (GB)	Machiavellian (USA)
		Helen Street
Zibelina (IRE)	Dansili (GB)	Danehill (USA)
		Hasili (IRE)
	Zaeema (GB)	Zafonic (USA)
		Talented (GB)

ROYAL DORNOCH (IRE)

Gleneagles (by Galileo) went to stud as one of the most exciting prospects of his year, a two-year-old star who became a dual classic-winning miler at three and whose pattern-winning dam is a full sister to champion racehorse and multiple US champion sire Giant's Causeway (by Storm Cat). Those in his initial crop have just turned four, and although he is yet to get a winner at the highest level, and his tally of eight stakes winners is disappointing for a horse of his credentials, there remains reason to hope that it is just a matter of time before his profile picks up and the top-level winners start to appear.

Two of his first-crop sons have won Group 2 contests and they got those wins as juveniles; another of his juvenile stakes winners, Southern Hills, starts his stallion career at March Hare Stud in 2021. Royal Lytham won the Group 2 July Stakes over six furlongs, finished third in the Group 1 Phoenix Stakes and is now in his first season as a sire at Clongiffen Stud in Ireland. Royal Dornoch, on the other hand, picked up the Group 2 Royal Lodge Stakes over a mile after finishing third in the Group 2 Richmond Stakes. He also won the Group 3 Desmond Stakes over a mile at Leopardstown at three, beating Ancient Spirit by a neck, although he finished well-beaten in each of the Group 1 2000 Guineas, Group 1 St James's Palace Stakes and Group 1 Queen Elizabeth II Stakes. His penultimate start of the year was in the Group 2 Clipper Logistics Boomerang Mile on the opening day of Irish Champions Weekend, and although he kept on well in the closing stages and pipped Century Dream for fourth place on the line, he never looked like getting to the principals. Safe Voyage short-headed Sinawann, there was a four-length gap back to Gleneagles's full brother Vatican City in third and that colt was another two and a half lengths clear of Royal Dornoch.

His final engagement of the year was at the Tattersalls Autumn Horses-in-Training Sale in late October when he fetched the surprisingly low price of 35,000 guineas, bought by Fathi Egziama. Royal Dornoch was bred by the famous Barronstown Stud in Ireland, he made 240,000 guineas at the Tattersalls December Yearling Sale in 2018, and he holds an official handicap mark of

110. As one might imagine, he has some talented relations, notably his half-sister Hawksmoor (by Azamour). She won the Group 3 Prestige Stakes in England at two, the Group 2 German 1000 Guineas at three, she was placed in the Group 1 Prix Saint-Alary and went on to become a US Grade 1-placed Grade 2 winner whose career earnings passed the $1.1 million mark. Their half-sister Magical Fire (by Dragon Pulse) was runner-up in the Group 2 Duchess of Cambridge Stakes as a two-year-old, their non-winning half-sister Qatar Princess (by Marju) is the dam of 2019's Group 3-placed juvenile sprint stakes winner Flaming Princess (by Hot Streak), and their dam, Bridal Dance (by Danehill Dancer), is a half-sister to the Grade 1-placed Grade 3 scorer Millennium Dragon (by Mark of Esteem). Canadian Grade 2 and multiple US Grade 3 winner J'Ray (by Distant View) is among those of note who appear under the third generation of the pedigree.

Royal Dornoch has left Ireland to join Musabbeh Al Mheiri in the United Arab Emirates and he has been entered in an ultra-valuable seven-furlong conditions race at Riyadh in late February.

SUMMARY DETAILS
Bred: Barronstown Stud
Owned: Michael Tabor, Derrick Smith & Mrs John Magnier
(now Abdulwahhab Misbah Rajab Altireeki)
Trained: Aidan O'Brien (now Musabbeh Al Mheiri)
Country: Ireland (now United Arab Emirates)
Race record: 0230101-00140-
Career highlights: 3 wins inc Juddmonte Royal Lodge Stakes (Gr2), Clipper Logistics Desmond Stakes (Gr3), 3rd Qatar Richmond Stakes (Gr2)

ROYAL DORNOCH (IRE) – 2017 bay colt

Gleneagles (IRE)	Galileo (IRE)	Sadler's Wells (USA)
		Urban Sea (USA)
	You'resothrilling (USA)	Storm Cat (USA)
		Mariah's Storm (USA)
Bridal Dance (IRE)	Danehill Dancer (IRE)	Danehill (USA)
		Mira Adonde (USA)
	Feather Bride (IRE)	Groom Dancer (USA)
		Bubbling Danseuse (USA)

RUSSIAN EMPEROR (IRE)

Russian Emperor was one of the more fancied of the six Aidan O'Brien-trained colts who ran in the Group 1 Investec Derby at Epsom in July. However, he finished fourth among them, seventh overall in the race itself, and was not seen out again. It was later reported that he had been exported to Hong Kong and, in January, a few weeks before this book went to print, he ran twice for the Douglas Whyte team, finishing unplaced in a seven-furlong handicap and a one-mile conditions race at Sha Tin.

The colt's career began with a third-place finish in a seven-furlong Curragh maiden in July 2019, his only start as a juvenile, and he kicked off his classic season with a short-head victory over a mile on ground described as soft-to-heavy at Naas in late March. He chased home half-length winner and stablemate Cormorant in the Group 3 Derrinstown Stud Derby Trial Stakes over ten furlongs on fast ground at Leopardstown on his next start, in early June, and then beat First Receiver by half a length to take the Group 3 Hampton Court Stakes over that same trip at Royal Ascot eight days later.

The son of Galileo (by Sadler's Wells) is out of Atlantic Jewel (by Fastnet Rock), a multiple clear-cut Group 1 star from seven to ten furlongs and whose only defeat in an eleven-race career came when short-headed by Dundeel in the Group 1 Underwood Stakes over nine furlongs at Caulfield on her penultimate start. Russian Emperor is her third foal, she had a Galileo filly in 2018—named Atlantic Emerald—a colt by the sire in 2019, but sadly died last August at Coolmore's Australian farm. She suffered a fatal haemorrhage after foaling a colt by the US Triple Crown star Justify (by Scat Daddy). The mare was a three-parts sister to the Group 1 Schweppes Thousand Guineas winner Commanding Jewel (by Commands), and the pair of them were out of Regard (by Zabeel), a winning mare with strong European connections.

Nanshan (by Nashwan), the grandam of Atlantic Jewel, is a half-sister to the Group 1 Cheveley Park Stakes winner and juvenile filly champion Embassy (by Cadeaux Genereux), who is the grandam of Group 1 Prix Maurice de Gheest scorer King's Apostle (by King's Best). Her siblings also include Puck's Castle (by Shirley Heights), the stakes-placed dam of the Group 2-placed sprint stakes winner Emerald Peace (by Green Desert) and ancestor of the classic-placed juvenile pattern scorer East (by Frankel). They are out of the classic-placed Group 1 Cheveley Park Stakes heroine Pass The Peace (by Alzao) and so can also count Tarfshi (by Mtoto) among their siblings. That multiple blacktype scorer got her best win in the Group 2 Pretty Polly Stakes over ten furlongs at the Curragh and she is the grandam of both the Group 3 John of Gaunt Stakes winner Absolutely So (by Acclamation) and the Grade 1-winning South African sprinter Pacific Trader (by Sail From Seattle).

SUMMARY DETAILS
Bred: Coolmore, Lauri Macri & Partners
Owned: Laurie Macri, Mrs J Magnier, et al (now Mike Cheung Shun Ching)
Trained: Aidan O'Brien (now Douglas White)
Country: Ireland (now Hong Kong)
Race record: 3-1210-00
Career highlights: 2 wins inc Hampton Court Stakes (Gr3), 2nd Derrinstown Stud Derby Trial Stakes (Gr3)

RUSSIAN EMPEROR (IRE) – 2017 bay colt

Galileo (IRE)	Sadler's Wells (USA)	Northern Dancer
		Fairy Bridge (USA)
	Urban Sea (USA)	Miswaki (USA)
		Allegretta
Atlantic Jewel (AUS)	Fastnet Rock (AUS)	Danehill (USA)
		Piccadilly Circus (AUS)
	Regard (AUS)	Zabeel (NZ)
		Nanshan (IRE)

SAFE VOYAGE (IRE)

Safe Voyage was well-beaten on his only start at two, gelded that autumn, and finished his three-year-old season with one win, three unplaced runs and an instance of 'unseated rider'. It would have been hard to imagine then that the seventy-five-rated bay would go on to become a leading seven-furlong performer who would enjoy Group 2 success at a mile and earn a trip to the Breeders' Cup.

The John Quinn-trainee won three from seven as a four-year-old but it was at five that he first moved into the triple-digit range of the handicap. He had kicked off that short campaign with a six-length score on soft ground at Haydock in late April but rose to 103 after a narrow win in the valuable Ahonoora Handicap at the Galway Festival. He finished well down the field in the one-mile Balmoral Handicap at Ascot on his only other run but returned at the age of six when his profile took a leap forward. That season began with a treble at Haydock: handicap success in April, a listed win in May and a one-and-three-quarter-length defeat of Suedois in the Group 3 Betway John of Gaunt Stakes, the latter on heavy ground. He then finished third to Romanised in the Group 2 Paddy Power Minstrel Stakes at the Curragh and fourth to One Master in the Group 1 Prix de la Foret at ParisLongchamp before putting up the best performance of his life to that point, taking third to King of Change and The Revenant in the Group 1 Queen Elizabeth II Stakes on heavy ground at Ascot. Despite the added pressure that the distance and ground placed on his stamina, he was staying on at the finish, only beaten by margins of one and a quarter lengths and one and a half lengths.

That fine effort, for which his rating moved up to 114, broadened the potential range of targets for him in 2020. Subsequent Group 1 scorer Space Blues beat him by a neck in the Listed Betway Spring Trophy Stakes over seven furlongs on good-to-soft ground at Haydock in early June and by three lengths when the pair finished first and fourth in the Group 2 Qatar Lennox Stakes on good at the end of July. Between those two runs, he beat Vale of Kent by a length and a half to take the Listed Investec Surrey Stakes at Epsom, and he followed the Goodwood defeat with an impressive effort at York. This was his day, his front-running performance earned a career-high mark of 116 and he posted a three-and-a-half-length victory in the Group 2 Sky Bet City of York Stakes. The ground was good-to-soft, the triple Group 1 Prix de la Foret heroine One Master did not show her best yet chased him home—she reasserted her superiority at ParisLongchamp six weeks later—Queen Jo Jo ran a big race in third and there was an over four-length gap back to Threat in fourth.

Safe Voyage was only beaten by a neck and a short head when third to One Master and Earthlight in the 2020 edition of the Group 1 Qatar Prix de la Foret, run on heavy ground, but went into that race following a notable performance in Ireland. The ground was good at Leopardstown on the opening day of Irish Champions Weekend, local riding star Colin Keane was on board the gelding for the first time, and the race turned into a two-way battle throughout the final furlong. Safe Voyage went to the front but was pursued by the talented three-year-old Sinawann, ridden by Ronan Whelan for the Michael Halford stable. The Aga Khan's colt, a pattern winner who had finished sixth in the Group 1 Irish 2,000 Guineas, got his nose in front in the closing stages but his older rival would not be denied and the pair flashed past the post together, four lengths clear of the regally bred but somewhat disappointing Group 1 Irish 2,000 Guineas runner-up Vatican City. The official margin was a short-head in Safe Voyage's favour and a stewards' enquiry made no alterations to the placings.

Now a winner of a dozen of his thirty starts and with over £520,000 in earnings, Safe Voyage is among the star representatives of his late sire, Fast Company (by Danehill Dancer). The lightly raced Group 1-placed juvenile Group 3 scorer spent five seasons at Rathasker Stud and one at Overbury Stud before joining the team at Kildangan Stud and he was in his fourth year at the latter when he died, aged fifteen. He had covered nineteen mares at the time so will have left behind one final but small crop, arriving this year. He also shuttled to Chile and it is there that his standout performer was born. Seven-figure earner Robert Bruce was a classic and multiple Grade 1 star there before moving north and adding the Grade 1 Arlington Million as well as

Grade 3 success and a couple of Grade 1 placings. Of his Europeans, Baitha Alga won the Group 2 Norfolk Stakes, Devonshire won the Group 2 Ridgewood Pearl Stakes and finished third in the Group 1 Irish 1,000 Guineas, whereas Jet Setting's trio of pattern-race wins featured victory in the 2016 edition of that same mile classic. It was a somewhat fortunate success given that odds-on favourite Minding suffered facial injuries when hitting her head in the stalls but only failed by a head to take the classic, although the pair finished ten lengths clear of the third, Now Or Later.

Shishangaan (by Mujadil), the dam of £52,000 DBS Premier Yearling Sale graduate Safe Voyage, is also responsible for the five-time middle-distance scorer Lyrica's Lion (by Dragon Pulse). She had a Cappella Sansevero (by Showcasing) filly in 2019 and was bred to Dansant (by Dansili)—by whom she had a filly in 2018—last season. She was listed-placed at six and seven furlongs in France and Italy, has two blacktype-placed half-brothers, and is a daughter of Irish Flower (by Zieten), a stakes-placed multiple winner in France at seven and eight furlongs. That mare has a string of winning siblings, headed by the mile Irish listed scorer Doreg (by Fools Holme), and she is out of a half-sister to Superlative (by Nebbiolo). He was a leading sprint juvenile of 1983 when he won the Group 2 Flying Childers Stakes and Group 3 July Stakes and was placed in both the Group 1 Middle Park Stakes and Group 1 Prix Robert-Papin. His overall record at stud was fairly average but he did give us the middle-distance German Group 1 scorer Kornado, juvenile Group 1 winner Superpower, the capable US sprinter Superstrike, Winter Derby winner Supreme Sound, and the Group 3 Sweet Solera Stakes winner Pearl Angel who picked up third place in the Group 1 Oaks at Epsom despite finishing twenty lengths behind the runner-up, All At Sea. That was the year that User Friendly landed the classic by three and a half lengths.

Safe Voyage finished last behind Order of Australia in the Grade 1 Breeders' Cup Mile on firm ground at Keeneland on his final start in early November. He is much better suited to some cut in the ground, although, as his Irish win demonstrates, is not the mudlark some have called him; he goes on most surfaces. He has now turned eight but having been better than ever at the age of seven there is every reason to hope that, presuming he's happy and well, he may have another rewarding season ahead of him. He has been something of a seven-furlong specialist in recent years but being a Group 1-placed pattern winner from just five starts over a mile, it would be interesting to see more of what he can do over that trip.

SUMMARY DETAILS
Bred: Adolf Schneider
Owned: Ross Harmon
Trained: John Quinn
Country: England
Race record: 0-001U0-1102414-110-1113343-2141130-
Career highlights: 12 wins inc Clipper Logistics Boomerang Mile (Gr2), Sky Bet City of York Stakes (Gr2), Betway John of Gaunt Stakes (Gr3), Investec Surrey Stakes (L), Pertemps Network Spring Trophy Stakes (L), 2nd Betway Spring Trophy Stakes (L), 3rd Queen Elizabeth II Stakes (Gr1), Qatar Prix de la Foret (Gr1), Unibet Hungerford Stakes (Gr2), Paddy Power Minstrel Stakes (Gr2)

SAFE VOYAGE (IRE) – 2013 bay gelding

Fast Company (IRE)	Danehill Dancer (IRE)	Danehill (USA)
		Mira Adonde (USA)
	Sheezalady (GB)	Zafonic (USA)
		Canadian Mill (USA)
Shishangaan (IRE)	Mujadil (USA)	Storm Bird (CAN)
		Vallee Secrete (USA)
	Irish Flower (IRE)	Zieten (USA)
		Sally St Clair

<h1 style="text-align:center">SAFFRON BEACH (IRE)</h1>

New Bay was runner-up in a one-mile conditions race on the Polytrack at Chantilly in late November on his only start as a two-year-old, so it is reasonable to expect that the Arc-placed classic star will become a sire whose best results are with his three-year-olds and older horses. Such a stallion typically gets a few autumn two-year-olds who catch the eye or do particularly well and so it was no surprise to see Ballylinch Stud's regally related son of Dubawi (by Dubai Millennium) have a successful freshman season. Four of his low double-digit number of winners earned blacktype, one of those was the Group 2 Royal Lodge Stakes and Listed Flying Scotsman Stakes scorer New Mandate, and the quartet also featured the unbeaten pattern winner Saffron Beach.

The chestnut sprang a surprise on her debut over seven furlongs of the Rowley Mile at Newmarket in late September but there was no hint of fluke about the way in which she stormed clear of her fourteen rivals to post a four-and-a-quarter-length win. Her five closest pursuers all had prior racecourse experience, and the third, Nebulosa, was a clear-cut maiden winner next time out. It is fair to say that the 2020 edition of the Group 3 Godolphin Lifetime Care Oh So Sharp Stakes did not look a strong one. Runner-up Thank You Next had plenty of experience—the nursery winner had been out of the frame in two prior blacktype events—and Saffron Beach was assigned a handicap mark of only 101 following her half-length victory here. The twice-raced Leicester winner Shine For You was a rapidly diminishing length and a quarter back in third, a half-length in front of the blacktype-placed pair Mamma Wamba and Setarhe, who had a dozen prior runs between them. However, the first three finishers picked up Group 3 blacktype, an especially valuable commodity for the winner.

The filly is a 55,000-guinea graduate of the Tattersalls December Foal Sale, she is the second foal of the lightly raced seven-furlong Lingfield maiden Falling Petals (by Raven's Pass) and Shadwell Estate Company had to go to 120,000 guineas to secure her now two-year-old Exceed And Excel (by Danehill) half-brother from the Tattersalls October Book 2 Yearling Sale.

The mare had an Australia (by Galileo) filly last year and was then bred back to New Bay. Five-length UAE 1000 Guineas winner Infinite Spirit (by Maria's Mon), the grandam of this year's potential classic contender, is also responsible for several multiple winners, including the prolific miler Vainglory (by Swain) who achieved a peak handicap mark of ninety-four. The full sister to mile listed scorer Moquette and half-sister to Royal Hunt Cup victor Invisible Man (by Elusive Quality) is, in turn, a daughter of the talented Eternal Reve (by Diesis), a Group 3 Matron Stakes winner who chased home Danish in the Grade 1 Queen Elizabeth II Challenge Cup over a furlong farther at Keeneland and was short-headed by the front-running Kissing Cousin—the first of Danehill's eighty-three Group 1 stars—in the Group 1 Coronation Stakes at Royal Ascot.

This means that the fourth dam of Saffron Beach is Northern Eternity (by Northern Dancer), the stakes winner and Group 2 Lowther Stakes runner-up whose Group 1-winning half-brother Miswaki (by Mr Prospector) was the prolific blacktype sire whose top-level stars featured Arc heroine and broodmare superstar Urban Sea.

Saffron Beach, who is trained by Jane Chapple-Hyam, holds entries in the Group 1 Tattersalls Irish 1,000 Guineas and Group 1 Emirates Poule d'Essai des Pouliches (French 1000 Guineas). She needs to step up considerably on what she showed at two if she is going to be able to hold her own at the top level, but this is a filly who is bred to be better at three than she was as a juvenile, which makes her an interesting prospect.

SUMMARY DETAILS

Bred: China Horse Club International Ltd
Owned: Mrs B V Sangster, J Wigan & O Sangster
Trained: Jane Chapple-Hyam
Country: England
Race record: 11-
Career highlights: 2 wins inc Godolphin Lifetime Care Oh So Sharp Stakes (Gr3)

SAFFRON BEACH (IRE) – 2018 chestnut filly

New Bay (GB)	Dubawi (IRE)	Dubai Millennium (GB)
		Zomaradah (GB)
	Cinnamon Bay (GB)	Zamindar (USA)
		Trellis Bay (GB)
Falling Petals (IRE)	Raven's Pass (USA)	Elusive Quality (USA)
		Ascutney (USA)
	Infinite Spirit (USA)	Maria's Mon (USA)
		Eternal Reve (USA)

SANTOSHA (IRE)

Santosha was a 50/1 long-shot on her first two starts and finished well-beaten in a pair of Group 2 races as her final two runs, but she is better than that sounds. The first-crop daughter of Rathasker Stud stallion Coulsty (by Kodiac) made a winning debut over six furlongs at Lingfield in late June, scoring by one and three-quarter lengths, and was then pitched straight into pattern company. The ground was soft on the July Course at Newmarket when she finished third in the Group 2 Duchess of Cambridge Stakes, and she was bumped at the start, but she stayed on well in the closing stages, only failing by margins of a head and half a length to beat Dandalla and Fev Rover. The winner had run away with the Group 3 Albany Stakes on her previous start, whereas the runner-up took a listed contest and the Group 2 Shadwell Prix du Calvados on her next two starts and rounded off her season with a fourth-place finish in the Group 1 Qatar Prix Marcel Boussac. Time Scale, who was a neck behind Santosha in fourth and four lengths clear of the fifth, Hala Hala Hala, had won a listed contest easily over the course and distance on her previous run. The bunched nature of the finish case a shade on the strength of the form, but at least the credentials of the principals were solid.

Sixteen days later, Santosha beat Hala Hala Hala and her own stablemate Caroline Dale by three-quarters of a lengths and the same to take the Group 3 Princess Margaret Betfred Stakes over six furlongs on good ground at Ascot. She had drifted to her left in the closing stages but kept on well. It was an eye-catching performance, as was that of the fourth-placed filly, Isabella Giles, who was staying on strongly, only failed to take third by a short head, and looked likely to be suited to a step up in trip. That rival would duly go on to easy Group 3 and Group 2 success over seven furlongs, the latter being the Shadwell Rockfel Stakes at Newmarket where Santosha finished last of the five runners. The David Loughnane-trained bay was also well-beaten behind Miss Amulet in the Group 2 Sky Bet Lowther Stakes at York.

Santosha is a May 6th-born daughter of a stallion whose best wins came at three and four and whose dam, Princess Zoffany (by Zoffany), was placed in ten-furlong handicaps on fast ground at

Brighton and Salisbury. Her dam's siblings include mile-placed dual sprint winner Tarsille (by Dansili) and the middle-distance flat winner and Towcester handicap hurdle scorer Timoca (by Marju), and the mare is out of Tara Gold (by Royal Academy), a ten-furlong-winning full sister to Listed Strensall Stakes scorer and Group 1 St James's Palace Stakes third Gold Academy. This suggests that Santosha may improve from two to three and, combined with the cadence of 2.37 she recorded on her debut, that she may stay a mile.

As for her sire, Coulsty had only a handful of first-crop runners compared to some of his cohorts but, in addition to this filly, supplied the Italian listed scorers Sopran Aragorn and Suicide Squad, Group 3 Round Tower Stakes third Coulthard and the listed-placed Coul Queen. He has only a dozen two-year-olds for this coming season, had three foals registered in 2020, and covered just nine mares last season. The 2021 fee of this well-related grandson of Danehill (by Danzig) has been advertised as €4,000 and his freshman results should give him a deserved and much-needed boost in support.

SUMMARY DETAILS
Bred: Paddy Murray
Owned: Ms S Lyons
Trained: David Loughnane
Country: England
Race record: 13100-
Career highlights: 2 wins inc Princess Margaret Betfred Stakes (Gr3), 3rd Duchess of Cambridge Stakes - sponsored by bet365 (Gr2)

SANTOSHA (IRE) – 2018 bay filly

Coulsty (IRE)	Kodiac (GB)	Danehill (USA)
		Rafha
	Hazium (IRE)	In The Wings
		Safe Care (IRE)
Princess Zoffany (RE)	Zoffany (IRE)	Dansili (GB)
		Tyranny (GB)
	Tara Gold (IRE)	Royal Academy (USA)
		Soha (USA)

SECRET ADVISOR (FR)

Secret Advisor (by Dubawi) won the valuable fourteen-furlong Melrose Handicap at York on his final start at three and two months after he finished third to Stradivarius and Count Octave, beaten by a neck and two lengths, in the Group 2 Queen's Vase over the same trip on fast ground at Ascot. He was then off the track for twenty-two months, had been gelded in the interim, and finished well-beaten on his only starts of 2019. However, Godolphin kept him in training as a six-year-old and the decision was rewarded with listed and Group 3 success. He was not disgraced in Group 1 company on his final outing.

He sprang something of a surprise when landing a fourteen-furlong listed handicap at Meydan in January but proved that was no fluke by following up in the Group 3 Nad Al Sheba Trophy over the same course and distance a month later. He hit the front a furlong and a half out that day and kept on well to the line to beat a trio of his owner's other contenders, headed by the Saeed bin Suroor-trained Dubai Future, the length-and-a-quarter runner-up. Although trained by Charlie Appleby, Secret Advisor's only run in England came at Newmarket in early June where he stayed on past First In Line in the final half-furlong to get within a length of the front-running Dashing Willoughby in the Listed Betfair Exchange Buckhounds Stakes over twelve furlongs. This was a notable effort as his group-race penalty meant he was giving the winner five pounds.

It would have been interesting to see him tackle further middle-distance races in England, but it was five months before he returned to action and that was in the Group 1 Allianz - Grosser Preis von Bayern on heavy ground at Munich in November. Although hitting the front a quarter of a mile from home, he was unable to sustain that effort to the finish and had to settle for fourth behind the three-year-olds Sunny Queen, Torquator Tasso and Dicaprio. The only other time he has ever raced on anything easier than good ground was when an unplaced favourite in a valuable Goodwood handicap as a three-year-old, on soft ground.

Secret Advisor is a half-brother to the Group 2 Prix du Conseil de Paris winner and Group 1 Champion Stakes third Subway Dancer (by Shamardal), who is well suited to very soft underfoot conditions, and he is out of Sub Rose (by Galileo). Both of her races were on soft, including her three-length defeat of Treat Gently in the Group 3 Prix de Royaumont, but her full sister, Astonishing, preferred a sounder surface and was a seven-length listed scorer at Newmarket, also over twelve furlongs. That sibling is also a successful broodmare, represented in 2020 by her Group 3 Gallinule Stakes runner-up, on good-to-firm, and Group 3 Diamond Stakes third Gold Maze (by Golden Horn) plus that one's younger half-brother Surprise Exhibit (by Showcasing), an easy Wolverhampton winner who finished third in a one-mile listed contest on good-to-soft, was well-beaten on soft and then gelded. Third dam Magic Gleam (by Danzig) trounced classic star Ensconse by four lengths in the Group 2 Child Stakes (now Falmouth Stakes) on good ground at Newmarket after finishing a half-length runner-up to Golden Opinion in the Group 1 Coronation Stakes on firm at Ascot.

Secret Advisor, a 114-rated gelding, clearly has plenty of ability and although he is now seven years old, he has only run a dozen times. It will be interesting to see how he fares if returning to action in Europe in 2021, especially if avoiding soft ground. He holds an entry in the ultra-valuable Red Sea Turf Handicap over fifteen furlongs at Riyadh in late February.

SUMMARY DETAILS
Bred: SCEA Haras de Saint Pair
Owned: Godolphin
Trained: Charlie Appleby
Country: England
Race record: -122301/00-1124-
Career highlights: 4 wins inc Nad Al Sheba Trophy sponsored by Mohammed Bin Rashid Al Maktoum City-District One (Gr3), Meydan Cup sponsored by P&O Marinas (L), 2nd Betfair Exchange Buckhounds Stakes (L), 3rd Queen's Vase (Gr2)

SECRET ADVISOR (FR) – 2014 bay gelding

Dubawi (IRE)	Dubai Millennium (GB)	Seeking The Gold (USA)
		Colorado Dancer
	Zomaradah (GB)	Deploy
		Jawaher (IRE)
Sub Rose (IRE)	Galileo (IRE)	Sadler's Wells (USA)
		Urban Sea (USA)
	Amazing Krisken (USA)	Kris S (USA)
		Magic Gleam (USA)

SINAWANN (IRE)

Kingman (by Invincible Spirit) was a brilliant miler and the young Banstead Manor Stud resident has made an exciting start to his stallion career. He has had three crops of racing age in action so far and has supplied twenty-nine stakes winners, three of them successful at the highest level. His first-crop standout Persian King won the Group 1 Poule d'Essai des Poulains (French 2000 Guineas) and was runner-up in the Group 1 Prix du Jockey Club (French Derby) in 2019 before returning to action at four to add the Group 1 Prix d'Ispahan and Group 1 Prix du Moulin de Longchamp and take third place in the Group 1 Prix de l'Arc de Triomphe. Like the Group 2-winning sprinter Calyx, who has already served a season for Coolmore, Persian King has joined the stallion ranks, new to Haras d'Etreham in 2021 and for a fee of €30,000. Kingman's second crop was lit up by Palace Pier, the John Gosden-trained star who won both the Group 1 St James's Palace Stakes and Group 1 Prix du Fresnay-le-Buffard Jacques le Marois and whose only defeat to date is his third-place finish to The Revenant and Roseman (by Kingman) in the Group 1 Queen Elizabeth II Stakes in October. Domestic Spending landed the Grade 1 Hollywood Derby in late November.

Sinawann is among the thirteen of his sire's progeny to have won at pattern level and although only a Group 3 scorer right now, there is every reason to hope that this colt can strike at a higher level in 2021. The 115-rated bay chased home Mogul in a one-mile Group 2 at Leopardstown on his final of three starts at two, was sixth to Siskin in the Group 1 Tattersalls Irish 2,000 Guineas on his seasonal reappearance, won the Group 3 Amethyst Stakes in promising style at Leopardstown, and then finished third in the Group 3 Irish Field Celebrating 150 Years Royal Whip Stakes over ten furlongs at the Curragh in mid-August, beaten a neck and a length, by Armory and Numerian. However, it is his final start that identified him as a potentially significant older horse this coming season.

The Group 2 Clipper Logistics Boomerang Stakes over a mile at Leopardstown on the opening day of Irish Champions Weekend brought together a competitive field, but from soon after they turned into the straight it was a two-horse race. Seven-year-old Safe Voyage moved into a narrow lead but Sinawann went with him and the pair battled all the way to the line. The younger colt definitely had his head in front at one point, but the veteran gelding would not be denied. The pair flashed past the post locked together, the official margin a short head and the result unaltered after a stewards' enquiry. They left the Group 1 Irish 2,000 Guineas runner-up Vatican City four lengths behind. He, in turn, was two and a half lengths and a nose clear of Royal Dornoch and Century Dream, the latter running below form.

The Michael Halford-trained Sinawann is the best of four blacktype horses out of the Aga Khan homebred Simawa (by Anabaa), who finished third in the Listed Martin Molony Stakes. His half-sister Summaya (by Azamour) was runner-up in the Group 3 Derrinstown Stud Derby Trial Stakes on the final of her four starts, Silwana (by Peintre Celebre) won the Listed Loughbrown Stakes over two miles at the Curragh before retiring to the paddocks in Japan, and stakes-placed half-brother Simsir (by Zoffany), who left the Halford stable to join Fawzi Abdulla Nass in Bahrain, won the valuable Bahrain International Trophy over ten furlongs at Sakhir in November. Their dam was sold for €210,000 at the Goffs November Mare Sale in 2018, she had a Gleneagles (by Galileo) filly about two and a half months later, a Motivator (by Montjeu) colt in 2020 and was then bred to Calyx (by Kingman).

Simawa is out of the stakes-winner Sinntara (by Lashkari) and that makes her a half-sister to the Prix de l'Arc de Triomphe and dual Derby hero Sinndar (by Grand Lodge). Their siblings also include Sinndiya (by Pharly), the winning dam of middle-distance listed scorer Sindirana (by Kalanisi) and ancestor of several other stakes winners, three of whom have been Group 1 placed. The stakes-winning sprinter Sonaiyla (by Dark Angel) and the pattern-winning sprinter-miler Marie's Diamond (by Footstepsinthesand) are the most notable of them in Europe. Sinndar, on the other hand, disappointed at stud given what he achieved on the track and yet his twenty stakes winners included the top-class middle-distance horse Youmzain (now a blacktype sire), classic-placed juvenile Group 1 scorer Rosanara, Arc-placed dual Group 1 star

Shareta, plus 2005's Group 1 Irish Oaks and Group 1 Prix Vermeille heroine Shawanda.

From what we have seen of him so far, Sinawann appears to be best at a mile. He remains a promising prospect.

SUMMARY DETAILS
Bred: His Highness The Aga Khan's Studs S C
Owned: H H Aga Khan
Trained: Michael Halford
Country: Ireland
Race record: 012-0132-
Career highlights: 2 wins inc Amethyst Stakes (Gr3), 2nd Clipper Logistics Boomerang Mile (Gr2), KPMG Champions Juvenile Stakes (Gr2), 3rd Irish Field Celebrating 150 Years Royal Whip Stakes (Gr3)

SINAWANN (IRE) – 2017 bay colt

Kingman (GB)	Invincible Spirit (IRE)	Green Desert (USA)
		Rafha
	Zenda (GB)	Zamindar (USA)
		Hope (IRE)
Simawa (IRE)	Anabaa (USA)	Danzig (USA)
		Balbonella (FR)
	Sinntara (IRE)	Lashkari
		Sidama (FR)

SNOW (IRE)

Snow cost 1,200,000 guineas as a yearling and although her form is some way below the best of her generation, she is worth her price, and arguably more, as a broodmare. The daughter of Galileo (by Sadler's Wells), yet another good horse bred by Barronstown Stud in Ireland, is out of the Group 1 scorer Chelsea Rose (by Desert King) and so is a full sister to Kew Gardens. That Group 1 St Leger and Group 1 Grand Prix de Paris scorer has joined Coolmore's National Hunt division and is standing his first season at Castlehyde Stud for a fee of €5,000. The two also have a contrasting half-sister in Thawaany (by Tamayuz), a stakes-winning miler who dropped to sprints for her final two starts, winning the Group 3 Prix de Ris-Orangis and finishing a half-length runner-up to Garswood in the Group 1 Prix Maurice de Gheest, both at Deauville. That talented chestnut had a Shamardal (by Giant's Causeway) colt last year and was then bred to Frankel (by Galileo). Snow will also be visiting elite stallions.

Snow was well-beaten on her only two runs as a two-year-old, both over a mile on yielding-to-soft ground, but won two from six last season, notably the Group 3 Munster Oaks Stakes over twelve furlongs on yielding at Cork in early July, beating Snapraeceps by a length and a quarter. She was only fifth to Even So in the Group 1 Juddmonte Irish Oaks, a long way last of three in the Group 2 Qatar Lillie Langtry Stakes on good-to-firm over fourteen furlongs at Goodwood in early August and then, in first-time blinkers, beat only one home behind Pista in the Group 2 bet365 Park Hill Fillies' Stakes over the St Leger course and distance at Doncaster. Her other outings of 2020 were her maiden success over ten furlongs at the Curragh in mid-June and when finishing a half-length runner-up to One Voice in the Group 3 Irish Stallion Farms EBF Blue Wind Stakes over ten furlongs at Leopardstown eight days later.

Her dam, Chelsea Rose, won the Group 1 Moyglare Stud Stakes, went on to be placed in the Group 1 Pretty Polly Stakes and Group 1 Premio Lydia Tesio and retired to stud as a four-time stakes winner. She is the grandam of the pattern-placed juvenile stakes winner Justifier (by Free Eagle), who has been exported to Hong Kong, she was bred to Galileo again last year, and her youngest racing-age representative is the now three-year-old Wordsworth (by Galileo). That classic-entered Aidan O'Brien-trained colt was a three-quarter-length runner-up to his stablemate and subsequent pattern star High Definition on their debut in a mile maiden on soft ground at the Curragh in August.

In addition to being a half-sister to the stakes-winning miler European (by Great Commotion), Chelsea Rose is a half-sister to the Group 2-placed, middle-distance pattern winner Downdraft (by Camelot). Her dam, Cinnamon Rose (by Trempolino), is a winning half-sister to a Grade 3 scorer and to the Grade 1-placed Group 2 Prix Eugene Adam winner River Warden (by Riverman). If you go back further on the page you will find that Senones (by Prince Bio), the Prix Penelope-winning fifth dam of Snow, was a full sister to 1951's Prix du Jockey Club (French Derby) and Grand Prix de Paris star Sicambre, who was a classic and leading sire. There are no guarantees, of course, but with her pedigree, racing record and connections it will be a disappointment if Snow fails to have a successful career at stud.

SUMMARY DETAILS

Bred: Barronstown Stud
Owned: Michael Tabor, Derrick Smith & Mrs John Magnier
Trained: Aidan O'Brien
Country: Ireland
Race record: 04-121030-
Career highlights: 2 wins inc Munster Oaks Stakes (Gr3), 2nd Irish Stallion Farms EBF Blue Wind Stakes (Gr3), 3rd Qatar Lillie Langtry Stakes (Gr2)

SNOW (IRE) – 2017 chestnut filly

Galileo (IRE)	Sadler's Wells (USA)	Northern Dancer
		Fairy Bridge (USA)
	Urban Sea (USA)	Miswaki (USA)
		Allegretta
Chelsea Rose (IRE)	Desert King (IRE)	Danehill (USA)
		Sabaah (USA)
	Cinnamon Rose (USA)	Trempolino (USA)
		Sweet Simone (FR)

SPANISH MISSION (USA)

Spanish Mission is a talented stayer and he shares the surprising distinction of being one of only two pattern winners, so far, by Frankel's multiple Group 1-winning full brother Noble Mission (by Galileo). That stallion is now in Japan having spent six seasons at Lane's End Farm in Kentucky, but only the classic-placed, Grade 1 Jockey Club Gold Cup and Grade 1 Travers Stakes victor Code of Honor has struck at stakes level across the Atlantic. Five of his other progeny have been blacktype placed, including the Group 1 Toorak Handicap runner-up Buffalo River. Perhaps books of mostly European-bred mares might have suited him better—we cannot know—and perhaps he will click with the bloodlines and families prevalent in his new home, a country in which his full brother has sired three top-level winners and, from 2021, has one son at stud: the seven-to-eight-furlong horse Mozu Ascot, the fastest Group 1-winning son of Frankel.

It is possible that both of Noble Mission's talented sons will become stallions. Code of Honor is pretty much guaranteed to secure a top opportunity, whereas for Spanish Mission it would surely be a National Hunt role. He beat Nayef Road by four lengths to take the Group 3 Bahrain Trophy over thirteen furlongs at Newmarket as a three-year-old and won a valuable twelve-furlong conditions race at Belmont Park that same year. His first three runs of 2020 were mixed, his second-place finish to Dashing Willoughby in the Group 3 Coral Henry II Stakes at Sandown in early July the standout effort, and he switched from the David Simcock stable to the Andrew Balding team in mid-August. He then won twice, beating Selino by three lengths each time, before finishing well down the field behind Trueshan in the Group 2 Qipco British Champions Long Distance Cup on soft ground at Ascot in October. All of his best form has been on ground ranging from good-to-soft up to good-to-firm.

Selino, whose record had been two wins and five placings from eight starts before he met Spanish Mission, moved to Australia after their second encounter. He has joined the Chris Waller stable and was unplaced in a twelve-and-a-half-furlong Group 2 contest at Moonee Valley on his debut for his new team. He stayed on well when chasing home Spanish Mission in the Listed Share Shop Chester Stakes over just short of fourteen and a half furlongs at Chester—the winner's first outing for the Balding stable—and although running another fine race in the Group 2 bet365 Doncaster Cup Stakes over almost two and a quarter miles next time, he had no chance with the winner. Spanish Mission again hit the front over a furlong from home, he went clear in the final half furlong and was eased before the line.

This victory suggests that the $125,000 Keeneland September Yearling Sale graduate could be a Cup horse in 2021, although with a rating of 110, further improvement will be necessary to become a top player and potential Group 1 horse. He is a half-brother to the listed scorer and Group 2 Gimcrack Stakes runner-up Mokarris (by More Than Ready) and out of Limonar (by Street Cry), a mile listed winner whose siblings feature the unfortunate Grade 1 Shoemaker Mile Stakes victor Talco (by Pivotal). He failed to recover from surgery just four months after his big win. The mare had a first-crop son of the lightly raced and undefeated juvenile Group 1 scorer Mastery (by Candy Ride) in 2019 and an Uncle Mo (by Indian Charlie) colt last year. Their dam, Trylko (by Diesis), is a half-sister to the Group 1 Irish 2,000 Guineas winner Bachelor Duke (by Miswaki), related to the ill-fated classic-placed Group 1 star Fatherland (by Sadler's Wells) and comes from a branch of the famous family of Nureyev (by Northern Dancer), Sadler's Wells (by Northern Dancer), among many others of note.

Spanish Mission is back in training as a five-year-old and he holds an entry in the ultra-valuable Red Sea Turf Handicap over fifteen furlongs at Riyadh in late February.

SUMMARY DETAILS
Bred: St Elias Stables LLC
Owned: Team Valor LLC & Gary Barber
Trained: Andrew Balding
Country: England
Race record: 31-02131-020110-
Career highlights: 5 wins inc bet365 Doncaster Cup Stakes (Gr2), Bahrain Trophy Stakes (Gr3), Share Shop Chester Stakes

(L), 2nd Coral Henry II Stakes (Gr3), British Stallion Studs EBF Cocked Hat Stakes (L), 3rd Qatar Gordon Stakes (Gr3)

SPANISH MISSION (USA) – 2016 bay colt

Noble Mission (GB)	Galileo (IRE)	Sadler's Wells (USA)
		Urban Sea (USA)
	Kind (IRE)	Danehill (USA)
		Rainbow Lake (GB)
Limonar (IRE)	Street Cry (IRE)	Machiavellian (USA)
		Helen Street
	Trylko (USA)	Diesis
		Gossamer (USA)

SPEAK IN COLOURS (GB)

This popular grey is one of the leading sprinters in Ireland and he looks sure to attract plenty of attention when he goes to stud, an opportunity one might have expected to see him land for 2021. Instead, he is back in training for another year, was runner-up in a three-horse conditions race at Dundalk shortly before this book went to print—his first ever run on an artificial track—and is due to travel to Saudi Arabia to challenge for a valuable prize there. Speak In Colours is by a star mile-son of Exceed And Excel (by Danehill), had a pattern-winning half-sister in action in 2020, it out of a half-sister to a notable miler and from a prolific blacktype family.

Speak In Colours, a vendor buy-back in Newmarket as a foal and yearling, was a stakes-winning juvenile sprinter at Doncaster on the last of three starts for the Marco Botti stable in 2017 and then crossed the Irish Sea to join the Joseph O'Brien team. He was short-headed in a listed contest at Navan first time out for his new connections, followed that with a third-place finish in the Group 3 Goffs Lacken Stakes at Naas and notched up his first pattern success three months later, beating Gordon Lord Byron by a length and a quarter in the Group 3 Qatar Racing & Equestrian Club Phoenix Sprint Stakes. He added the Group 3 AES Renaissance Stakes and a listed contest the following season, missed out on a Group 1 placing when fourth to Blue Point in the Diamond Jubilee Stakes at Royal Ascot but secured one when third to One Master in the second of her three victories in the Group 1 Qatar Prix de la Foret.

That ParisLongchamp race is over seven furlongs and, in 2020, he beat Surrounding easily by two and a quarter lengths over that trip to take the Group 3 Rybo Ballycorus Stakes at Fairyhouse in early July having chased home Lancaster House in the Group 3 Coolmore Calyx Gladness Stakes over the distance at the Curragh the month before. Between those two races he had finished a three-length fifth to Hello Youmzain in the Group 1 Diamond Jubilee Stakes and pipped Forever in Dreams by a head to take the Group 2 Weatherbys Ireland Greenlands Stakes at the Curragh, both over six furlongs. And he went very close in his attempt to win the Group 3 Rathasker Stud Phoenix Sprint Stakes over the latter course and distance in early August, going well behind horses a furlong and a half out, finding a gap and running on well but failing by margins of a neck, head and short head, pipped by Glen Shiel, Sonaiyla and Forever in Dreams, giving them all weight.

Speak In Colours can race prominently or come from behind, he is a proven six-furlong performer, is talented over seven and, given his pedigree, it would be interesting to see him try a mile. His sire, Excelebration, was top class over that trip and, although a generally disappointing stallion given what he achieved on the track, is the sire of the multiple Group 1 star Barney Roy.

The now six-year-old is the first foal of Maglietta Fina (by Verglas), whose late Group 1 sire was classic-placed at a mile, and both of his siblings to race are proven at the distance. Lady Bowthorpe (by Nathaniel), who has never raced beyond a mile, won the Group 3 Valiant Stakes over it by almost five lengths at Ascot in July, whereas Pretty In Grey (by Brazen Beau) has won three times over seven furlongs and is a stakes-placed winner at a mile. Their dam is a half-sister to the Group 1 Lockinge Stakes runner-up and dual Group 2 scorer Tullius (by Le Vie Dei Colori), and she is out of Meringue Pie (by Silent Screen), the multiple stakes-winning dam of the capable milers Monsagem (by Nureyev) and Pie In Your Eye (by Spend A Buck).

SUMMARY DETAILS

Bred: Scuderia Archi Romani
Owned: Mrs C C Regalado-Gonzalez
Trained: Joseph O'Brien
Country: Ireland
Race record: 311-230100-24144130-42011400-2
Career highlights: 7 wins inc Weatherbys Ireland Greenlands Stakes (Gr2), Rybo Ballycorus Stakes (Gr3), AES Renaissance Stakes (Gr3), Qatar Racing & Equestrian Club Phoenix Sprint Stakes (Gr3), Dubai Duty Free Tennis Championship Dash Stakes (L), Bet Through The Racing Post App Doncaster Stakes (L), 2nd Weatherbys Ireland Greenlands Stakes (Gr2), Coolmore

Calyx Gladness Stakes (Gr3), Committed Stakes (L), 3rd Qatar Prix de la Foret (Gr1), Goffs Lacken Stakes (Gr3)

SPEAK IN COLOURS (GB) – 2015 grey horse

Excelebration (IRE)	Exceed And Excel (AUS)	Danehill (USA)
		Patrona (USA)
	Sun Shower (IRE)	Indian Ridge
		Miss Kemble (IRE)
Maglietta Fina (IRE)	Verglas (IRE)	Highest Honor (FR)
		Rahaam (USA)
	Whipped Queen (USA)	Kingmambo (USA)
		Meringue Pie (USA)

STAR OF EMARAATY (IRE)

Coolmore's Australian juvenile Group 1 star Pride of Dubai (by Street Cry) served two reverse-shuttle seasons in Ireland and was a freshman of 2020. He is out of a somewhat close relation to Invincible Spirit (by Green Desert) and Kodiac (by Danehill), and the seven stakes winners in his global first crop include five who have achieved the feat from the northern hemisphere half. None is as yet highly rated, but Telepatic Glances (sic), Flying Visit and Star of Emaraaty won pattern races, whereas Fancy Man and Zaffy's Pride struck at listed level. The first named of those achieved the feat in Italy and is trained in that country, so that is why she is not listed under her sire at the back of the book or included in the freshman table in the introduction section.

Star of Emaraaty's big win came on her fifth start when she sprang a 66/1 shock to defeat Dubai Fountain by a length and a quarter in the Group 3 Betway Sweet Solera Stakes over seven furlongs on the July Course at Newmarket. She had been a well-beaten fourth to Fev Rover in a listed contest over the same trip at Sandown on her previous start, got her initial success at Ayr eight days before that, and was a suitably well-beaten 200/1 shot in the Group 2 Queen Mary Stakes at Royal Ascot. The €3,500 Goffs Sportsman's Yearling Sale graduate was sold privately after her pattern success and carried the famous black, yellow and red colours of Teruya Yoshida on her final two outings. She was unplaced in both, finishing fifth to Indigo Girl in the Group 2 bet365 May Hill Stakes and seventh to Pretty Gorgeous in the Group 1 bet365 Fillies' Mile.

The Kevin Ryan-trained chestnut is a half-sister to a winner and out of the unplaced La Grande Elisa (by Ad Valorem), a half-sister to the Group 1 Juddmonte International Stakes, Group 1 Queen Elizabeth II Stakes and Group 1 Sussex Stakes star Rip Van Winkle (by Galileo). He died in early August, aged fourteen, and although a blacktype sire from his days at Coolmore, he was disappointing despite getting an early Group 1 winner via Dick Whittington, who stands at stud in Ireland. However, as happens from time to time, he was having a breakthrough year at the time of his death at Windsor Park Stud in New Zealand.

His Group 2 mile scorer and Group 1 Cox Plate third Te Akau Shark blossomed into a dual Group 1 star, taking the seven-furlong Waikato Sprint at Te Rapa and the ATC Chipping Norton Stakes over a mile at Randwick. Meanwhile, his excellent daughter Jennifer Eccles, who had cost just NZ$5,000 as a weanling, was runner-up in the Group 1 New Zealand 1000 Guineas, won the Group 1 New Zealand Oaks and landed a trio of Group 2 contests from eight to ten furlongs.

La Grande Elisa's siblings also include the Italian Group 3 scorer Le Vie Infinite (by Le Vie Dei Colori) and A Star Is Born (by Galileo), the winning dam of Fleet Review (by War Front). He won the Listed Belgrave Stakes at the Curragh, was runner-up to U S Navy Flag in the Group 1 Middle Park Stakes and third to that same star in the Group 1 July Cup before moving to Australia. They are out of the listed-placed winner Looking Back (by Stravinsky) and come from a branch of the family of top-level winners such as Danish (by Danehill), African Story (by Pivotal), Kingsbarns (by Galileo), and Kameko (by Kitten's Joy).

Star of Emaraaty is only rated ninety-seven, down from a peak of 102, so has a lot of improvement to make if she is to become a filly of note in 2021. It is possible that seven furlongs is her trip, so perhaps she will show progress if returned to that distance, but she holds an entry in the Group 1 Emirates Poule d'Essai des Pouliches (French 1000 Guineas) so may start out on a classic path. Her long-term future is likely to lie as a broodmare in Japan.

SUMMARY DETAILS
Bred: Karis Bloodstock Ltd & Rathbarry Stud
Owned: Teruya Yoshida
Trained: Kevin Ryan
Country: England
Race record: 2014100-
Career highlights: 2 wins inc Betway Sweet Solera Stakes (Gr3)

STAR OF EMARAATY (IRE) – 2018 chestnut filly

Pride of Dubai (AUS)	Street Cry (IRE)	Machiavellian (USA)
		Helen Street
	Al Anood (AUS)	Danehill (USA)
		Eljazzi
La Grande Elisa (IRE)	Ad Valorem (USA)	Danzig (USA)
		Classy Women (USA)
	Looking Back (IRE)	Stravinsky (USA)
		Mustique Dream (GB)

STEEL BULL (IRE)

Steel Bull is the great-grandson of a Group 1 sprint star, and although it is in that division that his future may lie, he has a long way to go yet to match her exploits. He made a winning debut over five furlongs at Naas in July, three weeks after trainer Michael O'Callaghan snapped him up for £28,000 at the rescheduled Goffs UK Breeze-Up Sale. It was the colt's third time in the auction ring; he made only €5,000 as a foal at the Tattersalls Ireland Flat Bloodstock Sale and £15,000 at the Tattersalls Ascot Yearling Sale the following September. Just one week after his debut success, the colt went to Goodwood for the Group 3 Markel Insurance Molecomb Stakes where, having met with traffic problems in the race, he showed a turn of foot when finally having room and landed the top prize by three-quarters of a length from Ben Macdui. Internationaldream and Chief Little Hawk were one and a half lengths and a short head back in third and fourth.

He changed hands privately after that win but failed to make the frame in three subsequent outings. He was only seventh to Lucky Vega in the Group 1 Keeneland Phoenix Stakes over six furlongs, returned to the minimum trip and finished fifth in the Group 2 Flying Childers Stakes at Doncaster and was then beaten by a total of six and a half lengths when fifth to Frenetic in a five-furlong listed contest at Dundalk in October. He had received a bump early in that race and was under pressure a quarter of a mile from home, never looking dangerous. His Doncaster run, however, wasn't a bad effort and he was only beaten by a total of one and three-quarter lengths by the winner, Ubettabelieveit. The field had split into two groups, there were some minor traffic issues near the line, and he may have finished third but for the latter.

Steel Bull is among twenty-five stakes winners by the classic-winning miler and Rathasker Stud veteran Clodovil (by Danehill), a stallion who notched up his third Group 1 scorer last season: Prix Marcel Boussac winner Tiger Tanaka. His best representatives tend to be milers or seven furlongs horses, some stay farther, but they also include the Group 2-winning sprinter Shining Emerald and last season's talented German sprinter

Majestic Colt, plus the prolific Secret Asset who won ten of his 120 starts and was a surprise runner-up to Tangerine Trees in the Group 1 Prix de l'Abbaye de Longchamp in 2011.

Macarthurs Park, his once-placed dam, is a full sister to the five-time sprint winner Marietta Robusti and by the sprint ace and multiple Group 1 sire Equiano (by Acclamation), a long-time Newsells Park Stud resident who is now in his first season at the Irish National Stud. Her third foal is a Gregorian (by Clodovil) filly born in late March 2020, a three-parts sister to Steel Bull. The mare is a half-sister to Three Sea Captains (by Choisir), who won the Listed Marble Hill Stakes over five furlongs at the Curragh before going on to Class 3 six-furlong handicap success in Hong Kong under the name Hella Hedge, and also to a mare named Verra Lilley (by Verglas). She too was placed only once—fourth is finishing out of the frame, unplaced—and had a very low handicap rating, but her daughter Lil Grey (by Starspangledbanner) has been runner-up in the Group 3 Anglesey Stakes and third in the Listed Curragh Stakes.

It is their dam, one-time scorer La Tintoretta (by Desert Prince), who is the daughter of Lavinia Fontana (by Sharpo). She notched up nine wins including the Group 1 Sprint Cup at Haydock, the Group 3 Prix du Petit Couvert and three Italian Group 3 contests, she was a runner-up in the Group 2 Temple Stakes and Group 2 Goldene Peitsche and third in the Group 2 Prix Maurice de Gheest. Sadly, she only produced two winners from six foals. Her winning dam, Belle Origine (by Exclusive Native), had a couple of listed-race scorers among her nine winning siblings and she was out of Belle Sorella (by Ribot), a three-time winning full sister to 1968's Dewhurst Stakes and Champagne Stakes winner and two-year-old champion colt, Ribofilio.

Five furlongs on good ground appears to suit Steel Bull well and the 104-rated late-April-born colt could have a rewarding year in 2021 and/or 2022.

SUMMARY DETAILS
Bred: Macarthurs Park Partnership
Owned: Mrs C C Regalado-Gonzalez

Trained: Michael O'Callaghan
Country: Ireland
Race record: 11000-
Career highlights: 2 wins inc Markel Insurance Molecomb Stakes (Gr3)

STEEL BULL (IRE) – 2018 grey colt

Clodovil (IRE)	Danehill (USA)	Danzig (USA)
		Razyana (USA)
	Clodora (FR)	Linamix (FR)
		Cloche d'Or (FR)
Macarthurs Park (IRE)	Equiano (FR)	Acclamation (GB)
		Entente Cordiale (IRE)
	La Tintoretta (IRE)	Desert Prince (IRE)
		Lavinia Fontana (IRE)

SUMMER ROMANCE (IRE)

Summer Romance is bred to achieve anything, on the track and at stud, so it's hardly a surprise that she cost 300,000 guineas from Book 1 of the Tattersalls October Yearling Sale. The progress she made between then and when she reappeared at the Arqana May Breeze-Up Sale the following year was such that her price soared and Godolphin had to pay €800,000 to add her to their string. The Roundhill Stud-bred grey is trained by Charlie Appleby and although she had not acquired star status on the track, she is talented, a 109-rated filly who has both a Group 3 and listed win to her name.

Her career began in fine style, a two-length success on soft ground at Yarmouth followed by a six-length victory in the Listed Random Health Empress Fillies' Stakes on fast ground at the July Course in Newmarket. But she disappointed a month later when only sixth to Under The Stars in the Group 3 Princess Margaret Stakes at Ascot and again when finishing a four-and-a-half-length third to Dark Lady in the Group 3 Shadwell Dick Poole Fillies' Stakes at Salisbury in September. All of those races had been over six furlongs, whereas her trio of outings last season were at a mile. She was unplaced behind Love in the Group 1 Qipco 1000 Guineas and behind Watch Me in the Group 1 Prix Rothschild but, between those runs, she beat Cloak of Spirits by three-quarters of a length to take the Group 3 Princess Elizabeth Stakes at Epsom.

A daughter of Banstead Manor Stud's brilliant miler and exciting young classic sire Kingman (by Invincible Spirit), Summer Romance is out of Serena's Storm (by Statue of Liberty) and that makes her a half-sister to Rizeena (by Iffraaj). That sibling's victory in the Group 1 Moyglare Stud Stakes earned her the title of champion two-year-old filly in Ireland in 2013. The Clive Brittain-trained star also won the Group 2 Queen Mary Stakes and Listed National Stakes that year, was runner-up in the Group 1 Fillies' Mile and third in the Group 1 Prix Morny. She went on to add a Group 1 Coronation Stakes victory the following summer before also making the frame in Group 1 company in the Falmouth Stakes at Newmarket and Matron Stakes at

Leopardstown, runner-up in both. Rizeena's first foal is the classic-entered Latest Generation (by Frankel), a Doncaster maiden winner who disappointed when unplaced behind One Ruler in the Group 3 Emirates Autumn Stakes over a mile on soft ground at Newmarket in October. He is trained by Simon and Ed Crisford.

Serena's Queen (by Iffraaj), the year-younger half-sister to Summer Romance, is a full sister to Rizeena and in training with Ralph Beckett. She finished fourth in a mile novice race at Lingfield on her debut in early December and won a similar contest over the same trip at Chelmsford two weeks later, so she could be one to watch with interest in 2021. They also have a now two-year-old half-sister, Midnight Moll (by Dark Angel), who made 210,000 guineas from Book 1 of the Tattersalls October Yearling Sale. Their dam had a Dubawi (by Dubai Millennium) colt last year.

Serena's Storm is a half-sister to the Group 1 Prix d'Ispahan scorer Zabeel Prince (by Lope de Vega), Group 1-placed Australian Group 2 scorer and blacktype sire Puissance de Lune (by Shamardal) and the dual Group 2-placed listed winner Queen Power (by Shamardal). They are among the eight winners from eight runners produced by Princess Serena (by Unbridled's Song), a winning half-sister to the Grade 1-placed US Grade 2 scorer Doubles Partner (by Rock Hard Ten) and out of Serena's Sister (by Rahy), a full sister to the champion Serena's Song. That thirteen-time Grade 1 star has produced a string of stakes-winning offspring, headed by 2002's Group 1 Coronation Stakes heroine Sophisticat (by Storm Cat), and her descendants include the multiple pattern scorer and successful Redmondstown Stud stallion Vocalised (by Vindication), sire of the juvenile Group 1 winner Verbal Dexterity.

It will be fascinating to see what the future holds for Summer Romance. She finished fifth in the Group 2 Cape Verdi Stakes over a mile at Meydan shortly before this book went to print, her first run in almost six months.

SUMMARY DETAILS
Bred: Roundhill Stud

Owned: Godolphin
Trained: Charlie Appleby
Country: England
Race record: 1103-010-0
Career highlights: 3 wins inc Princess Elizabeth Stakes (sponsored by Investec) (Gr3), Randox Health Empress Fillies' Stakes (L), 3rd Shadwell Dick Poole Fillies' Stakes (Gr3)

SUMMER ROMANCE (IRE) – 2017 grey filly

Kingman (GB)	Invincible Spirit (IRE)	Green Desert (USA)
		Rafha
	Zenda (GB)	Zamindar (USA)
		Hope (IRE)
Serena's Storm (IRE)	Statue of Liberty (USA)	Storm Cat (USA)
		Charming Lassie (USA)
	Princess Serena (USA)	Unbridled's Song (USA)
		Serena's Sister (USA)

TABDEED (GB)

Tabdeed has looked like a potential pattern-race winner from the day he made a winning debut at Leicester as a two-year-old, beating Yafta by two and a quarter lengths. Sadly, he has been very lightly raced, he was gelded at the end of his four-year-old season but then made the breakthrough in another short campaign at five, beating The Tin Man by half a length to take the Group 3 bet365 Hackwood Stakes at Newbury. He had chased home Glen Shiel in a handicap at Newcastle the time before and was unsuited by the soft-to-heavy underfoot conditions when finishing last of thirteen in the Group 1 Betfair Sprint Cup Stakes on his final of three starts. His only defeats before 2020 had been when sixth to Cape Byron in the Group 3 John Guest Racing Bengough Stakes on soft at Ascot the previous October and when down the field behind Expert Eye in 2018's edition of the Group 3 Jersey Stakes on fast ground at Ascot, the one time in his career to date that he has not run over six furlongs.

The Owen Burrows-trained chestnut was bred by the partnership of Red House Stud and Ketton Ashwell Ltd and he is a 42,000-guinea graduate of the Tattersalls December Foal Sale. Like the Group 1-winning sprinter and popular young Whitsbury Manor Stud stallion Havana Grey, Tabdeed represents the first crop of the Group 1-winning miler Havana Gold. That Tweenhills Farm & Stud resident is an early stallion son for Teofilo (by Galileo), he is out of a pattern-winning sprinter and from a family of sprinters and milers and so it's no surprise that his best to date tend to show speed. The smart filly Treasuring, a pattern winner at five furlongs and at a mile, is also among his seven blacktype scorers.

Tabdeed is the second foal of a four-time placed mare called Puzzled (by Peintre Celebre) and that daughter of Group 1 Irish 1,000 Guineas scorer Classic Park (by Robellino) is also responsible for considerably lower-rated triple six-furlong scorer Aquarius (by Charm Spirit). Their now three-year-old half-brother Cash Machine (by Twilight Son) has run only once so far but that was a second-place finish over six furlongs at Kempton in late November. That colt had hit the front a furlong from home and kept on well to the line but was soon headed and then passed by the odds-on favourite Popmaster, a colt who had made a winning debut over the course and distance a month before. Classic Park is also the dam of the dual pattern-placed Killarney listed scorer Soon (by Galileo) and of Group 1 Derby runner-up and hugely popular National Hunt stallion Walk In The Park (by Montjeu), she is the grandam of the pattern-placed listed winner Crystal Gal (by Galileo) and she is a half-sister to the US Grade 2 scorer Rumpipumpy (by Shirley Heights).

On pedigree, Tabdeed could have been a miler. However, he has clearly inherited speed rather than stamina, and his dam appears to be developing a sprint branch of the family despite having done most of her racing over middle-distances. Cash Machine is by a Group 1 sprint star, as is the now two-year-old Profitable (by Invincible Spirit) colt for whom Shadwell Estate Company paid 130,000 guineas from Book 2 of the Tattersalls October Yearling Sale; he has been named Glengarra. The mare had a Zoffany (by Dansili) filly in 2020 and was then bred to U S Navy Flag (by War Front). Her lightly raced and 112-rated son could add further pattern success if returning to action this coming season.

SUMMARY DETAILS

Bred: Red House Stud & Ketton Ashwell Ltd
Owned: Hamdan Al Maktoum
Trained: Owen Burrows
Country: England
Race record: 1-101-10-210-
Career highlights: 5 wins inc bet365 Hackwood Stakes (Gr3)

TABDEED (GB) – 2015 chestnut gelding

Havana Gold (IRE)	Teofilo (IRE)	Galileo (IRE)
		Speirbhean (IRE)
	Jessica's Dream (IRE)	Desert Style (IRE)
		Ziffany (GB)
Puzzled (IRE)	Peintre Celebre (USA)	Nureyev (USA)
		Peinture Bleue (USA)
	Classic Park (GB)	Robellino (USA)
		Wanton

TACTICAL (GB)

Dual Derby and Breeders' Cup star High Chaparral (by Sadler's Wells) was a leading international sire who was only fifteen at the time of his death. The shuttle stallion supplied 130 stakes winners, of whom twenty-three struck at the highest level, and the successful southern hemisphere sires Dundeel and So You Think are among his sons at stud. Their level of success has not yet been matched by his handful of sons based at European farms, but it is still early in their careers. Free Eagle's (Irish National Stud) first crop is headed by 2020's Derby-placed stakes winner Khalifa Sat, whereas Toronado (Haras de Bouquetot) has five European-born stakes winners to go along with another five 'down under'. The latter includes the Group 1-placed Group 2 scorer Affair To Remember, whereas Tactical currently headlines the European-conceived ones.

He finished third in a five-furlong Newmarket maiden on his debut in early June, got off the mark with a length-and-a-quarter and short-head defeat of Yazaman and Muker in the Listed Windsor Castle Stakes over the same trip at Royal Ascot thirteen days later and then followed that a near repeat performance over six furlongs on good-to-soft at Newmarket, this time on the July Course. He hit the front half a furlong from home in the Group 2 Tattersalls July Stakes and again finished well to beat Yazaman by a length and a quarter. This time, however, there was a further gap of two and three-quarter lengths back to the third, Escape Route.

One might have expected to see a colt of his pedigree step up to seven furlongs at this point, perhaps going the Champagne Stakes-Dewhurst Stakes route, but he remained at six for his next two starts. He was a staying-on fifth to Campanelle on soft ground in the Group 1 Darley Prix Morny at Deauville and then finished a three-and-a-half-length fourth to Supremacy in the Group 1 Juddmonte Middle Park Stakes on good at Newmarket in late September. He had gone second a quarter of a mile from home in the latter but couldn't match the pace of the first three: Lucky Vega and Minzaal were the other pair who finished ahead of him there, whereas The Lir Jet and Lipizzaner were his closest pursuers. Then he stepped up in trip, but that run can be ignored if looking for a guide as to how far he might stay. He was always towards the rear, eventually passing the post thirteen and a half lengths behind St Mark's Basilica, and jockey Oisin Murphy reported that the colt was never travelling.

Tactical is the first foal of Make Fast (by Makfi), a mare who earned her blacktype when finishing third in the Listed Radley Stakes over seven furlongs at two and when runner-up in a listed contest over the same trip at Epsom as a three-year-old. His now two-year-old half-brother has been named Tack (by Iffraaj), the mare had a Recorder (by Galileo) filly in 2020 and was then bred to Zoffany (by Dansili), so there could be more good updates to the page in the next few seasons. Make Fast's dam, Raymi Coya (by Van Nistelrooy), won the Group 3 Oh So Sharp Stakes over seven at two and a one-mile listed contest at York at three, and that granddaughter of Storm Cat (by Storm Bird) is also notable as being a granddaughter of Try Something New (by Hail The Pirates). That mare won the Grade 1 Spinster Stakes over nine furlongs at four, was placed in the Grade 1 Vanity Handicap, Grade 1 Ruffian Handicap and Grade 1 Apple Blossom Handicap, and her star runner was Somethingdifferent (by Green Forest). A half-brother to Tactical's unraced third dam Something Mon (by Maria's Mon), he was a six-furlong Group 2 winner in Germany at two, was placed in the Group 2 Mill Reef Stakes and Group 3 Cornwallis Stakes, and went on to be Grade 2-placed over eight and a half furlongs in California.

Tactical, an Andrew Balding-trained bay, is owned and bred by Queen Elizabeth II. He finished the year on a rating of 107 and remains an interesting prospect for 2021, one who, on pedigree, could show plenty of improvement if stepping up to a mile. A potential St James's Palace Stakes contender, perhaps?

SUMMARY DETAILS

Bred: The Queen
Owned: The Queen
Trained: Andrew Balding
Country: England
Race record: 311040-

Career highlights: 2 wins inc Tattersalls July Stakes (Gr2), Windsor Castle Stakes (L)

TACTICAL (GB) – 2018 bay colt

Toronado (IRE)	High Chaparral (IRE)	Sadler's Wells (USA)
		Kasora (IRE)
	Wana Doo (USA)	Grand Slam (USA)
		Wedding Gift (FR)
Make Fast (GB)	Makfi (GB)	Dubawi (IRE)
		Dhelaal (GB)
	Raymi Coya (CAN)	Van Nistelrooy (USA)
		Something Mon (USA)

TELECASTER (GB)

Telecaster chased home Bangkok in a ten-furlong Doncaster maiden in March of his three-year-old season and ran away with a similar contest at Windsor two weeks later but it was his third start that showed him to be a colt of considerable potential. It is true that the extended ten furlongs at York was a bit beyond Too Darn Hot's comfort zone, but there was a lot to like in the way in which Telecaster beat the previously undefeated champion by a length in the Group 2 Dante Stakes. The ground was good-to-firm, there were further gaps of four lengths and three-quarters of a length back to to Surfman and Japan in third and fourth, and the performance saw Telecaster line-up as third-favourite in the following month's Group 1 Derby at Epsom.

He was edgy and sweating that day, raced prominently, was disputing third as the field swung around Tattenham Corner, looked briefly like he might play a major role but was soon under pressure and couldn't pick up as most of the field moved past him. He was eased in the closing stages and came home last of the thirteen runners. The colt disappointed again at Sandown a month later, when finishing a never-dangerous seventh to Enable in the Group 1 Coral-Eclipse Stakes, and he was not seen in action again for eleven months. He was third to Lord North in the Group 3 Betway Brigadier Gerard Stakes at Haydock on his seasonal reappearance at four, easily beat Romanciere by four lengths in the Group 3 La Coupe over the same trip at ParisLongchamp, but then disappointed when an almost five-length fourth to Aspetar in the Group 2 Sky Bet York Stakes a month later.

However, his next run was so impressive that he was being spoken of as a potential Group 1 Qatar Prix de l'Arc de Triomphe candidate. This time he set off in front and was never headed in the Group 2 Lucien Barriere Grand Prix de Deauville, beating Soft Light and Ziyad by six and a half lengths and three-quarters of a length over twelve and a half furlongs on heavy ground. Unfortunately, he missed that race and the rest of the season due to a setback. Then, in mid-November, it was announced that he had been sold to stand as a dual-purpose stallion at Haras du Mesnil in the west of France, also the home of the notably successful Doctor Dino. The Devin family, who own the stud, have stated their intention to support their new horse with some of their best mares, and given the pedigree and race record he takes with him to his new role, there is every reason to believe that Telecaster can become a sire of prominence, especially with National Hunt horses.

The son of Dalham Hall Stud's classic star and classic sire New Approach (by Galileo) was bred by Meon Valley Stud and represents a branch of one of their most famous families. He is a half-brother to the pattern-placed stakes winner Al Suhail (by Dubawi), his dam is the Group 1 Oaks and Group 1 Irish Oaks runner-up Shirocco Star (by Shirocco), his fourth dam is the dual stakes winner Hyabella (by Shirley Heights) and so the classic-placed Group 2 Prix de l'Opera winner Bella Colora (by Bellypha) is his fifth dam. Stagecraft (by Sadler's Wells), a triple Group 1-placed triple Group/Grade 2 scorer, was Bella Colora's best representative on the track and she has plenty of notable relations and descendants. Her half-brother Cezanne (by Ajdal) won the Group 1 Irish Champion Stakes but of greater note, especially with Telecaster's stallion career in mind, is that her half-sister Colorspin (by High Top) won the Group 1 Irish Oaks and that classic heroine's trio of Group 1-winning offspring featured star stayer and top National Hunt sire Kayf Tara (by Sadler's Wells).

Telecaster's actual relationship to Kayf Tara is distant—his sixth dam, Reprocolor (by Jimmy Reppin) is the grandam of Kayf Tara—but being a great-grandson of Sadler's Wells (by Northern Dancer), and of Monsun (by Konigsstuhl), and coming from the family of one of the all-time leading British National Hunt sires makes him a fascinating addition to the stallion ranks, especially as he is to stand in France and so will have easy access to that country's AQPS (*autre que pur sang*) mares.

SUMMARY DETAILS
Bred: Meon Valley Stud
Owned: Castle Down Racing
Trained: Hughie Morrison
Country: England
Race record: -21100-3141-

Career highlights: 4 wins inc Lucien Barriere Grand Prix de Deauville (Gr2), Al Basti Equiworld Dubai Dante Stakes (Gr2), La Coupe (Gr3), 3rd Betway Brigadier Gerard Stakes (Gr3)

TELECASTER (GB) – 2016 bay colt

New Approach (IRE)	Galileo (IRE)	Sadler's Wells (USA)
		Urban Sea (USA)
	Park Express	Ahonoora
		Matcher
Shirocco Star (GB)	Shirocco (GER)	Monsun (GER)
		So Sedulous (USA)
	Spectral Star (GB)	Unfuwain (USA)
		Hyperspectra (GB)

TEREBELLUM (IRE)

Gilltown Stud stallion and Timeform 140-rated superstar Sea The Stars (by Cape Cross) is well established as one of Europe's leading sires whose tally of seventy-three stakes winners includes fourteen who have struck at least once at the highest level. Terebellum came within a head of adding her name to that more select roll of honour when she failed narrowly to beat Circus Maximus in the Group 1 Queen Anne Stakes at Royal Ascot in June. It came ten days after her length-and-a-quarter defeat of Queen Power in the Group 2 Betfair Dahlia Stakes over quarter of a mile farther at Newmarket and was to remain her best performance of the year.

She was an odds-on favourite when beaten by a neck and the same by Nazeef and Billesdon Brook in the Group 1 Tattersalls Falmouth Stakes on soft ground at the July Course in Newmarket the following month, was only fifth to that same winning rival in the Group 1 Kingdom of Bahrain Sun Chariot Stakes on heavy ground over the nearby Rowley Mile course three months later and then beat only one home behind Audarya in the Grade 1 Breeders' Cup Filly & Mare Turf over nine and a half furlongs on firm ground at Keeneland in November. It was a disappointing end to the season for a filly for whom a mile was new territory; she spent all of her prior career running over ten furlongs.

Terebellum didn't race as a juvenile but advertised her blacktype potential when taking a Goodwood maiden by four and a half lengths on her debut. She was beaten by just over five lengths when third to Antonia de Vega in a listed contest at Newbury next time but then landed the Group 2 Shadwell Prix de la Nonette by almost two lengths from Mutamakina. Both of those blacktype events were run on soft ground and it was even softer when she lined up at ParisLongchamp on the first weekend in October. She hit the front with a furlong and a half to race in the Group 1 Prix de l'Opera Longines but was headed a furlong later and had no more to give, eventually passing the post in fifth position, albeit beaten by a total of a length and a quarter in a blanket finish in which Villa Marina got to the line first.

She was bred by Alan O'Flynn, made €400,000 at the Arqana Deauville August yearling sale and, as you might expect given the quality of mares that go to her sire, she represents a notably successful family. She is a half-sister to the multiple six- and seven-furlong scorer Mount Wellington (by Invincible Spirit) and her now three-year-old half-sister Miss Finland (by Invincible Spirit) got off the mark at the second attempt at two, narrowly winning a seven-furlong maiden at Chelmsford in early December. Their Frankel (by Galileo) half-sister made €440,000 at the delayed Goffs November Foal Sale (in late December), and it was no surprise to learn that their dam, Marvada (by Elusive City), was bred back to Sea The Stars in 2020.

Marvada won the Group 3 Brownstown Stakes over seven furlongs on heavy ground at Naas, she was only beaten by a neck when runner-up in the Group 3 Ballycorus Stakes over the same trip on good-to-soft at Leopardstown, she won once on the Polytrack at Dundalk and each of her other three wins, from six furlongs to a mile, came on ground described as good-to-firm. She is the best of six winners from fifteen foals out of Theory of Law (by Generous), a three-time winner whose handful of successful siblings—their dam had only three winners from thirteen foals—featured the Group 1 Prix Morny and triple US Grade 2 scorer Charges d'Affaires (by Kendor).

Lettre de Cachet (by Secreto), Terebellum's third dam, was a full sister to the Group 2 Premio Ellington victor and Group 2 King Edward VII Stakes runner-up Secret Haunt and they were among five winners from eleven foals out of the Grade 1-placed US Grade 3 scorer Royal Suite (by Majestic Prince). Some of the mares in this family have had low strike-rates at stud, but that does not mean that Terebellum will do the same. After all, her dam has already had three winners from five progeny of racing age and her half-sister Paint In Green (by Invincible Spirit), a stakes-placed seven-time winner, came up with three stakes winners from her first three foals. The first two of those, Drive To Hell (by Manduro) and Collateral Risk (by Duke of Marmalade), won at listed level in Italy. Sound Of Freedom (by Duke of Marmalade), on the other hand, won the Group 1 Premio Lydia Tesio and Group 3 Premio Regina Elena (Italian 1000 Guineas), she was runner-up in another edition of the Premio Lydia Tesio and she also picked up second place in the Group 2 Derby Italiano. Their siblings also include Smart Rag (by Gleneagles), who won two starts at two, in 2019, by an aggregate of nine lengths.

Terebellum is a high-class filly and she is among the array of notable older horses due to return to action again in 2021.

SUMMARY DETAILS
Bred: Alan O'Flynn
Owned: Godolphin
Trained: John Gosden
Country: England
Race record: -1310-12300-
Career highlights: 3 wins inc Betfair Dahlia Stakes (Gr2), Shadwell Prix de la Nonette (Gr2), 2nd Queen Anne Stakes (Gr1), 3rd Tattersalls Falmouth Stakes (Gr1), Johnnie Lewis Memorial British EBF Stakes (registered as the Abingdon Stakes) (L)

TEREBELLUM (IRE) – 2016 brown filly

Sea The Stars (IRE)	Cape Cross (IRE)	Green Desert (USA)
		Park Appeal
	Urban Sea (USA)	Miswaki (USA)
		Allegretta
Marvada (IRE)	Elusive City (USA)	Elusive Quality (USA)
		Star of Paris (USA)
	Theory Of Law (GB)	Generous (IRE)
		Lettre de Cachet (USA)

THE LIR JET (IRE)

Prince of Lir (by Kodiac) won the Group 2 Norfolk Stakes at Royal Ascot but retired to stud at the end of that season, covering his first mares as a three-year-old at Ballyhane Stud. He had a large first crop to represent him in 2020, supplied a low double-digit tally of winners and three who earned blacktype. Two of those were only listed-placed, but The Lir Jet emulated his sire by taking the same prestigious five-furlong pattern contest. The Michael Bell-trained colt landed the prize by a neck from the Wesley Ward-trained Golden Pal, but while that rival went on to become a front-running winner of the Grade 2 Breeders' Cup Juvenile Turf Sprint over five and a half furlongs at Keeneland in November and is being spoken of as a potential Group 1 King's Stand Stakes and Group 1 Nunthorpe Stakes challenger in 2021, The Lir Jet failed to win again in four subsequent outings.

Ventura Tormenta, who subsequently proved disappointing, short-headed him in the Group 2 Darley Prix Robert Papin a month after the Ascot race, he then chased home Lucky Vega in the Group 1 Keeneland Phoenix Stakes at the Curragh, beaten by three and a half lengths, but was only fifth to Supremacy in the Group 1 Juddmonte Middle Park Stakes and a running-on-but-never-dangerous seventh to Fire At Will in the Grade 1 Breeders' Cup Juvenile Turf. That race was run over a mile, a distance that suited or was even a bit short for all of his most notable relations.

His dam, Paper Dreams (by Green Desert), got both of her wins in six-furlong sellers and was never tried beyond an extended seven furlongs, but she is out of an unraced daughter of Singspiel (by In The Wings) and Papering (by Shaadi), one parent a middle-distance star on the international circuit and the other one a Group 2 Premio Lydia Tesio scorer who was runner-up in the Group 1 Yorkshire Oaks, the Group 1 Prix Vermeille and the Group 2 Nassau Stakes. The latter, who earned the title of champion older mare in Italy, is the dam of the Group 3 Premio St Leger Italiano scorer Donn Halling (by Halling) and the lightly raced Irish stakes winner Dossier (by Octagonal). She won the Listed Platinum Stakes over a mile at Cork and was placed in both the Group 2 Matron Stakes at Leopardstown and Group 3

Blandford Stakes at the Curragh. Papering was a daughter of the Group 1 Oaks d'Italia runner-up Wrapping (by Kris) and that full sister to the Group 2 Royal Lodge Stakes scorer and Group 2 Dante Stakes third Reach was, in turn, out of the Group 3 Lingfield Oaks Trial winner and Group 2 Queen Elizabeth II Stakes third Gift Wrapped (by Wolver Hollow).

If you go back another step on the page then you will find that this is a branch of the family of the classic and Arc hero and Group 1 sire Dylan Thomas (by Danehill), his classic-winning half-sister Homecoming Queen (by Holy Roman Emperor) and juvenile champion half-sister Queen's Logic (by Grand Lodge), among others of note, including 2020's front-running Group 1 Investec Derby star Serpentine (by Galileo).

The closer family connections make The Lir Jet an interesting prospect for 2021; those other Group 1 stars are too remote to have any relevance beyond academic interest. The bargain-basement colt, a €9,500 foal and £8,000 yearling, needs to improve considerably on his current figure of 106 if he is going to hold his own in Group 2 or Group 1 company, but most of the best horses in his family have done well as three-year-olds, so at least some improvement could be forthcoming. It would be good to see him try a mile again, and he does hold an entry in the Group 1 Emirates Poule d'Essai des Poulains (French 2000 Guineas), although it would not be a surprise to see him targeting something like the Group 1 Commonwealth Cup instead, or first.

SUMMARY DETAILS

Bred: Donal Boylan
Owned: Qatar Racing Ltd
Trained: Michael Bell
Country: England
Race record: 112200-
Career highlights: 2 wins inc Norfolk Stakes (Gr2), 2nd Keeneland Phoenix Stakes (Gr1), Darley Prix Robert Papin (Gr2)

THE LIR JET (IRE) – 2018 bay colt

Prince of Lir (IRE)	Kodiac (GB)	Danehill (USA)
		Rafha
	Esuvia (IRE)	Whipper (USA)
		Aoife (IRE)
Paper Dreams (IRE)	Green Desert (USA)	Danzig (USA)
		Foreign Courier (USA)
	Pickwick Papers (GB)	Singspiel (IRE)
		Papering (IRE)

THUNDERING NIGHTS (IRE)

Thundering Heights was beaten by an accumulated total of twenty-five lengths in her first two starts as a two-year-old, both mile maidens in heavy ground, and it would have required an active imagination to picture her then as a potential pattern winner. But she won a Galway maiden on her only subsequent run of 2019, was short-headed in a ten-furlong Curragh handicap first time out at three, and then began to work her way up through the rankings. She was raised to a mark of ninety-nine after beating Amma Grace by a length and a half in a nine-furlong conditions race on good ground at Leopardstown in early August and to her current mark of 105 after following that with a length-and-a-half defeat of Albigna in the Group 3 Snow Fairy Fillies Stakes over the same trip on soft ground at the Curragh three weeks later. She had hit the front over a furlong from home and kept on well when challenged, winning a shade comfortably. Epona Plays was another neck behind in third.

This filly comes from a famous Group 1-producing family and so adding pattern success to her name gave her future paddocks value a tremendous boost. She was beaten on her final two runs but remained on the same handicap figure and did not tarnish her reputation. First was the Group 2 Moyglare 'Jewels' Blandford Stakes over ten furlongs on good at the Curragh where, despite keeping on well in the closing stages, she never looked like improving on the third-place position into which she'd moved a furlong from home. Cayenne Pepper won in style by four lengths from Amma Grace and with Thundering Nights another length and a half behind. The Group 1 Qipco British Champions Fillies & Mares Stakes was an ambitious target for a horse of her level, but although outclassed on the day, she was not disgraced in finishing seventh of twelve, passing the post eleven and a quarter lengths adrift of the winner, Wonderful Tonight.

Thundering Nights represents the first crop of the classic-winning miler Night of Thunder (by Dubawi), a Kildangan Stud stallion whose global first two crops have so far yielded nineteen stakes winners. He has had Group 2 winners in Australia, England and Italy, but is awaiting his first Group 1 scorer. The filly was offered for sale in Goffs as a foal and Tattersalls Ireland as a yearling but failed to meet her modest reserve on both occasions, remarkable when you consider the family from which she comes.

She is the first foal of Cape Castle (by Cape Cross), a four-time winner from twelve to fourteen furlongs and out of a half-sister to several broodmares of note. Reverie Solitaire (by Nashwan) is the stakes-winning dam of the Group 1-placed German mile Group 2 scorer Royal Solitaire (by Shamardal), Samdaniya (by Machiavellian) is the winning dam of the Group 1-placed pattern winning filly Dabyah (by Sepoy), Queen's Best (by King's Best) is the pattern-winning dam of the Grade 1 Breeders' Cup Filly & Mare Turf heroine Queen's Trust (by Dansili), whereas November's Grade 1 Hollywood Derby winner Domestic Spending (by Kingman) is the only foal out of the late thirteen-furlong stakes winner Urban Castle (by Street Cry).

Cloud Castle (by In The Wings) is, therefore, the third dam of Thundering Nights. That Group 1 Prix Vermeille and Group 1 Yorkshire Oaks-placed Group 3 Nell Gwyn Stakes winner was, in turn, a daughter of Lucayan Princess (by High Line) and that makes her a half-sister to the Group 1-winning middle-distance stars Luso (by Salse) and Warrsan (by Caerleon) and their multiple Group 1-placed, Group 2-winning half-brother Needle Gun (by Sure Blade). Several of their half-sisters went on to produce or become the ancestor of stakes and pattern winners, with the dual classic heroine Avenir Certain (by Le Havre), last season's Group 2 Royal Lodge Stakes victor New Mandate (by New Bay) and 2020's champion freshman sire Mehmas (by Acclamation) just three examples.

It will be fascinating to see what the future holds for Thundering Nights and doubtful that she would fail to find a buyer should she ever reappear in an auction ring. She has remained in training as a four-year-old.

SUMMARY DETAILS
Bred: Manjri Farm
Owned: Shapoor Mistry
Trained: Joseph O'Brien
Country: Ireland

Race record: 041-21130-
Career highlights: 3 wins inc Snow Fairy Fillies Stakes (Gr3),
3rd Moyglare 'Jewels' Blandford Stakes (Gr2)

THUNDERING NIGHTS (IRE) – 2017 bay filly

Night of Thunder (IRE)	Dubawi (IRE)	Dubai Millennium (GB)
		Zomaradah (GB)
	Forest Storm (GB)	Galileo (IRE)
		Quiet Storm (IRE)
Cape Castle (IRE)	Cape Cross (IRE)	Green Desert (USA)
		Park Appeal
	Kaabari (USA)	Seeking The Gold (USA)
		Cloud Castle (GB)

THUNDEROUS (IRE)

This colt was an unbeaten stakes winner over seven furlongs at two and made just two appearances on the track at three, but he remains something of an unknown quantity. His only defeat came when chasing home Volkan Star in the Listed Betway Fairway Stakes over ten furlongs on good-to-firm ground at Newmarket in late June, his first outing for ten months, and then he won the Group 2 Al Basti Equiworld Dante Stakes at York. The condensed and reorganised early part of the 2020 season put that traditional Derby trial five days after the Epsom classic, both races taking place in early July, and he ended the unbeaten run of the well-regarded Highest Ground. His margin of victory was a neck, Juan Elcano and Cormorant were two lengths and a neck behind in third and fourth. The runner-up, a mid-May foal, ran only once more, disappointing on soft ground at Newmarket in October, but he could be a leading middle-distance horse in 2021.

Thunderous, a 70,000-guinea Tattersalls October Book 2 graduate trained by Mark Johnston, also remains a bright prospect. He is among nineteen stakes winners that have emerged so far from the global first two crops of Kildangan Stud's classic-winning miler Night of Thunder (by Dubawi) and he comes from the family of a filly who struck at Group 1 level in 2020.

His now three-year-old half-brother Unforgotten (by Exceed And Excel), a 150,000-guinea Book 2 graduate who was gelded last spring, was a half-length runner-up in a one-mile Lingfield novice race in mid-December and could be an interesting member of the John Gosden stable this coming season. Their dam, Souviens Toi (by Dalakhani), for whom Rabbah Bloodstock paid 230,000 guineas at the 2015 Tattersalls December Mare Sale, got her listed-race win in Italy. She was also placed at that level at Pontefract, Goodwood and Windsor, had a Frankel (by Galileo) filly in 2020, and she is the best of several winners out of the Grade 3-placed multiple US-based winner Diavla (by Bahri). Fourth dam Coastal Patrol (by Cornish Prince) had a trio of Louisiana Downs blacktype events among her eleven career wins, and she is the third dam of Donjah (by Teofilo), winner of the Group 1 Preis von Europa at Cologne in August. That Henk

Crewe-trained filly is reviewed in *Volume 1: European Group 1 Winners*.

It will be good to see Thunderous back in action in 2021. He is already rated 112, so would not have far to go to be up to good open Group 2 company. Whether or not he can be the first or an early Group 1 star for his promising young sire remains to be seen.

SUMMARY DETAILS
Bred: Rabbah Bloodstock Ltd
Owned: Highclere Thoroughbred Racing - George Stubbs
Trained: Mark Johnston
Country: England
Race record: 111-21-
Career highlights: 4 wins inc Al Basti Equiworld Dubai Dante Stakes (Gr2), Denford Stakes (L), 2nd Betway Fairway Stakes (L)

THUNDEROUS (IRE) – 2017 bay colt

		Dubai Millennium (GB)
	Dubawi (IRE)	Zomaradah (GB)
Night of Thunder (IRE)		Galileo (IRE)
	Forest Storm (GB)	Quiet Storm (IRE)
		Darshaan
	Dalakhani (IRE)	Daltawa (IRE)
Souviens Toi (GB)		Bahri (USA)
	Diavla (USA)	Change My Heart (USA)

TIGER MOTH (IRE)

Tiger Moth has only run five times to date but is a dual Group 1-placed pattern winner who came within a head of landing a classic. He has proven his ability to stay two miles yet is clearly talented at twelve furlongs, so there should be plenty of potential options for him this coming season.

He finished a three-quarter-length third in a seven-furlong Curragh maiden on soft ground on his only start at two and made a winning return to action over ten furlongs at Leopardstown in early June, beating Dawn Patrol by half a length in a maiden. The gap between them widened to five lengths when they met again in the Group 1 Dubai Duty Free Irish Derby just eighteen days later, the pair finishing second and third to the narrow winner Santiago and with the subsequent shock Grade 1 Breeders' Cup Mile star Order of Australia another length and a quarter back in fourth. Tiger Moth, whose partner Emmet McNamara would give Serpentine an outstanding front-running ride at Epsom a week later, chased the Group 2 Queen's Vase winner throughout the final furlong and was closing as the line approached but needed a few more strides. It was a one-two-three-four for the Ballydoyle team.

Tiger Moth was next seen in action at Leopardstown in mid-September when he impressed in the Group 3 Paddy Power 'Is It 2021 Yet?' Stakes over twelve furlongs, also on good ground, on the opening day of Irish Champions Weekend. His stablemate Cormorant led the field into the straight but was already being asked for more. To his credit, the grey kept going and was still in front well inside the final furlong, until Ryan Moore and the favourite went past, staying on strongly for an easy four-length win. The filly Silence Please ran on for second, a neck and a head in front of Up Helly Aa and Cormorant and with Buckhurst an aditional three-quarters of a length back in fifth.

A major international target looked sure to be on the cards but rather than travel to England or France, he went to Australia and almost won the Group 1 Lexus Melbourne Cup. He was always prominent throughout the famous two-mile handicap, under pressure from Kerrin McEvoy from a furlong and a half out, soon moved into second but just couldn't peg back the front-running Twilight Payment who held on by half a length. Prince of Arran was a head back in third, staying on strongly at the finish and thereby making it a one-two-three for the Europeans.

What makes Tiger Moth's performances at the Curragh and Flemington more noteworthy is that he is a May 16th foal and so could be open to further improvement as a four-year-old. The Coolmore homebred is a son of the phenomenal Galileo (by Sadler's Wells) and out of the Group 3 Ballyogan Stakes winner Lesson In Humility (by Mujadil). She is a sprinter by a sprinter and from a family of sprinters, but there are also seven-furlong and mile horses in there too as well as Milli Charm (by Deep Impact), an eight- and nine-furlong graded winner in Japan who chased home the great Almond Eye in the Grade 1 Shuka Sho—the final leg of the Fillies' Triple Crown—over ten furlongs at Kyoto in 2018. She appears under a branch of the fourth generation of Tiger Moth's family so is a distant connection at best.

Lesson In Humility has spent most of her stud career visiting Galileo, and the juvenile Group 3-placed filly Butterscotch is among those progeny, but she was bred to Oasis Dream (by Green Desert) in her first season and the result was Coach House. He raced only at two, won his maiden by six and a half lengths over the minimum trip at Tipperary in early May, followed-up with a near two-length score in the Listed Marble Hill Stakes on fast ground at the Curragh, chased home No Nay Never in the Group 2 Norfolk Stakes at Royal Ascot and finished third to the subsequent Group 1 scorer Sudirman in the Group 2 Railway Stakes over six furlongs at the Curragh. He stands at Chapel Stud, his eldest progeny are now five years old, his progeny earnings are closing in on the £1 million mark and the Group 1-placed juvenile stakes winner Summer Sands is the better of his two blacktype horses.

The mare's half-sister Poet's Vanity (by Poet's Voice) won the Group 3 Oh So Sharp Stakes over seven furlongs at two, her stakes-winning half-sister Boastful (by Clodovil) is the dam of the stakes-winning sprinter Stage Play (by Oasis Dream), and she is out of a half-sister to Ffestiniog (by Efisio), the seven-furlong Listed Radley Stakes winner was a five-length winner over a mile on soft ground at Leicester. That four-time scorer's offspring include the Group 3 Prix de Meautry scorer Eisteddfod (by Cadeaux Genereux), the mile Group 3 winners Boston Lodge (by Grand Lodge) and Border Patrol (by Selkirk), and also include Brecon Beacon (by Spectrum). He chased home Grey Swallow in a twelve-furlong Grade 2 handicap at Hollywood Park and was a two-length third to Aragorn in the Grade 2 Oak Tree Derby over nine furlongs.

It will be interesting to see what sort of programme is mapped out for Tiger Moth. His Melbourne Cup second may pigeon-hole him as a stayer, but his earlier form and his pedigree could make it worthwhile to try him again over twelve furlongs and perhaps even at ten.

SUMMARY DETAILS

Bred: Coolmore
Owned: Mrs John Magnier, Michael Tabor & Derrick Smith
Trained: Aidan O'Brien
Country: Ireland
Race record: 3-1212-
Career highlights: 2 wins inc Paddy Power 'Is It 2021 Yet?' Stakes (Gr3), 2nd Dubai Duty Free Irish Derby (Gr1), Lexus Melbourne Cup (Gr1)

TIGER MOTH (IRE) – 2017 bay colt

Galileo (IRE)	Sadler's Wells (USA)	Northern Dancer
		Fairy Bridge (USA)
	Urban Sea (USA)	Miswaki (USA)
		Allegretta
Lesson In Humility (IRE)	Mujadil (USA)	Storm Bird (CAN)
		Vallee Secrete (USA)
	Vanity (IRE)	Thatching
		Penny Fan (GB)

TILSIT (USA)

First Defence (by Unbridled's Song) was a talented sprinter-miler who won the Grade 1 Forego Handicap and was runner-up in the Grade 1 King's Bishop Stakes at Saratoga. However, his early years as part of the Juddmonte team did not yield a sufficiently large number of stakes winners to keep him on the roster—he had the prolific Grade 1 star Close Hatches but little else of real note—and he moved to Saudi Arabia in the autumn of 2016. His daughter Antonoe won the Grade 1 Just A Game Stakes over a mile at Belmont Park the following summer, after his final northern hemisphere crop of foals was on the ground. They include the juvenile Group 1 star and classic-winning miler Siskin, who has joined the team at the famous Shadai Stallion Station in Japan, and also the Charles Hills-trained Tilsit.

That Juddmonte homebred was unraced at two and beaten by a head over a mile at Newcastle on his debut in early June but announced his presence in some style just over three weeks later when beating thirteen rivals with rarely seen ease over the same course and distance. His winning margin was nineteen lengths and a step up to pattern company clearly imminent. One month later, he beat My Oberon and Khaloosy by margins of one and a half lengths and two and a half lengths in the Group 3 Bonhams Thoroughbred Stakes at Goodwood. This mile contest on good-to-firm ground was his turf debut, he ran green and badly hampered the eventual runner-up just inside the final furlong, but the placings remained unaltered after the inevitable stewards' enquiry. He again failed to keep straight under pressure in the Group 2 Shadwell Joel Stakes on the Rowley Mile at Newmarket in late September, this time going to his left, but still ran on in the closing stages to finish fourth to Kameko, Regal Reality and Benbatl. This was a good effort from such an inexperienced colt, one who was making only his second start on grass, and he remains a highly promising prospect.

Tilsit, who has been entered in the ultra-valuable Neom Turf Cup over ten and a half furlongs at Riyadh in late February, has Group 1 potential and fulfilling that would surely enable him to secure a good berth at stud. With the combination of his sire plus the family he represents he could be a particularly interesting one in Europe rather than across the Atlantic. He is the first foal of a mare called Multilingual (by Dansili) and she a half-sister to the brilliant miler and now Banstead Manor Stud-based classic sire Kingman (by Invincible Spirit). This makes the classic-winning Zenda (by Zamindar) his grandam, and in addition to being out of a full sister to the Group 1 Irish Oaks heroine Wemyss Bight (by Dancing Brave), that mile star is a half-sister to the sprint champion and leading international sire Oasis Dream (by Green Desert). It will be fascinating to see what the future holds for this colt.

SUMMARY DETAILS
Bred: Juddmonte Farms Inc
Owned: Khalid Abdullah
Trained: Charles Hills
Country: England
Race record: -2114-
Career highlights: 2 wins inc Bonhams Thoroughbred Stakes (Gr3)

TILSIT (USA) – 2017 bay colt

First Defence (USA)	Unbridled's Song (USA)	Unbridled (USA)
		Trolley Song (USA)
	Honest Lady (USA)	Seattle Slew (USA)
		Toussaud (USA)
Multilingual (GB)	Dansili (GB)	Danehill (USA)
		Hasili (IRE)
	Zenda (GB)	Zamindar (USA)
		Hope (IRE)

TOP RANK (IRE)

He has not yet lived up to his name, but this lightly raced grey clearly has plenty of ability and, if he returns to action in 2021, could be an interesting contender for some of the top mile events. The 26,000-guinea Tattersalls October Book 3 graduate has raced only over that distance to date, which is a little unusual for a son of Dark Angel (by Acclamation), but he has won five from seven and been placed once. He made a winning debut at Lingfield in late December of his juvenile year, won a Thirsk novice race and a Newmarket handicap by two lengths and two and three-quarter lengths respectively on his only outings as a three-year-old and extended his unbeaten record to four when making his reappearance at Thirsk in late July 2020. He followed that four-and-a-quarter-length handicap success with a one-length third in a heritage handicap at York in August, after which his rating rose to 106, and then he stepped up to pattern level.

The ground was soft at Haydock in early September, the only time he has encountered such conditions on the track, but Top Rank showed a lot of promise in winning the Group 3 Betfair Superior Mile Stakes by a length and a half and the same from My Oberon and Khaloosy, with Kinross a neck behind in fourth. That first pair had filled the same positions behind Tilset in a similar contest on their previous start, giving the form a solid look, so it was no surprise to see the winner's rating rise again, this time to 111. He had been under some pressure from two out but keeping up with the principals and then drawing level before hitting the front a half furlong out and running on well to the line, pulling clear in the final few yards. The Group 2 Shadwell Joel Stakes was a much tougher ask three weeks later. He raced prominently, came under pressure two out but this time weakened in the final furlong, passing the post last of the six runners. That said, he was certainly not disgraced and he was only five and three-quarter lengths behind the winner, Kameko, who was shouldering a five-pound penalty.

Top Rank is the best of three runners out of Countess Ferrama (by Authorized), a twelve-furlong winner whose siblings include the Group 1 Irish 2,000 Guineas star Indian Haven (by Indian

Ridge) and the juvenile mile Group 1 scorer Count Dubois (by Zafonic). Both of that pair have had some success at stud, with the latter's record in South Africa surpassing what his more highly rated sibling has achieved in Europe. Their stakes-placed half-sister Place de l'Opera (by Sadler's Wells) is the dam of the middle-distance pattern winners High Pitched (by Indian Ridge) and Imperial Stride (by Indian Ridge) and of Hala Bek (by Halling), the colt whose only defeat in a three-race career was when finishing a half-length fourth to Sir Percy in a blanket finish in 2006's Group 1 Derby at Epsom. Madame Dubois (by Legend of France), the grandam of Top Rank, won both the Group 2 Park Hill Stakes and Group 2 Prix de Royallieu and her siblings included Sun And Shade (by Ajdal), the once-raced winning dam of the Group 2 Champagne Stakes and Group 2 Richmond Stakes scorer and minor blacktype sire Daggers Drawn (by Diesis).

There are plenty of other talented horses within the various branches of the family, but what is closest on the page is what has the greatest potential influence on what this colt might achieve on the track and, if earning the opportunity, at stud. Top Rank is one his distaff line's talented milers and it will be interesting to see what the future holds for him.

SUMMARY DETAILS

Bred: Wicklow Bloodstock
Owned: Saeed Manana
Trained: James Tate
Country: England
Race record: 1-11-1310-
Career highlights: 5 wins inc Betfair Superior Mile Stakes (Gr3)

TOP RANK (IRE) – 2016 grey colt

Dark Angel (IRE)	Acclamation (GB)	Royal Applause (GB)
		Princess Athena
	Midnight Angel (GB)	Machiavellian (USA)
		Night At Sea
Countess Ferrama (GB)	Authorized (IRE)	Montjeu (IRE)
		Funsie (FR)
	Madame Dubois (GB)	Legend of France (USA)
		Shadywood

TRUE SELF (IRE)

Most National Hunt stallions are either 'failed' flat sires or horses who were deemed to be more commercially viable if serving large books for the jumps sector rather than smaller ones for the one in which they excelled as racehorses. And even the best of them will end up with much lower percentages of winners to runners than you would expect to see among their supposedly classier brethren. Despite this many are still surprised when a one of them comes up with a high-class flat horse. If the mare is flat-bred and related to plenty of horses who were successful on the level then why should it be unexpected that she might produce a stakes or pattern scorer on the level?

Accordion (by Sadler's Wells) achieved the feat. He was bred to be a Derby horse, his Group 1-winning half-brother Hawaiian Sound (by Hawaii) was runner-up to Shirley Heights at Epsom, but he never raced. He spent his career serving in the National Hunt sector, sired a string of Grade 1 stars but also got the flat middle-distance Group 1 scorer Yavana's Pace and his talented full sister Littlepacepaddocks. That pattern-placed stakes winner missed out on a classic placing when finishing fourth to Petrushka in the Group 1 Irish Oaks at the Curragh. Oscar is also a flat-bred son of Sadler's Wells (by Northern Dancer), he was classic-placed in France but marketed for the jumps market from the start of his second career. He became a star in that role, a top source of staying chasers, but as with Accordion, there was always a chance that he could end up with at least one talented flat horse.

True Self is that horse. She started off in bumpers, went on to become a Grade B-winning hurdler and then, at the age of five, made her debut on the flat. She was runner-up over fourteen furlongs at Bellewstown first time out, ran away with a twelve-furlong Cork maiden and then added listed success over fourteen furlongs at Bath and another one over ten furlongs at Newmarket. She has not jumped a hurdle in public since. She won a listed at Gowran Park and was Group 3-placed at Haydock at the start of her six-year-old season, finished a three-length sixth to Mustajeer in the Ebor Handicap and then made her first trip to Australia. She was a head runner-up to Prince of Arran in the Group 3

Geelong Cup, missed the Melbourne Cup and, instead, took in the Grade 3 Queen Elizabeth Stakes, a thirteen-furlong handicap at Flemington which she won by a length and a half. She finished mid-field in the Grade 1 Longines Hong Kong Vase at Sha Tin a month later, stayed in training as a seven-year-old and kicked off her 2020 campaign with a sixth-place finish in the ultra-valuable Longines Turf Handicap over fifteen furlongs at Riyadh at the end of February.

True Self made the frame only once more in five starts, when securing a repeat victory in that Group 3 handicap at Flemington in November, although she picked up some more prize money along the way. Those unplaced efforts included a nine-and-three-quarter-length fourth to Magical in the Group 1 Alwasmiyah Pretty Polly Stakes over ten furlongs at the Curragh in late June, a performance which earned €8,000 for her connections.

This talented, Don Cantillon-bred bay is out of an unraced mare named Good Thought (by Mukaddamah) and she is the only one of her dam's offspring to have won under National Hunt rules. However, her half-sister Shared Moment (by Tagula) won seven times on the flat and half-brother Sir Boss (by Tagula) won eleven. Beau Cyrano (by Cyrano de Bergerac) won once over hurdles but three times on the flat at eight and nine furlongs. Their dam, Only Great (by Simply Great), won over six furlongs, nine furlongs and two miles on the level and also landed a two-mile maiden hurdle, and in addition to a trio of one-time National Hunt winners, that mare's siblings included the seven-furlong and triple six-furlong scorer Thatchenne (by Thatching). Fourth dam Ceili More (by Irish Ball) was placed in the Pretty Polly Stakes at the Curragh in 1976, the next dam, Princess Ray (by Princely Gift), was placed in the Fred Darling Stakes.

This is a moderate pedigree for a flat pattern winner, but it is a flat one and it will make True Self an intriguing broodmare prospect, especially if she is given the chance to breed some flat horses. It appears that her class may be at least in part the result of something from a well-bred classic-placed son of Sadler's Wells combining with something from a well-bred broodmare sire Mukaddamah (by Storm Bird). She is back in training at the age of eight and has been entered in the ultra-valuable Neom Turf Cup due to be run over ten and a half furlongs at Riyadh at the end of February.

SUMMARY DETAILS
Bred: Don Cantillon
Owned: Three Mile House & Oti Partnership
Trained: Willie Mullins
Country: Ireland
Race record: *-2-11124F1-00*2111-1200210-040001-
(National Hunt form in italics)
Career highlights: 10 wins inc Queen Elizabeth Stakes (Gr3-twice), BetVictor Irish EBF Vintage Tipple Stakes (L), Weatherbys General Stud Book James Seymour Stakes (L), British Stallion Studs EBF Beckford Stakes (L), Killashee Handicap Hurdle (NH-B), 2nd bet365 Geelong Cup (Gr3), Betway Pinnacle Stakes (Gr3), Irish Stallion Farms EBF Boreen Belle Mares Novice Hurdle (NH-L)

TRUE SELF (IRE) – 2013 bay mare

Oscar (IRE)	Sadler's Wells (USA)	Northern Dancer
		Fairy Bridge (USA)
	Snow Day (FR)	Reliance II
		Vindaria (USA)
Good Thought (IRE)	Mukaddamah (USA)	Storm Bird (CAN)
		Tash (USA)
	Only Great (IRE)	Simply Great (FR)
		Enterprisor

TRUESHAN (FR)

Trueshan put up one of the most impressive performances of the year when running away with the Group 2 Qipco British Champions Long Distance Cup at Ascot in mid-October. It was a revelation on his eleventh career start, a leap forward from anything he had achieved before and yet there did not appear to be any element of fluke about it. This was a gelding who had been racing almost exclusively from twelve to fourteen furlongs, he had won on everything from good to heavy, he'd even won on the Tapeta at Wolverhampton, and he came into the race a 109-rated winner of six of his ten starts. That tally included a twelve-furlong listed contest at Haydock in July. But this was his first attempt at two miles and his pattern-race debut. Hollie Doyle sent him to the front a furlong from home and it was quickly apparent that nothing was going to catch him. The dual Group 1 Irish St Leger heroine Search For A Song took the runners-up spot, finishing half a length, a neck and half a length in front of Fujaira Prince, Morando, and Sovereign, but Trueshan was the winner by seven and a half lengths.

This French-bred, Alan King-trained gelding—a description you'd expect to be followed by reference to a hurdler or chaser of note—heads into the 2021 flat season as a 118-rated five-year-old who could become one of the leading lights of the Cup races. Stradivarius and the other established members of the division have a new contender to deal with and it will be fascinating to see how this new phase of Trueshan's career turns out.

King secured the €8,000 Osarus September Yearling Sale graduate for 31,000 guineas at the 2018 Tattersalls Guineas Breeze-Up Sale, and the horse was gelded before his sole juvenile run, an unplaced finish in a maiden over an extended mile on soft ground at Nottingham. He won both of his first two starts at three, with Doyle in the saddle, and as that partnership was not renewed until Ascot, the pair currently makes an undefeated team.

Trueshan is a second-crop son of the top-class middle-distance horse Planteur (by Danehill Dancer). The stallion spent five seasons at Haras de Bouquetot, two at Haras du Grand Courgeon, and the timing of his son's rise towards stardom is perfect for his new connections in England. He is now standing as a National Hunt stallion at Roisin Close's Chapel Stud, alongside the speed-oriented flat sires Hellvelyn, Coach House and Pearl Secret. Shao Line (by General Holme), the dam of Trueshan, was a claiming-class middle-distance winner, she has produced several other winners in France, and if you go back to the third generation of her pedigree you will find branches that lead to the Group 1 Derby Italiano scorer Houmayoun (by Shernazar) and the multiple Grade 1 chase star Sizing John (by Midnight Legend) among others of note.

SUMMARY DETAILS
Bred: Didier Blot
Owned: Barbury Lions 5
Trained: Alan King
Country: England
Race record: 0-11211-41011-
Career highlights: 7 wins inc Qipco British Champions Long Distance Cup (Gr2), Tapster Stakes (L)

TRUESHAN (FR) – 2016 bay gelding

Planteur (IRE)	Danehill Dancer (IRE)	Danehill (USA)
		Mira Adonde (USA)
	Plante Rare (IRE)	Giant's Causeway (USA)
		Palmeraie (USA)
Shao Line (FR)	General Holme (USA)	Noholme (AUS)
		General's Sister (USA)
	Marie d'Altoria (FR)	Roi de Rome (USA)
		Marie de Lempire (FR)

UBETTABELIEVEIT (IRE)

Derek Veitch's Co Offaly-based Ringfort Stud bred a remarkable crop of foals in 2018. They received only €1,000 for an early-April-born filly at the Goffs November Foal Sale that year, one February-born colt fetched 85,000 guineas when sold in Newmarket as a weanling, and another, born in late March, made €35,000 in Goffs and was consigned again from the stud the following October when selling for 50,000 guineas from Tattersalls' Book 1 Sale. We now know that trio as Miss Amulet, Minzaal and Ubettabelieveit. The first two are Group 1-placed Group 2 winners and the third is the Nigel Tinkler-trained bay who won the Group 2 Bombardier Flying Childers Stakes at Doncaster in September before finishing an honourable third to Golden Pal in the Grade 2 Breeders' Cup Juvenile Turf Sprint at Keeneland.

That colt had finished fourth on his debut at Doncaster in mid-June, won easily over the same course and distance seventeen days later and then added the Listed National Stakes at Sandown. He was visibly travelling well at halfway and moved up to the leaders two out at which point it was only a matter of when Oisin Murphy would ask him to go on to win his race. That was around the furlong pole and the colt made steady progress to pull a length and a half clear of Wings of A Dove by the line. Murphy reported that the colt ran too freely when finishing last of nine in the Group 2 Al Basti Equiworld Dubai Gimcrack Stakes at York next time.

Rowan Scott, who had ridden him on his debut, was back in the saddle for the colt's final two runs. The field split into two groups in the Flying Childers, Ubettabelieveit raced towards the rear, moved towards the front a furlong out and ran on well to the line, short-heading Sacred, who headed the near-side trio, at the post. Neither of the front two steered a straight line, him drifting to his right and the filly to her left, so they were racing upsides for the final yards. There was a gap of one and a quarter lengths to the Irish-trained Measure of Magic in third, with a head, neck and a neck back to Burning Cash, Steel Bull and Ventura Tormenta in fourth, fifth and sixth.

He was slowly into stride at Keeneland and brought up the rear in the early stages but then moved forward a few places, made further progress over two furlongs out and was challenging for second a furlong later. He was unable to find an extra kick when it mattered and had to settle for third as Cowan went a length past him in the final half-furlong while still finishing three-quarters of a length behind the front-running Golden Pal. That Wesley Ward-trained winner had been a neck runner-up to The Lir Jet in the Group 2 Norfolk Stakes at Royal Ascot in June and easily won a listed contest over five and a half furlongs at Saratoga on his only subsequent outing between Ascot and Keeneland.

It is possible that he and the English-based colt could meet again in 2021 as Ward is reportedly considering potential Group 1 King's Stand Stakes and Group 1 Nunthorpe Stakes challenges for his son of Uncle Mo (by Indian Charlie). Incidentally, that stallion's son Lipizzaner, an Aidan O'Brien-trained pattern-placed stakes winner, finished fourth in that Keeneland race, one and three-quarter lengths behind Ubettabelieveit.

Ubettabelieveit is among sixty-five stakes winners by Tally-Ho Stud's Kodiac (by Danehill) and one of four blacktype scorers for his dam, Ladylishandra (by Mujadil). Half-sister Tropical Paradise (by Verglas) won the Group 3 Oak Tree Stakes and Group 3 Supreme Stakes, both over seven furlongs at Goodwood, and is the dam of several winners plus a 500,000-guinea Tattersalls Book 1 colt from her early foals. Shenanigans (by Arcano), a multiple blacktype earner, was a pattern-placed stakes winner over ten furlongs and she visited Gleneagles (by Galileo) in 2020, her first season at stud, whereas their half-brother Harlem Shake (by Moss Vale) is a sprinter, a Group 3 and dual listed scorer who has accumulated a double-digit tally of wins. Their grandam, Mevlana (by Red Sunset), is a winning full sister to the Group 3 Royal Whip Stakes scorer and blacktype producer Dancing Sunset and out of Dance Partner (by Graustark), a Grade 1-placed full sister to the classic-placed Santa Anita Derby victor Jim French and Group 3 Prix de Royallieu winner Don't Sulk, the dam of Group 1 Prix Lupin scorer Gracioso (by Nureyev).

Ubettabelieveit is clearly a sprinter with a lot of promise. Although some of his relations have stayed farther, it is likely that the colt will be best at five and six furlongs as a three-year-old. The 110-rated colt has shown all of his best form on good or fast ground—his debut run was on good-to-soft—and there is every reason to hope that he will do well again in 2021.

SUMMARY DETAILS

Bred: Ringfort Stud
Owned: Martin Webb Racing
Trained: Nigel Tinker
Country: England
Race record: 411013-
Career highlights: 3 wins inc Bombardier Flying Childers Stakes (Gr2), National Stakes (L), 3rd Breeders' Cup Juvenile Turf Sprint (Gr2)

UBETTABELIEVEIT (IRE) – 2018 bay colt

Kodiac (GB)	Danehill (USA)	Danzig (USA)
		Razyana (USA)
	Rafha	Kris
		Eljazzi
Ladylishandra (IRE)	Mujadil (USA)	Storm Bird (CAN)
		Vallee Secrete (USA)
	Mevlana (IRE)	Red Sunset
		Dance Partner (USA)

UMM KULTHUM (IRE)

Tally-Ho Stud stallion Kodiac (by Danehill) had an excellent year with his two-year-olds and Umm Kulthum was among those who won at pattern level. The Richard Fahey-trained juvenile, who Tally-Ho bred and sold for £75,000 at the delayed Goffs UK Breeze-Up Sale on July 1st, won two of her four starts, was placed in the other two, and finished the year on a rating of 110. Her winning debut was over five furlongs at Thirsk in late July, she finished third to Miss Amulet and Sacred in the Group 2 Sky Bet Lowther Stakes, won the Group 3 Scotty Brand Firth of Clyde Stakes at Ayr and rounded off the season with a third-place finish in the Group 1 Juddmonte Cheveley Park Stakes.

She had been green and swerved to her left in the closing stages of her debut but showed plenty of promise, winning by margins of half a length and the same against more experienced rivals. If you paused the race at the two-furlong pole at York you would likely have thought her likely to finish well-beaten. However, although still a bit green, she began to run on for Paul Hanagan, was a clear third passing the furlong pole, and kept on behind the front pair, Miss Amulet and Sacred, without threatening to catch them. The final margins were a length and three and a quarter lengths, with the fourth, She's So Nice, another two lengths behind. The ground had been good-to-soft there, as it was at Ayr in September, and having made up a lot of ground from two out to the final furlong marker, where she started to fight it out with Scarlet Bear, she kept on well to the line for a one-length victory. Lullaby Moon was another length back in third, with Mamba Wamba fourth. The Cheveley Park Stakes was one week later. Once again, she did her best work in the final quarter mile but this time had to settle for third, unable to catch Alcohol Free and pipped in the final strides by Miss Amulet. The margins were half a length and a head, with a one-and-a-quarter-length gap back to Happy Romance in fourth.

Umm Kulthum is the first foal of Queen's Code (by Shamardal), her dam had a Vadamos (by Monsun) filly in 2019, another Kodiac filly in 2020 and was then bred to Galileo Gold (by Paco Boy). The mare was well-beaten in all three of her starts, including when third in a seven-furlong Chester maiden, but has winning siblings and is out of Dehbanu (by King's Best), an unraced full sister to the stakes-placed winner Cadre. That mare's half-sister Jakarta Jade (by Royal Abjar) was a listed-placed winner from eight to twelve furlongs and is a blacktype producer, whereas half-brother Dubai Prince (by Shamardal), who won the Group 3 Killavullan Stakes and Group 3 Strensall Stakes before embarking on a successful National Hunt career, could be described as being a three-parts brother to Dehbanu. Third dam Persian Frolic (by Persian Bold), who won five times, is a half-sister to the triple Group/Grade 1-winning middle-distance star and blacktype sire Storming Home (by Machiavellian).

Umm Kulthum clearly has ability. All of her racing so far has been over sprint trips, and it may be that is where her future lies, but her pedigree also gives her the potential to stay a mile and it catches the eye that she holds entries in the Group 1 Tattersalls Irish 1,000 Guineas and Group 1 Emirates Poule d'Essai des Pouliches (French 1000 Guineas). She remains a bright prospect.

SUMMARY DETAILS
Bred: Tally-Ho Stud
Owned: Saeed Bin Mohammed Al Qassimi
Trained: Richard Fahey
Country: England
Race record: 1313-
Career highlights: 2 wins inc Scotty Brand Firth of Clyde Fillies' Stakes (Gr3), 3rd Juddmonte Cheveley Park Stakes (Gr1), Sky Bet Lowther Stakes (Gr2)

UMM KULTHUM (IRE) – 2018 bay filly

		Danzig (USA)
	Danehill (USA)	Razyana (USA)
Kodiac (GB)		Kris
	Rafha	Eljazzi
	Shamardal (USA)	Giant's Causeway (USA)
		Helsinki (GB)
Queen's Code (IRE)	Dehbanu (IRE)	King's Best (USA)
		Desert Frolic (IRE)

VALERIA MESSALINA (IRE)

Airlie Stud has bred many top-class horses over the years, and although this filly is only rated 109 and so some way below the best of her age, she has a pattern win on her record. The daughter of Coolmore Stud's well-established classic sire Holy Roman Emperor (by Danehill) won a Naas maiden by a nose on her debut and was a neck runner-up to Rose of Kildare in the Group 3 Godolphin Lifetime Care Oh So Sharp Stakes from just two starts at two, both of them over seven furlongs. She bounced back from an unplaced classic effort first time out at three to take the Group 3 Irish Stallion Farms EBF Brownstown Stakes at Cork. That race was over seven furlongs, as is the Group 3 Saint Clair Oak Tree Stakes in which she was short-headed by the triple Group 1 Prix de la Foret heroine One Master. Her only other outing was in the Group 1 Coolmore 'Justify' Matron Stakes at Leopardstown on Irish Champions Weekend where, having met with some traffic problems in the straight, she finished sixth to Champers Elysees.

The Jessica Harrington-trained bay is a half-sister to several winners, notably the capable miler Pincheck (by Invincible Spirit) who has won the Group 3 Desmond Stakes and twice finished third in the Group 2 Clipper Logistics Boomerang Stakes. Their dam, Arty Crafty (by Arch), won four times from ten to twelve furlongs, three of them on Polytrack, and she is a full sister to Prince Arch who got his best win in the Grade 1 Gulfstream Breeders' Cup Handicap over eleven furlongs on turf. The mare's half-brother Kingsfort (by War Chant) narrowly won the Group 1 National Stakes at the Curragh when trained by Kevin Prendergast and later won a mile listed contest at Newmarket for the Saeed bin Suroor stable.

Princess Kris (by Kris), the grandam of Valeria Messalina, is a winning daughter of the pattern-placed dual French stakes winner As You Desire Me (by Kalamoun) and that makes her a half-sister to the Group 3 May Hill Stakes scorer Intimate Guest (by Be My Guest) and to several mares who became blacktype producers at stud. Luas Line (by Danehill Dancer), who won the Grade 1 Garden City Breeders' Cup Handicap and finished third in the Group 1 Irish 1,000 Guineas, is the most notable among the string of stakes winners that descend from them. As for their dam, As You Desire Me was a half-sister to 1977's Group 2 King Edward VII winner and Group 1 Irish Derby runner-up, Classic Example (by Run The Gantlet), and a daughter of the Fred Darling Stakes and Strensall Stakes winner and Coronation Stakes runner-up Royal Saint (by Saint Crespin), a full sister to the triple classic star Altesse Royale.

Valeria Messalina is a pattern winner by a notable sire and broodmare sire—his granddaughter Shale (by Galileo) was a Group 1 winner in 2020—and she comes from a family that has a long history of producing stakes and group-race winners, all of which will make her a valuable addition to the broodmare ranks. She has remained in training as a four-year-old.

SUMMARY DETAILS
Bred: Airlie Stud
Owned: Marc Chan
Trained: Jessica Harrington
Country: Ireland
Race record: 12-0120-
Career highlights: 2 wins inc Irish Stallion Farms EBF Brownstown Stakes (Gr3), 2nd Saint Clair Oak Tree Stakes (Gr3), Godolphin Lifetime Care Oh So Sharp Stakes (Gr3)

VALERIA MESSALINA (IRE) – 2017 bay filly

Holy Roman Emperor (IRE)	Danehill (USA)	Danzig (USA)
		Razyana (USA)
	L'On Vite (USA)	Secretariat (USA)
		Fanfreluche (CAN)
Arty Crafty (USA)	Arch (USA)	Kris S (USA)
		Aurora (USA)
	Princess Kris (GB)	Kris
		As You Desire Me

VENTURA REBEL (GB)

Ventura Rebel looked a potential pattern winner when finishing a neck runner-up to A'Ali in the Group 2 Norfolk Stakes on soft ground at Royal Ascot as a juvenile, but he had to wait over fifteen months before achieving the feat. He had won his two prior races, a Thirsk maiden and a conditions races at Ascot both run on fast ground, and he finished a two-length fourth to Bettys Hope in the valuable Weatherbys Super Sprint at Newbury a month after losing his perfect record, ending his juvenile season on a rating of 107.

His first run of 2020 looked a bit rusty. He was at the rear of the field for much of the Group 3 Betway Pavilion Stakes at Newcastle, started to move forward about a furlong from home and kept on into sixth. It was his first attempt over six furlongs and on that evidence the trip was likely more suitable than the shorter one over which he'd raced at two. It was no surprise to see him go off at 50/1 for the Group 1 Commonwealth Cup next time, but he outran those odds, again making progress in the final furlong and keeping on to the finish. This time he picked up third place, two and a half lengths behind the American filly Kimari who was a length and a half behind Golden Horde. Seven furlongs was worth a shot but he ran the same way in the Listed William Hill King Charles Stakes at York: slowly away, racing in rear, under pressure two out, running on at the finish. However, he was only fifth in a dead-heat with Royal Commando, the colt who had been just a head behind him at Ascot.

A return to six produced two more unplaced runs in listed races, one of them in a first-time visor, and his rating dropped to 101. The visor was replaced with cheekpieces for what turned out to be his final outing of the year: the Group 3 Qatar Racing and Equestrian Club Renaissance Stakes at the Curragh in late September. The ground was good, local rider Declan McDonagh was on board him for the first time and although it looked two out like this might be more of the same from the colt, he got his head in front in the final hundred yards and pulled half a length ahead of Forever In Dreams. Summerghand was a length and a half behind in third, denying Romantic Proposal a pattern-race placing by a short head.

Ventura Rebel, a £28,000 Tattersalls Ireland Ascot September Yearling Sale graduate, was catalogued for the Tattersalls Autumn Horses-in-Training Sale in late October but did not go through the ring. He is a son of the Group 1 July Cup winner and former National Stud stallion Pastoral Pursuits (by Bahamian Bounty), now in his fourth season at Norton Grove Stud. That horse has sired plenty of multiple and prolific winners but has only thirteen stakes winners to his name, four of whom have won Group 3 contests. Ten of his other offspring have been placed in pattern company and ten in listed company, and although some of his best stay a bit farther, most are effective in the five-to-seven-furlong range.

Finalize (by Firebreak), his dam, fell in a five-furlong Hamilton maiden on her only start, her first foal is the eight-time scorer Suitcase 'N' Taxi (by Major Cadeaux), her second is the sprint winner Compton's Finale (by Compton Place) and Ventura Rebel is her third. He has been followed by a trio of fillies—a Swiss Spirit (by Invincible Spirit) in 2018, a Fountain of Youth (by Oasis Dream) in 2019 and a Jungle Cat (by Iffraaj) in 2020—and the mare was bred to Mayson (by Invincible Spirit) last season. Finalize's siblings include multiple winners by the sires of those first two daughters but the most prolific is her half-brother Flying Pursuit (by Pastoral Pursuits). That Tim Easterby-trained gelding, who is also bred by Crossfields Bloodstock Ltd, has won eight times, earned almost £200,000, and his dozen placings include third in the Ayr Gold Cup in 2018, a race his grandam, Final Shot (by Dalsaan), won in 1990. He can be described as being a three-parts brother to Ventura Rebel. Fast Shot (by Fasliyev), an Easterby-trained seven-time winner who was a neck runner-up in 2013's Ayr Silver Cup, is a half-brother to Ventura Rebel's winning grandam, Choisette (by Choisir).

The colt's rating rose to 108 after his pattern success and although further progress is needed if he is to trouble the best, he could be one to watch in the sprinters' division in 2021. He is also something of a modern-day rarity in that he is a pattern winner who is an outcross, i.e., there are no duplicated ancestors within

the first five generations of his pedigree, and that could make him
an interesting prospect if he earns a berth at stud.

SUMMARY DETAILS
Bred: Crossfields Bloodstock Ltd
Owned: Abdullah Menahi
Trained: Richard Fahey
Country: England
Race record: 1124-030001-
Career highlights: 3 wins inc Qatar Racing And Equestrian
Club Renaissance Stakes (Gr3), 2nd Norfolk Stakes (Gr2), 3rd
Commonwealth Cup (Gr1)

VENTURA REBEL (GB) – 2017 bay colt

Pastoral Pursuits (GB)	Bahamian Bounty (GB)	Cadeaux Genereux
		Clarentia
	Star (GB)	Most Welcome
		Marista
Finalize (GB)	Firebreak (GB)	Charnwood Forest (IRE)
		Breakaway
	Choisette (GB)	Choisir (AUS)
		Final Pursuit (GB)

VENTURA TORMENTA (IRE)

Take out this colt's fourth race and you have a horse who won a Yarmouth novice race in early July but was unplaced in a string of pattern events, a potential candidate for being gelded and dropping to handicap level as a three-year-old. He was sixth in the Group 2 Norfolk Stakes on his debut, fifth in the Group 2 bet365 Superlative Stakes, sixth in the Group 2 Bombardier Flying Childers Stakes at Doncaster, and last in both the Group 1 Keeneland Phoenix Stakes and Group 3 Tattersalls Stakes. However, that fourth race was the Group 2 Darley Prix Robert Papin, run over six furlongs at Chantilly in 2020 rather than over its traditional five-and-a-half-furlong trip, and he made most of the running while short-heading The Lir Jet. Subsequent Group 1 scorer Tiger Tanaka was a neck behind in third and the only other runner was tailed off. Ventura Tormenta is by the sire of Dark Angel (by Acclamation), Harbour Watch, Mehmas and Expert Eye, so if he remains a colt and can pick up one or more pattern wins in 2021 there could be a stallion role in his future.

Both of his wins have come over six furlongs, he was only beaten by a total of two and a quarter lengths at Doncaster having been in a potential winning position a furlong out, and he was unplaced in both attempts at seven furlongs. All six of his older siblings are winners and George Bowen, his three-parts brother, has been the most successful of them. The Richard Fahey-trained grey has won eight of his sixty-nine starts, earned over £235,000, achieved a career-high mark of 107 after finishing fifth to Gifted Master in 2018's Stewards' Cup at Goodwood and finished 2020 on a mark of eighty-three. They are all out of Midnight Oasis (by Oasis Dream), her now two-year-old Starspangledbanner (by Choisir) colt made £55,000 at the Goffs UK Premier Yearling Sale, she had a son of Camacho (by Danehill) in 2020 and was then bred to both Australia (by Galileo) and Caravaggio (by Scat Daddy).

The mare showed little aptitude for racing in seven runs but it is not a surprise that she has done well as a broodmare. Her string of successful siblings includes the Group 3 Ballyogan Stakes winner Miss Anabaa (by Anabaa) and the talented handicappers

Move It (by Cadeaux Genereux) and Out After Dark (by Cadeaux Genereux), winners of the Shergar Cup Sprint and Portland Handicap respectively and who both achieved a career-high mark of 105. They are all out of Midnight Shift (by Night Shift), a winning half-sister to Owington (by Green Desert), which makes Midnight Oasis closely related to that Group 1 July Cup star and blacktype sire.

Ventura Tormenta, a £95,000 Goffs UK Premier Yearling Sale graduate, clearly has ability, so it will be interesting to see how he gets on in 2021 and what the future holds for him.

SUMMARY DETAILS
Bred: Kevin Blake
Owned: Middleham Park Racing IV
Trained: Richard Hannon
Country: England
Race record: 0101000-
Career highlights: 2 wins inc Darley Prix Robert Papin (Gr2)

VENTURA TORMENTA (IRE) – 2018 bay colt

Acclamation (GB)	Royal Applause (GB)	Waajib
		Flying Melody
	Princess Athena	Ahonoora
		Shopping Wise
Midnight Oasis (GB)	Oasis Dream (GB)	Green Desert (USA)
		Hope (IRE)
	Midnight Shift (IRE)	Night Shift (USA)
		Old Domesday Book

VOLKAN STAR (IRE)

Volkan Star, a €300,000 Goffs November Foal Sale purchase, is a one million-guinea graduate of Tattersalls' October Book 1 Sale but was gelded after his final juvenile run. He had been a neck runner-up over seven furlongs at Newmarket on his debut that August, won by six lengths over a mile at Goodwood a fortnight later but then finished only sixth to Max Vega in the Group 3 Godolphin Flying Start Zetland Stakes over an extra two furlongs. He chased home the subsequent classic star Mishriff in a listed contest over the same course and distance first time out in 2020, returned to the venue three weeks later to beat Thunderous by almost two lengths in the Listed Betway Fairway Stakes and then stepped up to twelve furlongs at ParisLongchamp where he landed the Group 3 Prix du Lys. He had only three rivals that day and made all to beat Ketil and Measure of Time by three-quarters of a length and a neck. He raced prominently in the Group 2 Prix Hocquart Longines over a half furlong farther at Deauville on his only subsequent outing but could finish only fifth as Port Guillaume beat Ketil by three lengths.

The son of Gilltown Stud's Timeform 140-rated Arc and multiple classic ace Sea The Stars (by Cape Cross) is the first foal of Chicago Dancer (by Azamour), who was unplaced in eight starts and retired with an official rating of just forty-four. Her half-sister Epatha (by Highest Honor) won a ten-and-a-half-furlong listed contest in France, half-brother Skins Game (by Diktat) won the Group 3 Prix Edmond Blanc over a mile and has sired winners under National Hunt rules, and they are out of Mouriyana (by Akarad), a winning granddaughter of the Group 2 Nassau Stakes third Mamouna (by Vaguely Noble). Mouriyana's half-sister Mouramara (by Kahyasi) won the Group 2 Prix de Royallieu and went on to produce three horses of note at stud. Her star son Mourayan (by Alhaarth) won the Group 1 Sydney Cup over two miles at Randwick and is the sire of last season's 300/1 Leopardstown maiden winner He Knows No Fear. Mourilyan (by Desert Prince) won the Listed March Stakes, was runner-up in the Group 2 Goodwood Cup and third in the Group 1 Melbourne

Cup, and Mourad (by Sinndar) was a multiple Grade 2-winning staying hurdler for the Willie Mullins stable.

Family connections like these raise the possibility that Volkan Star could be a Cup horse in the making, although the middle-distances over which he has proven effective so far could be just as suitable. His now two-year-old full sister has been named Infinite Wonder and that 350,000-guinea Book 1 graduate is followed by an Invincible Spirit (by Green Desert) colt who made €120,000 in Goffs in December. It will be interesting to see which of them has the most notable profile in the years to come.

SUMMARY DETAILS
Bred: Forenaghts Stud & S Mencoff
Owned: Godolphin
Trained: Charlie Appleby
Country: England
Race record: 210-2110-
Career highlights: 3 wins inc Prix du Lys (Gr3), Betway Fairway Stakes (L), 2nd Betfair Exchange Free Bet Streak Newmarket Stakes (L)

VOLKAN STAR (IRE) – 2017 bay gelding

		Green Desert (USA)
Sea The Stars (IRE)	Cape Cross (IRE)	Green Desert (USA)
		Park Appeal
	Urban Sea (USA)	Miswaki (USA)
		Allegretta
Chicago Dancer (IRE)	Azamour (IRE)	Night Shift (USA)
		Asmara (USA)
	Mouriyana (IRE)	Akarad (FR)
		Mamoura (IRE)

WICHITA (IRE)

The juvenile class of 2020 did not excite and left an impression that some of the brightest stars among its cohort may not yet have stepped into blacktype company or possibly even made it to the track. The class of 2019, on the other hand, produced some wide-margin performances in top races that generated much chatter and anticipation, headed by the spectacular juvenile champion Pinatubo's runaway victory in the Group 1 Goffs Vincent O'Brien National Stakes at the Curragh. Wichita was also among the highly rated members of that class.

The 140,000-guinea Tattersalls October Book 2 graduate only won by a head when making a successful debut over seven furlongs at the Curragh that August and then confirmed that he had ability when chasing home the half-length winner Molatham in a listed contest over the same trip at Doncaster three weeks later. Berlin Tango was another three-quarters of a lengths behind in third. But when he went to Newmarket next time, he ran away with the Group 3 Tattersalls Stakes over the trip, moving into the lead over two furlongs from home and storming clear for a seven-length victory, looking like a serious contender for the following spring's Group 1 Qipco 2000 Guineas. The ground was good for the Tattersalls Stakes but soft when he returned to the Rowley Mile course sixteen days later. This time he was unable to quicken when it mattered. The race was the Group 1 Darley Dewhurst Stakes in which Pinatubo closed out his season with a two-length score from Arizona and Wichita was another two and three-quarter lengths adrift in third.

The colt's pedigree and juvenile record suggested that he would likely stay a mile, though possibly no farther, and he duly ran well in the 2000 Guineas on his seasonal reappearance on the first Saturday in June. He hit the front a quarter of a mile from home, was only headed about half a furlong out and then kept on well to the line, failing by only a neck to beat Kameko and with the previously undefeated pair Pinatubo and Military March a length and two and a half lengths behind in third and fourth.

He set a steady pace when trying to make all in the Group 1 St James's Palace Stakes at the Royal Ascot meeting a fortnight later, and although finishing five lengths clear of his closest pursuer, he had to settle for third, beaten a length and a head by Palace Pier and Pinatubo. He finished just over five lengths off the winner when fifth in the Group 1 Qatar Sussex Stakes next time—Mohaather led home Circus Maximus, Siskin and Kameko—and seven and a half lengths behind Space Blues when unplaced in the Group 1 LARC Prix Maurice de Gheest at Deauville in early August, but then put up an excellent effort at Doncaster in mid-September on what would be his final start.

Wichita hit the front inside the final furlong of the Group 2 bet365 Park Stakes but was strongly challenged by the six-year-old mare One Master, running over her specialist distance of seven furlongs. It looked as though she would not get there in time but, close to the line, she got her nose in front only for the colt to take back the lead when it mattered most. The pair finished two lengths clear of Molatham, who was third.

Wichita was among the team of horses that Ballydoyle shipped to Australia for a series of big-race targets, with the Group 1 Kennedy Cantala Stakes and the AU$7.5 million Golden Eagle—the latter over seven and a half furlongs—under consideration for him. However, while working with Anthony Van Dyck on the track at Werribee in mid-October, he sustained a fracture to his right hind leg, an injury that was only discovered after he returned to his stable. He underwent surgery but there were complications during his recovery and, on October 23rd, he was put down. In a sad coincidence, Anthony Van Dyck also died a few weeks later.

Even if Wichita had been able to retire without a top-level win to his name, he would likely have been a popular addition to the stallion ranks given his good two-year-old form, his status as a classic-placed Group 2 scorer at three and being a good-looking son of Coolmore Stud's rising star No Nay Never (by Scat Daddy). He was out of Lumiere Noire (by Dashing Blade), a stakes-winning half-sister to the Grade 1 Manhattan Handicap scorer Desert Blanc (by Desert Style), related to the Group 1-placed juvenile seven-furlong Group 2 scorer Signe Divin (by Bering)—also a pattern winner over nine—and from the family of the Group 1 stars Satwa Queen (by Muhtathir), Spadoun (by

Kaldoun) and, more distantly, the stayer Mille Et Mille (by Muhtathir).

SUMMARY DETAILS
Bred: W Maxwell Ervine
Owned: Derrick Smith, Mrs John Magnier & Michael Tabor
Trained: Aidan O'Brien
Country: Ireland
Race record: 1213-23001-
Career highlights: 3 wins inc bet365 Park Stakes (Gr2), Tattersalls Stakes (Gr3), 2nd Qipco 2000 Guineas (Gr1), Weatherbys Global Stallions App Flying Scotsman Stakes (L), 3rd St James's Palace Stakes (Gr1), Darley Dewhurst Stakes (Gr1)

WICHITA (IRE) – 2017 bay colt

No Nay Never (USA)	Scat Daddy (USA)	Johannesburg (USA)
		Love Style (USA)
	Cat's Eye Witness (USA)	Elusive Quality (USA)
		Comical Cat (USA)
Lumiere Noire (FR)	Dashing Blade	Elegant Air
		Sharp Castan
	Lumiere Rouge (FR)	Indian Ridge
		Lumen Dei (USA)

WINTER POWER (IRE)

Winter Power had a busy first season. She did not get off the mark until her third start, she finished last of ten in the Group 2 Bombardier Flying Childers Stakes but then rounded off the year with a pair of blacktype wins and an official rating of 109. She is a capable sprinter who has only raced over the minimum trip.

Her first success was a near effortless five-length score in a Redcar nursery in late July, her second was by two lengths in a novice contest at Ripon and her third a half-length defeat of Nomadic Empire in the Listed Shadwell Stud/EBF Stallions Harry Rosebery Stakes on good-to-soft ground at Ayr, a performance that raised her handicap figure to ninety-five. She had been keen there and eventually hit the front a furlong out, but she made almost all the running at Newmarket on her final start and beat Method and Burning Cash by three lengths and a neck, hence the leap in her rating. The race was the Group 3 Newmarket Academy Godolphin Beacon Project Cornwallis Stakes and the ground on the Rowley Mile course was soft.

The Tim Easterby-trained bay was bred by Newlands House Stud, is a €90,000 Goffs Orby Sale graduate and one of five stakes winners for the Rathasker Stud stallion Bungle Inthejungle (by Exceed And Excel). Her siblings include the five-furlong listed winner Hay Chewed (by Camacho), stakes-placed winner Flying Sparkle (by Fast Company) and eight-time sprint scorer Imperial Legend (by Mujadil), and she is out of Titian Saga (by Titus Livius), a winning half-sister to Nova Tor (by Trans Island). That sibling won six times but what makes her particularly notable is that she too has produced three blacktype winners at stud. Devonshire (by Fast Company) won the Group 2 Lanwades Stud Stakes over a mile at the Curragh and finished third to Pleascach in the Group 1 Irish 1,000 Guineas, Hurryupharriet beat Mecca's Angel in a five-furlong listed contest at Ayr as a two-year-old, whereas Veneer of Charm (by Fast Company) won the Grade 3 Boodles Fred Winter Juvenile Handicap Hurdle at the 2018 Cheltenham Festival.

There are lots of opportunities available for Winter Power if she remains at five furlongs, although it would be interesting to see how she might get on over six. Looking further ahead, the only inbreeding in her pedigree is 5x5x5x5x4 to Northern Dancer (by Nearctic), so that will provide her connections with plenty of options when the time comes for her to go to stud.

SUMMARY DETAILS
Bred: Newlands House Stud
Owned: King Power Racing Co Ltd
Trained: Tim Easterby
Country: England
Race record: 331401011-
Career highlights: 4 wins inc Newmarket Academy Godolphin Beacon Project Cornwallis Stakes (Gr3), Shadwell Stud/EBF Stallions Harry Rosebery Stakes (L)

WINTER POWER (IRE) – 2018 bay filly

Bungle Inthejungle (GB)	Exceed And Excel (AUS)	Danehill (USA)
		Patrona (USA)
	Licence To Thrill (GB)	Wolfhound (USA)
		Crime of Passion
Titian Saga (IRE)	Titus Livius (FR)	Machiavellian (USA)
		Party Doll
	Nordic Living (IRE)	Nordico (USA)
		To Die For (USA)

WITH THANKS (IRE)

With Thanks was a €5,000 vendor buy-back in Goffs as a yearling but made such improvement over the winter and spring that she transformed into a €100,000 Tattersalls Ireland Goresbridge Breeze-Up filly. Her only race that year was over seven furlongs in heavy ground at Newmarket in early November, which she won by three-quarters of a length, and she was short-headed over six at Thirsk on her seasonal reappearance in late July. That was on good ground but all of her other starts have been over seven and on heavy. She ran away with a novice fillies' contest at Catterick in late August, failed by only half a length to beat Onassis in the Listed Tote/British EBF October Fillies' Stakes at Goodwood in October and then made a big impression at Naas in November. The race was the Group 3 Irish Stallion Farms EBF Athasi Stakes, which is usually run in the spring as a classic trial. She cruised to the lead a quarter of a mile from home, soon went clear and was eased near the finish while winning by five lengths and half a length from Silk Forest and Soul Search. Her official handicap figure leapt from ninety-six to 110.

The filly is one of six pattern winners among an overall tally of seventeen stakes winners by Yeomanstown Stud's veteran classic sire Camacho (by Danehill) and she is the best of several runners out of Thanks (by Kheleyf), an unraced mare with Group 1 relations. With Thanks has a now two-year-old half-sister by Belardo (by Lope de Vega), a yearling National Defense (by Invincible Spirit) half-brother and her dam was bred back to Camacho last season. Briviesca (by Peintre Celebre), the most notable of Thanks's siblings, won a listed contest over twelve furlongs in France before crossing the Atlantic where she was a neck runner-up in a pair of Grade 3 handicaps, and in 2019 her daughter Villa Marina (by Le Havre) won the Group 1 Prix de l'Opera at ParisLongchamp.

Kimono (by Machiavellian), the grandam of With Thanks, is a half-sister to Kiswahili (by Selkirk), the stakes-winning dam of a pattern-placed stakes winner for owner-breeder Kirsten Rausing. She is out of Kiliniski (by Niniski), the Group 3 Oaks Trial winner who was runner-up in the Group 1 Yorkshire Oaks and fourth to

Fillies' Triple Crown heroine Oh So Sharp in the Group 1 Oaks at Epsom in 1985, and a granddaughter of Special (by Forli). This makes the young Naas winner another talented representative of a branch of the famous family of Nureyev (by Northern Dancer), Sadler's Wells (by Northern Dancer) and so many others of note.

With Thanks has remained in training as a four-year-old and it will be fascinating to see how the season goes for her.

SUMMARY DETAILS
Bred: Mrs E Thompson
Owned: Sheikh Rashid Dalmook Al Maktoum
Trained: William Haggas
Country: England
Race record: 1-2121-
Career highlights: 3 wins inc Irish Stallion Farms EBF Athasi Stakes (Gr3), 2nd Tote/British EBF October Fillies' Stakes (L)

WITH THANKS (IRE) – 2017 bay filly

Camacho (GB)	Danehill (USA)	Danzig (USA)
		Razyana (USA)
	Arabesque (GB)	Zafonic (USA)
		Prophecy (IRE)
Thanks (IRE)	Kheleyf (USA)	Green Desert (USA)
		Society Lady (USA)
	Kimono (IRE)	Machiavellian (USA)
		Kiliniski

YOUNG RASCAL (FR)

Young Rascal did all of his racing of 2020 in Australia, the first two starts while still representing the William Haggas stable and the rest as a member of Archie Alexander's team. He gave Mugatoo eleven pounds and a half-length beating in a Group 3 handicap over twelve furlongs at Rosehill in March, finished down the field when favourite for the Group 1 Schweppes Sydney Cup over two miles at Randwick the following month, and was later unplaced at Caulfield and in a couple of middle-distance contests at Flemington. He won a listed race at Kempton in 2019, had been a triple Group 3 scorer as a three-year-old and was well-beaten when finishing seventh to Masar in the Group 1 Derby at Epsom.

The gelding is a €215,000 graduate of the Arqana Deauville August yearling sale and he is a son of Intello (by Galileo), the classic winning French champion who has been alternating his stallion career between Cheveley Park Stud in England and Haras du Quesnay in France. He is at the latter venue in 2021. The now eleven-year-old has not been as successful as one might have hoped of a horse with his credentials, with only Group 1 Prix Jean Prat scorer Intellogent successful at above Group 3 level and an overall tally of just thirteen stakes winners. Regal Reality, who is reviewed elsewhere in this volume, is one of those who have been Group 1 placed, and it is probably just a matter of time before the stallion gets his next winner at that level.

Young Rascal is out of the triple mile listed scorer Rock My Soul (by Clodovil), a mare whose siblings include the mile Group 3 winner Rock My Love (by Holy Roman Emperor), mile listed scorer and Group 1 Preis der Diana (German Oaks) fourth (no blacktype) Rock My Heart (by Sholokhov), and the John Gosden-trained and pattern-placed Run Wild (by Amaron) who was an impressive winner of the Listed Betfair EBF Pretty Polly Stakes over ten furlongs at Newmarket in June. Their dam, Rondinay (by Cadeaux Genereux), is a half-sister to the pattern-winning miler Touch My Soul (by Tiger Hill), whereas her dam, Topline (by Acatenango), is a winning half-sister to several horses of note. Turfkonig (by Anfield) was a Group 1 Deutsches Derby-placed middle-distance Group 1 scorer in Germany whose wins also included the Group 2 Mehl-Mülhens-Rennen (German 2000 Guineas), his three-parts sister Tryphosa (by Be My Guest) won the Group 2 German 1000 Guineas and was third in the Group 1 Prix de Diane (French Oaks), and Tiberius Caesar (by Zieten) was a mile Group 3 scorer before becoming the teaser that sired the Group 2 Grand Prix de Deauville winner Tiberian.

SUMMARY DETAILS

Bred: Ecurie Peregrine SAS
Owned: Oti Racing Syndicate (now Oti Racing, B Kantor, et al)
Trained: William Haggas (now Archie Alexander)
Country: England (now Australia)
Race record: 2-11011-0010-10000-0
Career highlights: 6 wins inc Iron Jack N E Manion Cup (Gr3), Teddington Royal British Legion (St Simon) Stakes (Gr3), Dubai Duty Free Legacy Cup Stakes (Gr3), Centennial Celebration - MBNA Chester Vase Stakes (Gr3), Matchbook Floodlit Stakes (L)

YOUNG RASCAL (FR) – 2015 bay gelding

		Sadler's Wells (USA)
Intello (GER)	Galileo (IRE)	Urban Sea (USA)
	Impressionnante (GB)	**Danehill (USA)**
		Occupandiste (IRE)
Rock My Soul (IRE)	Clodovil (IRE)	**Danehill (USA)**
		Clodora (FR)
	Rondinay (FR)	Cadeaux Genereux
		Topline (GER)

ZAKOUSKI (GB)

This gelding ended his four-year-old season as still something of a dark horse. He beat Headman by two lengths over seven furlongs on the Polytrack at Kempton on his only start at two, finished fifth to Skardu in the Group 3 Craven Stakes on his only run at three, was gelded that summer, made a winning return to action in a valuable one-mile handicap at Meydan in January and then beat Mythical Magic and Dream Castle by a neck and the same in the Group 2 Zabeel Mile at the same venue. That was in late February 2020 but he was not seen in action again until early October when he disappointed over seven furlongs on soft ground at Newmarket. The race was the Group 2 Godolphin Stud & Stable Staff Awards Challenge Stakes, he started slowly, took a while to catch up to the horse who was at the rear of the bunched field, was being pushed along from three out, and finished a six-and-a-half-length fourth to Happy Power.

His final start was much better. This time he raced prominently, made his challenge a quarter of a mile from home, hit the front inside the final furlong and fought to the line to short-head Modern Millie in the Listed Bet In-Play at MansionBet Ben Marshall Stakes over a mile on heavy ground at Newmarket at the end of October. His Group 3 Prix Thomas Bryon-winning half-brother King's Command (by Dubawi) was among those behind, finishing six and a quarter lengths adrift in fourth.

The Godolphin homebred is a son of the late and much-missed Shamardal (by Giant's Causeway), his siblings also include the Group 1-placed and pattern-winning sprinter Albrecht (by Redoute's Choice) and his Australian-bred dam, O'Giselle (by Octagonal) is a full sister to champion racehorse and champion sire Lonhro and his triple Group 1-winning brother Niello. Lonhro got his eleven Group 1 wins from seven to ten furlongs, all of Niello's were at or close to ten furlongs. Lonhro is closing in on the 100 stakes winners mark and his dozen Group 1 stars include Pierro, Impending, Bounding and Kementari. He stands at Darley Stud in Kelvinside, New South Wales. Niello, who sired a few stakes winners, died following an accident in August 2011. Their dam is the highly rated Group 1-placed pattern winner

Shadea (by Straight Strike) and her descendants also include the Group 1 New Zealand 2000 Guineas winner and champion Catalyst (by Darci Brahma), classic-placed Group 1 scorer Device (by Darci Brahma) and several others who won at stakes or pattern level.

Zakouski is one to watch in 2021 and, shortly before this book went to print, he was a three-length runner-up to Lord Glitters in the Group 2 Singspiel Stakes over nine furlongs on turf at Meydan and then beat that same rival (had a three-pound penalty) by three-quarters of a length and a nose in a steadily run edition of the Group 2 Al Rashidiya over the same course and distance. He has won on Polytrack, good ground and heavy, eight and nine furlongs suit him well and perhaps ten furlongs may be within his range. It would be no surprise to see him improve considerably on his current mark of 109.

SUMMARY DETAILS
Bred: Godolphin
Owned: Godolphin
Trained: Charlie Appleby
Country: England
Race record: 1-0-1141-21
Career highlights: 5 wins inc Al Rashidiya sponsored by emirates.com (Gr2), Zabeel Mile sponsored by Al Tayer Motors (Gr2), Bet In-Play at MansionBet Ben Marshall Stakes (L), 2nd Singspiel Stakes sponsored by Riviera By Azizi (Gr2)

ZAKOUSKI (GB) – 2016 bay gelding

Shamardal (USA)	Giant's Causeway (USA)	Storm Cat (USA)
		Mariah's Storm (USA)
	Helsinki (GB)	Machiavellian (USA)
		Helen Street
O'Giselle (AUS)	Octagonal (NZ)	Zabeel (NZ)
		Eight Carat
	Shadea (NZ)	Straight Strike (USA)
		Concia (NZ)

GROUP 2 & GROUP 3 WINNERS OF 2020
BY SIRE
(* freshman sire of 2020)

Acclamation (GB) – Ventura Tormenta (IRE)

Al Kazeem (GB) – Aspetar (FR)

American Pharoah (USA) – Pista (USA)

Australia (GB) – Buckhurst (IRE)
Australia (GB) – Cayenne Pepper (IRE)
Australia (GB) – Epona Plays (IRE)
Australia (GB) – Leo de Fury (IRE)
Australia (GB) – Patrick Sarsfield (FR)

Authorized (IRE) – Euchen Glen (GB)
Authorized (IRE) – Santiago (IRE)

Bated Breath (GB) – Breathtaking Look (GB)
Bated Breath (GB) – Cairn Gorm (GB)

*Belardo (IRE) – Elysium (IRE)
*Belardo (IRE) – Isabella Giles (IRE)
*Belardo (IRE) – Lullaby Moon (GB)

Brazen Beau (AUS) – Dubai Station (GB)

Bungle Inthejungle (GB) – Winter Power (IRE)

Camacho (GB) – With Thanks (IRE)

Camelot (GB) – Current Option (IRE)
Camelot (GB) – Lady Wannabe (IRE)

Cape Cross (IRE) – Century Dream (IRE)
Cape Cross (IRE) – Nkosikazi (GB)

Champs Elysees (GB) – Dame Malliot (GB)

Clodovil (IRE) – Certain Lad (GB)
Clodovil (IRE) – Steel Bull (IRE)

*Coulsty (IRE) – Santosha (IRE)

Dandy Man (IRE) – Dandalla (IRE)
Dandy Man (IRE) – Happy Romance (IRE)

Dansili (GB) – Berlin Tango (GB)
Dansili (GB) – Dubai Warrior (GB)

Dark Angel (IRE) – Art Power (IRE)
Dark Angel (IRE) – Battaash (IRE)
Dark Angel (IRE) – Happy Power (IRE)
Dark Angel (IRE) – Top Rank (IRE)

Dawn Approach (IRE) – Poetic Flare (IRE)

Dream Ahead (USA) – Dark Vision (IRE)
Dream Ahead (USA) – Dream of Dreams (IRE)

Dubawi (IRE) – Benbatl (GB)
Dubawi (IRE) – Ghaiyyath (IRE)
Dubawi (IRE) – Glorious Journey (GB)
Dubawi (IRE) – Indigo Girl (GB)
Dubawi (IRE) – Lazuli (IRE)
Dubawi (IRE) – Lord North (IRE)
Dubawi (IRE) – Maamora (IRE)
Dubawi (IRE) – Master of The Seas (IRE)
Dubawi (IRE) – One Ruler (IRE)
Dubawi (IRE) – Secret Advisor (FR)
Dubawi (IRE) – Space Blues (IRE)

Dutch Art (GB) – Bowerman (GB)
Dutch Art (GB) – Brad The Brief (GB)

Elzaam (AUS) – Champers Elysees (IRE)

Equiano (FR) – Dakota Gold (GB)

Excelebration (IRE) – Barney Roy (GB)
Excelebration (IRE) – Speak In Colours (GB)

Farhh (GB) – Far Above (IRE)

Fast Company (IRE) – Safe Voyage (IRE)

Fastnet Rock (AUS) – One Master (IRE)

First Defence (USA) – Tilsit (USA)

Foxwedge (AUS) – Foxtrot Lady (GB)

Frankel (GB) – Elarqam (GB)
Frankel (GB) – Frankly Darling (GB)

Galileo (IRE) – Anthony Van Dyck (IRE)
Galileo (IRE) – Armory (IRE)
Galileo (IRE) – Dawn Patrol (IRE)
Galileo (IRE) – Delphi (IRE)
Galileo (IRE) – Divinely (IRE)
Galileo (IRE) – High Definition (IRE)
Galileo (IRE) – Lancaster House (IRE)
Galileo (IRE) – Lone Eagle (IRE)
Galileo (IRE) – Magic Wand (IRE)
Galileo (IRE) – Mogul (GB)
Galileo (IRE) – Nayef Road (IRE)
Galileo (IRE) – Nobel Prize (IRE)
Galileo (IRE) – Pablo Escobarr (IRE)
Galileo (IRE) – Passion (IRE)
Galileo (IRE) – Russian Emperor (IRE)
Galileo (IRE) – Shale (IRE)
Galileo (IRE) – Snow (IRE)
Galileo (IRE) – Tiger Moth (IRE)

Gleneagles (IRE) – Royal Dornoch (IRE)

Gregorian (IRE) – Queen Jo Jo (GB)

Gutaifan (IRE) – Fev Rover (IRE)

Harbour Watch (IRE) – Baron Samedi (GB)
Harbour Watch (IRE) – Pyledriver (GB)

Havana Gold (IRE) – Tabdeed (GB)

Holy Roman Emperor (IRE) – Romanised (IRE)
Holy Roman Emperor (IRE) – Valeria Messalina (IRE)

Hot Streak (IRE) – A Case of You (IRE)

Iffraaj (GB) – Judicial (IRE)

Intello (GER) – Regal Reality (GB)
Intello (GER) – Young Rascal (FR)

Invincible Spirit (IRE) – Nazeef (GB)

Kendargent (FR) – Nickajack Cave (IRE)

Kingman (GB) – Cormorant (IRE)
Kingman (GB) – Sinawann (IRE)
Kingman (GB) – Summer Romance (IRE)

Kitten's Joy (USA) – Crossfirehurricane (USA)
Kitten's Joy (USA) – Kameko (USA)

Kodiac (GB) – Campanelle (IRE)
Kodiac (GB) – Nando Parrado (GB)
Kodiac (GB) – Ubettabelieveit (IRE)
Kodiac (GB) – Umm Kulthum (IRE)

Lawman (FR) – Pretty Gorgeous (FR)

Le Havre (IRE) – Wonderful Tonight (FR)

Lemon Drop Kid (USA) – Red Verdon (USA)

Lope de Vega (IRE) – Angel Power (GB)
Lope de Vega (IRE) – Antonia de Vega (IRE)
Lope de Vega (IRE) – Cadillac (IRE)
Lope de Vega (IRE) – La Barrosa (IRE)
Lope de Vega (IRE) – Manuela de Vega (IRE)

Lord Kanaloa (JPN) – Know It All (GB)

Make Believe (GB) – Believe In Love (IRE)
Make Believe (GB) – Mishriff (IRE)
Make Believe (GB) – Rose of Kildare (IRE)

Mastercraftsman (IRE) – Extra Elusive (GB)

Mayson (GB) – Oxted (GB)

*Mehmas (IRE) – Minzaal (IRE)
*Mehmas (IRE) – Supremacy (IRE)

Muhaarar (GB) – Mujbar (GB)

Nathaniel (IRE) – Dashing Willoughby (GB)
Nathaniel (IRE) – Enable (GB)
Nathaniel (IRE) – Lady Bowthorpe (GB)

New Approach (IRE) – Loxley (IRE)
New Approach (IRE) – Mac Swiney (IRE)
New Approach (IRE) – Magic Lily (GB)
New Approach (IRE) – New Treasure (IRE)
New Approach (IRE) – Telecaster (GB)

*New Bay (GB) – New Mandate (IRE)
*New Bay (GB) – Saffron Beach (IRE)

Night of Thunder (IRE) – Molatham (GB)
Night of Thunder (IRE) – Thundering Nights (IRE)
Night of Thunder (IRE) – Thunderous (IRE)

No Nay Never (USA) – Love Locket (IRE)
No Nay Never (USA) – Wichita (IRE)

Noble Mission (GB) – Spanish Mission (USA)

Olympic Glory (IRE) – Etonian (IRE)

Oscar (IRE) – True Self (IRE)

Pastoral Pursuits (GB) – Ventura Rebel (GB)

Pivotal (GB) – Glen Shiel (GB)

Planteur (IRE) – Trueshan (FR)

Poet's Voice (GB) – One Voice (IRE)

Power (GB) – Helvic Dream (IRE)
Power (GB) – Laws of Indices (IRE)

*Pride of Dubai (AUS) – Flying Visit (IRE)
*Pride of Dubai (AUS) – Star of Emaraaty (IRE)

*Prince of Lir (IRE) – The Lir Jet (IRE)

Raven's Pass (USA) – Lemista (IRE)

Redoute's Choice (AUS) – Enbihaar (IRE)

Sea The Stars (IRE) – Al Aasy (IRE)
Sea The Stars (IRE) – Eagles By Day (IRE)

Sea The Stars (IRE) – Fanny Logan (IRE)
Sea The Stars (IRE) – Hukum (IRE)
Sea The Stars (IRE) – Terebellum (IRE)
Sea The Stars (IRE) – Volkan Star (IRE)

Sepoy (AUS) – Mighty Gurkha (IRE)

Shamardal (USA) – Royal Crusade (GB)
Shamardal (USA) – Tarnawa (IRE)
Shamardal (USA) – Zakouski (GB)

Showcasing (GB) – Alkumait (GB)
Showcasing (GB) – Mohaather (GB)

Sir Prancealot (IRE) – Miss Amulet (IRE)

Society Rock (IRE) – A'Ali (IRE)

Starspangledbanner (AUS) – Aloha Star (IRE)
Starspangledbanner (AUS) – Millisle (IRE)

Tagula (IRE) – Limato (IRE)

Teofilo (IRE) – Gear Up (IRE)
Teofilo (IRE) – Subjectivist (GB)
Teofilo (IRE) – Twilight Payment (IRE)

Toronado (IRE) – Tactical (GB)

War Front (USA) – Battleground (USA)
War Front (USA) – Military Style (USA)

Wootton Bassett (GB) – Chindit (IRE)

Zoffany (IRE) – Minaun (IRE)
Zoffany (IRE) – Mother Earth (IRE)

**GROUP 2 & GROUP 3 WINNERS OF 2020
BY GRANDSIRE**

Acclamation (GB) – Art Power (IRE), by Dark Angel (IRE)
Acclamation (GB) – Baron Samedi (GB), by Harbour Watch
    (IRE)
Acclamation (GB) – Battaash (IRE), by Dark Angel (IRE)
Acclamation (GB) – Dakota Gold (GB), by Equiano (FR)
Acclamation (GB) – Happy Power (IRE), by Dark Angel (IRE)
Acclamation (GB) – Minzaal (IRE), by Mehmas (IRE)
Acclamation (GB) – Pyledriver (GB), by Harbour Watch (IRE)
Acclamation (GB) – Supremacy (IRE), by Mehmas (IRE)
Acclamation (GB) – Top Rank (IRE), by Dark Angel (IRE)

Bahamian Bounty (GB) – Ventura Rebel (GB), by Pastoral
    Pursuits (GB)

Cape Cross (IRE) – Al Aasy (IRE), by Sea The Stars (IRE)
Cape Cross (IRE) – Eagles By Day (IRE), by Sea The Stars
    (IRE)
Cape Cross (IRE) – Fanny Logan (IRE), by Sea The Stars (IRE)
Cape Cross (IRE) – Hukum (IRE), by Sea The Stars (IRE)
Cape Cross (IRE) – Terebellum (IRE), by Sea The Stars (IRE)
Cape Cross (IRE) – Volkan Star (IRE), by Sea The Stars (IRE)

Choisir (AUS) – Aloha Star (IRE), by Starspangledbanner (AUS)
Choisir (AUS) – Etonian (IRE), by Olympic Glory (IRE)
Choisir (AUS) – Millisle (IRE), by Starspangledbanner (AUS)

Clodovil (IRE) – Queen Jo Jo (GB), by Gregorian (IRE)

Danehill (USA) – Berlin Tango (GB), by Dansili (GB)
Danehill (USA) – Campanelle (IRE), by Kodiac (GB)
Danehill (USA) – Certain Lad (GB), by Clodovil (IRE)
Danehill (USA) – Dame Malliot (GB), by Champs Elysees (GB)
Danehill (USA) – Dubai Warrior (GB), by Dansili (GB)
Danehill (USA) – Enbihaar (IRE), by Redoute's Choice (AUS)
Danehill (USA) – Nando Parrado (GB), by Kodiac (GB)

456

Danehill (USA) – One Master (IRE), by Fastnet Rock (AUS)
Danehill (USA) – Romanised (IRE), by Holy Roman Emperor
    (IRE)
Danehill (USA) – Steel Bull (IRE), by Clodovil (IRE)
Danehill (USA) – Ubettabelieveit (IRE), by Kodiac (GB)
Danehill (USA) – Umm Kulthum (IRE), by Kodiac (GB)
Danehill (USA) – Valeria Messalina (IRE), by Holy Roman
    Emperor (IRE)
Danehill (USA) – With Thanks (IRE), by Camacho (GB)

Danehill Dancer (IRE) – Extra Elusive (GB), by
    Mastercraftsman (IRE)
Danehill Dancer (IRE) – Safe Voyage (IRE), by Fast Company
    (IRE)
Danehill Dancer (IRE) – Trueshan (FR), by Planteur (IRE)

Dansili (GB) – Breathtaking Look (GB), by Bated Breath (GB)
Dansili (GB) – Cairn Gorm (GB), by Bated Breath (GB)
Dansili (GB) – Minaun (IRE), by Zoffany (IRE)
Dansili (GB) – Mother Earth (IRE), by Zoffany (IRE)

Danzig (USA) – Battleground (USA), by War Front (USA)
Danzig (USA) – Military Style (USA), by War Front (USA)

Dark Angel (IRE) – Fev Rover (IRE), by Gutaifan (IRE)

Diktat (GB) – Dark Vision (IRE), by Dream Ahead (USA)
Diktat (GB) – Dream of Dreams (IRE), by Dream Ahead (USA)

Dubai Millennium (GB) – Benbatl (GB), by Dubawi (IRE)
Dubai Millennium (GB) – Ghaiyyath (IRE), by Dubawi (IRE)
Dubai Millennium (GB) – Glorious Journey (GB), by Dubawi
    (IRE)
Dubai Millennium (GB) – Indigo Girl (GB), by Dubawi (IRE)
Dubai Millennium (GB) – Lazuli (IRE), by Dubawi (IRE)
Dubai Millennium (GB) – Lord North (IRE), by Dubawi (IRE)
Dubai Millennium (GB) – Maamora (IRE), by Dubawi (IRE)

Dubai Millennium (GB) – Master of The Seas (IRE), by Dubawi (IRE)

Dubai Millennium (GB) – One Ruler (IRE), by Dubawi (IRE)

Dubai Millennium (GB) – Secret Advisor (FR), by Dubawi (IRE)

Dubai Millennium (GB) – Space Blues (IRE), by Dubawi (IRE)

Dubawi (IRE) – Aspetar (FR), by Al Kazeem (GB)

Dubawi (IRE) – Molatham (GB), by Night of Thunder (IRE)

Dubawi (IRE) – New Mandate (IRE), by New Bay (GB)

Dubawi (IRE) – One Voice (IRE), by Poet's Voice (GB)

Dubawi (IRE) – Saffron Beach (IRE), by New Bay (GB)

Dubawi (IRE) – Thundering Nights (IRE), by Night of Thunder (IRE)

Dubawi (IRE) – Thunderous (IRE), by Night of Thunder (IRE)

El Prado (IRE) – Crossfirehurricane (USA), by Kitten's Joy (USA)

El Prado (IRE) – Kameko (USA), by Kitten's Joy (USA)

Elusive Quality (USA) – Lemista (IRE), by Raven's Pass (USA)

Elusive Quality (USA) – Mighty Gurkha (IRE), by Sepoy (AUS)

Exceed And Excel (AUS) – Barney Roy (GB), by Excelebration (IRE)

Exceed And Excel (AUS) – Speak In Colours (GB), by Excelebration (IRE)

Exceed And Excel (AUS) – Winter Power (IRE), by Bungle Inthejungle (GB)

Fastnet Rock (AUS) – Foxtrot Lady (GB), by Foxwedge (AUS)

Galileo (IRE) – Buckhurst (IRE), by Australia (GB)

Galileo (IRE) – Cayenne Pepper (IRE), by Australia (GB)

Galileo (IRE) – Dashing Willoughby (GB), by Nathaniel (IRE)

Galileo (IRE) – Elarqam (GB), by Frankel (GB)

Galileo (IRE) – Enable (GB), by Nathaniel (IRE)

Galileo (IRE) – Epona Plays (IRE), by Australia (GB)

Galileo (IRE) – Frankly Darling (GB), by Frankel (GB)

Galileo (IRE) – Gear Up (IRE), by Teofilo (IRE)
Galileo (IRE) – Lady Bowthorpe (GB), by Nathaniel (IRE)
Galileo (IRE) – Leo de Fury (IRE), by Australia (GB)
Galileo (IRE) – Loxley (IRE), by New Approach (IRE)
Galileo (IRE) – Mac Swiney (IRE), by New Approach (IRE)
Galileo (IRE) – Magic Lily (GB), by New Approach (IRE)
Galileo (IRE) – New Treasure (IRE), by New Approach (IRE)
Galileo (IRE) – Patrick Sarsfield (FR), by Australia (GB)
Galileo (IRE) – Regal Reality (GB), by Intello (GER)
Galileo (IRE) – Royal Dornoch (IRE), by Gleneagles (IRE)
Galileo (IRE) – Spanish Mission (USA), by Noble Mission (GB)
Galileo (IRE) – Subjectivist (GB), by Teofilo (IRE)
Galileo (IRE) – Telecaster (GB), by New Approach (IRE)
Galileo (IRE) – Twilight Payment (IRE), by Teofilo (IRE)
Galileo (IRE) – Young Rascal (FR), by Intello (GER)

Giant's Causeway (USA) – Royal Crusade (GB), by Shamardal
    (USA)
Giant's Causeway (USA) – Tarnawa (IRE), by Shamardal (USA)
Giant's Causeway (USA) – Zakouski (GB), by Shamardal (USA)

Green Desert (USA) – Century Dream (IRE), by Cape Cross
    (IRE)
Green Desert (USA) – Nazeef (GB), by Invincible Spirit (IRE)
Green Desert (USA) – Nkosikazi (GB), by Cape Cross (IRE)

High Chaparral (IRE) – Tactical (GB), by Toronado (IRE)

I Am Invincible (AUS) – Dubai Station (GB), by Brazen Beau
    (AUS)

Iffraaj (GB) – A Case of You (IRE), by Hot Streak (IRE)
Iffraaj (GB) – Chindit (IRE), by Wootton Bassett (GB)

Invincible Spirit (IRE) – Cormorant (IRE), by Kingman (GB)
Invincible Spirit (IRE) – Oxted (GB), by Mayson (GB)
Invincible Spirit (IRE) – Pretty Gorgeous (FR), by Lawman (FR)
Invincible Spirit (IRE) – Sinawann (IRE), by Kingman (GB)

Invincible Spirit (IRE) – Summer Romance (IRE), by Kingman (GB)

Kendor (FR) – Nickajack Cave (IRE), by Kendargent (FR)
King Kamehameha (JPN) – Know It All (GB), by Lord Kanaloa (JPN)

Kingmambo (USA) – Red Verdon (USA), by Lemon Drop Kid (USA)

Kodiac (GB) – Santosha (IRE), by Coulsty (IRE)
Kodiac (GB) – The Lir Jet (IRE), by Prince of Lir (IRE)

Lope de Vega (IRE) – Elysium (IRE), by Belardo (IRE)
Lope de Vega (IRE) – Isabella Giles (IRE), by Belardo (IRE)
Lope de Vega (IRE) – Lullaby Moon (GB), by Belardo (IRE)

Makfi (GB) – Believe In Love (IRE), by Make Believe (GB)
Makfi (GB) – Mishriff (IRE), by Make Believe (GB)
Makfi (GB) – Rose of Kildare (IRE), by Make Believe (GB)

Medicean (GB) – Bowerman (GB), by Dutch Art (GB)
Medicean (GB) – Brad The Brief (GB), by Dutch Art (GB)

Montjeu (IRE) – Current Option (IRE), by Camelot (GB)
Montjeu (IRE) – Euchen Glen (GB), by Authorized (IRE)
Montjeu (IRE) – Lady Wannabe (IRE), by Camelot (GB)
Montjeu (IRE) – Santiago (IRE), by Authorized (IRE)

Mozart (IRE) – Dandalla (IRE), by Dandy Man (IRE)
Mozart (IRE) – Happy Romance (IRE), by Dandy Man (IRE)

New Approach (IRE) – Poetic Flare (IRE), by Dawn Approach (IRE)

Noverre (USA) – Wonderful Tonight (FR), by Le Havre (IRE)

Oasis Dream (GB) – Alkumait (GB), by Showcasing (GB)

Oasis Dream (GB) – Helvic Dream (IRE), by Power (GB)
Oasis Dream (GB) – Laws of Indices (IRE), by Power (GB)
Oasis Dream (GB) – Mohaather (GB), by Showcasing (GB)
Oasis Dream (GB) – Mujbar (GB), by Muhaarar (GB)

Pioneerof The Nile (USA) – Pista (USA), by American Pharoah (USA)

Pivotal (GB) – Far Above (IRE), by Farhh (GB)

Polar Falcon (USA) – Glen Shiel (GB), by Pivotal (GB)

Redoute's Choice (AUS) – Champers Elysees (IRE), by Elzaam (AUS)

Rock of Gibraltar (IRE) – A'Ali (IRE), by Society Rock (IRE)

Royal Applause (GB) – Ventura Tormenta (IRE), by Acclamation (GB)

Sadler's Wells (USA) – Anthony Van Dyck (IRE), by Galileo (IRE)
Sadler's Wells (USA) – Armory (IRE), by Galileo (IRE)
Sadler's Wells (USA) – Dawn Patrol (IRE), by Galileo (IRE)
Sadler's Wells (USA) – Delphi (IRE), by Galileo (IRE)
Sadler's Wells (USA) – Divinely (IRE), by Galileo (IRE)
Sadler's Wells (USA) – High Definition (IRE), by Galileo (IRE)
Sadler's Wells (USA) – Lancaster House (IRE), by Galileo (IRE)
Sadler's Wells (USA) – Lone Eagle (IRE), by Galileo (IRE)
Sadler's Wells (USA) – Magic Wand (IRE), by Galileo (IRE)
Sadler's Wells (USA) – Mogul (GB), by Galileo (IRE)
Sadler's Wells (USA) – Nayef Road (IRE), by Galileo (IRE)
Sadler's Wells (USA) – Nobel Prize (IRE), by Galileo (IRE)
Sadler's Wells (USA) – Pablo Escobarr (IRE), by Galileo (IRE)
Sadler's Wells (USA) – Passion (IRE), by Galileo (IRE)
Sadler's Wells (USA) – Russian Emperor (IRE), by Galileo (IRE)
Sadler's Wells (USA) – Shale (IRE), by Galileo (IRE)
Sadler's Wells (USA) – Snow (IRE), by Galileo (IRE)

Sadler's Wells (USA) – Tiger Moth (IRE), by Galileo (IRE)
Sadler's Wells (USA) – True Self (IRE), by Oscar (IRE)

Scat Daddy (USA) – Love Locket (IRE), by No Nay Never
      (USA)
Scat Daddy (USA) – Wichita (IRE), by No Nay Never (USA)

Shamardal (USA) – Angel Power (GB), by Lope de Vega (IRE)
Shamardal (USA) – Antonia de Vega (IRE), by Lope de Vega
      (IRE)
Shamardal (USA) – Cadillac (IRE), by Lope de Vega (IRE)
Shamardal (USA) – La Barrosa (IRE), by Lope de Vega (IRE)
Shamardal (USA) – Manuela de Vega (IRE), by Lope de Vega
      (IRE)

Street Cry (IRE) – Flying Visit (IRE), by Pride of Dubai (AUS)
Street Cry (IRE) – Star of Emaraaty (IRE), by Pride of Dubai
      (AUS)

Tamayuz (GB) – Miss Amulet (IRE), by Sir Prancealot (IRE)

Taufan (USA) – Limato (IRE), by Tagula (IRE)

Teofilo (IRE) – Tabdeed (GB), by Havana Gold (IRE)

Unbridled's Song (USA) – Tilsit (USA), by First Defence (USA)

Zafonic (USA) – Judicial (IRE), by Iffraaj (GB)

GROUP 2 & GROUP 3 WINNERS OF 2020
BY GREAT-GRANDSIRE

Acclamation (GB) – Fev Rover (IRE), by Gutaifan (IRE), by
Dark Angel (IRE)

Cadeaux Genereux – Ventura Rebel (GB), by Pastoral Pursuits
(GB), by Bahamian Bounty (GB)

Danehill (USA) – A'Ali (IRE), by Society Rock (IRE), by Rock
of Gibraltar (IRE)

Danehill (USA) – Barney Roy (GB), by Excelebration (IRE), by
Exceed And Excel (AUS)

Danehill (USA) – Breathtaking Look (GB), by Bated Breath
(GB), by Dansili (GB)

Danehill (USA) – Cairn Gorm (GB), by Bated Breath (GB), by
Dansili (GB)

Danehill (USA) – Champers Elysees (IRE), by Elzaam (AUS), by
Redoute's Choice (AUS)

Danehill (USA) – Dandalla (IRE), by Dandy Man (IRE), by
Mozart (IRE)

Danehill (USA) – Extra Elusive (GB), by Mastercraftsman
(IRE), by Danehill Dancer (IRE)

Danehill (USA) – Foxtrot Lady (GB), by Foxwedge (AUS), by
Fastnet Rock (AUS)

Danehill (USA) – Happy Romance (IRE), by Dandy Man (IRE),
by Mozart (IRE)

Danehill (USA) – Minaun (IRE), by Zoffany (IRE), by Dansili
(GB)

Danehill (USA) – Mother Earth (IRE), by Zoffany (IRE), by
Dansili (GB)

Danehill (USA) – Queen Jo Jo (GB), by Gregorian (IRE), by
Clodovil (IRE)

Danehill (USA) – Safe Voyage (IRE), by Fast Company (IRE),
by Danehill Dancer (IRE)

Danehill (USA) – Santosha (IRE), by Coulsty (IRE), by Kodiac
(GB)

Danehill (USA) – Speak In Colours (GB), by Excelebration (IRE), by Exceed And Excel (AUS)
Danehill (USA) – The Lir Jet (IRE), by Prince of Lir (IRE), by Kodiac (GB)
Danehill (USA) – Trueshan (FR), by Planteur (IRE), by Danehill Dancer (IRE)
Danehill (USA) – Winter Power (IRE), by Bungle Inthejungle (GB), by Exceed And Excel (AUS)

Danehill Dancer (IRE) – Aloha Star (IRE), by Starspangledbanner (AUS), by Choisir (AUS)
Danehill Dancer (IRE) – Etonian (IRE), by Olympic Glory (IRE), by Choisir (AUS)
Danehill Dancer (IRE) – Millisle (IRE), by Starspangledbanner (AUS), by Choisir (AUS)

Danzig (USA) – Berlin Tango (GB), by Dansili (GB), by Danehill (USA)
Danzig (USA) – Campanelle (IRE), by Kodiac (GB), by Danehill (USA)
Danzig (USA) – Century Dream (IRE), by Cape Cross (IRE), by Green Desert (USA)
Danzig (USA) – Certain Lad (GB), by Clodovil (IRE), by Danehill (USA)
Danzig (USA) – Dame Malliot (GB), by Champs Elysees (GB), by Danehill (USA)
Danzig (USA) – Dubai Warrior (GB), by Dansili (GB), by Danehill (USA)
Danzig (USA) – Enbihaar (IRE), by Redoute's Choice (AUS), by Danehill (USA)
Danzig (USA) – Nando Parrado (GB), by Kodiac (GB), by Danehill (USA)
Danzig (USA) – Nazeef (GB), by Invincible Spirit (IRE), by Green Desert (USA)
Danzig (USA) – Nkosikazi (GB), by Cape Cross (IRE), by Green Desert (USA)
Danzig (USA) – One Master (IRE), by Fastnet Rock (AUS), by Danehill (USA)

Danzig (USA) – Romanised (IRE), by Holy Roman Emperor (IRE), by Danehill (USA)

Danzig (USA) – Steel Bull (IRE), by Clodovil (IRE), by Danehill (USA)

Danzig (USA) – Ubettabelieveit (IRE), by Kodiac (GB), by Danehill (USA)

Danzig (USA) – Umm Kulthum (IRE), by Kodiac (GB), by Danehill (USA)

Danzig (USA) – Valeria Messalina (IRE), by Holy Roman Emperor (IRE), by Danehill (USA)

Danzig (USA) – With Thanks (IRE), by Camacho (GB), by Danehill (USA)

Dubai Millennium (GB) – Aspetar (FR), by Al Kazeem (GB), by Dubawi (IRE)

Dubai Millennium (GB) – Molatham (GB), by Night of Thunder (IRE), by Dubawi (IRE)

Dubai Millennium (GB) – New Mandate (IRE), by New Bay (GB), by Dubawi (IRE)

Dubai Millennium (GB) – One Voice (IRE), by Poet's Voice (GB), by Dubawi (IRE)

Dubai Millennium (GB) – Saffron Beach (IRE), by New Bay (GB), by Dubawi (IRE)

Dubai Millennium (GB) – Thundering Nights (IRE), by Night of Thunder (IRE), by Dubawi (IRE)

Dubai Millennium (GB) – Thunderous (IRE), by Night of Thunder (IRE), by Dubawi (IRE)

Dubawi (IRE) – Believe In Love (IRE), by Make Believe (GB), by Makfi (GB)

Dubawi (IRE) – Mishriff (IRE), by Make Believe (GB), by Makfi (GB)

Dubawi (IRE) – Rose of Kildare (IRE), by Make Believe (GB), by Makfi (GB)

Empire Maker (USA) – Pista (USA), by American Pharoah (USA), by Pioneerof The Nile (USA)

Galileo (IRE) – Poetic Flare (IRE), by Dawn Approach (IRE), by New Approach (IRE)

Galileo (IRE) – Tabdeed (GB), by Havana Gold (IRE), by Teofilo (IRE)

Giant's Causeway (USA) – Angel Power (GB), by Lope de Vega (IRE), by Shamardal (USA)

Giant's Causeway (USA) – Antonia de Vega (IRE), by Lope de Vega (IRE), by Shamardal (USA)

Giant's Causeway (USA) – Cadillac (IRE), by Lope de Vega (IRE), by Shamardal (USA)

Giant's Causeway (USA) – La Barrosa (IRE), by Lope de Vega (IRE), by Shamardal (USA)

Giant's Causeway (USA) – Manuela de Vega (IRE), by Lope de Vega (IRE), by Shamardal (USA)

Gone West (USA) – Judicial (IRE), by Iffraaj (GB), by Zafonic (USA)

Gone West (USA) – Lemista (IRE), by Raven's Pass (USA), by Elusive Quality (USA)

Gone West (USA) – Mighty Gurkha (IRE), by Sepoy (AUS), by Elusive Quality (USA)

Green Desert (USA) – Al Aasy (IRE), by Sea The Stars (IRE), by Cape Cross (IRE)

Green Desert (USA) – Alkumait (GB), by Showcasing (GB), by Oasis Dream (GB)

Green Desert (USA) – Cormorant (IRE), by Kingman (GB), by Invincible Spirit (IRE)

Green Desert (USA) – Eagles By Day (IRE), by Sea The Stars (IRE), by Cape Cross (IRE)

Green Desert (USA) – Fanny Logan (IRE), by Sea The Stars (IRE), by Cape Cross (IRE)

Green Desert (USA) – Helvic Dream (IRE), by Power (GB), by Oasis Dream (GB)

Green Desert (USA) – Hukum (IRE), by Sea The Stars (IRE), by Cape Cross (IRE)

Green Desert (USA) – Laws of Indices (IRE), by Power (GB),
by Oasis Dream (GB)

Green Desert (USA) – Mohaather (GB), by Showcasing (GB), by
Oasis Dream (GB)

Green Desert (USA) – Mujbar (GB), by Muhaarar (GB), by
Oasis Dream (GB)

Green Desert (USA) – Oxted (GB), by Mayson (GB), by
Invincible Spirit (IRE)

Green Desert (USA) – Pretty Gorgeous (FR), by Lawman (FR),
by Invincible Spirit (IRE)

Green Desert (USA) – Sinawann (IRE), by Kingman (GB), by
Invincible Spirit (IRE)

Green Desert (USA) – Summer Romance (IRE), by Kingman
(GB), by Invincible Spirit (IRE)

Green Desert (USA) – Terebellum (IRE), by Sea The Stars
(IRE), by Cape Cross (IRE)

Green Desert (USA) – Volkan Star (IRE), by Sea The Stars
(IRE), by Cape Cross (IRE)

Invincible Spirit (IRE) – Dubai Station (GB), by Brazen Beau
(AUS), by I Am Invincible (AUS)

Johannesburg (USA) – Love Locket (IRE), by No Nay Never
(USA), by Scat Daddy (USA)

Johannesburg (USA) – Wichita (IRE), by No Nay Never (USA),
by Scat Daddy (USA)

Kenmare (FR) – Nickajack Cave (IRE), by Kendargent (FR), by
Kendor (FR)

Kingmambo (USA) – Know It All (GB), by Lord Kanaloa
(JPN), by King Kamehameha (JPN)

Machiavellian (USA) – Bowerman (GB), by Dutch Art (GB), by
Medicean (GB)

Machiavellian (USA) – Brad The Brief (GB), by Dutch Art (GB),
by Medicean (GB)

Machiavellian (USA) – Flying Visit (IRE), by Pride of Dubai
    (AUS), by Street Cry (IRE)
Machiavellian (USA) – Star of Emaraaty (IRE), by Pride of
    Dubai (AUS), by Street Cry (IRE)

Mr Prospector (USA) – Red Verdon (USA), by Lemon Drop
    Kid (USA), by Kingmambo (USA)

Nayef (USA) – Miss Amulet (IRE), by Sir Prancealot (IRE), by
    Tamayuz (GB)

Northern Dancer – Anthony Van Dyck (IRE), by Galileo (IRE),
    by Sadler's Wells (USA)
Northern Dancer – Armory (IRE), by Galileo (IRE), by Sadler's
    Wells (USA)
Northern Dancer – Battleground (USA), by War Front (USA),
    by Danzig (USA)
Northern Dancer – Dawn Patrol (IRE), by Galileo (IRE), by
    Sadler's Wells (USA)
Northern Dancer – Delphi (IRE), by Galileo (IRE), by Sadler's
    Wells (USA)
Northern Dancer – Divinely (IRE), by Galileo (IRE), by Sadler's
    Wells (USA)
Northern Dancer – High Definition (IRE), by Galileo (IRE), by
    Sadler's Wells (USA)
Northern Dancer – Lancaster House (IRE), by Galileo (IRE), by
    Sadler's Wells (USA)
Northern Dancer – Lone Eagle (IRE), by Galileo (IRE), by
    Sadler's Wells (USA)
Northern Dancer – Magic Wand (IRE), by Galileo (IRE), by
    Sadler's Wells (USA)
Northern Dancer – Military Style (USA), by War Front (USA),
    by Danzig (USA)
Northern Dancer – Mogul (GB), by Galileo (IRE), by Sadler's
    Wells (USA)
Northern Dancer – Nayef Road (IRE), by Galileo (IRE), by
    Sadler's Wells (USA)

Northern Dancer – Nobel Prize (IRE), by Galileo (IRE), by
   Sadler's Wells (USA)
Northern Dancer – Pablo Escobarr (IRE), by Galileo (IRE), by
   Sadler's Wells (USA)
Northern Dancer – Passion (IRE), by Galileo (IRE), by Sadler's
   Wells (USA)
Northern Dancer – Russian Emperor (IRE), by Galileo (IRE),
   by Sadler's Wells (USA)
Northern Dancer – Shale (IRE), by Galileo (IRE), by Sadler's
   Wells (USA)
Northern Dancer – Snow (IRE), by Galileo (IRE), by Sadler's
   Wells (USA)
Northern Dancer – Tiger Moth (IRE), by Galileo (IRE), by
   Sadler's Wells (USA)
Northern Dancer – True Self (IRE), by Oscar (IRE), by Sadler's
   Wells (USA)

Nureyev (USA) – Glen Shiel (GB), by Pivotal (GB), by Polar
   Falcon (USA)

Polar Falcon (USA) – Far Above (IRE), by Farhh (GB), by
   Pivotal (GB)

Rahy (USA) – Wonderful Tonight (FR), by Le Havre (IRE), by
   Noverre (USA)

Royal Applause (GB) – Art Power (IRE), by Dark Angel (IRE),
   by Acclamation (GB)
Royal Applause (GB) – Baron Samedi (GB), by Harbour Watch
   (IRE), by Acclamation (GB)
Royal Applause (GB) – Battaash (IRE), by Dark Angel (IRE), by
   Acclamation (GB)
Royal Applause (GB) – Dakota Gold (GB), by Equiano (FR), by
   Acclamation (GB)
Royal Applause (GB) – Happy Power (IRE), by Dark Angel
   (IRE), by Acclamation (GB)
Royal Applause (GB) – Minzaal (IRE), by Mehmas (IRE), by
   Acclamation (GB)

Royal Applause (GB) – Pyledriver (GB), by Harbour Watch (IRE), by Acclamation (GB)
Royal Applause (GB) – Supremacy (IRE), by Mehmas (IRE), by Acclamation (GB)
Royal Applause (GB) – Top Rank (IRE), by Dark Angel (IRE), by Acclamation (GB)

Sadler's Wells (USA) – Buckhurst (IRE), by Australia (GB), by Galileo (IRE)
Sadler's Wells (USA) – Cayenne Pepper (IRE), by Australia (GB), by Galileo (IRE)
Sadler's Wells (USA) – Crossfirehurricane (USA), by Kitten's Joy (USA), by El Prado (IRE)
Sadler's Wells (USA) – Current Option (IRE), by Camelot (GB), by Montjeu (IRE)
Sadler's Wells (USA) – Dashing Willoughby (GB), by Nathaniel (IRE), by Galileo (IRE)
Sadler's Wells (USA) – Elarqam (GB), by Frankel (GB), by Galileo (IRE)
Sadler's Wells (USA) – Enable (GB), by Nathaniel (IRE), by Galileo (IRE)
Sadler's Wells (USA) – Epona Plays (IRE), by Australia (GB), by Galileo (IRE)
Sadler's Wells (USA) – Euchen Glen (GB), by Authorized (IRE), by Montjeu (IRE)
Sadler's Wells (USA) – Frankly Darling (GB), by Frankel (GB), by Galileo (IRE)
Sadler's Wells (USA) – Gear Up (IRE), by Teofilo (IRE), by Galileo (IRE)
Sadler's Wells (USA) – Kameko (USA), by Kitten's Joy (USA), by El Prado (IRE)
Sadler's Wells (USA) – Lady Bowthorpe (GB), by Nathaniel (IRE), by Galileo (IRE)
Sadler's Wells (USA) – Lady Wannabe (IRE), by Camelot (GB), by Montjeu (IRE)
Sadler's Wells (USA) – Leo de Fury (IRE), by Australia (GB), by Galileo (IRE)

Sadler's Wells (USA) – Loxley (IRE), by New Approach (IRE),
    by Galileo (IRE)
Sadler's Wells (USA) – Mac Swiney (IRE), by New Approach
    (IRE), by Galileo (IRE)
Sadler's Wells (USA) – Magic Lily (GB), by New Approach
    (IRE), by Galileo (IRE)
Sadler's Wells (USA) – New Treasure (IRE), by New Approach
    (IRE), by Galileo (IRE)
Sadler's Wells (USA) – Patrick Sarsfield (FR), by Australia (GB),
    by Galileo (IRE)
Sadler's Wells (USA) – Regal Reality (GB), by Intello (GER), by
    Galileo (IRE)
Sadler's Wells (USA) – Royal Dornoch (IRE), by Gleneagles
    (IRE), by Galileo (IRE)
Sadler's Wells (USA) – Santiago (IRE), by Authorized (IRE), by
    Montjeu (IRE)
Sadler's Wells (USA) – Spanish Mission (USA), by Noble
    Mission (GB), by Galileo (IRE)
Sadler's Wells (USA) – Subjectivist (GB), by Teofilo (IRE), by
    Galileo (IRE)
Sadler's Wells (USA) – Tactical (GB), by Toronado (IRE), by
    High Chaparral (IRE)
Sadler's Wells (USA) – Telecaster (GB), by New Approach
    (IRE), by Galileo (IRE)
Sadler's Wells (USA) – Twilight Payment (IRE), by Teofilo
    (IRE), by Galileo (IRE)
Sadler's Wells (USA) – Young Rascal (FR), by Intello (GER)

Seeking The Gold (USA) – Benbatl (GB), by Dubawi (IRE), by
    Dubai Millennium (GB)
Seeking The Gold (USA) – Ghaiyyath (IRE), by Dubawi (IRE),
    by Dubai Millennium (GB)
Seeking The Gold (USA) – Glorious Journey (GB), by Dubawi
    (IRE), by Dubai Millennium (GB)
Seeking The Gold (USA) – Indigo Girl (GB), by Dubawi (IRE),
    by Dubai Millennium (GB)
Seeking The Gold (USA) – Lazuli (IRE), by Dubawi (IRE), by
    Dubai Millennium (GB)

Seeking The Gold (USA) – Lord North (IRE), by Dubawi (IRE),
by Dubai Millennium (GB)
Seeking The Gold (USA) – Maamora (IRE), by Dubawi (IRE),
by Dubai Millennium (GB)
Seeking The Gold (USA) – Master of The Seas (IRE), by
Dubawi (IRE), by Dubai Millennium (GB)
Seeking The Gold (USA) – One Ruler (IRE), by Dubawi (IRE),
by Dubai Millennium (GB)
Seeking The Gold (USA) – Secret Advisor (FR), by Dubawi
(IRE), by Dubai Millennium (GB)
Seeking The Gold (USA) – Space Blues (IRE), by Dubawi (IRE),
by Dubai Millennium (GB)

Shamardal (USA) – Elysium (IRE), by Belardo (IRE), by Lope
de Vega (IRE)
Shamardal (USA) – Isabella Giles (IRE), by Belardo (IRE), by
Lope de Vega (IRE)
Shamardal (USA) – Lullaby Moon (GB), by Belardo (IRE), by
Lope de Vega (IRE)

Stop The Music (USA) – Limato (IRE), by Tagula (IRE), by
Taufan (USA)

Storm Cat (USA) – Royal Crusade (GB), by Shamardal (USA),
by Giant's Causeway (USA)
Storm Cat (USA) – Tarnawa (IRE), by Shamardal (USA), by
Giant's Causeway (USA)
Storm Cat (USA) – Zakouski (GB), by Shamardal (USA), by
Giant's Causeway (USA)

Unbridled (USA) – Tilsit (USA), by First Defence (USA), by
Unbridled's Song (USA)

Waajib – Ventura Tormenta (IRE), by Acclamation (GB), by
Royal Applause (GB)

Warning – Dark Vision (IRE), by Dream Ahead (USA), by
Diktat (GB)

Warning – Dream of Dreams (IRE), by Dream Ahead (GB), by
  Diktat (GB)

Zafonic (USA) – A Case of You (IRE), by Hot Streak (IRE), by
  Iffraaj (GB)
Zafonic (USA) – Chindit (IRE), by Wootton Bassett (GB), by
  Iffraaj (GB)

GROUP 2 & GROUP 3 WINNERS OF 2020
BY DAM

After (IRE) – Armory (IRE), by Galileo (IRE)

Aghareed (USA) – Hukum (IRE), by Sea The Stars (IRE)

Alina (IRE) – Barney Roy (GB), by Excelebration (IRE)

Always A Dream (GB) – Chindit (IRE), by Wootton Bassett
(GB)

Anna Law (IRE) – Battaash (IRE), by Dark Angel (IRE)

Artful (IRE) – Buckhurst (IRE), by Australia (GB)

Arty Crafty (USA) – Valeria Messalina (IRE), by Holy Roman
Emperor (IRE)

Atlantic Jewel (AUS) – Russian Emperor (IRE), by Galileo (IRE)

Attire (IRE) – Leo de Fury (IRE), by Australia (GB)

Attraction (GB) – Elarqam (GB), by Frankel (GB)

Bee Eater (IRE) – Minaun (IRE), by Zoffany (IRE)

Believe'n'Succeed (AUS) – Anthony Van Dyck (IRE), by Galileo
(IRE)

Bella Qatara (IRE) – Aspetar (FR), by Al Kazeem (GB)

Bewitched (IRE) – Pablo Escobarr (IRE), by Galileo (IRE)

Bikini Babe (IRE) – La Barrosa (IRE), by Lope de Vega (IRE)

Black Dahlia (GB) – Dark Vision (IRE), by Dream Ahead (USA)

Bold Bidder (GB) – Lullaby Moon (GB), by Belardo (IRE)

Bridal Dance (IRE) – Royal Dornoch (IRE), by Gleneagles (IRE)

Burning Rules (IRE) – Angel Power (GB), by Lope de Vega (IRE)

Bye Bye Birdie (IRE) – Delphi (IRE), by Galileo (IRE)

Cantal (GB) – Molatham (GB), by Night of Thunder (IRE)

Cape Castle (IRE) – Thundering Nights (IRE), by Night of Thunder (IRE)

Chanterelle (FR) – Enbihaar (IRE), by Redoute's Choice (AUS)

Charlotte Rosina (GB) – Oxted (GB), by Mayson (GB)

Chellalla (GB) – Dandalla (IRE), by Dandy Man (IRE)

Chelsea Rose (IRE) – Snow (IRE), by Galileo (IRE)

Chelsey Jayne (IRE) – Certain Lad (GB), by Clodovil (IRE)

Chibola (ARG) – Nando Parrado (GB), by Kodiac (GB)

Chicago Dancer (IRE) – Volkan Star (IRE), by Sea The Stars (IRE)

Come April (GB) – Limato (IRE), by Tagula (IRE)

Common Knowledge (GB) – Know It All (GB), by Lord Kanaloa (JPN)

Concentric (GB) – Enable (GB), by Nathaniel (IRE)

Contradict (GB) – Mishriff (IRE), by Make Believe (GB)

Coppertop (IRE) – Current Option (IRE), by Camelot (GB)

Could You Be Loved (IRE) – Nickajack Cave (IRE), by Kendargent (FR)

Countess Ferrama (GB) – Top Rank (IRE), by Dark Angel (IRE)

Cruck Realta (GB) – Rose of Kildare (IRE), by Make Believe (GB)

Dame Shirley (GB) – Baron Samedi (GB), by Harbour Watch (IRE)

Dancing Rain (IRE) – Magic Lily (GB), by New Approach (IRE)

Dialafara (FR) – Passion (IRE), by Galileo (IRE)

Dorraar (IRE) – Far Above (IRE), by Farhh (GB)

Dream On Buddy (IRE) – Twilight Payment (IRE), by Teofilo (IRE)

Enticing (IRE) – One Master (IRE), by Fastnet Rock (AUS)

Evening Time (IRE) – Art Power (IRE), by Dark Angel (IRE)

Fallen For You (GB) – Glorious Journey (GB), by Dubawi (IRE)

Falling Petals (IRE) – Saffron Beach (IRE), by New Bay (GB)

Fantasia (GB) – Berlin Tango (GB), by Dansili (GB)

Finalize (GB) – Ventura Rebel (GB), by Pastoral Pursuits (GB)

Fintry (IRE) – One Ruler (IRE), by Dubawi (IRE)

Firth of Lorne (IRE) – Master of The Seas (IRE), by Dubawi (IRE)

Floristry (GB) – Lazuli (IRE), by Dubawi (IRE)

Fionnuar (IRE) – Flying Visit (IRE), by Pride of Dubai (AUS)

Found (IRE) – Battleground (USA), by War Front (USA)

Gearanai (USA) – Gear Up (IRE), by Teofilo (IRE)

Gonfilia (GER) – Glen Shiel (GB), by Pivotal (GB)

Good Thought (IRE) – True Self (IRE), by Oscar (IRE)

Green Castle (IRE) – Millisle (IRE), by Starspangledbanner (AUS)

Gwynn (IRE) – Dawn Patrol (IRE), by Galileo (IRE)

Halla Na Saoire (IRE) – Mac Swiney (IRE), by New Approach (IRE)

Handassa (GB) – Nazeef (GB), by Invincible Spirit (IRE)

Hidden Hope (GB) – Frankly Darling (GB), by Frankel (GB)

Homecoming Queen (IRE) – Shale (IRE), by Galileo (IRE)

Hveger (AUS) – Nobel Prize (IRE), by Galileo (IRE)

In Your Time (GB) – Cairn Gorm (GB), by Bated Breath (GB)

Jabbara (IRE) – Euchen Glen (GB), by Authorized (IRE)

Jamboretta (IRE) – Bowerman (GB), by Dutch Art (GB)

Janina (GB) – Campanelle (IRE), by Kodiac (GB)

Joyeaux (GB) – Dakota Gold (GB), by Equiano (FR)

Karjera (IRE) – A Case of You (IRE), by Hot Streak (IRE)

Kenzadargent (FR) – Brad The Brief (GB), by Dutch Art (GB)

Kitcara (GB) – Al Aasy (IRE), by Sea The Stars (IRE)

La Cuvee (GB) – Champers Elysees (IRE), by Elzaam (AUS)

La Grande Elisa (IRE) – Star of Emaraaty (IRE), by Pride of Dubai (AUS)

La Pyle (FR) – Pyledriver (GB), by Harbour Watch (IRE)

Lady Gorgeous (GB) – Pretty Gorgeous (FR), by Lawman (FR)

Lady Marian (GER) – Loxley (IRE), by New Approach (IRE)

Ladylishandra (IRE) – Ubettabelieveit (IRE), by Kodiac (GB)

Laurelita (IRE) – Fev Rover (IRE), by Gutaifan (IRE)

Lesson In Humility (IRE) – Tiger Moth (IRE), by Galileo (IRE)

Limonar (IRE) – Spanish Mission (USA), by Noble Mission (GB)

Linda Radlett (IRE) – Fanny Logan (IRE), by Sea The Stars (IRE)

Louvakhova (USA) – Crossfirehurricane (USA), by Kitten's Joy (USA)

Love Your Looks (GB) – Breathtaking Look (GB), by Bated Breath (GB)

Lumiere Noire (FR) – Wichita (IRE), by No Nay Never (USA)

Macarthurs Park (IRE) – Steel Bull (IRE), by Clodovil (IRE)

Madany (IRE) – Mujbar (GB), by Muhaarar (GB)

Maglietta Fina (IRE) – Lady Bowthorpe (GB), by Nathaniel (IRE)

Maglietta Fina (IRE) – Speak In Colours (GB), by Excelebration (IRE)

Mahbooba (AUS) – Dubai Warrior (GB), by Dansili (GB)

Majestic Dubawi (IRE) – Isabella Giles (IRE), by Belardo (IRE)

Make Fast (GB) – Tactical (GB), by Toronado (IRE)

Many Colours (GB) – Mother Earth (IRE), by Zoffany (IRE)

Maoineach (USA) – New Treasure (IRE), by New Approach (IRE)

Maria Lee (IRE) – Poetic Flare (IRE), by Dawn Approach (IRE)

Marlinka (GB) – Judicial (IRE), by Iffraaj (GB)

Marvada (IRE) – Terebellum (IRE), by Sea The Stars (IRE)

Midnight Oasis (GB) – Ventura Tormenta (IRE), by Acclamation (GB)

Mishhar (IRE) – New Mandate (IRE), by New Bay (GB)

Miss Dashwood (GB) – Dashing Willoughby (GB), by Nathaniel (IRE)

Miss Lucifer (FR) – Space Blues (IRE), by Dubawi (IRE)

Missunited (IRE) – Eagles By Day (IRE), by Sea The Stars (IRE)

Modernstone (GB) – Lone Eagle (IRE), by Galileo (IRE)

Mohini (IRE) – Pista (USA), by American Pharoah (USA)

Montare (IRE) – Indigo Girl (GB), by Dubawi (IRE)

Motion Lass (GB) – A'Ali (IRE), by Society Rock (IRE)

Multilingual (GB) – Tilsit (USA), by First Defence (USA)

Muwakaba (USA) – Cayenne Pepper (IRE), by Australia (GB)

Naan (IRE) – Etonian (IRE), by Olympic Glory (IRE)

Nahrain (GB) – Benbatl (GB), by Dubawi (IRE)

Najoum (USA) – Lord North (IRE), by Dubawi (IRE)

Nessina (USA) – Extra Elusive (GB), by Mastercraftsman (IRE)

New Plays (IRE) – Epona Plays (IRE), by Australia (GB)

Nightime (IRE) – Ghaiyyath (IRE), by Dubawi (IRE)

O'Giselle (AUS) – Zakouski (GB), by Shamardal (USA)

Palace (IRE) – High Definition (IRE), by Galileo (IRE)

Paper Dreams (IRE) – The Lir Jet (IRE), by Prince of Lir (IRE)

Pardoven (IRE) – Minzaal (IRE), by Mehmas (IRE)

Porto Marmay (IRE) – Red Verdon (USA), by Lemon Drop Kid (USA)

Princess Guest (IRE) – Dubai Station (GB), by Brazen Beau (AUS)

Princess Zoffany (IRE) – Santosha (IRE), by Coulsty (IRE)

Prudenzia (IRE) – Magic Wand (IRE), by Galileo (IRE)

Puzzled (IRE) – Tabdeed (GB), by Havana Gold (IRE)

Queen's Code (IRE) – Umm Kulthum (IRE), by Kodiac (GB)

Quiet Oasis (IRE) – Lancaster House (IRE), by Galileo (IRE)

Rachevie (IRE) – Helvic Dream (IRE), by Power (GB)

Reckoning (IRE) – Subjectivist (GB), by Teofilo (IRE)

Red Evie (IRE) – Divinely (IRE), by Galileo (IRE)

Regal Realm (GB) – Regal Reality (GB), by Intello (GER)

River Song (USA) – Queen Jo Jo (GB), by Gregorian (IRE)

Rock My Soul (IRE) – Young Rascal (FR), by Intello (GER)

Romantic Venture (IRE) – Romanised (IRE), by Holy Roman Emperor (IRE)

Roodeye (GB) – Mohaather (GB), by Showcasing (GB)

Roscoff (IRE) – Manuela de Vega (IRE), by Lope de Vega (IRE)

Rose Bonheur (GB) – Nayef Road (IRE), by Galileo (IRE)

Royal Debt (GB) – Mighty Gurkha (IRE), by Sepoy (AUS)

Rugged Up (IRE) – Happy Romance (IRE), by Dandy Man (IRE)

Salacia (IRE) – Century Dream (IRE), by Cape Cross (IRE)

Salvation (GB) – Wonderful Tonight (FR), by Le Havre (IRE)

Sampers (IRE) – Laws of Indices (IRE), by Power (GB)

Seas of Wells (IRE) – Cadillac (IRE), by Lope de Vega (IRE)

Serena's Storm (IRE) – Summer Romance (IRE), by Kingman (GB)

Shao Line (FR) – Trueshan (FR), by Planteur (IRE)

Shastye (IRE) – Mogul (GB), by Galileo (IRE)

Shemya (FR) – Cormorant (IRE), by Kingman (GB)

Shena's Dream (IRE) – Miss Amulet (IRE), by Sir Prancealot (IRE)

Shirocco Star (GB) – Telecaster (GB), by New Approach (IRE)

Shishangaan (IRE) – Safe Voyage (IRE), by Fast Company (IRE)

Shortmile Lady (IRE) – Lemista (IRE), by Raven's Pass (USA)

Simawa (IRE) – Sinawann (IRE), by Kingman (GB)

Sonning Rose (IRE) – Elysium (IRE), by Belardo (IRE)

Souviens Toi (GB) – Thunderous (IRE), by Night of Thunder (IRE)

Starlet (IRE) – Love Locket (IRE), by No Nay Never (USA)

Stars In Your Eyes (GB) – Dame Malliot (GB), by Champs Elysees (GB)

Strictly Dancing (IRE) – Foxtrot Lady (GB), by Foxwedge (AUS)

Sub Rose (IRE) – Secret Advisor (FR), by Dubawi (IRE)

Suelita (GB) – Alkumait (GB), by Showcasing (GB)

Sweeter Still (IRE) – Kameko (USA), by Kitten's Joy (USA)

Tamarisk (GER) – Happy Power (IRE), by Dark Angel (IRE)

Tarana (IRE) – Tarnawa (IRE), by Shamardal (USA)

Thanks (IRE) – With Thanks (IRE), by Camacho (GB)

Titian Saga (IRE) – Winter Power (IRE), by Bungle Inthejungle (GB)

Together Forever (IRE) – Military Style (USA), by War Front (USA)

Topka (FR) – Believe In Love (IRE), by Make Believe (GB)

Triggers Broom (IRE) – Supremacy (IRE), by Mehmas (IRE)

Ultra Appeal (IRE) – Patrick Sarsfield (FR), by Australia (GB)

Vasilia (GB) – Dream of Dreams (IRE), by Dream Ahead (USA)

Wadyhatta (GB) – Santiago (IRE), by Authorized (IRE)

Wannabe Better (IRE) – Lady Wannabe (IRE), by Camelot (GB)

Whatami (GB) – Nkosikazi (GB), by Cape Cross (IRE)

Witches Brew (IRE) – Antonia de Vega (IRE), by Lope de Vega (IRE)

Zaaqya (GB) – One Voice (IRE), by Poet's Voice (GB)

Zain Art (IRE) – Aloha Star (IRE), by Starspangledbanner (AUS)

Zibelina (IRE) – Royal Crusade (GB), by Shamardal (USA)

Zoowraa (GB) – Maamora (IRE), by Dubawi (IRE)

Acclamation (GB) – Mujbar (GB), by Muhaarar (GB)

Ad Valorem (USA) – Star of Emaraaty (IRE), by Pride of Dubai
(AUS)

Anabaa (USA) – Passion (IRE), by Galileo (IRE)
Anabaa (USA) – Sinawann (IRE), by Kingman (GB)

Arcano (IRE) – Lemista (IRE), by Raven's Pass (USA)
Arcano (IRE) – Supremacy (IRE), by Mehmas (IRE)

Arch (USA) – Valeria Messalina (IRE), by Holy Roman Emperor
(IRE)

Aussie Rules (USA) – Angel Power (GB), by Lope de Vega
(IRE)

Authorized (IRE) – New Mandate (IRE), by New Bay (GB)
Authorized (IRE) – Top Rank (IRE), by Dark Angel (IRE)

Azamour (IRE) – Maamora (IRE), by Dubawi (IRE)
Azamour (IRE) – Volkan Star (IRE), by Sea The Stars (IRE)

Big Shuffle (USA) – Glen Shiel (GB), by Pivotal (GB)

Cape Cross (IRE) – Santiago (IRE), by Authorized (IRE)
Cape Cross (IRE) – Tarnawa (IRE), by Shamardal (USA)
Cape Cross (IRE) – Thundering Nights (IRE), by Night of
Thunder (IRE)

Choisir (AUS) – Oxted (GB), by Mayson (GB)
Choisir (AUS) – Red Verdon (USA), by Lemon Drop Kid (USA)

Clodovil (IRE) – Minzaal (IRE), by Mehmas (IRE)
Clodovil (IRE) – Young Rascal (FR), by Intello (GER)

Compton Place (GB) – Pretty Gorgeous (FR), by Lawman (FR)

Congaree (USA) – New Treasure (IRE), by New Approach (IRE)

Dalakhani (IRE) – Cairn Gorm (GB), by Bated Breath (GB)
Dalakhani (IRE) – Thunderous (IRE), by Night of Thunder (IRE)

Danehill (USA) – Bowerman (GB), by Dutch Art (GB)
Danehill (USA) – Master of The Seas (IRE), by Dubawi (IRE)
Danehill (USA) – Mogul (GB), by Galileo (IRE)
Danehill (USA) – Nobel Prize (IRE), by Galileo (IRE)

Danehill Dancer (IRE) – Armory (IRE), by Galileo (IRE)
Danehill Dancer (IRE) – Foxtrot Lady (GB), by Foxwedge (AUS)
Danehill Dancer (IRE) – Helvic Dream (IRE), by Power (GB)
Danehill Dancer (IRE) – Leo de Fury (IRE), by Australia (GB)
Danehill Dancer (IRE) – Magic Lily (GB), by New Approach (IRE)
Danehill Dancer (IRE) – Nayef Road (IRE), by Galileo (IRE)
Danehill Dancer (IRE) – Royal Dornoch (IRE), by Gleneagles (IRE)
Danehill Dancer (IRE) – Subjectivist (GB), by Teofilo (IRE)

Dansili (GB) – Aspetar (FR), by Al Kazeem (GB)
Dansili (GB) – Cadillac (IRE), by Lope de Vega (IRE)
Dansili (GB) – Cormorant (IRE), by Kingman (GB)
Dansili (GB) – Dark Vision (IRE), by Dream Ahead (USA)
Dansili (GB) – Dream of Dreams (IRE), by Dream Ahead (USA)
Dansili (GB) – Glorious Journey (GB), by Dubawi (IRE)
Dansili (GB) – Magic Wand (IRE), by Galileo (IRE)
Dansili (GB) – Pablo Escobarr (IRE), by Galileo (IRE)
Dansili (GB) – Royal Crusade (GB), by Shamardal (USA)
Dansili (GB) – Tilsit (USA), by First Defence (USA)

Darshaan – Dawn Patrol (IRE), by Galileo (IRE)

Dashing Blade – Wichita (IRE), by No Nay Never (USA)

Daylami (IRE) – Frankly Darling (GB), by Frankel (GB)
Daylami (IRE) – Manuela de Vega (IRE), by Lope de Vega
    (IRE)
Daylami (IRE) – Nkosikazi (GB), by Cape Cross (IRE)

Desert King (IRE) – Snow (IRE), by Galileo (IRE)

Dubawi (IRE) – Isabella Giles (IRE), by Belardo (IRE)
Dubawi (IRE) – Nazeef (GB), by Invincible Spirit (IRE)

Duke of Marmalade (IRE) – Antonia de Vega (IRE), by Lope de
    Vega (IRE)
Duke of Marmalade (IRE) – Lady Wannabe (IRE), by Camelot
    (GB)
Duke of Marmalade (IRE) – Lone Eagle (IRE), by Galileo (IRE)

Dutch Art (GB) – Alkumait (GB), by Showcasing (GB)

Dylan Thomas (IRE) – Dashing Willoughby (GB), by Nathaniel
    (IRE)

Echo of Light (GB) – Century Dream (IRE), by Cape Cross
    (IRE)

Efisio – Elarqam (GB), by Frankel (GB)

Elnadim (USA) – Dandalla (IRE), by Dandy Man (IRE)

Elusive City (USA) – Terebellum (IRE), by Sea The Stars (IRE)

Elusive Quality (USA) – Cayenne Pepper (IRE), by Australia
    (GB)

Equiano (FR) – Steel Bull (IRE), by Clodovil (IRE)

Exceed And Excel (AUS) – Anthony Van Dyck (IRE), by
    Galileo (IRE)
Exceed And Excel (AUS) – Current Option (IRE), by Camelot
    (GB)
Exceed And Excel (AUS) – Laws of Indices (IRE), by Power
    (GB)

Excellent Art (GB) – Aloha Star (IRE), by Starspangledbanner
    (AUS)

Fasliyev (USA) – Lazuli (IRE), by Dubawi (IRE)

Fastnet Rock (AUS) – High Definition (IRE), by Galileo (IRE)
Fastnet Rock (AUS) – Russian Emperor (IRE), by Galileo (IRE)

Firebreak (GB) – Ventura Rebel (GB), by Pastoral Pursuits (GB)

Galileo (IRE) – Barney Roy (GB), by Excelebration (IRE)
Galileo (IRE) – Battleground (USA), by War Front (USA)
Galileo (IRE) – Certain Lad (GB), by Clodovil (IRE)
Galileo (IRE) – Dame Malliot (GB), by Champs Elysees (GB)
Galileo (IRE) – Dubai Warrior (GB), by Dansili (GB)
Galileo (IRE) – Ghaiyyath (IRE), by Dubawi (IRE)
Galileo (IRE) – Military Style (USA), by War Front (USA)
Galileo (IRE) – Pista (USA), by American Pharoah (USA)
Galileo (IRE) – Secret Advisor (FR), by Dubawi (IRE)

General Holme (USA) – Trueshan (FR), by Planteur (IRE)

Giant's Causeway (USA) – Lord North (IRE), by Dubawi (IRE)

Golan (IRE) – Eagles By Day (IRE), by Sea The Stars (IRE)

Green Desert (USA) – Buckhurst (IRE), by Australia (GB)
Green Desert (USA) – Minaun (IRE), by Zoffany (IRE)
Green Desert (USA) – Mother Earth (IRE), by Zoffany (IRE)

Green Desert (USA) – The Lir Jet (IRE), by Prince of Lir (IRE)

Haafhd (GB) – Baron Samedi (GB), by Harbour Watch (IRE)

Hawk Wing (USA) – Elysium (IRE), by Belardo (IRE)

Hennessy (USA) – Extra Elusive (GB), by Mastercraftsman (IRE)

High Chaparral (IRE) – Fev Rover (IRE), by Gutaifan (IRE)

Holy Roman Emperor (IRE) – Shale (IRE), by Galileo (IRE)

Iffraaj (GB) – Breathtaking Look (GB), by Bated Breath (GB)
Iffraaj (GB) – Dubai Station (GB), by Brazen Beau (AUS)

Inchinor (GB) – Mohaather (GB), by Showcasing (GB)

Indesatchel (IRE) – Lullaby Moon (GB), by Belardo (IRE)

Indian Charlie (USA) – Etonian (IRE), by Olympic Glory (IRE)

Indian Ridge – Millisle (IRE), by Starspangledbanner (AUS)
Indian Ridge – Romanised (IRE), by Holy Roman Emperor (IRE)

Intikhab (USA) – Divinely (IRE), by Galileo (IRE)

Kahyasi – Believe In Love (IRE), by Make Believe (GB)

Keltos (FR) – Art Power (IRE), by Dark Angel (IRE)

Kendargent (FR) – Brad The Brief (GB), by Dutch Art (GB)

Key of Luck (USA) – A Case of You (IRE), by Hot Streak (IRE)

Kheleyf (USA) – With Thanks (IRE), by Camacho (GB)

Kingmambo (USA) – Euchen Glen (GB), by Authorized (IRE)
Kingmambo (USA) – Hukum (IRE), by Sea The Stars (IRE)

Lawman (FR) – Battaash (IRE), by Dark Angel (IRE)
Lawman (FR) – Patrick Sarsfield (FR), by Australia (GB)

Le Havre (IRE) – Pyledriver (GB), by Harbour Watch (IRE)

Makfi (GB) – Tactical (GB), by Toronado (IRE)

Manduro (GER) – Fanny Logan (IRE), by Sea The Stars (IRE)

Maria's Mon (USA) – Crossfirehurricane (USA), by Kitten's Joy
    (USA)

Mark of Esteem (IRE) – Dakota Gold (GB), by Equiano (FR)

Marju (IRE) – Happy Romance (IRE), by Dandy Man (IRE)
Marju (IRE) – Judicial (IRE), by Iffraaj (GB)

Mark of Esteem (IRE) – Champers Elysees (IRE), by Elzaam
    (AUS)

Medicean (GB) – Regal Reality (GB), by Intello (GER)

Montjeu (IRE) – Indigo Girl (GB), by Dubawi (IRE)
Montjeu (IRE) – La Barrosa (IRE), by Lope de Vega (IRE)
Montjeu (IRE) – Nickajack Cave (IRE), by Kendargent (FR)
Montjeu (IRE) – Wonderful Tonight (FR), by Le Havre (IRE)

Motivator (GB) – A'Ali (IRE), by Society Rock (IRE)

Mujadil (USA) – Safe Voyage (IRE), by Fast Company (IRE)
Mujadil (USA) – Tiger Moth (IRE), by Galileo (IRE)
Mujadil (USA) – Ubettabelieveit (IRE), by Kodiac (GB)

Mukaddamah (USA) – True Self (IRE), by Oscar (IRE)

Namid (GB) – Campanelle (IRE), by Kodiac (GB)

Nayef (USA) – Loxley (IRE), by New Approach (IRE)
Nayef (USA) – One Voice (IRE), by Poet's Voice (GB)

Noverre (USA) – Space Blues (IRE), by Dubawi (IRE)

Oasis Dream (GB) – Chindit (IRE), by Wootton Bassett (GB)
Oasis Dream (GB) – Delphi (IRE), by Galileo (IRE)
Oasis Dream (GB) – Lancaster House (IRE), by Galileo (IRE)
Oasis Dream (GB) – Miss Amulet (IRE), by Sir Prancealot (IRE)
Oasis Dream (GB) – Twilight Payment (IRE), by Teofilo (IRE)
Oasis Dream (GB) – Ventura Tormenta (IRE), by Acclamation (GB)

Octagonal (NZ) – Zakouski (GB), by Shamardal (USA)

Oratorio (IRE) – Epona Plays (IRE), by Australia (GB)

Peintre Celebre (USA) – Tabdeed (GB), by Havana Gold (IRE)

Pivotal (GB) – Molatham (GB), by Night of Thunder (IRE)
Pivotal (GB) – One Master (IRE), by Fastnet Rock (AUS)

Raven's Pass (USA) – Mishriff (IRE), by Make Believe (GB)
Raven's Pass (USA) – Saffron Beach (IRE), by New Bay (GB)

Rainbow Quest (USA) – Know It All (GB), by Lord Kanaloa (JPN)

Rock of Gibraltar (IRE) – Kameko (USA), by Kitten's Joy (USA)
Rock of Gibraltar (IRE) – Poetic Flare (IRE), by Dawn Approach (IRE)

Roy (USA) – Nando Parrado (GB), by Kodiac (GB)

Royal Applause (GB) – Mighty Gurkha (IRE), by Sepoy (AUS)

Sadler's Wells (USA) – Berlin Tango (GB), by Dansili (GB)
Sadler's Wells (USA) – Enable (GB), by Nathaniel (IRE)

Sea The Stars (IRE) – Love Locket (IRE), by No Nay Never (USA)

Selkirk (USA) – Benbatl (GB), by Dubawi (IRE)
Selkirk (USA) – Happy Power (IRE), by Dark Angel (IRE)

Shamardal (USA) – Al Aasy (IRE), by Sea The Stars (IRE)
Shamardal (USA) – Far Above (IRE), by Farhh (GB)
Shamardal (USA) – One Ruler (IRE), by Dubawi (IRE)
Shamardal (USA) – Umm Kulthum (IRE), by Kodiac (GB)

Shirocco (GER) – Telecaster (GB), by New Approach (IRE)

Singspiel (IRE) – Limato (IRE), by Tagula (IRE)

Siphon (BRZ) – Queen Jo Jo (GB), by Gregorian (IRE)

Sixties Icon (GB) – Rose of Kildare (IRE), by Make Believe (GB)

Statue of Liberty (USA) – Summer Romance (IRE), by Kingman (GB)

Street Cry (IRE) – Spanish Mission (USA), by Noble Mission (GB)

Teofilo (IRE) – Flying Visit (IRE), by Pride of Dubai (AUS)
Teofilo (IRE) – Mac Swiney (IRE), by New Approach (IRE)

Titus Livius (FR) – Winter Power (IRE), by Bungle Inthejungle (GB)

Toccet (USA) – Gear Up (IRE), by Teofilo (IRE)

Trempolino (USA) – Enbihaar (IRE), by Redoute's Choice (AUS)

Verglas (IRE) – Lady Bowthorpe (GB), by Nathaniel (IRE)
Verglas (IRE) – Speak In Colours (GB), by Excelebration (IRE)

Zoffany (IRE) – Santosha (IRE), by Coulsty (IRE)

GROUP 2 & GROUP 3 WINNERS OF 2020
BY MATERNAL GRANDSIRE
(Sire of the broodmare sire)

Acclamation (GB) – Steel Bull (IRE), by Clodovil (IRE), dam by Equiano (FR)

Ahonoora – Millisle (IRE), by Starspangledbanner (AUS), dam by Indian Ridge

Ahonoora – Mohaather (GB), by Showcasing (GB), dam by Inchinor (GB)

Ahonoora – Romanised (IRE), by Holy Roman Emperor (IRE), dam by Indian Ridge

Alhaarth (IRE) – Baron Samedi (GB), by Harbour Watch (IRE), dam by Haafhd (GB)

Arazi (USA) – New Treasure (IRE), by New Approach (IRE), dam by Congaree (USA)

Awesome Again (CAN) – Gear Up (IRE), by Teofilo (IRE), dam by Toccet (USA)

Blushing Groom (FR) – Know It All (GB), by Lord Kanaloa (JPN), dam by Rainbow Quest (USA)

Cape Cross (IRE) – Love Locket (IRE), by No Nay Never (USA), dam by Sea The Stars (IRE)

Charnwood Forest (IRE) – Ventura Rebel (GB), by Pastoral Pursuits (GB), dam by Firebreak (GB)

Chief's Crown (USA) – A Case of You (IRE), by Hot Streak (IRE), dam by Key of Luck (USA)

Danehill (USA) – Angel Power (GB), by Lope de Vega (IRE), dam by Aussie Rules (USA)

Danehill (USA) – Anthony Van Dyck (IRE), by Galileo (IRE), dam by Exceed And Excel (AUS)

Danehill (USA) – Antonia de Vega (IRE), by Lope de Vega (IRE), dam by Duke of Marmalade (IRE)

Danehill (USA) – Armory (IRE), by Galileo (IRE), dam by Danehill Dancer (IRE)

Danehill (USA) – Aspetar (FR), by Al Kazeem (GB), dam by Dansili (GB)

Danehill (USA) – Cadillac (IRE), by Lope de Vega (IRE), dam by Dansili (GB)

Danehill (USA) – Cormorant (IRE), by Kingman (GB), dam by Dansili (GB)

Danehill (USA) – Current Option (IRE), by Camelot (GB), dam by Exceed And Excel (AUS)

Danehill (USA) – Dark Vision (IRE), by Dream Ahead (USA), dam by Dansili (GB)

Danehill (USA) – Dashing Willoughby (GB), by Nathaniel (IRE), dam by Dylan Thomas (IRE)

Danehill (USA) – Dream of Dreams (IRE), by Dream Ahead (USA), dam by Dansili (GB)

Danehill (USA) – Epona Plays (IRE), by Australia (GB), dam by Oratorio (IRE)

Danehill (USA) – Foxtrot Lady (GB), by Foxwedge (AUS), dam by Danehill Dancer (IRE)

Danehill (USA) – Glorious Journey (GB), by Dubawi (IRE), dam by Dansili (GB)

Danehill (USA) – Helvic Dream (IRE), by Power (GB), dam by Danehill Dancer (IRE)

Danehill (USA) – High Definition (IRE), by Galileo (IRE), dam by Fastnet Rock (AUS)

Danehill (USA) – Kameko (USA), by Kitten's Joy (USA), dam by Rock of Gibraltar (IRE)

Danehill (USA) – Lady Wannabe (IRE), by Camelot (GB), dam by Duke of Marmalade (IRE)

Danehill (USA) – Laws of Indices (IRE), by Power (GB), dam by Exceed And Excel (AUS)

Danehill (USA) – Leo de Fury (IRE), by Australia (GB), dam by Danehill Dancer (IRE)

Danehill (USA) – Lone Eagle (IRE), by Galileo (IRE), dam by
Duke of Marmalade (IRE)
Danehill (USA) – Magic Lily (GB), by New Approach (IRE),
dam by Danehill Dancer (IRE)
Danehill (USA) – Magic Wand (IRE), by Galileo (IRE), dam by
Dansili (GB)
Danehill (USA) – Minzaal (IRE), by Mehmas (IRE), dam by
Clodovil (IRE)
Danehill (USA) – Nayef Road (IRE), by Galileo (IRE), dam by
Danehill Dancer (IRE)
Danehill (USA) – Pablo Escobarr (IRE), by Galileo (IRE), dam
by Dansili (GB)
Danehill (USA) – Poetic Flare (IRE), by Dawn Approach (IRE),
dam by Rock of Gibraltar (IRE)
Danehill (USA) – Royal Crusade (GB), by Shamardal (USA),
dam by Dansili (GB)
Danehill (USA) – Royal Dornoch (IRE), by Gleneagles (IRE),
dam by Danehill Dancer (IRE)
Danehill (USA) – Russian Emperor (IRE), by Galileo (IRE),
dam by Fastnet Rock (AUS)
Danehill (USA) – Shale (IRE), by Galileo (IRE), dam by Holy
Roman Emperor (IRE)
Danehill (USA) – Snow (IRE), by Galileo (IRE), dam by Desert
King (IRE)
Danehill (USA) – Subjectivist (GB), by Teofilo (IRE), dam by
Danehill Dancer (IRE)
Danehill (USA) – Tilsit (USA), by First Defence (USA), dam by
Dansili (GB)
Danehill (USA) – Young Rascal (FR), by Intello (GER), dam by
Clodovil (IRE)

Danehill Dancer (IRE) – Lullaby Moon (GB), by Belardo (IRE),
dam by Indesatchel (IRE)
Danehill Dancer (IRE) – Oxted (GB), by Mayson (GB), dam by
Choisir (AUS)
Danehill Dancer (IRE) – Red Verdon (USA), by Lemon Drop
Kid (USA), dam by Choisir (AUS)

Dansili (GB) – Santosha (IRE), by Coulsty (IRE), dam by
Zoffany (IRE)

Danzig (USA) – Bowerman (GB), by Dutch Art (GB), dam by
Danehill (USA)
Danzig (USA) – Buckhurst (IRE), by Australia (GB), dam by
Green Desert (USA)
Danzig (USA) – Dandalla (IRE), by Dandy Man (IRE), dam by
Elnadim (USA)
Danzig (USA) – Master of The Seas (IRE), by Dubawi (IRE),
dam by Danehill (USA)
Danzig (USA) – Minaun (IRE), by Zoffany (IRE), dam by Green
Desert (USA)
Danzig (USA) – Mogul (GB), by Galileo (IRE), dam by Danehill
(USA)
Danzig (USA) – Mother Earth (IRE), by Zoffany (IRE), dam by
Green Desert (USA)
Danzig (USA) – Nobel Prize (IRE), by Galileo (IRE), dam by
Danehill (USA)
Danzig (USA) – Passion (IRE), by Galileo (IRE), dam by
Anabaa (USA)
Danzig (USA) – Sinawann (IRE), by Kingman (GB), dam by
Anabaa (USA)
Danzig (USA) – Star of Emaraaty (IRE), by Pride of Dubai
(AUS), dam by Ad Valorem (USA)
Danzig (USA) – The Lir Jet (IRE), by Prince of Lir (IRE), dam
by Green Desert (USA)

Darshaan – Cairn Gorm (GB), by Bated Breath (GB), dam by
Dalakhani (IRE)
Darshaan – Champers Elysees (IRE), by Elzaam (AUS), dam by
Mark of Esteem (IRE)
Darshaan – Dakota Gold (GB), by Equiano (FR), dam by Mark
of Esteem (IRE)
Darshaan – Thunderous (IRE), by Night of Thunder (IRE), dam
by Dalakhani (IRE)

Doyoun – Frankly Darling (GB), by Frankel (GB), dam by
    Daylami (IRE)
Doyoun – Manuela de Vega (IRE), by Lope de Vega (IRE), dam
    by Daylami (IRE)
Doyoun – Nkosikazi (GB), by Cape Cross (IRE), dam by
    Daylami (IRE)

Dubai Millennium (GB) – Century Dream (IRE), by Cape Cross
    (IRE), dam by Echo of Light (GB)
Dubai Millennium (GB) – Isabella Giles (IRE), by Belardo
    (IRE), dam by Dubawi (IRE)
Dubai Millennium (GB) – Nazeef (GB), by Invincible Spirit
    (IRE), dam by Dubawi (IRE)

Dubawi (IRE) – Tactical (GB), by Toronado (IRE), dam by
    Makfi (GB)

Elegant Air – Wichita (IRE), by No Nay Never (USA), dam by
    Dashing Blade

Elusive Quality (USA) – Mishriff (IRE), by Make Believe (GB),
    dam by Raven's Pass (USA)
Elusive Quality (USA) – Saffron Beach (IRE), by New Bay (GB),
    dam by Raven's Pass (USA)
Elusive Quality (USA) – Terebellum (IRE), by Sea The Stars
    (IRE), dam by Elusive City (USA)

Fappiano (USA) – Nando Parrado (GB), by Kodiac (GB), dam
    by Roy (USA)

Formidable (USA) – Elarqam (GB), by Frankel (GB), dam by
    Efisio

Galileo (IRE) – Flying Visit (IRE), by Pride of Dubai (AUS),
    dam by Teofilo (IRE)
Galileo (IRE) – Mac Swiney (IRE), by New Approach (IRE),
    dam by Teofilo (IRE)

Galileo (IRE) – Rose of Kildare (IRE), by Make Believe (GB), dam by Sixties Icon (GB)

Giant's Causeway (USA) – Al Aasy (IRE), by Sea The Stars (IRE), dam by Shamardal (USA)

Giant's Causeway (USA) – Far Above (IRE), by Farhh (GB), dam by Shamardal (USA)

Giant's Causeway (USA) – One Ruler (IRE), by Dubawi (IRE), dam by Shamardal (USA)

Giant's Causeway (USA) – Umm Kulthum (IRE), by Kodiac (GB), dam by Shamardal (USA)

Gone West (USA) – Cayenne Pepper (IRE), by Australia (GB), dam by Elusive Quality (USA)

Green Desert (USA) – Chindit (IRE), by Wootton Bassett (GB), dam by Oasis Dream (GB)

Green Desert (USA) – Delphi (IRE), by Galileo (IRE), dam by Oasis Dream (GB)

Green Desert (USA) – Lancaster House (IRE), by Galileo (IRE), dam by Oasis Dream (GB)

Green Desert (USA) – Miss Amulet (IRE), by Sir Prancealot (IRE), dam by Oasis Dream (GB)

Green Desert (USA) – Santiago (IRE), by Authorized (IRE), dam by Cape Cross (IRE)

Green Desert (USA) – Tarnawa (IRE), by Shamardal (USA), dam by Cape Cross (IRE)

Green Desert (USA) – Thundering Nights (IRE), by Night of Thunder (IRE), dam by Cape Cross (IRE)

Green Desert (USA) – Twilight Payment (IRE), by Teofilo (IRE), dam by Oasis Dream (GB)

Green Desert (USA) – Ventura Tormenta (IRE), by Acclamation (GB), dam by Oasis Dream (GB)

Green Desert (USA) – With Thanks (IRE), by Camacho (GB), dam by Kheleyf (USA)

Gulch (USA) – Loxley (IRE), by New Approach (IRE), dam by Nayef (USA)

Gulch (USA) – One Voice (IRE), by Poet's Voice (GB), dam by
Nayef (USA)

Highest Honor (FR) – Lady Bowthorpe (GB), by Nathaniel
(IRE), dam by Verglas (IRE)
Highest Honor (FR) – Speak In Colours (GB), by Excelebration
(IRE), dam by Verglas (IRE)

Ile de Bourbon (USA) – Believe In Love (IRE), by Make Believe
(GB), dam by Kahyasi

In Excess – Etonian (IRE), by Olympic Glory (IRE), dam by
Indian Charlie (USA)

In The Wings – Limato (IRE), by Tagula (IRE), dam by
Singspiel (IRE)

Indian Ridge – Campanelle (IRE), by Kodiac (GB), dam by
Namid (GB)
Indian Ridge – Pretty Gorgeous (FR), by Lawman (FR), dam by
Compton Place (GB)

Invincible Spirit (IRE) – Battaash (IRE), by Dark Angel (IRE),
dam by Lawman (FR)
Invincible Spirit (IRE) – Patrick Sarsfield (FR), by Australia
(GB), dam by Lawman (FR)

Itajara (BRZ) – Queen Jo Jo (GB), by Gregorian (IRE), dam by
Siphon (BRZ)

Kendor (FR) – Art Power (IRE), by Dark Angel (IRE), dam by
Keltos (FR)
Kendor (FR) – Brad The Brief (GB), by Dutch Art (GB), dam
by Kendargent (FR)

Kris S (USA) – Valeria Messalina (IRE), by Holy Roman
Emperor (IRE), dam by Arch (USA)

Last Tycoon – Happy Romance (IRE), by Dandy Man (IRE),
    dam by Marju (IRE)
Last Tycoon – Judicial (IRE), by Iffraaj (GB), dam by Marju
    (IRE)

Machiavellian (USA) – Regal Reality (GB), by Intello (GER),
    dam by Medicean (GB)
Machiavellian (USA) – Spanish Mission (USA), by Noble
    Mission (GB), dam by Street Cry (IRE)
Machiavellian (USA) – Winter Power (IRE), by Bungle
    Inthejungle (GB), dam by Titus Livius (FR)

Medicean (GB) – Alkumait (GB), by Showcasing (GB), dam by
    Dutch Art (GB)

Monsun (GER) – Fanny Logan (IRE), by Sea The Stars (IRE),
    dam by Manduro (GER)
Monsun (GER) – Telecaster (GB), by New Approach (IRE),
    dam by Shirocco (GER)

Montjeu (IRE) – A'Ali (IRE), by Society Rock (IRE), dam by
    Motivator (GB)
Montjeu (IRE) – New Mandate (IRE), by New Bay (GB), dam
    by Authorized (IRE)
Montjeu (IRE) – Top Rank (IRE), by Dark Angel (IRE), dam by
    Authorized (IRE)

Mr Prospector (USA) – Euchen Glen (GB), by Authorized
    (IRE), dam by Kingmambo (USA)
Mr Prospector (USA) – Hukum (IRE), by Sea The Stars (IRE),
    dam by Kingmambo (USA)

Night Shift (USA) – Maamora (IRE), by Dubawi (IRE), dam by
    Azamour (IRE)
Night Shift (USA) – Volkan Star (IRE), by Sea The Stars (IRE),
    dam by Azamour (IRE)

Noholme (AUS) – Trueshan (FR), by Planteur (IRE), dam by General Holme (USA)

Northern Dancer – Berlin Tango (GB), by Dansili (GB), dam by Sadler's Wells (USA)
Northern Dancer – Enable (GB), by Nathaniel (IRE), dam by Sadler's Wells (USA)

Noverre (USA) – Pyledriver (GB), by Harbour Watch (IRE), dam by Le Havre (IRE)

Nureyev (USA) – Lazuli (IRE), by Dubawi (IRE), dam by Fasliyev (USA)
Nureyev (USA) – Tabdeed (GB), by Havana Gold (IRE), dam by Peintre Celebre (USA)

Oasis Dream (GB) – Lemista (IRE), by Raven's Pass (USA), dam by Arcano (IRE)
Oasis Dream (GB) – Supremacy (IRE), by Mehmas (IRE), dam by Arcano (IRE)

Pivotal (GB) – Aloha Star (IRE), by Starspangledbanner (AUS), dam by Excellent Art (GB)

Polar Falcon (USA) – Molatham (GB), by Night of Thunder (IRE), dam by Pivotal (GB)
Polar Falcon (USA) – One Master (IRE), by Fastnet Rock (AUS), dam by Pivotal (GB)

Rahy (USA) – Space Blues (IRE), by Dubawi (IRE), dam by Noverre (USA)

Red Ransom (USA) – Divinely (IRE), by Galileo (IRE), dam by Intikhab (USA)

Royal Applause (GB) – Mujbar (GB), by Muhaarar (GB), dam by Acclamation (GB)

Sadler's Wells (USA) – Barney Roy (GB), by Excelebration
(IRE), dam by Galileo (IRE)
Sadler's Wells (USA) – Battleground (USA), by War Front
(USA), dam by Galileo (IRE)
Sadler's Wells (USA) – Certain Lad (GB), by Clodovil (IRE),
dam by Galileo (IRE)
Sadler's Wells (USA) – Dame Malliot (GB), by Champs Elysees
(GB), dam by Galileo (IRE)
Sadler's Wells (USA) – Dubai Warrior (GB), by Dansili (GB),
dam by Galileo (IRE)
Sadler's Wells (USA) – Fev Rover (IRE), by Gutaifan (IRE), dam
by High Chaparral (IRE)
Sadler's Wells (USA) – Ghaiyyath (IRE), by Dubawi (IRE), dam
by Galileo (IRE)
Sadler's Wells (USA) – Indigo Girl (GB), by Dubawi (IRE), dam
by Montjeu (IRE)
Sadler's Wells (USA) – La Barrosa (IRE), by Lope de Vega
(IRE), dam by Montjeu (IRE)
Sadler's Wells (USA) – Military Style (USA), by War Front
(USA), dam by Galileo (IRE)
Sadler's Wells (USA) – Nickajack Cave (IRE), by Kendargent
(FR), dam by Montjeu (IRE)
Sadler's Wells (USA) – Pista (USA), by American Pharoah
(USA), dam by Galileo (IRE)
Sadler's Wells (USA) – Secret Advisor (FR), by Dubawi (IRE),
dam by Galileo (IRE)
Sadler's Wells (USA) – Wonderful Tonight (FR), by Le Havre
(IRE), dam by Montjeu (IRE)

Shamardal (USA) – Lord North (IRE), by Dubawi (IRE), dam
by Giant's Causeway (USA)

Sharpen Up – Benbatl (GB), by Dubawi (IRE), dam by Selkirk
(USA)
Sharpen Up – Enbihaar (IRE), by Redoute's Choice (AUS), dam
by Trempolino (USA)
Sharpen Up – Happy Power (IRE), by Dark Angel (IRE), dam
by Selkirk (USA)

Shirley Heights – Dawn Patrol (IRE), by Galileo (IRE), dam by
    Darshaan

Spectrum (IRE) – Eagles By Day (IRE), by Sea The Stars (IRE),
    dam by Golan (IRE)

Storm Bird (CAN) – Safe Voyage (IRE), by Fast Company
    (IRE), dam by Mujadil (USA)
Storm Bird (CAN) – Tiger Moth (IRE), by Galileo (IRE), dam
    by Mujadil (USA)
Storm Bird (CAN) – True Self (IRE), by Oscar (IRE), dam by
    Mukaddamah (USA)
Storm Bird (CAN) – Ubettabelieveit (IRE), by Kodiac (GB),
    dam by Mujadil (USA)

Storm Cat (USA) – Extra Elusive (GB), by Mastercraftsman
    (IRE), dam by Hennessy (USA)
Storm Cat (USA) – Summer Romance (IRE), by Kingman (GB),
    dam by Statue of Liberty (USA)

Super Concorde (USA) – Glen Shiel (GB), by Pivotal (GB), dam
    by Big Shuffle (USA)

Waajib – Mighty Gurkha (IRE), by Sepoy (AUS), dam by Royal
    Applause (GB)

Wavering Monarch (USA) – Crossfirehurricane (USA), by
    Kitten's Joy (USA), dam by Maria's Mon (USA)

Woodman (USA) – Elysium (IRE), by Belardo (IRE), dam by
    Hawk Wing (USA)

Zabeel (NZ) – Zakouski (GB), by Shamardal (USA), dam by
    Octagonal (NZ)

Zafonic (USA) – Breathtaking Look (GB), by Bated Breath
    (GB), dam by Iffraaj (GB)

Zafonic (USA) – Dubai Station (GB), by Brazen Beau (AUS), dam by Iffraaj (GB)

Abbatiale (FR) – Pablo Escobarr (IRE), by Galileo (IRE), out of Bewitched (IRE)

Acts of Grace (USA) – Mishriff (IRE), by Make Believe (GB), out of Contradict (GB)

Alexandrova (IRE) – Aspetar (FR), by Al Kazeem (GB), out of Bella Qatara (IRE)

Always Remembered (IRE) – Chindit (IRE), by Wootton Bassett (GB), out of Always A Dream (GB)

Amazing Krisken (USA) – Secret Advisor (FR), by Dubawi (IRE), out of Sub Rose (IRE)

Apache Star (GB) – Dame Malliot (GB), by Champs Elysees (GB), out of Stars In Your Eyes (GB)

Apogee (GB) – Enable (GB), by Nathaniel (IRE), out of Concentric (GB)

Arctic Drift (USA) – Anthony Van Dyck (IRE), by Galileo (IRE), out of Believe'N'Succeed (AUS)

Asnieres (USA) – Leo de Fury (IRE), by Australia (GB), out of Attire (IRE)

Bahr (GB) – Benbatl (GB), by Dubawi (IRE), out of Nahrain (GB)

Baralinka (IRE) – Judicial (IRE), by Iffraaj (GB), out of Marlinka (GB)

Belle de Cadix (IRE) – Mujbar (GB), by Muhaarar (GB), out of Madany (IRE)

Beltisaal (FR) – Kameko (USA), by Kitten's Joy (USA), out of Sweeter Still (IRE)

Beraysim (GB) – Maamora (IRE), by Dubawi (IRE), out of Zoowraa (GB)

Birdie (GB) – Wonderful Tonight (FR), by Le Havre (IRE), out of Salvation (GB)

Blue Symphony (GB) – Berlin Tango (GB), by Dansili (GB), out of Fantasia (GB)

Burning Heights (GER) – Angel Power (GB), by Lope de Vega (IRE), out of Burning Rules (IRE)

Caldy Dancer (IRE) – Mighty Gurkha (IRE), by Sepoy (AUS), out of Royal Debt (GB)

Campsie Fells (UAE) – One Ruler (IRE), by Dubawi (IRE), out of Fintry (IRE)

Canda (USA) – Molatham (GB), by Night of Thunder (IRE), out of Cantal (GB)

Caumshinaun (IRE) – Ghaiyyath (IRE), by Dubawi (IRE), out of Nightime (IRE)

Cayman Sunset (IRE) – Pretty Gorgeous (FR), by Lawman (FR), out of Lady Gorgeous (GB)

Challow Hills (USA) – Helvic Dream (IRE), by Power (GB), out of Rachevie (IRE)

Cheloca (GB) – Dandalla (IRE), by Dandy Man (IRE), out of Chellalla (GB)

Chervil (GB) – Fev Rover (IRE), by Gutaifan (IRE), out of
Laurelita (IRE)

Cheyenne Star (IRE) – Barney Roy (GB), by Excelebration
(IRE), out of Alina (IRE)

Choice (ARG) – Nando Parrado (GB), by Kodiac (GB), out of
Chibola (ARG)

Choisette (GB) – Ventura Rebel (GB), by Pastoral Pursuits
(GB), out of Finalize (GB)

Cinnamon Rose (USA) – Snow (IRE), by Galileo (IRE), out of
Chelsea Rose (IRE)

Circles of Gold (AUS) – Nobel Prize (IRE), by Galileo (IRE),
out of Hveger (AUS)

Classic Park (GB) – Tabdeed (GB), by Havana Gold (IRE), out
of Puzzled (IRE)

Classical Dancer (GB) – One Voice (IRE), by Poet's Voice (GB),
out of Zaaqya (GB)

Contare (GB) – Indigo Girl (GB), by Dubawi (IRE), out of
Montare (IRE)

Dancing Prize (IRE) – Minzaal (IRE), by Mehmas (IRE), out of
Pardoven (IRE)

Dash To The Front (GB) – Dashing Willoughby (GB), by
Nathaniel (IRE), out of Miss Dashwood (GB)

Dehbanu (IRE) – Umm Kulthum (IRE), by Kodiac (GB), out of
Queen's Code (IRE)

Denebola (USA) – Pista (USA), by American Pharoah (USA),
out of Mohini (IRE)

Devil's Imp (IRE) – Space Blues (IRE), by Dubawi (IRE), out of
  Miss Lucifer (FR)

Diamilina (FR) – Passion (IRE), by Galileo (IRE), out of
  Dialafara (FR)

Diavla (USA) – Thunderous (IRE), by Night of Thunder (IRE),
  out of Souviens Toi (GB)

Didina (GB) – Extra Elusive (GB), by Mastercraftsman (GB),
  out of Nessina (USA)

Divine Dixie (USA) – Lord North (IRE), by Dubawi (IRE), out
  of Najoum (USA)

Divine Secret (GB) – Dakota Gold (GB), by Equiano (FR), out
  of Joyeaux (GB)

Dorrati (USA) – Far Above (IRE), by Farhh (GB), out of
  Dorraar (IRE)

Elida (IRE) – Poetic Flare (IRE), by Dawn Approach (IRE), out
  of Maria Lee (IRE)

Fallen Star (GB) – Glorious Journey (GB), by Dubawi (IRE), out
  of Fallen For You (GB)

Feather Bride (IRE) – Royal Dornoch (IRE), by Gleneagles
  (IRE), out of Bridal Dance (IRE)

First of Many (GB) – Mother Earth (IRE), by Zoffany (IRE),
  out of Many Colours (GB)

Flirtation (GB) – Elarqam (GB), by Frankel (GB), out of
  Attraction (GB)

For Evva Silca (GB) – Happy Romance (IRE), by Dandy Man (IRE), out of Rugged Up (IRE)

Fresh Mint (IRE) – Current Option (IRE), by Camelot (GB), out of Coppertop (IRE)

Global World (GER) – Patrick Sarsfield (FR), by Australia (GB), out of Ultra Appeal (IRE)

Gold Dodger (USA) – Buckhurst (IRE), by Australia (GB), out of Artful (IRE)

Gonfalon (GB) – Glen Shiel (GB), by Pivotal (GB), out of Gonfilia (GER)

Great Hope (IRE) – Subjectivist (GB), by Teofilo (IRE), out of Reckoning (IRE)

Great Joy (IRE) – Supremacy (IRE), by Mehmas (IRE), out of Triggers Broom (IRE)

Green Lucia – Millisle (IRE), by Starspangledbanner (AUS), out of Green Castle (IRE)

Green Room (USA) – Military Style (USA), by War Front (USA), out of Together Forever (IRE)

Gujarat (USA) – Laws of Indices (IRE), by Power (GB), out of Sampers (IRE)

Highbrow – Know It All (GB), by Lord Kanaloa (JPN), out of Common Knowledge (GB)

Infinite Spirit (USA) – Saffron Beach (IRE), by New Bay (GB), out of Falling Petals (IRE)

Intriguing Glimpse (GB) – Oxted (GB), by Mayson (GB), out of Charlotte Rosina (GB)

Irish Flower (IRE) – Safe Voyage (IRE), by Fast Company (IRE), out of Shishangaan (IRE)

Isle de France (USA) – Euchen Glen (GB), by Authorized (IRE), out of Jabbara (IRE)

Jakarta (IRE) – New Mandate (IRE), by New Bay (GB), out of Mishhar (IRE)

Jinsiyah (USA) – Lemista (IRE), by Raven's Pass (USA), out of Shortmile Lady (IRE)

Jiving (GB) – Bowerman (GB), by Dutch Art (GB), out of Jamboretta (IRE)

Kaabari (USA) – Thundering Nights (IRE), by Night of Thunder (IRE), out of Cape Castle (IRE)

Kangra Valley (GB) – Dream of Dreams (IRE), by Dream Ahead (USA), out of Vasilia (GB)

Kerrera – Master of The Seas (IRE), by Dubawi (IRE), out of Firth of Lorne (IRE)

Kimono (IRE) – With Thanks (IRE), by Camacho (GB), out of Thanks (IRE)

Kitcat (GER) – Al Aasy (IRE), by Sea The Stars (IRE), out of Kitcara (GB)

Kiyra Wells (IRE) – Cadillac (IRE), by Lope de Vega (IRE), out of Seas of Wells (IRE)

La Felicita (GB) – Loxley (IRE), by New Approach (IRE), out of Lady Marian (GER)

La Tintoretta (IRE) – Steel Bull (IRE), by Clodovil (IRE), out of Macarthurs Park (IRE)

Lady Dominatrix (IRE) – Campanelle (IRE), by Kodiac (GB), out of Janina (GB)

Lady Icarus (GB) – High Definition (IRE), by Galileo (IRE), out of Palace (IRE)

Lady Lahar (GB) – Certain Lad (GB), by Clodovil (IRE), out of Chelsey Jayne (IRE)

Lagrion (USA) – Shale (IRE), by Galileo (IRE), out of Homecoming Queen (IRE)

Lahudood (GB) – Hukum (IRE), by Sea The Stars (IRE), out of Aghareed (USA)

Lets Clic Together (IRE) – Eagles By Day (IRE), by Sea The Stars (IRE), out of Missunited (IRE)

Lidana (IRE) – Pyledriver (GB), by Harbour Watch (IRE), out of La Pyle (FR)

Light My Way (IRE) – Nickajack Cave (IRE), by Kendargent (FR), out of Could You Be Loved (IRE)

Littlefeather (IRE) – Minaun (IRE), by Zoffany (IRE), out of Bee Eater (IRE)

Lochangel (GB) – Foxtrot Lady (GB), by Foxwedge (AUS), out of Strictly Dancing (IRE)

Lock's Heath (CAN) – A Case of You (IRE), by Hot Streak (IRE), out of Karjera (IRE)

Looking Back (IRE) – Star of Emaraaty (IRE), by Pride of Dubai (AUS), out of La Grande Elisa (IRE)

Louvain (IRE) – Crossfirehurricane (USA), by Kitten's Joy (USA), out of Louvakhova (USA)

Lumiere Rouge (FR) – Wichita (IRE), by No Nay Never (USA), out of Lumiere Noire (FR)

Macheera (IRE) – Antonia de Vega (IRE), by Lope de Vega (IRE), out of Witches Brew (IRE)

Madame Dubois – Top Rank (IRE), by Dark Angel (IRE), out of Countess Ferrama (GB)

Malafemmena (IRE) – Divinely (IRE), by Galileo (IRE), out of Red Evie (IRE)

Mangala (USA) – Queen Jo Jo (GB), by Gregorian (IRE), out of River Song (USA)

Maria d'Altoria (FR) – Trueshan (FR), by Planteur (IRE), out of Shao Line (FR)

Mevlana (IRE) – Ubettabelieveit (IRE), by Kodiac (GB), out of Ladylishandra (IRE)

Midnight Shift (IRE) – Ventura Tormenta (IRE), by Acclamation (GB), out of Midnight Oasis (GB)

Mouriyana (IRE) – Volkan Star (IRE), by Sea The Stars (IRE), out of Chicago Dancer (IRE)

My Renee (USA) – Twilight Payment (IRE), by Teofilo (IRE), out of Dream On Buddy (IRE)

Neptune's Bride (USA) – Century Dream (IRE), by Cape Cross (IRE), out of Salacia (IRE)

Noahs Ark (IRE) – Armory (IRE), by Galileo (IRE), out of After (IRE)

Nordic Living (IRE) – Winter Power (IRE), by Bungle Inthejungle (GB), out of Titian Saga (IRE)

Nordicolini (IRE) – Red Verdon (USA), by Lemon Drop Kid (USA), out of Porto Marmay (IRE)

Not Before Time (IRE) – Cairn Gorm (GB), by Bated Breath (GB), out of In Your Time (GB)

Nuryana – Frankly Darling (GB), by Frankel (GB), out of Hidden Hope (GB)

Only Great – True Self (IRE), by Oscar (IRE), out of Good Thought (IRE)

Pickwick Papers (GB) – The Lir Jet (IRE), by Prince of Lir (IRE), out of Paper Dreams (IRE)

Plaintiff (USA) – Gear Up (IRE), by Teofilo (IRE), out of Gearanai (USA)

Platonic (GB) – Magic Wand (IRE), by Galileo (IRE), out of Prudenzia (IRE)

Play Around (IRE) – Breathtaking Look (GB), by Bated Breath (GB), out of Love Your Looks (GB)

Portelet (GB) – Battaash (IRE), by Dark Angel (IRE), out of Anna Law (IRE)

Portmanteau (GB) – Fanny Logan (IRE), by Sea The Stars (IRE), out of Linda Radlett (IRE)

Post Modern (USA) – Lone Eagle (IRE), by Galileo (IRE), out of Modernstone (GB)

Premiere Cuvee – Champers Elysees (IRE), by Elzaam (AUS), out of La Cuvee (GB)

Princess Kris (GB) – Valeria Messalina (IRE), by Holy Roman Emperor (IRE), out of Arty Crafty (USA)

Princess Serena (USA) – Summer Romance (IRE), by Kingman (GB), out of Serena's Storm (IRE)

Princess Speedfit (FR) – Dubai Station (GB), by Brazen Beau (AUS), out of Princess Guest (IRE)

Quiz Show (GB) – Lullaby Moon (GB), by Belardo (IRE), out of Bold Bidder (GB)

Quiza Bere (FR) – Brad The Brief (GB), by Dutch Art (GB), out of Kenzadargent (FR)

Rain Flower (IRE) – Magic Lily (GB), by New Approach (IRE), out of Dancing Rain (IRE)

Raymi Coya (CAN) – Tactical (GB), by Toronado (IRE), out of Make Fast (GB)

Red Evie (IRE) – Battleground (USA), by War Front (USA), out of Found (IRE)

Red Feather (IRE) – Nayef Road (IRE), by Galileo (IRE), out of Rose Bonheur (GB)

Regal Riband (GB) – Regal Reality (GB), by Intello (GER), out of Regal Realm (GB)

Regard (AUS) – Russian Emperor (IRE), by Galileo (IRE), out of Atlantic Jewel (AUS)

Rondinay (FR) – Young Rascal (FR), by Intello (GER), out of
Rock My Soul (IRE)

Roo (GB) – Mohaather (GB), by Showcasing (GB), out of
Roodeye (GB)

Sagamartha (GB) – Epona Plays (IRE), by Australia (GB), out of
New Plays (IRE)

Saganeca (USA) – Mogul (GB), by Galileo (IRE), out of Shastye
(IRE)

Saleela (USA) – Cayenne Pepper (IRE), by Australia (GB), out of
Muwakaba (USA)

Sallanches (USA) – Miss Amulet (IRE), by Sir Prancealot (IRE),
out of Shena's Dream (IRE)

Shadea (NZ) – Zakouski (GB), by Shamardal (USA), out of
O'Giselle (AUS)

Shadow Casting (GB) – Art Power (IRE), by Dark Angel (IRE),
out of Evening Time (IRE)

Shemima (GB) – Cormorant (IRE), by Kingman (GB), out of
Shemya (FR)

Shinkoh Rose (FR) – Elysium (IRE), by Belardo (IRE), out of
Sonning Rose (IRE)

Siamsa (USA) – Mac Swiney (IRE), by New Approach (IRE),
out of Halla Na Saoire (IRE)

Silent Heir (AUS) – Lancaster House (IRE), by Galileo (IRE),
out of Quiet Oasis (IRE)

Sinntara (IRE) – Sinawann (IRE), by Kingman (GB), out of
Simawa (IRE)

Six Nations (USA) – Flying Visit (IRE), by Pride of Dubai (AUS), out of Fionnuar (IRE)

Slink (GB) – Delphi (IRE), by Galileo (IRE), out of Bye Bye Birdie (IRE)

So Admirable (GB) – Limato (IRE), by Tagula (IRE), out of Come April (GB)

Sogha (AUS) – Dubai Warrior (GB), by Dansili (GB), out of Mahbooba (AUS)

South Rock (GB) – Dark Vision (IRE), by Dream Ahead (USA), out of Black Dahlia (GB)

Spectacular Joke (USA) – Enbihaar (IRE), by Redoute's Choice (AUS), out of Chanterelle (FR)

Spectral Star (GB) – Telecaster (GB), by New Approach (IRE), out of Shirocco Star (GB)

Starstone (GB) – Nazeef (GB), by Invincible Spirit (IRE), out of Handassa (GB)

Summer Trysting (USA) – Romanised (IRE), by Holy Roman Emperor (IRE), out of Romantic Venture (IRE)

Superstar Leo (IRE) – One Master (IRE), by Fastnet Rock (AUS), out of Enticing (IRE)

Tanami (GB) – Happy Power (IRE), by Dark Angel (IRE), out of Tamarisk (GER)

Tara Gold (IRE) – Santosha (IRE), by Coulsty (IRE), out of Princess Zoffany (IRE)

Tarakala (IRE) – Tarnawa (IRE), by Shamardal (USA), out of Tarana (IRE)

Tarneem (USA) – A'Ali (IRE), by Society Rock (IRE), out of Motion Lass (GB)

Thamarat (GB) – Santiago (IRE), by Authorized (IRE), out of Wadyhatta (GB)

Theory of Law (GB) – Terebellum (IRE), by Sea The Stars (IRE), out of Marvada (IRE)

Tidal Chorus (GB) – Isabella Giles (IRE), by Belardo (IRE), out of Majestic Dubawi (GB)

Tipsy Topsy (GB) – Believe In Love (IRE), by Make Believe (GB), out of Topka (FR)

Traou Mad (IRE) – Manuela de Vega (IRE), by Lope de Vega (IRE), out of Roscoff (IRE)

Treasure The Lady (IRE) – Love Locket (IRE), by No Nay Never (USA), out of Starlet (IRE)

Trepidation (USA) – New Treasure (IRE), by New Approach (IRE), out of Maoineach (USA)

Trylko (USA) – Spanish Mission (USA), by Noble Mission (GB), out of Limonar (IRE)

Vanity (IRE) – Tiger Moth (IRE), by Galileo (IRE), out of Lesson In Humility (IRE)

Venoge (IRE) – Alkumait (GB), by Showcasing (GB), out of Suelita (GB)

Victoress (USA) – Dawn Patrol (IRE), by Galileo (IRE), out of Gwynn (IRE)

Wannabe (GB) – Lady Wannabe (IRE), by Camelot (GB), out of
Wannabe Better (IRE)

Wansdyke Lass (GB) – Rose of Kildare (IRE), by Make Believe
(GB), out of Cruck Realta (GB)

Welsh Diva (GB) – Baron Samedi (GB), by Harbour Watch
(IRE), out of Dame Shirley (GB)

Whipped Queen (USA) – Lady Bowthorpe (GB), by Nathaniel
(IRE), out of Maglietta Fina (IRE)
Whipped Queen (USA) – Speak In Colours (GB), by
Excelebration (IRE), out of Maglietta Fina (IRE)

Wingspan (USA) – Etonian (IRE), by Olympic Glory (IRE), out
of Naan (IRE)

Wosaita (GB) – Nkosikazi (GB), by Cape Cross (IRE), out of
Whatami (GB)

Zaeema (GB) – Lazuli (IRE), by Dubawi (IRE), out of Floristry
(GB)
Zaeema (GB) – Royal Crusade (GB), by Shamardal (USA), out
of Zibelina (IRE)

Zeiting (IRE) – La Barrosa (IRE), by Lope de Vega (IRE), out
of Bikini Babe (IRE)

Zenda (GB) – Tilsit (USA), by First Defence (USA), out of
Multilingual (GB)

Zigarra (GB) – Aloha Star (IRE), by Starspangledbanner (AUS),
out of Zain Art (IRE)

GROUP 2 & GROUP 3 WINNERS OF 2020
BY THIRD DAM

Abstraction (GB) – Armory (IRE), by Galileo (IRE), out of After (IRE), out of Noahs Ark (IRE)

Aim For The Top (USA) – Minzaal (IRE), by Mehmas (IRE), out of Pardoven (IRE), out of Dancing Prize (IRE)

Al Ishq (FR) – Santiago (IRE), by Authorized (IRE), out of Wadyhatta (GB), out of Thamarat (GB)

Albertine (FR) – Leo de Fury (IRE), by Australia (GB), out of Attire (IRE), out of Asnieres (USA)

Allegretta – Cayenne Pepper (IRE), by Australia (GB), out of Muwakaba (USA), out of Saleela (USA)

Amoura (USA) – Mac Swiney (IRE), by New Approach (IRE), out of Halla Na Saoire (IRE), out of Siamsa (USA)

Anna Edes (FR) – Pablo Escobarr (IRE), by Galileo (IRE), out of Bewitched (IRE), out of Abbatiale (FR)

Aryaf (CAN) – Lullaby Moon (GB), by Belardo (IRE), out of Bold Bidder (GB), out of Quiz Show (GB)

As You Desire Me – Valeria Messalina (IRE), by Holy Roman Emperor (IRE), out of Arty Crafty (USA), out of Princess Kris (GB)

Aspiration (IRE) – Subjectivist (GB), by Teofilo (IRE), out of Reckoning (IRE), out of Great Hope (IRE)

Bahr (GB) – Far Above (IRE), by Farhh (GB), out of Dorraar (IRE), out of Dorrati (USA)

Balenare – Indigo Girl (GB), by Dubawi (IRE), out of Montare (IRE), out of Contare (GB)

Belisonde (FR) – Brad The Brief (GB), by Dutch Art (GB), out of Kenzadargent (FR), out of Quiza Bere (FR)

Belle de Cadix (IRE) – La Barrosa (IRE), by Lope de Vega (IRE), out of Bikini Babe (IRE), out of Zeiting (IRE)

Blue Duster (USA) – Berlin Tango (GB), by Dansili (GB), out of Fantasia (GB), out of Blue Symphony (GB)

Bougainvillea (GER) – Angel Power (GB), by Lope de Vega (IRE), out of Burning Rules (IRE), out of Burning Heights (GER)

Bourbon Girl – Enable (GB), by Nathaniel (IRE), out of Concentric (GB), out of Apogee (GB)

Brigadiers Bird (IRE) – Certain Lad (GB), by Clodovil (IRE), out of Chelsey Jayne (IRE), out of Lady Lahar (GB)

Broad Pennant (USA) – Etonian (IRE), by Olympic Glory (IRE), out of Naan (IRE), out of Wingspan (USA)

Brooklyn's Dance (FR) – Buckhurst (IRE), by Australia (GB), out of Artful (IRE), out of Gold Dodger (USA)

Bubbling Danseuse (USA) – Royal Dornoch (IRE), by Gleneagles (IRE), out of Bridal Dance (IRE), out of Feather Bride (IRE)

Caerlina (IRE) – Antonia de Vega (IRE), by Lope de Vega (IRE), out of Witches Brew (IRE), out of Macheera (IRE)

Cascassi (USA) – Helvic Dream (IRE), by Power (GB), out of Rachevie (IRE), out of Challow Hills (USA)

Chain Fern (USA) – Military Style (USA), by War Front (USA), out of Together Forever (IRE), out of Green Room (USA)

Change My Heart (USA) – Thunderous (IRE), by Night of Thunder (IRE), out of Souviens Toi (GB), out of Diavla (USA)

Charita (IRE) – Barney Roy (GB), by Excelebration (IRE), out of Alina (IRE), out of Cheyenne Star (IRE)

Che Constanza (ARG) – Nando Parrado (GB), by Kodiac (GB), out of Chibola (ARG), out of Choice (ARG)

Cheese Soup (USA) – Supremacy (IRE), by Mehmas (IRE), out of Triggers Broom (IRE), out of Great Joy (IRE)

City Centre (IRE) – Dandalla (IRE), by Dandy Man (IRE), out of Chellalla (GB), out of Cheloca (GB)

Clicquot – Champers Elysees (IRE), by Elzaam (AUS), out of La Cuvee (GB), out of Premiere Cuvee

Cloud Castle (GB) – Thundering Nights (IRE), by Night of Thunder (IRE), out of Kaabari (USA), out of Cape Castle (IRE)

Cockade – Millisle (IRE), by Starspangledbanner (AUS), out of Green Castle (IRE), out of Green Lucia

Concia (NZ) – Zakouski (GB), by Shamardal (USA), out of O'Giselle (AUS), out of Shadea (NZ)

Council Rock – One Master (IRE), by Fastnet Rock (AUS), out of Enticing (IRE), out of Superstar Leo (IRE)

Coup de Genie (USA) – Pista (USA), by American Pharoah (USA), out of Mohini (IRE), out of Denebola (USA)

Dance Partner (USA) – Ubettabelieveit (IRE), by Kodiac (GB), out of Ladylishandra (IRE), out of Mevlana (IRE)

Danzigaway (USA) – Aloha Star (IRE), by Starspangledbanner (AUS), out of Zain Art (IRE), out of Zigarra (GB)

Dayanata – Fanny Logan (IRE), by Sea The Stars (IRE), out of Linda Radlett (IRE), out of Portmanteau (GB)

Desert Frolic (IRE) – Umm Kulthum (IRE), by Kodiac (GB), out of Queen's Code (IRE), out of Dehbanu (IRE)

Diamonaka (FR) – Passion (IRE), by Galileo (IRE), out of Dialafara (FR), out of Diamilina (FR)

Didicoy (USA) – Extra Elusive (GB), by Mastercraftsman (IRE), out of Nessina (USA), out of Didina (GB)

Dispute (USA) – Gear Up (IRE), by Teofilo (IRE), out of Gearanai (USA), out of Plaintiff (USA)

East of The Moon (USA) – Molatham (GB), by Night of Thunder (IRE), out of Cantal (GB), out of Canda (USA)

Eastern Shore – Elarqam (GB), by Frankel (GB), out of Attraction (GB), out of Flirtation (GB)

Eljazzi – Nkosikazi (GB), by Cape Cross (IRE), out of Whatami (GB), out of Wosaita (GB)

Enterprisor – True Self (IRE), by Oscar (IRE), out of Good Thought (IRE), out of Only Great

Eternal Reve (USA) – Saffron Beach (IRE), by New Bay (GB), out of Falling Petals (IRE), out of Infinite Spirit (USA)

Fade (GB) – Wonderful Tonight (FR), by Le Havre (IRE), out of Salvation (GB), out of Birdie (GB)

Fanciful (FR) – Art Power (IRE), by Dark Angel (IRE), out of
Evening Time (IRE), out of Shadow Casting (GB)

Final Pursuit (GB) – Ventura Rebel (GB), by Pastoral Pursuits
(GB), out of Finalize (GB), out of Choisette (GB)

Flanders (IRE) – Crossfirehurricane (USA), by Kitten's Joy
(USA), out of Louvakhova (USA), out of Louvain (IRE)

Galyph (USA) – Nayef Road (IRE), by Galileo (IRE), out of
Rose Bonheur (GB), out of Red Feather (IRE)

Goonda (GB) – Patrick Sarsfield (FR), by Australia (GB), out of
Ultra Appeal (IRE), out of Global World (GER)

Gorgeous Dancer (IRE) – One Voice (IRE), by Poet's Voice
(GB), out of Zaaqya (GB), out of Classical Dancer (GB)

Gossamer (USA) – Spanish Mission (USA), by Noble Mission
(GB), out of Limonar (IRE), out of Trylko (USA)

Gourgandine – Mujbar (GB), by Muhaarar (GB), out of Madany
(IRE), out of Belle de Cadix (IRE)

Grimpola (GER) – Glen Shiel (GB), by Pivotal (GB), out of
Gonfilia (GER), out of Gonfalon (GB)

Haglette – Mogul (GB), by Galileo (IRE), out of Shastye (IRE),
out of Saganeca (USA)

Hail Atlantis (USA) – Lord North (IRE), by Dubawi (IRE), out
of Najoum (USA), out of Divine Dixie (USA)

Heady (GB) – Believe In Love (IRE), by Make Believe (GB), out
of Topka (FR), out of Tipsy Topsy (GB)

High Spirited – Space Blues (IRE), by Dubawi (IRE), out of
Miss Lucifer (FR), out of Devil's Imp (IRE)

Highclere – Know It All (GB), by Lord Kanaloa (JPN), out of
Common Knowledge (GB), out of Highbrow

Hope (IRE) – Tilsit (USA), by First Defence (USA), out of
Multilingual (GB), out of Zenda (GB)

Horatia (IRE) – Alkumait (GB), by Showcasing (GB), out of
Suelita (GB), out of Venoge (IRE)

Hyperspectra (GB) – Telecaster (GB), by New Approach (IRE),
out of Shirocco Star (GB), out of Spectral Star (GB)

Ittisaal – Kameko (USA), by Kitten's Joy (USA), out of Sweeter
Still (IRE), out of Beltisaal (FR)

Kalinka (IRE) – Judicial (IRE), by Iffraaj (GB), out of Marlinka
(GB), out of Baralinka (IRE)

Kasora (IRE) – Love Locket (IRE), by No Nay Never (USA),
out of Starlet (IRE), out of Treasure The Lady (IRE)

Kerali – Bowerman (GB), by Dutch Art (GB), out of Jamboretta
(IRE), out of Jiving (GB)

Khuzba (GB) – Baron Samedi (GB), by Harbour Watch (IRE),
out of Dame Shirley (GB), out of Welsh Diva (GB)

Kiliniski – With Thanks (IRE), by Camacho (GB), out of Thanks
(IRE), out of Kimono (IRE)

Kittiwake (GB) – Al Aasy (IRE), by Sea The Stars (IRE), out of
Kitcara (GB), out of Kitcat (GER)

La Concordia (GER) – Loxley (IRE), by New Approach (IRE),
out of Lady Marian (GER), out of La Felicita (GB)

Lady of The Sea – Benbatl (GB), by Dubawi (IRE), out of
Nahrain (GB), out of Bahr (GB)

Lavinia Fontana (IRE) – Steel Bull (IRE), by Clodovil (IRE), out
of Macarthurs Park (IRE), out of La Tintoretta (IRE)

Lettre de Cachet (USA) – Terebellum (IRE), by Sea The Stars
(IRE), out of Marvada (IRE), out of Theory of Law (GB)

Lidakiya (IRE) – Pyledriver (GB), by Harbour Watch (IRE), out
of La Pyle (FR), out of Lidana (IRE)

Lock's Dream (USA) – A Case of You (IRE), by Hot Streak
(IRE), out of Karjera (IRE), out of Lock's Heath (CAN)

Loralane – Frankly Darling (GB), by Frankel (GB), out of
Hidden Hope (GB), out of Nuryana

Lovealoch (IRE) – Epona Plays (IRE), by Australia (GB), out of
New Plays (IRE), out of Sagamartha (GB)

Lumen Dei (USA) – Wichita (IRE), by No Nay Never (USA),
out of Lumiere Noire (FR), out of Lumiere Rouge (FR)

Lunda (IRE) – New Mandate (IRE), by New Bay (GB), out of
Mishhar (IRE), out of Jakarta (IRE)

Magic Gleam (USA) – Secret Advisor (FR), by Dubawi (IRE),
out of Sub Rose (IRE), out of Amazing Krisken (USA)

Malafemmena (IRE) – Battleground (USA), by War Front
(USA), out of Found (IRE), out of Red Evie (IRE)

Mamoura (IRE) – Volkan Star (IRE), by Sea The Stars (IRE),
out of Chicago Dancer (IRE), out of Mouriyana (IRE)

Marie de Lempire (FR) – Trueshan (FR), by Planteur (IRE), out of Shao Line (FR), out of Marie d'Altoria (FR)

Marple (GB) – Dubai Warrior (GB), by Dansili (GB), out of Mahbooba (AUS), out of Sogha (AUS)

Martinova – Divinely (IRE), by Galileo (IRE), out of Red Evie (IRE), out of Malafemmena (IRE)

Marwell – Minaun (IRE), by Zoffany (IRE), out of Bee Eater (IRE), out of Littlefeather (IRE)

Masskana (IRE) – Delphi (IRE), by Galileo (IRE), out of Bye Bye Birdie (IRE), out of Slink (GB)

Mayenne (USA) – Twilight Payment (IRE), by Teofilo (IRE), out of Dream On Buddy (IRE), out of My Renee (USA)

Meadow Blue (USA) – Queen Jo Jo (GB), by Gregorian (IRE), out of River Song (USA), out of Mangala (USA)

Meringue Pie (USA) – Lady Bowthorpe (GB), by Nathaniel (IRE), out of Maglietta Fina (IRE), out of Whipped Queen (USA)
Meringue Pie (USA) – Speak In Colours (GB), by Excelebration (IRE), out of Maglietta Fina (IRE), out of Whipped Queen (USA)

Millennium Dash (GB) – Dashing Willoughby (GB), by Nathaniel (IRE), out of Miss Dashwood (GB), out of Dash To The Front (GB)

Minifah (USA) – Lemista (IRE), by Raven's Pass (USA), out of Shortmile Lady (IRE), out of Jinsiyah (USA)

Modena (USA) – Lone Eagle (IRE), by Galileo (IRE), out of Modernstone (GB), out of Post Modern (USA)

Mombones – Eagles By Day (IRE), by Sea The Stars (IRE), out of Missunited (IRE), out of Lets Clic Together (IRE)

Mustique Dream (GB) – Star of Emaraaty (IRE), by Pride of Dubai (AUS), out of La Grande Elisa (IRE), out of Looking Back (IRE)

Mysterious Plans (IRE) – Dakota Gold (GB), by Equiano (FR), out of Joyeaux (GB), out of Divine Secret (IRE)

Nanshan (IRE) – Russian Emperor (IRE), by Galileo (IRE), out of Atlantic Jewel (AUS), out of Regard (AUS)

Nashmeel (USA) – Fev Rover (IRE), by Gutaifan (IRE), out of Laurelita (IRE), out of Chervil (GB)

No Joke (USA) – Enbihaar (IRE), by Redoute's Choice (AUS), out of Chanterelle (FR), out of Spectacular Joke (USA)

Noirmant – Battaash (IRE), by Dark Angel (IRE), out of Anna Law (IRE), out of Portelet (GB)

November Snow (USA) – Anthony Van Dyck (IRE), by Galileo (IRE), out of Believe'N'Succeed (AUS), out of Arctic Drift (USA)

Old Domesday Book – Ventura Tormenta (IRE), by Acclamation (GB), out of Midnight Oasis (GB), out of Midnight Shift (IRE)

Olympic Aim (NZ) – Nobel Prize (IRE), by Galileo (IRE), out of Hveger (AUS), out of Circles of Gold (AUS)

Out West (USA) – Chindit (IRE), by Wootton Bassett (GB), out of Always A Dream (GB), out of Always Remembered (IRE)

Papering (IRE) – The Lir Jet (IRE), by Prince of Lir (IRE), out of Paper Dreams (IRE), out of Pickwick Papers (GB)

Park Heiress (IRE) – Lancaster House (IRE), by Galileo (IRE), out of Quiet Oasis (IRE), out of Silent Heir (AUS)

Peckitts Well – Foxtrot Lady (GB), by Foxwedge (AUS), out of Strictly Dancing (IRE), out of Lochangel (GB)

Penny Fan (GB) – Tiger Moth (IRE), by Galileo (IRE), out of Lesson In Humility (IRE), out of Vanity (IRE)

Perfect Sister (USA) – Dubai Station (GB), by Brazen Beau (AUS), out of Princess Guest (IRE), out of Princess Speedfit (FR)

Play Or Pay (USA) – Breathtaking Look (GB), Bated Breath (GB), out of Love Your Looks (GB), out of Play Around (IRE)

Pont-Aven – Manuela de Vega (IRE), by Lope de Vega (IRE), out of Roscoff (IRE), out of Traou Mad (IRE)

Privity (USA) – Laws of Indices (IRE), by Power (GB), out of Sampers (IRE), out of Gujarat (USA)

Propensity – Happy Power (IRE), by Dark Angel (IRE), out of Tamarisk (GER), out of Tanami (GB)
Propensity – Lady Wannabe (IRE), by Camelot (GB), out of Wannabe Better (IRE), out of Wannabe (GB)

Puce (GB) – Magic Wand (IRE), by Galileo (IRE), out of Prudenzia (IRE), out of Platonic (GB)

Queen's View (FR) – One Ruler (IRE), by Dubawi (IRE), out of Fintry (IRE), out of Campsie Fells (UAE)

Rafha – Mishriff (IRE), by Make Believe (GB), out of Contradict (GB), out of Acts of Grace (USA)

Rahayeb (GB) – Hukum (IRE), by Sea The Stars (IRE), out of Aghareed (USA), out of Lahudood (GB)

Regal Rose (GB) – Regal Reality (GB), by Intello (GER), out of Regal Realm (GB), out of Regal Riband (GB)

Ridge Pool (IRE) – Ghaiyyath (IRE), by Dubawi (IRE), out of Nightime (IRE), out of Caumshinaun (IRE)

Rimosa's Pet – Master of The Seas (IRE), by Dubawi (IRE), out of Firth of Lorne (IRE), out of Kerrera

Rise And Fall – Glorious Journey (GB), by Dubawi (IRE), out of Fallen For You (GB), out of Fallen Star (GB)

Robinia (USA) – Pretty Gorgeous (FR), by Lawman (FR), out of Lady Gorgeous (GB), out of Cayman Sunset (IRE)

Rose of Jericho (USA) – Magic Lily (GB), by New Approach (IRE), out of Dancing Rain (IRE), out of Rain Flower (IRE)

Royal Statute – Dawn Patrol (IRE), by Galileo (IRE), out of Gwynn (IRE), out of Victoress (USA)

Running Glimpse (IRE) – Oxted (GB), by Mayson (GB), out of Charlotte Rosina (GB), out of Intriguing Glimpse (GB)

Sally St Clair – Safe Voyage (IRE), by Fast Company (IRE), out of Shishangaan (IRE), out of Irish Flower (IRE)

Sandpiper's Dream (USA) – Elysium (IRE), by Belardo (IRE), out of Sonning Rose (IRE), out of Shinkoh Rose (FR)

Saviour (USA) – Poetic Flare (IRE), by Dawn Approach (IRE), out of Maria Lee (IRE), out of Elida (IRE)

Seasonal Pickup (USA) – Romanised (IRE), by Holy Roman Emperor (IRE), out of Romantic Venture (IRE), out of Summer Trysting (USA)

Serena's Sister (USA) – Summer Romance (IRE), by Kingman (GB), out of Serena's Storm (IRE), out of Princess Serena (USA)

Shadywood – Top Rank (IRE), by Dark Angel (IRE), out of Countess Ferrama (GB), out of Madame Dubois

Shall We Run – Mohaather (GB), by Showcasing (GB), out of Roodeye (GB), out of Roo (GB)

Shemaka (IRE) – Cormorant (IRE), by Kingman (GB), out of Shemya (FR), out of Shemima (GB)

Shouk (GB) – Aspetar (FR), by Al Kazeem (GB), out of Bella Qatara (IRE), out of Alexandrova (IRE)

Sidama (FR) – Sinawann (IRE), by Kingman (GB), out of Simawa (IRE), out of Sinntara (IRE)

Silankka (GB) – Rose of Kildare (IRE), by Make Believe (GB), out of Cruck Realta (GB), out of Wansdyke Lass (GB)

Silca-Cisa (GB) – Happy Romance (IRE), by Dandy Man (IRE), out of Rugged Up (IRE), out of For Evva Silca (GB)

Silk Braid (USA) – Maamora (IRE), by Dubawi (IRE), out of Zoowraa (GB), out of Beraysim (GB)

Six Crowns (USA) – Flying Visit (IRE), by Pride of Dubai (AUS), out of Fionnuar (IRE), out of Six Nations (USA)

Smile Awhile (USA) – Mighty Gurkha (IRE), by Sepoy (AUS), out of Royal Debt (GB), out of Caldy Dancer (IRE)

Soha (USA) – Santosha (IRE), by Coulsty (IRE), out of Princess
    Zoffany (IRE), out of Tara Gold (IRE)

Something Mon (USA) – Tactical (GB), by Toronado (IRE), out
    of Make Fast (GB), out of Raymi Coya (CAN)

Sonic Lady (USA) – High Definition (IRE), by Galileo (IRE),
    out of Palace (IRE), out of Lady Icarus (GB)

South Shore – Dark Vision (IRE), by Dream Ahead (USA), out
    of Black Dahlia (GB), out of South Rock (GB)
South Shore – Isabella Giles (IRE), by Belardo (IRE), out of
    Majestic Dubawi (IRE), out of Tidal Chorus (GB)

Specificity (USA) – Nickajack Cave (IRE), by Kendargent (FR),
    out of Could You Be Loved (IRE), out of Light My Way
    (IRE)

Spout House (IRE) – Campanelle (IRE), by Kodiac (GB), out of
    Janina (GB), out of Lady Dominatrix (IRE)

Star (GB) – Nazeef (GB), by Invincible Spirit (IRE), out of
    Handassa (GB), out of Starstone (GB)

Star Profile (IRE) – Mother Earth (IRE), by Zoffany (IRE), out
    of Many Colours (GB), out of First of Many (GB)

Stella Madrid (USA) – Euchen Glen (GB), by Authorized (IRE),
    out of Jabbara (IRE), out of Isle de France (USA)

Stresa – Miss Amulet (IRE), by Sir Prancealot (IRE), out of
    Shena's Dream (IRE), out of Sallanches (USA)

Sumoto (GB) – Limato (IRE), by Tagula (IRE), out of Come
    April (GB), out of So Admirable (GB)

Sweet Simone (FR) – Snow (IRE), by Galileo (IRE), out of
    Chelsea Rose (IRE), out of Cinnamon Rose (USA)

Tadkiyra (IRE) – Cadillac (IRE), by Lope de Vega (IRE), out of
 Seas of Wells (IRE), out of Kiyra Wells (IRE)

Talented (GB) – Lazuli (IRE), by Dubawi (IRE), out of Floristry
 (GB), out of Zaeema (GB)
Talented (GB) – Royal Crusade (GB), by Shamardal (USA), out
 of Zibelina (IRE), out of Zaeema (GB)

Tarakana (USA) – Tarnawa (IRE), by Shamardal (USA), out of
 Tarana (IRE), out of Tarakala (IRE)

Thorner Lane – Dream of Dreams (IRE), by Dream Ahead
 (USA), out of Vasilia (GB), out of Kangra Valley (GB)

Time Charter – Cairn Gorm (GB), by Bated Breath (GB), out of
 In Your Time (GB), out of Not Before Time (IRE)

To Die For (USA) – Winter Power (IRE), by Bungle Inthejungle
 (GB), out of Titian Saga (IRE), out of Nordic Living (IRE)

Topline (GER) – Young Rascal (FR), by Intello (GER), out of
 Rock My Soul (IRE), out of Rondinay (FR)

Troubling (USA) – New Treasure (IRE), by New Approach
 (IRE), out of Maoineach (USA), out of Trepidation (USA)

Tuyenu – Red Verdon (USA), by Lemon Drop Kid (USA), out
 of Porto Marmay (IRE), out of Nordicolini (IRE)

Valley of Song (GB) – Current Option (IRE), by Camelot (GB),
 out of Coppertop (IRE), out of Fresh Mint (IRE)

Wanton – Tabdeed (GB), by Havana Gold (IRE), out of Puzzled
 (IRE), out of Classic Park (GB)

Wedding of The Sea (USA) – Century Dream (IRE), by Cape Cross (IRE), out of Salacia (IRE), out of Neptune's Bride (USA)

Wild Pavane (GB) – Dame Malliot (GB), by Champs Elysees (GB), out of Stars In Your Eyes (GB), out of Apache Star (GB)

Willowy Mood (USA) – A'Ali (IRE), by Society Rock (IRE), out of Motion Lass (GB), out of Tarneem (USA)

Wrap It Up – Shale (IRE), by Galileo (IRE), out of Homecoming Queen (IRE), out of Lagrion (USA)

GROUP 2 & GROUP 3 WINNERS OF 2020
BY BREEDER

Aherne, Monica – Romanised (IRE)

Airlie Stud – Valeria Messalina (IRE)

Al Homaizi, Saleh & Imad Al Sagar – Extra Elusive (GB)

Alkas, Emir – Etonian (IRE)

Ballylinch Stud – Isabella Giles (IRE)
Ballylinch Stud – Lone Eagle (IRE)

Ballyphilip Stud – Battaash (IRE)

Barronstown Stud – Lancaster House (IRE)
Barronstown Stud – Royal Dornoch (IRE)
Barronstown Stud – Snow (IRE)

Bearstone Stud – Lullaby Moon (GB)
Bearstone Stud – Queen Jo Jo (GB)

Beirne (jnr), Patrick – Aloha Star (IRE)

Bin Khalifa Al Thani, H H Sheikh Mohammed – Aspetar (FR)

Blake, Kevin – Ventura Tormenta (IRE)

Blot, Didier – Trueshan (FR)

Bolger, J S – Flying Visit (IRE)
Bolger, J S – Gear Up (IRE)
Bolger, J S – Mac Swiney (IRE)
Bolger, J S – New Treasure (IRE)
Bolger, J S – Poetic Flare (IRE)
Bolger, J S – Twilight Payment (IRE)

Bowen, Karl – Champers Elysees (IRE)

Boylan, Donal – The Lir Jet (IRE)

Brown, D J & Mrs – Nkosikazi (GB)

Calumet Farm – Kameko (USA)

Cantillon, Don – True Self (IRE)

Chasemore Farm – Brad The Brief (GB)

Cheveley Park Stud Ltd – Bowerman (GB)
Cheveley Park Stud Ltd – Molatham (GB)
Cheveley Park Stud Ltd – Regal Reality (GB)

China Horse Club International Ltd – Patrick Sarsfield (FR)
China Horse Club International Ltd – Saffron Beach (IRE)

Churchtown House Stud – Lady Wannabe (IRE)

Coolmore – Armory (IRE)
Coolmore – Delphi (IRE)
Coolmore – Divinely (IRE)
Coolmore – Nobel Prize (IRE)
Coolmore – Shale (IRE)
Coolmore – Tiger Moth (IRE)

Coolmore, Lauri Macri & Partners – Russian Emperor (IRE)

Crossfields Bloodstock Ltd – Ventura Rebel (GB)

Darley – Benbatl (GB)
Darley – Glen Shiel (GB)

Denford Stud Ltd – Buckhurst (IRE)

Drumlin Bloodstock – Lemista (IRE)

Ecurie Des Monceaux & Skymarc Farm Inc – Magic Wand
    (IRE)

Ecurie Haras du Cadran, E Ciampi, SAS I.E.I., Ecurie La Boetie
    – Pretty Gorgeous (FR)

Ecurie Peregrine SAS – Young Rascal (FR)

Ecurie Taos – Wonderful Tonight (FR)

Elite Racing Club – Judicial (IRE)

Eliza Park International Pty Ltd – Barney Roy (GB)

Ellis Stud and Bellow Hill Stud – Breathtaking Look (GB)

Ervine, W Maxwell – Wichita (IRE)

Essafinaat Ltd – Dubai Warrior (GB)

Fermoir Ltd – Antonia de Vega (IRE)

Floors Farming – Elarqam (GB)

Forenaghts Stud & S Mencoff – Volkan Star (IRE)

Forni, Renzo – Epona Plays (IRE)

G H S Bloodstock & J C Bloodstock – Cayenne Pepper (IRE)

Glen Hill Farm & Scott C Heider – Crossfirehurricane (USA)

Godolphin – Fanny Logan (IRE)
Godolphin – Lazuli (IRE)
Godolphin – Lord North (IRE)
Godolphin – Loxley (IRE)
Godolphin – Maamora (IRE)

Godolphin – Magic Lily (GB)
Godolphin – Master of The Seas (IRE)
Godolphin – One Ruler (IRE)
Godolphin – Royal Crusade (GB)
Godolphin – Space Blues (IRE)
Godolphin – Zakouski (GB)

Grangecon Holdings Ltd – Current Option (IRE)

Grenane House Stud – Mother Earth (IRE)

Hall Of Fame Stud – Dubai Station (GB)

Haras Du Mezeray – Enbihaar (IRE)

Hartery, N – Laws of Indices (IRE)

Hascombe & Valiant Studs – Dame Malliot (GB)
Hascombe & Valiant Stud – Frankly Darling (GB)

His Highness The Aga Khan's Studs S C – Sinawann (IRE)
His Highness The Aga Khan's Studs S C – Tarnawa (IRE)

Homecroft Wealth Racing – Oxted (GB)

Hunscote Stud – Cairn Gorm (GB)

Hutch, Vanessa – Eagles By Day (IRE)

J C Bloodstock & R Mahon – Chindit (IRE)

Johnson Houghton, Mrs R F – Mohaather (GB)

Johnstone, W M – Euchen Glen (GB)

Juddmonte Farms Ltd – Enable (GB)
Juddmonte Farms Inc – Tilsit (USA)

Kangyu International Racing – Supremacy (IRE)

Karis Bloodstock Ltd & Rathbarry Stud – Star of Emaraaty (IRE)

Kenilworth House Stud – Believe In Love (IRE)

Knocktoran Stud – La Barrosa (IRE)

Knox & Wells Ltd & R Devlin – Pyledriver (GB)

Lael Stables – One Master (IRE)

Lenihan, J – One Voice (IRE)

Liberty Road Stables – Red Verdon (USA)

Limestone and Tara Studs – A Case of You (IRE)

Littleton Stud – Foxtrot Lady (GB)

Loder, Sir E J – Minaun (IRE)

Lynch Bages Ltd – Dawn Patrol (IRE)
Lynch Bages Ltd – Pista (USA)
Lynch Bages Ltd – Santiago (IRE)

Lynch Bages Ltd & Camas Park Stud – Passion (IRE)

Macarthurs Park Partnership – Steel Bull (IRE)

Malik, Mohammed Abdul – Far Above (IRE)

Manister House Stud – Fev Rover (IRE)

Manjri Farm – Thundering Nights (IRE)

Mascalls Stud – Subjectivist (GB)

Meon Valley Stud – Dashing Willoughby (GB)
Meon Valley Stud – Telecaster (GB)

Merriebelle Irish Farm Ltd – Manuela de Vega (IRE)

Mishhar Syndicate – New Mandate (IRE)

Murray, Paddy – Santosha (IRE)

Nawara Stud Ltd – Mishriff (IRE)

Newlands House Stud – Winter Power (IRE)

Newsells Park Stud – Mogul (GB)

Normandie Stud Ltd – Glorious Journey (GB)

Norton, Robert – Dandalla (IRE)

O'Dwyer, Tony & Keith O'Brien – Helvic Dream (IRE)

O'Flynn, Alan – Terebellum (IRE)

Orpendale, Chelston & Wynatt – Anthony Van Dyck (IRE)
Orpendale, Chelston & Wynatt – Battleground (USA)
Orpendale, Chelston & Wynatt – Military Style (USA)

Owenstown Bloodstock Ltd – Art Power (IRE)

Phelan, Seamus – Limato (IRE)

Prostock Ltd – Dream of Dreams (IRE)

Qatar Bloodstock Ltd – Know It All (GB)

Queen, The – Tactical (GB)

Rabbah Bloodstock Ltd – Century Dream (IRE)
Rabbah Bloodstock Ltd – Mighty Gurkha (IRE)
Rabbah Bloodstock Ltd – Thunderous (IRE)

Red House Stud & Ketton Ashwell Ltd – Tabdeed (GB)

Redgate Bloodstock & Peter Bottowley Bloodstock – Dakota
    Gold (GB)

Redpender Stud Ltd – Happy Romance (IRE)

Ringfort Stud – Minzaal (IRE)
Ringfort Stud – Miss Amulet (IRE)
Ringfort Stud – Ubettabelieveit (IRE)

Roundhill Stud – Summer Romance (IRE)

S F Bloodstock LLC – Dark Vision (IRE)

Sangster, B V – Leo de Fury (IRE)
Sangster, B V – Nayef Road (IRE)

Scarborough, R & Carradale – Pablo Escobarr (IRE)

SCEA Haras de Saint Pair – Secret Advisor (FR)

SCEA Team Hogdala France – Nickajack Cave (IRE)

Schneider, Adolf – Safe Voyage (IRE)

Scuderia Archi Romani – Lady Bowthorpe (GB)
Scuderia Archi Romani – Speak In Colours (GB)

Shadwell Estate Company Ltd – Hukum (IRE)
Shadwell Estate Company Ltd – Mujbar (GB)
Shadwell Estate Company Ltd – Nazeef (GB)

Springbank Way Stud – Ghaiyyath (IRE)

Springbank Way Stud – Love Locket (IRE)

St Elias Stables LLC – Spanish Mission (USA)

Stonethorn Stud Farms Ltd – Millisle (IRE)

Strawbridge, George – Berlin Tango (GB)
Strawbridge, George – Indigo Girl (GB)

Sunderland Holdings Inc – Al Aasy (IRE)
Sunderland Holdings Inc – Cadillac (IRE)

Tally-Ho Stud – A'Ali (IRE)
Tally-Ho Stud – Campanelle (IRE)
Tally-Ho Stud – Umm Kulthum (IRE)

Thompson, Mrs E – With Thanks (IRE)

Tullpark Ltd – Elysium (IRE)

Usk Valley Stud – Baron Samedi (GB)

Walters, Barry – Certain Lad (GB)

Wansdyke Farms Ltd – Rose of Kildare (IRE)

Wates, Michael E – Cormorant (IRE)

Whisperview Trading Ltd – High Definition (IRE)

Whitsbury Manor Stud – Alkumait (GB)

Wicklow Bloodstock – Top Rank (IRE)

Wigan. Mrs Anita – Angel Power (GB)
Wigan, Mrs Anita – Nando Parrado (GB)

Yeomanstown Stud – Happy Power (IRE)

GROUP 2 & GROUP 3 WINNERS OF 2020
BY OWNER

Abdullah, Khalid – Enable (GB)
Abdullah, Khalid – Tilsit (USA)

H H Aga Khan – Sinawann (IRE)
H H Aga Khan – Tarnawa (IRE)

Ahmad Alshaikh & Co – Dubai Station (GB)

Al Khalifa, Shaikh Duaij – A'Ali (IRE)

Al Maktoum, Sheikh Ahmed – Maamora (IRE)

Al Maktoum, Hamdan – Al Aasy (IRE)
Al Maktoum, Hamdan – Alkumait (GB)
Al Maktoum, Hamdan – Battaash (IRE)
Al Maktoum, Hamdan – Elarqam (GB)
Al Maktoum, Hamdan – Enbihaar (IRE)
Al Maktoum, Hamdan – Hukum (IRE)
Al Maktoum, Hamdan – Minzaal (IRE)
Al Maktoum, Hamdan – Mohaather (GB)
Al Maktoum, Hamdan – Molatham (GB)
Al Maktoum, Hamdan – Mujbar (GB)
Al Maktoum, Hamdan – Nazeef (GB)
Al Maktoum, Hamdan – Tabdeed (GB)

Al Maktoum, Sheikh Rashid Dalmook – Far Above (IRE)
Al Maktoum, Sheikh Rashid Dalmook – With Thanks (IRE)

Al Sagar, Imad – Extra Elusive (GB)

Alpha Racing 2020 – Cadillac (IRE)

Amo Racing Ltd & Co – Lullaby Moon (GB)

Arculli, The Hon R J – Red Verdon (USA)

Ballylinch Stud & Aquis Farm – Lone Eagle (IRE)

Banks, Ms E L – Lady Bowthorpe (GB)

Barbury Lions 5 – Trueshan (FR)

Belhabb, Abdulla – Century Dream (IRE)

Bernick, Craig – One Voice (IRE)

Bin Khalifa Al Maktoum, Sheikh Mohammed – Dubai Warrior (GB)

Bin Khalifa Al Thani, H H Sheikh Mohammed – Aspetar (FR)

Bin Mohammed Al Qassimi, Saeed – Umm Kulthum (IRE)

Bolger, Mrs J S – Flying Visit (IRE)
Bolger, Mrs J S – Mac Swiney (IRE)
Bolger, Mrs J S – New Treasure (IRE)
Bolger, Mrs J S – Poetic Flare (IRE)

Brant, Peter M – Lemista (IRE)

Castle Down Racing – Telecaster (GB)

Chan, Marc – New Mandate (IRE)
Chan, Marc – Valeria Messalina (IRE)

Chasemore Farm – Brad The Brief (GB)

Cheveley Park Stud – Regal Reality (GB)

Clipper Logistics – Eagles By Day (IRE)

Coolmore, Moffitt & Meduri Syndicate – Nobel Prize (IRE)

Dooley Thoroughbreds, Shamrock Thoroughbreds & B T
    O'Sullivan – Current Option (IRE)

Elite Racing Club – Judicial (IRE)

Faisal, Prince A A – Mishriff (IRE)

Forni, Renzo – Epona Plays (IRE)

Gaffney, Mrs T & Mrs Barbara Murphy – Lady Wannabe (IRE)

Glenn, Sir Owen & Mick and Janice Mariscotti – Dashing
    Willoughby (GB)

Goddard, J – Supremacy (IRE)

Godolphin – Barney Roy (GB)
Godolphin – Benbatl (GB)
Godolphin – Dark Vision (IRE)
Godolphin – Ghaiyyath (IRE)
Godolphin – La Barrosa (IRE)
Godolphin – Lazuli (IRE)
Godolphin – Loxley (IRE)
Godolphin – Magic Lily (GB)
Godolphin – Master of The Seas (IRE)
Godolphin – One Ruler (IRE)
Godolphin – Royal Crusade (GB)
Godolphin – Secret Advisor (FR)
Godolphin – Space Blues (IRE)
Godolphin – Summer Romance (IRE)
Godolphin – Terebellum (IRE)
Godolphin – Volkan Star (IRE)
Godolphin – Zakouski (GB)

Graham, Doug, Ian Davison & Alan Drysdale – Dakota Gold
    (GB)

H H Sheikh Zayed bin Mohammed Racing – Lord North (IRE)

Hambleton Racing XXXVI & Partner – Glen Shiel (GB)

Harmon, Ross – Safe Voyage (IRE)

Heider, Scott C – Crossfirehurricane (USA)
Heider, Scott C – Pista (USA)

Hendron, Mrs Caroline & Mrs M Cahill – Helvic Dream (IRE)

HH Sheikha Al Jalila Racing – Fanny Logan (IRE)
HH Sheikha Al Jalila Racing – Glorious Journey (GB)

Highclere Thoroughbred Racing - George Stubbs – Thunderous
    (IRE)

Hirst, C R – Certain Lad (GB)

Hoare, Olivia – Nkosikazi (GB)

Holmes, Miss C R – Laws of Indices (IRE)

Hunscote Stud Ltd and Partner – Cairn Gorm (GB)

Jacobs, Paul G – Limato (IRE)

Johnstone, W M – Euchen Glen (GB)

Kelly, Mrs S – Cayenne Pepper (IRE)

King Power Racing Co Ltd – Angel Power (GB)
King Power Racing Co Ltd – Art Power (IRE)
King Power Racing Co Ltd – Happy Power (IRE)
King Power Racing Co Ltd – Winter Power (IRE)

La Pyle Partnership – Pyledriver (GB)

Lael Stable – One Master (IRE)

LECH Racing Ltd – Baron Samedi (GB)

LNJ Foxwoods – Aloha Star (IRE)

Lootah, Hussain Alabbas – Pablo Escobarr (IRE)

Lyons, Ms S – Santosha (IRE)

Macri, Laurie, Mrs J Magnier, et al – Russian Emperor (IRE)

Maeda, Koji – Believe In Love (IRE)

Magnier, Mrs John, Michael Tabor & Derrick Smith – Anthony Van Dyck (IRE)
Magnier, Mrs John, Michael Tabor & Derrick Smith – Armory (IRE)
Magnier, Mrs John, Michael Tabor & Derrick Smith – Divinely (IRE)
Magnier, Mrs John, Michael Tabor & Derrick Smith – Love Locket (IRE)
Magnier, Mrs John, Michael Tabor & Derrick Smith – Military Style (USA)
Magnier, Mrs John, Michael Tabor & Derrick Smith – Passion (IRE)
Magnier, Mrs John, Michael Tabor & Derrick Smith – Tiger Moth (IRE)

Manana, Saeed – Top Rank (IRE)

Martin Webb Racing – Ubettabelieveit (IRE)

McCartan, Marie – Nando Parrado (GB)

McCarthy, Stephen E – Minaun (IRE)

McConnell, John C – A Case of You (IRE)

McMurray Family, The – Happy Romance (IRE)

Menahi, Abdullah – Ventura Rebel (GB)

Middleham Park Racing IV – Ventura Tormenta (IRE)

Mistry, Shapoor – Thundering Nights (IRE)

Ng, Robert – Romanised (IRE)

Nick Bradley Racing 28 & E Burke – Dandalla (IRE)

Nick Bradley Racing 43 & Partner – Fev Rover (IRE)

Obaida, Mohamed – Nayef Road (IRE)

Oppenheimer, A E – Dame Malliot (GB)
Oppenheimer, A E – Frankly Darling (GB)

Oti Racing Syndicate – Young Rascal (FR)

Oxley, John C – Pretty Gorgeous (FR)

Parry, J W – Breathtaking Look (GB)

Peel, Roger & Clipper Logistics – Queen Jo Jo (GB)

Pescod, Michael – Chindit (IRE)

Piper, S, T Hirschfeld, D Fish & J Collins – Oxted (GB)

Qatar Racing Ltd – Kameko (USA)
Qatar Racing Ltd – Know It All (GB)
Qatar Racing Ltd – Rose of Kildare (IRE)
Qatar Racing Ltd – The Lir Jet (IRE)

Queen, The – Tactical (GB)

Rashid, Mohammed – Mighty Gurkha (IRE)

Regalado-Gonzalez, Mrs C C – Patrick Sarsfield (FR)
Regalado-Gonzalez, Mrs C C – Speak In Colours (GB)
Regalado-Gonzalez, Mrs C C – Steel Bull (IRE)

Rooney, Paul & Clare – Isabella Giles (IRE)

Sangster, Mrs B V, J Wigan & O Sangster – Saffron Beach (IRE)

Smith, Derrick, Mrs John Magnier & Michael Tabor – Delphi
    (IRE)
Smith, Derrick, Mrs John Magnier & Michael Tabor – Mother
    Earth (IRE)
Smith, Derrick, Mrs John Magnier & Michael Tabor – Shale
    (IRE)
Smith, Derrick, Mrs John Magnier & Michael Tabor – Wichita
    (IRE)

Smith, Derrick, Mrs John Magnier, Michael Tabor & Mrs A M
    O'Brien – High Definition (IRE)

Smith, J C – Foxtrot Lady (GB)

Spratt, David, Sean Jones & Mrs Lynne Lyons – Nickajack Cave
    (IRE)

Stonestreet Stables LLC – Campanelle (IRE)

Stonethorn Stud Farms Ltd – Millisle (IRE)

Strawbridge, George – Berlin Tango (GB)
Strawbridge, George – Indigo Girl (GB)

Suhail, Saeed – Dream of Dreams (IRE)

Tabor, Doreen – Miss Amulet (IRE)

Tabor, Michael, Derrick Smith & Mrs John Magnier –
    Battleground (USA)
Tabor, Michael, Derrick Smith & Mrs John Magnier –
    Cormorant (IRE)
Tabor, Michael, Derrick Smith & Mrs John Magnier – Dawn
    Patrol (IRE)
Tabor, Michael, Derrick Smith & Mrs John Magnier – Lancaster
    House (IRE)
Tabor, Michael, Derrick Smith & Mrs John Magnier – Magic
    Wand (IRE)
Tabor, Michael, Derrick Smith & Mrs John Magnier – Mogul
    (GB)
Tabor, Michael, Derrick Smith & Mrs John Magnier – Royal
    Dornoch (IRE)
Tabor, Michael, Derrick Smith & Mrs John Magnier – Santiago
    (IRE)
Tabor, Michael, Derrick Smith & Mrs John Magnier – Snow
    (IRE)

Team Valor LLC & Gary Barber – Spanish Mission (USA)

Teme Valley 2 – Gear Up (IRE)

The London Racing Partnership – Elysium (IRE)

Three Mile House & OTI Partnership – True Self (IRE)

Total Recall Racing Club – Bowerman (GB)

Walker, Dr J – Subjectivist (GB)

Waverley Racing – Antonia de Vega (IRE)
Waverley Racing – Manuela de Vega (IRE)

Williams, Lloyd J – Buckhurst (IRE)
Williams, Lloyd J – Twilight Payment (IRE)

Wood, Mrs J – Etonian (IRE)

Wright, Christopher – Wonderful Tonight (FR)

Yoshida, Teruya – Champers Elysees (IRE)
Yoshida, Teruya – Star of Emaraaty (IRE)

Yuesheng, Zhang – Leo de Fury (IRE)

GROUP 2 & GROUP 3 WINNERS OF 2020
BY TRAINER

Ireland
Bolger, Jim – Flying Visit (IRE)
Bolger, Jim – Mac Swiney (IRE)
Bolger, Jim – New Treasure (IRE)
Bolger, Jim – Poetic Flare (IRE)

Condon, Ken – Laws of Indices (IRE)
Condon, Ken – Miss Amulet (IRE)
Condon, Ken – Romanised (IRE)

de Bromhead, Henry – Minaun (IRE)

Halford, Michael – Sinawann (IRE)

Harrington, Jessica – Cadillac (IRE)
Harrington, Jessica – Cayenne Pepper (IRE)
Harrington, Jessica – Leo de Fury (IRE)
Harrington, Jessica – Millisle (IRE)
Harrington, Jessica – One Voice (IRE)
Harrington, Jessica – Valeria Messalina (IRE)

Lyons, Ger – Lemista (IRE)
Lyons, Ger – Nickajack Cave (IRE)

McConnell, John C – A Case of You (IRE)

McCreery, Willie – Epona Plays (IRE)

McGuinness, Adrian (Ado) – Bowerman (GB)
McGuinness, Adrian (Ado) – Current Option (IRE)

Meade, Noel – Elysium (IRE)
Meade, Noel – Helvic Dream (IRE)

Mullins, Willie – True Self (IRE)

Murtagh, Johnny – Champers Elysees (IRE)
Murtagh, Johnny – Know It All (GB)

O'Brien, Aidan – Anthony Van Dyck (IRE)
O'Brien, Aidan – Armoury (IRE)
O'Brien, Aidan – Battleground (USA)
O'Brien, Aidan – Cormorant (IRE)
O'Brien, Aidan – Dawn Patrol (IRE)
O'Brien, Aidan – Delphi (IRE)
O'Brien, Aidan – Divinely (IRE)
O'Brien, Aidan – High Definition (IRE)
O'Brien, Aidan – Lancaster House (IRE)
O'Brien, Aidan – Love Locket (IRE)
O'Brien, Aidan – Magic Wand (IRE)
O'Brien, Aidan – Military Style (USA)
O'Brien, Aidan – Mogul (GB)
O'Brien, Aidan – Mother Earth (IRE)
O'Brien, Aidan – Nobel Prize (IRE)
O'Brien, Aidan – Passion (IRE)
O'Brien, Aidan – Royal Dornoch (IRE)
O'Brien, Aidan – Russian Emperor (IRE)
O'Brien, Aidan – Santiago (IRE)
O'Brien, Aidan – Snow (IRE)
O'Brien, Aidan – Tiger Moth (IRE)
O'Brien, Aidan – Wichita (IRE)

O'Brien, Donnacha – Shale (IRE)

O'Brien, Joseph – Baron Samedi (GB)
O'Brien, Joseph – Buckhurst (IRE)
O'Brien, Joseph – Crossfirehurricane (USA)
O'Brien, Joseph – Pretty Gorgeous (FR)
O'Brien, Joseph – Patrick Sarsfield (FR)
O'Brien, Joseph – Pista (USA)
O'Brien, Joseph – Speak In Colours (GB)
O'Brien, Joseph – Thundering Nights (IRE)
O'Brien, Joseph – Twilight Payment (IRE)

O'Callaghan, Michael – Steel Bull (IRE)

Stack, James (Fozzy) – Aloha Star (IRE)
Stack, James (Fozzy) – Lady Wannabe (IRE)

Weld, Dermot – Tarnawa (IRE)

Great Britain
Appleby, Charlie – Barney Roy (GB)
Appleby, Charlie – Ghaiyyath (IRE)
Appleby, Charlie – Glorious Journey (GB)
Appleby, Charlie – La Barrosa (IRE)
Appleby, Charlie – Lazuli (IRE)
Appleby, Charlie – Loxley (IRE)
Appleby, Charlie – Magic Lily (GB)
Appleby, Charlie – Master of The Seas (IRE)
Appleby, Charlie – One Ruler (IRE)
Appleby, Charlie – Royal Crusade (GB)
Appleby, Charlie – Secret Advisor (FR)
Appleby, Charlie – Space Blues (IRE)
Appleby, Charlie – Summer Romance (IRE)
Appleby, Charlie – Volkan Star (IRE)
Appleby, Charlie – Zakouski (GB)

Balding, Andrew – Berlin Tango (GB)
Balding, Andrew – Dashing Willoughby (GB)
Balding, Andrew – Foxtrot Lady (GB)
Balding, Andrew – Happy Power (IRE)
Balding, Andrew – Kameko (USA)
Balding, Andrew – Spanish Mission (USA)
Balding, Andrew – Tactical (GB)

Beckett, Ralph – Antonia de Vega (IRE)
Beckett, Ralph – Lullaby Moon (GB)
Beckett, Ralph – Manuela de Vega (IRE)
Beckett, Ralph – New Mandate (IRE)

Bell, Michael – The Lir Jet (IRE)

Bin Suroor, Saeed – Benbatl (GB)

Burke, Karl – Dandalla (IRE)
Burke, Karl – Dubai Station (GB)

Burrows, Owen – Hukum (IRE)
Burrows, Owen – Minzaal (IRE)
Burrows, Owen – Tabdeed (GB)

Camacho, Julie – Judicial (IRE)

Candy, Henry – Limato (IRE)

Channon, Mick – Cairn Gorm (GB)
Channon, Mick – Certain Lad (GB)

Chapple-Hyam, Jane – Saffron Beach (IRE)

Charlton, Roger – Aspetar (FR)
Charlton, Roger – Extra Elusive (GB)

Cox, Clive – Isabella Giles (IRE)
Cox, Clive – Nando Parrado (GB)
Cox, Clive – Supremacy (IRE)

Crisford, Simon & Ed – A'Ali (IRE)
Crisford, Simon & Ed – Century Dream (IRE)
Crisford, Simon & Ed – Maamora (IRE)

Dascombe, Tom – Brad The Brief (GB)

Dods, Michael – Dakota Gold (GB)

Dunlop, Ed – Red Verdon (USA)

Easterby, Tim – Art Power (IRE)

Easterby, Tim – Winter Power (IRE)

Fahey, Richard – Fev Rover (IRE)
Fahey, Richard – Umm Kulthum (IRE)
Fahey, Richard – Ventura Rebel (GB)

Goldie, Jim – Euchen Glen (GB)

Gosden, John – Dubai Warrior (GB)
Gosden, John – Enable (GB)
Gosden, John – Enbihaar (IRE)
Gosden, John – Fanny Logan (IRE)
Gosden, John – Frankly Darling (GB)
Gosden, John – Indigo Girl (GB)
Gosden, John – Lord North (IRE)
Gosden, John – Mishriff (IRE)
Gosden, John – Nazeef (GB)
Gosden, John – Terebellum (IRE)

Hannon, Richard – Chindit (IRE)
Hannon, Richard – Etonian (IRE)
Hannon, Richard – Happy Romance (IRE)
Hannon, Richard – Ventura Tormenta (IRE)

Haggas, William – Al Aasy (IRE)
Haggas, William – Nkosikazi (GB)
Haggas, William – One Master (IRE)
Haggas, William – Pablo Escobarr (IRE)
Haggas, William – With Thanks (IRE)
Haggas, William – Young Rascal (FR)

Hills, Charles – Battaash (IRE)
Hills, Charles – Mujbar (GB)
Hills, Charles – Tilsit (USA)

Jarvis, William – Lady Bowthorpe (GB)

Johnston, Mark – Dark Vision (IRE)

Johnston, Mark – Elarqam (GB)
Johnston, Mark – Gear Up (IRE)
Johnston, Mark – Nayef Road (IRE)
Johnston, Mark – Rose of Kildare (IRE)
Johnston, Mark – Subjectivist (GB)
Johnston, Mark – Thunderous (IRE)

King, Alan – Trueshan (FR)

Loughnane, David – Santosha (IRE)

Meade, Martyn – Lone Eagle (IRE)

Menuisier, David – Wonderful Tonight (FR)

Morrison, Hughie – Telecaster (GB)

Muir, William – Pyledriver (GB)

O'Meara, David – Eagles By Day (IRE)

Quinn, John – Safe Voyage (IRE)

Ryan, Kevin – Queen Jo Jo (GB)
Ryan, Kevin – Star of Emaraaty (IRE)

Stoute, Sir Michael – Dream of Dreams (IRE)
Stoute, Sir Michael – Regal Reality (GB)

Tate, James – Far Above (IRE)
Tate, James – Top Rank (IRE)

Teal, Roger – Oxted (GB)

Tinkler, Nigel – Ubettabelieveit (IRE)

Tregoning, Marcus – Alkumait (GB)
Tregoning, Marcus – Mohaather (GB)

Varian, Roger – Angel Power (GB)
Varian, Roger – Believe In Love (IRE)
Varian, Roger – Molatham (GB)

Vaughan, Ed – Dame Malliot (GB)

Watson, Archie – Glen Shiel (GB)
Watson, Archie – Mighty Gurkha (IRE)

Williams, Stuart – Breathtaking Look (GB)

United States of America
Ward, Wesley – Campanelle (IRE)

GROUP 2 & GROUP 3 WINNERS OF 2020
AUCTION PRICES
(where relevant; excluding vendor buy-backs)

Ireland
Goffs
Aloha Star (IRE) – 2018 November Foals – €42,000 – Vendor: Cornagher House from Collegelands – Purchaser: Grove Stud

Antonia de Vega (IRE) – 2017 Orby – €130,000 – Vendor: Ballylinch Stud – Purchaser: Ralph Beckett

Art Power (IRE) – 2018 Orby – €110,000 – Vendor: Owenstown Stud – Purchaser: SackvilleDonald

Cadillac (IRE) – 2019 Orby – €40,000 – Vendor: The Castlebridge Consignment – Purchaser: BBA Ireland

Dandalla (IRE) – 2018 November Foals – €15,500 – Vendor: Robert Norton from Newtown Barry House Stud – Purchaser: LS Bloodstock

Dark Vision (IRE) – 2016 November Foals – €15,000 – Vendor: Baroda & Colbinstown Studs – Purchaser: Limefield Stud

Elysium (IRE) – 2019 Autumn Yearlings – €15,000 – Vendor: Tullpark Ltd from Stanley Lodge – Purchaser: Noel Meade

Etonian (IRE) – 2018 November Foals – €14,000 – Vendor: Whitethorn Bloodstock – Purchaser: Woodstock

Gear Up (IRE) – 2019 Orby – €52,000 – Vendor: Redmondstown Stud – Purchaser: Johnston Racing

Ghaiyyath (IRE) – 2015 November Foals – €1,100,000 – Vendor: The Castlebridge Consignment – Purchaser: John Ferguson

Isabella Giles (IRE) – 2019 Sportsman's Yearlings – €45,000 – Vendor: Ballylinch Stud – Purchaser: Kevin Ross Bloodstock

Laws of Indices (IRE) – 2019 Autumn Yearlings – €8,000 – Vendor: Rathasker Stud – Purchaser: Dermot Farrington

Lemista (IRE) – 2017 November Foals – €16,000 – Vendor: Yellowform Farm – Purchaser: Gaelic Bloodstock

Leo de Fury (IRE) – 2017 Orby – €25,000 – Vendor: Glenvale Stud – Purchaser: BBA Ireland

Love Locket (IRE) – 2017 November Foals – €52,000 – Vendor:
    The Castlebridge Consignment – Purchaser: Glenvale Stud
Love Locket (IRE) – 2018 Orby – €700,000 – Vendor: Glenvale
    Stud – Purchaser: M V Magnier
Manuela de Vega (IRE) – 2017 Orby – €100,000 – Vendor:
    Mount Coote Stud – Purchaser: Ralph Beckett
Minaun (IRE) – 2019 Sportsman's Yearlings – €8,000 – Vendor:
    The Castlebridge Consignment – Purchaser: Leamore Horses
Miss Amulet (IRE) – 2018 November Foals – €1,000 – Vendor:
    Ringfort Stud – Purchaser: P.D. Bloodstock
Mother Earth (IRE) – 2019 Orby – €150,000 – Vendor:
    Whitehall Stud – Purchaser: MV Magnier
One Voice (IRE) – 2018 Sportsman's Yearlings – €55,000 –
    Vendor: Ballyogue Stud from Kilmoney Cottage Stud –
    Purchaser: BBA Ireland
Star of Emaraaty (IRE) – 2019 Sportsman's Yearlings – €3,500 –
    Vendor: Rathbarry Stud – Purchaser: Robson Aguiar
Twilight Payment (IRE) – 2018 November Horses-in-Training –
    €200,000 – Vendor: Glebe House Stables – Purchaser: Kerr
    & Co Ltd, Agent
Ubettabelieveit (IRE) – 2018 November Foals – €35,000 –
    Vendor: Ringfort Stud – Purchaser: Barclay Bloodstock
Volkan Star (IRE) – 2017 November Foals – €330,000 –
    Vendor: Tinnakill House – Purchaser: Dromoland Farm
Winter Power (IRE) – 2019 Orby – €90,000 – Vendor:
    Newlands House Stud – Purchaser: SackvilleDonald

Goresbridge
With Thanks (IRE) – 2019 Breeze-Up – €100,000 – Vendor:
    Meadowview Stables – Purchaser: Blandford Bloodstock

Tattersalls Ireland
Aloha Star (IRE) – 2019 September Yearlings – €67,000 –
    Vendor: Grove Stud – Purchaser: de Burgh Equine / F Stack
Champers Elysees (IRE) – 2017 November Flat – €12,500 –
    Vendor: Archway Stud from Mantlehill Stud – Purchaser:
    Aughamore Stud

Champers Elysees (IRE) – 2018 September Yearlings Part 2 – €28,000 – Vendor: Aughamore Stud – Purchaser: Johnny Murtagh

Dandalla (IRE) – 2019 September Yearlings – €22,000 – Vendor: The Castlebridge Consignment – Purchaser: Kelly Burke

Helvic Dream (IRE) – 2018 September Yearlings Part 2 – €12,000 – Vendor: Portlester Stud – Purchaser: Peter Nolan Bloodstock

Rose of Kildare (IRE) – 2018 September Yearlings – €3,000 – Vendor: Oghill House Stud – Purchaser: Johnston Racing

Steel Bull (IRE) – 2018 Flat Bloodstock – €5,000 – Vendor: Rathasker Stud – Purchaser: Madeline Burns

The Lir Jet (IRE) – 2018 November Flat Bloodstock – €9,500 – Vendor: Rockton Stud – Purchaser: Joe Foley

Great Britain
DBS

Barney Roy (GB) – 2015 Premier Yearlings – £70,000 – Vendor: Castletown Quarry Stud, Ireland – Purchaser: Peter & Ross Doyle Bloodstock

Limato (IRE) – 2013 Premier Yearlings – £41,000 – Vendor: Weylands Stud, Ireland – Purchaser: Peter & Ross Doyle Bloodstock

Safe Voyage (IRE) – 2014 Premier Yearlings – £52,000 – Vendor: Owenstown Stud, Ireland – Purchaser: Richard Knight Bloodstock Agent/Quinn

Goffs UK

A'Ali (IRE) – 2018 Premier Yearlings – £35,000 (p/s) – Vendor: Tally-Ho Stud, Ireland – Purchaser: Star BS Ltd

A'Ali (IRE) – 2019 Breeze-Up – £135,000 – Vendor: Star Bloodstock – Purchaser: Stroud Coleman Bloodstock

Fev Rover (IRE) – 2019 Premier Yearlings – £20,000 – Vendor: Manister House Stud, Ireland – Purchaser: Howson & Houldsworth/N Bradley

Glen Shiel (GB) – 2019 Spring Horses-in-Training – £45,000 – Vendor: Godolphin – Purchaser: Blandford Bloodstock

Happy Romance (IRE) – 2019 Premier Yearlings – £25,000 – Vendor: Redpender Stud, Ireland – Purchaser: Peter & Ross Doyle Bloodstock

Nickajack Cave (IRE) – 2017 Premier Yearlings – £65,000 – Vendor: Coulances Sales (Anna Sundstrom) – Purchaser: Gaelic Bloodstock

Queen Jo Jo (GB) – 2017 Premier Yearlings – £11,000 – Vendor: Bearstone Stud – Purchaser: Marcio Aguiar

Steel Bull (IRE) – 2020 Breeze-Up – £28,000 – Vendor: Kilbrew Stakes, Ireland – Purchaser: Michael O'Callaghan

Supremacy (IRE) – 2019 Premier Yearlings – £65,000 – Vendor: Owenstown Stud, Ireland – Purchaser: Clive Cox Racing

The Lir Jet (IRE) – 2019 Premier Yearlings – £8,000 – Vendor: Ballyhane Stud, Ireland – Purchaser: Robson Agular

Umm Kulthum (IRE) – 2020 Breeze-Up - £75,000 – Vendor: Tally-Ho Stud, Ireland – Purchaser: Blandford Bloodstock

Ventura Tormenta (IRE) – 2019 Premier Yearlings – £95,000 – Vendor: Tinnakill House, Ireland – Purchaser: Peter & Ross Doyle Bloodstock

Tattersalls

Al Aasy (IRE) – 2018 October Book 1 – 300,000gns – Vendor: Mount Coote Stud, Ireland – Purchaser: Shadwell Estate Company

Alkumait (GB) – 2018 December Foals – 150,000gns – Vendor: Whitsbury Manor Stud – Purchaser: West Park Farm

Alkumait (GB) – 2019 October Book 1 – 220,000gns – Vendor: Baroda Stud, Ireland – Purchaser: Shadwell Estate Company

Angel Power (GB) – 2017 December Foals – 35,000gns – Vendor: Setwood Bloodstock – Purchaser: Glidawn Stud

Angel Power (GB) – 2018 October Book 1 – 150,000gns – Vendor: Glidawn Stud, Ireland – Purchaser: SackvilleDonald

Barney Roy (GB) – 2014 December Foals – 30,000gns – Vendor: Irish National Stud – Purchaser: A T Bloodstock

Baron Samedi (GB) – 2017 December Foals – 3,500gns – Vendor: Usk Valley Stud – Purchaser: LECH Racing/Sussex Stud

Battaash (IRE) – 2015 October Book 2 – 200,000gns – Vendor: Ballyphilip Stud, Ireland – Purchaser: Shadwell Estate Company

Believe In Love (IRE) – 2017 December Foals – 42,000gns – Vendor: Kenilworth House Stud, Ireland – Purchaser: Voute Sales/Nawara Stud

Believe In Love (IRE) – 2018 October Book 1 – 55,000gns – Vendor: Voute Sales Ltd (Agent) – Purchaser: North Hills Co Ltd

Bowerman (GB) – 2015 October Book 2 – 150,000gns – Vendor: Cheveley Park Stud Ltd – Purchaser: C Gordon-Watson Bloodstock/Paul Smith

Bowerman (GB) – 2019 July Horse-in-Training – 52,000gns – Vendor: Carlsburg Stables (R Varian) – Purchaser: EAM Bloodstock

Breathtaking Look (GB) – 2016 October Book 3 – 42,000gns – Vendor: A Partnership from Mickley Stud – Purchaser: Stuart Williams

Breathtaking Look (GB) – 2020 December Mare Sale – 400,000gns – Vendor: Mr J W Parry from Diomed Stables (S Williams) – Purchaser: Katsumi Yoshida

Buckhurst (IRE) – 2017 October Book 1 – 70,000gns – Vendor: The Castlebridge Consignment – Purchaser: Joseph O'Brien

Campanelle (IRE) – 2019 October Book 1 – 190,000gns – Vendor: Tally-Ho Stud, Ireland – Purchaser: Ben McElroy Agent

Cayenne Pepper (IRE) – 2017 December Foals – 195,000gns – Vendor: Bumble Mitchell – Purchaser: Harriet Jellet for Jon S Kelly

Certain Lad (GB) – 2017 October Book 3 – 13,000gns – Vendor: Hillwood Stud – Purchaser: Gill Richardson Bloodstock

Chindit (IRE) – 2019 October Book 2 – 65,000gns – Vendor: Kilminfoyle House Stud, Ireland (Agent) – Purchaser: Peter & Ross Doyle Bloodstock

Cormorant (IRE) – 2017 December Foals – 135,000gns – Vendor: Langton Stud – Purchaser: JC Bloodstock

Cormorant (IRE) – 2018 October Book 1 – 1,050,000gns –
Vendor: Kilminfoyle House Stud, Ireland (Agent) –
Purchaser: M V Magnier

Current Option (IRE) – 2017 October Book 2 – 62,000gns –
Vendor: The Castlebridge Consignment – Purchaser: Stroud
Coleman Bloodstock

Current Option (IRE) – 2019 July Horses-in-Training –
85,000gns – Vendor: Somerville Lodge Ltd (W Haggas),
Agent – Purchaser: Shamrock Thoroughbreds

Dakota Gold (GB) – 2015 October Book 2 – 26,000gns –
Vendor: Redgate Bloodstock Ltd – Purchaser: Michael Dods

Dark Vision (IRE) – 2018 October Book 2 – 15,000gns –
Vendor: Ballylinch Stud, Ireland – Purchaser: Mark Johnston
Racing

Dashing Willoughby (GB) – 2017 October Book 1 – 70,000gns
– Vendor: A Partnership of Meon Valley Stud from Meon
Valley Stud – Purchaser: Andrew Balding

Dream of Dreams (IRE) – 2014 December Foals – 37,000gns –
Vendor: Bumble Mitchell – Purchaser: Mick Flanagan, Agent

Dubai Station (GB) – 2018 October Book 2 – 30,000gns –
Vendor: Manister House Stud, Ireland – Purchaser: Ahmad
Al Shaikh

Dubai Station (GB) – 2020 Autumn Horses-in-Training –
150,000gns – Vendor: Mr Ahmad Alshaikh from Spigot
Lodge Stakes (K Burke) – Purchaser: Robert Cowell

Eagles By Day (IRE) – 2016 December Foals – 125,000gns –
Vendor: Whispering Grass Stud, Ireland – Purchaser: Joe
Foley

Elarqam (GB) – 2016 October Book 1 – 1,600,000gns – Vendor:
Floors Stud – Purchaser: Shadwell Estate Company

Extra Elusive (GB) – 2018 Autumn Horses-in-Training –
300,000gns – Vendor: From Beckhampton House Stables (R
Charlton) – Purchaser: Blue Diamond Stud Farm UK

Far Above (IRE) – 2017 October Book 3 – 18,000gns – Vendor:
Jamie Railton (Agent) – Purchaser: Matt Whyte

Far Above (IRE) – 2018 Guineas Breeze-Up – 105,000gns –
Vendor: Bushypark Stables, Ireland – Purchaser: Blandford
Bloodstock

Glorious Journey (GB) – 2016 October Book 1 – 2,600,000gns – Vendor: Normandie Stud from Norris Bloodstock – Purchaser: John Ferguson Bloodstock

Happy Power (IRE) – 2017 October Book 1 – 625,000gns – Vendor: Yeomanstown Stud, Ireland – Purchaser: SackvilleDonald

La Barrosa (IRE) – 2019 October Book 1 – 750,000gns – Vendor: Ballyphilip Stud, Ireland – Purchaser: Godolphin

Lady Bowthorpe (GB) – 2017 October Book 2 – 82,000gns – Vendor: John Troy (Agent) – Purchaser: James Toller

Long Eagle (IRE) – 2019 October Book 1 – 500,000gns – Vendor: Ballylinch Stud, Ireland – Purchaser: Aquis Farm

Lullaby Moon (IRE) – 2019 October Book 2 – 16,000gns – Vendor: Bearstone Stud – Purchaser: D Tunmore/GB Horseracing

Minzaal (IRE) – 2018 December Foals – 85,000gns – Vendor: Ringfort Stud, Ireland – Purchaser: Shadwell Estate Company

Mogul (GB) – 2018 October Book 1 – 3,400,000gns – Vendor: Newsells Park Stud Ltd – Purchaser: MV Magnier

Mohaather (GB) – 2017 October Book 2 – 110,000gns – Vendor: Hillwood Stud – Purchaser: Shadwell Estate Company

Molatham (GB) – 2018 October Book 2 – 160,000gns – Vendor: Cheveley Park Stud – Purchaser: Shadwell Estate Company

Nando Parrado (GB) – 2018 December Foals – 165,000gns – Vendor: Whatton Manor Stud – Purchaser: Ballyphilip Stud

Nayef Road (IRE) – 2017 October Book 1 – 100,000gns – Vendor: Oaks Farm Stables – Purchaser: Rabbah Bloodstock

Nkosikazi (GB) – 2016 October Book 2 – 25,000gns – Vendor: Courtleigh Stud from Furnace Mill Stud – Purchaser: McKeever Bloodstock

Nkosikazi (GB) – 2018 December Mares – 30,000gns – Vendor: The Castlebridge Consignment – Purchaser: Avenue Bloodstock

Nkosikazi (GB) – 2019 December Mares – 220,000gns – Vendor: A Partnership from Somerville Lodge Ltd (W Haggas), Agent – Purchaser: Kern/Lillingston Association

Nobel Prize (IRE) – 2020 Autumn Horses-in-Training –
170,000gns – Vendor: From Ballydoyle Stables, Ireland (A.
O'Brien) – Purchaser: J Walsh Bloodstock

Passion (IRE) – 2018 October Book 1 – 800,000gns – Vendor:
Camas Park Stud, Ireland – Purchaser: SackvilleDonald

Patrick Sarsfield (FR) – 2019 July Horses-in-Training –
230,000gns – Vendor: The Castlebridge Consignment –
Purchaser: Joseph O'Brien

Pretty Gorgeous (FR) – 2019 October Book 1 – 525,000gns –
Vendor: Glenvale Stud, Ireland – Purchaser: Joseph O'Brien

Queen Jo Jo (GB) – 2018 Craven Breeze-Up – 68,000gns –
Vendor: Hyde Park Stud, Ireland – Purchaser: Federico
Barberini

Queen Jo Jo (GB) – 2020 December Mare Sale – 360,000gns –
Vendor: The Castlebridge Consignment – Purchaser:
Hurworth Bloodstock

Red Verdon (USA) – 2015 Craven Breeze-Up – 90,000gns –
Vendor: Mocklershill, Ireland – Purchaser: C Gordon
Watson-Bloodstock

Royal Dornoch (IRE) – 2018 December Yearlings – 240,000gns
– Vendor: Barronstown Stud, Ireland – Purchaser: Amanda
Skiffington

Royal Dornoch (IRE) – 2020 Autumn Horses-in-Training –
35,000gns – Vendor: From Ballydoyle Stables, Ireland (A.
O'Brien) – Purchaser: Fathi Egziama

Saffron Beach (IRE) – 2018 December Foals – 55,000gns –
Vendor: Ballylinch Stud, Ireland – Purchaser:
Norris/Huntingdon

Snow (IRE) – 2018 October Book 1 – 1,200,000gns – Vendor:
Barronstown Stud, Ireland – Purchaser: MV Magnier

Subjectivist (GB) – 2018 October Book 2 – 62,000gns – Vendor:
New England Stud – Purchaser: Mark Johnston Racing

Summer Romance (IRE) – 2018 October Book 1 – 300,000gns –
Vendor: Round Hill Stud, Ireland – Purchaser: Oceanic
Bloodstock for D Farm

Tabdeed (GB) – 2015 December Foals – 42,000gns – Vendor:
Ketton Ashwell Ltd from Red House Stud – Purchaser:
Shadwell Estate Company

Thunderous (IRE) – 2018 October Book 2 – 70,000gns – Vendor: Genesis Green Stud – Purchaser: John & Jake Warren

Top Rank (IRE) – 2017 October Book 3 – 26,000gns – Vendor: Cooneen Stud, Ireland – Purchaser: Rabbah Bloodstock

Trueshan (FR) – 2018 Guineas Breeze-Up – 31,000gns – Vendor: Knockanglass Stables, Ireland – Purchaser: Highflyer Bloodstock/A King

Ubettabelieveit (IRE) – 2019 October Book 1 – 50,000gns – Vendor: Ringfort Stud, Ireland – Purchaser: Church Farm/Horse Park Stud

Volkan Star (IRE) – 2018 October Book 1 – 1,000,000gns – Vendor: Longview Stud – Purchaser: Stroud Coleman Bloodstock

Wichita (IRE) – 2018 October Book 2 – 140,000gns – Vendor: Max Ervine from Keith Harte (Agent) – Purchaser: Amanda Skiffington/MV Magnier

Tattersalls Ascot

Miss Amulet (IRE) – 2019 Yearling Sale – £7,500 – Vendor: Rockview Stables, Ireland – Purchaser: BBA Ireland

Steel Bull (IRE) – 2019 Yearling Sale – £15,000 – Vendor: Rathasker Stud, Ireland – Purchaser: Kilbrew Stables

Tattersalls Ireland Ascot

Ventura Rebel (GB) – 2018 September Yearlings – £28,000 – Vendor: Bearstone Stud – Purchaser: Barberini Bloodstock

France
Arqana

Enbihaar (IRE) – 2016 Deauville August (yearlings) – €500,000 – Vendor: Mezeray – Purchaser: Shadwell France SNC

Magic Wand (IRE) – 2016 Deauville August (yearlings) – €1,400,000 – Vendor: Monceaux – Purchaser: P & R Doyle / MV Magnier / Mayfair Speculators

New Mandate (IRE) – 2019 Deauville August (yearlings) – €35,000 – Vendor: Hotellerie – Purchaser: Elliott Bloodstock Services Ltd

Pablo Escobarr (IRE) – 2017 Deauville August (yearlings) – €200,000 – Vendor: Capucines – Purchaser: Richard Knight Bloodstock Agent Ltd

Patrick Sarsfield (FR) – 2017 Deauville August (yearlings) – €140,000 – Vendor: Monceaux – Purchaser: David Myerscough

Pretty Gorgeous (FR) – 2018 December Breeding Stock – €55,000 – Vendor: Cadran – Purchaser: Margaret O'Toole

Summer Romance (IRE) – May Breeze-Up – €800,000 – Vendor: Mocklershill – Purchaser: Godolphin SNC

Terebellum (IRE) – 2017 Deauville August (yearlings) – €400,000 – Vendor: Grove Stud – Purchaser: Godolphin SNC

Wonderful Tonight (FR) – 2018 Deauville August (yearlings) – €40,000 – Vendor: Coulonces Sales – Purchaser: Private Sale

Young Rascal (FR) – 2016 Deauville August (yearlings) – €215,000 – Vendor: Mezeray – Purchaser: Stroud Coleman Bloodstock Ltd

Osarus

Trueshan (FR) – 2017 September Yearlings – €8,000 – Vendor: Haras de Clairefontaine – Purchaser: Pegasus

USA
Keeneland

Kameko (USA) – 2018 September Yearlings – $90,000 – Vendor: Paramount Sales – Purchaser: David Redvers

Pista (USA) – 2018 September Yearlings – $675,000 – Vendor: Gainesway – Purchaser: Heider Family Stables

Red Verdon (USA) – 2014 September Yearlings – $85,000 – Vendor: Gainesway – Purchaser: Jim McCartan

Spanish Mission (USA) – 2017 September Yearlings – $125,000 – Vendor: Lane's End – Purchaser: Lynch Bloodstock

**GROUP 2 & GROUP 3 WINNERS OF 2020
BY MONTH OF BIRTH**

January
08 – Armory (IRE)
12 – Lemista (IRE)
17 – Pablo Escobarr (IRE)
19 – Happy Power (IRE)
22 – Ventura Rebel (GB)
25 – Maamora (IRE)
26 – Tabdeed (GB)
27 – One Voice (IRE)
29 – Barney Roy (GB)
30 – Summer Romance (IRE)
31 – Delphi (IRE)

February
01 – With Thanks (IRE)
03 – Century Dream (IRE)
05 – Romanised (IRE)
05 – Tilsit (USA)
06 – Foxtrot Lady (GB)
07 – Dream of Dreams (IRE)
08 – Limato (IRE)
08 – Military Style (USA)
09 – Fanny Logan (IRE)
09 – Glorious Journey (GB)
09 – Lord North (IRE)
09 – Nando Parrado (GB)
09 – Tarnawa (IRE)
09 – Telecaster (GB)
09 – Terebellum (IRE)
10 – Battaash (IRE)
10 – Cadillac (IRE)
10 – Flying Visit (IRE)
10 – Minzaal (IRE)
10 – Ventura Tormenta (IRE)
11 – Angel Power (GB)
11 – Loxley (IRE)

11 – Magic Lily (GB)
12 – Baron Samedi (GB)
12 – Cayenne Pepper (IRE)
12 – Enable (GB)
12 – Space Blues (IRE)
13 – Lancaster House (IRE)
14 – Fev Rover (IRE)
14 – Mighty Gurkha (IRE)
14 – Saffron Beach (IRE)
14 – Tactical (GB)
14 – Young Rascal (FR)
15 – Benbatl (GB)
15 – Snow (IRE)
16 – Dark Vision (IRE)
17 – Star of Emaraaty (IRE)
18 – Alkumait (GB)
19 – Dubai Station (GB)
20 – Bowerman (GB)
20 – Regal Reality (GB)
22 – Judicial (IRE)
23 – Elarqam (GB)
23 – Mac Swiney (IRE)
24 – Dame Malliot (GB)
24 – Minaun (IRE)
24 – Pretty Gorgeous (FR)
25 – Royal Crusade (GB)
25 – Volkan Star (IRE)
26 – Passion (IRE)
26 – Patrick Sarsfield (FR)
26 – Thunderous (IRE)
26 – Trueshan (FR)
27 – Secret Advisor (FR)
28 – Aspetar (FR)
28 – La Barrosa (IRE)
29 – Lady Wannabe (IRE)

March

03 – Al Aasy (IRE)
03 – Isabella Giles (IRE)
03 – Rose of Kildare (IRE)
04 – Dubai Warrior (GB)
04 – Master of The Seas (IRE)
04 – Queen Jo Jo (GB)
05 – Chindit (IRE)
05 – Cormorant (IRE)
06 – Oxted (GB)
07 – Buckhurst (IRE)
07 – Etonian (IRE)
07 – The Lir Jet (IRE)
07 – Wonderful Tonight (FR)
08 – Gear Up (IRE)
09 – Antonia de Vega (IRE)
09 – Dandalla (IRE)
09 – Leo de Fury (IRE)
09 – Nickajack Cave (IRE)
11 – Santiago (IRE)
11 – Speak In Colours (GB)
12 – Happy Romance (IRE)
12 – Helvic Dream (IRE)
12 – Mujbar (GB)
12 – Zakouski (GB)
13 – Magic Wand (IRE)
14 – Pyledriver (GB)
15 – Aloha Star (IRE)
16 – Winter Power (IRE)
17 – True Self (IRE)
19 – Thundering Nights (IRE)
20 – Champers Elysees (IRE)
21 – Love Locket (IRE)
21 – Manuela de Vega (IRE)
22 – Enbihaar (IRE)
22 – Lone Eagle (IRE)
23 – A'Ali (IRE)
23 – Euchen Glen (GB)
24 – Red Verdon (USA)

25 – Nkosikazi (GB)
25 – Ubettabelieveit (IRE)
26 – Poetic Flare (IRE)
26 – Shale (IRE)
27 – A Case of You (IRE)
28 – Elysium (IRE)
28 – Supremacy (IRE)
30 – Pista (USA)
30 – Subjectivist (GB)
31 – Laws of Indices (IRE)

April

01 – Know It All (GB)
01 – Mishriff (IRE)
01 – One Master (IRE)
01 – Royal Dornoch (IRE)
01 – Sinawann (IRE)
02 – Hukum (IRE)
03 – Breathtaking Look
03 – Mogul (GB)
04 – Current Option (IRE)
04 – Lullaby Moon (GB)
05 – Dakota Gold (GB)
05 – Umm Kulthum (IRE)
06 – Berlin Tango (GB)
06 – Miss Amulet (IRE)
06 – Russian Emperor (IRE)
06 – Spanish Mission (USA)
07 – Epona Plays (IRE)
07 – Kameko (USA)
08 – Indigo Girl (GB)
09 – Molatham (GB)
10 – Extra Elusive (GB)
12 – Far Above (IRE)
13 – Nazeef (GB)
13 – Valeria Messalina (IRE)
14 – Lazuli (IRE)
14 – New Treasure (IRE)
15 – Safe Voyage (IRE)

16 – Cairn Gorm (GB)
16 – Campanelle (IRE)
16 – One Ruler (IRE)
19 – Frankly Darling (GB)
19 – Ghaiyyath (IRE)
20 – Crossfirehurricane (USA)
22 – Lady Bowthorpe (GB)
24 – Mother Earth (IRE)
26 – Mohaather (GB)
26 – Steel Bull (IRE)
28 – Dashing Willoughby
28 – Eagles By Day (IRE)
28 – Wichita (IRE)
29 – Certain Lad (GB)
30 – Believe In Love (IRE)

May
03 – Nayef Road (IRE)
04 – Art Power (IRE)
04 – New Mandate (IRE)
05 – Divinely (IRE)
06 – Santosha (IRE)
06 – Twilight Payment
07 – Brad The Brief (GB)
07 – Glen Shiel (GB)
07 – Nobel Prize (IRE)
07 – Top Rank (IRE)
10 – Battleground (USA)
11 – Millisle (IRE)
15 – Dawn Patrol (IRE)
16 – Tiger Moth (IRE)
18 – High Definition (IRE)
19 – Anthony Van Dyck

March

11 – Believe In Love (IRE) – 1m3f handicap on standard–to–slow at Kempton, England – 3yo

23 – Poetic Flare (IRE) – 5f maiden on soft–to–heavy at Naas, Ireland – 2yo

23 – Russian Emperor (IRE) – 1m maiden on soft–to–heavy at Naas, Ireland – 3yo

April

02 – Benbatl (GB) – 7f maiden on good at Doncaster, England – 3yo

03 – Tarnawa (IRE) – 1m2f maiden on good–to–yielding at Leopardstown, Ireland – 3yo

05 – Bowerman (GB) – 1m maiden on standard at Kempton, England – 3yo

06 – Buckhurst (IRE) – 1m maiden on soft at Leopardstown, Ireland – 3yo

07 – Lady Wannabe (IRE) – 1m100y maiden on good at Cork, Ireland – 3yo

07 – Nickajack Cave (IRE) – 1m2f maiden on good at Cork, Ireland – 3yo

13 – Ventura Rebel (GB) – 5f maiden on good–to–firm at Thirsk, England – 2yo

15 – Telecaster (GB) – 1m2f novice on good at Windsor, England – 3yo

18 – Far Above (IRE) – 7f maiden on good–to–firm at Newmarket, England – 3yo

21 – Young Rascal (FR) – 1m3f maiden on good–to–soft at Newbury, England – 3yo

24 – Romanised (IRE) – 6f maiden on good at Naas, Ireland – 2yo

28 – Eagles By Day (IRE) – 1m4f maiden on good–to–firm at Salisbury, England – 3yo

28 – Fanny Logan (IRE) – 1m2f novice on good at Wetherby, England – 3yo

28 – Oxted (GB) – 7f novice on good–to–firm at Salisbury, England – 3yo

30 – Aspetar (FR) – 1m2f maiden on good at Windsor, England – 3yo

30 – Secret Advisor (FR) – 1m maiden on good at Thirsk, England – 3yo

May

09 – Magic Wand (IRE) – 1m3f75y listed on good at Chester, England – 3yo

18 – Battaash (IRE) – 5f novice on good at Bath, England – 2yo

20 – Rose of Kildare (IRE) – 6f novice auction on good–to–firm at Redcar, England – 2yo

21 – Certain Lad (GB) – 6f novice auction on good–to–firm at Redcar, England – 2yo

23 – Terebellum (IRE) – 1m2f maiden on good at Goodwood, England – 3yo

26 – Foxtrot Lady (GB) – 6f handicap on good at Chester, England – 3yo

27 – Dream of Dreams (IRE) – 6f notice on good–to–soft at Haydock, England – 2yo

31 – Campanelle (IRE) – 5f maiden special weight on firm at Gulfstream Park, USA – 2yo

June

01 – Frankly Darling (GB) – 1m2f maiden on standard–to–slow at Newcastle, England – 3yo

02 – Dandalla (IRE) – 5f maiden on slow–to–standard at Newcastle, England – 2yo

03 – Euchen Glen (GB) – 1m4f handicap on good–to–firm at Doncaster, England – 3yo

03 – The Lir Jet (IRE) – 5f novice auction on good–to–firm at Yarmouth, England – 2yo

05 – Mighty Gurkha (IRE) – 6f maiden auction on standard–to–slow at Lingfield, England – 2yo

06 – Cayenne Pepper (IRE) – 7f maiden on good at Leopardstown, Ireland – 2yo

06 – Dubai Station (GB) – 5f novice on soft at Haydock, England – 2yo

06 – Maamora (IRE) – 1m maiden on good at Ripon, England – 3yo

08 – Angel Power (GB) – 1m novice on standard at Chelmsford, England – 2yo

09 – Tiger Moth (IRE) – 1m2f maiden on good–to–firm at Leopardstown, Ireland – 3yo

10 – Glorious Journey (GB) – 6f novice on good at Newmarket, England – 2yo

11 – Limato (IRE) – 6f maiden on standard at Kempton, England – 2yo

13 – Happy Romance (IRE) – 5f maiden on good at Sandown, England – 2yo

13 – Isabella Giles (IRE) – 6f maiden on good at Leicester, England – 2yo

13 – Snow (IRE) – 1m2f maiden on good–to–firm at Curragh, Ireland – 3yo

13 – Summer Romance (IRE) – 6f maiden on soft at Yarmouth, England – 2yo

14 – Lullaby Moon (GB) – 5f novice on good at Goodwood, England – 2yo

15 – Crossfirehurricane (USA) – 7f maiden on yielding at Limerick, Ireland – 2yo

17 – Tactical (GB) – 5f Listed on good at Ascot, England – 2yo

18 – Al Aasy (IRE) – 1m4f novice on soft at Newmarket, England – 3yo

18 – Battleground (USA) – 7f Listed on soft at Ascot, England – 2yo

18 – Current Option (IRE) – 7f novice on good–to–soft at Thirsk, England – 3yo

18 – Master of The Seas (IRE) – 7f novice on soft at Newmarket, England – 2yo

20 – A'Ali (IRE) – 5f Group 2 on soft at Ascot, England – 2yo

20 – Military Style (USA) – 6f maiden on good–to–yielding at Naas, Ireland – 2yo

20 – Nando Parrado (GB) – 6f Group 2 on good at Ascot, England – 2yo

22 – Cairn Gorm (GB) – 6f maiden on good at Windsor, England – 2yo

23 – Elysium (IRE) – 5f164y auction maiden on yielding at Navan, Ireland – 2yo

23 – Laws of Indices (IRE) – 5f164y auction maiden on yielding at Navan, Ireland – 2yo

26 – Delphi (IRE) – 1m maiden on good at Curragh, Ireland – 3yo

26 – Santosha (IRE) – 6f novice auction on good at Lingfield, England – 2yo

27 – Armory (IRE) – 7f maiden on good–to–yielding at Curragh, Ireland – 2yo

27 – Leo de Fury (IRE) – 1m2f maiden on good at Curragh, Ireland – 3yo

27 – Nazeef (GB) – 7f maiden on good at Newmarket, England – 3yo

28 – Thunderous (IRE) – 7f novice on good at Doncaster, England – 2yo

30 – Ubettabelieveit (IRE) – 5f novice on good–to–firm at Doncaster, England – 2yo

July

01 – Cadillac (IRE) – 7f maiden on good at Leopardstown, Ireland – 2yo

02 – Aloha Star (IRE) – 5f maiden on yielding at Bellewstown, Ireland – 2yo

02 – Pretty Gorgeous (FR) – 1m maiden on yielding at Bellewstown, Ireland – 2yo

03 – Judicial (IRE) – 5f maiden on good at Newbury, England – 2yo

04 – Millisle (IRE) – 5f maiden on good at Bellewstown, Ireland – 2yo

04 – Mother Earth (IRE) – 6f Group 3 on yielding–to–soft at Naas, Ireland – 2yo

04 – Ventura Tormenta (IRE) – 6f novice on good–to–firm at Yarmouth, England – 2yo

05 – Chindit (IRE) – 7f maiden on good at Doncaster, England – 2yo

05 – Dark Vision (IRE) – 6f novice on good–to–firm at Yarmouth, England – 2yo

05 – Minaun (IRE) – 6f Group 3 on good at Cork, Ireland – 2yo

05 – Miss Amulet (IRE) – 5f maiden on good at Cork, Ireland – 2yo

05 – Subjectivist (GB) – 7f novice on standard at Chelmsford, England – 2yo

06 – Supremacy (IRE) – 6f maiden on good–to–firm at Windsor, England – 2yo

08 – Shale (IRE) – 1m maiden on soft–to–heavy at Gowran Park, Ireland – 2yo

13 – Pyledriver (GB) – 7f novice on firm at Salisbury, England – 2yo

13 – Star of Emaraaty (IRE) – 7f novice auction on good at Ayr, Scotland – 2yo

14 – Antonia de Vega (IRE) – 7f maiden on good–to–firm at Newmarket, England – 2yo

15 – Anthony Van Dyck (IRE) – 1m maiden on good at Killarney, Ireland – 2yo

16 – Twilight Payment (IRE) – 1m4f maiden on good at Curragh, Ireland – 3yo

18 – Mac Swiney (IRE) – 7f maiden on yielding at Curragh, Ireland – 2yo

21 – Fev Rover (IRE) – 7f Listed on good–to–firm at Sandown, England – 2yo

22 – Dawn Patrol (IRE) – 1m2f maiden on good at Naas, Ireland – 3yo

22 – Nkosikazi (GB) – 1m handicap on good–to–firm at Redcar, England – 3yo

22 – Steel Bull (IRE) – 5f maiden on good at Naas, Ireland – 2yo

23 – Etonian (IRE) – 7f maiden on good–to–firm at Sandown, England – 2yo

23 – Queen Jo Jo (GB) – 5f novice on good–to–firm at Beverley, England – 2yo

25 – Epona Plays (IRE) – 1m maiden on yielding at Gowran Park, Ireland – 3yo

25 – Gear Up (IRE) – 7f novice action on good at York, England – 2yo

25 – Kameko (USA) – 7f maiden on good at Sandown, England – 2yo

25 – One Voice (IRE) – 7f maiden on good at Leopardstown, Ireland – 2yo

27 – Winter Power (IRE) – 5f handicap on good–to–firm at Redcar, England – 2yo

28 – Alkumait (GB) – 6f maiden on good at Goodwood, England – 2yo

29 – Berlin Tango (GB) – 7f 80y novice on good–to–firm at Ffos Las, Wales – 2yo

29 – Safe Voyage (IRE) – 6f handicap on good–to–soft at Thirsk, England – 3yo

29 – Umm Kulthum (IRE) – 5f maiden on good at Thirsk, England – 2yo

August

02 – Lazuli (IRE) – 6f novice on good–to–firm at Newmarket, England – 2yo

02 – Pista (USA) – 1m4f maiden on soft at Galway, Ireland – 3yo

02 – Tabdeed (GB) – 6f novice on good at Leicester, England – 2yo

02 – Trueshan (FR) – 1m4f novice on standard at Wolverhampton, England – 3yo

03 – Lancaster House (IRE) – 1m73y maiden on good at Galway, Ireland – 3yo

05 – True Self (IRE) – 2m bumper (INH Flat Race) on soft at Galway, Ireland – 4yo

08 – Cormorant (IRE) – 1m maiden on good–to–firm at Leopardstown, Ireland – 2yo

09 – Know It All (GB) – 7f conditions on soft at Curragh, Ireland – 2yo

09 – Minzaal (IRE) – 6f novice on good–to–firm at Salisbury, England – 2yo

10 – Nayef Road (IRE) – 7f novice on good–to–firm at Haydock, England – 2yo

17 – Dashing Willoughby (GB) – 1m142y maiden on standard at Wolverhampton, England – 2yo

19 – Helvic Dream (IRE) – 7f89y auction on soft at Roscommon, Ireland – 2yo

19 – Lady Bowthorpe (GB) – 7f novice on standard at Lingfield, England – 2yo

21 – Brad The Brief (GB) – 5f maiden on good at Bath, England – 2yo

21 – Happy Power (IRE) – 6f maiden on good at Hamilton, Scotland – 2yo

22 – High Definition (IRE) – 1m maiden on soft at Curragh, Ireland – 2yo

23 – Molatham (GB) – 7f maiden on good–to–firm at York, England – 2yo

23 – New Mandate (IRE) – 7f handicap on good at Sandown, England – 2yo

23 – One Ruler (IRE) – 7f maiden on good at Sandown, England – 2yo

23 – Royal Crusade (GB) – 7f novice on good–to–firm at Newmarket, England – 2yo

23 – Sinawann (IRE) – 1m maiden on yielding at Curragh, Ireland – 2yo

23 – Volkan Star (IRE) – 1m novice on good at Goodwood, England – 2yo

23 – Wichita (IRE) – 7f maiden on yielding at Curragh, Ireland – 2yo

25 – Baron Samedi (GB) – 1m2f handicap on heavy at Cork, Ireland – 3yo

27 – Tilsit (USA) – 1m novice auction on standard at Newcastle, England – 3yo

28 – Divinely (IRE) – 1m Group 3 on heavy at Curragh, Ireland – 2yo

28 – Lone Eagle (IRE) – 1m novice on soft at Goodwood, England – 2yo

28 – Mujbar (GB) – 7f novice on soft at Newmarket, England – 2yo

28 – New Treasure (IRE) – 6f Group 3 on heavy at Curragh, Ireland – 2yo

30 – Dakota Gold (GB) – 6f maiden on good–to–firm at Hamilton, Scotland – 2yo

30 – Indigo Girl (GB) – 1m novice on soft at Yarmouth, England – 2yo

30 – Mogul (GB) – 1m maiden on good–to–yielding at Curragh, Ireland – 2yo

September

01 – Passion (IRE) – 1m maiden on yielding at Cork, Ireland – 2yo

04 – A Case of You (IRE) – 7f maiden on soft at Down Royal, Northern Ireland – 2yo

04 – La Barrosa (IRE) – 7f maiden on good at Ascot, England – 2yo

04 – Royal Dornoch (IRE) – 7f maiden on yielding at Gowran Park, Ireland – 2yo

06 – Manuela de Vega (IRE) – 7f maiden on good–to–firm at Salisbury, England – 2yo

08 – Speak In Colours (GB) – 6f novice auction on soft at Ascot, England – 2yo

10 – Elarqam (GB) – 7f novice on good–to–soft at York, England – 2yo

12 – Santiago (IRE) – 1m maiden on soft at Listowel, Ireland – 2yo

15 – Enbihaar (IRE) – 1m3f novice on standard–to–slow at Kempton, England – 3yo

18 – Breathtaking Look (GB) – 6f novice on good–to–firm at Yarmouth, England – 3yo

18 – Valeria Messalina (IRE) – 7f maiden on good at Naas, Ireland – 2yo

19 – One Master (IRE) – 6f maiden on soft at Yarmouth, England – 3yo

20 – Regal Reality (GB) – 7f maiden on soft at Yarmouth, England – 2yo

23 – Magic Lily (GB) – 1m novice on good at Newmarket, England – 2yo

24 – Barney Roy (GB) – 1m maiden on good at Haydock, England – 2yo

24 – Flying Visit (IRE) – 1m maiden on heavy at Listowel, Ireland – 2yo

26 – Pablo Escobarr (IRE) – 1m2f maiden on good–to–soft at Goodwood, England – 2yo

26 – Saffron Beach (IRE) – 7f maiden on good at Newmarket, England – 2yo

28 – Ghaiyyath (IRE) – 1m maiden on good–to–soft at Newmarket, England – 2yo

29 – Champers Elysees (IRE) – 6f auction on heavy at Curragh, Ireland – 2yo

October

10 – Mohaather (GB) – 6f novice on good at Nottingham, England – 2yo

11 – Art Power (IRE) – 5f novice on soft at York, England – 2yo

12 – Century Dream (IRE) – 1m75y maiden on good–to–soft at Nottingham, England – 2yo

14 – Lemista (IRE) – 1m maiden on heavy at Gowran Park, Ireland – 2yo

15 – Loxley (IRE) – 1m1f novice at Goodwood, England – 2yo

19 – Lord North (IRE) – 1m novice on soft at Redcar, England – 2yo

20 – Love Locket (IRE) – 6f maiden on soft–to–heavy at Naas, Ireland – 2yo

22 – Patrick Sarsfield (FR) – 1m maiden on soft at Curragh, Ireland – 3yo

27 – Extra Elusive (GB) – 1m novice on soft at Newbury, England – 2yo

28 – Thundering Nights (IRE) – 1m73y maiden on soft–to–heavy at Galway, Ireland – 2yo

November

02 – With Thanks (IRE) – 7f novice on heavy at Newmarket, England – 2yo

03 – Nobel Prize (IRE) – 1m maiden on heavy at Naas, Ireland – 2yo

06 – Mishriff (IRE) – 1m75y maiden on heavy at Nottingham, England – 2yo

07 – Space Blues (IRE) – 1m75y maiden on good–to–soft at Nottingham, England – 2yo

08 – Dubai Warrior (GB) – 1m novice on standard at Chelmsford, England – 2yo

10 – Spanish Mission (USA) – 1m2f conditions on standard at Chelmsford, England – 2yo

16 – Glen Shiel (GB) – 7f110y newcomers on heavy at Saint–Cloud, France – 2yo

19 – Hukum (IRE) – 1m novice on standard–to–slow at Kempton, England – 2yo

21 – Zakouski (GB) – 7f novice on standard–to–slow at Kempton, England – 2yo

22 – Wonderful Tonight (FR) – 1m2f maiden on heavy at Saint–Cloud, France – 2yo

28 – Enable (GB) – 1m maiden on standard at Newcastle, England – 2yo

December

05 – Red Verdon (USA) – 1m142y maiden on standard at Wolverhampton, England – 2yo

17 – Dame Malliot (GB) – 1m1f104y novice median auction on standard at Wolverhampton, England – 2yo

22 – Top Rank (IRE) – 1m novice auction on standard at Lingfield, England – 2yo

GROUP 2 & GROUP 3 WINNERS OF 2020
BY DISTANCE OF THE WINS

5f
A'Ali (IRE)
Battaash (IRE)
Campanelle (IRE)
Far Above (IRE)
Lazuli (IRE)
Steel Bull (IRE)
The Lir Jet (IRE)
Ubettabelieveit (IRE)
Winter Power (IRE)

6f
Alkumait (GB)
Aloha Star (IRE)
Art Power (IRE)
Brad The Brief (GB)
Breathtaking Look (GB)
Cairn Gorm (GB)
Dakota Gold (GB)
Dandalla (IRE)
Dubai Station (GB)
Glen Shiel (GB)
Happy Romance (IRE)
Judicial (IRE)
Laws of Indices (IRE)
Mighty Gurkha (IRE)
Millisle (IRE)
Minaun (IRE)
Minzaal (IRE)
Miss Amulet (IRE)
Mother Earth (IRE)
Nando Parrado (GB)
New Treasure (IRE)
Oxted (GB)
Queen Jo Jo (GB)
Royal Crusade (GB)

Santosha (IRE)
Speak In Colours (GB)
Supremacy (IRE)
Tabdeed (GB)
Tactical (GB)
Umm Kulthum (IRE)
Ventura Rebel (GB)
Ventura Tormenta (IRE)

6.25f
A Case of You (IRE)

7f
Battleground (USA)
Chindit (IRE)
Dream of Dreams (IRE)
Elysium (IRE)
Etonian (IRE)
Fev Rover (IRE)
Foxtrot Lady (GB)
Gear Up (IRE)
Glorious Journey (GB)
Happy Power (IRE)
Isabella Giles (IRE)
La Barrosa (IRE)
Lancaster House (IRE)
Limato (IRE)
Love Locket (IRE)
Lullaby Moon (GB)
Mac Swiney (IRE)
Master of The Seas (IRE)
Military Style (USA)
Molatham (GB)
Mujbar (GB)
One Master (IRE)
Poetic Flare (IRE)

Pretty Gorgeous (FR)
Romanised (IRE)
Safe Voyage (IRE)
Saffron Beach (IRE)
Shale (IRE)
Space Blues (IRE)
Speak In Colours (GB)
Star of Emaraaty (IRE)
Valeria Messalina (IRE)
Wichita (IRE)
With Thanks (IRE)

7.5f
Champers Elysees (IRE)
Current Option (IRE)

1m
Cadillac (IRE)
Century Dream (IRE)
Dark Vision (IRE)
Divinely (IRE)
High Definition (IRE)
Indigo Girl (GB)
Kameko (USA)
Know It All (GB)
Lady Bowthorpe (GB)
Lemista (IRE)
Maamora (IRE)
Magic Lily (GB)
Magic Wand (IRE)
Mohaather (GB)
Nazeef (GB)
New Mandate (IRE)
One Ruler (IRE)
Regal Reality (GB)
Royal Dornoch (IRE)
Safe Voyage (IRE)
Sinawann (IRE)
Tilsit (USA)

Top Rank (IRE)
Zakouski (GB)

1m0.5f
Summer Romance (IRE)

1m0.75f
Certain Lad (GB)

1m1f
Barney Roy (GB)
Benbatl (GB)
Flying Visit (IRE)
Lady Wannabe (IRE)
Lemista (IRE)
Magic Lily (GB)
Patrick Sarsfield (FR)
Thundering Nights (IRE)

1m1.5f
Benbatl (GB)
Epona Plays (IRE)

1m2f
Angel Power (GB)
Armory (IRE)
Berlin Tango (GB)
Buckhurst (IRE)
Cayenne Pepper (IRE)
Cormorant (IRE)
Crossfirehurricane (USA)
Dubai Warrior (GB)
Extra Elusive (GB)
Ghaiyyath (IRE)
Helvic Dream (IRE)
Long Eagle (IRE)
Lord North (IRE)
Mishriff (IRE)
Nkosikazi (GB)

One Voice (IRE)
Russian Emperor (IRE)
Telecaster (GB)
Terebellum (IRE)

1m2.25f
Aspetar (FR)
Rose of Kildare (IRE)
Thunderous (IRE)

1m2.5f
Bowerman (GB)
Leo de Fury (IRE)
Nobel Prize (IRE)

1m3f
Baron Samedi (GB)
Elarqam (GB)

1m3.5f
Manuela de Vega (IRE)

1m4f
Anthony Van Dyck (IRE)
Antonia de Vega (IRE)
Dame Malliot (GB)
Enable (GB)
Euchen Glen (GB)
Fanny Logan (IRE)
Frankly Darling (GB)
Loxley (IRE)
Manuela de Vega (IRE)
Mogul (GB)
Nickajack Cave (IRE)
Pablo Escobarr (IRE)
Pyledriver (GB)
Snow (IRE)
Tarnawa (IRE)
Tiger Moth (IRE)

Volkan Star (IRE)
Young Rascal (FR)

1m4.5f
Telecaster (GB)
Wonderful Tonight (FR)

1m5f
Al Aasy (IRE)
True Self (IRE)

1m5.5f
Hukum (IRE)

1m6f
Believe In Love (IRE)
Delphi (IRE)
Eagles By Day (IRE)
Enbihaar (IRE)
Passion (IRE)
Red Verdon (USA)
Santiago (IRE)
Secret Advisor (FR)
Subjectivist (GB)
Twilight Payment (IRE)

1m6.5f
Pista (USA)

2m
Dashing Willoughby (GB)
Dawn Patrol (IRE)
Nayef Road (IRE)
Trueshan (FR)
2m0.25f
Enbihaar (IRE)

2m2f
Spanish Mission (USA)

GROUP 2 & GROUP 3 WINNERS OF 2020 BY GOING DESCRIPTION FOR THE GROUP WINS

TURF

Good-to-firm

Battaash (IRE)
Cormorant (IRE)
Crossfirehurricane (USA)
Enbihaar (IRE)
Far Above (IRE)
Lancaster House (IRE)
Leo de Fury (IRE)
Limato (IRE)
Love Locket (IRE)
Magic Wand (IRE)
One Master (IRE)
Oxted (GB)
Pablo Escobarr (IRE)
Regal Reality (GB)
Star of Emaraaty (IRE)
Terebellum (IRE)
Tilsit (USA)

Good

A'Ali (IRE)
Alkumait (GB)
Anthony Van Dyck (IRE)
Antonia de Vega (IRE)
Armory (IRE)
Aspetar (FR)
Barney Roy (GB)
Battleground (USA)
Benbatl (GB)
Buckhurst (IRE)
Cadillac (IRE)
Cairn Gorm (GB)
Campanelle (IRE)
Cayenne Pepper (IRE)

Century Dream (IRE)
Chindit (IRE)
Dark Vision (IRE)
Dashing Willoughby (GB)
Delphi (IRE)
Eagles By Day (IRE)
Elarqam (GB)
Enbihaar (IRE)
Epona Plays (IRE)
Etonian (IRE)
Extra Elusive (GB)
Foxtrot Lady (GB)
Gear Up (IRE)
Ghaiyyath (IRE)
Glorious Journey (GB)
Happy Romance (IRE)
Indigo Girl (GB)
Isabella Giles (IRE)
Kameko (USA)
Know It All (GB)
La Barrosa (IRE)
Lady Bowthorpe (GB)
Lazuli (IRE)
Lemista (IRE)
Loxley (IRE)
Maamora (IRE)
Magic Lily (GB)
Master of The Seas (IRE)
Military Style (USA)
Millisle (IRE)
Minaun (IRE)
Minzaal (IRE)
Mogul (GB)
Mohaather (GB)
Nando Parrado (GB)

Nazeef (GB)
New Mandate (IRE)
Nickajack Cave (IRE)
One Voice (IRE)
Patrick Sarsfield (FR)
Pista (USA)
Pyledriver (GB)
Queen Jo Jo (GB)
Royal Crusade (GB)
Royal Dornoch (IRE)
Russian Emperor (IRE)
Safe Voyage (IRE)
Santosha (IRE)
Secret Advisor (FR)
Shale (IRE)
Sinawann (IRE)
Space Blues (IRE)
Spanish Mission (USA)
Steel Bull (IRE)
Summer Romance (IRE)
Supremacy (IRE)
Tabdeed (GB)
Tarnawa (IRE)
Tiger Moth (IRE)
True Self (IRE)
Twilight Payment (IRE)
Ubettabelieveit (IRE)
Valeria Messalina (IRE)
Ventura Rebel (GB)
Wichita (IRE)
Zakouski (GB)

Good-to-yielding
A'Ali (IRE)
Aloha Star (IRE)
Dawn Patrol (IRE)
Glen Shiel (GB)
High Definition (IRE)
Speak In Colours (GB)

Twilight Payment (IRE)

Good-to-soft
Al Aasy (IRE)
Certain Lad (GB)
Dandalla (IRE)
Dream of Dreams (IRE)
Frankly Darling (GB)
Happy Power (IRE)
Hukum (IRE)
Lord North (IRE)
Manuela de Vega (IRE)
Miss Amulet (IRE)
Pyledriver (GB)
Red Verdon (USA)
Rose of Kildare (IRE)
Safe Voyage (IRE)
Tactical (GB)
Telecaster (GB)
The Lir Jet (IRE)
Thunderous (IRE)
Umm Kulthum (IRE)
Ventura Tormenta (IRE)
Volkan Star (IRE)
Young Rascal (FR)

Yielding
Elysium (IRE)
Laws of Indices (IRE)
Romanised (IRE)
Snow (IRE)
Speak In Colours (GB)

Yielding-to-soft
Art Power (IRE)
Current Option (IRE)
Mother Earth (IRE)
Poetic Flare (IRE)

Soft
A Case of You (IRE)
Angel Power (GB)
Century Dream (IRE)
Dakota Gold (GB)
Dame Malliot (GB)
Dandalla (IRE)
Euchen Glen (GB)
Extra Elusive (GB)
Fanny Logan (IRE)
Happy Power (IRE)
Helvic Dream (IRE)
Isabella Giles (IRE)
Lady Wannabe (IRE)
Lone Eagle (IRE)
Mac Swiney (IRE)
Manuela de Vega (IRE)
Molatham (GB)
One Ruler (IRE)
Passion (IRE)
Pretty Gorgeous (FR)
Saffron Beach (IRE)
Santiago (IRE)
Subjectivist (GB)
Thundering Nights (IRE)
Top Rank (IRE)
Trueshan (FR)
Winer Power (IRE)

Very soft
Fev Rover (IRE)

Soft-to-heavy
Champers Elysees (IRE)
Flying Visit (IRE)
Lemista (IRE)

Heavy
Baron Samedi (GB)
Believe In Love (IRE)
Brad The Brief (GB)
Breathtaking Look (GB)
Divinely (IRE)
Lullaby Moon (GB)
Mishriff (IRE)
Mujbar (GB)
New Treasure (IRE)
Telecaster (GB)
With Thanks (IRE)
Wonderful Tonight (FR)

POLYTRACK
Standard
Bowerman (GB)
Dubai Warrior (GB)
Nobel Prize (IRE)

Standard-to-slow
Berlin Tango (GB)
Enable (GB)
Mighty Gurkha (IRE)

TAPETA
Standard
Dubai Station (GB)
Judicial (IRE)
Nayef Road (IRE)
Nkosikazi (GB)

DIRT
Fast
Benbatl (GB)

GROUP 2 & GROUP 3 WINNERS OF 2020
BY WINNERS OF TWO OR MORE
GROUP RACES (ANY LEVEL)

Winners of four
Barney Roy (GB)***
Ghaiyyath (IRE)***
Tarnawa (IRE)***

Winners of three
Battaash (IRE)**
Nazeef (GB)**
Space Blues (IRE)*
Twilight Payment (IRE)*
Wonderful Tonight (FR)**

Winners of two
A'Ali (IRE)
Angel Power (GB)
Benbatl (GB)
Campanelle (IRE)*
Century Dream (IRE)
Champers Elysees (IRE)*
Dandalla (IRE)
Dream of Dreams (IRE)*
Enbihaar (IRE)
Euchen Glen (GB)
Extra Elusive (GB)

Gear Up (IRE)*
Glen Shiel (GB)*
Happy Power (IRE)
Isabella Giles (IRE)
Kameko (USA)*
Lemista (IRE)
Lord North (IRE)*
Mac Swiney (IRE)*
Magic Lily (GB)
Manuela de Vega (IRE)
Mishriff (IRE)*
Mogul (GB)*
Mohaather (GB)*
One Master (GB)*
Oxted (GB)*
Pretty Gorgeous (FR)*
Pyledriver (GB)
Safe Voyage (IRE)
Santiago (IRE)*
Shale (IRE)*
Speak In Colours (GB)
Subjectivist (GB)*
Supremacy (IRE)*
Telecaster (GB)

* including one Group 1 win
** including two Group 1 wins
*** including three Group 1 wins

Ireland
Group 2

Coolmore Magna Grecia Irish EBF Mooresbridge Stakes
(1m2f110y, Curragh, 4yo+) – Leo de Fury (IRE)

Lanwades Stud Stakes (1m, Curragh, 4yo+ fillies & mares) –
Magic Wand (IRE)

Weatherbys Ireland Greenlands Stakes (6f, Curragh, 4yo+) –
Speak In Colours (GB)

Comer Group International Curragh Cup (1m6f, Curragh, 3yo+)
– Twilight Payment (IRE)

Paddy Power Minstrel Stakes (7f, Curragh, 3yo+) – Romanised
(IRE)

GAIN Railway Stakes (6f, Curragh, 2yo) – Laws of Indices (IRE)

Airlie Stud Stakes (6f, Curragh, 2yo fillies) – Aloha Star (IRE)

Holden Plant Rentals Sapphire Stakes (5f, Curragh, 3yo+) –
A'Ali (IRE)

Kilboy Estate Stakes (1m1f, Curragh, 3yo+ fillies & mares) –
Lemista (IRE)

A.R.M. Holding Debutante Stakes (7f, Curragh, 2yo fillies) –
Pretty Gorgeous (FR)

Galileo Irish EBF Futurity Stakes (7f, Curragh, 2yo) – Mac
Swiney (IRE)

KPMG Champions Juvenile Stakes (1m, Leopardstown, 2yo) –
Cadillac (IRE)

Clipper Logistics Boomerang Mile (1m, Leopardstown, 3yo+) –
Safe Voyage (IRE)

Moyglare 'Jewels' Blandford Stakes (1m2f, Curragh, 3yo+ fillies
& mares) – Cayenne Pepper (IRE)

Alan Smurfit Memorial Beresford Stakes (1m, Curragh, 2yo) –
High Definition (IRE)

Group 3

Lodge Park Stud Irish EBF Park Express Stakes (1m, Naas,
3yo+ fillies & mares) – Lemista (IRE)

Derrinstown Stud Derby Trial Stakes (1m2f, Leopardstown, 3yo)
– Cormorant (IRE)

Leopardstown Fillies Trial Stakes (7f, Leopardstown, 3yo fillies)
– Love Locket (IRE)

Coolmore Ten Sovereigns Gallinule Stakes (1m2f, Curragh, 3yo)
– Crossfirehurricane (USA)

Coolmore Calyx Gladness Stakes (7f, Curragh, 4yo+) –
Lancaster House (IRE)

Irish Stallion Farms EBF Blue Wind Stakes (1m2f, Curragh, 3yo
fillies) – One Voice (IRE)

Dubai Duty Free Jumeirah Creekside Hotel Alleged Stakes
(1m2f, Curragh, 4yo+) – Buckhurst (IRE)

Comer Group International Vintage Crop Stakes (1m6f,
Curragh, 4yo+) – Twilight Payment (IRE)

Derrinstown Stud Fillies Stakes (1m, Leopardstown, 3yo fillies) –
Know It All (GB)

Amethyst Stakes (1m, Leopardstown, 3yo colts & geldings) –
Sinawann (IRE)

Coolmore Stud Irish EBF Fillies' Sprint Stakes (6f, Naas, 2yo
fillies) – Mother Earth (IRE)

Coolmore Sioux Nation Lacken Stakes (6f, Naas, 3yo) – Art
Power (IRE)

Marble Hill Stakes (6f, Cork, 2yo) – Minaun (IRE)

Munster Oaks Stakes (1m4f, Cork, 3yo+ fillies & mares) – Snow
(IRE)

Rybo Ballycorus Stakes (7f, Fairyhouse, 3yo+) – Speak In
Colours (GB)

'Green Room' Meld Stakes (1m1f, Leopardstown, 3yo+) –
Patrick Sarsfield (FR)

Irish Stallion Farms EBF Brownstown Stakes (7f, Cork, 3yo+
fillies & mares) – Valeria Messalina (IRE)

Woodford Reserve Ballysax Stakes (1m2f150y, Dundalk–AW,
3yo) – Nobel Prize (IRE)

Yeomanstown Stud Ballyogan Stakes (6f, Naas, 3yo+ fillies &
mares) – Millisle (IRE)

Frank Conroy Silver Flash Stakes (7f, Leopardstown, 2yo fillies)
– Shale (IRE)

Japan Racing Association Tyros Stakes (7f, Leopardstown, 2yo)
– Military Style (USA)

Bahrain International Ballyroan Stakes (1m4f, Leopardstown,
3yo+) – Nickajack Cave (IRE)

Irish Stallion Farms EBF Give Thanks Stakes (1m4f, Cork, 3yo+
fillies & mares) – Tarnawa (IRE)

Rathasker Stud Phoenix Sprint Stakes (6f, Curragh, 3yo+) –
Glen Shiel (GB)

Clipper Logistics Desmond Stakes (1m, Leopardstown, 3yo+) –
Royal Dornoch (IRE)

Comer Group International Irish St Leger Trial Stakes (1m6f,
Curragh, 3yo+) – Delphi (IRE)

Irish Field Celebrating 150 Years Royal Whip Stakes (1m2f,
Curragh, 3yo+) – Armory (IRE)

Irish Stallion Farms EBF Stanerra Stakes (1m6f, Naas, 3yo+
fillies & mares) – Passion (IRE)

Kilcarn Stud Flame of Tara Irish EBF Stakes (1m, Curragh, 2yo
fillies) – Divinely (IRE)

Snow Fairy Fillies Stakes (1m1f, Curragh, 3yo+ fillies & mares) –
Thundering Nights (IRE)

Heider Family Stables Round Tower Stakes (6f, Curragh, 2yo) –
New Treasure (IRE)

Coolmore Stud No Nay Never Fairy Bridge Stakes (7f110y,
Gowran Park, 3yo+ fillies & mares) – Champers Elysees
(IRE)

Paddy Power 'Is It 2021 Yet?' Stakes (1m4f, Leopardstown,
3yo+) – Tiger Moth (IRE)

Denny Cordell Lavarack & Lanwades Stud Fillies Stakes
(1m1f100y, Gowran Park, 3yo+ fillies & mares) – Epona
Plays (IRE)

Al Basti Equiworld, Dubai Diamond Stakes (1m1f150y,
Dundalk–AW, 3yo+) – Bowerman (GB)

Qatar Racing And Equestrian Club Renaissance Stakes (6f,
Curragh, 3yo+) – Ventura Rebel (GB)

Weld Park Stakes (7f, Curragh, 2yo fillies) – Elysium (IRE)

Comer Group International Loughbrown Stakes (2m, Curragh,
3yo+) – Dawn Patrol (IRE)

Coolmore U S Navy Flag Concorde Stakes (7f100y, Tipperary, 3yo+) – Current Option (IRE)
Jebel Ali Racecourse And Stables Anglesey Stakes (6f63y, Curragh, 2yo) – A Case of You (IRE)
Novi IT Services International Stakes (1m2f, Curragh, 3yo+) – Helvic Dream (IRE)
Killavullan Stakes (7f, Leopardstown, 2yo) – Poetic Flare (IRE)
Eyrefield Stakes (1m1f, Leopardstown, 2yo) – Flying Visit (IRE)
Irish Stallion Farms EBF Athasi Stakes (7f, Naas, 3yo+ fillies & mares) – With Thanks (IRE)

Great Britain
Group 2
Betfair Dahlia Fillies' Stakes (1m2f, Newmarket, 4yo+ fillies & mares) – Terebellum (IRE)
Ribblesdale Stakes (1m4f, Ascot, 3yo fillies) – Frankly Darling (GB)
King Edward VII Stakes (1m4f, Ascot, 3yo colts & geldings) – Pyledriver (GB)
Duke of Cambridge Stakes (1m, Ascot, 4yo+ fillies & mares) – Nazeef (GB)
Norfolk Stakes (5f, Ascot, 2yo) – The Lir Jet (IRE)
Hardwicke Stakes (1m4f, Ascot, 4yo+) – Fanny Logan (IRE)
Queen's Vase (1m6f, Ascot, 3yo) – Santiago (IRE)
Queen Mary Stakes (5f, Ascot, 2yo fillies) – Campanelle (IRE)
Coventry Stakes (6f, Ascot, 2yo) – Nando Parrado (GB)
Bet365 Lancashire Oaks (1m3f175y, Haydock, 3yo+ fillies & mares) – Manuela de Vega (IRE)
Tattersalls July Stakes (6f, Newmarket, 2yo colts & geldings) – Tactical (GB)
Princess of Wales's Tattersalls Stakes (1m4f, Newmarket, 3yo+) – Dame Malliot (GB)
Al Basti Equiworld Dubai Dante Stakes (1m2f56y, York, 3yo) – Thunderous (IRE)
Duchess of Cambridge Stakes - sponsored by bet365 (6f, Newmarket, 2yo fillies) – Dandalla (IRE)
Bet365 Superlative Stakes (7f, Newmarket, 2yo) – Master of The Seas (IRE)

Betfred Summer Mile Stakes (1m, Ascot, 4yo+) – Mohaather (GB)

Sky Bet York Stakes (1m2f56y, York, 3yo+) – Aspetar (FR)

Veuve Clicquot Vintage Stakes (7f, Goodwood, 2yo) – Battleground (USA)

Qatar Lennox Stakes (7f, Goodwood, 3yo+) – Space Blues (IRE)

Qatar Richmond Stakes (6f, Goodwood, 2yo colts & geldings) – Supremacy (IRE)

King George Qatar Stakes (5f, Goodwood, 3yo+) – Battaash (IRE)

Qatar Lillie Langtry Stakes (1m6f, Goodwood, 3yo+ fillies & mares) – Enbihaar (IRE)

Unibet Hungerford Stakes (7f, Newbury, 3yo+) – Dream of Dreams (IRE)

Sky Bet Great Voltigeur Stakes (1m4f, York, 3yo colts & geldings) – Pyledriver (GB)

Sky Bet Lowther Stakes (6f, York, 2yo fillies) – Miss Amulet (IRE)

Weatherbys Hamilton Lonsdale Cup Stakes (2m56y, York, 3yo+) – Enbihaar (IRE)

Al Basti Equiworld Dubai Gimcrack Stakes (6f, York, 2yo colts & geldings) – Minzaal (IRE)

Sky Bet City of York Stakes (7f, York, 3yo+) – Safe Voyage (IRE)

Ladbrokes Celebration Mile Stakes (1m, Goodwood, 3yo+) – Century Dream (IRE)

Bet365 May Hill Stakes (1m, Doncaster, 2yo fillies) – Indigo Girl (GB)

Bet365 Park Hill Fillies' Stakes (1m6f115y, Doncaster, 3yo+ fillies & mares) – Pista (USA)

Bombardier Flying Childers Stakes (5f, Doncaster, 2yo) – Ubettabelieveit (IRE)

Bet365 Doncaster Cup Stakes (2m1f197y, Doncaster, 3yo+) – Spanish Mission (USA)

Bet365 Champagne Stakes (7f, Doncaster, 2yo colts & geldings) – Chindit (IRE)

Bet365 Park Stakes (7f, Doncaster, 3yo+) – Wichita (IRE)

Dubai Duty Free Mill Reef Stakes (6f, Newbury, 2yo) – Alkumait (GB)

Shadwell Rockfel Stakes (7f, Newmarket, 2yo fillies) – Isabella Giles (IRE)

Shadwell Joel Stakes (1m, Newmarket, 3yo+) – Kameko (USA)

Juddmonte Royal Lodge Stakes (1m, Newmarket, 2yo colts & geldings) – New Mandate (IRE)

Qipco British Champions Long Distance Cup (1m7f209y, Ascot, 3yo+) – Trueshan (FR)

Group 3

Betway Winter Derby Stakes (1m2f, Lingfield-AW, 4yo+) – Dubai Warrior (GB)

Unibet Classic Trial Stakes (1m2f, Kempton-AW, 3yo) – Berlin Tango (GB)

Betway Pavilion Stakes (6f, Newcastle-AW, 3yo) – Dubai Station (GB)

Betway Abernant Stakes (6f, Newmarket, 3yo+) – Oxted (GB)

Betfair Supports Racing Welfare Palace House Stakes (5f, Newmarket, 3yo+) – Far Above (IRE)

Betway Sagaro Stakes (2m56y, Newcastle-AW, 4yo+) – Nayef Road (IRE)

Betway Pinnacle Stakes (1m3f140y, Haydock, 4yo+ fillies & mares) – Manuela de Vega (IRE)

Betway Brigadier Gerard Stakes (1m2f, Haydock, 4yo+) – Lord North (IRE)

MansionBet's Beaten By A Head Diomed Stakes (1m, Newbury, 3yo+) – Century Dream (IRE)

Hampton Court Stakes (1m2f, Ascot, 3yo) – Russian Emperor (IRE)

Jersey Stakes (7f, Ascot, 3yo) – Molatham (GB)

Albany Stakes (6f, Ascot, 2yo fillies) – Dandalla (IRE)

Betfair Backs Racing Welfare Chipchase Stakes (6f, Newcastle-AW, 3yo+) – Judicial (IRE)

Betfair Exchange Hoppings Fillies' Stakes (1m2f, Newcastle-AW, 3yo+ fillies & mares) – Nkosikazi (GB)

Betway Criterion Stakes (7f, Newcastle-AW, 3yo+) – Limato (IRE)

Princess Elizabeth Stakes - sponsored by Investec (1m113y, Epsom, 3yo fillies) – Summer Romance (IRE)

Coral Charge (registered as the Sprint Stakes) (5f, Sandown, 3yo+) – A'Ali (IRE)

Coral Henry II Stakes (2m50y, Sandown, 4yo+) – Dashing Willoughby (GB)

Bahrain Trophy Stakes (1m5f, Newmarket, 3yo) – Al Aasy (IRE)

Tattersalls Musidora Stakes (1m2f56y, York, 3yo fillies) – Rose of Kildare (IRE)

John Smith's Silver Cup Stakes (1m5f188y, York, 4yo+) – Eagles By Day (IRE)

Bet365 Hackwood Stakes (6f, Newbury, 3yo+) – Tabdeed (GB)

William Hill Summer Fillies' Stakes (6f, York, 3yo+ fillies & mares) – Queen Jo Jo (GB)

Betfred Valiant Fillies' Stakes (1m, Ascot, 3yo+) – Lady Bowthorpe (GB)

Princess Margaret Betfred Stakes (6f, Ascot, 2yo fillies) – Santosha (IRE)

Markel Insurance Molecomb Stakes (5f, Goodwood, 2yo) – Steel Bull (IRE)

John Pearce Racing Gordon Stakes (1m4f, Goodwood, 3yo) – Mogul (GB)

Saint Clair Oak Tree Stakes (7f, Goodwood, 3yo+ fillies & mares) – One Master (IRE)

Bonhams Thoroughbred Stakes (1m, Goodwood, 3yo) – Tilsit (USA)

L'Ormarins Queen's Plate Glorious Stakes (1m4f, Goodwood, 4yo+) – Pablo Escobarr (IRE)

BetVictor Rose of Lancaster Stakes (1m2f, Haydock, 3yo+) – Extra Elusive (GB)

Betway Sweet Solera Stakes (7f, Newmarket, 2yo fillies) – Star of Emaraaty (IRE)

AJN Steelstock Sovereign Stakes (1m, Salisbury, 3yo+ colts & geldings) – Regal Reality (GB)

Irish Thoroughbred Marketing Geoffrey Freer Stakes (1m5f61y, Newbury, 3yo+) – Hukum (IRE)

Tattersalls Acomb Stakes (7f, York, 2yo) – Gear Up (IRE)

Sky Bet And Symphony Group Strensall Stakes (1m177y, York, 3yo+) – Certain Lad (GB)

Betway Atalanta Stakes (1m, Sandown, 3yo+ fillies & mares) – Maamora (IRE)

Betway Solario Stakes (7f, Sandown, 2yo) – Etonian (IRE)

Ladbrokes Prestige Stakes (7f, Goodwood, 2yo fillies) – Isabella Giles (IRE)

Ladbrokes March Stakes (In Memory of John Dunlop) (1m6f, Goodwood, 3yo) – Subjectivist (GB)

Gallagher Group Winter Hill Stakes (1m2f, Windsor, 3yo+) – Extra Elusive (GB)

Ladbrokes Supreme Stakes (7f, Goodwood, 3yo+) – Happy Power (IRE)

Shadwell Dick Poole Fillies' Stakes (6f, Salisbury, 2yo fillies) – Happy Romance (IRE)

Betfair Superior Mile Stakes (1m, Haydock, 3yo+) – Top Rank (IRE)

Unibet 3 Uniboosts A Day Sirenia Stakes (6f, Kempton-AW, 2yo) – Mighty Gurkha (IRE)

Unibet September Stakes (1m4f, Kempton-AW, 3yo+) – Enable (GB)

Bet365 Sceptre Fillies' Stakes (7f, Doncaster, 3yo+) – Foxtrot Lady (GB)

Dubai International Airport World Trophy Stakes (5f, Newbury, 3yo+) – Lazuli (IRE)

Dubai Duty Free Legacy Cup Stakes (1m3f, Newbury, 3yo+) – Elarqam (GB)

Scotty Brand Firth of Clyde Fillies' Stakes (6f, Ayr, 2yo fillies) – Umm Kulthum (IRE)

Tattersalls Stakes (registered as the Somerville Tattersall Stakes) (7f, Newmarket, 2yo colts & geldings) – La Barrosa (IRE)

Princess Royal Muhaarar Stakes (1m4f, Newmarket, 3yo+ fillies & mares) – Antonia de Vega (IRE)

Betsafe Cumberland Lodge Stakes (1m3f188y, York, 3yo+) – Euchen Glen (GB)

Newmarket Academy Godolphin Beacon Project Cornwallis Stakes (5f, Newmarket, 2yo) – Winter Power (IRE)

Godolphin Lifetime Care Oh So Sharp Stakes (7f, Newmarket, 2yo fillies) – Saffron Beach (IRE)
Darley Pride Stakes (1m2f, Newmarket, 3yo+ fillies & mares) – Angel Power (GB)
Coral Bengough Stakes (6f, York, 3yo+) – Dakota Gold (GB)
Godolphin Flying Start Zetland Stakes (1m2f, Newmarket, 2yo) – Lone Eagle (IRE)
Emirates Autumn Stakes (1m, Newmarket, 2yo) – One Ruler (IRE)
Emirates Darley Stakes (1m1f, Newmarket, 3yo+) – Lady Wannabe (IRE)
Molson Coors Beverage Company Stakes (registered as the Horris Hill Stakes) (7f, Newbury, 2yo colts & geldings) – Mujbar (GB)
Pravha Stakes (registered as the St Simon Stakes) (1m4f, Newbury, 3yo+) – Euchen Glen (GB)

GREAT BRITAIN & IRELAND'S
GROUP 2 & GROUP 3 WINNERS OF 2020
IN OTHER COUNTRIES

Australia
Group 3
Iron Jack N E Manion Cup (1m4f, Rosehill, 3yo+) – Young
Rascal (FR)
Queen Elizabeth Stakes (1m5f, Flemington, 3yo+) – True Self
(IRE)

France
Group 2
Prix Maurice de Nieuil (1m6f, ParisLongchamp, 4yo+) – Red
Verdon (USA)
Darley Prix Robert Papin (6f, Chantilly, 2yo) – Ventura
Tormenta (IRE)
Prix Guillaume d'Ornano - Haras du Logis Saint Germain (1m2f,
Deauville, 3yo) – Mishriff (IRE)
Shadwell Prix du Calvados (7f, Deauville, 2yo fillies) – Fev Rover
(IRE)
Lucien Barriere Grand Prix de Deauville (1m4f110y, Deauville,
3yo+) – Telecaster (GB)
Qatar Prix Foy (1m4f, ParisLongchamp, 4yo+) – Anthony Van
Dyck (IRE)
Prix du Conseil de Paris (1m3f, ParisLongchamp, 3yo+) – Baron
Samedi (GB)

Group 3
La Coupe (1m2f, ParisLongchamp, 4yo+) – Telecaster (GB)
Prix de la Porte Maillot (7f, ParisLongchamp, 3yo+) – Space
Blues (IRE)
Qatar Pris de Ris-Orangis (6f, Deauville, 3yo+) – Royal Crusade
(GB)
Prix du Lys (1m4f, ParisLongchamp, 3yo) – Volkan Star (IRE)
Darley Prix de Cabourg (6f, Deauville, 2yo) – Cairn Gorm (GB)
Prix Minerve (1m4f110y, Deauville, 3yo fillies) – Wonderful
Tonight (FR)

Barriere Prix de Meautry (6f, Deauville, 3yo+) – Breathtaking
Look (GB)
Prix Belle de Nuit (1m6f, Saint-Cloud, 3yo+ fillies & mares) –
Believe In Love (IRE)
Prix Miesque (7f, Chantilly, 2yo fillies) – Lullaby Moon (GB)
Prix de Seine-et-Oise (6f, Chantilly, 3yo+) – Brad The Brief
(GB)

Germany
Group 2
87th Kronimus Oettingen-Rennen (1m, Baden-Baden, 3yo+) –
Dark Vision (IRE)

Italy
Group 2
Premio Lydia Tesio (1m2f, Capannelle, 3yo+ fillies & mares) –
Angel Power (GB)

United Arab Emirates
Group 2
Singspiel Stakes presented by Longines Master Collection (1m1f,
Meydan, 3yo+) – Benbatl (IRE)
Cape Verdi sponsored by Creek Views (1m, Meydan, 3yo+ fillies
& mares) – Magic Lily (GB)
Al Fahidi Fort sponsored by DP World UAE Region (7f,
Meydan, 3yo+) – Glorious Journey (GB)
Al Rashidiya sponsored by Hamdan Bin Mohammed Cruise
Terminal (1m1f, Meydan, 3yo+) – Barney Roy (GB)
Al Maktoum Challenge R2 sponsored by Mubadala (1m1f110y,
Meydan, 3yo+) – Benbatl (GB)
Balanchine sponsored by Gulf News (1m1f, Meydan, 3yo+ fillies
& mares) – Magic Lily (GB)
Zabeel Mile sponsored by Al Tayer Motors (1m, Meydan, 3yo+)
– Zakouski (GB)
Dubai City of Gold sponsored by Emirates SkyCargo (1m4f,
Meydan, 3yo+) – Loxley (IRE)

Group 3

Dubai Millennium Stakes sponsored by Jaguar (1m2f, Meydan, 3yo+) – Ghaiyyath (IRE)

Nad Al Sheba Trophy sponsored by Mohammed Bin Rashid Al Maktoum City - District One (1m6f, Meydan, 3yo+) – Secret Advisor (FR)

Aurora, 430

Aussie Rules, 53-4, 128, 485, 494

Australia, 10, 18-20, 23-5, 27, 91, 93, 95, 102-3, 166-8, 172, 240, 242, 244, 319, 325-6, 328, 352, 366, 434, 449, 458-9, 470-1, 474, 480, 483, 486-8, 490-1, 495, 497, 499-500, 506, 510, 516, 520-1, 524, 526

Authorized, 9-10, 25, 49, 172, 174, 229, 301, 303, 417-8, 449, 460, 470-1, 477, 483, 485, 490, 499, 501, 511, 518, 520, 532

Avenir Certain, 302, 314, 408

Avilius, 56

Awesome Again, 494

Awesome Rock, 262

Awtaad, 111, 252

Azamour, 259-60, 358, 374, 436-7, 485, 501

Bachelor Duke, 379

Bahamian Bounty, 71, 432-3, 456, 463

Bahr, 78-9, 182, 506, 520, 526

Bahri, 314, 410-1

Bairam, 324

Balbonella, 36, 324, 375

Balenare, 212, 521

Balidaress, 107, 311

Ballad Rock, 273

Balladonia, 113

Baltic Baroness, 53

Bangkok, 148-9, 343, 398

Banks Hill, 83

Baralinka, 217-8, 506, 525

Barathea, 42, 128, 179-80, 217-8, 266, 268, 270

Barney Roy, 1, 8, 13, 15, 24, 30, 59, 124, 261, 325, 382, 451, 458, 463, 474, 488, 503, 508, 522, 537, 545, 554, 561-2, 569, 579, 583, 585, 588, 599

Baron Samedi, 14, 27 70-2, 335, 452, 456, 469, 476, 489, 494, 519, 525, 542, 547, 552, 562, 569, 578, 584, 587, 598

Barrington Court, 138

Bated Breath, 53, 63, 88-9, 98-9, 111, 176, 211, 240, 449, 457, 463, 477-8, 486, 489, 497, 504, 514, 529, 533

Gabrial, 104

Galileo, 9-11, 18-9, 21-5, 28, 44, 46, 49, 55, 57, 60, 62, 65, 73, 75, 80, 83, 91, 93, 102-3, 109-10, 112-3, 125-6, 128, 135-43, 145, 149-50, 154, 156-7, 166-8, 172, 178-9, 186-7, 190, 192, 205-6, 214, 217, 225, 227 230, 232-3, 240, 242, 244, 249-51, 253, 255-6, 261-5, 267, 276-8, 289, 300, 305-6, 311-3, 319-25, 327-8, 330 333-4, 337, 346-7, 352-3, 355, 357-60, 366, 371-2, 374, 376-8, 380, 384-5, 393-4, 396, 399-400, 402, 405, 409-11, 413-4, 425, 430, 434, 445-6, 451, 458-9, 461-2, 466, 468-71, 474-8, 480-2, 485-91, 495-9, 502-4, 506, 508-9, 512-8, 520, 523-4, 527-30, 532, 534

Galileo Chrome, 14, 20, 23, 25, 71, 91, 138, 166, 207, 242, 325, 336

Galileo Gold, 427

Galiway, 30, 49

Gallant Romeo, 174

Galyph, 300, 524

Gamut, 128

Gay Gallanta, 229

Gear Up, 1, 11, 15, 20, 88, , 186, 191, 301, 305, 333, 455, 459, 470, 477, 492, 494, 514, 523, 535, 550, 557, 559, 570, 576 582, 585, 588, 595

Gearanai, 477, 514, 523

General Holme, 423, 488, 502

General's Sister, 423

Generous, 78-9, 83-4, 179, 182, 220, 310-1, 402-3

Ghaiyyath, 1, 8, 13, 15, 18-9, 23-4, 27-8, 56, 61-2, 108, 252, 265, 351, 450, 457, 471, 480, 488, 503, 507, 530, 541, 545, 554, 559, 571, 580, 583, 585, 588, 600

Giant's Causeway, 23, 43, 54, 59, 97, 182, 201, 224, 234, 246, 262, 270, 277, 315, 327, 354, 356-7, 376, 423, 428, 447-8, 459, 466, 472, 488, 499, 503

Gilt Edge Girl, 96

Give Thanks, 314

Glass Slippers, 11, 38, 132

Glatisant, 202, 235

Macheera, 59, 513, 521

Machiavellian, 45, 59, 67, 84, 86, 88, 102, 119, 126, 187, 191, 197, 205, 282, 284, 292, 302-3, 330, 347, 355-6, 380, 386, 408, 418, 428, 442-4, 448, 467-8, 501

Madame Dubois, 418, 513, 531

Madany, 223, 294-5, 479, 506, 524

Made of Gold, 51, 280

Madhmoon, 95, 325, 331

Magic Gleam, 371-2, 526

Magic Lily, 9, 13, 16, 19-20, 22, 24-5, 259, 261-4, 453, 459, 471, 476, 486, 496, 515, 530, 538, 545, 554, 569, 579, 583, 585, 588, 599

Magic Wand, 13, 18-9, 24-5, 28, 101, 172, 228, 265-7, 316, 451, 461, 468, 481, 486, 496, 514, 529, 537, 550, 553, 567, 570, 573, 583, 585, 589

Magical, 10, 12, 17, 19, 23, 25, 61-2, 90, 100-1, 137, 205, 242, 346, 351, 420

Magical Romance, 266

Maglietta Fina, 226-7, 382-3, 479, 519, 527

Magna Grecia, 105, 130, 134, 320, 332

Magnificient Style, 136, 227

Magny Cours, 68, 148

Mahbooba, 23, 149-50, 479, 517, 527

Mahrah, 168

Majestic Colt, 109, 214, 388

Majestic Dubawi, 214-5, 479, 518, 532

Majestic Light, 333, 341

Majestic Prince, 341, 402

Majinskaya, 160, 215, 258

Major Emblem, 157

Makaloun, 88

Make A Challenge, 38

Make Believe, 27, 30, 76-7, 311, 351, 353, 453, 460, 465, 475-6, 483, 489, 491-2, 498-500, 506, 518-9, 524, 529, 531

Make Fast, 396-7, 479, 515, 532

Makfi, 76-7, 91, 156, 351, 353, 396-7, 460, 465, 490, 498

Makybe Diva, 35, 262

Malafemmena, 75, 145, 513, 526-7

Master of Reality, 140

Master of The Seas, 9, 13, 16, 18-9, 24-5, 69, 271-3, 450, 458, 472, 477, 486, 497, 511, 530, 538, 545, 554, 570, 574, 582, 585, 592

Mastercraftsman, 9, 49, 176-7 229, 249, 253, 289, 311, 453, 457, 463, 480, 489, 504, 509, 523

Mastery, 379

Matcher, 256, 264, 306, 400

Mathaayl, 185

Matterhorn, 240

Max Vega, 207, 248, 436

Maximum Security, 78, 265

Maybe, 263

Mayenne, 527

Mayson, 217, 226, 432, 453, 459, 467 475, 485, 496, 510, 530

Mecca's Angel, 245, 441

Medaglia d'Oro, 164

Medicean, 47, 83-6, 283, 346-7 460, 467, 490, 501

Mehdaayih, 125, 269, 323

Mehmas, 11, 21-2, 284, 302, 408, 434, 453, 456, 469-70, 480 483, 485, 496, 502, 508, 510, 520, 522

Mendez, 293

Meringue Pie, 226-7, 382-3, 527

Mevlana, 425-6, 513, 523

Mia Karina, 136, 227

Midday, 140, 249-50

Midnight Angel, 67, 185, 197 418

Midnight Bisou, 78, 341

Midnight Legend, 423

Midnight Oasis, 434-5, 479, 513, 528

Midnight Shift, 435, 513, 528

Midships, 64

Miesque, 73, 135, 174, 209, 288 345

Mighty Gurkha, 11, 274-5, 455, 458, 466, 481, 491 504, 507, 531, 541, 549, 558, 569, 573, 582, 587, 596

Mildenberger, 299

Military March, 438

Misty For Me, 78

Miswaki, 43, 57, 65, 100, 139, 142, 145, 153, 180, 206, 209, 233, 251, 267, 300, 313, 321, 324, 340, 360, 366, 377, 379, 403, 414, 437

Mizzen Mast, 64

Modena, 249-51, 527

Modernstone, 249, 251, 480, 514, 527

Mogul, 1, 13, 18-9, 24-5, 28, 42, 95, 114, 312, 336, 373, 451, 461, 468, 482,, 486, 497, 516, 524, 540, 550, 554, 565, 579, 584-5, 588, 595

Mohaather, 1, 16, 44, 439, 455, 461, 467, 481, 489, 494, 516, 531, 538, 543, 557, 565, 571, 580, 583, 585, 588, 593

Mohini, 330, 480, 508, 522

Molatham, 11, 16, 25, 130, 245, 288-9, 438-9, 454, 458, 465, 475, 491, 502, 507, 523, 536, 543, 558, 565, 570, 578, 582, 587, 594

Mombones, 152-3, 528

Mona Em, 287

Monsieur Bond, 96

Monsun, 42-3, 92, 180, 399-400, 427, 501

Mont Ormel, 337, 343

Montare, 23, 208, 210-2, 480, 508, 521

Montelimar, 110

Montjeu, 23-5, 40, 53-4, 80, 99, 109, 112, 118, 120, 125, 135, 138 156, 172, 174, 202, 210, 212, 222, 224, 228, 230, 266, 294, 301, 303, 309, 325, 374, 394, 418, 460, 470-1, 490, 501, 503

Moon Search, 31

Morando, 207, 307, 422

More Than Ready, 311, 379

Morning Line, 55

Moss Vale, 425

Most Welcome, 433

Mother Earth, 13, 17, 24-5, 48, 127, 285, 290-2, 455, 457, 463, 479, 488, 497, 509, 532, 538, 549, 553, 560, 571, 575, 582, 586, 590

Motion Lass, 38, 40, 480, 518, 534

Motivator, 38, 40, 112, 374, 490, 501

Mourayan, 436

SOURCES

Many sources were consulted during the writing of this book. The main ones were:

arion.co.nz
attheraces.com
bloodhorse.com/stallion-register/
bloodstockreports.co.uk
European Group 1 Winners of 2018
European Group 1 Winners of 2019
france-galop.com
irishfield.ie
pedigreequery.com
racenet.com.au
racingpost.com
racingtv.com
timeform.com
Timeform's *Racehorses* annuals
Twitter
Weatherbys/BloodHorse Global Stallions app
Weatherbys' *Return of Mares 2019* & supplement
Weatherbys' *Return of Mares 2020* & supplement
wikipedia.org

Thank you for reading *Best Racehorses of 2020 – Volume 2: Great Britain & Ireland's Group 2 & Group 3 Winners of 2020.*

If you enjoyed this book, please spread the word and perhaps leave a review on Amazon, Goodreads or another book-review site.

Even a single line will do.

Reviews help authors!